Dominion
of Bears

Dominion
of Bears
Living with Wildlife
in Alaska

Sherry Simpson

 University Press of Kansas

Published by the

University Press of Kansas

(Lawrence, Kansas 66045),

which was organized by the

Kansas Board of Regents and

is operated and funded by

Emporia State University,

Fort Hays State University,

Kansas State University,

Pittsburg State University,

the University of Kansas, and

Wichita State University

Photo on pages ii–iii by bobby20/Shutterstock.com

Photos on pages vi and viii by David Rasmus
/Shutterstock.com

Photo on page xii by Nina B/Shutterstock.com

Library of Congress Cataloging-in-Publication Data

Simpson, Sherry.

   Dominion of bears : living with wildlife in Alaska /
Sherry Simpson.

      pages cm

   Includes bibliographical references and index.

   ISBN 978-0-7006-1935-1 (cloth : alkaline paper)

1. Bears—Alaska. 2. Brown bear—Alaska. 3. Black bear—
Alaska. 4. Polar bear—Alaska. 5. Bears—Behavior—
Alaska. 6. Bears—Ecology—Alaska. 7. Human-animal
relationships—Alaska. 8. Nature—Effect of human
beings on—Alaska. 9. Simpson, Sherry—Travel—Alaska.
10. Alaska—Description and travel.

I. Title.

   QL737.C27S564 2013

   599.78409798—dc23

                                        2013031248

British Library Cataloguing-in-Publication Data is available.

Printed in the United States of America

10 9 8 7 6 5 4 3 2 1

The paper used in this publication is recycled and
contains 30 percent postconsumer waste. It is acid free
and meets the minimum requirements of the American
National Standard for Permanence of Paper for Printed
Library Materials Z39.48–1992.

For Barb and Ray Farnworth,

and for bear people everywhere.

contents

acknowledgments

So many of the people I met and interviewed during this project could and should write their own books about bears. I hope they do. In the meantime, I'm grateful to them for sharing their time, work, research, ideas, stories, and opinions. Some of their names appear in this book, and some don't. My urge to consult every single bear researcher or expert on the planet was curtailed only by the constraints of time and space, but I could not have finished this book without relying on the work of many, many people I have never met.

I'm especially grateful to Larry Aumiller, Brian Barnes, Neil Barten, Bruce Bartley, Pete Buist, Jessy Coltrane, Pat Costello, Ken and Chris Day, Fred Dean, Terry DeBruyn, Andrew Derocher, Tom Evans, Craig George, Tom Griffin, Kathie Harms, Ernestine Hayes, John Hechtel, Grant Hilderbrand, Nick Jans, Charlie Johnson, Perry Matumeak, Joe Meehan, Susanne Miller, Patricia Owen, Josh and Kellie Peirce, Harry Reynolds, Mark Richards, John Schoen, Rick Sinnott, Derek Stonorov, and Vic Van Ballenberghe. Thank you to John Toppenberg of the Alaska Wildlife Alliance and Rod Arno and Patrick Valkenburg of the Alaska Outdoor Council for explaining their organizations' positions. I owe a lot to Kim Titus and Vern Beier for allowing me to accompany them on a bear-tagging expedition on Admiralty Island years ago; they ignited my interest in the secret lives of bears. Sterling Miller's expertise in bear science and his editorial suggestions were immensely important, and I can't thank him enough for his careful and thorough review. I especially appreciate his permission to dispense with the unworthy terms "sow" and "boar" when referring to bears. John Hechtel, Vic Van Ballenberghe, and Mark Richards made helpful suggestions on specific sections. I also thank Andrew Derocher, Terry DeBruyn, Derek Stonorov, Richard Ellis, Nancy Lord, and Bill Sherwonit for reading the entire manuscript and providing comments. Any factual errors or misinterpretations are, of course, mine. My apologies to anyone I've inadvertently forgotten to thank; you can be sure I am grateful for your help.

Merry Ellefson generously shared her treasure trove of interviews with me, and Doug Fesler gave me an invaluable collection of historical newspaper articles that deserve their own chapter. Robyn Russell at the Elmer Rasmuson Library in Fairbanks and Justine Bishop at the Alaska State Archives in Juneau were very helpful. Thank you to Gary Porter for taking me to Geographic Harbor, and to Maurizio Zanin, Claudio Groff, and Piero Genovesi for letting me attend the sixteenth annual conference of the International Association for Bear Research and Management in Riva del Garda, Italy. I appreciate the generosity of photographers Kenneth Gill and Alan Wilson in sharing their images. Andri Grishkowsky and Robert Meyerowitz deserve special thanks for their encouragement and contributions. I appreciate the work of the many news reporters who provided valuable information. I'm also obligated to Stephen Colbert and his regular inclusion of bears in his "Threat Down" segments for providing years of laughs and periodic reminders of why a book like this is necessary.

Michael Briggs of the University Press of Kansas was unfailingly supportive and unbelievably patient; I cannot thank him enough for his keen insights and his hard work on behalf of this book. I was buoyed in the final stages by the encouragement, professionalism (and patience!) of Kelly Chrisman Jacques, Susan Schott, and Rebecca Murray Schuler. Linda Lotz performed heroic work as a copyeditor and saved me from myself many times.

I'm painfully aware of what's not included in this book—enough to write another two or three books, really. Two perspectives in particular deserve more attention. For a deeper understanding of historical and contemporary relationships between Alaska Natives and bears, I recommend starting with Richard Nelson's ethnographic studies, in particular *Make Prayers to the Raven: A Koyukon View of the Northern Forest*. And two remarkable new books beautifully describe the firsthand experience of the aftermath of a bear attack: *Beyond the Bear: How I Learned to Live and Love Again after Being Blinded by a Bear* by Dan Bigley and Debra McKinney (Lyons Press, 2013), and *North of Hope: A Daughter's Arctic Journey* by Shannon Huffman Polson (Zondervan/Harper Collins, 2013).

Finally, I am beyond grateful to friends and family for years of help and encouragement. People who endured my various fits of despair and excitement and yet never expressed doubts (openly) about my sanity include Aisha Barnes, David Stevenson, Jo-Ann Mapson, Stewart Allison, and the Simpson, Hulbert, Monagle, and Kiefer clans. I promise never to inflict another lecture on the wonders of bears and marine nitrogen cycles on them again. A multitude of friends, students, and acquaintances shared stories and information; their interest in bears sustained me.

Frankly, I consider it a miracle that I remain married. Scott Kiefer has done more housework, dog walking, listening, soothing, proofreading, and chocolate procuring than anybody should have to, and he did it with grace and love. I can't repay him for this great gift, but I intend to try.

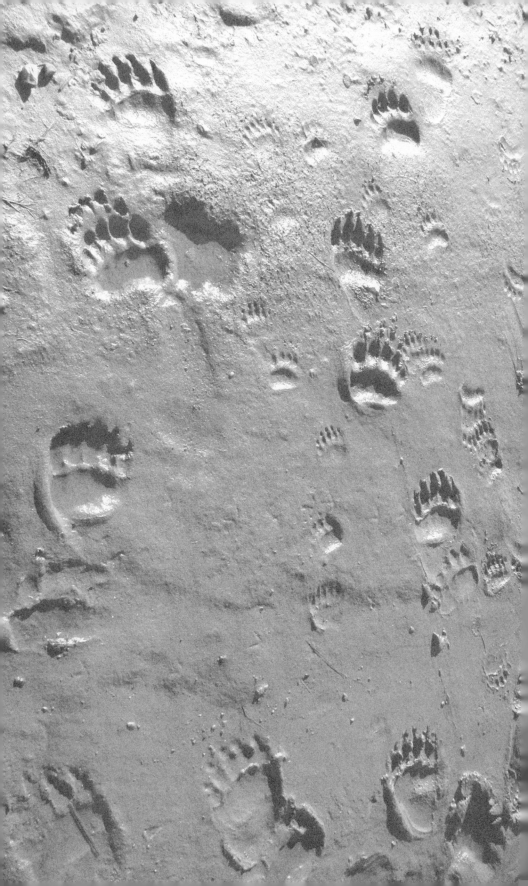

the metaphorical
bear

At first I didn't notice the tracks pressed into the muddy trail. My dog and I were walking in the fading warmth of an October sun through an aspen forest not far from my house. Several paces beyond the prints, I stopped, suddenly aware of the image percolating through my thoughts. I retraced my steps to sort through a collage of impressions: the waffle tread of my boots, the deep crescents of moose hooves, the dog's skidding feet, and there, beneath a confetti of golden tamarack needles, the crisp, familiar outlines of a bear's front and rear paws.

That bears dwell in the wildlands edging Anchorage's eastern flank didn't surprise me. Thirty minutes of walking would take me into the foothills of the western Chugach Mountains, where black and brown bears den on alpine slopes and in the valleys. At least twenty brown bears regularly venture into the city's margins, drawn by spawning salmon, vulnerable moose calves, berries galore. A few years before, a brown bear had killed and cached a moose within a hundred yards of where I stood. Knowing all this, I straightened from studying the trail to scan the surrounding forest. Leaves and needles scattered across the prints suggested there was no need for high alert, that a day or so had passed since the bear had paced along this path, head swinging, muzzle twitching. Yet even the air seemed charged by its presence, a lingering reminder that bears don't live *out there*. They live *here*, with us. Nothing had changed, and everything had changed.

The slightest evidence that bears share your world—or that you share theirs—can alter not only your sense of the landscape but also your sense of yourself within that landscape. You look around hopefully, fearfully, expectantly, uncertainly, trying to decide if you feel threatened or enlarged, alarmed or invigorated, if you should retreat or press on. Once, after a friend and I noticed the fresh grooves of a bear's claws scoring the tender cambium of a spruce tree, she confessed, "I just want to know how to *be* around bears." On this October day I looked at the bear tracks one more time, called to my dog, and kept walking because, like most Alaskans, I want to know how to be around bears, too.

Spending time outdoors in Alaska means cultivating an awareness of bears that is almost psychologically organic, a way of thinking and behaving that approaches the autonomic. I didn't realize this until I lived for a few months in New Zealand, where the absence of snakes, scorpions, predators, or anything larger than feral swine and goats makes it one of the world's most benign natural landscapes. Hiking there seemed no riskier than strolling the grounds of Buckingham Palace, yet I caught myself constantly on the verge of calling out, "Hey, bear!" at blind spots and in brushy corridors. Some part of me was always listening for the sound of breaking twigs, thudding paws, popping teeth. It wasn't paranoia that I couldn't relinquish, but a habit of mind developed in a place where bears are ever present in the wilderness and in our backyards.

Not only present, but a presence. They inhabit our conversations, headlines, stories, history, cultural practices, art, politics, imaginations. To catalog all the ways the ideas and images of bears invade daily life in Alaska would require a separate book. Once I counted twenty different bear images between the front doors of the Ted Stevens International Airport and my boarding gate. They appeared on socks and T-shirts, book covers and snack wrappers, notecards and an entire wall of McDonald's. The state's souvenir industry might collapse without bears. The *Dictionary of Alaska Place Names* lists more than 150 geographic features named after bears, including 69 different Bear Creeks. A silent menagerie of taxidermied brown, black, and polar bears populates hotel and bank lobbies, restaurants, libraries, stores, and airports (last time I counted, the airport in Anchorage had six bears, and the airports in Fairbanks and Juneau had four each). The state's largest newspaper, the *Anchorage Daily News*, hosts an online gallery of bear photos submitted by readers—part of an entire section devoted to bear sightings, videos, and articles. At home, a polar bear greets me each day on a fridge magnet advertising a law office. They are the most coveted of animal endorsements in business names: Brown Bear Plumbing and Heating, Bear's Nest Café, and Bear Asphalt and Construction are a few among hundreds. They lend ferocity to the Juneau-Douglas High Crimson Bears and the University of Alaska–Fairbanks Nanooks. And what else would

Kodiak High School choose as a mascot? Look around almost any Alaskan street, and somewhere a metaphorical or merchandised bear will be looking back at you.

Even the state flag acknowledges the dominion of bears. Against a deep blue background, the golden stars of the Big Dipper point toward the North Star. "The Dipper is for the Great Bear—symbolizing strength," explained thirteen-year-old Benny Benson, whose flag design won a 1926 competition. Few Alaskans today recognize the Great Bear as the nymph Callisto, who was impregnated by Zeus and transmogrified into a bear by his jealous wife, Hera. Sixteen years later Callisto's son, Arcas, nearly speared his unrecognizable bear-mother before Zeus took pity and fixed them both in the sky as the constellations Ursa Major and Ursa Minor. Hera's final revenge ensured that neither would ever dip below the horizon for a drink or a bath. Thus, by stars and by flag, by night and by day, Alaskans live under the sign of the bear.

Today, Alaska serves as a refugium for intact populations of bears and for ideas about bears. More than 70 percent of North America's brown bears live in Alaska. Altogether an estimated 31,000 brown bears, maybe 100,000 black bears, and perhaps 3,500 polar bears inhabit the state, according to the Alaska Department of Fish and Game. (Brown bears and grizzly bears are actually the same species, Ursus arctos, but the coastal bears that grow so large from eating salmon are generally called brown bears, and the smaller, inland dwellers are called grizzlies.) Place and animal are bound so tightly that they amplify each other, transform into metaphors of each other, fuse into a mythos in which one could not exist without the other. Nearly every aspect of northern society reflects this dynamic, from tourism marketing to wildlife management to urban planning. As the most mega of the charismatic megafauna, bears radiate a pure animal glamour of grandness, power, and beauty, tinged by the irresistible aura of danger. We admire them, photograph them, hunt them, fear them, tell stories about them. We notice how we resemble them, and vice versa, in our shared ability to stand on two legs, preference for an omnivorous diet, sense of curiosity, and adaptable intelligence. Alaska Native peoples recall an older way of knowing bears—as a living mercantile that supplied hides, bones, and flesh, and as a spiritual go-between that shifted between the physical and the cosmic dimensions. To borrow shamelessly from the lexicon of conservation biology, bears function as a keystone species in northern cultural ecologies both indigenous and transplanted. They're so critical to the whole that if they were removed, an important system of beliefs and values would collapse.

Historians continue to debate whether Alaska deserves to be considered "exceptional" or merely "different." It's true that nearly 85 percent of the state's residents live in urban communities where the likes of Home Depot, Netflix, and Costco continue to colonize the Last Frontier of merchandising. It's also true that many other states take pride in their mountains, forests, wildlife, salmon, glaciers, and harsh winter weather. But almost nowhere else do so many people live in such close quarters with so many bears, and maybe this qualifies as the ultimate measure of exceptionalism.

"It is difficult to envision what the popular image of Alaska might be, or how Alaskans would see themselves, or what would happen to their unique sense of place, if there were no more bears in the state," observes Morgan Sherwood in his history of wildlife management, *Big Game in Alaska*. Alaskans certainly don't hesitate to indulge in self-exceptionalism when it comes to bears. Residency allows everyone to play two easy cards: one that says, *Eh, it's no big deal to live in bear country*, and another that declares, *No kidding, you could die almost anytime you step outside your front door*. Without the threat of bears, what true dangers would a pioneer face, now that weather satellites, cell phones, snowblowers, central heating, and annual Permanent Fund dividend checks have eased the frontier's privations?

So cherished is the notion of the rugged Alaskan that an entire genre of reality TV has been developed to prop up this northern mythology with such shows as *Deadliest Catch*, *Flying Wild Alaska*, *Gold Rush Alaska*, *Alaska Wing Men*, *Ice Road Truckers*, *Tougher in Alaska*, *Cowboys of the Sea*, and *Extreme Alaska*. A series tentatively titled *The Frontiersmen* will drop contestants into the boonies to battle for survival. Discovery Channel president and general manager Clark Bunting explained the appeal in an *Anchorage Daily News* article: "So many people today drive to the office in an economy car. Then they work in a cubicle. And then they go to the big box stores on the weekend," he said. "What Alaska really represents for a lot of people right now, is the true pioneer spirit."

The most unreal of these reality shows, *Sarah Palin's Alaska*, didn't miss the opportunity to demonstrate this spirit by using bears as a dramatic foil. "Our ruggedness is really a mystery in the Lower 48 states,"

Palin explained to the camera. During that episode she abandoned the family's RV to take fellow celebrity Kate Gosselin and her eight children camping. Gosselin's deep alarm upon learning that bears live in the wilderness was a cue for the self-styled "Mama Grizzly" to shepherd Gosselin through a bear safety class and to visit a gun shop for advice on the best bear-stopping weapon (a shotgun, she learned). "If you are unarmed and you're out in the wilderness, well, you're putting yourself and your family in danger," Palin warned. Personally, I can't imagine why any self-respecting bear would go near ten children, several adults, and a camera crew out in the "wilderness," even if the expedition did leave inviting coolers of food outside.

But we can hardly blame Palin for mouthing the sentiments Alaskans have worked so industriously to keep alive, or for invoking some of the most potent elements of American frontier identity as inventoried by historian Frederick Jackson Turner—independence, resourcefulness, self-reliance, adventurousness, the determination to pursue every opportunity and conquer any obstacle. This is how Merle Colby characterized northerners in his 1939 guide to Alaska: "Bestriding two worlds of time, often isolated from his fellow citizens of the United States and even from his fellow Alaskans, the white frontiersman has something of the character of a westerner of Andrew Jackson's day, but without the Jacksonian's provincialism." During World War II Colby produced the pamphlet *What Has Alaska to Offer Postwar Pioneers?* Nothing less than challenge and opportunity, he assured veterans, reminding them in a stirring introduction that "pioneer is a magic word in American history," and "the frontier is bred into our bones." In 1965 *Life* magazine published this description of a homesteader who had arrived four decades earlier: "There is the look of the frontier about Alaska, and you see it too in the faces of her old-time residents like Shorty Bradley—men whose migration into the north country was a natural extension of the movement into the American West." Those who built Alaska were men "who drew strength from the struggle with nature," the article added.

Teasing out the multiple meanings of the words *wildness, wilderness, nature,* and *frontier* remains the fractious work of cultural and historical scholars—the splitters, in taxonomic jargon. In contrast, we lumpers toss about these words and concepts as we please, glibly substituting them for one another, happily unconcerned with intellectual lineages and philosophical debates. Is wildness a condition or a concept? Are we supposed to tame nature, enshrine it, or infuse ourselves with it? We do know, however, that the quickest way to figure out the difference between wilderness and civilization is to locate the bears. "Question— Why do we tolerate bears in Anchorage?" a resident asked in response to an *Alaska Dispatch* story about bear safety. "Would an African city, comparable in size to Anchorage, tolerate lions within the core of their city? If within 10 minutes a person can be eating a Big Mac, watching the latest IMAX movie, and/or shopping at a mall, then they DO NOT LIVE IN THE WILD." Bears, oddly enough, don't seem to follow the same criteria.

Sharp-eyed scholars rummaging through the past have located the hulking figure of the bear loitering at the corner of wilderness and frontier. "From the nineteenth century on, bears symbolized the power, strangeness, extravagance, and wildness of the West," historian Patricia Nelson Limerick remarks in *The Legacy of Conquest*. As it turned out, settlers loved the idea of renewing and reinventing themselves in the frontier's open expanses, but they didn't care for some of its inhabitants. They feared grizzly bears as a danger to themselves, a threat to their livestock, and an impediment to the orderly development of a new agricultural empire. As the twentieth century approached, anxiety over the rapid depletion of wilderness, wildlife, and natural resources only amplified the suspicion that the frontier era was over, as Frederick Jackson Turner argued in 1893. Gold rushes in Alaska and the Yukon redirected the nation's gaze toward the distant, perilous North as a place where people could still live out that old dream of natural riches and abundant animals there for the taking. "While the sourdough with his pick and pan personified the go-getter on the Last Frontier, wild animals just as surely symbolized the Alaskan wilderness," writes historian Theodore Catton in *Inhabited Wilderness*.

Few wilderness symbols serve as many different aims as the brown bear, so easily incarnated as commodity and killer, trophy and impediment, victim and vermin. As Edward Hoagland once wrote, "Animals are stylized characters in a kind of old saga—stylized because even the most acute of them have little leeway as they play out their parts." Neither do people, apparently. As the wilderness ideals of Outsiders butted against the frontier mentality of Alaska's pioneers, bears became a convenient symbol of either old mistakes or future obstacles. Then, as now, Alaskans were aggravated by game policies intended to prevent a recurrence of past excesses or to make up for them. People who had chewed up their own wilderness and spit it out had a lot of nerve asking for a do-over in Alaska, the thinking went. "The conservation associations look upon the brown bear as a unique animal, his last stamping ground as Alaska, and wish him preserved. They are very silly about it, and never having been to Alaska, you can realize how they visualize the country," wrote Governor Thomas Riggs Jr. to *The Western Sportsman* in 1920.

Most Alaskans considered bears a dangerous hindrance to progress for the same reasons that inspired westerners to cull bears and other predators from their lands. "If Alaska is ever to become a country of homes it is high time to commence to exterminate their greatest enemy and also at the same time the greatest enemy to the increase of other game animals which are not destructive," Fairbanks resident George Wilson wrote in support of Riggs's campaign to exterminate bears. The governor's crusade failed, yet in 1938 a biologist for the Alaska Game Commission still harbored the delusion that a cattle industry could succeed in Alaska "were it not for the presence of the bear in such quantities." As late as 1963, Kodiak cattle ranchers were so sure—and so wrong—that brown bears had foiled their success that they methodically tried to wipe them out using poison, bait, snares, and a semiautomatic weapon mounted on a small plane. "Civilization is moving north, and the bear is going to have to give way," explained a rancher with an instinctive grasp of manifest destiny.

By then, the grizzly had given way almost entirely in the Lower 48. An estimated 700 to 800 bears persisted in isolated pockets of Wyoming, Montana, Idaho, and Washington when the species was assigned federal "threatened" status. Even as outdoors-minded Americans were stampeding into national parks, hungry for natural experiences and "untouched" landscapes, bears seemed bound for the realm of the passenger pigeon. "The grandest and most powerful living symbol of wilderness in America is struggling for survival," nature writer David Petersen wrote in *Mother Earth News* in 1985. Lose all the bears, and we'll lose a necessary humility, bear researcher and author Doug Peacock told him. "The grizzly bear offers us one of our very few remaining opportunities to sample a little of the wild and woolly flavor of the American West our forefathers knew."

A similar symbolic transaction occurs in Alaska not because there are too few bears but because there are so many. It works something like this: bears equal wildness, wildness equals wilderness, wilderness equals Alaska, therefore bears equal Alaska and Alaska equals bears. Alaska Airlines' in-flight magazine explained it like this: "Land of Bears.

At home amid ice floes, crystal rivers or dark forests, bears make Alaska wild." Three separate photographs of brown bears illustrate the "Experience Alaska" page on the state's official travel site. Try googling any variety of "Alaska pristine wilderness bear" to see how tightly these ideas are knotted together. Sometimes the words *frontier* and *wilderness* are treated interchangeably, as in the National Geographic series *Bears of the Last Frontier*. Nevertheless, host Chris Morgan made the connection between bears and Alaska perfectly clear: "Bears conjure up a sense of wild. And for just about everyone, Alaska does the same thing." For a hunter whose online identity is ".338 mag," it's as simple as this: "The Brown/Grizzly bears of Alaska are what makes this the Last Frontier."

This idea was minted—literally—in 2007 with the unveiling of a commemorative quarter celebrating the fiftieth anniversary of statehood. Alaskans could vote informally for the image they preferred—a sled dog team, a gold panner, a polar bear, or a brown bear—but then-governor Sarah Palin made the final choice: the brown bear. "I think nothing could be more Alaskan," she said. These were wilderness words concealing frontier meanings. Two weeks after she announced the quarter's design, she introduced a bill to allow the aerial shooting of brown bears, wolves, and wolverines in areas where the Board of Game had approved predator control as a way to boost harvests of moose and caribou for hunters. (The bill died in committee.) The following year she sued the federal government for listing polar bears as "threatened" under the Endangered Species Act. Protecting polar bears, she said, would have a "significant adverse impact on Alaska by deterring activities such as commercial fisheries, oil and gas exploration and development, transportation, and tourism within and off-shore of Alaska." The frontier philosophy of territorial governor Thomas Riggs Jr. lives on.

When I first began thinking about bears, I harbored the misty-eyed notion that Alaskans were changing the way they thought about bears and therefore about wilderness. Maybe, I thought, we're figuring out that we can coexist with bears rather than subdue or eliminate or fear them. Two trends intrigued me. The first was a boom in bear viewing throughout coastal Alaska. Ever-growing numbers of visitors paid hundreds of dollars to watch bears they had no desire to shoot with anything but cameras. Surely people were finally realizing that bears aren't the crazed killers of hunting tales and folklore. The second important change occurred in my hometown, Juneau. As a newspaper reporter there, I had once watched a wildlife official shoot a black bear in the head because it had repeatedly raided garbage bins. Years of earnest discussion and halfhearted attempts to change the community's habits led only to more dead bears. Finally, a couple of admirable gadflies pestered municipal officials into an unusually prolonged bout of common sense, and the community worked out successful strategies to better protect black bears and people from each other.

I never imagined that Alaska would somehow develop a postfrontier, postcolonial enlightenment, but I failed to understand how powerful some old habits were. For decades, the public scrum over predator control focused on wolves, until it dawned on people that bears also eat moose and caribou calves before the youngsters grow into their legs and can outrace them. Now the wilderness is parceled into "predator control areas," where hunting ethics don't apply and the clock is rolled back to the good old territorial days, circa 1900, and you can shoot as many bears as you like, kill cubs and mothers, trap bears, and sell hides. This wildlife policy is pure frontierism—bears are eating moose and caribou that belong to people!—but it's a policy enshrined in a state statute and supported more by wishful thinking than solid science. "The current attitude toward grizzly bears in Alaska is akin to attitudes that existed 100 years ago in the 48 U.S. states and poses a threat to the largest population of grizzly bears in North America," blogged former Alaska bear biologist Sterling Miller in 2012. Miller is one of several retired wildlife biologists who have criticized the state's practices as complacent, applied as if there were an endless supply of bears emanating from some underground conduit secreted in the wilderness. In the meantime, although bears may be eating more moose and caribou calves in some places, the Board of Game hasn't eased off killing wolves.

Nobody can seriously argue that Alaska is in immediate danger of running out of bears. Hunters kill an average of 2,800 black bears and 1,450 brown bears each year. Most are killed for sport, some are eaten, and some are dispatched for predator control. A few score are shot by frightened home owners, struck by cars and trains, exterminated as nuisance bears, and wounded or killed by armed backcountry travelers. Still, it's impossible to ignore the gradual recapitulation of the West, the persistent attitude that bears are less a necessity than a dangerous nuisance or even a hindrance. "Alaska is being chopped, minced, and grated," wrote one of the state's first professional wildlife biologists in 1975. Frederick Dean pointed out that the range of grizzly bears in the Lower 48 had shriveled from a substantial territory to "remnant ribbons, islands and pockets" in just fifty years. He recognized the threats that would inevitably affect Alaska's bears, too: resource development and extraction, the expansion of towns and the establishment of new settlements in wildlife habitat, and the "skyrocketing" recreational use of the backcountry, a factor too easily overlooked by wilderness lovers. "Bears will be killed directly, and bear range will be challenged and converted," Dean wrote. "The pressure will come from the periphery and will also propagate in the manner of frost cracks, dissecting the broad expanses of bear range." More of us means less of everything else, so far. This is the modern methodology of a modern frontier: not wholesale slaughter, but attrition, inattention, ignorance, expediency, inevitability.

Some things have changed since the old frontier became the Last Frontier. Many people recognize the truth as stated by retired bear biologist John Hechtel: "The bottom line is we are competitors with large carnivores, and humans won the competition. Humans must now decide where and how to conserve carnivores and how much of their habitat we are willing to protect." This is true even in Alaska, where enormous blocks of national parklands and designated wilderness areas protect habitat and blunt some effects of human development. But as Dean pointed out decades ago, bears don't recognize park boundaries, and many preserves, refuges, and state parks allow hunting. Outside of predator control areas, wildlife officials manage most bear populations to maintain their numbers, or at least to prevent them from declining too precipitously, even if no one's sure what those numbers are. Many communities are working to reduce conflicts with bears, and maybe someday reducing the bear population won't be the solution by default. Some hunters are genuine conservationists who want to protect bears. Other people who enjoy hunting bears would never want to eradicate all of them: what would be the fun in that?

Yet there is something deeply emblematic in the way frontier thinking persists. Take the story of the "ghost grizzly" told by legendary trapper and predator killer Frank Glaser. He believed the enormous bear denned not far from his cabin, in what was then known as Mount McKinley National Park. In nine years, Glaser had spotted its tracks many times but had seen the bear itself just twice—once when he killed the bear's mate, and again when he crossed its trail one October. He shot the half-ton bear numerous times before it died. "It was my ghost grizzly all right, for

I never saw those big tracks heading cross-country again," he recalled. And then he added, "I missed him."

There you have the story of the frontier in two sentences—the impulse to kill a predator, because that's what you do with predators, followed by lasting regret at its absence, because that absence erodes the wilderness and your own idea of yourself. In this way, we turn the bear into a symbol for everything we've lost—or, rather, everything we've given away—in the landscape and in ourselves. "Why does our fascination with grizzlies continue?" asked *Outdoor Life* editor Todd Smith. "Perhaps it's because they remind us of that secret part of ourselves that longs to be something the grizzly bear has always been . . . indomitable, wild and free." It's quite a burden for one animal, forcing it to represent both wilderness and the loss of wilderness, the wildness of Mother Nature and the wildness of our hidden natures.

I'm not a scholar, historian, wildlife biologist, or politician. I'm merely an Alaskan who, like many others, has encountered bears in situations both frightening and mind-blowing. Yet how little I still know about this animal with which I share a home. As a backcountry traveler and a responsible citizen of the urban-wild interface, as it's so awkwardly called, I'm eager to understand bear behavior and human behavior around bears. I want to know what they eat, how they survive, how they shape the landscape itself.

Our way of thinking about bears interests me, too. We recruit them into a kind of metaphorical servitude, using them to represent how we regard the land, remember the past, imagine the future, see ourselves. In Alaska, people encounter bears in a multitude of situations, and how we create or react to those encounters tends to cast bears into preordained roles. What's so difficult is looking past labels and beyond images to see the living animal within the imagined bear, the individual bear rather than the caricatured species. "Most folks can never really see a bear for what it is—their view is obstructed by their vantage point," Alaska bear researcher Terry DeBruyn told his colleagues at a workshop on bear-people conflicts. "We must recognize that every second of every day can be a life or death matter to a bear. And, while that may sound trite, nothing I know of is truer."

At one time I imagined this book as an inquiry into relationships between people and bears in Alaska. The fundamental flaw in this idea is that a one-way transaction is not a relationship. We can get along without bears—billions of us do every day—and surely they'd be better off without us. Even if I mounted some novel argument on behalf of bears that had not already been made by people far smarter and more eloquent, I'd really be arguing only for myself. In *The Fallacy of Wildlife Conservation*, the brilliant naturalist John Livingston gently dismantles every rationale for championing conservation because all such assertions are inherently a matter of self-interest, no matter how well-intentioned or desirable the outcome. "Argument, it seems to me, is never going to help wildlife," he wrote. "It rarely has, and there is little to persuade me that it ever will, appreciably. . . . I believe that wildlife preservation is entirely dependent upon *individual human experience*."

So this is not a book about relationships with bears. It's a book about experiences with bears, as they are part of my world and part of me. Some experiences are wholly mine (though Livingston would say that gathering the experiences of others makes those mine, too). Some are from people with far greater knowledge and more intimate experience than I will ever have. And some of these experiences come from bears, because they experience us, too.

When I ask people why they like bears, they say the usual sorts of things—they're magnificent, they make me feel humble, they remind me of who we used to be, they're just plain cool—not because their ideas are trite but because words can't express these experiences very well. Words are beside the point, anyway. The presence of a wild bear, the experience of a wild bear, sizzles through the nerves, jolts the heart, startles the brain; it strips away that filter that separates us from the world and allows us to become part of that world more completely. My friend Jennifer said it first: I just want to know how to *be* around bears. Maybe it's more essential than that. Maybe we're drawn to bears because we just want to know how to be.

the unseen bear

In the clear light of a June morning, we walked like bears toward a gathering of bears on a skinny trail made by bears, and with every step we looked and listened for bears. Derek Stonorov led the way, ambling beside the shallow creek that spills into Chenik Lagoon two miles away. A golden-crowned sparrow pierced the air with a three-note descant. Sometimes we tunneled through wiry alders and grass so dense that our feet had to feel their way along a muddy path we couldn't see. Our rain pants gathered dew as they whisked through the brush. Now and then Derek clapped his hands, calling out an amiable "Hey, bear. Ho, bear."

Walking like a bear was the first slow thing I'd seen Derek do since the previous evening, when my friend Nora Gruner and I arrived at his bear-viewing camp at Chenik Lake on the Alaska Peninsula. Derek is in his early sixties, one of those good-looking bearded guys who is rarely seen without a ball cap. As our floatplane chugged to shore, he toted gear down to the beach for two professional photographers who would be leaving on the return flight. They'd been at the camp for two weeks, which made me envious in an unseemly way. Nora and I joined the human chain to help unload supplies, and then we delivered pizza and beer to the Weir Boys. That's what Derek called the pair of scruffy fisheries students who lived in a lakeside shack all summer and counted migrating salmon when they weren't playing poker or fixing the weir because some bear had busted it. After we ate, we pitched our tent in a fragrant meadow purpled with iris. Derek showed us how to switch on the waist-high electric fence that would discourage curious bears. Meanwhile, trying to decide whether we should go look for bears right then or wait until morning, we all collapsed into sleep.

Derek talks like a fast river, stories and asides rushing over one another, an idea sometimes eddying out before swirling back into the torrent. From previous conversations, I knew my notes would consist mostly of scribbled half sentences that lurched from topic to topic as my pen struggled to keep up. So I'd learned to wave a recorder near his face to capture whatever he said that was interesting or funny, which is almost everything. But this morning, his natural urgency contained itself as we hiked toward the lagoon. He was open to the world, and so the world seemed to open before him.

Walking like a bear does not mean swaggering like a bully or creeping about like a cat burglar. It means adopting an attentive, deliberate gait. It means paying attention—hallooing before rounding a blind corner, listening for unusual sounds like a cough or a chuff, watching for movement that may or may not be wind swishing through leaves. Most important, it means avoiding a disrespectful pace that might cause you to accidentally breach that invisible barrier of personal space that surrounds every bear. Bears don't rush around, Derek said, because they don't like surprising other bears either. "I try to go through my entire day never scaring a bear," he said. Most of us who poke around the backcountry clap our hands and holler a lot because we try to go through an entire day never being scared by a bear. But Derek doesn't like to frighten bears for reasons beyond personal safety. If you walk slowly, he told us, you'll have more time to recognize that humming sound in the brush as the distinctive purr of cubs suckling their mother. "It's probably not a good idea to stumble upon a mother nursing her cubs," Derek explained, "because you would interrupt the nursing session and she would probably be completely upset and run away."

In bear country, it's hard for the mind not to regard the body as Spam with legs, especially on the Alaska Peninsula, home to one of the world's densest brown bear populations. So when Derek said this, I couldn't help but suspect that what he really meant was, "It's probably not a good idea to stumble upon a mother nursing her cubs because you would interrupt the nursing session and she would probably be completely upset and run toward you, attack you, kill you, and eat you." But that was never what Derek meant. "Any fool can scare a bear," he liked to say, paraphrasing John Muir's admonition about cutting down trees. "It's real easy to run bears off. They're timid animals. It takes all their courage to come up and look at you. Lots and lots of people that I take out do not have a clue that the bears are not comfortable around us."

Many times I've seen bears bolt like nervous poultry from people, from other bears, even from me. It took a moment to absorb the idea that we should avoid surprising bears not only because the bears might react poorly toward us but also because it's wrong to blunder around alarming wild animals who are just trying to make an honest living. Most people find it hard to ignore the amygdala's primal assumption that a creature that *can* kill you *will* kill you, so you'd best run away or maybe even attack first—the old fight-or-flight strategy that has served the human race so well. The cerebrum, more modern and measured in its responses, doesn't always help matters. It is disturbingly efficient at digging through its extensive files and calling up every mauling story you have ever heard or read.

"People are terrified of bears," veteran bear-watching guide Ken Day told me. "And it's just because we've all been brought up to say that they're mad, blood-thirsty, vicious killers. And they're not." He and his wife, Chris, are Derek's friends, and they have spent almost thirty summers in close quarters with bears. That kind of familiarity gives Ken the authority to say, "They're very gentle, quiet, accepting, respectful animals. And if you can return the same to them, you can get along fine with them."

Most people never experience live bears outside of a zoo, so Ken's characterization bucks a collective judgment based on scary movies and sensational headlines. There's no denying that, on rare occasions, bears do attack and even kill people, almost always because they've been surprised or feel threatened. Yet it's nearly impossible to frame the risk of a bear mauling rationally, no matter how many statistics you trot out: Faulty Christmas lights kill more people each year than bears do. Moose harm more Alaskans than bears do. "Every year more people are injured by toilets than they are injured by bears," the National Park Service assures us.

Your amygdala knows better: Christmas lights, moose, and toilets don't have claws and incisors, and they don't eat your flesh. "Among the earliest forms of human self-awareness was the awareness of being meat," writes David Quammen in *Monster of God*, his study of man-eating predators. Who wants to be meat? That's a fear we haven't had much time to shed, evolutionarily speaking. Nor does technology help, when news of any bear incident spreads the alarm instantaneously to millions of meat-people. Once, a young man in upstate New York asked me, "Which are more vicious, brown bears or grizzly bears?" It's easy enough to explain that the two bears are actually one species, *Ursus arctos*, but how to begin rescuing the reputation of bears?

So indelible are the accounts of grizzly bears supplied by Lewis and Clark's Corps of Discovery Expedition that after two centuries we still haven't shaken off their thrilling effect. "They have a gospel-like value in the popular bear lore," observes Paul Schullery, a historian and former ranger with the National Park Service. Members of the expedition were not the first to see or mention grizzlies in North America, but their 1804–1806 journals recorded the first anatomical details of what they usually called the "white bear" or some version of "grizly." Meriwether Lewis speculated that all the white, red, black, brown, and grizzly bears were the same species. They penned other descriptions too, including "monster," "monstrous," "ferocious," and "a bear of the large vicious species."

The gospel of Lewis and Clark captured the tension between the awe and the fear the grizzly evoked—particularly a wounded one. "The wonderful power of life which these animals possess renders them dreadful," observed Lewis. Who wouldn't be impressed, as Lewis was, when two members of the expedition killed the largest bear they had seen to date: "it was a most tremendious looking anamal, and extreemly hard to kill notwithstanding he had five balls through his lungs and five others in various parts he swam more than half the distance across the river to a sandbar & it was at least twenty minutes before he died; he did not attempt to attact, but fled and made the most tremendous roaring from the moment he was shot." The durability of grizzlies intimidated the men, even when the men were intimidating the bears. Lewis wrote this account of the first fellow in the expedition to spot a grizzly: "he wounded him, but being alarmed at the formidable appearance of the bear he left his tomahalk and gun; but shortly after returned and found that the bear had taken the oposit rout." (Later that day the same man shot a buffalo that did chase him, forcing him to hide in a small ravine.) The more dramatic episodes involved lots of bullets and fleeing and close calls, not to mention numerous wounded bears and forty-three dead ones, according to biologist Raymond Darwin Burroughs in *The Natural History of the Lewis and Clark Expedition*.

When well-known bear biologist Barrie Gilbert examined the journals' accounts of thirty-seven bear encounters, he concluded that the men were the aggressors in most cases, the bears in none. What some historians and scholars have misinterpreted as attacks are better characterized as defensive behavior, he observed during a presentation at the 2002 International Bear Association conference. It seems easy enough to recognize the instigator when, for example, the journals describe six men sneaking up on a bear and plugging it with four bullets. Instantly, the "monster" gave chase, forcing two men to throw themselves into the river before the last of eight bullets stopped it. "Even when it's written in very plain English, we get it altogether wrong," Gilbert told his colleagues.

The expedition's published journals were "so widely read in early America that they became a kind of nineteenth-century guidebook for how to think about the West and its inhabitants," writes historian Dan Flores. In the absence of any other information, the journals supplied many naturalists and explorers with an exciting and thoroughly misguided template for thinking about grizzlies. After reading them, New York governor De Witt Clinton speechified about the "ferocious tyrant of the American woods." The expedition's experiences led writer Henry Marie Brackenridge to conclude about the grizzly, "He is the enemy of man; and literally thirsts for human blood." (Speaking of bloodthirsty, while journeying up the Missouri River, Brackenridge and his party chopped down a tree providing refuge to a black bear and her three cubs, then used an axe to kill "Madam Cuff" and, presumably, her offspring.) Naturalist George Ord quoted Brackenridge's description in the 1815 edition of Guthrie's Geography and assigned the scientific name that stuck: Ursus arctos horribilis.

Most biologists estimate that at least 50,000 grizzlies inhabited the American West before the frontier opened. Traps, guns, poison, and the relentless appropriation of habitat had so efficiently eliminated the bears that a century after Lewis and Clark gazed on the Pacific, zoologist William Hornaday wrote that sportsmen had largely given up hunting grizzlies outside of Yellowstone National Park and the Bitterroot Mountains because so few remained. (This is also why hunters began supporting bear protection in Alaska—so there would be bears to kill somewhere.) Four decades of hard work by government agencies and bear advocates nearly doubled the grizzly population south of Canada to between 1,400 and 1,700 animals. Keep in mind that since 1970, the human population in the Greater Yellowstone ecosystem has ballooned by more than 60 percent.

As grizzlies slowly return to parts of the West, so does fear. In 2005

CBS News sent reporter Lesley Stahl to interview folks about the number of grizzly bears expanding from Yellowstone National Park into neighboring communities. "It's one thing to appreciate and protect the grizzly bear as an American icon," the program began. "It's another thing when a giant brown predator with those big teeth and those big claws shows up in your backyard looking for a snack."

A woman whose family had relocated from California to Wapiti, Wyoming, told Stahl, "My worst fear would be that—to see a bear running away with my little Claire in his mouth."

"Telling you that they haven't killed anybody in these kinds of communities is not comforting enough?" Stahl asked.

"Not when you hear about people getting their scalps sewed back on, and things like that," replied the woman. Her family had moved to downtown Cody after bears chewed on their hot tub, tangled with the barbecue, and tore siding off the house.

A local rancher asked, "Why do I have to live with them in the constant fear that they might grab one of my kids or myself or my wife and kill them?" Americans have answered that question once before: you don't—if you kill most of them first.

Meanwhile, local wildlife officials try to educate home owners about the importance of reducing food sources that draw bears into neighborhoods—garbage, fruit trees, birdseed, and chicken coops. And though some things have changed in the West, others haven't. A 2010 report, "Hazards Affecting Bear Survival in the Greater Yellowstone Ecosystem," synthesized more than two decades of data into a scientifically proven, historically documented, predictably inevitable truth: "Humans are the primary agent of death in grizzly bears."

One lovely thing about bear country is that it's wonderful people country, too. Derek led us from the brush across a plateau of plush tundra that opened beneath green hills roller-coastering against the sky. We paused to study twisted wolf scat and strip off rain gear before crossing the creek and climbing onto the grassy bluff overlooking the tidal flats of Chenik Lagoon. There we dropped our packs and settled ourselves above the creek's south bank. The bears know they have exclusive rights to the opposite bank, though many don't hesitate to use the peopled side whenever they wish.

Sunlight dazzled the landscape into blinding shards of blues and greens. The tide was out, and two seiners floated at the lagoon's entrance, waiting for official word to begin fishing for sockeye salmon. Beyond them, the living volcano of Mount Augustine smoldered on its island like a sleepy old uncle puffing on a half-lit pipe. All these things I noticed later. Below the bluff three golden bears nosed along the shoreline. A fourth bear plodded across the mudflats.

The sight of bears moving through the landscape always stirs something primal in me, as if ancient synapses start firing anew, waking the part of the brain that was accustomed to inhabiting a world where large animals moved around freely. Nora, a professional photographer, had never been around bears before. She kept lowering her camera so she could verify with her own eyes what the lens reported. These bears were waiting for the flood tide to sluice salmon into the lagoon. There, the fish would mill at the creek mouth before sprinting over the mild falls, bound for Chenik Lake. The salmon tend to blast up the creek in thick pulses—safety in numbers, and all that. Their mission is to spawn and die (and, therefore, to avoid dying before they spawn). The bears' mission is to bulk up before denning for winter, to stuff themselves with fatty eggs and brains and firm, red flesh.

Derek identified the trio nosing along the beach as Solstice and her offspring. He and the Days had named the bear so they could share information about her from season to season. The cubs were two and a half years old and nearly as large as their mother. "Solstice is still nursing these big lugs," Derek said fondly. "She looks sort of old. About half the time she doesn't know what she's doing. She just sort of follows her cubs around." She must be doing something right, though. Two subadults who appeared later that day were also Solstice's offspring, Spanky and Scrappy. In some parts of Southwest Alaska, about 70 percent of cubs die before they're weaned. If Solstice's cubs survived until next summer, she would push them out on their own, leaving her free to mate again.

As the tide eased in and salmon pooled near the falls, several other bears emerged from the alders and descended the bluffs to loiter beside the stream. The appearance of each animal rippled through the group of bears in a subtle and constant refinement of social standing. They took note of one another, paused to read the situation, moved away, or ignored new bears, based on some mutual understanding. "My guess is all these bears know each other and there's a discernible hierarchy," Derek said. Most were young subadults or females with cubs. Big males tend to feed two coves south at McNeil River State Game Sanctuary, where the chum salmon run is bigger, the falls mightier, and the river-banks more expansive. The lone male commonly seen feeding at Chenik Lagoon—Buddy, the guides called him—didn't cause trouble for people or for other bears. He was solid but lithe, not like those massive, droopy-lipped older males that drag their bellies and lumber around like bearosaurs upon the earth. Still, when Buddy ambled down to the creek in the early afternoon, some bears evaporated into the brush, and others shifted out of his way. It reminded me of a junior high lunchroom when that one kid showed up and everyone else suddenly found something better to do.

It was harder to gauge the effect of our presence on the animals. Many bears on the Katmai coast and elsewhere have grown accustomed to sharing rivers and coastlines with fishermen, photographers, and bear watchers, especially when people follow routines, keep quiet, move slowly. People say bears are unpredictable, but really we're the ones liable to do something wacky with no warning. Responsible bear-viewing guides make sure their groups arrive and leave at about the same time each day and sit in the same places so the bears know what to expect. So mannerly is this understanding that you can eat your lunch without fear while watching the bears eat theirs. Scientists describe this neutral response as *habituation*, meaning the bears don't overtly react to humans either positively (by shaking us down for food rewards, like Yogi Bear) or negatively (by charging us or fleeing). Habituation doesn't mean they're tame; it means that their response to a repeated stimulus diminishes. Recent research suggests that because coastal brown bears learn to tolerate other bears nearby, often fishing within a few feet of one another, they find it possible to tolerate people, too.

Just because the bears at Chenik Lagoon didn't disappear immediately doesn't mean they didn't notice us or change their behavior, perhaps imperceptibly. Some bears might not emerge to feed until the humans departed. Others might leave early. "All the signals they put off to us, sometimes they're really slight," Derek said. In the 1970s he wrote a master's thesis identifying about forty different visual signals used by McNeil River bears to communicate with one another, signals that offer people clues about how to behave around bears. Most of this repertoire functions to avoid conflict. Bears can't afford to waste valuable chow time fighting among themselves. Like dogs, they display dominance and subordination through the way they stand, the position of their ears, the movement of their mouths, and the sounds they utter. It's possible that bears can intuit human body language quickly because their survival depends on reading other bears. This is one reason a person's physical response during a bear encounter is so important. Holding your ground confidently signals *Don't mess with me, pal.* Running away suggests *Why not chase me? I might be good to eat.*

"You just have to really look at what they're doing," Derek said. "But the cool thing is, if you go about doing everything right, then they will come close to us and will go about leading their lives. When we watch bears, I think the best thing about it is that we want to watch bears being bears. We don't want to watch bears reacting to the people in the group or to us being there, although we obviously are going to have an influence on them. But it's fun to watch them playing together or nursing their cubs or catching fish or grazing. That's what everybody really wants to see."

Experienced guides like Stonorov and the Days can distinguish curiosity from a dominance display. They know when to stop moving because a bear is nervous or uncertain and when it's unwise to let a bear push you around. Twice in the past four days, young bears had "put little rushes" on Derek and the two professional photographers who had just left. The bears were not exactly aggressive, but more like blustery teenagers testing their own powers. Such behavior doesn't worry Derek. Three or four people will nearly always out-intimidate a bear simply by standing their ground. A single person can do that, too. Derek doesn't carry a gun or even bear spray, a highly effective deterrent that blasts a burning dose of aerosolized capsaicin, the substance that makes peppers hot. "It's not brains in a can," he explained, a quote from Yellowstone researcher Stephen French that's become a credo among bear experts. He doesn't oppose defensive measures; he just doesn't need them. The electric fence keeps nosey parkers out of camp while he's gone, and his experience and awareness keep him sharp while he's in the backcountry.

"I'm as careful as I can be," he said. "And nobody I know that has half a brain has ever had problems with a bear." (He meant careless people who should know better, not those who find themselves in bad situations through no fault of their own.)

Bears don't stress him out, but people can, as we saw that afternoon when a floatplane dropped off five clients on a day trip from Homer, Derek's hometown on the other side of Cook Inlet. By the time Derek had helped a rickety older man up the bluffs, settled everybody beside the creek to eat lunch, answered a multitude of questions, explained several times to an overamped little boy the virtues of being quiet around bears, and finally farewelled them onto their return flight to Homer, he was so drained that he sprawled in the warm grass to nap, arms outflung and his cap covering his face.

While he dozed, Nora returned from answering nature's call and whispered, "There's a big bear coming!" Derek didn't wake. A few moments later, Buddy paced toward us on the trail that edges the bluff and drops into the creek. Nora and I kneeled, and I began snapping photographs. Then I stopped so I could see him better. He was so close that every picture was out of focus anyway. We rocked back on our heels as the bear passed within a few yards, never sparing us a direct glance and yet somehow taut with the knowledge of our presence, as we were with his.

I wanted to press a pause button so I could study every inch of him, understand the mechanics of that muscular stride, discover whatever his eyes might reveal, if anything. But the bear walked past, intent on his destination, willing to risk that moment of shared existence not because he wanted to but because he had come to understand something about the way people behave. Later it came to me that Derek had been teaching us not only a different way of thinking about bears but also a different way of being human.

People have been thinking about bears for a long time, so long that we judge what it means to be human by the presence of bears. Archaeologists investigating France's Régourdou Cave in the 1960s found what Eugène Bonifay called an "ensemble sepulchral": the skull and arm bones of a brown bear buried beneath a stone slab and beside the entombed remains of a Neanderthal. Among other bear bones found at the site were two tibias arranged at the foot of the Neanderthal skeleton. "Régourdou constitutes a convincing case for some kind of bear-centered animal cult some 60,000–70,000 years ago," concludes archaeologist Brian Hayden in his book *Shamans, Sorcerers, and Saints*. Not everyone agrees, but whether such interpretations are correct is beside the point. Modern human brains see hominin and ursine bones together and immediately start wondering whether this indicates ritual or supernatural thinking, whether our ancient kin also thought about the afterlife. Because we regard bears as somehow special, we assume Neanderthals did, too.

This kind of attention to bears appears in other forms, other places, other times, and we tease ourselves with provocative possibilities. In Chauvet Cave, where a visual bestiary represents the oldest known Paleolithic rock art, images of cave bears shimmer on the walls in urgent strokes of red pigment, the ancient color of blood and magic. Scattered throughout the chambers are what remains of actual cave bears—claw marks scoring the walls, paw prints impressed in the soft floor, and the bones and skulls of at least 190 animals that once hibernated there. Scientists sequencing ancient DNA from these *Ursus spelaeus* bones helped confirm that many paintings are at least 35,000 years old. But what seizes the imagination is a single massive bear skull resting on a large limestone block, hollow eyes staring into the darkness. Thanks to Werner Herzog's 2010 documentary *Cave of Forgotten Dreams*, you can judge whether the skull's position is an accident of nature or a human gesture that recognizes the sacred, as Herzog suggests: "The strongest hint of something spiritual, some religious ceremony in the cave, is this bear skull. It has been placed dead center on a rock resembling an altar. The staging seems deliberate."

Few animals have roamed through our psyches as intimately or as continuously as bears. Even as scientists rummage through our bones and genomes trying to sort out our origins, they're doing the same for bears. Across 5 million years, evolution has whittled the Ursidae family into eight modern species—brown bears, American black bears, Asiatic black bears, sun bears, Andean spectacled bears, sloth bears, polar bears, and giant pandas. Of these, the brown bear's long lope through time most resembles our own journey through the world. *Ursus arctos* likely appeared in Asia about a half million years ago, eventually inhabiting China, Russia, Japan, Europe, the Middle East, North Africa, and, about 70,000 years ago, North America.

As intelligent generalists and flexible omnivores, brown bears and humans alike dodged the tumultuous grind of the Pleistocene to join the Holocene about 10,000 years ago, outsurviving their competitors the cave bear, the giant short-faced bear, the Neanderthal, and a newly identified human relative, the Denisovan. The parallel passages of bear and human across space and time are even now altering the stories we tell ourselves about the peopling of the New World. Limestone caves hollowing the southernmost islands of Southeast Alaska have yielded the remains of a 10,300-year-old young male whose bones reveal the maritime nature of his short life. Nearby, natural catacombs shelter fossilized brown and black bear bones whose ages span the past 50,000 years.

Their existence suggests that the northwest coast may not have been completely locked in ice during the last spasm of the Pleistocene.

The significance is this: recent archaeological discoveries along the coastlines of North and South America, coupled with advances in geology, glaciology, maritime archaeology, and especially molecular genetics, are radically changing our notions of who settled the Western Hemisphere, when they came, and how they arrived. The prevailing theory that mammoth hunters marched across the Bering land bridge, through a gap in the continental ice sheets, and into the great Pleistocene plains of North America (think *National Geographic*) is being fractured by evidence that the first immigrants actually paddled down the Pacific coast before the ice sheets had fully retreated. One reason this coastal migration seems more likely is that those ancient island bears apparently outlasted the Ice Age in refugia along Alaska's southeasterly rim. It's as true now as it was 10,000, 12,000, even 13,000 years ago: wherever bears live, people can, too.

Because of their range and flexibility, some consider brown bears one of the most successful land mammals that ever lived. Even now, a few brown bears persist in surprising nooks of the Old World—Greece, Pakistan, Romania, Mongolia, Hokkaido, Iraq, and Italy among them. But culturally—and these days, geographically—brown bears are mostly a creature of northern realms in Eurasia and North America. "Not surprisingly, human societies in the boreal zone apparently very early developed the idea that the bear is actually a human, clad in bearskin," wrote Juha Janhunen in a survey of bear myths in Northeast Asia. That disconcertingly familiar shape is only one reason bears are the most readily anthropomorphized of all boreal animals, observed A. Irving Hallowell in his seminal study of how northern indigenous peoples regarded bears. "Bears do, first of all, seem to possess sagacious qualities," he wrote. We can't help but see ourselves in the way they walk on hind legs, leave footprints that resemble ours, prop themselves against trees, and eat—and compete for—the same foods we do.

At a time when the distinction between bear and human was malleable, when the world was not yet divided between the everyday and the divine, bears mediated between the human and nonhuman worlds, bridging the pitilessness of our corporeal existence and our perpetual reach for the divine, according to Alaska anthropologist Lydia Black. Examples of this to-and-fro between the domains of persons and nonhuman persons are legion. The Saami people of northern Sweden interred bears in graves, sometimes hiding them beneath cairns or arranging their bones in circles and rays. In ancient China women shrugged themselves into bearskins, the better to speak as oracles. The Ainu of Hokkaido and Sakhalin and the Siberian Ket raised cubs in their homes for a year or more, feeding them and sometimes even suckling them, before they killed the beloved animal in the joyful, mournful ceremony of the Bear Festival. By bestowing the slain bear's soul with gifts and honor, they hoped to be rewarded later with meat and fur.

Hallowell's survey of customs and beliefs led him to conclude that "no other animal was found to attain such universal prominence as the bear, nor to have associated with it, over such a wide geographical area, such a large series of customs." So similar were the ways Native American and Eurasian peoples hunted and killed bears, spoke about them, and treated them after death that Hallowell wondered whether these ideas had developed on each continent separately but in parallel or whether they shared a common source. He suspected the latter. "In short, I think it more than likely that a bear cult was one of the characteristic features of an ancient Boreal culture, Old World in origin and closely associated with the pursuit of the reindeer," he wrote.

Not every culture, tribe, or clan in the Old World or the New regarded bears with the same degree of veneration, but bears actual and symbolic have participated in almost every human endeavor: hunting, dancing, art making, dreaming, healing, storytelling, soothsaying, eating, praying, birthing, dying—so many that Paul Shepard and Barry Sanders wrote *The Sacred Paw* to describe these pervasive ties. Today, Alaska Native peoples are among the last to still recognize the old, complicated relationships between people and bears. Specific practices have differed among the major cultural groups, but the importance of treating bears properly before a hunt and after death has lingered.

Speaking carefully to or about bears to avoid giving offense remains important to some Native people. Elders throughout the North understand that bears really do not like being laughed at or mocked, and there are plenty of sorry tales about a boastful or indiscreet hunter who was later mauled. Researchers interested in learning how the Inupiat of Northwest Alaska think about bears discovered that even mentioning the name, *aklaq*, made villagers uneasy: "After describing the study, the researchers subsequently referred to the brown bear as 'that animal' to ease people's discomfort." Tlingits sometimes referred to bears as Big Ears, The Strong One, The One Going Around in the Woods, My

Brother-in-Law, or Town Person, according to anthropologist Thomas Thornton. Koyukon Athabascans, who are skilled hunters of black bears, almost never use their name, sis; instead, they use phrases describing a type of bear. For example, "That Which Went Away" refers to a one- or two-year-old bear, and women call bears hulzinh, or "black place."

This practice is nearly as old as language itself. In the unwritten ancestral language known as Proto-Indo-European, the root word for bear spawned arktos in Greek, ursus in Latin, and even arth in Welsh, according to the Encyclopedia of Indo-European Culture. Think of Arthur, the once and future king, or Saint Ursula, martyred with 11,000 virgins. However, northern cultures acknowledged the bear's power by avoiding its true name. Thus, the Germanic circumlocution beron, or "the brown one," eventually produced bear, bär, bruin, björn, bero, and Berne. Bears shadow our very words.

Today, the Tlingits of Southeast Alaska maintain a formal kinship with brown bears through their social structure. The bear is brother to those of the Eagle-Wolf moiety and brother-in-law to members of the Raven moiety, Thornton noted, and the bear crests displayed by the Teikweidee and Kaagwaantaan clans identify a specific historical relationship described in clan stories. Writer Ernestine Hayes, a Kaagwaantaan woman, learned from her grandmother that the wind spoke to her, spiders talked to her, and the bear was her cousin. These weren't fancies; they were implicit connections with a world that was always aware of her. "If I saw a bear, I would just tell him who I was, the way I think you're supposed to," she explained to me. "Because even though he's aware of you, it's just like any respect, just like a person, you introduce yourself. I would introduce myself. And cite how we're related, which is what Native people do. 'How do you do, who's your mother?' Or 'What clan are you with? Who are you related to? Are we related in some way?' We do the same thing with a bear."

Sharing a cosmos with bears, shaping your thoughts and words and deeds because of bears, is a worldview with resonances and meanings that are beyond the ken of most of us. We can gaze across the broad savannah of history and understand intuitively how the bear's magical ability to burrow into the ground and emerge each spring came to represent so many big ideas: the changing seasons, the portal from death to life, the mysteries of birth and resurrection, the watchfulness of the

Lord of the Animals. We continue to recruit and respond to bears in stories, folklore, entertainment, and art. But what's missing from contemporary understanding is the dimension that Hallowell recognized in indigenous cultures nearly two decades after his original study of people and bears: "Man and animals, instead of being separate categories of being, are deeply rooted in a world of nature that is unified."

Over and over, Derek startled me into recognizing my own stubborn preconceptions, those lazy assumptions about what bears are and what they do and what it all means. He'd say things like, "When somebody tells me that bears are solitary, I never even bother to finish the conversation or try to be polite to them or read the rest of the article or the book. Because bears are not solitary. They're not social like lions or dogs. They're something else. They're bears."

I remembered four splendid days I'd spent one summer at McNeil River State Game Sanctuary, eight miles south of Chenik Lagoon. There, all around our tiny band of people, bears fished and fought and shepherded their cubs carefully through the crowd of big males. They greeted one another, beat up on one another, and ignored one another. They walked within ten feet of us, occasionally plopping down nearby for a rest. Once a pair of bears coupled fifteen feet away, which was a little embarrassing. Sometimes two dozen bears clustered around the falls, outnumbering the people two to one, yet never bothering to do the math. And recalling that time, I thought, *Of course bears aren't solitary animals. Where did I get that stupid idea?* Derek would describe the highly individual nature of bears, and he'd joke, "I'm sure if you stayed out here for a week you'd probably see a bear stand on its head. Whether it can stand on its head, I'm not sure. I have seen them do somersaults." How fervently I wished to see a bear do a headstand—or at the very least, a somersault.

Now and then he delivered some amazing fact or anecdote to illustrate the expansive range of bear behavior: a female bear at Hallo Bay who became expert at swimming to a nearby island and eating puffins, or the bear who miscalculated the distance between its snout and Ken Day's outstretched hand, making Ken maybe the only person in the world who has poked a finger into a bear's nostril and lived (no harm done to either the surprised bear or Ken). Or there was the time Derek saw a big old male, weighing maybe 1,200 pounds, lying submissively on its back while a young bear playfully worried its throat, like two dogs fooling around, which made him wonder, *How did that subadult ever get close enough to the big male to start playing?*

I'd try to memorize these morsels so I could astound other people with my secondhand knowledge. "Hey," I'd say casually, "did you know bears eat puffins? Rassle like dogs? Flip somersaults?" But to Derek, who spends thirty-five or forty days in the field each summer gathering firsthand experience, these were not party stories but bits of information that illuminate a larger truth: nobody really understands bears completely. "I don't know everything about them," he said. "Every day I spend with bears I learn something new. There's just so much—they've got so many secrets that I haven't been able to figure out." And I'd think, *He's been doing this for forty-five years and he's still learning about bears?* It made me want to clear my calendar for the next fifty.

Barrie Gilbert lost an eye after being mauled by a Yellowstone bear in 1977, so it seems counterintuitive that he has spent most of his career trying to recalibrate our thinking about bears. Even as he was being medevaced to a hospital, according to newspaper reports, he told a paramedic he didn't want anyone to kill the bear because the incident had been an accident, probably triggered when he and his field assistant surprised what may have been a female with cubs. "I guess I constantly attempt to stop them from being demonized," he said during a presentation to other bear biologists.

He's picked an endless battle. "Articles that Demonize Bears" is exactly how researchers at the North American Bear Center described the 1998 centennial edition of *Outdoor Life*. The cover illustration depicts a helpless, agonized outdoorsman dangling from the jaws of a maddened brown bear. The headline: "Killer Bears: 100 Years of Wild Adventures." In 2011 the magazine's website posted a gallery of "The 30 Best *Outdoor Life* Bear Attack Covers of All Time." A grizzly had recently mauled a Nome hunter who was following it by snowmachine (the Alaskan term for a snowmobile), leading the magazine to conclude that "with a growing grizzly bear population in the West and ever-shrinking wilderness areas, most bear experts expect to see a rise in grizzly attacks this summer and fall." (No experts were cited.)

If we can't locate demon bears, we'll invent them. A 2007 episode of the Discovery Channel's reality series *Man vs. Wild* featured Edward "Bear" Grylls pitching camp somewhere in the Rockies and informing viewers that the nearby woods were "packed with grizzly bears." That night he fled his shelter after hearing something and filming a dark shape moving around camp. The *Daily Mail* later reported that the producers had scripted the scene beforehand and used a crewmember in a bear costume when they couldn't find a tame bear to play the role of scary beast. The Discovery Channel insisted that the bear costume—of which there were photographs—was merely a prank. Also, that dead badger Grylls cooked and ate? It was really a steak tucked inside a badger skin. Welcome to reality TV.

Even real bears transmogrify into monsters by the time we get through with them. In 2001, e-mails about the death of a man-eating Alaska bear weighing 1,600 or even 1,800 pounds began circling the globe. They still are. Most versions claim that a Forest Service employee was out deer hunting when he was charged by a ludicrously huge brown bear from about fifty yards. "The guy unloaded a 7mm Mag Semi-auto into the bear and it dropped a few feet from him," reported the e-mail, reading much like a tale told by a bar braggart. "The thing was still alive so he reloaded and capped it in the head. It was over one thousand six hundred pounds, 12′ 6″ high at the shoulder. . . . It's a world record. The bear had killed a couple of other people. Of course, the game department did not let him keep it. . . . Think about it. This thing on it's [sic] hind legs could walk up to the average single story house and could look on the roof at eye level."

This breathless message often includes photographs, sometimes accompanied by a warning guaranteed to make you look: "Do not view these photos if you get queasy at the sight of blood and bodies. This is not an 'urban legend.' REAL life, REAL danger, WILD ALASKA." One shows a young man posing with a bear carcass so enormous that a paw nearly spans the width of the hunter's chest. These photographs are real, despite the exaggerated perspective commonly employed in trophy pictures. But sometimes the message includes a gruesome picture of a dead person with a leg gnawed to the bone. These are the remains of the "unlucky nature buff" found in the bear's gut, according to the hoaxer. Most people don't notice the palm fronds in the background; in a National Geographic special *Search for the Ultimate Bear*, bear expert Tom Smith suggests that this particular nature buff was more likely killed by a tiger. Never mind that, though. The tall tale elicits responses like this one posted to a website: "I am happy that guy took that terrorist bear out. Usually they are afraid of humans. The ones in the wild in CA (except Yosemite) usually leave you alone. But I had heard that those Alaskan Grizzlies were vicious." Nobody pointed out that the only grizzly to show its face in California since 1922 has been the one jazzing up the state flag.

The facts will never defeat this splendid mythical bear: Ted Winnen, a twenty-two-year-old airman stationed at Eielson Air Force Base near Fairbanks, shot the bear in October 2001 while hunting deer on Hinchinbrook Island in Prince William Sound. The bear was seeking salmon in a nearby creek and wandered within ten yards of the hunter and his partner, but it's not clear whether it ever saw them, Winnen told an Anchorage news reporter a few months later. He took careful aim and shot it several times, dropping it instantly. Though no world record, the bear was indeed large, measuring over ten feet from nose to tail and weighing between 1,000 and 1,200 pounds.

The desire to reincarnate a bear that wasn't bothering anybody into a vicious man-killer reveals how hard it is to relinquish our deepest fears. Once I got into an argument with a tourist who was reading a printout of this well-traveled e-mail tacked to a bulletin board in the tiny community of McCarthy. When I told her the story had been debunked, she simply refused to believe me. She could not surrender that gigantic monster to truth. As late as 2006, an outdoor correspondent for the *Oklahoma Sun* published the urban legend as news, prompting another round of excited Internet postings from the gullible, followed by letters to the editor from beleaguered wildlife officials in Alaska and elsewhere. "I have been trying to kill this urban myth since early 2002, and I receive both phone calls and e-mails almost daily from individuals and media from all over the world about this story," wrote Ray Massey, an assistant director in the US Forest Service's Alaska region.

Good luck, Mr. Massey. We will never turn our gaze away from the "terrible teeth" of predators that still haunt our monkey dreams, noted the late Paul Shepard, a profound thinker about nature and culture. "Images of the great bear remind us that the ecological contract, celebrated in ceremonial feasts, includes the possibility of being eaten," he added. We broke that contract long ago, but our fears remain so embedded—so treasured—that we will conjure them from the bloody carcass of some poor old bear hoping for a few more meals before winter.

The Hinchinbrook bear's next appearance as a taxidermy mount remained truer to reality. The National Geographic special filmed the bear in Winnen's house, where it stood on four feet with mouth closed and a mild expression on its face. Somehow it avoided being molded into a crazed beast slavering for human flesh, but its imaginary doppelganger will live forever on the World Wide Web and in our imaginations.

When Derek was an undergraduate at Goddard College, he spent two summers and falls studying bears at Becharof Lake on the Alaska Peninsula with his wife, Molly. He'd never seen a brown bear before. "I didn't know what was going to happen if I just sat down and watched them," he said. This is what happened: the bears got used to him, walked up and looked at him, fished near him. His undergraduate thesis earned him a graduate assistantship with Allen Stokes at Utah State University. Together they started bear projects that would involve several students in Alaska research. He and Stokes spent the summer of 1970 observing bears at the McNeil River falls, where up to thirty or more bears (even higher numbers in recent years) gathered each day in late July to eat salmon. They wanted to figure out how bears create a social structure that allows them to share resources just when each individual needs to pack on as much weight as possible. Researchers are still trying to understand this.

Since then, Derek has worked at McNeil River, taught university courses about bear behavior, written reports and booklets about bear safety and conservation, and guided photographers, filmmakers, and bear viewers to places where they can spend hours watching bears safely and without disturbing them. Wildlife biologists respect his expertise; several of them referred me to Derek when I had questions about play and other bear behavior. In turn, he probes his researcher friends for their ideas about nutrition, life history, and bear management. Why hasn't anybody designed a study of olfactory cues? How important is vocalization as a method of communication? What would a good DNA study reveal about family relationships? What is the shape of bear society?

"Sometimes you see things with bears that are really hard to understand," he said. "You see two big males playing with each other but they won't play with other males. Some big males won't ever play with other males. They've got their buddies they play with." Bears behave differently at different times of the year, too. "We've seen as many as ten subadult bears in just a very small area all playing with each other interchangeably. Very, very social. All fat and full of fish, and social tensions have really sort of disappeared."

Working at McNeil River also allowed Derek to study human behavior in the presence of wild animals. "I saw everybody's demeanor change at McNeil," he said. The bears at McNeil have learned over generations to accommodate groups of ten or so visitors who come each summer to sit unobtrusively in the same spots by the river. People who believe a mother bear with cubs will tear apart any person who looks at her sideways or who think firing a gun is the logical response to any bear encounter soon realize that the bears living in their heads are not the same creatures walking the world around them.

"I'm really convinced we can get along with bears," Derek said. "I don't think a subadult bear wandering through Anchorage would be a danger if everybody really understood bears. Which is huge wishful thinking on my part."

Most of us don't understand bears, of course. This was nicely illustrated by a video of a "charging" brown bear that surfaced on YouTube in early 2012 and quickly went viral, appearing in international headlines and on television newscasts. I first saw it in a Chicago hotel room on cable news. The footage was taken in Katmai National Park by a visitor who, along with his wife and eight others, was watching bears fish for salmon. Suddenly a rangy young brown bear burst into a gallop and headed directly toward the seated group, stopping a few yards away. Everyone kept their cool, undoubtedly coached by a guide. The bear shook water off like a dog, cautiously sniffed at someone's hood, and then wandered away. Britain's *Daily Mail* titled the footage "Angry Bear" and captioned the dramatic still, "Ferocious: The bear's razor-sharp claws are seen as he breaks away from the main grizzly group and fearlessly approaches the invaders." Most coverage breathlessly remarked on how lucky the bear watchers had been to escape death or maiming.

Longtime bear guide Brad Josephs of Homer chided the paper's description in the comments section. He had been taking people to the same location for a dozen years, he wrote, and had witnessed numerous similar events. "I am 100% sure this bear was frightened by another bear, and just ran close to the people, although it wasn't really that close," he commented. "This article, and many of the comments below are mired in ignorance. The people were not in danger, and the stories and quotes are embarrassingly inaccurate." Katmai guide Clint Hiebechuk offered this interpretation of the video: "You will notice the bear casting serious backward glances as it is running, worried more about the dominant bear pursuing and hardly paying attention to the direction it is running.

Calling this a charging bear is something that could only be created in someone's wildest imagination and [serves] only to give bears a bad reputation causing the untimely death of many bears who were just going about their business." Anyone who watched the footage again in this context could clearly see that the bear had bolted from another bear, only to find itself blocked by the bear watchers. The people weren't the only frightened creatures who kept their composure.

Few people would know how to interpret a bear's actions, but inexperience isn't the real problem. Unfortunately, the old Lewis and Clark attitude serves as the standard default in our thinking. In an online discussion about whether Alaska still represents the frontier, one contributor wrote, "Alaska is a place where nature can intrude violently at any moment (there's a picture somewhere out on the web of a trio of black bears playing on the swing and slide set one couple set up in their back yard) and anyone not living in downtown Anchorage should consider carrying a .357 or .45 handgun, lest they come face to face with a wolf pack or hungry bear (black, grizzly, or polar)."

The photograph mentioned is one of a series circulating on the Internet, where all good bear stories go to live. The images could not be more charming: four sleek black bears goof around on the slide, dangle from the swings, climb in the fort, wrestle on hind legs. Some messages claim the photos were taken in Milford, Pennsylvania, or Petoskey, Michigan, but the rumor-debunking website Snopes.com traced them to an Anchorage woman who photographed the bears in August 2006. "After about twenty minutes, I figured I had better scare them off so they wouldn't think our playset was a good place to return," she told Snopes. "I threw rocks and dirt clods at them. At first they just sniffed the rocks and looked at me. I actually connected with one of them (finally) and they sauntered away." She and her husband didn't respond to this intrusion by strapping on guns. Instead, they mounted an air horn outside for their two children, ages three and four. "That way, the boys can alert me if a moose or bear or porcupine or any other critter comes around," she said.

The online commenter perceived bears playing on a swing set as a violent intrusion that automatically called for a frontier solution. The home owners understood that bears don't care about an imaginary line we've drawn between wilderness and society, but everything usually works out fine with nothing more than common sense, tolerance, and restraint.

All afternoon, the bears at Chenik Creek galloped in the shallows or waded neck deep in a silvery penumbra of salmon. A couple of fishermen skiffed over from the seiners to photograph the bears fishing, offering a kind of professional respect, I thought. Gulls flapped and shrieked as they snatched fish scraps from distracted bears. The bears, the fishermen, the gulls, the watchful eagle on the bluff behind us, and the harbor seals gliding underwater—all of us were here because of the salmon. Derek tried to remember a German word that means "the joy of bears" but finally gave up. "I think part of the joy of watching bears is watching other things going on in the country," he explained.

When we returned to camp in the early evening, we drank some beer and noodled around a question that Nora had raised. "Who cares about bears?" she'd asked, not for herself but on behalf of the legions of people who do not feel an absence of bears in their lives, who are indifferent or hostile to bears as individuals or as a species, who cannot conceive of any response to bears other than fear. Yes, why do bears matter? There are lots of ways to answer such a question: Bear make us humble. Bears help us feel alive. Bears have an ancient relationship with people all over the world. Bears are an apex predator. Bears are smart. Bears are cute. Bears are cool. Bears are an umbrella, keystone, indicator, or flagship species. Bears are cosmic, primal, iconic, spiritual, noble, sacred, profane. Bears are like us, only better. Bears are like us, only worse.

So many possible answers, yet I fumbled for something that didn't sound obvious, trite, or abstract. In the end, the best I could muster was an embarrassingly utilitarian argument. Researchers are learning how bears improve stream habitats just by eating salmon, I said, throwing in some important-sounding stuff about nitrogen and marine isotopes and ecosystem engineers, which I figured Nora would appreciate since she teaches science to schoolkids. Derek talked about how much he likes looking at bears and thinking about bears and pondering all their mysteries. Between us, we unwittingly endorsed the famous assertion by anthropologist Claude Levi-Strauss that some animals are "good to eat" and "some are good to think." But in truth, Derek and I had cobbled together reasons why bears matter to us, not why they should matter to anybody else. Clearly, most of the world has no problem chugging along without bears, and some people wouldn't mind ridding themselves of those that remain.

Later, deeply unsatisfied with my feeble answer, I thought about a moment at Chenik Lagoon. In late afternoon the bear we called Solstice stopped fishing. She waded across the creek with her offspring trailing behind, and the three of them walked past us as we sat beside the creek. With a few powerful strides, she climbed the bluff trail and disappeared over the edge. One of the young bears followed at her rump, but just before cresting the top, the other paused and looked down at us. There is no way to interpret its look. I could not say whether it was curious or fearful, contemplating mayhem or play, or simply gathering another bit of knowledge that might come in handy during its life. My companions had turned back to the creek, so no one else saw the cub. It looked at us, and I looked back. Then the bear was gone.

Sometimes I try to imagine that young bear still living on the Alaska Peninsula. Perhaps it's shoveling a den from the alpine tundra with those long, curved claws. Maybe it's walking a ridge into another valley, placing its steps along the worn trail as precisely as every bear before it. It could be nibbling grass or chasing salmon or doing somersaults. It could be dead. I suppose I'll never know. The fate of any bear is a mystery, except to those who pull the trigger or drive the car or launch the arrow. As for the fate of most bears—well, if you believe that history is destiny, then there's no mystery at all.

Maybe this is all we can say about the meaning of Alaska's bears: Some have individual names and known histories. Others exist as data points or in population models. Some people call them "killer"; others call them "cousin." Some are trophies, some are meat. Some are predators, some are prey. Some are noble, some are nuisances, some are clowns. Some bears, it must be said, are more equal than other bears. Most difficult to understand are those that are just bears, animals whose purposes and desires and lives belong only to themselves. Those are the bears most of us never see.

the hungry bear

The grizzly could not have been long out of the den when a helicopter swooped overhead and a biologist leaned out and shot him with a
tranquilizing dart. A few hours later he was no longer just another bear
roaming the foothills of the Brooks Range. Now he was Z.B., the star of
his own reality show.

Z.B. weighed 350 pounds and was 14.5 years old when researcher
Spencer Linderman and his partner strapped a radio-transmitting collar on him near the headwaters of the Canning River in arctic Alaska.
They planned to follow him around the clock, seven days on and two
off, to learn about his daily life—what he ate, where he went, what he
did all day. The treeless landscape and perpetual light of a midnight
sun helped, but to spot him more easily as he roamed the broad valley
floor and the tundra slopes, they attached six-inch-long red and yellow
streamers to his collar.

Shadowing a bear isn't easy, no matter how you decorate it. "Visual
ground tracking of a grizzly bear on a 24 hour basis was a demanding,
sometimes monotonous, and often difficult task," Linderman wrote in
his 1974 report. From the slopes, the researchers peered at Z.B. through
binoculars and a spotting scope, relying on the electronic tether only
when rain, snow, fog, or the topography interfered. When Z.B. was on
the move, the spies broke camp and trailed behind, never drawing closer
than a half mile to avoid spooking him. They'd hoped to follow him all
summer, but the collar malfunctioned on June 17. Still, in the few weeks
since collaring him on May 14, they had captured a snapshot of Z.B.'s
habits as he traveled a twenty-seven-mile circuit of the braided river and
ventured out on side trips once the tundra greened up.

So what does a wild grizzly bear do all day with its top-of-the-food-
chain attitude, its good fortune in the evolutionary lottery, its rock-star
status as charismatic megafauna? Mostly, it looks for something to eat.

"Z.B.'s movements appeared to be controlled almost exclusively by food availability," Linderman wrote. Because a brown or black bear in the North spends maybe half its life awake and aboveground, it can't afford to dawdle on idle pursuits. By October or November a bear must enter its den prepared to survive six or seven months without food or water. Impregnated females will need to eat for two, three, or four bears. During hibernation bears can lose 15 to 40 percent of their body mass, so if they're not sufficiently sheathed in fat, they can starve to death.

Bears, like people, eat lots of different things, depending on where they live: plants, fish, fowl, anything from wasps to whales, really. "Every habitat has foods of interest to bears," wrote biologist John Hechtel, who spent four summers studying barren-ground grizzlies in the western Brooks Range, and "though general patterns were evident, bears could be encountered in any habitat at any time." To say that a bear is an omnivore that eats sedges and salmon, caribou and blueberries, roots and goose eggs, doesn't say enough. To say that the world is the bear's larder goes a bit further. To say that the world shapes the bear, and the bear shapes the world—now we're getting somewhere.

Living in the North takes an extraordinary amount of work for any creature. When male bears in the Brooks Range emerge around mid-April, the snow-covered landscape offers little except leftovers. Often they don't eat for a week or two until their appetites wake up. Z.B. grazed on overwintered bearberries that had sweetened since fall. Over two days in mid-May, he filched two caribou carcasses from the same lone gray wolf. He slept on or beside the carrion and endured a plague of ravens until he'd stripped the remains. As the ground thawed, he found it easier to excavate the thick, ropy roots of *Hedysarum alpinum*, also known as Eskimo potato and alpine sweetvetch. This is a staple favored by bears all over Alaska, particularly in the spring and fall when it gains protein. (People eat it, too.) In June the flush of new vegetation added wispy horsetails, grasses, and sedges to Z.B.'s diet. Now and then he balanced on his hind legs to tug willow branches tipped with tender buds to his mouth. Sometimes he leaned against brushy trunks and pawed the branches. "This position also permitted him the advantage of being able to scratch his back in between bites," Linderman noticed.

Everywhere, bears make the most of whatever's in season. Calling black and brown bears "omnivorous carnivores" is another way of saying they have the palate and sensibility of a French chef. Himalayan brown bears depend on golden marmots for meat. In central Sweden brown bears can hoover up as many as 4,000 to 5,000 ants in an average meal; the insects supply about a fifth of their diet. Slovakian brown bears can eat so much fermenting fruit that travelers are warned about encounters with drunken bruins. In Yellowstone National Park grizzlies steal whitebark pinecones from bird and squirrel caches; in a good year, seeds can provide 30 to 50 percent of their fat. Yellowstone bears slurp earthworms, sometimes graze on pondweed, occasionally fish for trout, and, in late summer, scrabble at talus slopes for army cutworm moths, eating as many as 40,000 of the little fat bombs at a time.

While Z.B. gnawed on carrion and roots, newly emerged brown bears in the Eden of Southeast Alaska foraged heavily in avalanche chutes and tidal meadows for succulents and herbaceous vegetation. Eating sedges, grasses, and forbs is a quick way to regain mass in the spring because these plants are highly digestible and loaded with protein. Coastal bears eat skunk cabbage roots, horsetail, and voles. They chase deer, dine on intertidal creatures, dig out sand lances, and lap up herring eggs. Glacier Bay's black and brown bears eat more than forty kinds of plants from spring to fall, a poetic litany of oxytrope and angelica, sweetvetch and groundcone, strawberries, salmonberries, soapberries, bearberries. They eat paper wasps and wasp nests, too. When the snow disappears from Kodiak Island's alpine slopes in late June or early July, bears graze like cattle on luscious and digestible stands of long-awn sedge, tugging mouthfuls free before chewing. They're also partial to the flowers of pushki (cow parsnip), purple lupine, and cream-colored angelica. A "crittercam" attached to a young female brown bear in Southeast Alaska recorded her nibbling devil's club berries, tearing at grass, and gulping toads as she wandered through the rainforest with her mother and siblings. A photograph taken somewhere in Alaska shows a beached whale carcass surrounded by about forty brown bears; they must have felt as if a Safeway had dropped from the heavens.

Grocery lists don't convey how a bear learns about the world through its mouth, the way it can live globally but eat locally. I'm oversimplifying the importance of what bears eat and why. Being ecologically nimble allows them to rummage through almost any landscape and find something to eat. All sorts of factors enter into a bear's eating patterns: when food is available; what nutrients they need; which foods offer the most energy, protein, or fat, and when; what foods are most easily digested and metabolized. In the spring, for example, they eat to replenish themselves and regain muscle mass. In the fall, during what's known as *hyperphagia*, black bears may accelerate their caloric intake from 8,000 to between 15,000 and 20,000 calories a day—even more for brown bears, according to researcher Ralph Nelson.

The way bears adapt to an unreliable world reminds me of a visit to Vladivostok at the end of the Cold War, where I learned how citizens survived the Soviet system: they made the rounds of stores hoping to find staples but prepared to pounce on any providential delivery of goods. For similar reasons, bears living in stingy habitats need an expansive territory to survive. One of the largest home ranges ever documented belonged to a male brown bear that roamed 2,287 square miles in Southcentral Alaska—larger than the state of Rhode Island, noted retired state biologist John Schoen. Bears constricted to small, fragmented areas risk betrayal from forced or natural changes in the landscape. A prime example is the West's whitebark pine, which the US Fish and Wildlife Service considers in danger of imminent extinction due to the ravages of blister rust, mountain pine beetles, fire suppression, and climate change. The loss of pine seeds as a major food source means fewer food choices for grizzlies. Another kind of threat can emerge when natural food sources fail: hungry bears near urban areas are more likely to partake of livestock or garbage, usually the quickest route to a bullet.

So, then, what was a typical day for Z.B.? He ate. He rested. He traveled. Calculate the hours devoted to each, and you have data: "Z.B. spent 31 percent of his time feeding, 59 percent resting, and 10 percent traveling." But those numbers don't convey a sense of a particular animal living his life moment to moment. "Z.B. had been up from a nap for a half hour, defecated and was traveling steadily upstream, poking about, scratching himself on willows but not yet feeding," Linderman wrote. (This description reminds me of some of my backpacking partners.) Or: "After feeding on a caribou carcass, Z.B. trudged up the mountainside to a large snowbank at the foot of a talus slope, scooped out a hole and flopped into it in the hot, early afternoon."

Linderman's report suggests that Z.B. was a mellow bear, rarely bothering to do more than raise his head when aircraft passed over. He was perfectly happy to nap on the open tundra after eating, because being at the top of the food chain has its perks. Sometimes he scraped away a few inches of dirt in a riverbed or hollowed out a bed in a snowdrift. He was a restless sleeper, frequently changing positions. Often he moseyed along as he grazed, but when he decided to go somewhere, he set out purposefully. This usually occurred between 9:00 p.m. and 4:00 a.m., after resting. His pace was about as fast as the average suburban exerciser, around three to four miles per hour. Once he covered sixteen miles in ten hours. "His travels often lasted for several hours, and obstacles such as deep, rotten snow, thin ice and open creeks did not slow him, much less divert or stop his march," Linderman wrote. (This sentence reminds me of a troublesome river crossing near Glacier Bay during a weeklong backpacking trip. After much drama, my friends and I were warming ourselves by a fire when a brown bear approached the mouth of the river. Without pausing for a moment, it walked into the turbulent current and swam across, accomplishing in a few minutes what had taken us four hours.)

Z.B.'s loose schedule may have some connection to his gender. In a similar study, graduate student James Gebhard followed a grizzly and her two new cubs as they roamed the northern foothills of the Brooks Range in 1977. Over the summer, she rested about 36 percent of the time, and more than 90 percent of her active hours were devoted to finding and eating food. As winter pressed closer, she spent twenty hours a day foraging. Rearing cubs added the nutritional stress of nursing, and it also made life more dangerous. I speed-read through Gebhard's account of the family's desperate attempt to outrace a male grizzly that was gaining on them. The boar came within forty feet of snatching the little female cub as the group dashed up a slope of Meat Mountain and disappeared. The male either retreated due to the mother's defense or surrendered to the exertion of running uphill, because a few minutes later he strolled down the hill, leaving the family intact. Whew.

If Z.B. had been born elsewhere, would his life have been different? In its details, yes, but in its scope, not really. A bear is the Swiss army knife of mammals, tooled with the physiology, life history, and behavioral plasticity that allow it to survive in the generosity of the temperate rain forest or the austerity of the Gobi Desert. Brown bears are evolving the apparatus of herbivores—longer claws and broader molars, for example—while retaining the digestive efficiency of carnivores, according to bear biologists Ian Stirling and Andrew Derocher. A bear can tear the throat from a caribou calf, slice open a clamshell, pit a peach, plow a field of roots, or lip a cluster of blueberries from a twig. It can run faster than an Olympic sprinter and tread as quietly as a burglar. It can climb mountains, cross glaciers, swim oceans, and tuck itself into the cold earth to revolve through space and time as patiently as an astronaut.

To accomplish all this, a bear relies on senses that range from adequate to amazing. In what may be the only hearing tests conducted on bears thus far, polar bears demonstrated an ability to hear frequencies over a wider range than people can. Naturalist Adolph Murie studied grizzlies in Denali National Park for twenty-five summers and reported that bears could hear him making slight noises from 200 yards away. Experiments with captive polar bears and black bears showed that they—and presumably brown bears as well—can see color and distinguish between hues as closely aligned as blue-gray and blue-green. The researchers who studied black bears' ability to discriminate between colors speculated that good visual acuity may help them locate foods such as berries, insects, and scattered acorns. (They also noted that the bears in their study learned faster than chimpanzees and as quickly as dogs used in similar experiments.)

Despite conventional wisdom, bears are not nearsighted; their vision is as good as ours, says Kodiak wildlife biologist Larry Van Daele. "They just don't trust it," he told me. "They trust their nose." This is where "amazing" comes in. Flatten the olfactory structures known as turbinates across a surface, according to Van Daele, and a human's would cover a postage stamp; a dog's, an area the size of a regular sheet of paper; a bear's, three or four pieces of paper. "So a bear's sense of smell is so incredibly different than ours, I would guess they can 'see' smells," he said.

The nose is embedded with tiny muscles that can flex the nostrils to an unusual degree, according to neurosurgeon George Stevenson. He has devoted his retirement to investigating the brains and olfactory systems of bears, with the goal of creating a brain atlas. Smells waft through the long nasal chambers, activate a dense network of nerves and receptor cells, and light up an olfactory bulb that Stevenson once described as resembling a golf ball with quills. This amplified ability allows bears to locate distant sources of food, which is especially critical in the spring, when meals are scarce. "I think they smell their way through life," Stevenson told the *Hungry Horse News*.

More important, bears can extend this knowledge across time and space because their hippocampus archives memories of scents and experiences. "A bear's got this incredible map in their brain that relates to food, location, and time," says naturalist and bear-viewing guide Chris Day. As a doctoral student, biologist Tamara Olson observed an adult female in Katmai National Park that returned to the Brooks River to eat salmon on the same day each fall for three years in a row. On the Alaska Peninsula, bears reliably visit salmon streams about ninety minutes before high tide, when the fish start pulsing upstream to spawn—even though the peak of high tide shifts by about fifty minutes each day. Ken Day likes to tell the story of a boat that ran aground one winter loaded with crabs. In the spring the bears discovered the boat, tore it open, and feasted. Until someone finally torched the wreck, the bears returned every spring to check the boat, just in case it had been miraculously replenished with free crabs.

"Now if a rufus [sic] hummingbird, which weighs 2 dimes, can build a map on its forehead of the location of its food stuffs, and use that map to keep finding those food stuffs, we should not be surprised at what a grizzly can do," commented Fred Bunnell at a Canadian symposium on managing bear-people conflicts. This ability to remember, to adapt, and to learn helps bears succeed at a long-term strategy that, according to bear biologist Harry Reynolds, is basically this: "To live for a long time and be ready to exploit high levels of food resources one way or another." If you think about it, this is a useful mission statement for people, too.

Barren-ground grizzlies aren't devoted vegans, of course, but Z.B. was something of a pacifist who ignored migrating caribou and neighborhood moose. "Although other grizzlies in the study were commonly found on moose carcasses early in the spring, Z.B. appeared to peacefully co-exist with the 8–12 moose inhabiting the high willows of the 10-mile length of the upper Canning which was his most frequented section of range," Linderman noted. Even when Z.B. ventured into willow thickets occupied by cows and calves, he emerged unbloodied. Once he napped on a slope near one of his stolen caribou carcasses, apparently oblivious to a group of nineteen caribou feeding within fifty yards. He startled one into a sprint only when he stretched out a leg in his sleep.

Plenty of grizzlies do chase ungulates, given the opportunity. A population of grizzlies in Canada's central arctic ate mostly caribou, apparently because the bears lived near a migratory route that conveniently channeled caribou back and forth across the plains. One study of brown bears in east-central Alaska calculated that adult male bears killed an average of three to four moose each year, while adult females averaged less than one per year. However, lone adult females were more successful at killing moose calves. Black bears have been known to take down an adult moose now and then. With the doggedness of TV detectives, Ontario biologists once deciphered a kill scene in which a black bear had apparently clung to the back of a moose that attempted to dislodge it by bashing into a couple of trees before succumbing. I've also seen more than one photograph of an enraged moose pursuing a brown bear.

Bears take most advantage of calves that are too young to outrace them. But by the time a caribou calf is ten days old, bears might as well not bother chasing it unless they enjoy pointless exercise. Newborn moose aren't as speedy and are most vulnerable for their first few weeks of life, although they're at risk of becoming a meal for a hungry bear until winter. Studies conducted in various parts of Alaska have calculated black and brown bear predation rates at anywhere between 2 and 52 percent of newborn ungulates and occasionally higher, according to the Alaska Department of Fish and Game. Not all bears kill calves, though; some seem to specialize in it, while others ignore them—a fact that complicates predator control efforts in Alaska.

Bears don't exclude their own kind from their diet. Biologists have documented numerous instances of males killing bear cubs, brown and black. Occasionally a brown bear kills an adult black bear or a subadult brown bear and eats it. US Fish and Wildlife Service biologists Mark Bertram and Michael Vivion discovered two cases of female black bears denning with cubs on the Yukon Flats that died after immense ruckuses that tore up the landscape. Grizzlies were probably responsible. Likewise, one August a sixteen-year-old male black bear was killed and eaten after a violent struggle with a grizzly. (Technically speaking, all struggles with grizzlies are violent, I suppose.) Bears have also reportedly eaten wolf pups in their den while the adults were away.

Some bears learn to expand their menus, which means they were curious or hungry enough to try to kill something strange to them and smart enough to figure out how to do it. Canadian polar bear biologist Mitch Taylor once spotted a 700-pound male grizzly near the remains of two seal pups 300 miles out on the ice pack. "From tracks it was apparent that the grizzly bear had been hunting seal pups in birth lairs," he reported. A few days later hunters saw what was presumably the same bear near the carcass of a two-year-old polar bear. It was clear that the grizzly had attacked and killed the seven-foot polar bear. Some Alaskan grizzlies have become adept at killing musk oxen, which average 800 pounds as adults. Musk oxen were reintroduced into the Arctic National Wildlife Refuge in 1969, and eighteen years later, Patricia Reynolds and her colleagues documented the first bear kill. In at least ten instances, bears hunting singly or in families have killed more than one musk ox at a time, overcoming the beasts' dangerous horns and a group defense. A few are especially skilled hunters. In 2000 a fifteen-year-old radio-collared male bear killed five musk oxen in one rampage on the Canning River. The following year he killed three in another incident.

When large meat isn't available, small will do. One year in the Arctic, recalled Harry Reynolds, "There were so many lemmings available that some of the bears we captured had recognizable muscle masses and little tiny furry feet in their feces. You've seen bear scats full of berries—they look like pie filling? Well, these looked like four and twenty lemmings baked in a pie." John Hechtel concluded that in the meat-poor regions of the Brooks Range, the most important fall food was ground squirrel. Bear No. 1086 in his study was a squirrel connoisseur who spent nearly half her time chasing ground squirrels; she caught somewhere between 170 and 241 of them one autumn. A Canadian bear was once recorded eating 357 squirrels in six weeks. Anyone who has ever watched a bear shoveling through great scoops of earth in pursuit of a two-pound squirrel has to wonder if a few bites of squirrel protein—the human equivalent of Cheez-whiz on a Ritz cracker—is worth the effort. Hechtel concluded that it may be, depending on the local population density of squirrels and the ease of digging. The squirrels' own behavior can affect their chances, too. He once saw a bear abandon a squirrel burrow only to tear back and resume digging after the squirrel emerged and emitted an alarm call, which apparently sounded like a dinner bell to the bear.

Bird colonies also offer a generous buffet, one feathery bite at a time. Researchers surveying seabirds along the Katmai coast counted more than forty bears, mostly females and cubs, swimming among the offshore islands. They damaged or destroyed numerous puffin and gull colonies by excavating nesting burrows, strewing feathers and eggshells in their wake. On some islands they eliminated nesting birds altogether. After the 1964 earthquake lifted the wetlands of the Copper River delta, bears became a major predator of dusky Canada goose eggs, which were more vulnerable on the higher ground. People have also seen bears raiding the nests of trumpeter swans, foraging for eggs laid by ground-nesting bald eagles, and picking their way along narrow ledges to eat hundreds of murre eggs and chicks clinging to the cliffs of Cape Lisburne on Alaska's northwest coast.

Certainly a bear is not above appropriating the work of others. Mystified by the digging style of a couple of bears, John Hechtel peeled back the tundra and discovered they'd been gobbling caches of roots and seeds collected by lemmings and voles. Adolph Murie noted that such caches can produce two or three quarts of roots. On Kodiak Island, where Sitka black-tailed deer thrived after being transplanted in the 1920s and 1930s, bears are widely believed to respond to deer calls and gunshots because they've figured out that these signals often produce a gut pile or a carcass. This has also been reported on Admiralty Island and with elk in Montana (Larry Van Daele has his doubts, though). One survey found that as many as 26 percent of Kodiak hunters reported losing deer meat in camp or in the field to bears.

The bromide "when the tide is out, the table is set" applies to bears, too. Before the salmon runs appear in Katmai coast's Hallo Bay, as many as 150 bears forage each spring and early summer along a six-mile stretch of salt marshes and tidal flats. There, researchers Tom Smith and Steven Partridge watched bears rummage through exposed clam beds at low tide, excavating soft-shell and Pacific razor clams so swiftly and expertly that the researchers couldn't record how many they ate. The availability of mussels, clams, seaweed, algae, peanut worms, and nutritious gardens of sedges and forbs may offer bears a quick way to regain weight once they emerge from the den—especially females with cubs—influencing the population's productivity, the researchers suggested.

In the glacial fjords of Tracy Arm in Southeast Alaska, I once watched a black bear scraping at a field of barnacles and lapping up the innards with its long tongue, unconcerned about our boat hovering a few yards away. How does a bear even know that a barnacle is worth risking the steep climb down the fjord's stone walls? How did it learn to scratch open those bony plates? The same way, I suppose, that bears learned to pluck salmon from set nets strung across the mouth of the Alsek River by wading alongside the nets or dragging them ashore. The same way that those swimming bears figured out they should paddle several miles to reach a bird colony. The same way that some bear in Glacier Bay eyed the first moose or the first salmon that wandered into the fjords newly released from ice. One of us, after all, was the first to sauté a snail in butter and tell everyone else it tasted good.

Well, everything eats. But only recently has it become clear how much bears' everyday habits affect ecological processes. One term for this effect is *ecosystem engineering*, a concept developed since the mid-1990s to describe how organisms physically create, change, or maintain habitats. Some alterations are obvious—think about beavers or, for that matter, people. Engineering by bears is both subtle and profound. Of course, a bear doesn't regard the landscape as if it were a do-it-yourself project. But individually and collectively, bears influence the invisible universe of nutrient flux and energy cycles, of chemical call and response, of community dynamics and competition. A bear is a fisher, a grazer, a hunter, a soil tiller, a sower, a trail maker. A bear can change its environment simply because it's hungry.

Z.B., for example, was spotted grazing heavily in late summer and fall on soapberries, an orangish fruit that grows in clusters on bushes. Maybe he found some crowberries, low-bush cranberries, or blueberries, too. If soapberries weren't available, he might have eaten mostly bearberries, as Hechtel's subjects did in the western range. During the high season, bears sometimes spend seventeen or eighteen hours a day working a berry patch. In good years, observed researcher Christy Welch and her colleagues, bears tend to crop away at clusters as they move, rather than pausing to strip off every last berry (a technique many people adopt, too). Brown bears on Chichagof Island may harvest 16,000 or more berries daily, according to Alaska botanist Mary Willson. She notes that other researchers have calculated that grizzlies can shovel in as many as 200,000 soapberries, or eighty-eight pounds, each day. That makes them less grazer than living combine.

Wild fruit is so important that bears living near salmon streams spend several hours a day grazing on berries by choice, even though coho salmon would produce seven times the digestible energy per hour. Based on simple models of energy efficiency, bears should devote 100 percent of their time to eating salmon when they can. Why would they bother with berries when they could catch a coho in just a few minutes? They're not looking for dessert, concluded Charles Robbins and other researchers. Nor were the bears they studied tired of salmon and craving variety, looking for nutrients they couldn't obtain from fish, satisfying a need for fibrous bulk (the way some of us require Metamucil), crowded off salmon streams by people or bigger bears, or unable to spend enough time fishing. As it turns out, bears face a kind of Goldilocks scenario when it comes to metabolizing protein. If they eat either too little or too much protein, it's harder for them to maintain their weight. A bear that eats a high-carbohydrate, low-protein diet gains more fat and loses lean mass—something Atkins dieters understand. But studies of captive bears revealed that when they voluntarily ate just the right amount of protein combined with fruit, they gained more body mass than if they ate only fruit or only protein. The optimal ratio changes all the time and varies with the size of the bear. The bigger the bear, the more protein it needs.

Could a bear like Z.B. survive mostly on berries? For several years, bear biologist Bruce McLellan investigated the cuisine and body conditions of 490 grizzly and black bears in the Flathead and upper Columbia River drainages in British Columbia. (He also analyzed nearly 1,400 scats.) Bears are nearly vegetarian there, eating little meat aside from ants and the occasional ungulate. More than 85 percent of their summer diet consists of low-protein fruit like huckleberries and soapberries (also called buffalo berries). "Bears rapidly gained fat but lost lean tissues while feeding on fruit," McLellan wrote in 2011, "suggesting that lean tissues were used to buffer seasonal protein shortages." These inland grizzly females were much smaller in mass but fatter than salmon-eating females on the Kenai Peninsula in Alaska. Black bears gorging themselves on berries—perhaps with the occasional side dish of ants— can also pack on the weight. One female who weighed a svelte 125 pounds on June 23 was a chubby 255 by October 10, McLellan reported.

Bears throughout Alaska depend on berries, but some berries also depend on bears as one member of a league of rodents, birds, and other mammals that disperse seeds away from the original plant. Bears work in bulk, though; graduate student Laura Patten calculated that a large brown bear could eat more than 15 million blueberry seeds a day. Thanks to an active digestive system, bears are unwitting Johnny Appleseeds, scattering most of their seed-studded scat a third to a half mile away in Southeast Alaska forests, but sometimes as far as a couple of miles. These scats sprout clusters of seedlings that Mary Willson calls "bear gardens." The trails of droppings they leave while trundling through the forest help spread the seeds over a wide area, reducing competition among seedlings and improving the likelihood that they'll land in a favorable microhabitat. Rodents or birds often add another leg to the journey by hauling away undigested berries and seeds from the treasure trove of bear scat.

Bears perform an additional service for some plant species. The seeds of salmonberry, elderberry, and cow parsnip germinate more quickly and in greater percentages if they've completed the long voyage through a bear gut. Bear dung is also a rich source of fertilizer for seedlings. The other kinds of food that bears consume can alter these complex mechanisms. Researchers Anna Traveset and her colleagues performed the brave task of gathering and sieving brown bear scat from Chichagof Island and discovered that when bears digested salmonberries along with animal matter—in this case, mostly deer—more seeds germinated. For salmonberry and blueberry seeds, being eaten by a bear improved their chances of entering winter as bigger, more established plants.

By tilling the earth with their long claws, bears are capable of influencing plant growth and altering plant communities. In Montana's Glacier National Park grizzlies trowel subalpine meadows looking for glacier lily bulbs year after year. The large patches of bare, disturbed soil they create are favored by the plant's seedlings. Lilies overlooked by the bears in these plowed fields produced twice as many seeds as lilies growing in undisturbed meadows, according to researchers Sandra Tardiff and Jack Stanford, and their bulbs had increased levels of nitrogen and carbohydrates. Bears also made "modest but significant" changes in alpine plant communities after excavating arctic squirrel burrows in Alaska's Chugach and Wrangell Mountains. When bears dig dens or seek roots, bulbs, squirrels, and insects, they're regular bulldozers, or what geographer David Butler calls "powerful geomorphic agents." An estimated population of 332 grizzlies in Glacier National Park can excavate almost 3,000 cubic yards of soil each year, he calculated, displacing sediment and affecting slope hydrology and river systems.

We humans remain the champions of change, of course, having rearranged much of the architecture and ecological workings of the continent. But as Butler points out, we've also eliminated widespread populations of bears, prairie dogs, bison, and beavers—creatures that once bioengineered the West's landscape and ecosystems. "It is already too late to truly quantify the geomorphic impact of pre-Contact bison or beaver," Butler noted. He has urged his colleagues to get busy and study how animals alter the natural world before climate change, overpopulation, and other human influences scramble things even more. Maybe someone could begin with Alaska's bears, who even now are yanking back tundra mats, tugging ground squirrels and Eskimo potato tubers from the soil, or sleeping in the very earth itself.

For a mature male representative of *Ursus arctos*, Z.B. wasn't very large. Compare his 350 pounds to the 787 pounds carried by an average male coastal bear on the Alaska Peninsula. The size differences among brown bears are so expansive that in 1918 zoologist C. Hart Merriam diligently named eighty-six species or subspecies based on skull measurements, five on Admiralty Island alone. Merriam christened many after the wealthy hunters who had sent him specimens or the places where the specimens had been collected. Some identifications he based on a single skull. His enthusiasm for sorting bears into narrow taxonomic categories prompted the great paleontologist and evolutionist George Gaylord Simpson to remark, "On such a system twin bear cubs could be of different species." Similarly, Dirk Pieter Erdbrink proposed 232 recent and 39 fossil species and subspecies in his 1953 *Review of Fossil and Recent Bears of the Old World*, a "waste of systematic effort which, as far as we know, is unparalleled," judged Pleistocene experts Björn Kurtén and Elaine Anderson.

Others had whittled the number of subspecies to five by the time Alaska biologist Robert Rausch began streamlining this unwieldy taxonomy in the 1950s and 1960s. After studying 357 bear skulls from across North America, he shrank Merriam's menagerie into *Ursus arctos*, with two subspecies: *U. arctos horribilis* includes most bears in North America, and *U. arctos middendorffi* covers the bears from the Kodiak Island archipelago, a population physically and genetically isolated from the mainland. Bear taxonomy has been recomplicated by advancements in mitochondrial DNA analysis, which can identify broad lineages of brown bears worldwide, known as clades. This work also collapses support for subspecies such as *horribilis* and *middendorffi*. Fortunately, geneticists recognize that without more analysis, rejiggering the taxonomy would only create needless confusion. Several of the black bear's sixteen subspecies occur in Alaska, including on the Kenai Peninsula, on some of the islands in the Alexander Archipelago, and on the mainland of Southeast Alaska.

Bear skulls do display a surprising range of shapes, according to biologists Ian Stirling and Andrew Derocher. They noticed that some brown bear skulls in a group of Eurasian bears resembled the broader faces of pandas, while others had a more streamlined wolf shape. McNeil River biologists describe local bears broadly as "monkey-faced"or "horse-faced," while the narrow-faced, long-snouted bears at Katmai National Park are called "dog faces." Bears seem so morphologically diverse because of differences between the sexes and among age classes, Rausch explained, but they also display interesting individual variations, such as pelt color and body shape. The environment itself seems to influence a bear's appearance, he suggested. Harry Reynolds and other wildlife biologists have observed that the pelage of Alaska's brown bears seems to be related to their predominant habitat. Bears in the primeval, dim rain forests of coastal Alaska trend toward darker browns, while subarctic or arctic brown bears often display golden heads and shoulders with darker legs, backs, and flanks—a color scheme that some call a "Toklat" bear. The light grizzle of Z.B.'s pelt offered him exceptional camouflage against the tawny tundra, which is why Linderman flagged him with bright streamers. Similarly, black bears can be cinnamon, saffron, chocolate, or even blue or white, but good old-fashioned black bears are more common in temperate and boreal forests and the montane, trending toward lighter colors in open forests or deserts.

The confounding distinction between a brown bear and a grizzly bear highlights the most obvious example of environmental influence. Calling coastal bears "brown" and inland bears "grizzly" is based on a size difference due almost entirely to the availability of meat—that is, salmon. "Salmon was the most important source of meat for the largest, most carnivorous bears and most productive populations," reported Alaska biologist Grant Hilderbrand and his colleagues. Adult female brown bears on the Kenai Peninsula consumed an average of twenty-four pounds of salmon each day and more than a ton each year—60 percent of their diet when the fish were running. "Because salmon was available through successive runs for as long as 110 days, large wild bears were able to increase their body mass by as much as 50%," they found. By the end of fall, some bears bulge with enormous bellies. "It looks more like a hippopotamus than a bear," John Schoen once remarked about a photograph of a particularly healthy eater. In southwestern Alaska a ten-year study showed that salmon was the most important component of brown bear diets, representing 42 percent of the total. Berries accounted for 24.5 percent, mammals 13.5 percent, vegetation almost 9 percent, and freshwater fish about 11 percent. Pity poor Z.B., making the most of his spare diet of roots, greens, berries, carrion, and ground squirrels.

What's good for individuals is good for the population. Entering the den in top condition matters tremendously for female bears and their offspring. The average adult female brown bear on the Kenai Peninsula gains about 140 pounds by eating salmon, Hilderbrand determined, 80 percent of it fat. "Fat is the essential currency of successful hibernation and cub production," Robbins and his colleagues explained. Those living in meat-rich habitats give birth at a younger age, produce litters at shorter intervals, and produce more cubs per litter, Hilderbrand's studies showed. (This is also true for urban black bears in Nevada compared with their wilder counterparts.) Fatter mothers gave birth earlier in winter than their leaner counterparts, according to a 2012 study of captive brown bears, giving the cubs more time to nurse and grow before entering the outside world. Twins born to the fattest mothers emerged from their dens up to 80 percent bigger than those born to the skinniest mothers, making them less vulnerable to cannibalistic males and better able to keep up with their mothers. Females with less than 20 percent body fat failed to produce any cubs at all, even after mating repeatedly.

More meat also means more bears. The population density of fish-eating coastal bears can be as much as eighty times greater than that of inland vegetarians. There were between 191 and 551 bears per thousand square kilometers living in parts of Katmai National Park, Kodiak Island, Admiralty Island, and other places where salmon were plentiful, according to a comprehensive study by Sterling Miller and colleagues using refined survey techniques. In contrast, densities in Interior and northern Alaska ranged from 7 to 32 bears per thousand square kilometers. Salmon are so valuable to coastal bear populations and ecosystems that state and federal wildlife biologists have recommended that fisheries managers consider allocating a share of spawning salmon to wildlife, just as they do for sport, commercial, and subsistence fishermen.

However, the mere presence of salmon streams doesn't mean that every bear eats salmon. On Admiralty Island, for example, some females never leave the alpine slopes to gorge on salmon just a few miles away (similar to Z.B. ignoring those nearby caribou). This happens on Kodiak Island too, where any bear could travel from one end to the other in a couple of days. Instead, bears demonstrate "ecological flexibility," according to Larry Van Daele and colleagues. Rather than each bear seeking the very best habitat, the population infiltrates the entire landscape and specializes in eating whatever is available locally. This strategy makes sense and can protect an entire population from crashing if, for example, a salmon run fails. Kodiak bears are so flexible that when

Van Daele's group examined data collected over fifteen years, they found that bears inhabited several types of habitat—rock and ice, grasslands, heath, wetlands, alpine, freshwater, high and low shrub—with a varying abundance of salmon, berries, and other foods. Yet females in all study areas produced similar litter sizes and weaned similar numbers of cubs. Arctic grizzlies living in Canada's Mackenzie River delta fell into three distinct foraging groups when researchers examined the proportion of seven food groups in their diets: vegetation, beavers, moose, broad whitefish, snow goose eggs, muskrats, and lemmings. Even within the same population, bear diets varied from almost fully herbivorous to nearly completely carnivorous, as documented by Mark Edwards and his colleagues. For example, some diets were 80 percent herbaceous foods or 80 percent small mammals, while others consisted of more than 60 percent snow goose eggs or whitefish.

A bear's size can affect its choices. Females basically stop growing when they begin channeling their energy toward reproduction, but males continue to gain mass and size. The largest animals can't sustain themselves on berries alone, although subadults or females might do just fine on that diet. So in regions where bears can't count on a thundering herd of calving caribou to present itself regularly, it's better for a male bear to remain at a smaller size that it can maintain with a mostly vegetarian diet. Even in a rich environment, males often choose foods that offer the most calories while requiring the least amount of energy to locate and eat. For example, Smith and Partridge noticed that most bears foraging in Hallo Bay's intertidal zones were subadults and females with one- or two-year-old cubs. A few hours of clam digging wouldn't pay off metabolically for large males, whose size requires them to eat more efficiently.

Deciding what to eat and where to eat it can be tricky. A mother bear that wants to reduce the risk of a male eating her cubs for dinner might forage for seaweed or berries rather than joining the crowd at a salmon river. Some females with spring cubs avoided eating salmon altogether on Admiralty and Chichagof Islands, as reported by Merav Ben-David and coauthors. Bears fishing at Chenik River tend to be subadults or females with cubs, Derek Stonorov told me, while big males congregate several miles south at McNeil River, suggesting that some microhabitats provide "nurseries" where families can feed more safely. Similarly, Jennifer Fortin and her colleagues found that black bears generally don't fish in streams dominated by brown bears. Some meals just aren't worth dying for.

When a bear does eat a salmon, it matters not only to the eater and the eaten but also to the entire watershed. Salmon are the gift that keeps on giving. Five species of Pacific salmon circulate in the ocean before returning to their natal waters to spawn: chinook, sockeye, chum, pink, and coho. Once the salmon find the rivers where their internal clocks will tick-tock away their final days, they face a daunting array of predators, including people with fishing poles and bears with empty bellies. On shallow creeks in Southeast Alaska, bears might claim nearly half a returning run. In big rivers flooded by millions of sockeyes or pinks, bears don't make much of a dent unless waterfalls slow the spawners.

A salmon may seem like a neatly packaged slab of energy, but to a bear, not all parts are equal, and not every salmon offers the same package. In years of plenty, brown and black bears don't bother eating an entire fish; it makes more sense physiologically to gorge on only the yummy, fattening lipids that saturate the eggs and brains. Bears love salmon roe so much that sometimes after slicing open a belly or stepping on a carcass to squirt out the eggs, they'll lick the orange globes off the rocks before moving on. They're rewarded with almost twice the calories that meat offers. "Multiplied over the course of the run, the energetic advantage for bears targeting high-energy body parts would be immense," notes ecologist Scott Gende, whose team documented the 20,230 bear-killed salmon necessary to reach this conclusion.

When salmon aren't as abundant, bears are less picky. They eat more of each fish and may even resort to eating spawned-out carcasses (horrors!), sniffing out dead females for their remaining eggs. Bears can probably detect a salmon's state by such cues as its color shift from ocean-bright silver to olive green or red or by the amount of fungus colonizing it. "It is easy for humans to estimate the length of time a salmon has been in the stream and it would not be surprising if a bear could do likewise," Gende and colleagues observed. Like zombies, bears seem to know that brains are good food no matter how old the carcass is.

Salmon choice also depends on the size of the waterway. In shallow channels where it's easier to catch a salmon rippling through the water, bears clearly prefer fish that have just entered the stream, and for good reason: new arrivals have more fat. Some salmon spend weeks or months in freshwater systems trying to reach their spawning grounds, never eating. Once they arrive, another three weeks may pass while they fertilize or lay eggs. By the time they die, they've lost 80 to 95 percent of their fat reserves and up to half of their total energy. Eating an old, spawned-out salmon is like settling for a low-fat snack bar when you really wanted a marbled T-bone. But in deeper, wider rivers, where woody debris can protect fish, bears often choose older salmon even when plenty of younger spawners are present, probably because vigorous fish can escape more easily. It can take a bear three times longer to catch a salmon in a big river than in a small stream, Gende has reported. So it's more efficient to eat a slow, less nourishing, but easily caught fish than to waste energy galloping after a fast salmon—particularly if you're a subdominant bear trying to grab a bite before a bigger bear steals it.

Once a bear catches and eats a salmon, it triggers chemical responses that cascade throughout the ecosystem. No one understood bears' importance in streamside, or riparian, habitats until the development of stable isotope analysis, which has been called "the single greatest breakthrough in the nutritional ecology field during the past 20 years." This technique allows researchers to trace a form of marine nitrogen, N15, as it migrates into freshwater and terrestrial systems. Nitrogen acts as a fertilizer for plants, and it is delivered mostly through the atmosphere or in collaboration with organisms that help "fix" it—that is, make it available to plants.

The distribution chain works like this: Salmon absorb marine nitrogen, carbon, and phosphorus during their oceangoing years and then transfer these critical elements into freshwater rivers and lakes when they lay eggs and die, helpfully leaving behind their rotting carcasses. Some nutrients return to the ocean after the dead salmon decay, but a significant amount enters the terrestrial cycle, thanks partially to bears. They excrete most of the nitrogen they absorb from salmon when they urinate and defecate. They also redistribute nitrogen when they carry fish into the brush or trees to eat, usually to avoid losing their catch to another bear. And bears can move a lot of salmon. Ecologist Tom Reimchen found that black bears on Haida Gwaii in British Columbia caught as many as 700 salmon apiece over six weeks. They hauled most of the fish into the trees, where they usually left at least half the carcasses. On several streams in Southeast and Southwest Alaska, bears carried 42 to 68 percent of their kills into the forest, sometimes more than 300 feet from the water, according to Thomas Quinn and his colleagues.

Scavengers take their share, but nitrogen also seeps into the forest floor as the fish mulches itself.

The flow of marine nitrogen continues as some plants absorb it. Ferns, Sitka spruce, devil's club, and other plants growing near spawning streams may obtain anywhere from 18 to 26 percent of their nitrogen from salmon. Grant Hilderbrand calculated that spruce trees buffering salmon streams received nearly 85 percent of their marine nitrogen from bear urine. Researchers are still trying to tease out a cause-and-effect relationship between salmon-borne nitrogen and plant growth—and a few studies suggest that such a relationship exists—but a tangle of factors makes it difficult to quantify. That's partly because the nitrogen cycle is like a spirograph, with lines of energy and nutrients weaving intricate patterns of give-and-take as organisms eat, live, move through the environment, and expire.

If salmon-derived nitrogen does help streamside plants grow faster, researchers James Helfield and Robert Naiman suggest that a feedback loop exists between salmon and forests, aided by bears. As vegetation and trees die and decompose, for example, they release nitrogen back into streams. Logs and other organic debris help protect eggs and juvenile salmon from the high water that can scour embryos from streambeds or wash away fry. Leaf litter from nitrogen-enhanced trees increases the nutrients available to aquatic insects, an important food for juvenile salmon. Tree canopies provide valuable shade, which can protect developing salmon embryos, while root systems stabilize banks and filter sediments that can reduce the oxygen flow in gravel and imperil developing eggs. It's an elegant waltz: thanks to bears, salmon contribute nitrogen to the forest, which helps create favorable conditions for young salmon, which ultimately leads to more fish returning to streams to feed bears (and everybody else) in subsequent years.

I like to think of bears fertilizing our forests and river systems, much as American Indians taught the early colonists the benefits of burying fish among rows of corn. Still, sorting out these complex relationships is a bit like studying the moon and hoping it explains the universe. "For every question you answer, you raise five or six more," Hilderbrand once told me. What's known about the interplay between salmon and bears and their shared ecology is still rudimentary, partly because the effects are so far-reaching. Gende and colleagues point out the expansive potential of the marine nitrogen cycle this way: "Southeast Alaska has over 5000 salmon streams; initial estimates have found that over 90%

of this forested area falls within 5 kilometers (km) of a salmon stream." Consider that commercial fisheries in some areas harvest 60 percent or more of salmon before they ever reach their spawning grounds, and that hunters harvest bears, and it's clear that until recently, this bear-operated conveyor belt transferred far more salmon from rivers to land. People have altered forest and stream ecosystems in ways more subtle than chopping down trees.

At least we now have an answer to the age-old question: does a bear poop (and eat and pee) in the woods? Yes, and it's a good thing it does.

Based on just a month of watching Z.B., it would be hard to pinpoint how he influenced his own habitat. It's easier to trace such effects on a larger scale by examining the links between bears and other species. For example, bears may be altering the evolutionary development of salmon, according to at least three studies. Brown and black bears tend to eat more male than female salmon, perhaps because males are bigger and, in some species, develop a prominent hump that acts as a convenient handle. Several researchers believe that such selective predation on bigger fish may affect the body size and shape of salmon. In addition, it may influence salmon's evasive techniques, spawning strategies, and genetic variability. Bears can also drive the aging process in salmon. In streams where bears prefer senescent fish—older salmon that deteriorate quickly after spawning—salmon age more slowly than in streams where bears eat newcomers. Female salmon tend to have shorter life spans in streams crowded by bears because they spawn more quickly to avoid surrendering their genetic legacy to a bear's taste for eggs. "Where bear activity was high, the strategy seemed to be 'breed as soon as you get in the creek,'" researcher Stephanie Carlson told science writer Ned Rozell.

A bear's influence extends throughout all trophic levels (levels of consumption) in the food web. The simple decision whether to eat its catch in the stream or carry it into the forest has important consequences for the aquatic or terrestrial ecosystem. Bears that eat the good stuff and then abandon a salmon carcass to the stream bequeath the remaining nutrients and biomass to aquatic invertebrates and other fish. Fish leftovers feed smaller carnivores such as weasels, martens, and minks. Dead salmon also feed a multitude of insects and birds. Blowflies laid more eggs on bear-killed fish than on those that died a natural death on three Southwest Alaska salmon streams, according to Erin Meehan and colleagues. Nearly 51,000 maggots colonized full carcasses found in the forest. Multiply that by the hundreds or thousands of salmon abandoned by bears, and as many as 10 million maggots exist in a creek with 400 dead salmon, they calculated. Caddis flies also strongly prefer laying eggs in salmon killed by bears in Alaska's Wood River system, possibly because the bear's teeth perforate the fish, making them easier to colonize. Death by bear also leaves carcasses with more energy and nutrition than death by senescence.

Really, it's one big pay-it-forward scheme. Flies, midges, and other invertebrates colonize salmon carcasses and attract breeding songbirds such as the golden-crowned kinglet, Swainson's thrush, varied thrush, Pacific-slope flycatcher, and winter wren. All these bird species are more abundant in forests next to salmon-bearing streams in British Columbia, according to a study by Katie Christie and Thomas Reimchen. The presence of more birds may protect vegetation because insectivorous birds can reduce plant-eating insects. Fruit-eating birds such as thrushes benefit from the lush growth of salmonberry and blueberry bushes along salmon streams. Bears also profit from productive berry bushes— another example of how a bear's hunger ultimately helps itself.

It's possible to reverse-engineer bears' effects on ecosystems by considering what would happen if they weren't around. Gende suggested one possibility, noting that "without salmon, bear densities would be lower and seed dispersal patterns could be altered, with unknown consequences." We can also look to the Greater Yellowstone ecosystem for clues, where Joel Berger and others traced an important link between the absence of predators and the shrinking populations of some neotropical migratory birds. These birds winter in Central and South America and fly to North America to breed. The local extirpation of bears and wolves since the 1930s meant that more moose calves survived in Grand Teton National Park, until the moose population in the park was five times that in adjacent lands that were open to hunting. That many moose browsing on riparian willows dramatically altered the vegetation structure, which was important to nesting neotropical songbirds. Consequently, half of the twelve local neotropical species shrank in number in heavily grazed thickets. Two species, gray catbirds and MacGillivray's warblers, disappeared completely. Eliminating natural predators had triggered a trophic cascade that reduced biodiversity in this particular bird community.

Such losses add up across North America, where at least 127 of 341 neo-tropical bird species are declining, according to a 2007 National Audubon Society report.

Bears also suffer when other species succeed at their expense. Biologist Steeve Côté suspects that white-tailed deer introduced to a Quebec island in 1896 extirpated the black bear population within five to seven decades by overbrowsing berry shrubs and nearly eliminating the bears' most important fall food. It's a good lesson for us. In some places, land managers have realized they need to restrict people from important berry patches so bears can take their cut.

An emerging field of study known as conservation physiology allows us to see how bears respond internally to human changes in their environments by examining their metabolism, nutrition, and endocrine responses, according to Martin Wikelski and Steven Cooke. Minnesota researchers studying the recent expansion of black bears into agricultural areas, where they eat mostly corn and sunflowers, used a combination of GPS technology and implanted cardiac monitors to track the bears' movements and activities in relationship to food availability. "Landscape fragmentation had a large influence on movement and heart rate for the two male bears: movement and heart [rate] increased with increasing fragmentation, likely due to the longer travel between patches of available natural foods and non-natural landscape," according to a report in *International Bear News*. In a different study, researchers monitoring the heart rates of fifteen wild bears (one released from captivity as a cub) happened to record the responses of two bears that were legally killed by hunters. One bear's heart rate exceeded 200 beats per minute seventeen times during the three hours before it was shot, even though it didn't appear at the bait station where it was killed until moments before it died, "suggesting that the bear was in the area of the hunter's bait and sensed danger." I can't help but wish it had paid better attention to its instincts.

The complexity of individual responses to ecological relationships means that rewilding the West is not as straightforward as plopping a few bears in parks and hoping everything works out. Nor can we assume that displaced bears in Alaska can always make do in some other habitat, because that other habitat is probably already occupied by perfectly content bears. Alaska wildlife biologist John Schoen, who was instrumental in outlining the relationships between brown bears and logging, mining, and development in Southeast Alaska, believes we should think bigger when it comes to bears. Consider bears as "wide-ranging creatures of landscape" rather than occupants of habitats, and plan with a time horizon of at least a century, he urges. That's a tough task for a species that is only now discovering what happens when a bear catches a salmon and eats it in the forest.

For Z.B. and his kind, eating their way through spring, summer, and fall makes it possible to fast through winter. Faced with the season's privations, other animals migrate, store food, make do with less desirable fare, or, in the case of Alaskans, vacation in Hawaii. But northern bears survive by spending half their lives sealed away, consuming only their own bodies. Researcher Ralph Nelson once called hibernation "the most amazing metabolic feat in the animal kingdom." In effect, bears become a different kind of animal entirely.

Z.B.'s chroniclers never saw the den where he underwent his transformation. If he was like most of the Brooks Range bears followed by Harry Reynolds, he probably excavated his winter chamber from a steep, south-facing slope several hundred feet above the valley floor, where the soil was easier to dig and the snow melted earlier in the spring. Bears everywhere make do with whatever terrain, climate, and resources they inherit, creating an astonishing array of strategies. Among polar bears, only pregnant females den. In the circumpolar north, brown and black bears may spend up to seven months in hibernation, while Tennessee black bears emerge after only three months, according to an overview by John D. C. Linnell and colleagues. Some male black bears denned for as many as 247 days near the Susitna River, Charles Schwartz and associates reported. Generally, male bears everywhere are the last to den and the first to emerge, while impregnated females and those with cubs enter earliest and reappear last. Van Daele recorded lone females leaving dens in late March at one end of Kodiak Island and in early May at the other end—a spread of two and a half months.

The availability of food helps determine hibernation patterns. Sometimes bears linger until late November or December to feed on late salmon runs or if they haven't eaten enough—because a berry crop failed, for example, or the fishing competition was too heavy. Zoo bears don't hibernate as long as the meals keep coming. Almost a quarter of the males Van Daele followed on Kodiak Island never denned. In one area, three-quarters of the males remained active all winter, thanks to bountiful supplies of bull kelp, sea lettuce, beach hoppers, whale carcasses, and other marine food.

Flooded dens, human disturbance, sudden warm spells, and starvation can wake bears and set them roaming. Inland Nunamiuts believed that winter bears dipped themselves into springs to form a frozen armor and conserve warmth, Robert Rausch reported. Kutchin Athabascans told anthropologist Richard Nelson that they consider winter bears especially dangerous because they are driven by hunger and will attack men unprovoked. Wiseman resident Jack Reakoff told me about an extremely emaciated bear in his neighborhood that attacked a trapper's dog team and killed eight of the nine dogs in November 1998. Reakoff and a friend tracked the bear and shot it. He estimated its age at twenty-eight or twenty-nine. "It had a tough, tough life," Reakoff said. "We did him a big favor."

Bears can hibernate almost anywhere: crevices, hollow snags, excavated dirt chambers, snow caverns, root wads, caves, rock piles, even open ground. A Wisconsin black bear once denned in an eagle's nest cradled in an aspen, *International Bear News* reported. Others snooze undetected in urban neighborhoods. Black bears living in Southeast Alaska's rain forests preferred stands protected from frequent windstorms, where it's easier to find attractive quarters in large, old trees emptied by heart fungi. Brown bears on Chichagof Island prefer old-growth forest, but John Schoen found that almost 80 percent of brown bear dens he examined on neighboring Admiralty Island were in rock cavities, some of them mere crevices beneath boulders. "Some cave dens are rubbed smooth like marble, so we assume the bears have been using them for centuries," he wrote in *Natural History* magazine. Yet one young male settled for lying at the base of a big tree near the beach. Schoen's colleague, LaVern Beier, has also located alpine dens buried beneath as much as fourteen feet of snow.

On the seemingly featureless tundra plains of Alaska's North Slope, wildlife biologist Richard Shideler found grizzly dens in "microsites" such as stream banks, ancient sand dunes, and especially pingos, the domed eruptions of tundra formed around an ice lens. One enterprising bear tucked itself into a pipe casing, and another denned less than a kilometer from the Beaufort Sea; some food-conditioned bears bedded down in active oilfields, presumably for convenience. But no matter where bears excavated their winter dwellings, at least 60 percent of them faced between 181 and 270 degrees north, the better to collect insulating snow.

Black bears are flexible about their winter accommodations. In South-central Alaska black bears often tuck themselves inside the hollowed stubs of dead cottonwoods. On the Kenai Peninsula bears excavated all but 4 percent of the dens that Charles Schwartz and his coinvestigators examined. Farther north in the Susitna Basin, they found that some bears dug dens and others settled into caves or rock piles. Interior bears often den on forested hillsides at the base of trees, but some curl up on open ground and simply let the snow cover them, according to John Hechtel. He once located a mother and her three two-year-olds buried beneath a yurt-like heap of grass. "A lot of times you couldn't even tell a den was there," he told a writer for *Alaska Fish & Wildlife News*. "It makes you wonder what you've walked by. Scattered through the landscape under the snow these bears are tucked away—and you'd never know."

That is, you'd never know without radio collars to help locate them. Researchers have long tracked bears to their dens so they can gather information about cubs, for example. Black bears are amazingly mild tempered when biologists interrupt their winter snoozes, as well-known Minnesota bear expert David Garshelis noted in an interview. "We've done over a thousand [radio collars] and we've never had an issue with a bear attacking," he said. "You're lying there at the front of the den with a little stick with a syringe on the end. They could come out and bite your head off, but they don't." More recent technological advances have made it possible to see what goes on when no one's around. Researchers at the North American Bear Center in Ely, Minnesota, installed webcams in the dens of cooperative females, allowing people around the world to watch the birth of cubs and the daily drama of maternal care.

Other considerations may influence den choices. Most Kodiak bears preferred to winter close to where they foraged for food, Van Daele observed, even if that meant excavating dens in tundra hummocks vulnerable to flooding or collapse. That instability may be the reason 20 percent of female bears in the area occupied more than one den during a winter. Females in Denali National Park den at higher elevations and on steeper grades than males, leading Nathan Libal and coauthors to hypothesize that females with cubs are attempting to avoid potentially infanticidal males.

Bears often renovate their quarters with piles of branches or foliage—up to a foot thick in northern Alaska. But it's hard to know what to make of one den found by a Tlingit bear guide while deer hunting on Chichagof Island. "It was a cave, but that bear had woven all the branches and stuff like a mat to close the den entrance," he told interviewer Merry Ellefson. "We saw it, we thought it was a human being that did it." Inside they found berries lying on skunk cabbage leaves, as if the bear were storing them.

The way bears disappear with the waning year and reemerge each spring impressed early observers, according to Paul Shepard and Barry Sanders: "Clearly the bear was master of renewal and the wheel of the seasons, of the knowledge of when to die and when to be re-born." Today, scientists are still gripped by the intricate mysteries of hibernation. Brian Barnes, an expert in arctic hibernation, regards this cyclical shift in a bear's life as profound. For part of the year, Barnes said, bears are "sensory junkies"—curious, aware, sometimes aggressive. All that changes when they enter hibernation. They lose their appetites, and they don't need to defecate or urinate, yet they seem content, according to Barnes. "They must have a driving urge to withdraw and live in a snow-enclosed dark den that essentially provides sensory deprivation. Can you imagine sitting in a dark box for six months? And then it reverses itself in the spring."

Barnes has peered into the dark box of the den and into the bear's brain by creating artificial hibernacula at the Institute of Arctic Biology at the University of Alaska–Fairbanks, where he and researcher Øivind Tøien studied hibernating black bears. Barnes, the institute's director, is a zoophysiologist who first investigated hibernation in wood frogs and arctic ground squirrels. He describes hibernation like this: "An organism withdraws from the environment, stops interacting, stops becoming dependent on a day-to-day basis on the environment for food or water and goes into a lethargic state with decreased metabolism." Powering down for prolonged periods conserves energy during the hungry season, but not all hibernators are alike. Ground squirrels, for example, slow their metabolism radically and allow their core temperature to cool to near freezing during six months of hibernation. Their brains essentially flat-line as they become what Barnes calls "little ice cubes."

"Imagine that in you or me," Barnes said. "They would declare us dead and cut us up for parts. But these ground squirrels aren't dead. In fact, they're just fine." Like other small hibernators, squirrels rewarm themselves about every three weeks, meaning their winter is actually eleven nights long. Barnes's hypothesis is that hibernating squirrels become progressively sleep-deprived, so they rewarm their brains to get a good night's sleep, which is critical for maintaining memories. "If they didn't warm up to sleep, they would lose their minds," Barnes said. Some studies show that neurons retract when ground squirrels fall into torpor and then regrow when they rouse themselves.

Barnes and his associates wondered about hibernators that maintain brain function without turning into popsicles. Enter the black bear—a research subject not as small and cuddly or as easily obtained and housed as ground squirrels. The scientists acquired otherwise doomed nuisance bears from state wildlife biologists and surgically implanted tiny devices to record their core temperature, heart rate, and muscle activity. In the fall the bears entered outdoor wood boxes outfitted with cameras, microphones, and antennae. The researchers measured the bears' metabolism by recording how much oxygen they absorbed and how much carbon dioxide they emitted.

"We can tell everything the bear does," Barnes said, "including—I got asked by some high school students the other day—whether they fart."

"And the answer was?" I asked.

"No. No farting." They do, however, snore.

The study produced some unexpected results. The bears' metabolic rate slowed to about 25 percent of normal, even though their core temperature dropped by just seven to ten degrees Fahrenheit, as the researchers reported in *Science* in 2011. The exception was a pregnant female whose temperature didn't drop until after she gave birth to a cub that died of congenital defects. Another surprise: after the bears left hibernation, their temperature returned to normal, but their metabolism remained at half throttle for a few weeks. Thus, in bears, body temperature seems less linked to the induction of torpor than in other hibernators.

Bear brains operate differently, too. "We did measure sleep in these bears with EEG electrodes and found out that, unlike ground squirrels who have to warm up to sleep and sleep only once every few weeks, black bears for the most part sleep all the time," Barnes said. "In fact, we're astounded by how much they can sleep—as much as 80 percent of the time, which is pretty hard to do." Like humans and other animals, Barnes said, bears cycle through different types of sleep: slow wave, paradoxical, and rapid eye movement (REM), when bears enter a "dream state." As with people, muscle paralysis prevents their slumbering bodies from reacting during this state.

Bears are not inert heaps trapped in dreamland, however. Every few hours to every couple of days, they rise, stretch, turn over, maybe scratch themselves, and circle like a dog before lying down again—locomotion that could help allay muscle loss, Barnes said. Rather like myself, ground squirrels take about half a day to emerge from their torpor. But hibernating bears can wake quickly when they're disturbed, as their brain waves revealed whenever researchers approached the dens. During the study of fifteen wild Minnesota bears implanted with monitors, Tim Laske and his coinvestigators discovered that although the bears seemed fairly undisturbed when the researchers approached quietly, their elevated heart rates demonstrated "the alertness of the bear while in a state of hibernation to potential dangers outside the den."

This self-protective response can lead to unfortunate consequences when it comes to brown bears. Oil companies on the Kenai Peninsula hired guards to protect their crews after one man was killed in 1998 by a skull-crushing bite from a hibernating brown bear that was inadvertently awakened. Six years later a guard was mauled by a female who erupted from her den when a seismic crew passed by. He shot her as she charged, and the wounded bear was later tracked and killed. Her two cubs disappeared. There's a good reason researchers almost never annoy hibernating brown bears.

A bear's ability to jolt itself into action after months of barely stirring depends on a suite of mechanisms that prevent muscle atrophy, bone loss, heart problems, and organ damage under conditions that would harm or kill a human being. Researchers describe these functions as "amazing" and "phenomenal" and "incredibly fascinating." Compare a hibernating bear to an astronaut in space: Absent the forces of gravity, the astronaut's muscles begin to atrophy and weaken within days. During brief missions an astronaut may lose 10 to 20 percent of muscle mass and as much as 50 percent on extended flights. Likewise, the bones of some space jockeys are eroded by 20 percent after six months in space. (Unlike human bones, bear bones become stronger as they age.)

Hibernating bears avoid such problems by living in slow motion, conserving energy, and altering their physiological processes in ways that are impossible in summer. They don't bother growing hair, for example. Between breaths, thirteen or fourteen seconds may pass without a heartbeat, bioengineer Tim Laske explained in a presentation to science students. "Your body will not allow your heart to go that long without beating," he said. "You'll faint for about three seconds, and other parts of your heart will contract." Yet after six months without food or water, bear hearts show no change in mass or electrical function. Meanwhile, the black bears Laske and his colleagues studied minimized their weight loss to an average of 12 percent over six months. (Grizzlies lose between 24 and 43 percent of their body mass, according to *Wild Mammals of North America*.) Despite months of inactivity, bears retain most of their strength, as measured by a biomechanical device that stimulates the muscles of hibernating wild black bears. "We find that overwintering black bears lose less than 23% of their strength over 130 days—unlike humans, who are weakened by a predicted 90% strength loss over the same period," reported Henry Harlow and coauthors in *Nature*. Harlow's later work suggests that daily bouts of shivering and other muscle contractions act like isometric exercises to help bears tone and strengthen their muscles.

Hibernating bears don't urinate; they avoid poisoning themselves with urea by recycling it. Work since the early 1970s by the late Ralph Nelson and others determined that urea moves from the bladder through the blood and into the gut, where specialized microbes reduce it to nitrogen and carbon dioxide. The bear exhales the carbon dioxide, and the nitrogen finds a new purpose as amino acids, the building blocks of the protein used in muscle, among other tasks.

For medical researchers, bears represent a cabinet of wonders whose secrets could cure what ails us. As they slept, their powerful immune systems actually expelled the transmitters that had been implanted beneath their skin, reported Paul Iaizzo and colleagues. Despite being powered down, the bears also displayed a remarkable ability to heal themselves. Their blood plasma contains hormones and other compounds that can induce torpor, reduce the damage from heart attacks, and extend the life of donor organs in pigs and other animals, Iaizzo told science students. Ursodiol, first identified in bear bile and produced by other mammals as well, can be used to treat gallstones and liver disease. (Although a synthetic version is available, the demand for raw bear bile in traditional Chinese medicine has created an industry that milks bile from thousands of captive Asiatic bears in one of the crueler expressions of human exploitation.)

What bears do is "seemingly impossible," Laske said, yet the study of bears offers tantalizing possibilities in terms of treating human ailments, preserving donor organs longer, and improving the prospects for prolonged space travel. Identifying the hormones that regulate a bear's appetite has obvious applications for the treatment of obesity or anorexia. Stimulating the metabolic pathways or administering parathyroid hormones that conserve bone mass could help prevent or reverse osteoporosis in aging or bedridden patients. Learning how bears handle urea could help kidney patients and reduce the need for dialysis. Being able to induce metabolic torpor and decrease blood flow to the brain would be a real breakthrough. As Barnes said, "Wow, if you could induce that state of protection in the brain at will, then it would be an acute treatment for stroke or heart attack or shock or hemorrhaging that you would immediately use to stabilize somebody before you could get them to advanced medical care."

Patents have been acquired, companies formed, and funding obtained from interested parties such as NASA. But what I want to know probably won't be explored for some time: What do bears dream about? Flashes of quicksilver in salmon streams? Fields of bushes thick with sweet berries? I wonder how it feels when they shake off their dreams, push their way out of their chambers, smell the clean air, and feel the sun for the first time in months. It must seem like the world reinvents itself each year just for them, until the earth tilts away from the sun and winter reclaims them once again.

Examining the cogs and wheels in an old-fashioned watch doesn't necessarily tell us that its purpose is to tell time. What, then, is the function of a bear? That's the question ecologist Daniel Simberloff posed to bear biologists in 1999. "So if some people think bears are not important to save in their own right, it seems that a justification for them might be that they serve unique functions in their respective ecosystems," he wrote. Ecologists deploy a range of metaphors to describe these functions. Are they a "keystone" species like salmon—that is, an organism with an outsized influence on other species in its ecosystem? They do make an excellent "flagship" species, according to Simberloff, providing an archetypal symbol for people to rally behind. But with so few species inhabiting the planet, bears offer a meager contribution to biodiversity, he concluded. (Bear specialists with the International Union for Conservation of Nature consider the survival of six of the eight species under threat—all but brown and black bears.) If bears were managed as an "umbrella" species, their need for large tracts of land would automatically help protect the multitude of other species inhabiting the same areas. But without more data on entire communities as well as the umbrella species, "all we have are clever ideas," Simberloff lamented.

The use of so many metaphors suggests that a bear's purpose is largely symbolic, an allegory for one way to think about how the world operates. But let us always remember that a bear doesn't live metaphorically. Z.B. wasn't a keystone, an umbrella, or a flagship. He was himself. Writer Ernestine Hayes explained this concept to me from a Tlingit perspective, which understands bears not as a different species but as fellow residents of a shared existence. "They're conducting their lives, you know. And I think that that's an important thing for people, maybe even especially for people who observe and study bears, to know, that that bear is conducting its life. And it's just as important. It's important to the bear. That's the bear's life."

Z.B. is, of course, long dead, and it saddened me to learn that his chronicler, Spencer Linderman, died in a plane crash the summer after his bear study, while he was surveying Dall sheep. He was twenty-nine. I consider his report a fine tribute to both human and ursine curiosity and persistence. He recorded a brief but intimate account of a bear's life that now seems rare, since field research has largely given way to data gathered by GPS, radiotelemetry, isotope analysis, genetic investigations, and field cameras. Surely Linderman understood something about how landscapes make bears, and how bears make landscapes. Maybe he saw that bears *are* a kind of living landscape that pinions earth and river, darkness and sunlight, plant and animal, fish and bird. And still we know so little about any bear's existence from day to day and season to season, from root to berry to fish to squirrel to caribou. The details of Z.B.'s birth, the rhythms of his life, and the manner of his death will always remain hidden from us—but this is true of almost every nameless, unnumbered bear in the North.

the social bear

Walking the two miles from camp to the McNeil River falls takes an hour, maybe two, depending on whether high tide is slopping into the lagoon and how many brown bears you encounter along the way. We had no reason to rush, even if that were possible swaddled in bulky rain gear, hip boots, and daypacks while lugging cameras, tripods, and telephoto lenses. This was our first full day of watching bears at McNeil River State Game Sanctuary, and a nervous thrill charged the small talk, as if the ten of us were bound for the Land That Time Forgot with its wondrous, dangerous beasts.

That had not seemed far from the truth the night before. Strange bellows drifted across the lagoon into camp, and in the midnight dimness, mysterious shapes trudged along the distant shore. Bears placidly cropped sedges near our camp, but it was still difficult to grasp that they weren't much interested in people. I'd almost drifted asleep when a chain of wheezy snorts outside the tent electrified me. I bolted upright, clutching the air horn supplied by staff biologists so we could signal if a bear wandered by. After holding my breath, I realized a snoring camper was supplying the soundtrack that had jump-started my imagination.

During the morning briefing, sanctuary manager Larry Aumiller dampened our anxiety with smart remarks and a relaxed demeanor. It was his day off, but he'd dropped by the cook cabin to scavenge lunch from the groceries left by previous visitors. "You'll be in camp today?" somebody asked. "Yep, so hide all your cookies," he said. When a couple from Hawaii announced, "We just saw four bears brushing our teeth!" Larry replied, "Where'd they get the toothbrushes?" This was his thirtieth—and final—summer managing the sanctuary. He knows more about brown bear behavior than almost anybody, but he also understands human nature.

"Don't you ever just want to screw with people's minds?" I asked him once, certain that if he announced bears could fly, we'd believe him.

"What makes you think I'm not?" he said.

Before we set out for the falls, Tom Griffin explained how we'd travel. "Stay in a group," he told us. "Ask before you stop. If we see a bear, we may watch it, or I might ask the group to tighten up. On the flats it's nice to walk in a cluster rather than a line." Some people might have assumed he was advising us to huddle for our own safety, so the bears couldn't cull individuals from the herd, but he really hoped to minimize the commotion created by a dozen people scattered hither and yon. A bear that stops fishing or nursing or mating because a person approaches too closely is a bear that's wasting time, energy, and purpose. We clomped along the path toward the lagoon for a few minutes before Tom said, offhandedly, "There's a little bear sleeping on the beach, but I think we're going to carry on." There's no such thing as tiptoeing in hip boots. The dozing bear woke, stood, and wandered away without any sign of alarm. Two yearlings eyed us and returned to grazing as a pair of young bears wrestled in Mikfik Creek. We paused so an approaching bear could pass between us and another adult barely visible in the meadow.

The new arrival plopped beside the creek and nibbled on a delicate sedge known as angel hair pasta, prompting Tom to school us briefly in bear cuisine. In the hungry weeks of early June, before chum salmon start running in McNeil River, bears fish Mikfik Creek for red salmon and browse in the greening sedge flats. They like Lyngbye's sedge and succulent goosetongue, Tom said, but they don't care much for beach greens. "They're pretty selective about what they eat," he added. With his dark beard and solid frame, he seemed somewhat ursine himself—a common trait among male bear biologists. Even Larry had commented on the distinctive morphologies of bear experts—from the burly, bearded types like Tom to the lean, quick models like him.

The tide was out, so we formed a human amoeba to cross the mudflats. There was too much to look at, really. A female galloped toward a fin slicing through the lagoon's rivulets as a tiny cub gamely rollicked behind her. A gangly bear wheeled around at the sudden thrash of a salmon and swung its head to locate breakfast. In the distance, a young bear pounced and trapped a wriggling fish between its paws. "All right!" people cheered. In the ongoing skirmish of bear versus salmon, humans like to root for bears.

"Is that Simba?" biologist Polly Hessing asked Tom. She pointed at a bear padding across the mudflats with a fluffy pelt and a nose scar in the shape of a plus sign. Simba had been one of Rollie's spring cubs in 1998, she explained. In lieu of identifying them with ear tags or radio collars, McNeil staff members assign names to the individual bears that frequent the sanctuary each summer—from as many as 144 to as few as 58 in years past. This was Polly's day off, but she wanted to work on identifying bears and counting fish. She joked about the need for "murder and mayhem" bug dope as we walked. Like her colleagues, she was calm, knowledgeable, and good-natured; she had the open, aware face and the bright eyes of someone who preferred to spend most of her time under the sky and around animals. This was her tenth season at the sanctuary, although she'd been away for a few years, working for Fish and Game in Juneau.

When the bears fishing the lagoon drifted into a looser constellation, Tom said this was our chance to wade a shallow channel cutting through the mud. We made an embarrassing production of it, with people sinking into the muck and abandoning the amoeba, letting their cameras distract them. Somehow, without hollering at anybody, Tom managed to corral and aim us toward the trailhead. (The staff avoids herding bears, but clearly, people need it.) He shepherded us past daybeds dimpling the shore beneath the bluffs and onto a rutted path seaming a meadow.

As we dodged bear scat and thudded over planks covering mud holes, Tom kept up a stream of conversation, talking to the bears so they'd know we were coming. "Hey monkeyflower," he called as casually as if he were greeting a colleague at the office. "Hey alder alder. Hey buddy buddy." The biologists' attentiveness demonstrated how much the rest of us didn't see—a flash of red Sitka burnet, moose pellets whitening in the moss, a fat bear browsing grass and ignoring us as we slipped by. Polly mentioned that the bear was female, and I asked how she knew. "If you look under the tail you can see the vulva," she said. I took her word for it.

A rushing sound whisked through the grass as we approached the falls. We topped a rise, and the screech of gulls and thrum of the cataracts swept through me. Turquoise water bucketed over the falls and pooled around broad platters of rock where a group of enormous bears—eleven, twelve?—stood in and beside the river. The collective noun for bears is actually "sleuth," but until then, I'd had no reason to use such a word. More remarkable than their number was the lack of any obvious reaction to our appearance. None galloped away or charged toward us or paid much attention at all. It was the damnedest sight.

I'd probably still be standing there with mouth agape, but the sanctuary's bear-watching protocol is a bit like clocking into work. People arrive and depart in one group about the same time every day, never claiming more than the tiny principality of two gravel pads—one overlooking the river from a bluff, and the other at the foot of the bluff about twenty yards from the river. Our job was to remain as boring as cardboard, avoiding any loud talk or jerky movements. If a bear approached, we were supposed to stand slowly to remind it of well-established guidelines: Viewing pads belong to people. Everything else belongs to bears.

Tom sorted us into two groups so we could take our places with minimal fuss. I joined the lower pad's first shift, which included the Hawaiian couple and two employees from Katmai National Park—acting chief ranger Missy Epping and chief of interpretation Roy Wood. We pulled camp chairs from a shallow cave in the bluff and lofted them to the group above us before seating ourselves. Moments later a largish male bear chased a smallish female bear across the river and directly toward us. Missy and I stood up abruptly. The blonde female dashed up the slope beside Roy. The male veered toward the river.

"I moved too fast," Missy said.

"So did I," I admitted.

Roy hoisted his camera and peered through his new telephoto lens at the blonde bear, who stood a few yards away watching the male depart. "I hate it when they're so close you can't photograph them," he deadpanned.

Some of the most astonishing bear photographs in the world are captured at McNeil River—a good number of them taken by Larry Aumiller and published in *The Way of the Grizzly* by Tom Walker. But during the next three days, I continually reminded myself to lower my rinky-dink camera and simply watch bears living their lives. Everything I knew about bears came from secondhand sources or from animals that had ventured into human territory and automatically assumed some unfortunate role conceived for them: interlopers, threats, dangerous beasts rupturing the boundary between wilderness and civilization. That boundary is far more permeable at McNeil River, where spawning salmon attract the largest gathering of brown bears in the world—eighty of them at one time in 2011. This place has become a sanctuary for people, too, since its establishment in 1967. Here the mental and physical distance between animals and humans narrows, allowing people an intimate glimpse into how wild bears conduct themselves as individuals, as a species, and as a self-organizing society engaged in all of life's important business: feeding, playing, fighting, mating, mothering, dying.

Some biologists and hunters would balk at calling this congregation a society, but I don't know how else to characterize a regular gathering of large, powerful animals who have worked out ways to accommodate one another (and us) so they can concentrate on eating salmon rather than tearing one another (or us) into tiny bits. Bears are notable for their plasticity, which one biologist defines as the "ability to respond to environmental circumstances, to assess complex situations, and to learn." They display behaviors we can reasonably interpret as curiosity, aggression, indifference, dominance, boldness, shyness, fear, playfulness, patience, submissiveness. It's a mind-shattering experience, reconciling the bears living in your head with the bears living in the wild. The bears themselves make it possible by tolerating daily incursions of people who park themselves beside the river for hours and expect to survive largely by comporting themselves properly. McNeil River asks us to demonstrate our own behavioral plasticity—the ability to respond to environmental circumstances, to assess complex situations, to learn.

On the first morning a dozen bears hunkered on the opposite shore within ten feet of one another, peering intently into the river as if reading runes. The scene seemed to be composed mostly of large bears staring at the water and people staring at large bears, but a closer look revealed that something interesting was unfolding at nearly every moment. "I think of it like the cutaway of an apartment building, and we're watching what everyone's doing," Polly said. All through the day, dramas large and small erupted as bears waded into the churning falls, lunged after salmon, chased other bears, napped in the brush, wrestled in the deeper pools, went and came, came and went. Harder to see were the subtle dynamics that inflected every bear's choices about where to stand, how to fish, when to run, who to approach, who to avoid.

A happy collusion of geology, natural history, and bear evolution made it possible for us to observe such goings-on. The river supports a major chum run and small runs of red, pink, silver, and king salmon—mobile bundles of fat and protein that are invaluable to big animals that don't eat for half their lives. Clear water sluices over a 150-yard-wide rock shelf in white-water chutes, slowing the migrating salmon and making them easier targets for hungry bears. The water is too deep for fishing below and above the falls, so the bears bunch up around the prime holes, the most dominant animals claiming the sweet spots. The river's architecture and ecology created the cafeteria, but the bears' social structure helps them survive one another's presence.

"We think of them as asocial animals, we have it in our mind that they can't really stand to be around each other," Larry said one afternoon as we watched bears fishing. "But all over the state we see exceptions to that. The reality is that they're plenty capable of putting up with each other if the reward is worth it. I've seen eight or ten bears on the same rock instead of three. They're very good about doing the right body language to accomplish all that with very little physical contact."

Habituation allows people to watch this hierarchy in action. "It means there's an absence of a response," Larry explained. "If you were there or you weren't there, they would be doing the exact same thing." Every time a bear sees a human and nothing particularly bad happens, it becomes less interested in avoiding or challenging people. A recent theory proposed by Stephen Herrero and other experts suggests that bears in dense populations learn to habituate to one another when they aggregate in places with important food sources, such as salmon rivers, sedge flats, and dumps. This ability seems to make it possible for them to accept our presence without any overt reaction, although they may react internally. Habituated bears aren't tame, though. They choose how closely to approach people. Aumiller and his staff have spent decades fostering bear-human habituation by treating every interaction as a learning experience, both for the bears and for us. This works best if people behave consistently and predictably. The sanctuary's small compound has remained in the same place for decades, and the number of visitors in each four-day window never exceeds ten people, who are chosen by lottery. The staff's success at ensuring that human food and garbage are unavailable to the bears means that they aren't rewarded by our presence; thus we could eat lunch at the river without being mugged. "We don't feed them, we don't control them, we try to have as little impact as possible," Larry said. "We try not to be part of their lives."

Not all bears become habituated. Each individual's response to the nearness of people depends on its own genetic predisposition, experiences, and learned behavior. "Wolfie, it took him two years to get used to people," Derek Stonorov said of a McNeil regular. "He used to stand in the alders, stand up and get down, wouldn't come down in the open.

Finally he got at ease and would come around people." Bears also exhibit varying degrees of habituation. Generally, females accept the presence of humans more easily than the big males do. Some spring cubs relax around people within a few days because their mothers remain unconcerned, creating generations of habituated bears at McNeil. A highly habituated female named White reared a daughter, Teddy, who became the UN ambassador of bears and probably one of the most photographed brown bears in history. Teddy felt comfortable nursing her cubs, napping, and hanging out a few feet from the viewing pads. "The ultimate compliment," Polly said, "is when a bear turns its back on you."

Nor does habituation to other bears mean that they sing "Kumbaya" and pass the fish. A sensitive hierarchy of dominance and subordination determines who fishes where, who mates with whom, and who had better hustle out of the way pronto. This social architecture helps avoid conflicts, particularly in a place where as many as 70 percent of the bears are adult males. The value of this pragmatic approach becomes obvious when you see the damage bears can inflict on one another—broken jaws, gaping wounds, peeled hides, even death. The authors of The Grizzly Bears of Yellowstone studied a similar process of habituation at the Trout Creek dump and concluded that these behaviors are neither rare nor recent. "The ability to recognize and remember a large number of ever-changing social relationships, and the existence of various and complex social signals expressing threat and submission, are all evidence of a long history of natural selection for socially adaptive traits among bears gathering in aggregations at natural ecocenters in pristine, presettlement environments," they wrote—a perfect description of McNeil River.

Derek Stonorov was one of the first to study social interactions among McNeil's bears. While a student at Utah State University, Derek worked with Professor Allen Stokes, who supervised several graduate projects on social and fishing behavior at McNeil. During the summer of 1970 Stonorov and Stokes observed about 600 aggressive encounters, which they defined as "any situation where two or more bears reacted with each other in such a way as to disrupt their ongoing patterns of moving, feeding or resting." Fighting, threatening, escaping, and appeasement through submission are all elements of agonistic behavior. McNeil bears were most likely to fight or threaten one another during four situations: violating another animal's critical space, competing for a fishing spot, losing an encounter to one bear and taking it out on a third bear, and encountering a strange bear for the first time.

After observing twenty-two different bears in at least seven encounters each, Stonorov and Stokes devised a sort of fight card to rank the bears. The biggest males were most dominant, followed by females with offspring a year or older, single females and small males, and finally subadults and siblings traveling together. The socially inferior subadults rarely bested anyone and tended to avoid the falls, as did females protecting their spring cubs. Two top males, identified as Bear A and Bear B, never lost a major altercation with another bear, but they evidently duked it out in private, because Bear A disappeared the day before the researchers first saw Bear B.

Bear communication includes the use of threats as a way to avoid harm. Because bears lack expressive ears and long tails that can convey signals, they employ body orientation, stance, head posture, and other gestures to scmaphore their intentions. In many cases, this body language indicates either "Back off!" or "No need to bother with me." Stonorov and Stokes identified almost two dozen behavioral components—such as raising ears, lowering heads, opening mouths, showing canines, twisting muzzles, charging, and biting—that, in combination, represent recognizable patterns. Bears also communicate by huffing, woofing, growling, bawling, roaring, and "chuffing," which biologist Maria Pasitschniak-Arts describes as a friendly combination of popping and forceful exhalations used in "greeting, coaxing, appeasement, during courting and mating, and between a female and her young."

Some signals even I noticed. In one confrontation, two bears stood in opposition, facing slightly away with their heads lowered. One worked its mouth as if talking, a behavior Stonorov labeled "jawing." In response, the other animal stepped sideways. Suddenly, all was copacetic. In such encounters, the "loser" is generally the bear that drops its head, faces away, backs up, walks off, or runs away. Less than 3 percent of agonistic encounters witnessed by doctoral student Allan Egbert at McNeil River included fighting; 75 percent of these incidents involved one bear attacking while the other (usually a subadult) fended off blows and bites. "Sometimes they make all the right moves and still get whomped," Larry said. "Who knows why?"

Most of the males we watched had already negotiated their social standing and knew where they could fish and who had first dibs on courting the females. On several occasions a bear confiscated another's salmon without any protest (to our eyes, anyway). Sometimes, so much was happening simultaneously that it was hard to unravel who did what to whom. One afternoon a huge snaggletoothed male named Earl eyed us as he followed a female in estrus through the meadow behind us. He was "cowboy walking"—a distinctive stiff-legged, deliberate pace. "Because he doesn't like us, he can't come as close to us as she can," Polly explained. "He has to work his way around us. He doesn't like us very much so he's not very happy about it." Earl's arrival was like a cue ball breaking a rack. Suddenly, eight bears were striding up the bluff trails, swerving away from one another, shifting toward us, loping back to the river. When the excitement subsided, Polly said, "There are about 4,000 things happening that we missed because we're not quick enough to get all the subtleties."

This particular year, the salmon run was weak, which can influence behavior. In a study by Egbert and Stokes, "a decline in salmon numbers was reflected by an immediate increase in intolerance among the bears." The more salmon there are to go around, the less frequently the bears threaten one another. Temperament and experience also influence whether an encounter escalates. One day, staff biologist Josh Peirce and I watched a female swipe a salmon from a bigger male. The male wasn't timid, according to Josh; though less of a scrapper than some of the others, he managed to hold his own. The female had simply outbossed him. "In the bear world, attitude is nine-tenths and size is the other tenth," he said. When an enormous bear known as McDougall joined the fishing line, the other bears ignored him. "They know he's just here to fish, even though he's huge," Josh said. Egbert reported that in nearly 60 percent of the interactions he witnessed, one bear simply deferred to another by changing its path or waiting for an open fishing spot.

It was easy to see which bear owned McNeil River that summer. A muscled hulk appeared one day on the opposite bank, moving with the careless authority of one who is certain that nobody would dare challenge him. No one did. Bears eased out of his way or evaporated into the alders as he followed a female who was nearly trotting in an effort to stay a fair distance ahead. His name was Fred, Polly said. She preferred that to his original horror-movie name: Freddy Krueger. His flanks and legs were nearly hairless, and his skin appeared almost black. A crest of fur bristled along his spine like a Mohawk. "He's really shed out,"

Polly commented. (Bears molt annually, some more dramatically than others.)

Fred's chiseled muscles moved like living granite. White scars on his shoulders, flanks, and head mapped a history of conflicts. "It's hard to tell, but that's the biggest bear in the world," Larry said. A McNeil bear tagged during an early research program weighed a thousand pounds, he said, but Fred probably weighed least a third again as much. The combination of Fred's size and attitude must have been overwhelming; one bear plunged into the rapids to avoid him.

Another afternoon, a male named Reo (short for Right Ear Off) confronted a bear dangling a salmon from its mouth. They reared up to swat at each other, and Reo grabbed the dropped salmon. But when Fred padded over, Reo instantly surrendered the fish and skedaddled. A half-ton bear named Woofie also backed away, clearly signaling, "Leave me out of this." Woofie was once the biggest, baddest bear on the river, Larry said. Not anymore.

Food seemed like an afterthought to Fred, though. He spent afternoons plodding after females on long circuits up and down and across the river. On his first loop past the viewing pads, he gave us a sidelong look, his eyes small and reddish in his colossal head. I didn't want to ascribe any malice to him, but we all agreed that his gargantuan size, his dramatic scars, and the almost physical force of his glance made him especially imposing—and by imposing we meant scary as hell. The female sensed an opportunity to ditch him and suddenly sprinted up the trail beside the pad. By now, we novices recognized that a bear running *toward* us wasn't running *at* us. Fred peeled away, reluctant to follow her so close to people. The female's gambit reminded me of a basketball move called a "pick-and-roll," which uses another player's body position to deflect an opponent.

"Sometimes we're the path of least resistance," Polly commented.

"Pretty smart strategy," I said.

"Here, yes," she said. "Somewhere else, probably not."

An hour later Fred popped from the alders on the opposite bank. A bear named Weird was attempting to mount Dolly, but when she glimpsed Fred, she freed herself from Weird's clasp and bolted. Fred lumbered after her, pausing to steal another bear's partially eaten fish. (Larry later joked, "Freddy, if he were a human, he'd be serving forty life sentences in a row for sexual harassment, date rape. . . .") Fred followed

Dolly across the river, and we stood up when Polly did. This time he passed so closely that I took an involuntary step back. Polly said, "When a big one comes by, you want to move slowly. Your heart can move quickly." Which it did, for quite a while.

The constant swirl of bears moving along the river and beside the viewing pads became so familiar that we took for granted the biologists' quick readings of bear behavior. With small gestures they reminded distracted bears that the gravel pads were off-limits. A tip of a cap, a shift in stance, a handclap, or a sharp "hey" usually worked. It was harder for us newbies to learn when to stand up and when to keep still, when to move slowly and when to act quickly. The man most responsible for developing a repertoire of bear communications is Larry Aumiller, the only guy there without a degree in wildlife science. "Larry knows more about bear behavior from up close and personal experience than anyone else in the world and has the mind of a scientist so that his observations fit together to reveal the whole picture of why McNeil bears behave as they do," says retired biologist Sterling Miller. Terry DeBruyn told me, "You can get it just from osmosis from that guy. I don't have many heroes but if I did, Larry'd be pretty close to it. You can watch his eyes sparkle when he talks about bears."

I saw Larry's keen understanding in action one day when two bears began mating beside the lower viewing pad. They faced away from us, completely uninterested in our presence, but the potential for trouble increased exponentially when another male wandered over. These two males had erupted into a raging fight earlier over the same female, and it was easy to imagine chaos in our ranks should they reignite their competition. Larry stood closest to the bears and casually propped his shotgun stock against his hip, barrel pointing upward. To encourage the lone bear to leave, he raised his ball cap and shifted ever so subtly toward him when the preoccupied male wasn't looking. Unbeknownst to us, Polly held a rock and a chair ready above us. "I would have used them only if things went to hell because I didn't have my gun with me," she explained later. Soon the unrequited bear drifted away.

Larry's early years taught him how little is required to alter a bear's behavior. "We've done everything you can imagine to get bears out of camp, starting with bird shot, slingshots, rubber bullets—all of these very heavy-handed things," he said. "Through the years, we've evolved into [using] a little can of rocks. And that's all that's needed. You don't ever want to overdo anything. Especially here, because we're trying to get them to like us and feel comfortable with us and trust us." Usually the biologists can deter an inattentive bear from approaching too closely by stepping off the pad, holding up a hand, flashing a notebook, or occasionally tossing a rock to attract its attention. "We're very careful about the rock thing because we don't want everybody and their mother to go out rocking bears," Polly said. "Because there's so much we can do up to that point."

They've each learned how easy it is to overreact. On his first day guiding visitors alone at Mikfik Creek, Josh stood abruptly to warn away a subadult approaching the group. "That bear just about fell over backward," he said. "It acted like I was Freddy." Once, an unfamiliar bear was surprised to discover people sitting on the bluff above Mikfik Creek and charged the group. Polly threw a chair at it and hollered so loudly that even the bears fishing below froze. "I was really mortified because there was no modulation at all," she said. "I ended up apologizing to the group: 'I'm sorry, that was really extreme.'" Derek Stonorov remembers when a male bear tried to cut between Rollie and her cubs at the falls. "She went towards him and drove him towards where all the people were," he said. "People were all backed up against the rock. I took my chair and threw it at him. Those bears—he stopped, she stopped. What we perceive as an aggressive, horrible thing, it obviously isn't the same thing to a bear."

This isn't to say that McNeil bears haven't occasionally asserted themselves with humans. Fred delivered a lesson in power and restraint one day as he followed a female in estrus. Five of us stood up on the lower pad when the female paused about fifteen feet away, as if she were trying to decide whether to continue or to turn up the slope beside us. As Fred approached her, Josh came below and clapped to encourage her to move. We clapped, too. As she dashed uphill, Fred slapped the ground twice and huffed forcefully. Then he followed her, arcing widely to avoid us. About fifteen minutes later the pair repeated their approach; the female bolted, and again Fred signaled his displeasure with a double-paw swat that was slightly less intense.

"Was that aimed at her or at us?" I asked Josh later.

"We got rushed twice," he said. He had almost chambered a round at this second display. But again Fred followed the female uphill and "put himself on time-out," Josh said.

I didn't understand the seriousness of Fred's reaction until the biologists discussed the day's events over a dinner of red salmon and rice in Larry's cabin. Josh pointed out that Fred never would have approached our group if he weren't following a female. She had used us to ditch Fred, they agreed. If another bear had tried to thwart Fred, Fred most likely would have "throttled" him, Josh predicted. "I think he treats us like a dominant bear," Polly said, "but he doesn't know what to do with us because we don't look like a dominant bear." When we didn't run away, as any sensible bear would have, it created a real conflict for Fred, who was strongly attracted to the female but equally repelled by us. Hence, his agitation. "In a lot of places, Freddy would have been a dead bear today," Josh said. Larry decided to accompany Polly the following day to help keep an eye on Fred.

This discussion illuminated how attentive the biologists were to bear behavior, despite their casual demeanor. When I asked Larry about this at the river the next day, he said, "Even now as I'm sitting here, we're looking, we're talking, I'm thinking about safety. Where people are, what the bears are doing." By constantly scanning the river and paying special attention to unfamiliar bears, females with cubs, and males following females, the biologists anticipate situations that might accidentally embroil viewers. "If a bear's stressed, we're alert, is sort of the bottom line," Larry said. "Any bear anywhere for any reason." Few problems have occurred over the decades, despite situations that many would consider volatile elsewhere. Staff recorded thirteen charges in the sanctuary's first thirty years, most of them from partially habituated bears. No staff member has ever fired a shot. No people have been injured. No bears have been killed since the permit system began. Think of this as a testament to the behavioral plasticity of bears and people alike.

One afternoon two bears swam back and forth downriver, where the current flattened into a pool. I couldn't figure out why until Polly explained that they were consorting—courting and mating. Mid-July was a bit late in the breeding season, although McNeil bears have been seen mating in August. Several bears were trailing the scent of at least three females in estrus, Teddy, Dolly, and Jennifer. Teddy finally let Reo catch up and mount her beside the river, maybe twenty yards from us voyeurs. "I hope we're not giving him performance anxiety," Polly remarked.

One way or another, most bear behavior we saw at McNeil revolved around the fundamental imperative to make more bears and contribute gencs to offspring. Because studying the sex lives of wild bears presents obvious difficulties, what we know about the mating system of brown bears is that we don't know enough, researcher Sam Steyært and his colleagues noted in a 2012 review. "We determined that many aspects of the reproduction of the brown bear remain unclear, including (i) biological aspects such as hormone and oestrous cycling, sperm competition, mate choice, sexually selected infanticide, etc. and (ii) human impacts on the mating system, occurring when humans alter population size and structure, through, for example, hunting or habitat degradation." In other words, basically everything.

The flexibility of life history and behavior in different populations is one reason for the uncertainty. For example, as Charles Schwartz and coauthors reported in a detailed overview of grizzly bears in *Wild Mammals of North America*, the mean age of sexual maturity in males is five and a half years in the Lower 48, but some mature as early as three and a half or as late as seven years. Females are usually sexually mature by three and a half years, but they produce their first litters between four and nine years of age. In northern Alaska females might not breed until they're eleven or twelve if conditions are poor, state bear biologist Harry Reynolds told me.

Researchers do know that both sexes breed with multiple partners, a situation described variously as polygyny (one male, many females), polyandry (one female, many males), and promiscuity, which even in its scientific connotation sounds slightly judgmental. Steyært suggested classifying bears as broadly polygamous: an individual bear can mate a variable number of times with a variable number of mates. One Yellowstone female mated ten times with four different males within two hours. Once males have donated DNA, their obligations are over. In *Polar Bears*, biologist Andrew Derocher called them "deadbeat dads," which is true of black and brown bears, too. Females tend to be choosier when it comes to mates because they invest so much time, energy, and resources in producing ova, gestating, birthing, nursing, and rearing cubs. Their mate choices favor certain traits that can drive sexual selection, which is "among the most powerful of all evolutionary forces," explained Stephen Shuster. "It occurs when individuals within one sex secure mates and produce offspring at the expense of other individuals within the same sex."

Teddy had refused other bears, but as I watched Reo snorting in her ear, I wondered what she saw in him. Occasionally she turned her head to snap at him, and sometimes he bit her neck and shoulders. "It can't be very comfortable," Polly said. "He's probably twice as heavy as she is. I'm sure she's thinking, 'It's for the good of the species, it's for the good of the species.'" How do females know whether a partner is a good genetic choice? Apparently, size matters. Females stop growing once they start reproducing, but males don't approach full size until they're around fourteen or fifteen years old, when they can be as much as 2.2 times larger than females. Scientists call this difference sexual dimorphism. Judging by which males tend to win breeding rights, females evidently regard big males as survivors who are more likely to produce healthy offspring—hence selection that encourages dimorphism. "The apparent success of larger, older or more aggressive male brown bears might be explained, in part, by female choice for these traits as signs of genetic quality," according to Steyært and coauthors. This seems borne out by a three-year study that identified the three largest and oldest males in an Appalachian black bear population as the fathers of 91 percent of the cubs. Body size, "superior fighting ability," and better search tactics allowed them to monitor and mate with females while keeping smaller males away, according to Adrienne Kovach and Roger Powell.

That size difference may be keenly felt in a species whose mating is, as described by Schwartz and colleagues, "vigorous and prolonged." Most breeding sessions between brown bears take from ten to forty minutes, although a heroic sixty minutes is on the record books. In contrast, William Boone and colleagues timed sixty-one black bear matings in captivity and reported a mean of about fifty-two seconds, although others have witnessed sessions in the wild lasting from five to forty-three minutes. Afterward, the pair may feed, rest, roughhouse, and travel together for hours, days, or weeks. Reo and Teddy's encounter ended less congenially when Teddy bit Reo and he growled, flipped her over, and left. Later, when we noticed a big gash on Dolly's flank, Larry said, "See the trouble love can cause?"

Sex doesn't necessarily end sexual competition. Males that mated frequently didn't always produce offspring in a study of mate selection in Scandinavian female brown bears. Eva Bellemain and her colleagues hypothesized that after mating with multiple males, the females may internally "choose" the best sperm, or the battle for genetic supremacy may continue as "sperm competition." In the sperm Olympics, the number, size, shape, and swimming speed can affect the race to fertilize an ovum. Both brown bears and black bears can produce litters sired by more than one father, which some biologists consider evidence of sperm competition (in this case, apparently ending in a tie).

No matter which male fertilizes a female's eggs, she's not exactly pregnant yet. In a clever survival strategy known as delayed implantation, the fertilized ova develop into blastocysts of about a hundred cells each that loiter in the oviduct until the female enters hibernation, usually around October. Only if she has eaten enough by then will the blastocysts burrow into her uterine wall in November or December and undertake the process of becoming cubs in six to eight weeks. If she isn't fat enough, the blastocysts don't attach, ensuring that her own survival is not at risk.

During one of our morning treks to the falls, a caramel-colored female with a darker spring cub climbed into the grassy meadow overlooking the lagoon. She lay belly up, head raised vigilantly, as the tiny cub nursed for several minutes until the mother rolled to her feet and it tumbled off. In their first two months out of the den, brown bear cubs drink about forty-five ounces of milk a day, consisting of 20 to 25 percent fat, according to Fish and Game research scientist Sean Farley. (Polar bear milk is about twice as fatty, and human milk is about 3 to 5 percent fat.) Bear researcher LaVern Beier tasted bear milk while assisting Farley and reported, in case you were wondering, "It was sweet, like that Eagle brand canned condensed milk." As summer proceeds, mothers shift cubs to other foods, but they continue nursing for a couple of years. This prolonged nursing may supply fatty acids or critical micronutrients, but a more important reason, Farley suspects, is that "extended lactation provides a strong behavioral bond between mother and cub, which allows her to keep them close, protect them, and train them."

When food is scarce, females sometimes lose their young. And if habitat conditions don't improve, years may pass before a female becomes healthy enough to breed again. Imagine the energy it takes, inside and out, to care for multiple cubs. Brown and black bears usually produce two offspring, sometimes one or three, and rarely four. A brown bear named Red Collar brought five cubs to the falls in 1974; three survived to become the Marx Brothers. Black bears with five cubs have been photographed in New Hampshire and filmed in videos posted on BearsForever.org. The champion of mothers must be the brown bear with six cubs spotted on the Alaska Peninsula in 1983 and 1984. "It may have been the result of orphaned or abandoned cubs being adopted, or an extremely rare occurrence of a litter of sextuplets," Randall Wilk and his colleagues reported.

As we left the falls one evening, a female with three small cubs popped her head over a nearby knoll, looked at the cluster of feeding bears, and vamoosed. The only other offspring we saw at the falls were a couple of rangy two-and-a-half-year-olds accompanying their mother in a wary phalanx. These were the Holdermanns. They headed for the deep pool below the falls, where Mrs. Holdermann spent a couple of hours upending herself, hind legs paddling absurdly in the air as she groped for salmon carcasses. Her youngsters fought her for scraps whenever she went ashore. Eating leftovers was better than risking trouble from the big males at the falls. Bears kill and sometimes eat other bears of all ages and sexes, but young cubs are especially vulnerable to adult males. Biologists have several hypotheses but few answers to explain this behavior. Some might be hungry. Some might overreact when a cub fails to signal submission and then opportunistically cannibalize the carcass—a sort of "Oops—oh well, no sense wasting a meal" kind of response.

One controversial hypothesis known as sexually selected infanticide (SSI) proposes that because females usually don't breed while lactating, a male may kill cubs unrelated to him so the female will become sexually receptive, mate with him, and produce his progeny. Bears are induced ovulators, which means they require copulation to release ova, and they can enter estrus between two and seven days after losing cubs, so this strategy could benefit infanticidal males. Presumably, they somehow recognize which females they've bred, so they don't kill their own cubs.

Some hunters and game managers consider SSI a rationale for killing big males and thus improving cub survival. But wildlife biologist Sterling Miller has cautioned that "managers should not count on such magical mechanisms to make everything come out right in the end." Conversely, in predator control areas, hunters sometimes argue that older males should be spared, in the hope they'll suppress the population by eating young. However, causes of cub mortality are seldom confirmed, and studies in Canada, Sweden, and Alaska have reported equivocal or conflicting information about the relationship between hunting and infanticide. "Convincing evidence of SSI in North American bear populations is lacking," Sophie Czetwertynski and coauthors reported in 2007.

When Miller and his colleagues examined four Alaska bear populations, hunted and unhunted, they found no evidence that removing males by hunting affected cub survival or litter size. Cub survivorship in Denali and Katmai National Parks was 34 percent, compared with 67 percent survivorship in the adjacent Susitna area, where hunting is heavy. At Black Lake on the Alaska Peninsula, where hunting seasons open in alternate years, there was no difference in cub mortality in hunting versus nonhunting years. The researchers suggested that a likelier reason for the difference in survivorship is that the Denali and Katmai populations have reached their carrying capacity—the maximum number of animals the environment can sustain at once. If there are too many bears, the competition for food, constraints on a mother's health, and increased predation can take a high toll on cubs as a way of regulating the population density. Despite high cub mortality, for example, Katmai also has the highest known bear density in North America.

"I have no doubt in my mind that male bears kill cubs, but with what frequency, I have no idea," Denali wildlife biologist Pat Owen told me. Cause of death is the biggest blank spot in her mortality data. Each spring she and her staff collar females, count cubs, and check on the families periodically with radio-tracking flights to record how many offspring remain before the females den. One such flight located the mother of two spring cubs standing alone on a rock pile. After she ran off, the researchers discovered a dead cub whose injuries implicated a rockslide. That was the only cub in their study whose manner of death was determined. They never located the second cub, which may have been buried in the rubble. The Grim Reaper of Denali bear cubs works overtime, but the park's overall bear population is stable or perhaps in slight decline, Owen said.

Confounding matters is the fact that female brown bears also kill cubs. In a 2005 study on SSI, researcher Bruce McLellan documented thirteen instances of cubs killed by males and seven by females. McNeil observers have reported several such incidents. Polly Hessing witnessed an episode in which one of White's cubs, known as WC, joined two cubs belonging to another nearby female. All three cubs ran toward that female, which struck WC and then killed him when he slipped while trying to get away. The staff named her Idi Amin. Another bear called McBride killed two cubs while fighting with their mother. The following year she killed another female's spring cub. "Nature is a messy thing," Josh Peirce observed. "It's not always neat and clean."

Bear cubs in Alaska die in many ways. At McNeil, several have drowned in the nearby Paint River falls. Teddy lost two cubs in 1992 within two days of each other while crossing the lagoon at high tide. Injuries, abandonment, falls from cliffs, starvation, flooded or collapsed dens, avalanches, vehicles—it's a long list made longer by everything that eats baby bears. "If you come out of the den and you weigh ten pounds, a lot of things will try to eat you," Sean Farley remarked—including wolverines, eagles, and presumably coyotes. As the bear-viewing season on the Alaska Peninsula extends into September, more people report wolves killing cubs, says Derek Stonorov. "I think wolves might be a significant predator on bear cubs," he added. "A wolf pack is pretty formidable. There's no way a mother can watch three cubs at a time."

The life histories of White and Teddy illustrate the challenge of rearing cubs successfully. In her twenty-five years, White produced eleven cubs, and seven survived to weaning. By 2004, Teddy had given birth to ten cubs, six of which lived until weaned. About 31 percent of McNeil cubs observed between 1978 and 1991 disappeared by their second summer, according to Richard Sellers and Larry Aumiller. As with humans, some bears are more adept at mothering than others. Perhaps they are fiercer, stricter, wiser, better providers, more attentive, more mature, or just plain luckier. Experience seems important. Farley has noticed that first-time mothers on the Kenai Peninsula nearly always lose their litters. "They're terrible moms. They don't know what they're doing," he said. Steven Kovach and colleagues found that as females grew older, they weaned their young more successfully. Still, even a skilled, healthy mother may give birth to just four or five litters if she reproduces every three years during the prime of her life. This is what makes survival of the species so dicey in some places.

Occasionally, distracted mothers lose, swap, and adopt cubs. Wildlife biologist Tom Bledsoe, the author of *Brown Bear Summer*, observed several cub mix-ups at McNeil in 1974. A female named Lady Bird once left the falls with twelve cubs, three of which belonged to Lanky. Lanky frantically searched for the cub pack, fought with Lady Bird, collected her offspring, and split, never to cross the river into cub-swapping territory again. A trio of mothers that fished near one another provoked great confusion among their ten youngsters, who often mingled, napped in pig piles, and huddled for comfort. Various configurations of befuddled offspring followed whichever mother caught a salmon and carried it into the brush to eat. Often several minutes passed before the other oblivious mothers realized their cubs were missing and began to search for them. Sometimes they fought for custody with a particularly nurturing female named Goldie, who inherited the entire pack for a time. She was once seen nursing nine of them, and she kept two cubs who weren't hers for at least three days. Goldie also ended the summer with an extra cub. Bledsoe suggested that these weren't cases of cub stealing but rather "sow-swapping" by offspring that were uncertain who Mom was. Maybe mother bears can't count very well.

Mixed-age litters are another oddity of bear motherhood. In Denali National Park in 1986, bear biologist Fred Dean and National Park Service ranger Rick McIntyre repeatedly saw a grizzly traveling with a spring cub and a juvenile female who was probably three and a half. They observed the juvenile bear nursing twice, once by herself, as well as playing with the cub and sometimes displaying more maternal interest in it than the mother did. Retired state biologist Richard Sellers photographed an adult traveling with two cubs and two apparent yearlings while flying near McNeil River in 1991. He spotted the group again a week later. "While the aircraft circled for a third pass, the adult lay down and rolled onto her back; all four young climbed onto her belly in nursing position," he and his coauthors wrote. Mixed-age litters in Sweden and Yellowstone were reported by Jon Swenson and Mark Haroldson in 2008. This unusual arrangement also occurs in black bears. A video on BearsForever.org shows a mother with a yearling and two spring cubs, and in 2011 a den webcam streamed intimate views of a mixed-age litter belonging to a wild but habituated bear named Lily, who cooperated with researchers at the North American Bear Center in Minnesota. The yearling, Hope, played with the newborns, nursed alongside them, and occasionally engaged in a tug-of-war with her mother for possession of them. She remained with her mother and the surviving cub the following summer.

Sometimes siblings travel and even den together after their mothers have sent them packing. One day at the falls we saw a young bear approach a little blonde female named Rena. They sniffed each other and then nuzzled. It was Reno, her sibling. They'd been on their own since the previous summer. For young bears, life without maternal protection is risky at first. When they were part of a family, other bears usually ran away, perhaps instilling an overinflated sense of power. "I think they think, 'I come and they go,'" John Hechtel told me. Surely it's bewildering to discover that, all this time, the other bears were deferring to your mother, not you.

Some bears make their way through the world with more confidence or chutzpah or whatever you want to call it. Rena seemed extraordinarily brave as she loitered near the river trying to snag a salmon, despite the presence of bears three or four times her size. "It would be really unusual for a three-and-a-half-year-old to hang out if it wasn't here a lot as a cub," Larry said. "Even if it was, this is unusual. If you ever have occasion to go down there and stand in the depression, it's very intimidating. You can't hear anything. You can't see anything behind you. For a little, sort of shy bear, that's a very, very tough thing to do." Rena seemed to have no illusions about her social status; she scooted away whenever a larger bear approached, but she was clever at nabbing leftovers and the occasional abandoned fish. One day she even caught her own salmon along a deserted stretch. Josh Peirce attributed Rena's boldness to her mother. "Rollie was a very dominant female," he said. "She would hang in there with the big boys."

So do bears learn from their mothers or teach themselves? "Both," Larry said. Later I realized how obvious the answer was. Behavior in animals is a combination of genetic traits and social learning. Female bears devote a lot of time and effort to raising cubs, suggesting that one purpose is to teach them enough skills to survive on their own: what to eat, where to find it, when to run away, and how to behave around other bears. Black bears usually push their young into the world at sixteen or seventeen months old. Brown bears tend to keep their offspring close for two summers before separating from them in the third, although some cubs in Sweden emancipate as yearlings. A long-term study in Northwest Alaska documented a few offspring weaned as yearlings, most as two-year-olds, and a fair number as three-year-olds. Denali bears typically raise their cubs until they are three, according to park biologist Pat Owen, but she knew of one mother who kept a cub until he was four and another one who jammed herself into a den with three male cubs through four winters. "I don't know how she tolerated them as long as she did," Owen said.

Some bears achieve self-sufficiency when they're quite young, as early as six months for Scandinavian brown bears. In 1970 two Alaska game biologists decided to test whether a seven-month-old cub could survive alone after a hunter killed its mother. They tattooed its upper lip for identification, flew it to the Kenai Peninsula, and released it. Almost a year later, a landowner about fifty miles away illegally killed the bear. Its survival until then seemed especially remarkable because it had been removed from the familiar landscape of its mother's home range. Who knows how long it could have lived in a world without guns?

If brown bears can become independent that early, why do mothers keep their cubs so long? Wouldn't it be more advantageous to produce more cubs sooner? Norwegian researcher Jiska van Dijk answered this question in a paper on the rehabilitation and release of bears: "Apparently taking care of the cubs longer than necessary is more profitable than reproducing a new litter again. Within this period the sow is able to give extra protection to and teach her cubs bear-specific behavior skills necessary for survival in the wild." The notion that a bear exhibits flexibility in deciding when to emancipate her offspring recalls a comment by British Columbia researcher Fred Bunnell at a symposium on bear-people conflicts. "Generally if an animal does something we call it instinct," he said. "If a person does the same thing for the same reason we call it intelligence." The Minnesota bear named Hope demonstrated strong instincts or intelligence (or both) when she was temporarily abandoned at four months of age. Biologists Lynn Rogers and Sue Mansfield left her alone but set out formula, mealworms, grapes, and nuts to supplement natural foods. Despite her limited experience, Hope foraged for vegetation, berries, crayfish, ants, insects, and even freshwater clams. The wary cub also had enough sense to sleep in trees. Watching this natural drama unfold online through daily photographs, video, and Facebook notes was nerve-racking for thousands of devoted followers (including me), but it was a fascinating lesson in the resourcefulness of bears and a happy conclusion when mother Lily and Hope were reunited. A bear's knowledge has limits, though. The following year a hunter legally shot Hope at a bait station.

Evidence of social learning is tricky to observe and quantify, but researcher Barrie Gilbert thinks one clear example is displayed by Katmai bears that swim to islands in Shelikof Strait to forage on burrowing seabirds. The ornithologists who originally noticed these bears counted more than forty swimming as far as ten miles. Many were females and cubs. "While one cannot exclude the possibility that each adult bear independently discovered the islands (perhaps by smell, or vision if the islands were high above the sea surface), it seems more likely that these traditions were learned by the young while accompanying their mothers," Gilbert wrote in a paper about social learning in mammals.

Bears also seem capable of independent learning. A young brown bear in Glacier Bay was seen manipulating and grooming itself with rocks by Volker Deecke, a vacationing senior lecturer from the University of Cambria's Centre for Wildlife Conservation. He photographed the bear successively picking up three underwater, barnacle-covered rocks and rubbing them against its neck and muzzle for several minutes, possibly to relieve the itch of molting. In a 2012 paper he described it as the first example of tool use in wild brown bears. The intelligence and motor skills necessary to manipulate objects such as salmon, clams, and rocks could explain why bears have the largest brain relative to body size among carnivores, Deecke noted. I eagerly await further sightings of exfoliating bears as evidence of behavioral learning.

At McNeil River it's impossible to gauge the ratio of nature to nurture when it comes to fishing skills, but the range of techniques clearly illustrates plasticity. Bears demonstrated wildly different styles as divers, snorkelers, submariners, waders, plungers, pouncers, thieves, and bullies. Monkeyface spent an entire afternoon submerging his head in one of the deeper pools to look for fish. "For three or four years he often had his own parasite that would follow him around and take the fish away," Polly commented. Across the river, Dusty launched himself into spectacular belly flops that seemed to yield a meal only occasionally. Bears sometimes stood in freezing water for hours waiting for a careless salmon. One male planted his butt in the main channel and let the white water froth around his shoulders and create an eddy. Another ducked his upper body into the river while his hind legs and stupendous rump anchored him to shore. One resourceful bear skipped the tedium of fishing and simply chased a luckier bear across and up the river to appropriate its salmon. Once the same salmon exchanged owners three times. I also saw a quick-witted female snatch a salmon in midair as a male copulated with her.

Some bears become tricksters. Researchers Robert and Johanna Fagen described a brown bear at Pack Creek Game Sanctuary named SJ who learned that if she provoked an aggressive encounter with a successful angler, it would roar at her and drop the salmon. "SJ would immediately pull the fish towards her with her paw and pick it up," they wrote. "Then SJ would trot away carrying the fish."

McNeil's free-for-all is actually on-the-job learning. Utah State

University researcher Michael Luque spent a total of fifty days in 1972 and 1973 observing fishing bears. In his thesis he identified three steps in a bear's fishing technique, each associated with specific components: search (walking, standing, sitting), approach (loping, head underwater, plunging), and capture (forepaws, forepaws and mouth, mouth, one forepaw, one forepaw and mouth). Of ninety possible combinations, standing proved most successful. Also profitable were plunging and trapping the salmon with forepaws and mouth. Some bears switched tactics immediately if they were skunked, a strategy I've often favored myself. Others attempted the same method more than thirty times before shifting to a new spot or a new approach—loping instead of plunging, say. A bear's physical and intellectual skills can be as important as social dominance in fishing success, according to Western Washington University researchers Ian Gill and James Helfield. Assisted by Larry Aumiller, Gill tracked four dominant behaviors in twenty-six McNeil bears: displacing competitors from a fishing spot, fishing in a popular spot, fishing in hot spots, and stealing. Some dominant bears were highly efficient anglers, but some nondominant bears fished just as successfully by adapting different strategies.

The year I visited, a low chum return meant that, on average, seven salmon became bear chow every half hour, by Josh Peirce's count—slim pickings for twenty or more bears. "It's pretty hard for us humans, who have never been hungry, to know what it's like," Larry said. Every catch seemed like a triumph during that lean season. You could almost feel the bears' pleasure as they gulped the briny red flesh. One good-sized male dropped a writhing salmon on the shore, shook himself like a dog, anchored the fish with a paw on its head, and chomped the belly. He ate deliberately, lapping up the orange eggs that spilled out before stripping off the skin, nibbling the stiff tail, ignoring the head, and then slurping water from the river. "He ate the center of that salmon the way you eat an Oreo cookie," commented Talkeetna photographer Rollie Ostermick, who shares his name with the bear Rollie ("a nice bear named after a strange person," Larry joked). Eventually, a smaller bear retrieved the salmon's head. Between the eagles, gulls, and younger bears, nothing was wasted. Bears come to McNeil to feed themselves, but in the process, they help feed the world, too.

Life isn't all about food and sex, even for bears. One afternoon two animals bobbed into a deep eddy on our side of the river and began playing.

In a ritual that combined waltzing and wrestling, they stood upright in shoulder-high water, one throwing a foreleg over the other's leg or shoulder, heads swaying as they mouthed each other's necks. "Sometimes you see a head swagger, like a bobblehead," Polly said. "That's a key-in on playing." This particular bout was unusual because one bear was female and smaller than the other. Females do play, although they're less likely to goof around than males, Polly said. Bears' playmates are usually roughly equal in size and status; however, Derek Stonorov has seen large adult males roughhousing with younger and smaller bears. Old bears play, too; Larry once watched two twenty-eight-year-olds wrestling. Another day, a pair of males about eight or nine years old grappled in the pool, gently tugging on each other's ears. Playing bears often rear up and paw at each other, biting necks and shoulders, using restrained versions of the same motions they'd use when fighting—what ethologists call "self-handicapping." Footage of "fighting" bears often depicts playtime ginned up with fake roars and growls. "When they do it seriously, it's a whole different level," Polly commented.

Ask different biologists why bears play, and they'll offer different answers. "I'm a lumper and simplifier," Tom Griffin said. "I just see it as playing. Some people think they're practicing their mojo." Larry said, "It's fun. It's satisfying a need. Probably helps determine which animal is more dominant." Bears begin life immersed in play, rassling and scrapping with siblings, pouncing on mothers and mouthing their faces. For them, the world is one big amusement park strewn with rocks, sticks, and other toys. John Hechtel once saw a bear balancing a stick on its head for fun. In his book *Into Brown Bear Country*, retired biologist Will Troyer described bears playing with sticks and repeatedly flinging dead salmon into the air. Grown bears like bigger toys such as kayaks, rafts, boats, and planes. A video posted at GrizzlyBay.org captured several minutes of a Katmai bear repeatedly lowering her muzzle just beneath the water's surface before exhaling a percolation of bubbles.

Few sights are as charming or entertaining as playful bears, but many ethologists consider play a confounding element of social behavior. "No behavioral concept has proved as ill-defined, elusive, controversial, and even unfashionable as play," E. O. Wilson observed. Robert Fagen framed the essential puzzle like this: Why would animals spend valuable time and energy playing unless it extends some biological or evolutionary benefit? What might those benefits be? Fagen and Fagen believe that playing can contribute to short-term survival in brown bears. After studying the play behavior of nineteen cubs at Pack Creek on Admiralty Island, they concluded, "Cubs who played more during their first summer survived better from their first summer to the end of their second summer." The sample was small, and the specific mechanisms were unknown, but they speculated that play might improve resistance to stress by allowing cubs to rehearse and recover from demanding situations. "Play involves both control and loss of control, both predictability and unpredictability, both novelty and familiarity," they wrote in 2004.

Ethologists have long recognized that almost all mammals play—some more than others, according to Suzanne Held and Marek Špinka. Maybe play helps animals develop physical abilities such as running, jumping, and twisting, some ethologists hypothesize. Perhaps it strengthens kinship bonds, stretches cognitive functions, and improves skills in predation, fighting, and mating. Maybe it just makes animals feel good. Researcher Jaak Panksepp discovered that rats like being tickled, and behaviorist Marc Bekoff has pointed out that neurochemicals known as opioids (similar to opiates) increase with rodents' playfulness. Play behavior signals an animal's well-being, but play's contagious effects may also improve the welfare of individuals and groups, posited Held and Špinka. Perhaps we can't prove exactly why bears play, but I'm pleased to report the results of my own observations: 100 percent of people who watch bears playing think it's a ton of fun.

At McNeil everybody commented on the personality traits of particular bears. Rena was bold. Fred was aggressive. McDougall was easygoing. "Reggie was just an exceptional bear," Polly once remarked. But would we say Fred was "mean" or Teddy was "nice"? Do bears really have personalities, or do we project our own emotions onto certain behaviors? Such inquiries edge perilously close to anthropomorphism, the third rail of animal studies. "Scientists have been reluctant to ascribe personality traits, emotions, and cognitions to animals, even though they readily accept that the anatomy and physiology of humans is similar to that of animals," observed psychology professors Samuel Gosling and Oliver John in 1999. "Yet there is nothing in evolutionary theory to suggest that only physical traits are subject to selection pressures, and Darwin argued that emotions exist in both human and non-human animals."

Zoologist Donald Griffin helped make it possible for us to discuss animal behavior, consciousness, and thought without smirking with his 1976 book *The Question of Animal Awareness*. He considered it silly for humans to insist that animals can't possibly experience an emotional and mental existence. "The prevailing view implies that only our species can have any sort of conscious awareness, or that, should animals have mental experiences, they must be identical with ours, since there can be no other kind," Griffin wrote. "This conceit is truly anthropomorphic, because it assumes a species monopoly of an important quality." Instead of manufacturing elaborate theories to explain animal behavior as something other than the product of self-awareness or personality, he thought that, in the absence of contrary information, it made more sense to assume that animals are capable of thought and behavior beyond simple mechanistic reactions to stimuli. Most nonscientists certainly don't hesitate to assign personalities to animals. When ABC News published a web story titled "Do Pets Really Have Personality?" many readers agreed with the commenter who wrote: "Well duh." Another response: "I'm more interested in determining why scientists don't have personalities." Not until the 1960s did researchers start investigating whether people have personalities, much less scientists. They mustered enough evidence over the next twenty years to declare that we do (though we can all probably think of someone who is an exception).

Researchers generally define animal personality in roughly the same way as human personality: patterns of behavior that are distinctive to individuals, repeatable, and consistent across time and in different situations. They continue to try to devise standard ways to observe, describe, measure, and test personality traits in animals both domestic and wild—the donkey, hedgehog, trout, rhesus monkey, hyena, octopus, and rhinoceros, among others. One challenge is to develop a common, useful lexicon; phrases such as *temperament, personality,* and *coping style* often refer to the same concept. Some researchers have adapted an instrument known as the five-factor model, which identifies major dimensions of human personality that are common across cultures. The five dimensions are openness to experience, conscientiousness, extroversion, agreeableness, and neuroticism (sometimes two additional dimensions, activity and dominance, are included). Each dimension is bundled with numerous related traits that can be tested experimentally, such as excitability, shyness, fearfulness, playfulness, curiosity, sociability, and aggressiveness. Gosling and John reviewed nineteen studies of a dozen species ranging from guppies to chimpanzees and found that nearly all the tested species demonstrated traits related to extroversion, neuroticism, and agreeableness. Most exhibited qualities associated with openness. Only chimpanzees displayed elements of conscientiousness (thinking before acting, impulse control, following norms and rules). Personality traits can also be linked in suites. For example, an animal that is bold may also be open to exploring its environment.

"There is strong evidence that personality does exist in animals," Samuel Gosling and Simine Vazire concluded. An important test is whether personality traits have real-world outcomes—whether researchers can predict how animals will behave, based on their traits. One example they cited is a study in which rhinos previously identified by their zookeepers as "more fearful" did indeed take longer to approach a new object than those rated "less fearful." Another criterion is whether personality traits are clearly inheritable. This has been demonstrated in studies on octopus, goats, fish, and chimpanzees, among others. One experiment selected and bred minks for "fearfulness," based on their reactions to people. In the resulting lineage, 90 percent of minks were "fearful," a trait expressed in only 30 percent of the original group. Studies that can demonstrate such connections, according to Gosling, "suggest that observer ratings reflect genuine attributes of individuals, not merely anthropomorphic projections."

One study of brown bear personality demonstrates how complicated describing their behavior can be. Over three summers, Robert and Johanna Fagen independently rated seven bears at Pack Creek using sixty-nine different behavioral definitions. After comparing their assessments, they identified twenty-one traits as statistically reliable and significant, including nosy, has an attitude, impulsive, irritable, show-off, and sparkly, the last of which they defined as "bubbly, cheerful, and full of sprightly movements." Some researchers might resist these terms, but I can recall seeing a sparkly bear or two.

Still, identifying individual personality traits can help explain why some animals behave in ways that don't make sense in ecological or evolutionary terms. Natural selection favors traits that ensure successful reproduction, so why wouldn't all members of a species exhibit exactly the same useful personality traits, such as boldness? Research on creatures such as Europe's great tit (a bird) suggests that shuffling a variety of inheritable personality traits may give a species a better overall chance of survival, allowing individual animals to react differently to fluctuations in food sources, weather, habitat, and population. Great tits identified as "bold" in one study consistently approached novel objects more quickly, were less stressed by handling, and recovered from surprises faster. Selectively breeding for those traits produced bolder or shyer birds.

Particular personality traits don't always guarantee survivability. For example, McNeil's staff informally characterized Rollie as "bold" because she was not afraid to fish near big males. Her boldness (not necessarily the same as aggressiveness) meant that she might eat more salmon than other females. Better nutrition would encourage more cubs, more litters, and therefore a better chance that Rollie's genes would persist. Her daughter, Rena, might have learned the value of boldness or she might have inherited that trait, or there might be some combination of social learning and genetics at work. Boldness could favor survivability in terms of Rena's nutritional health, but it might also increase the chance of another bear killing her before she could reproduce. Similarly, a young bear's openness to novelty—neophilia—could help it discover new sources of food (puffin eggs, anybody?) or lead it into dangerous urban areas, resulting in an early death and a squelching of those particular genes before they can be distributed. Some scientists investigate such trade-offs in animals to better understand them in humans. For example, in a study of British adults, researcher Daniel Nettle determined that extroverts tend to have more sex partners and are also more likely to be hospitalized.

When I asked wildlife biologists whether bears are endowed with personalities, they displayed little boldness. Most said something rather tame, like this observation from a 1990 paper on the behavioral ecology of bears: "In general, biologists who have worked with bears have been impressed with how variable the behavior of individuals appears to be." But in his fascinating study *Walking with Bears*, biologist Terry DeBruyn wasn't afraid to acknowledge that different animals display different emotions. "Bears get moody," he told me. "They get upset. They get flat-out pissed off if they don't get something. If they don't get their way, they get huffy." And a description of brown bears by the Alaska Department of Fish and Game was surprisingly open-minded: "By all indications, bears are extremely intelligent and most have individual personalities." This makes me wonder which bears don't have personalities, and how one would know. In the meantime, as scientists try to tease out the links among personality traits, genetics, experience, and survivability, I'll settle for LaVern Beier's assessment: "They are not punched out of a mold."

Because Polly Hessing had been away from McNeil for a few years, she wanted to refamiliarize herself with old bears and identify new ones. Throughout the day I listened to her exchanges with Tom Griffin:

"Is the bear upstream from Rocky Ricky or Needles?"

"Roofie just walked in. I guess that's Dolly."

"Let's stick with Mousehead. Forget about Sheila."

Usually, McNeil staff didn't tell us a bear's name unless we asked. Naming bears has always been a touchy subject. Years before, a department supervisor had objected when he heard the biologists referring to bears as Ralph, Woofie, and the like. "In his world," Larry said, "he really didn't want that to go forward because it really does get people riled up . . . about shooting them [bears] if you think about them as individuals." McNeil bears are no longer tagged or collared, so it took a certain amount of bureaucratic wrangling to allow staff to continue naming bears based on their physical quirks—size, permanent scars, toenail colors, missing ears, broken jaws, droopy lips, monkey faces, horse faces, and so on.

Entire maternal lineages have become familiar through such methods: the Melody clan, the Holdermann clan, the Rollie clan, the Teddy clan. Their lives overlap those of attentive humans for several weeks each summer, year after year, so McNeil staff members know which bears are attentive mothers, which bears share a mother, which bears return every season, which bears are missing. Like us, bears live their days from moment to moment, but radiating from every action and every relationship are grander patterns we can barely discern. Some biologists regard bears as "hardwired," meaning their behavior is more a matter of instinct than intelligence. Others suspect that the perpetual search for food explains their life history and population demographics.

Research into home ranges suggests a social structure that is more complex and intimate than previously recognized. Saying that bears have home ranges is a way of saying that they prefer familiar places with enough food, shelter, and potential mates to survive and reproduce. Bears don't stake out territories and defend them against intruders in the classic sense. They expand and contract their ranges in response to seasonal fluctuations in food, the search for mates, and the encroachments of human society. Their ranges overlap, so they must somehow accommodate one another. Bears on Admiralty Island, where food is abundant but space is not, make do with ranges that average 15 square miles for females, 70 for males. In the expansive but lean landscape of Northwest Alaska, a female may consider 600 square miles sufficient and a male closer to 900 square miles. Each male's area overlaps the ranges of several females and offers more resources to sustain his larger bulk. Bears that are abducted and relocated often make their own incredible journeys home. At least twelve of twenty radio-marked adults transplanted from the Susitna River area in 1979 returned. One traveled 160 miles, according to Sterling Miller and Warren Ballard. A Yukon grizzly trekked 70 miles in three days to return home, and a male brown bear captured near Cordova on Alaska's mainland and moved 58 miles to Montague Island reappeared within a month, having swum at least 6 miles of strong ocean currents.

The one-dimensional nature of such measurements doesn't express how fidelity to a familiar terrain requires an intellectual relationship with a place, a cognitive map that can navigate time and space. This internal guidance system tells a bear when to visit this berry patch, those clam beds, that patch of forest where moose give birth. "Yeah, how does that work—how a bear just knows?" asked Terry DeBruyn. "If you're going to beeline from here to there, you not only need to know what here and there is, but you have to know about what's in between. That amazes me, how an animal does that."

Some answers may lie in how bears arrange themselves within a habitat. Young brown and black bears tend to linger near their mother's home range after they separate, exhibiting what scientists call *natal philopatry*. Dwelling in familiar landscapes for even a short period means they can take advantage of known food sources and avoid conflicts with other bears or people. Two-year-old brown bears of both sexes dispersed about the same distances in a study conducted by Bruce McLellan and Frederick Hovey in British Columbia, but during the next two years, the males moved farther and farther away, easing into independence. Among black bears, more than 95 percent of juvenile females live in their mother's range, gradually expanding and sometimes claiming adjacent habitats or inheriting their mother's realm if she dies. Roaming in search of a good neighborhood is risky, particularly when the journey takes bears near roads and human settlements. Half of the eighteen male black bear yearlings that dispersed in a study on the Kenai Peninsula died the year they left, as did the only female who ventured away. Then again, the three males who stuck around died too, reported Charles Schwartz and Albert Franzmann. Although males were two to three times less likely to reach adulthood than females, survival wasn't easy for any of them. Of the original fifty-one subadults, just two males and nine females were alive at the end of the study. Humans caused nearly all the deaths.

Based on his experience following multiple generations of female black bears through the woods, Terry DeBruyn believes that mother bears impart some final lessons that clarify the limits of their range. "In the spring before family breakup, there was a lot of traveling around, big jumps from here to there," he told me. "I think it may have to do with females showing daughters around, maybe marking the territory." Derek Stonorov has always wanted to sort out the genetic relationships among bears that return annually to places like Chenik Lagoon or Mc-Neil River. I'm curious, too: if the same breeding females at McNeil tend to mate with bears that return to the river each year, how does that influence local kinship patterns? Researchers who combined field data with DNA samples from nearly a thousand Scandinavian brown bears reported that some females formed "matrilinear assemblages" in which every female within about twenty-five miles was closely related: mothers, daughters, sisters, nieces, grandmothers, granddaughters, aunts. Overlapping home ranges occurred most often between closely related females. "Our results thus indicate that brown bears discriminated between kin and nonkin with regard to sharing space," wrote Ole-Gunnar Støen and associates. For females, being related to their neighbors might mean they wasted less energy avoiding or confronting strangers. The distance between two females' home ranges might also influence reproduction. Among Scandinavian bears, females who lived within six miles of another female were less likely to have cubs if her neighbor did. Andrés Ordiz and coauthors speculated that dominant females may suppress estrus in subordinate females, possibly representing a form of population regulation.

Derek Stonorov became a little wistful when we talked about the possible shape and tenor of bear society not only genetically but also behaviorally. "If I had all the money in the world and I could figure out a way to do it," he said, "my ideal bear study would be to collect DNA samples from all the bears in an area [and] be able to watch all the cubs play, and watch them play through their adolescence, and then see if these special relationships that came from subadults that played together when they were younger, whether this lasted through their lives and would explain some of the things we find unexplainable when they get to be older." He was thinking of big males that play only with certain other males, for example, or about the two female brown bears his neighbor watched eating halibut from a pickup bed while their six cubs crowded around. Were they sisters, or just friendly acquaintances? Researchers who tracked bears with overlapping ranges in Alberta concluded in a 2005 paper that most associations between male and female bears likely involved breeding, but same-sex bears also spent time together. One summer, two sisters associated with each other on thirteen separate occasions, and two years later they met seven times.

So what does it mean to classify bears as solitary when females spend so much of their lives in the company of their offspring? What does *solitary* mean to eight giant males standing in a half circle and staring at the frothy blue waters of McNeil River—so close together they could form a conga line if they were so inclined? How solitary is a bear that mates each summer with several other bears, sometimes spending companionable days or weeks with a temporary beloved? If you've seen several young male bears grazing peaceably in a field of blueberries, as Stonorov has, is *solitary* the best word to describe the scene?

Yukon biologist Arthur Pearson once suggested that bear societies have matriarchal overtones, but "how one would prove this," Derek noted, "I don't know." He wonders what we're really seeing when we watch groups of bears, especially when wild females can live into their thirties. "If there was a constant food supply, you could have these matriarchs, and their families would be surrounded by cubs from other litters," he said. "I like to think of myself as a scientist, so it's just pure, pure, pure conjecture. But sometimes you just sort of think, God, these big . . . powerful beings, and the females wandering through the landscape, and everybody's just sort of following them. . . ." His voice trailed away as we imagined matriarchies unfolding among generations of bears.

"The one thing you have to remember is that bears are capable of extraordinary behavior," he once told me. I saw that at McNeil River, thanks to the extraordinary behavior of both biologists and bears. Our narrow vision of bear behavior is understandable because people started to think about bears in new ways only about thirty years ago. In human terms, that's the length of Larry Aumiller's career at Mc-Neil River, all those summers spent learning from bears and teaching humans—something he has continued to do at the sanctuary since he retired. Convert that into bear time, and we're talking about the life span of a single long-lived female brown bear in the wild, a bear who began as a shadow in her mother's womb, survived a perilous youth, learned her way through a landscape both inconstant and predictable, dreamed away half her life in the dark earth, and spent most of her days in the company of kin. Imagine how much more we'll understand just one bear's lifetime from now.

the urban bear

Pat Costello hunched into a driver's seat too small for his solid frame and peered out the windshield, one ear bent to the police scanner muttering on the dashboard. We were looking for black bears. It was a quiet September evening in Juneau, raining (as usual) in a way best described as a mizzle. A canopy of clouds muffled the mountains stooping over the town, sealing us beneath a gray dome of brooding light.

Costello was pretty sure we'd see bears in some neighborhood or other, if only because we'd see garbage too. "Bears are literally active everywhere in town," he said. "There is no place that does not have bears. The fact that people don't know that is astounding to me." The Juneau Police Department's weekly log backed him up. On a single day the previous week, callers had reported bears eating from garbage cans in an open garage, scattering trash through yards, hanging around a bus stop making people nervous, and dragging trash bags from a shed into the trees. Someone reported a bear killed by a Chevy. Kids pelted a treed bear with spruce cones. A man said he couldn't get rid of a female and her two cubs ("Caller was advised to clean up litter and warned about his threats to harm the bear").

Costello played high school basketball for the Juneau-Douglas Crimson Bears (class of '79), and I saw something of the intensity of the star player in the way he drove confidently through the town where he was born and I grew up. People who remain in their birthplaces can develop cataracts through sheer familiarity, but Costello is one of those rare people who sticks around and looks even harder. As a photographer, he wants people to see what he sees, so for years he posted a new landscape or wildlife photograph on his website every other day, images of natural beauty so luminous that they attracted 1.5 million hits a month.

One summer evening on a street near his house, Costello photographed a black bear with a shimmering pelt highlighted with hues of blue, gray, and silver. It was a glacier bear, a rare color phase usually associated with the Yakutat and Glacier Bay regions of Southeast Alaska. This bear had been eating tortillas from a garbage bin. In the photograph it stares at the camera wearing a mask of whipped cream, refuse piled around its feet. A week later a police officer killed the bear when it reared on its hind legs after a tug-of-war over a trash can. The officer didn't know that a two-legged bear is just gathering information, trying to see or smell better, not preparing to maul humans Hollywood style. This occurred during one of those summers when Juneau police received more than a thousand calls about bears digging through garbage, climbing on decks, snatching pork chops from the kitchen counters of mobile homes, prying open car doors to steal scones left on the dashboard, and wandering through backyards. By year's end, police, wildlife biologists, and residents had killed nine bears judged to be too food-conditioned or too bold around people. Cars struck and killed another seven.

Pat Costello was not the only resident upset by the number of bear deaths, but he was one of the few who did something about it. After the glacier bear died, he formed the Urban Bear Patrol with another bear advocate/civic pain in the ass/hometown hero named Mark Farmer, who had once run for mayor on a platform that called for reforming Juneau's garbage policy—not that it had much of a policy. They created a website to track bear news and drove around the town's streets and neighborhoods to document where garbage attracted bears. Some nights they counted eight or ten black bears downtown cruising for litter and startling tourists. They took reporters on rides to point out problems, such as bears eating placentas from the garbage at a birthing clinic, and they shared photographs of bike-riding kids pestering a bear. They served on the mayor's ad hoc bear committee and later resigned in a public hoorah to protest the city's inaction. They also wrote scathing editorials.

In 2001 Costello photographed a chubby black bear dashing past the popular Red Dog Saloon with a McDonald's bag dangling from its mouth. The bear had raided a city-owned trash can. The *Juneau Empire* published the embarrassing picture on the front page, and it seemed so emblematic of the community's problem that it became a tipping point, according to the city's special projects officer at the time. "It really did take Pat Costello's picture to remind people that every night, every night while you are sleeping, bears are getting into gallons and gallons and gallons of garbage," Maria Gladziszewski told me. The mayor's interest was also revived after a bear invaded her Dumpster despite wires and clips meant to secure it, the newspaper reported.

The connection between garbage and bears was no mystery (exhibit A: Yellowstone National Park). Since the 1970s Juneau officials and state management biologists had tried to educate, cajole, and guilt-trip residents into securing their garbage. Then came what local wildlife biologists started calling the "Great Shootout of 1987," when police, biologists, and residents killed twenty-one food-conditioned bears. As a newspaper reporter at the Empire, I had written numerous stories about the issue in the early 1990s, including a long account of state wildlife biologists agonizing over the fate of two bears live-trapped in a trailer park that served as an all-you-can-steal cafeteria. One of the biologists told me it broke his heart to kill a bear that had done nothing more than to act on its own nature. I was mortified when I lowered my camera and looked away at the very moment a state trooper fired a bullet into the head of a drugged black bear lying wet and dirty in a parking lot, unable to photograph the final loss of dignity for an animal now stilled from its wheezing struggle to waken. Predictably, my highly informative and incredibly moving story had no effect whatsoever.

But thanks to the Urban Bear Patrol and public pressure, a galvanized Juneau Assembly finally decided that the best approach was aggressive behavior modification—not for the bears, for the people. There would be no more fooling around with ineffective and rarely enforced measures such as lashing bungee cords across trash-can lids, which slows any self-respecting bear by only nanoseconds. New ordinances forced Dumpster owners to replace flimsy plastic lids with locking metal covers or to store bins behind bear-resistant barricades. Home owners were required to use bear-resistant containers or to store garbage in secure structures until 4:00 a.m. on trash pickup day. Most important, the city realized the ordinances would be useless until an enforcement officer was assigned to actually cite violators instead of issuing toothless warnings. "They don't chase bears around, they chase people around," is how Gladziszewski explained the philosophy shift to me. Fines that began at $50 and increased to $300 with repeat offenses proved quite motivating. "It's just like speeding," she said. "You can do all the campaigns you want on how speeding is dangerous and here's the ten reasons why it's bad. For most of us, the reason we don't speed is we don't want to get a ticket."

The problem is that there are always more speeders than ticket givers. The ticket giver in this case, a community service officer assigned to patrol trash, was also hindered by privacy laws that prevented him from examining anyone's trash can unless it was at the curb. This made it difficult to cite people before a bear proved their trash wasn't properly stored. Costello was discouraged because the city was phasing in the Dumpster rule over three years, and despite a full-on publicity campaign and increased enforcement, many people still didn't get the message. As we drove, he pointed out stuffed garbage cans without lids, a flimsy shed with a gaping door, garbage bags piled against a mobile home. "The sum total of all these little mistakes is keeping the bears here," he said—and killing them. We passed condominiums where Fish and Game had recently trapped and killed a 400-pound bear that had repeatedly raided the building's Dumpster. A few days later that same bin was outfitted with a locking metal lid that would have prevented the two-year-old bear from feeding there.

By the end of our circumnavigation of Juneau's neighborhoods, we'd followed a scanner report to a trailer court, where a pair of cubs wobbled at the top of tall spruce trees. We'd also seen two glacier bears. One, a yearling with a plush coat the shade of gunmetal, was pawing through mounds of spilled garbage with its coal-black mother. A family of four watched from their porch a few feet away and beckoned us over when we stopped. They were thrilled about their close-up view until the yearling's curious advance forced all of us to retreat inside. The bears had come by the previous evening, and the father had deliberately left the trash out, hoping they'd return. Within a few days a motorist would report hitting a light-colored bear, most likely the glacier yearling. The bear ran off into the woods. When I phoned Costello later to ask about it, he said, "It's just this little furry goofball out there that's unfortunately maybe dead already." He paused. "You do understand when you see these animals that they're doomed." The yearling survived the collision, though, because the following year a police officer shot it in a trailer park after it could not be discouraged from eating garbage there.

The other glacier bear, an adult, stood in a carport nosing through a potato chip bag it had plucked from an open can. That house belonged to one of Costello's former classmates, Steve, who chatted from a partly opened door as the bear ignored us. He had assumed a dog had been getting into his garbage for the past three weeks. "Well, I guess I'm going to have to move my garbage can inside for a while, now that I definitely know what's going on," Steve said as the bear waddled across the street and hoisted itself over a fence. "There's a police officer living upstairs."

"Don't worry, they don't fine people anyway," Costello said. After we left to follow the bear's perambulations through yards filled with children's swings and tricycles, he said, "I'm wondering, okay, who are these people who don't get it? And now I know. They are people who say, 'Yeah, this is the third straight week, and now I'll have to put my garbage away.'"

Even after he and Farmer ended the Urban Bear Patrol, Costello continued his private campaign to change people's ideas about black bears. (Brown bears are rarely seen near Juneau.) In August he'd experienced a felicitous conjunction of time and place that sometimes favors photographers when he hiked to a remote salmon stream to look for bears eating what they're supposed to eat. While he was there, a ghostly bear stepped from the forest. Its coat was the color of the moon, or old bone, or snow in late winter. Charcoal-colored fur clouded its face and smudged its ears. Costello sold the picture to the Associated Press for a few bucks, and the image flitted around the globe, prompting almost 2,000 e-mails. Hoping to protect the bear during hunting season, he called it "Juneau's spirit bear," deliberately adopting the term used for a rare subspecies of black bear found in parts of British Columbia. These bears, sometimes known as Kermode bears, carry a recessive gene that can produce a pelage of cream, orange, or white. The Alaska Board of Game approved his emergency petition and exempted white-colored black bears in the area from legal hunts.

By calling attention to this singular creature, an animal made unusual through genetic whimsy, he hoped to revive interest in all the other black bears that have stepped from the forests around Juneau: the bears burrowing their heads deep in garbage bins, the bears trapped and tranquilized so they can be moved or euthanized, the bears crossing that narrowing margin between what we call civilization and what we call nature, the bears that make no distinction between the two.

"While the white bear generated world-wide attention, no such luck for bears and garbage . . . unfortunately garbage is not a very sexy subject," he e-mailed me. "And while I can get away with calling a white bear a 'Spirit Bear,' it has proven exponentially more difficult to overcome the name 'garbage bear.'" Calling an animal a garbage bear, he argued, is like saying this bear is disposable, it's ruined, it has become garbage itself. He'd seen kids throwing rocks and screaming at bears. He'd watched a drunk lean out a window, point a gun at a bear, and advise, "Look at this gun and learn. Grow up and learn to fear men." He saw a man walk up to a bear eating garbage and blast it in the face with a fire extinguisher. That was the heart of the problem: the inability to see a black bear as something more than a nuisance or a hazard, the difficulty in remembering what a bear is meant to be.

Communities throughout Alaska and across North America are learning—or ignoring—Juneau's lessons as black bear populations continue to recover from the widespread loss of habitat and indiscriminate slaughter that followed settlers. Bears began reclaiming much of their range after game laws and conservation measures replaced bounties and unlimited hunting, according to researchers Hank Hristienko and John McDonald Jr. Their habitat has expanded as maturing forests have replaced farmlands in places like New Jersey and as settlements have produced easy sources of food such as garbage and birdseed. Today, an estimated 850,000 to 950,000 black bears live in North America—more than double the number of the seven other bear species put together, say scientists with the International Union for Conservation of Nature (IUCN). Black bears inhabit forty-one states and are sometimes seen in another three; in the absence of reliable estimates, most authorities say Alaska has 100,000 to 200,000 black bears. They also occupy all of Canada's provinces, except for Prince Edward Island, and are returning to northern Mexico. The population appears to be increasing in 60 percent of states and provinces. Researchers caution, however, that most population estimates provided by wildlife agencies aren't precise or rigorous enough to determine trends accurately.

Alaska bear biologist Terry DeBruyn reminds us not to mistake this comeback as an unmitigated triumph for black bears. "It just keeps getting tighter and tighter for them," he told me. "It's one of my pet peeves. People say black bears are adaptable. I hate that word, being used like that. Because what it says to people is that they get along just as well. And what's true is, they don't. Cope. Cope might be a better word." When people outcompete bears for habitat, and the bears respond by having fewer cubs or living shorter lives, that's not adaptation. He doesn't like it when people say bears are expanding their range, either. "Particularly in my home state of Michigan, people say that because now, all of a sudden, we have bears south of Saginaw Bay," he said. "It's like, come on!

They covered the whole state at one time. They're not expanding, they're reclaiming a birthright."

As humans continue to expand their range, black bears are forced to inhabit what land planners call the urban-wildland interface—and what many of us call home. People are building houses and roads in what used to be bear habitat, and their recreational pursuits are crowding bears in whatever natural landscapes remain. More bears plus more humans is a recipe for more bear-human conflicts, which are rarely resolved in favor of bears. In 1992, for example, 83 black bears were killed in British Columbia, according to the province's Conservation Officer Service; three years later, annual deaths averaged 814. (In 2011, 665 bears were killed.) "Managing bear-human conflict is arguably one of the most challenging priorities wildlife managers face today because black bears occur throughout most of North America, have a high tolerance for anthropogenic activities, and readily adapt to artificial food sources," wrote Rocky Spencer and colleagues in 2007. More than 80 percent of wildlife managers surveyed reported that human-bear conflicts range from "common" to a "serious problem."

Luring bears into human settlements with food and garbage is, of course, the biggest problem. If there's one thing people produce endlessly and copiously, it's garbage. Bird feed, pet food, beehives, compost, barbecue grills, livestock, fruit trees, and other delicious temptations contribute to the ever-replenishing bear buffet, which is especially appealing when local berry or mast crops fail and bears are intent on gaining weight for the winter. Other conflicts include crop destruction, killing of livestock or pets, vehicle collisions, property damage, and occasionally human injury or death. Pick almost any day in summer, and Google will be reporting human-bear conflicts from around the country, such as these headlines from May 22, 2010: in Colorado, "Wildlife Officers to Aspen: Shut Doors to Bears"; in Florida, "Black Bear Killed by Vehicle"; in Tennessee, "Bear Attack Leads to Euthanasia, Controversy." Even amusing stories reflect the underlying problem, such as the night in 2012 when Vermont governor Peter Shumlin dashed naked into his backyard to holler at four black bears raiding his bird feeders. He had assumed bears wouldn't appear within walking distance of downtown Montpelier, he said.

Even as we're adjusting our perceptions of where bears can live, we're altering how they live and how they die. In Nevada's Lake Tahoe basin, the population density of black bears dropped tenfold in the 1990s as black bears moved from the wildlands into urban centers, according to research ecologists Jon Beckmann and Joel Berger. In an uncomfortable parallel with lazy humans, urban bears eating garbage gained 30 percent in body mass, used much smaller home ranges, and were far less active than their wild counterparts. The high-calorie diet allowed females to reproduce earlier and to produce more cubs than wild bears did. Urban dwellers also became creatures of the night, presumably to avoid people and take better advantage of food sources. They denned later and spent less time in dens than did their wild counterparts. Some hibernated beneath house decks; some didn't den at all.

Urban life may have been easy, but it was not safe. Humans killed every one of the 240 bears that died of known causes between 1997 and 2008, Beckmann reported. The toll included 129 killed by vehicles and 85 eliminated by wildlife managers for reasons of public safety or livestock depredations. Because urban bears aren't repopulating the surrounding wildlands, the Lake Tahoe basin settlements are a population sink, a term that means just what it sounds like.

Bears aren't necessarily hopeless addicts jonesing for garbage, though. In the late 1980s Juneau wildlife biologist Tom McCarthy and his colleagues were among the first to investigate the habits of urban bears by tagging them and tracking their movements. Only a fairly small percentage of the local population became food-conditioned, they discovered. Years later an electronic collaring study in Juneau confirmed that some bears might raid garbage bins one night but return to natural foods the next. Researchers investigating the ecology of urban bears in Aspen, Colorado, found that the abundance of natural foods greatly influenced whether bears foraged for human-connected food sources, confirming the conclusions of previous studies. Bears that adopted the urban lifestyle—including becoming more nocturnal—returned to "normal" activities and wilder landscapes once their natural foods returned. However, garbage-eating females sometimes teach their cubs to scrounge in urban settings, a pattern that can persist through generations, assuming the offspring survive the perils of civilization long enough to breed. Other factors that can influence the number of urban bears include the local density of inexperienced young bears and the number of bears killed in a prior year.

Given how difficult it is to change human behavior, wildlife managers have long experimented with ways to dissuade bears from moving in or persuade them to move on. Juneau bears were early test subjects for aversive conditioning, a behavioral approach that tries to teach bears to associate people and their food with unpleasant experiences, such as scary noises or upset stomachs. Biologists Tom McCarthy and Roger Seavoy baited trash with peanut butter laced with thiabendazole, a non-toxic chemical that causes nausea. Then they sprinkled the trash cans with Pine Sol. Instead of avoiding garbage that smelled like Pine Sol, the bears avoided the peanut butter. Applying the proper dose and instilling the right negative associations in food-conditioned bears has proved tricky elsewhere, too. Minnesota black bears stopped eating MREs (meals ready to eat) after experiencing the effects of thiabendazole, but they continued to seek other human foods. Whistler black bears that ate spiked apples later avoided the fruit, dosed or not. But thiabendazole didn't ruin doughnuts for bears in southeastern Utah. Ammonia or pepper sauce sprayed on a mixture of dog food, oats, and molasses didn't bother black bears one bit on the Hoopa Valley Indian Reservation in California; only bear-resistant containers and electric fences foiled them. Still, nobody should count on any deterrent to be 100 percent successful. Of the ten bears that tested electric fences surrounding bait, one managed to remove the ground wire (we'll assume by accident), and two particularly persistent bears somehow squeezed under the charged fence without shocking themselves.

Two summers of experimentation in Juneau showed Tom McCarthy and his colleagues that sirens, rubber bullets, and harmless but loud cracker shells fired from a twelve-gauge shotgun almost never permanently discouraged an animal that was enthusiastic about garbage. Bears that didn't return to the original site usually moved to a nearby house, sometimes within five minutes. Bears aren't stupid; some bolted whenever they saw a police car or heard the distinctive sound of a shotgun being loaded. But after experiencing the explosive bang of cracker shells and the firecrackers known as seal bombs a few times, many bears realized that nothing particularly bad was happening, and their flight response diminished quickly. "Only 1 bear treated with physical aversives was thought to have permanently left the area," McCarthy and Seavoy noted. And that bear wasn't food-conditioned in the first place.

Even the full-on approach known as "bearmageddon" didn't impress urban bears in the Lake Tahoe basin. Jon Beckmann and his collaborators captured sixty-two food-conditioned bears and released twenty-one with no fuss. They hazed the others with yelling, pepper spray, rubber buckshot, rubber slugs, and cracker shells—all at the same time. Dogs also chased twenty of this group. The result? All but five returned to the spot where they had been captured, more than half within thirty days. The question wasn't *if* the bears would return but *when*, the researchers noted. "Our study suggests that bears that were human-food (i.e. garbage) conditioned and habituated to living near or in urban-wildland interface areas were unlikely to alter their behavior in response to the deterrent techniques currently adopted by most state and federal agencies," they concluded. After hazing wild and food-conditioned bears just over a thousand times during a four-year study in California's Sequoia National Park, Rachel Mazur found that aversive conditioning worked best with bears that never or rarely obtained human food. In fact, twenty-nine of the thirty-six bears subjected to hazing became food-conditioned *during* the study. The challenge is maintaining the constant vigilance necessary to apply aversive conditioning before bears ever taste human food, Mazur wrote.

Some techniques seem promising in this long-running battle. Officers and biologists with the Washington Department of Fish and Wildlife have hazed more than 150 urban black bears with specially trained Karelian bear dogs and estimate that about 80 percent don't become repeat offenders. Alaska Department of Fish and Game wildlife technician Larry Lewis of Soldotna began researching the use of Tasers as a bear deterrent after an incident with a moose cow. The protective female wouldn't let rescuers retrieve her calves from an open house foundation. Rubber slugs, roman candles, flares, and noisemakers didn't scare her, but when an Alaska state trooper delivered a brief charge with the Taser's electrodes, she dropped, jumped up immediately, and ran off. She showed no ill effects when she returned later to collect her offspring. Lewis worked with Taser International to develop an electronic control device for wildlife, which he and others have since used to remove a chicken feeder from a moose's head, extract a confused mountain goat from a garage, and discourage food-conditioned bears from frequenting a waste transfer facility, a garbage dump, and a fish hatchery. So striking is the device's ability to temporarily incapacitate big animals that Fish and Game asked the Board of Game to ban the general use of electronic control devices on wildlife, prompting headlines like "Bears to Humans: Don't Tase Me, Bro!" Research continues on its value for aversive conditioning and its long-term effects.

A nonlethal tactic that satisfies bear lovers but rarely works is relocating urban bears or translocating them far from their home ranges.

Among wildlife agencies surveyed by Spencer and coauthors, three-quarters said they relocated bears, usually because of public pressure or policies that gave bears two or three chances to stay out of town. Only 15 percent thought it was the best approach. Between 1986 and 1997, Alaska Department of Fish and Game staff transported ninety Juneau bears elsewhere, hoping the adults would return to natural foods and the cubs would never learn anything different. One swam twelve miles to return to its Juneau feeding grounds. Two bears removed from Petersburg's dump returned within three weeks after crossing Frederick Sound, a seven-mile stretch of cold ocean at its narrowest point. "They seemed to have enjoyed the experience and were last seen filling out frequent flyer applications," McCarthy and a colleague wrote in the department's magazine.

Eventually, the department limited its relocation efforts to females, which are more likely than males to remain in a new area, and young bears or cubs that had not yet developed an affinity for garbage. Moving bears is expensive, is not always successful, and does little to solve the core problem. The effect of plopping new bears into habitat that's probably already occupied is not clear, either. As long as people are careless with attractants, there will always be bears willing to indulge in the bounty. For this reason, Neil Barten, Juneau's area management biologist, tried to convince residents that his department would not constantly bail out the community. "We are not in the bear-moving business," Barten told the Juneau Empire in 2002. "It would be a warm, fuzzy world if we could move every bear that was causing a problem. We just don't have the staff or the time. Plus we are not going to get in the business of moving bears so that people can be messy with their garbage."

Educating people as well as bears is part of the mission for programs like Bear Aware, Bear Smart, and Bear Wise across the continent. Now researchers are starting to investigate whether such teachable moments make a difference. Studies testing the effects of educational campaigns in New York, Manitoba, and Aspen corroborate what officials in Juneau figured out: education without enforcement doesn't accomplish much. How to measure success is another problem. Gauging progress simply by tracking complaints ignores other factors, such as a bad berry year or a drought, noted Meredith Gore and coauthors in a 2006 review of six education programs. For example, Nevada's Division of Wildlife reported that bear complaints peaked at 1,500 in 2007 and plummeted by more than 1,200 the following year, yet the number of bears killed as a result of management actions increased from seventeen to twenty-four (although vehicular deaths dropped by thirty). Despite the favorable effects of stronger trash ordinances in several communities, state wildlife officials attributed the decrease in complaints largely to a wet spring that produced berries, grasses, and other important natural foods. Other wildlife managers have also learned that counting up complaints isn't an accurate measure because a single bear wreaking havoc in a neighborhood can produce multiple complaints, and because people often don't bother to contact authorities or don't want to complain because they fear the bear will be killed.

Although some states use hunting seasons to help reduce local bear populations, there is little scientific evidence that hunting reduces nuisance complaints. This shouldn't be too surprising, given that few bear hunts occur close to where people—and therefore bears—live. Researchers who analyzed a decade's worth of bear hunting and nuisance complaints in Wisconsin concluded that the "bear-hunting season did not show clear evidence of reducing nuisance complaints during 1995–2004, probably because hunting was not effectively designed for that goal." Several similar studies discussed at the Fourth International Human-Bear Conflicts Workshop didn't demonstrate a relationship between public hunting and bear conflicts, although Wyoming's Game and Fish Department found that opening a hunting season in specific problem areas succeeded in removing bears with a history of trouble.

The most immediate solution—killing the bear—is no solution at all. "That's by far the worst part of dealing with the whole bear issue," Neil Barten told me over coffee one day. "Somebody—usually me—is at the end of the whole train of things happening and all these phone calls of people going 'Get rid of these bears! They're worthless!' and 'Just haul them away' and all of that. Eventually, somebody at the very end—being me—has to put a bullet in their heads. And the people where you caught the bear, half of them are screaming at you because you killed this poor bear. The other half says, 'Good riddance, you should have killed them all.'" But most of the time, killing one bear just makes room for another at the feeding trough.

When I asked what it was like for someone working in wildlife conservation to have to regularly euthanize bears, Barten told this story: One August night a home owner near Thunder Mountain was awakened by his barking huskies. A bear was in the fenced yard chasing the dogs.

The home owner called the police, who arrived to find yelling people, crazed dogs, and a bear that seemed aggressive. The officers tossed a seal bomb near the bear to frighten it away with a concussive blast, but the bear only growled. So they shot it. In the morning they discovered why the bear had refused to leave: her cub was clinging to a nearby tree. That's when someone called Fish and Game. Barten asked Costello to photograph the dead female and the tranquilized cub as a way of publicizing the grim consequences of food-conditioning bears. Then he tried to find a zoo to take the cub, but zoos everywhere are full up with black bears these days. "We could have released it, but the chances of it surviving were zero," he later told the newspaper. The orphan was hardly bigger than a cocker spaniel.

Barten knew he would have to kill the cub. The proper procedure is to inject a drug, such as phenobarbital, into the animal's heart. Here's the difficulty, though: Tranquilized cubs often cry, a kind of mewling sound, emanating from whatever altered state they're in. Their eyes are closed, they seem to be asleep, but they cry no matter how much tranquilizer you administer. "Well, the whole time this cub's crying, and I'm crying," Barten said. "I'm sitting in the lab at 7:00 at night by myself, trying to kill this cub, and I was talking to it and petting it, and I was like, 'I shouldn't have to do this. And I'll never do it again.' And I never did it again. It was such a terrible thing. It was a terrible experience. This poor cub, I wanted so bad to pull the needle out and let it wake up and take it someplace, but you know, I couldn't. Anyway. That was the last time I've ever done that." After a moment he added, "Now what I do is, I put 'em to sleep and I shoot them with a shotgun in the head. Which is a lot better but it's still . . . it's awful."

Within a week of this incident—and after a vigorous bout of public criticism—the police department rethought its policy, and the chief announced that officers would no longer shoot bears unless there was "extreme danger" to human life. "Basically, bears were being destroyed in defense of people's garbage," he told the newspaper. "Garbage is not a valuable commodity."

Neil Barten didn't describe killing the cub because he's sentimental about animals or because he wanted me to feel sorry for him. He is a hunter, an outdoorsman who once trapped for a living, and a professional charged with managing the black bear hunt in his unit. But there's hunting, and then there's extinguishing. He was telling the other half of a common story, the half almost nobody sees. He's merely the agent of humanity, the hand that wields the needle or pulls the trigger. A person like Pat Costello is the witness. I can't say who the rest of us are.

During our tour of Juneau's neighborhoods, Pat Costello and I passed an empty suburban lot where, the previous year, a bear wounded by an arrow had lain moaning and crying all night until it finally died. The cruelty of this act seems impossible to understand unless you accept that some people truly believe that hostility or contempt is a rational response to bears. "Bears are without virtue or any redeeming social value," a longtime Juneau resident wrote in a letter to the editor. "Not only are they hazardous to your health, but their stools are black and tarry. Years ago we shot the excess and gave the meat to charities. That's still a logical solution."

When the letter appeared, you could almost hear the outraged bear lovers framing responses in their heads. No virtue? No redeeming social value? These days, some people load bears with virtue and value. To summarize: The presence of bears among us suggests that we are not the biggest, most dominant of creatures. They introduce humility into the prevailing American mind-set toward predators, toward the uncontrollable and elemental wilderness the colonists encountered when they first ventured into this dark and forested continent. Furthermore, bears were here first, and it's our responsibility to share the wilderness—or what's left of it. "Sure, it's inconvenient to keep the garbage inside until garbage day, but what makes us think it's OK to kill bears just to make our lives more convenient? It's self-centered and cruel," wrote someone from the pro-bear faction. "We all have to get our acts together and be responsible. Use that big human brain."

The dilemma has always been agreeing on what the right thing is and, more important, who's in charge of making everyone do it. In each village, town, and city in Alaska, you can locate every attitude toward bears: fear, reverence, indifference, respect, intolerance, unconditional love, antagonism. Kill bears. Save bears. Use your brain. Use your heart. Do the right thing. Don't do anything. The real discussion is not simply about whether killing garbage-eating bears is wrong and, if so, what can be done to stop it. It's also about what kind of people Alaskans want to be, what kind of wilderness they intend to live in.

It would be hard to find a place hovering more uncertainly in the vague margin between artifice and nature, civilization and wilderness, than

Anchorage. Here on the bleeding edge of the Last Frontier, the short list of urban hazards includes traffic accidents, gang shootings, moose stompings, and bear attacks. Almost 300,000 people inhabit a municipality larger than Rhode Island. Most squeeze into the 100 square miles of the Anchorage Bowl, a splendid landscape wedged between the tidal mudflats of Cook Inlet and the Chugach Mountains jigsawing above the city's eastern flank. The ragged edges of suburbia and the outlying communities press against the wilderness of Chugach State Park, making it easy for animals to permeate big tracts of undeveloped land and follow greenbelts into the city. Almost 40 percent of the state's population lives here, and many other Alaskans think of it as "Los Anchorage." In 2007, perhaps in an attempt to reinforce its bonds with Alaska—the "real" Alaska where everyone else lives—civic leaders and advertising agencies crafted a new brand for the city: Big Wild Life.

Nobody knows precisely how many big wild animals live in the municipality, but in the past, Alaska Fish and Game has estimated populations of about 1,700 moose, 4 or 5 wolf packs, 200 to 300 black bears, and 65 to 75 brown bears. Anchorage is not the only community in North America frequented by brown bears, but it may be the largest. The presence of so much wildlife tests everyone's perception of where people and animals belong and how we should comport ourselves around each other. When anthropologist Patricia Partnow examined how Anchorage residents responded to local wildlife incidents, including a man fatally trampled by a moose on the University of Alaska campus in 1995, one of her conclusions was that "far more important to Anchorage residents than rules for proper behavior toward animals—a paramount issue in Native cultures—are the rules for proper animal behavior toward humans." She added, "Anchorageites cannot seem to resist, in spite of their wish to be as Alaskan as the next guy, the temptation to civilize wild animals." This explains why someone who lives on the edge of a mountainous wilderness feels aggrieved when a bear has the nerve to eat his chickens, or why a home owner who witnesses a bear killing a moose calf says, "I know that's what bears do. But they don't do it in your driveway." People staked their claims; it was the bears that didn't honor the boundaries.

These philosophical and cultural distinctions are overshadowed by practical differences for wildlife biologist Rick Sinnott. "People and wildlife don't think alike at all in most cases," he said. "So I'm sort of in the middle, and I'm trying to explain the rules to both sides. Sometimes the people get it. The wildlife almost never do. So you're just trying to work out the details and making sure the game goes on." Until he retired in 2010, his job title at the Alaska Department of Fish and Game was Anchorage area management biologist, but I always thought of him as the mayor of Wild Kingdom. He was popular with the press for his lively and candid comments, the go-to guy who wore rubber XtraTuf boots to the office because he might need to haul a decomposing moose away from a bear's cache, trap a beaver, or rescue a squalling orphaned brown bear cub by climbing a spindly tree, net in hand. ("They're just bundles of sharp instruments," he said of cubs. "It's like handling a hand grenade or something.") The animals made his job interesting. The tough part was the baffling, unpredictable, and exasperating behavior of people. "You'd think I'd be an expert on human nature by now," he said in a radio interview once. "Bears are easier."

Because people often asked for his help or demanded explanations or delivered opinions about how he should be doing his job, Sinnott was a good listener. "He's got a quarter million people as his constituents, and he still manages to make each one feel important when they call," said colleague Larry Van Daele. But Sinnott could also be critical of the less intellectually gifted among the hominids, and who could blame him? When someone dumped rotting fish guts in a neighborhood frequented by bears, he told a reporter, "I'd like to catch the assholes who did it and beat the crap out of them." After the comment appeared in the newspaper, the Fish and Game commissioner told him not to talk to the press about bear matters for awhile. Letters poured in about the gag order. Some called Sinnott an "unsung hero" and a "fantastic public servant," but one guy welcomed Sinnott's muzzling and said he needed to just do his job and "stop bad-mouthing everyone else."

Sinnott had been doing his job for years. The difficulty was convincing everyone else to do theirs. He and his assistant, wildlife biologist Jessy Coltrane, fought the same battles as Neil Barten and their counterparts everywhere—not against bears but against oblivious or lazy home owners, city officials uninterested in enforcing trash ordinances or writing better ones, law enforcement officers too busy to hand out tickets for creating attractive nuisances with garbage or birdseed. By educating some people and aggravating others, the Anchorage biologists made incremental progress over the years. The department had formed the Anchorage Bear Committee to coordinate efforts among city officials, state agencies, educators, environmental organizations, and enforcement officers. Alaska Waste made bear-resistant roll carts available for only a few dollars more than regular garbage bins, developed a lightweight but bear-resistant Dumpster lid, and announced plans to retrofit commercial Dumpsters in three neighborhoods with persistent bear problems. The mayor agreed that garbage trucks could make their rounds later in the day so home owners would be less likely to set their cans out the night before pickup. Some neighborhoods rallied to better police themselves. Eventually the city began to replace open trash cans at parks and ballfields with bear-resistant containers.

Without the unqualified support of municipal and law enforcement officials, though, these efforts were a bit like patching the leaks in a dam—there were always more leaks than patches, particularly with only two biologists among nearly 300,000 residents. "I'd like to say Juneau is light years ahead of Anchorage," Sinnott told the Alaska Board of Game in 2007, "but they may only be ten or twenty years ahead." Complicating matters in Anchorage is the significant presence of brown bears. Although they are fewer in number and less likely to become food-conditioned or habituated than black bears, brown bears have a tendency to react more aggressively in dicey situations.

Like Barten and other urban biologists, Sinnott restated the obvious about bears and food year after year, and he made the hard decisions when others didn't listen. People could argue about where the boundaries between wilderness and society were, but to him, those distinctions were blurry. "We're moving in on the bears' habitat, and they're moving in on ours," he told me. Many Anchorage residents still don't grasp this simple truth and probably never will. One spring, he and Coltrane shot and killed a three-year-old brown bear that had been prying open a bird feeder in someone's backyard. In previous weeks the bear had generated more than a hundred complaints from the same subdivision as it raided garbage cans, helped itself to barbecue leftovers, and killed two moose calves in two days, one in the driveway of a home near the local Walmart. Coltrane later told an interviewer, "You think, 'Oh my gosh, all of the education we have done in this neighborhood, all of the begging, all the pleading, all the nights we patrolled, the citations, everything, and there's still someone with a bird feeder.'" The man who had been feeding the birds (and the bear) told a reporter, "I was hoping they would just dart it." In fifteen years he had never experienced this problem, he said: "I'm in the center of the neighborhood, not the periphery. The bear just wasn't afraid of people."

Sinnott was not delicate about assigning blame: "I didn't kill this bear. The people that are feeding it garbage and birdseed did," he told a reporter. When I asked him about the home owner's insistence that his house was firmly embraced by civilization, Sinnott snorted. "He was literally two blocks from the Eagle River greenbelt. It's not like the center of Anchorage," he said. "Maybe he sort of had to believe that." A few days later the Anchorage Daily News printed several letters from residents, rehashing all the arguments that appear after every such incident. A woman angry at Sinnott's comments wrote: "Yes, this area used to be bear habitat, but now there are homes with families, and we cannot co-exist with bears. For all of us who heard or witnessed the killing of a moose calf the morning of June 23, we are glad the bear has finally been put down." One man blamed Fish and Game for allowing problem bears to live in communities. What we need, he wrote, is respect for bears in wild areas and intolerance for bears in backyards. And a reader chastising irresponsible home owners concluded (as such letters often do), "If you don't want wilderness and wild animals, move to Los Angeles."

All these writers were trying to establish not only who was to blame but also who was responsible for the bears among us. Sinnott was accustomed to snotty comments from people who thought he was that person. His wife once pointed out that within a couple of weeks he'd been labeled a "bear lover" and a "bear hater" in the newspaper, neither term intended as a compliment. ("And I loved that," he said.) But beyond fixing blame and responsibility, these folks were also expressing their own notions about where bears do and don't belong and, by extension, where people do and don't belong.

Sinnott also knew that he usually heard only from the disgruntled and the worried, not from those who love having wildlife in their hometown. And, as he likes to point out, most residents belong to the latter group, judging from the results of public opinion surveys commissioned by the Alaska Department of Fish and Game in 1997 and 2009. In the more recent survey, 84 percent agreed with the statement "I take pride in the amount of wildlife in Anchorage, even if they cause some problems or hazards." Similar majorities believed that, despite occasional danger, wildlife encounters make life in Anchorage "interesting and special" and that people should learn to live with conflicts, including such annoyances as moose munching ornamental trees and creating safety hazards on roads.

People felt more ambivalent about the presence of bears, particularly brown bears. Only about one in twenty reported having any problems with brown or black bears, and most of those involved garbage. Still, the number of people who considered the possibility of encountering a brown bear a positive aspect of living in Anchorage (47 percent) was almost matched by those who didn't (44 percent). A third of respondents said the prospect of seeing a brown bear prevented them from using local parks and trails as much as they would have liked."What's the purpose of having them near people, of taking the chance?" asked a participant in a related focus group. Others found it difficult to separate the bears from the place. "Maybe I'm simple-minded, but I like [the idea of] running into bears because you live in Alaska," a trail user said. "This is Alaska—it's not San Francisco or Seattle or Chicago. Most of us are here because it's Anchorage, Alaska. I'm sorry people have been hurt or killed, but if you're worried, there are other trails and areas to use." These questions and answers folded into a larger, more complicated inquiry: is Anchorage the blunt instrument of the frontier, pacifying nature into civilization, or is it still part of the wilderness surrounding it?

The survey asked lots of questions about people's attitudes toward bears and trails for a good reason. The previous summer, brown bears had mauled two women in separate incidents on a popular trail in town. These were the most serious attacks in Anchorage since 1995, when a bear killed two well-known runners, a mother and son, on a Chugach State Park trail a few miles south of town. The evidence suggested that the bear had been feeding on a moose carcass a few yards from the trail. The 1995 incident was a classic case of being in the wrong place at the wrong time, but it spooked residents. Fish and Game biologist Sterling Miller even told the *Anchorage Daily News* that he might carry a gun the next time he hiked the trail. (He was also worried that nervous hikers with firearms might overreact and shoot harmless bears or accidentally injure people. Now that bear spray is available, he'd probably choose that instead of a gun.)

What alarmed many people about the more recent incidents was that they had occurred in the city's Far North Bicentennial Park, 4,000 acres of largely undeveloped woodlands adjoining big tracts owned by the military and the Bureau of Land Management and connecting with the wild, half-million-acre expanse of Chugach State Park. This prime bear habitat lies about seven miles from downtown Anchorage, which is seamed with greenbelts and riven with salmon streams. In 2007 a police officer shot a young brown bear that had been wandering through the city's downtown neighborhoods for weeks without incident until it attracted a Fourth of July crowd; the following year a car struck a 730-pound brown bear dashing across a busy street near a car dealership.

That brown bears live so close to people seemed like an aberration only to those who weren't privy to the results of a three-year study by Alaska Fish and Game research biologist Sean Farley. "One of the most startling findings of the study is that large numbers of brown bears are foraging, rearing young, and denning in close proximity to human development and human presence," Farley's 2007 report stated. After gathering hair samples for DNA analysis and tracking eleven animals with GPS collars, he identified at least thirty-six bears—not including cubs—that lived in the city's margins. Hair from four collared animals didn't turn up at snag sites, however, meaning that the true population of resident bears is surely larger.

The study's bears denned in the Chugach Mountains, and all but a few descended into the Anchorage Bowl to eat vegetation, moose calves, berries, and salmon from several streams. They regularly traveled along stream corridors, beside airstrips on military land, through a golf course, and occasionally across four lanes of Tudor Road. At least twenty bears commonly used trails in Bicentennial Park and the adjoining Campbell Tract—the same trails frequented by runners, day hikers, dog walkers, mountain bikers, and black bears. The study's findings caused Farley to reconsider his own ideas about brown bears. "They're not really a wilderness species like we once thought," he said in a public meeting.

Some bears lived weeks at a time within a kilometer of Campbell Creek, a clear, forked stream that pours from the mountains and through the city. "Within any given day those bears often are less than 10 meters from streamside," the report noted. And no wonder. The sport fisheries division of the Department of Fish and Game has boosted the creek's small run of sockeye salmon with stocked king and silver salmon. Fishing regulations prevent most anglers from catching anything but silvers. That leaves the rest for bears, and they appreciate it. Salmon formed 43 percent of the average diet among those visiting the stream, according to stable isotope analysis. Terrestrial meat—most likely moose calves and gut piles and carcasses left by hunters—contributed 29 percent of the average diet.

The gist of the report was this: These bears aren't occasional visitors to the Anchorage Bowl. They spend most of their summers living among people so secretively that few ever see them. Sinnott has seen how carefully and quietly bears can travel along stretches of Campbell Creek as it winds through neighborhoods on its way to Cook Inlet. "One big brown bear, he cruises among the homeless people and the midnight fishermen," he told me. "He loves fishing for salmon. When someone comes along he sort of fades into the brush and then he fades back."

A salmon stream plus brown bears plus recreationists: what could go wrong? In the summer of 2008 a few runners and bikers reported being chased by a brown bear with two cubs on Bicentennial Park trails, but no one was injured. In retrospect, locating Rover's Run trail beside two miles of Campbell Creek didn't seem like such a good idea after a brown bear seriously mauled a fifteen-year-old girl who was competing in a twenty-four-hour bike race that coursed through the park. The dim light of midnight and windy conditions made it difficult for biker and bear to detect each other on the brushy trail. She either slammed into the animal or surprised it into a defensive attack—she doesn't remember. She managed to call 9-1-1 despite a crushed larynx and a deflated lung, among other injuries severe enough that the next biker who came along, her coach, didn't recognize her. (She made a near-full recovery.)

The city closed the trail, which had originally been created for winter skijorers, not mountain bikers and hikers. There were public calls to destroy the animal responsible for injuring the teenager, but there was no way to know which of the park's twenty or so bears was responsible, Sinnott said at the time. "We're not going to just go shoot a bear and bring it back into town and say, 'There you go—there's a dead bear,'" he told the *Anchorage Daily News*. "It's just not going to do any good."

Five weeks later a fifty-one-year-old jogger misread a warning about a recent bear sighting on Rover's Run and ducked under tape blocking the trail. Two young brown bears chased her and her dog, and then the mother bear attacked, biting the woman's head and neck and collapsing a lung. Police sergeant Pablo Paiz expressed a common sentiment to a reporter: "This is Alaska: big, wild life. You have to be careful when you're out here in the woods. There's always a possibility that something's gonna jump out and grab you. You get between a sow and its cubs and a sow's gonna do what a sow's gonna do." The jogger, who recovered, acknowledged her own faulty judgment in running on a trail closed because of bear activity.

This mauling, coupled with the previous episodes involving a female and cubs, clinched the decision to find and kill the bear. Sinnott and

Coltrane had always taken action when it became clear that a bear represented a higher-than-usual risk to people, even if people had helped create that risk. Eleven days after the jogger was mauled, Sinnott shot an especially aggressive bear in a neighborhood where she was feeding with her cubs on a bull moose carcass. DNA tests showed that this bear had injured the jogger but not the teenage biker; that bear was never identified. The dead bear's two cubs, a male and a female, were eventually captured and sent to the Indianapolis Zoo, which changed their names from Rosie and Rover to K'etnu and Kiak. Rover's Run remained closed for the summer, although trail cams captured at least three mountain bikers using the trail shortly after the attacks, sometimes within hours of a bear's presence.

Several months after the maulings, Rick Sinnott and Sean Farley spoke to a standing-room-only crowd at a meeting of the Anchorage Waterways Council. Farley pointed out that stocking salmon in Campbell Creek may be good for stream health, but it can't help but attract hungry bears. "The bears are not here because they like us," he said. One old-timer said his piece, stating that he and his wife had seen more bears in their neighborhood than ever before. Somebody needed to do away with all these bears wandering through populated areas, he said: "I think we've got plenty of bears to spare." Sinnott responded to the suggestion that he was unwilling to dispatch food-conditioned animals by saying, "I, personally, have shot more bears in Anchorage than anyone else." He was quite familiar with the bear problems in the old-timer's neighborhood, he said, because a resident there consistently left piles of garbage bags in the driveway. Maybe the neighbors ought to do something about *that*, Sinnott suggested, which was not the answer the old-timer wanted.

Whether Anchorage has bears to spare is questionable. Between 2000 and 2009, home owners or authorities killed twenty-five brown bears locally, according to Fish and Game statistics. Seventy black bears died from 2007 to 2010 alone. The department estimates three to six black bear shootings go unreported each year, and cars or trains kill a few more annually. In response to the park maulings in 2008, the state Board of Game opened more of Chugach State Park to brown bear hunters; Sinnott thought this might relieve some pressure by removing a couple of the bolder, front-range bears each year, but hunters killed a record six in 2011. The average annual harvest of about fifty black bears in recent years is also a historic high, he wrote in his *Alaska Dispatch* column. Between hunting, roadkill, and bears shot in defense of life and property, humans remove an average of seven brown bears and sixty-eight black bears annually, he said, "too high to sustain, based on existing population estimates."

Before, during, and after these incidents, Sinnott repeated some version of this refrain: "The only way to reduce brown bear attacks to zero is to kill all the bears." Tolerating twenty bears in Bicentennial Park is much less risky than driving, he noted (fourteen people died in Anchorage traffic accidents in 2008). And if anyone could talk about the relative risks, he could. While driving home from his fifty-sixth birthday party in 2006, somebody in the next lane opened fire on another car, and a stray bullet pierced Sinnott's door and his thigh. He returned to work two days later, suffering no permanent damage.

Police couldn't say for sure if the gunfire was gang related, but I was surprised to learn that 130 known gang members and about 100 gang associates lived in Anchorage at the time. Yet nobody was publishing *Alaska's Gang Shooting Tales*. Instead, writers like Larry Kaniut have found a wide readership by publishing collections of gory bear attack stories. Sinnott sighed when I asked about these books' effect on the collective Alaskan psyche. "My whole professional goal has been set back thirty years by Larry," he said. After the Bicentennial Park episodes, Kaniut wrote a newspaper commentary complaining about the growing bear numbers in "Los Anchorage" and wildlife managers' failure to remedy that situation. Put him in charge of managing bears, Kaniut suggested, and any bear sighted in town would be killed, the edible bits given to charity, and the hide and claws auctioned. "I'll hire biologists who manage game, not biologists who manage people," he wrote. "I'll rid the department of spineless people who fear criticism from fairy-dust sniffers."

Sinnott responded by quoting a famous Alaskan who had written that sensationalistic accounts of bear attacks are often exaggerated and cause unnecessary anxiety about the wilderness. Bears are known to hang around towns, and when maulings occur, people should make sure not to blame bears unnecessarily, this Alaskan had advised. "We should respect these animals for the wild creatures they are," he urged. Who was the author of these soothing statements? Larry Kaniut, Sinnott revealed. "Was he always so intolerant of bears," Sinnott asked, "and if so, why do his books feign respect while titillating readers with 'sensationalistic accounts' he claims are 'exaggerated'—or has his mind become more unhinged by seeing a few bears 'around his house' in recent summers?"

Sinnott considers moose more dangerous than bears, and in fact, the ungulates have killed as many people in Anchorage as bears have: two. They've attacked and injured many more residents than bears have, yet people tend to think of moose as garden pests and traffic hazards rather than threats. It must be the long eyelashes and the big brown eyes, Sinnott suggests. He has tried to provide some perspective to people's fears about urban bears by investigating whether there's any validity to the claim that present-day Anchorage is besieged by more bears than in days of yore. He found comments mentioning the presence of numerous bears in multiple recollections of old-timers, even from a century ago. "Numbers of bears fluctuate from year to year, but most of the evidence I'm familiar with doesn't support the contention that bear numbers are increasing," he wrote in the *Alaska Dispatch*. "The only evidence that suggests black and brown bear populations have been growing for decades is that more bears are being seen. However, the best explanation for that appears to be more people, more trails, more attractants, more food-conditioned bears, and more coverage."

Considering how regularly people and bears encounter each other on the fringes of Anchorage and in the nearby wildlands, remarkably few attacks have occurred. Jessy Coltrane, who took Sinnott's place after he retired, compiled statistics for a spring 2012 medical meeting. Since 1908, she found, five black bears have delivered a swat or a bite. Of the area's sixteen brown bear maulings, two were the 1995 fatalities, and about a third of the rest were minor scratches or bites. Several took place in the Eagle River Valley, where trails pass near or through bear fishing grounds. This pattern continued in the summer of 2012, when brown bears injured another four hikers, three on Eagle River trails and one south of Anchorage. Each incident was a defensive response from a startled bear—one was guarding a moose carcass, and the others were females with cubs. In two of the incidents, the people ran after seeing the bear, possibly triggering the attack. As is typical, three of the bears vamoosed once they'd knocked the person down. One hiker fought back—generally not recommended in a defensive attack by a brown bear—but he broke free during the mauling and climbed a tree. Some of the injuries required hospitalization, but none were horrifically damaging—at least not physically.

Even in Juneau, where thousands of black bear sightings and

encounters have occurred in the past fifteen years, I found reports of only three minor injuries inflicted by bears. All were surprised animals that swiped at someone before running away. Although black bears are more likely than brown bears to seek out anthropogenic food, they are far less aggressive, according to bear expert Stephen Herrero. Wild black bears killed sixty-three people in North America from 1900 to 2009, forty-nine of them in Canada and Alaska, he and his coauthors reported in 2011. Eighty-six percent of these fatalities occurred since 1960, leading the researchers to hypothesize that population growth in both species has increased their chances of encountering each other, especially as more people work, play, and live in bear habitat. Another key factor: human food or garbage was present in almost 40 percent of fatal incidents. "Our experience with bear behavior and attacks leads us to speculate that black bears that become increasingly aggressive in going after people's food or garbage have an increased chance of initiating a serious or fatal attack." They were not suggesting that the availability of food or garbage "usually contributes" to an attack, although it has occasionally. (Predatory bears were responsible for most deaths.) Nevertheless, "the risk of fatal black bear attacks on people in our study area was extremely low," the researchers noted. "Each year, millions of interactions between people and black bears occur without any injury to a person, although by 2 years of age most black bears have the physical capacity to kill a person."

That's not to say that bears don't occasionally alarm people, bust into houses, damage cars, or kill dogs. Even so, given the opportunity, bears often refrain from causing trouble. A Swedish foreign-exchange student sunning himself on a Juneau deck opened his eyes to discover that the furry creature nuzzling and licking him was a young bear, which promptly ran into the woods after the startled student startled it. A bear that ventured through an open front door went into the bathroom, drank from the toilet, climbed in the shower, and somehow turned it on. It ignored cheese pinwheels cooling on the counter and passed the home owner on its way out. A twenty-two-year-old Juneau hairdresser made national news in 2011 when she punched a black bear that was carrying off her dachshund, Fudge. The surprised bear surrendered the unharmed dog. "I wasn't in my right mind at the moment but I would never think of doing it again," she told the newspaper.

Chance encounters with humans can escalate into serious incidents when people overreact. Bears that simply stumble into the wrong place at the wrong time often draw excited crowds, giving authorities little choice but to kill the agitated bear, as it's not considered good public policy to fire warning shots at citizens. Few people have experience interpreting bear behavior, so a bear that doesn't give ground, ignores you, or even moves toward you is a bear that provokes intense anxiety. Is it posturing? Bluffing? Curious? Will it charge? People with guns often don't wait to find out. State law allows bears to be killed in defense of life or property, and although garbage isn't considered defensible property, sheds and chickens and dogs are. And good luck trying to discern, after the fact, whether a home owner's decision to shoot was the result of fear, recklessness, or good judgment.

Wildlife managers, park officials, and enforcement officers are keenly aware of the liability issues that come with their jobs. Panels at the past two Bear-Human Conflicts Workshops have discussed US and Canadian case law and hashed over possible legal problems when it comes to tolerating habituated bears, handling food-conditioned animals, and warning park or campground visitors about potentially dangerous animals. Some of this concern stems from a 1996 incident near Tucson, Arizona, in which a nuisance bear that had been relocated after slightly injuring a Girl Scout returned within two days and severely mauled a teenage girl. The family sued Arizona's Game and Fish Department and the US Forest Service; both agencies settled out of court— Arizona for $2.5 million. The family's lawyers faulted wildlife managers for not killing the bear or relocating it farther away, for not closing the campground or warning other campers, and for not adequately enforcing food and garbage regulations. More recently, the family of an eleven-year-old Utah boy dragged from his tent and killed by a black bear at a primitive campsite in 2007 sued the US Forest Service and the state wildlife agency for negligence and won a $1.95 million judgment. A federal judge determined that the Forest Service was 65 percent responsible for the boy's death because it had failed to warn the public about an incident twelve hours earlier in the same campground, during which a bear had slashed through a tent and swatted at the occupant. The judge assigned 25 percent of the blame to the Utah Division of Wildlife Services because it had failed to tell the Forest Service that it was searching for the bear from the earlier incident. The family received 10 percent of the blame because a granola wrapper and half a can of Coke Zero were found in the tent. (In late 2011 a Utah district court ruled that the state was immune from a wrongful-death suit because black bears are native to Utah, exist in nature, and are therefore a "natural condition" on the land.)

The conclusion worth drawing is not that bears are becoming more dangerous or that the government can or should protect everyone in bear country. Rather, people who live or play anywhere near bear habitat need to know how to handle food and garbage and how to understand bear behavior. Neil Barten has pointed out that we train our dogs, however crudely, to read our behavior, and we can usually tell when a dog is frightened, happy, hungry, comfortable, or unfriendly. Otherwise, we could never expect to maintain any sort of living arrangement with a canine. Certainly, we understand the danger of behaving unpredictably around dogs. Yet most people's understanding of bears—an animal we instinctively regard as far more dangerous than a dog—remains vague or distorted. People are frequently just as confused about the lessons we teach bears as the bears are: help yourself to this, don't eat that, just ignore people, run away! The irony is that dogs have injured and killed more people in Alaska than bears have, if irony is the right word.

Human-bear conflicts are an excellent way to inspire human-human conflicts, it turns out. Wildlife agencies, public safety officers, activists, citizens, and officials from every level of government often become mired in disagreements over who's responsible for dealing with urban bears and what the best course of action might be. Dumps in the remote communities of Yakutat and Angoon serve as local brown bear–viewing (and –shooting) sites, as efforts to enclose them falter year after year from a lack of money or interest. Sometimes, though, people pull together and clean up their towns. Several communities in Southeast Alaska, on Kodiak Island, and on the Kenai Peninsula have adopted measures to enforce trash ordinances, distribute bear-resistant garbage containers, install electric fences at landfills, or ship out their waste. In Sitka, where each year an average of nine brown bears are killed in defense of life and property, a local Brown Bear Task Force successfully lobbied for a garbage ordinance with fines that are even stiffer than Juneau's. Residents can also post sightings on Facebook's Sitka Bear Report. (Sample update: "Bear is frequenting Old Harbor Mountain Road . . . so far he is only interested in garbage cans, so don't put them out until Friday morning.")

Perhaps because of its unwieldy size or its uneasy position as a frontier town teetering on the edge of wilderness, Anchorage tends to settle for the simplest response: do nothing. When it comes to urban bears, brown or black, residents often display a blinding disconnect between where they think they live (Suburbia, USA) and where they actually live (Suburbia, Alaska). Even as the city was still fixated on the young biker's mauling in Bicentennial Park, Sinnott spoke out against a plan to create a recreational trail along a well-traveled brown bear corridor in the bedroom community of Eagle River. "I can think of few worse places to build trails in the Anchorage area," he said. And he warned that encouraging more runners, bikers, and walkers to use this bear route would only invite trouble. The community's assemblywoman supported the trail, under the rationale that people and bears would share the route anyway. (Planners later decided to reevaluate part of the trail design.) As if to underscore Sinnott's argument, in late July a brown bear with cubs knocked down and bit an eighteen-year-old Eagle River man walking at 2:00 a.m. near a salmon creek in that corridor. Trail cameras later photographed bears visiting the creek several times a week at night.

Sinnott also took on Anchorage's new mayor, Dan Sullivan, over how to handle Rover's Run. The trail remained closed in 2009, which proved to be a quiet year in Anchorage bear-wise, perhaps because people were only slowly returning to Bicentennial Park. The following year a biker rode up on a brown bear with a cub at the intersection of Rover's Run and a connecting trail. The mother bear reacted by slapping the biker around and then retreating. Sullivan refused to do anything beyond posting a few warning signs, despite recommendations to close the trail from the Department of Fish and Game, the Anchorage Bear Committee, two municipal advisory boards, and the mayor's own parks department, Sinnott wrote in his column for the *Alaska Dispatch*. Restricting human activity along a salmon stream during the spawning season was only common sense, he argued, citing the Abbott Loop Trail near Eagle River: brown bears had injured several people there before state park managers started closing the trail seasonally once the salmon arrived. People will always do what they want, Sinnott acknowledged, but limiting access to known problem areas protects not only people but also bears, which are often killed simply for behaving like bears.

Mayor Sullivan's position was that people are responsible for educating themselves about potential dangers. "Do we want our urban parks to be brown bear sanctuaries or do we want them to be places where people can recreate?" he asked in the *Anchorage Daily News*. He'd actually answered that question the previous day when he first commented on the incident: "Sullivan said he would probably be armed if he was on Rover's Run," the paper reported. "Asked what kind of gun he would carry, he said, 'A big one.'"

As for long-term planning that could diminish citizens' need to arm themselves in parks, the city that branded itself Big Wild Life apparently has little regard for actual wildlife. The municipality began the long and tortuous process of revising its land-use codes in 2002, working from a comprehensive plan that described Anchorage as a place that values its spectacular natural setting and its wildlife. The Anchorage Bear Committee understood that visions weren't enough, and the group submitted guidelines to protect bear habitat and reduce conflicts. "It's time to do it," Sinnott said, "because they won't do it again [revise the codes] for another twenty years." The committee's plan was both rational and radical. It extended beyond trash handling to propose measures that would make coexistence more than a hollow buzzword. The plan recommended zoning for bears, similar to the way the city zones for floods. "Like floods, bears are a force of nature," said the accompanying memo. "Building houses in high-quality bear habitat is tantamount to building houses on a floodplain. Like floods, bears will continue to flow from their source in the mountains east of the city into the Anchorage Bowl and other developed areas. The municipality needs planning and zoning that accommodates bears, like floods." The plan recommended zoning for four different types of bear habitat that are especially vulnerable to human activity; for example, bear habitat 1 would include salmon spawning streams and surrounding land, and bear habitat 4 would incorporate neighborhoods located in important bear-movement corridors. The overall idea was to keep development from further encroaching on bear habitat and to regulate, eliminate, or bear-proof anything that would tempt bears to linger as they moved around the city—garbage, pet food, chicken coops, beehives, compost, livestock.

I asked Rick if this document was actually calling for mutual habituation between bears and people. "It is," he said. "It is." Ideally, bears and people would accept each other's presence but mind their own business, making life safer for everybody. But Sinnott knew better than anyone that success depends on a fundamental, shared belief that bears matter, that bears are something more than a convenient but empty symbol of wilderness or of Alaska.

That is the hard part—too hard for Anchorage city planners, as it turned out. Almost none of the committee's suggestions surfaced in the next version of the land-use codes. The notion of conserving wildlife habitat as part of urban planning lost even more ground after the election of pro-development mayor Dan Sullivan in 2009. Only one, limited provision addressed garbage and bears (and the city wanted to delete it from the final draft): Bear-resistant receptacles would be required at a few facilities in Girdwood, a tiny ski community south of town, and in wildlife management corridors. These corridors would span 200 feet on either side of certain streams, even though buffers on salmon-bearing streams on the Kenai Peninsula are as wide as 750 feet, the Bear Committee noted, and even that is "just a fraction of the habitat actually used by salmon-feeding bears."

City officials not only ignored human-bear conflicts; they actually contributed to them by allowing people to raise chickens and rabbits in their backyards—as if people needed one more reason to shoot marauding bears they themselves had baited. Within a couple of months, chickens had lured five black bears to their deaths. Of the eight bears killed by home owners in Anchorage in 2012, four were shot over chickens and one over a llama, Coltrane told the *Alaska Dispatch*. In late fall a home owner wounded a brown bear trying to eat his chickens, forcing Coltrane and others to track the injured, bleeding bear in the middle of the night. They never found it. "I don't understand people who won't shoot a bear over a garbage can, but they will shoot a bear over the chicken they paid 50 cents for," she commented during the Human-Bear Conflicts Workshop in Missoula, Montana. A national obsession for hobby coops means that people are choosing chickens over bears in Montana, New Jersey, and elsewhere. "Five years ago all we talked about was garbage, garbage, garbage," Jamie Jonkel of the Montana Department of Fish, Wildlife, and Parks told the *New York Times*. "Now it's chickens, chickens, chickens." This was how the West was lost: one chicken at a time.

Rather than require chicken ranchers to protect their poultry with something sensible like electric fences or bear-resistant sheds, a couple of Anchorage assembly members suggested opening a hunt in the well-populated flanks of the city to trim the brown bear population. Perhaps they hadn't bothered to read the resolution they'd approved in 2011 to encourage people to "foster a sense of personal responsibility for our bears and all wildlife"—a resolution packed with "whereases" enumerating the value of minimizing bear attractants and the importance of stewardship for "our bears" and so on and so forth, amen. Meanwhile, the state predicts that another 56,000 people will cram themselves into Anchorage by 2030. They'll be building new houses, making more garbage, crowding into parks, raising chickens, and maybe wondering where all the bears went.

Juneau's trash ordinances didn't solve all its problems permanently, but no one ever claimed they would. When I check in with my hometown newspaper, I still see the occasional story about urban bears, like those I once wrote. But people like Pat Costello and Neil Barten helped the city government understand that bears are the community's responsibility, not just the state's. "We actually have gained some ground that we're never going to lose back," Barten told me. Apparently, it takes a village to save a bear. Now, every kid in town learns about bear safety in school. Ernestine Hayes also wrote a children's book that was translated into Tlingit, *The Story of the Town Bear and the Forest Bear*. My favorite part is the end, when the Forest Bear returns to the woods rather than face the perils of town. We never learn what happened to the Town Bear, but we can hope for the best: "Maybe he came back to live with his relative in the forest, and up to now they're happy there, always digging roots, eating berries, and catching fish."

Not long ago, I learned that wistful hope or a simmering sense of outrage doesn't fix anything. Jessy Coltrane was forced to kill a female black bear raising her offspring in my neighborhood, a mile from Bicentennial Park. The bear had been hanging around Baxter Bog, directly behind my house, and making regular sorties on trash cans as her three cubs trailed behind. Maybe she was the same glossy animal I'd once seen pushing through the understory out back. After she died, the cubs spent about a day at the zoo before they were euthanized. The world has enough black bears in its zoos, and too many elsewhere, I suppose. When I thought about the neighbors I'd seen dragging their trash cans outside the night before pickup or leaving their bird feeders up all summer, I felt ashamed of myself. A phone call to ask the home owners' association to help, a polite conversation with the folks next door—would that have been so hard?

Even as these questions percolate, I fear that slowly, slowly, bears are disappearing again. By this, I don't mean the erosion of a population as much as the sense that bears are fading away to be replaced by an entirely new species: *Ursus rubbishii*. Our language reveals the presence of this other, degraded species: nuisance bears, trash bears, problem bears, garbage bears, fed bears that will become dead bears, potentially dangerous bears. They are repeat offenders, freeloaders, Dumpster divers, lazy bears, addicted bears, interlopers, ruined bears not worth saving. If bears need wilderness, and wilderness exists only in the realm of "out there," if bears are wild and we are not, then it's nearly impossible to imagine how we'll share the same trails, streams, forests, neighborhoods. To do that, we'd have to change the way we think about ourselves and where we belong, too.

On one of those still evenings when the light grows heavier as it falters, I stood in a meadow not far from the creek where the white bear had appeared to Pat Costello. It was late summer, and the smell of decomposing salmon was so strong it was more like a mizzle. Fog eased through the grass, and my feet sank into wet moss. For a few minutes, I tried willing the phantom bear to step out of the forest. After a time, this effort seemed beside the point. It was only one bear, after all, a moon-colored bear, but no more remarkable than all the other bears around us: the bear the color of obsidian, the bear a dusky blue like twilight, the bear as gold as autumn grass, the bear that wears the brown of forest loam, the bear that wears the color of night as it paces among the silent houses where people sleep in the deep embrace of civilization, even their dreams blank to the shadowy bear walking through their world.

the fearsome bear

Anyone who travels in the backcountry of Alaska carries, consciously or not, a rucksack of beliefs that constitute The Bear Rules. Some come from experience, some from hearsay and conventional wisdom; some come from experts, some from a personal cosmology about how bears should operate. Always carry a gun. No, carry bear spray instead. Or wait, what about bear bells? Look a bear in the eye. Whatever you do, never stare at a bear. Pitch your tent in the open. Hide your tent in the brush. Don't fight back if a bear mauls you, except for when you should fight back. When you're trying to sort out what you should and shouldn't worry about in bear country, simply knowing some rules— any rules!—can seem more important than what the rules mean.

"Nine times out of ten, bears won't maul you if you know the rules," a former Alaska state trooper told the authors of *Bear Attacks of the Century*. This common sentiment is meant to reassure people that maulings are rare (and they are) as long as you've memorized the rules. But who's in charge of dispensing these famous rules? What if there are different rules for different situations—or for different bears? What if you break some rules and nothing bad happens? What if the rules change? Even if you follow the rules as if Moses himself had hand-delivered them, what makes you think bears observe them, too? And that tenth time—whose fault is that?

A collective faith in the power of rules weakened a bit in late June 2005 after a grizzly entered Richard and Kathy Huffman's camp beside the Hulahula River in the Arctic National Wildlife Refuge. The bear killed the couple while they were in their tent. It ransacked their camp, chomped on their inflatable kayaks, and tore up their gear. Not long after, a guide from Kaktovik and his two clients rafted past and spotted the tawny bear standing on a beach near the wrecked camp. Nobody was around. The rafters beached on the opposite bank to investigate. The guide suspected something was wrong and used his satellite phone to ask a friend to contact the search-and-rescue unit stationed in Barrow. As the group was leaving, the bear crossed the braided river, and they paused to watch it until they realized it was stalking them. They scrambled to shove off as the bear charged toward them, crashed across the river, and veered up the steep riverbank in pursuit. It came within twenty feet, but they managed to evade it through quick maneuvering and finally outdistanced it. The helicopter pilots who arrived near midnight spotted the bear near the wrecked campsite. They also saw that there was no one left alive to rescue. When they returned hours later with a Kaktovik police officer to recover the Huffmans' bodies, the bear bolted at first. When it sidled back toward camp, one of the pilots shot the grizzly from the air.

Fifty-eight-year-old Kathy and sixty-one-year-old Richard were Anchorage residents and experienced outdoorsmen who had planned thoroughly for their kayak trip through the wilderness. The Huffmans knew how to behave in bear country. They had eaten dinner upriver to avoid creating food odors at their sleeping site. The state biologist who inspected the camp found the couple's food and even their toothpaste stored in bear-resistant containers far from the tent, newspapers reported. Their gear included an emergency radio beacon, two canisters of bear spray, and a .45–70 Co-Pilot rifle. The rifle was in the tent and the lever action had been worked, but apparently there hadn't been time to chamber a round. A necropsy showed that the male bear was seven years old, 300 pounds, and healthy.

No one knew quite what to make of these circumstances. "All indications now are it was a predatory attack," a spokesman for the Alaska Department of Fish and Game told the *Anchorage Daily News*. "It just hardly ever happens. Even more baffling is that these people had taken all the precautions." A department biologist described the camp as "a model of how to do it right." *National Geographic Adventure* magazine later ran a story titled "ANWR Grizzly Attacks: They Did Everything Right." And that was a common attitude following the incident: the Huffmans had followed the rules faithfully, yet something terrible had happened anyway.

Except that nobody really knows what happened, says John Hechtel, a retired state bear biologist and safety expert. Alaska doesn't have a "CSI: Bears" unit to dispatch to mauling scenes, much less any formal protocol for gathering information. We may know what the Huffmans did right, but we'll never know what went wrong. Did it matter that a bear had been digging in the ground squirrel colony near the campsite? Would the outcome have been different if a round had been chambered? Was the bear somehow food-conditioned? Beyond the speculation, what remains is a story both tragic and unsettling, one that still raises questions when the topic of bear attacks comes up. Nobody wants to accept that such experienced people had observed the rules but died anyway.

News coverage of any mauling incident immediately tries to fix on some obvious explanation: there was food in the tent, the hikers surprised a mother with cubs, a hunter was hauling a slab of bloody deer meat. Determining the cause means that maybe we can avoid the same fate. When a wounded brown bear in Glacier Bay mangled guide Allen Hasselborg's arm in 1912, a Tlingit elder knew the proper response: "I told you so." He'd warned Hasselborg the night before: *Don't brag about not fearing bears. It makes them angry.* And look what happened—Hasselborg's disrespect brought on the attack.

We tell bear stories to learn from them, but often the lessons are tied to a darker impulse loitering beneath: the compulsion to wonder what it feels like as a bear bites into flesh, to imagine the strength of will it takes to stagger away alive after being riven by a predator. We can't help it. "We're not just afraid of predators, we're transfixed by them, prone to weave stories and chatter endlessly about them, because fascination creates preparedness, and preparedness, survival," wrote sociobiologist E. O. Wilson. "In a deeply tribal sense, we love our monsters."

Oh, how we love our monsters. We adore freaking each other out with terrifying stories, and then we struggle to forget the details when we venture into the monsterland of wilderness, a place that feels wildest in the presence of animals that can kill you, animals with appetites. Yet we embed even our most fanciful tales with rules explaining how to defeat the monster: shoot it with a silver bullet, drive a stake through its heart, blow it out the airlock. Rules help us feel as if we're in control and operating under a karmic quid pro quo: Follow the rules, and you'll live. Break the rules, and you'll die.

Nobody wants to die, but compare the idea of perishing in a car accident with that of being reduced to meat by teeth and claws. The prospect seems not only horrific but also profoundly wrong because it fractures our idea of ourselves as the apex species, the creatures who ascended above all others by virtue of our top-notch intellect, opposable thumbs, superior technology, and established moral standing in the universe.

For two millennia, people have used wild predators to symbolize evil and demonology. "Hell's jaws are a picket fence of terrible teeth like those of snakes, wolves, and lions, not the dull dentures of cows," Paul Shepard observed. "Our fear of monsters in the night probably has its origins far back in the evolution of our primate ancestors, whose tribes were pruned by horrors whose shadows continue to elicit our monkey screams in dark theaters." Like E. O. Wilson, he recognized the exquisite irony in our uneasiness: "Yet we are endlessly attracted to the symbolic role of slavering monsters as evil." Without the bad guys to prove it, how would we know that we're the good guys?

After a solid 10,000 years of shared tenancy in the Northern Hemisphere, it's beginning to dawn on us—some of us, anyway—that, as a species, bears are not unadulterated monsters relentlessly dedicated to killing and eating people. Otherwise, many more of us would be strewn about the landscape as carcasses, and so would the bears. Let's be honest: we would never tolerate a dedicated predator among us. "The bottom line is, bears aren't hanging out waiting to kick human butt," Hechtel once told an audience of Alaskans. But our attitudes toward bears expose some of the polarities in how we think of ourselves in the wilder world. We're the alpha predator that doesn't put up with crap from anybody or anything. Or we're the bare-skinned weaklings of the animal kingdom, discriminated against by unfair laws of nature that we had no part in writing. Or maybe we're so insulated from the fierce demands of the wilderness that it's no longer clear what a reasonable risk might be, leaving us pickled in fear that's both hardwired and manufactured. "For a person who neither loves nor understands the grizzly any risk of injury is too great," wrote bear expert Stephen Herrero. Many people like rules not because they need a manual but because they expect a warranty.

John Hechtel is not much on parroting rules. He knows that an incomplete understanding of a bear encounter can cause even greater problems. "It's tough because everybody wants a simple answer: 'What do I do if I meet a bear?'" he said. "And it's not so complex and unpredictable that there aren't good insights and rules that can really make a big difference, but it's also not one size fits all. You want it simple, but you don't want it simplistic, and the problem is that people are following what they think is a rule with no concept of why." A different kind of complacency sets in because the risk of a mauling is small, so people make a lot of mistakes around bears without suffering any consequences. These are the folks who listen to bear advice and say, "Well,

I've lived in Alaska for twenty years and I never do that stuff, and I've never had a problem." There's a fancy psychological term for this kind of rationalization, but Hechtel makes a simple comparison: "You know, another thing that's BS is seat belts. I've been driving for thirty-five years, and I never buckle seat belts because they haven't done crap for me." That's the thing about seat belts or pepper spray or safety training—you don't need them until the moment you *really* need them.

Over the years, wildlife biologists have evolved from making lists of do's and don'ts into helping people understand how bears behave and why. Most situations aren't random events that unfold haphazardly no matter what you do, Hechtel says. "You do have a fair amount of control," he assures people in safety talks. Knowing the basics of bear behavior and ecology can make you smarter at avoiding dangerous situations, and learning to decipher what's happening can help you negotiate your way out of confrontations that otherwise might end badly for you, the bear, or both.

This approach also helps protect the very animal that could easily rend us limb from limb but almost never does. On the frontier, people think they don't need to bother with understanding bear behavior (or their own) as long as they have a gun. But if you prize the wilderness, then you're probably out there *because* bears live there, because the presence of bears is how we define wilderness now. As it turns out, the tools humans have employed so successfully to evade predators—our brains, our social skills, our technology—are the same tools we're using to protect some predators from us.

Hechtel is a wisecracking, fast-talking guy who can give you mental whiplash if you try to keep up. He's also deeply earnest and extremely knowledgeable about bears. His former colleague Rick Sinnott once told me, "He's forgotten more about bears than most people will ever know." Hechtel was a kid living in Chicago when he saw a National Geographic special about twins John and Frank Craighead, who conducted the first long-term study of grizzlies beginning in 1959 in Yellowstone National Park. "And for whatever reason, I thought, 'That is the coolest thing I've ever seen, and I want to go work with the Craigheads,'" he told me one day in his office. "And everybody said, 'That's stupid, you can't do that, you've never even been camping.' At the time I was too dumb to know that was an unrealistic dream, I guess."

In a series of those weird coincidences that can shape a life,

Hechtel attended the University of Montana and worked in the wildlife unit headed by John Craighead. He aged grizzly and elk teeth, spent the summer of his junior year working for the Interagency Grizzly Bear Study Team, joined the Peace Corps, went to West Africa, lost his spleen when a drunk driver smashed into his motorcycle, learned he could never return to the tropics and risk malaria, and had to surrender plans for his master's thesis. Well, long story short, the next thing you know, it's the spring of 1977 and Hechtel is flying in a small plane through the Brooks Range, peering into a big white nothing. Somewhere out there was a bear project already under way and the grizzlies that would be the subject of his future thesis. "And we land on this strip in the middle of the snow with a couple of wall tents and a few people there, and I think, 'What the heck did I do?'" he said. "So that's how I came up to Alaska."

He spent the next few summers tracking a grizzly family to collect data about their eating and activity habits, followed by decades of working with bears at the Alaska Department of Fish and Game and elsewhere. He consulted on a National Geographic documentary that followed up on the original film that had seized his imagination, studied grizzlies at Prudhoe Bay and on the North Slope, crawled into black bear dens on the Tanana Flats, and filled in at McNeil River State Game Sanctuary. Even though he's technically retired, he's still active in bear conservation and safety. Hechtel thinks Alaska is a better place because it has bears, and he believes those who agree should give something back. "For a long time, my passion and my emphasis was me understanding bears as much as I could and me learning about them," he said. "I wasn't too good about passing on my insights, and I even had a few friends of mine who said that with all the problems bears are facing, to spend all this time sitting on mountains and watching them is kind of self-indulgent."

He started focusing more on bear safety during a two-and-a-half-year stint as a wildlife biologist in the Yukon Territory. In the summer of 1999 a black bear entered a Dawson City campground for seasonal workers and approached two college-age women, one on crutches. As they backed up, the bear followed them, "getting kind of pushy," Hechtel said. The woman on crutches went for help. The other lay down and played dead. The bear tentatively approached, sniffed her, and started chewing her left calf. She continued to play dead. A landscaper who was working nearby used a four-foot club to beat on the bear and force it away (the Carnegie Hero Fund awarded him a medal the following year).

By then, she had almost lost her leg, Hechtel said. She later explained, "I was afraid to make noise or do anything because I didn't want to make the bear angry." Shortly after, Hechtel visited a Dawson City coffee shop and eavesdropped on conversations about the incident. What he heard dismayed him. Most people had no idea what the woman should have done differently. "I guess I even naively expected them to say, 'Well, you know, she's from eastern Canada, she doesn't understand you should never play dead with a black bear or in this kind of context,'" he told me. "But people were arguing about whether or not she did the right thing." He thought, *We're doing a bad job of getting the word out.*

Northerners continue to argue about what the right thing is for several reasons. Information about maulings usually appears first in newspapers and other media, where the focus is on drama rather than facts. "And a lot of times," Hechtel said, "a reporter will grab the closest person nearby who has a uniform or some kind of title and say, 'Why did this happen?' and the person will say, 'I don't know.' And [the story] will say, 'Experts are baffled.'" Without a survivor, he points out, it's nearly impossible to figure out what unfolded between bear and human. Did the bear approach first? Was it curious or aggressive? How did the person respond? Even firsthand accounts are often inaccurate—few of us are good at gauging distance or size, much less determining whether a bear is a subadult or fully grown. The Hulahula rafters understandably overestimated that bear's weight at 500 pounds, not 300. As wildlife researcher Tom Smith once noted in a public lecture, "When you're working with bear attacks, you're dealing with people who are excited, people who were under tremendous stress, so there is a limit to what can reasonably be true. Not to mention that old saying, 'If a story's not worth embellishing, it's not worth telling.' I notice a lot of men, they never get beat up by little females. It's always the biggest male on the block. Guys don't want to get trashed by a little bear."

The study of bear behavior doesn't involve testable hypotheses and repeatable experiments, and information extracted from anecdotal accounts may be sketchy or incomplete, Hechtel said. "You can say certain things," he said, "but as far as the fine points of 'Joe Blow did this and the bear did this, and this is why, and if you do this, then you wouldn't get attacked'—you probably can't tease that kind of information very easily out of bear attack data." It can be more useful to watch how bears interact with other bears and prevent their own conflicts, to gather insights on bear behavior based on experience, to think about

The Lower River Platform is one of three elevated viewing stands along the Brooks River in Katmai National Park and Preserve. The platforms allow visitors to watch bears fishing for sockeye salmon while reducing the effects of their presence on bears. These visitors are watching one bear chase another off-camera. Courtesy of National Park Service.

A brown bear allows a photographer to approach closely at Lake Clark National Park—perhaps closer than most experts would recommend. Photo by Nancy Vreuls/Shutterstock .com.

An archaeology student practices using bear pepper spray at Bureau of Land Management headquarters in Fairbanks, Alaska, to prepare for fieldwork in the Arctic. Photo by Karl Horeis (PolarTREC 2010), Courtesy of ARCUS.

These Katmai brown bears focus on fishing rather than fighting, which allows them to put on weight before winter rather than waste energy. Researchers believe this behavior predisposes them to accept the presence of people. Photo by Galyna Andrushko/Shutterstock.com.

A Denali grizzly bear displays the long, curved claws that make efficient digging tools for roots, ground squirrels, mice and vole nests, and other tundra foods. Courtesy of National Park Service.

A brown bear investigates Brooks Lodge in Katmai National Park. Park staff remind visitors that they may encounter bears anywhere at Brooks Camp. Photo by Gail Johnson/Shutterstock.com.

Electric fences are a safe and relatively inexpensive way to deter bears from tents, garbage containers, fish camps, compost piles, food supplies, airplanes, remote cabins, and chickens, beehives, and other domestic livestock. Photo by DPS/Shutterstock.com.

Ice seals, particularly ringed and bearded seals, are the primary food source for polar bears. This polar bear was feeding as the icebreaker USCGC Healy passed by on an Arctic research mission. Photo by Ute Kaden (TREC 2005), Courtesy of ARCUS.

The carcass of a forty-one-foot humpback whale fed bears, wolves, eagles, and other scavengers for months after it washed up on a beach in Glacier Bay National Park in 2010. Researchers used remote cameras to monitor wildlife behavior at the site and counted as many as six brown bears feasting on the calorie-rich blubber at a time. Courtesy of National Park Service.

These bears were killed in 1906 on the Snow River near Seward. The photograph identifies the hunters as Emswyler and Dupont Bill. Courtesy of Frank and Frances Carpenter Collection, Library of Congress.

Fishermen run away from a brown bear at Chilkoot River in Haines, a tactic discouraged by bear experts. Photo by ©iStockphoto.com/Pierre Chouinard.

A black bear strolls past delighted visitors at the Mendenhall Glacier in Juneau, where a bear-viewing area has become established in recent years. Photography by Gillfoto.

A determined young black bear investigates whether a trash bin in Hatcher Pass really is bear-resistant. Photo by ©iStockphoto.com/Suzann Julien Photography.

Coastal brown bears are one-and-a-half to three times larger than bears elsewhere, thanks to the fatty richness of salmon. A 2013 study calculated that Kodiak adult males like this one eat an average of 6,146 pounds of salmon annually. Bears can gain three to six pounds of fat daily in late summer and fall. Photo by bobby20/Shutterstock.com.

Young black bears play near Valdez. Many bears, particularly male brown bears, continue playing throughout their lives. Behaviorists and bear experts speculate that play may allow bears to develop physical abilities, build kinship bonds, practice skills useful in fighting, predation, and mating, and maybe just have some fun. Photo by Mighty Sequoia Studio/Shutterstock.com.

Polar bears depend on ice as a platform for traveling, catching seals and other prey, and sometimes denning. As sea ice continues thinning and retreating to new extremes during Arctic summers, researchers are documenting long swims between ice and land, poorer body conditions, lower cub survival, a loss of access to feeding areas and denning sites, declining populations in some areas, and other problems that make their future increasingly uncertain. Photo by Vladimir Melnick/Shutterstock.com.

This young polar bear visited the remains of bowhead whales caught by subsistence whalers in Kaktovik, an Inupiaq village on Barter Island. Whale carcasses can be a significant source of food for polar bears waiting on land for the sea ice to return in fall so they can reach their offshore seal-hunting grounds. Image courtesy Alan D. Wilson, www.naturespicsonline.com.

A successful hunter packs out his trophy in the Kodiak National Wildlife Refuge in 1957. Courtesy of William Troyer, U.S. Fish and Wildlife Service.

Habituated brown bears at McNeil River State Game Sanctuary are more interested in salmon and in each other than they are in people and their sandwiches. Photo by Sherry Simpson.

The world's largest society of brown bears assembles each July and August at McNeil River on the Alaska Peninsula during the salmon run. As many as 144 individual bears have been identified feeding at the river during a single summer. Visitor access is limited by lottery and carefully managed at the state game sanctuary. Photo by Sherry Simpson.

Female brown bears are extremely protective of their young, but only about 34 percent of cubs in Katmai National Park survive, according to one study. Photo by Tony Campbell/Shutterstock.com.

Black and brown bears eat an enormous variety of foods, including leaves, sedges, roots, berries, mollusks, fish, insects, eggs, and mammals large and small. Inland grizzlies tend to be smaller than their coastal cousins because food is scarcer. Photo by Eric Wang/Shutterstock.com.

Bears develop individual fishing techniques, including lunging, plunging, diving, snorkeling, and pouncing. Photo by Antoni Murcia/Shutterstock.com.

Humans have long recognized similarities with bears in the way they eat, walk, care for their young, and behave. Photo by David Rasmus/Shutterstock.com.

Bears gathered in places like Brooks Falls communicate with each other with threat displays as a way of establishing dominance and avoiding brutal fights. Photo by Tony Campbell/Shutterstock.com.

People kill 90 percent or more of adult bears in many places, usually through hunting, in defense of life or property, or as management actions to remove bears causing problems in human settlements. Other reasons include malicious shootings and collisions with vehicles. Photo by Louise Cukrov/Shutterstock.com.

what happens when people get into trouble with bears and how they get out of it. "For the most part, I think you can come up with pretty good insights," he said. "But is it hard science? No."

Hechtel likes writer Douglas Chadwick's observation that what people know about bears often has more to do with the nature of stories than the nature of bears. "Most of the knowledge that they have about animals doesn't come from interacting and observing them," Hechtel said. That sounds familiar. Even growing up on the cusp of wilderness in Juneau, I saw just two black bears before I was twenty: one loitering outside a house where I was babysitting, and the other hanging dead in a garage. The secondhand stories remain unforgettable, though: the black bear that chased a neighbor boy down a nearby trail, and the brown bear that killed and ate a camper in Glacier Bay's East Arm, leaving behind only a skeleton, a hand, the feet still in his boots, and a camera containing two final images of an apparently undernourished animal. (Sample paragraph from a 1976 *Juneau Empire* story: "It's been nearly two months now since [Alan] Precup's partially-eaten body was discovered buried under twigs near his camp, and still the killer bear is at large.") And I saw what a bear could do when I met a man who, at age seventeen, had been mauled and blinded on a local creek where he'd been trout fishing.

Nothing stuck like the B-movie classic *Claws*, made by a Juneau filmmaker and starring a crazed eleven-foot-tall bear. (The film *Grizzly* was released more widely and just as terrible.) One gory scene shows the savage beast dragging some poor Boy Scout from his tent. When I camped with girlfriends, that scene distilled everything I knew deep down about bears, and it was the reason I never, ever slept well out in the woods. Nor did I ever take the most basic precautions, because nobody had ever explained what those were. The only take-away message was: be afraid.

"The trouble is," Hechtel told me, "you've got the people who think you're crazy for going to your outhouse without your .44 strapped to your waist. Then you've got the other people who think they can walk through the woods radiating goodwill and they would never hurt a bear, so a bear would never hurt them. And you know, they're both silly." There's a third group, too—those who avoid risk by not going outside at all. About a third of Alaskans surveyed in 1992 admitted they were afraid to venture into the backcountry because of bears, reported Suzanne Miller and coauthors.

Bear experts often wield numbers to correct the distorted perception of risk. Tom Smith and Stephen Herrero combed through newspapers, books, and other sources and found records of fifty-six mauling fatalities in Alaska between 1900 and 2002. (Six more people have died since then, including the Huffmans.) In a public lecture, Smith reeled off a string of statistics comparing bears with bison, deer, snakes, and domestic dogs, all of them responsible for more deaths and injuries than bears were. "I'm not trying to trivialize bears and their impact," Smith said, "but they're really bush league when it comes to things that give us a hard time." Out of curiosity, I looked up this number myself: in Alaska, moose-vehicle collisions killed thirty-four people and injured a couple of thousand more between 1977 and 2007.

One statistic lies beyond our reach, though. "The interesting number we'll never get is how many times these things resolve and we just don't know about it," Smith said in his public talk. You may or may not find it reassuring to know that far more bears see you than you'll ever see. Several researchers have witnessed bears ducking or fading away when they hear people approaching on a nearby trail. Once the coast is clear, the bears return to their business.

Still, we can recite facts and figures all day long about the relative odds of death by bee sting, snakebite, lightning strike, or falling satellite, but I know what the irrational fear of death by predator feels like. Three unusual shark attacks took place within weeks of each other along my favorite stretch of Mexican coastline, and I never returned there. I really don't care how unlikely a shark attack is, and thanks to *Jaws*, you can't make me care. A shark attack seems more random, less controllable, less survivable, and more probable than a bear attack any day, and true or not, that's good enough for me. But it's also true that my rational brain couldn't overcome my overactive imagination until my eyeballs finally witnessed what usually happens when people and bears cross paths: the bear disappears as fast as it can.

Some of the most persistent myths about bears remain difficult to dispel because inexperienced people can't see past their preconceived notions. Yes, brown bears can climb trees, although they're not really built for it like black bears are. No, there's still no evidence that bears are particularly attracted to menstruating women. Yes, bears most certainly can run downhill, and fast. No, bears are not unpredictable. "In fact, bears are very predictable in the way they do things, if you understand how they perceive the world and how they deal with each other," Kodiak bear biologist Larry Van Daele told me. Assuming that bears are wacky ad-libbers suggests, incorrectly, that no matter what you do, there's no telling how they'll respond.

Neither are they furry automatons operating by a single set of rote responses, Hechtel said. Bears may respond differently depending on their age, their class, their species, and perhaps even their habitat. Mothers are naturally defensive, for example. Young, newly emancipated bears can be bold or pushy as they try to make their way in the world without a protective mother. Brown bears are more aggressive than black bears. Stephen Herrero attributes that difference to evolution in his landmark book *Bear Attacks: Their Causes and Avoidance*. As creatures of the forest, black bears learned to escape predators by hiding or climbing trees rather than risking injury or death in combat, while the open tundra and plains inhabited by brown bears made aggression a better self-defense strategy.

Brown bears also may react differently to people depending on population density, according to a 2005 paper by Smith, Herrero, and Terry DeBruyn. Because coastal bears learn to habituate to the presence of other bears on salmon streams, they hypothesize, this predisposes them to tolerate people at closer quarters, too. These bears tend to display a short "overt reaction distance" (ORD)—the range at which they physically react to other bears or people. "The shorter the ORD, the less likely a person will violate a bear's personal space and prompt an aggressive response; hence, bears at aggregations such as Brooks [River] are safely viewed throughout Alaska," they wrote. In low-density bear areas such as Interior Alaska, where food is scarce and ranges are bigger, ORDs are much longer, and inland bears seem to react to people from farther distances than coastal bears do.

Like humans, bears tend to behave in certain ways under certain circumstances, but each individual animal is also shaped by its own instincts, environment, experiences, and temperament. Still, it's wrong to attribute human emotions such as revenge or bloodlust to them, Hechtel says. Exhibit A: a hunting magazine article titled "Black Bears—Simple Fools or Cunning Killers" ("We know about the black bear's dark side," the author warns). Given our own thirst for what David Quammen calls "predator pornography," it's no wonder that people tend to forget the matter-of-fact advice in safety brochures and dwell on what happens in television programs like *Bear Feeding Frenzy*, which used misleading footage to reinforce the notion of bears as ruthless killers. This particular show first aired on Discovery's Animal Planet channel in late 2008, and clips still play on the network's website. Some scenes depict brown bears happening upon a mannequin named Billy and enthusiastically dismantling it, as if that's normal behavior from any wild bear that meets a human. Host Chris Douglas sits nearby in a clear Plexiglas box called a "predator shield" and gives the play-by-play: "This female tears through these jeans like wet paper. . . . If Billy wasn't plastic, his legs would be a bloody ruin. . . . If Billy were flesh and bone, his rib cage would be completely shattered and he'd be split in half."

If Billy were alive, he'd be participating in a deceptive setup. The show's producers didn't disclose that they had staged these scenes and others using captive and possibly bored animals at the Alaska Wildlife Conservation Center near Anchorage. Tom Smith participated in the filming but complained to the producers when he saw a rough cut. Several state biologists publicly criticized the program's inaccurate portrayal of bear behavior, its lack of safety information, and its overwhelming message that bears are vicious and camping in the wilderness is an open invitation to death by tooth and claw. Captive bears behave quite differently from wild bears, and the featured bears treated the mannequin like a toy, not a human, Van Daele said in a news release from the Alaska Department of Fish and Game. "It's like they made a program called, 'Don't Wear Seat Belts,'" he commented, "with footage of people drowning in cars, or burning up in cars, all because of their seat belts." The show's producers agreed to clarify that the bears filmed were not "free-ranging," but that's not what viewers will remember. They'll remember what happened to poor Billy the mannequin.

Fear can be a useful survival instinct, but excessive fear can lead to bigger trouble. "If your mind is primed to think if you bump into a bear there's a high probability that you're in danger, it could cause a problem you might not have had if you were just calm and didn't freak out," Hechtel said. Most people know that running from a bear can prompt it to give chase in a footrace you have little chance of winning. But if your knowledge of bears comes mostly from a story titled "Scalped Alive," sometimes it can be hard to stop your feet from fleeing no matter what rule your brain dredges up.

"People love bear stories, and the bears are campfire bogeymen," Hechtel said, "but a lot of this stuff has consequences."

The field of bear safety emerged by necessity as people seeking wilderness experiences began invading bear habitat in the late 1960s and 1970s without understanding how to conduct themselves. "Wilderness was suddenly 'in,'" wrote historian Roderick Frazier Nash in *Wilderness and the American Mind.* "An increasingly urban population turned to the nation's remaining empty places in unprecedented numbers." The same people eager to explore ever-shrinking wildlands only increased the pressure on what remained. In 1911, for example, about 4,000 people visited the newly created Glacier National Park, but by 1966, more than 900,000 arrived each summer like a seasonal flash flood. About 30,000 of them tromped through the backcountry, exhibiting a new enthusiasm for backpacking and "wilderness values"—the desire to experience the natural world, find solitude, and rediscover a deeper connection with an old way of being. The National Park Service had yet to resolve an ongoing philosophical debate about whether national parks should entertain recreationists (the anthropocentric approach) or protect wilderness and wildlife (the biocentric argument), according to Nash. By 1975, the population of grizzlies in the American West had eroded so severely that the US Fish and Wildlife Service listed them as threatened.

Many park lovers didn't want to leave bears alone—they wanted to lure them closer. Yellowstone National Park long acted as a petri dish for what happens when people and bears forge a relationship through food, as described by Alice Wondrak Biel in *Do (Not) Feed the Bears.* Today it's impossible to look at historical photographs of black bears posing on their hind legs and plucking food from people's hands without wincing. The National Park Service encouraged bear-feeding shows at park hotels and even built a concrete feeding platform in 1931 that included amphitheater seating on log benches for 250 visitors. Between fifty and seventy grizzlics thrilled visitors each evening by gorging on garbage and tussling with one another.

Predictably, bears injured dozens of people each year in Yellowstone. Expert Stephen Herrero found that before 1970 the park's grizzlies accounted for more than half of all bear-inflicted injuries in national parks. Instead of addressing the role of garbage and food, park rangers killed 354 "criminal" bears between 1930 and 1941, when the feeding platform closed. The following summer a bear killed a woman on her way to the campground bathroom at night, and rangers killed another 55 black bears and 21 grizzlies. Bears still found easy access to trash and food at open-pit dumps and campgrounds, and park managers struggled for another thirty years to convince people to stop feeding bears, deliberately or otherwise. The split between those who wanted to discipline people and those who blamed the bears usually resolved in favor of people, Biel observed. Between 1955 and 1965 rangers removed 349 bears, nearly all of them black bears.

The situation wasn't nearly as dire at Glacier National Park, where grizzlies had injured only two people since its 1911 opening. Then, on August 13, 1967, two different grizzlies attacked and killed two nineteen-year-old women in separate incidents. Both were camping with friends—one near a chalet and the other at Trout Lake—when the bears dragged them off in their sleeping bags. People grasped at explanations for this widely publicized and bizarre conjunction of events: the victims had been sleeping without shelter, the weather was hot, lightning or sonic booms had aggravated the bears, one of the women was menstruating, food in both camps had attracted the bears, the bears had eaten LSD or some plant hallucinogen.

That both bears had been eating garbage was never mentioned in a 1967 *Sports Illustrated* article titled "Menace in Our Northern Parks." The investigation hadn't reached a conclusion, the article reported, because "no one has even approached a solution to the problem of why the bears attacked. Perhaps no one ever will." But *Night of the Grizzlies*, a factual and thorough account by Jack Olsen published in 1969, made a point of describing how bears had visited the chalet nightly to eat and fight over table scraps intentionally set out so people could watch them, despite the Park Service's halfhearted efforts to stop such activity. The Trout Lake grizzly had regularly marauded campsites for food and frightened visitors, with no intervention by authorities.

Following the attacks, a Maryland biology professor named Gairdner B. Moment used these deaths and other incidents to launch a novel argument: grizzlies don't belong in national parks at all. In a paper titled "Bears: The Need for a New Sanity in Wildlife Conservation," Moment tried to establish the "highly dangerous character" of bears by citing comments from bear researchers Frank and John Craighead. His damning evidence: bears don't like being disturbed while sleeping, they don't like being startled, and they don't want you coming near their food. Moment argued that the Park Service's mission to preserve bears and to keep visitors safe was contradictory. He called for a reexamination of some "dogmatic, if well-intentioned philosophies of wildlife conservation," one being the assumption that people are obliged to save every species from extinction.

Stephen Herrero had recently earned a Ph.D. in animal behavior, and he responded to Moment's "shocking" proposal to eliminate grizzlies from Glacier and Yellowstone parks by using the radical technique of gathering facts. In a 1970 forum on whether bears and people can coexist, he reported that since 1872, grizzlies had killed a total of five people in the eleven national parks where bears lived in North America, a death rate he calculated as one per 30 million visitors. Sudden encounters likely caused most attacks on hikers, he concluded, but an association between people and food seemed to be an important factor in campground injuries. "Probably the most dangerous type of garbage feeding is when grizzlies have fed in campgrounds and have become habituated to the odor of man, and thus lost some of their natural avoidance of man," he wrote. (Herrero's research has convinced me to avoid public campgrounds whenever possible, because you have no control over how other people handle food, and you rarely know anything about the local bears' state of habituation or food conditioning.)

Herrero believed that helping people understand and relate to grizzlies was important for both species. "We should preserve grizzly bear populations, not because their ecological function is critical, but because of what they can do for human imagination, thought and experience," he wrote in 1974. He continued analyzing bear incidents, crunching numbers, and conducting fieldwork to produce *Bear Attacks*, the first comprehensive attempt to scientifically frame bear-human conflicts. The book explains bear ecology, describes behavior patterns, and identifies human practices that can increase or lower risks. Avoiding conflict in the first place is key, which is why Herrero and other experts emphasize basic, commonsense measures such as the proper handling of food, garbage, and other attractants; making noise while hiking to avoid surprising bears; never approaching bears to take pictures; never camping on bear trails; and so on. By the time he published a revised edition in 2002, useful deterrents such as bear spray and electric fences had appeared, but his fundamental philosophy remained the same: "Your best defense in bear country is still your brain—your knowledge and understanding of bears."

Nearly thirty years after Herrero's book first appeared, biologists recognize that there are better and worse ways to behave around bears, and most agree on what those practices are, Hechtel said. "It's not like 100 percent of the time you do the right thing, and you have no problems—it's more like 80/20." But often your response can help determine whether you emerge from an encounter with a story or with stitches.

After years of delivering talks, Hechtel realized that showing people these principles would be more effective than describing them. One night he and a few colleagues gathered to drink beer and discuss reediting an old training video from British Columbia. By evening's end, they had decided to make their own safety video. "So that's the problem with beer and things," Hechtel said. "We didn't know what the hell we were doing." Thus was born the Safety in Bear Country Society. To create the best script and the most useful scenarios possible, the group developed a consensus about what advice to offer viewers based on their own experiences, observations, insights, and research. Then they circulated the script among other bear experts with a wide range of experience and perspectives. The result was *Staying Safe in Bear Country: A Behavioral-Based Approach to Reducing Risk*.

A collaborator who had worked at a salmon weir thought they could safely film scenes using wild bears, which is how one woman earned $100 a day (Canadian) being charged by bears for a week, Hechtel joked. (Her nickname in the credits is "Bear Bait.") As a result, the video includes remarkable footage of people and bears responding to each other in specific situations and natural settings, allowing viewers to recognize what a disinterested or an agitated bear looks like and to better understand how a person's actions can influence a bear's behavior. Three more videos followed: *Working in Bear Country*, *Living in Bear Country*, and *Polar Bears: A Guide to Safety*. They all demonstrate the importance of using your brain to plan ahead, think rationally, and recognize when to be either humble or assertive in the presence of a bear.

The videos attempt to remedy the problem of swamping people with too much contradictory, confusing, or outdated safety information. "It's hard to get good information to them because they think they've heard it all or know it all," Hechtel said, "yet I've seen tragedies that were the result of bad information—people who didn't understand what they were doing." For example, early advice emphasized that the only safe bear is a distant bear, a fear-based message that Hechtel considers an overreaction to "people being stupid in Yellowstone about food." A 1981 Canadian pamphlet ominously titled "Bears Are Dangerous!" offers a perfect example: the cover illustration portrays the standard badass bear bristling with prominent fangs and claws. In contrast, Derek Stonorov's contemporary guide is titled *Living in Harmony with Bears*, and its cover features a photograph of a brown bear cub resting its head on its mother's back.

Much of the Canadian pamphlet's advice is common sense—stay alert, make noise while hiking, don't sleep in bloody clothes, and so on. Other suggestions are considered misguided these days. "Continually face the animal and growl or roar in a loud, low-pitched voice," it advises. "Drop your pack or any article of clothing and back away. This may distract the bear. Drop any food you may be carrying." Although it's understandable why a frightened hiker would surrender food or a pack, it's also an excellent way to train bears to threaten people.

"What would happen," Hechtel said, "is a subadult bear would be walking down the trail, somebody would bump into it, freak out, lob their pack at the bear, go running away, and the bear would be like, 'What's this?' find some food [in the pack], and become a mugger waiting along trails for people to toss packs at it." Bears quickly connect people with food in other situations that offer rewards. On popular Alaska fishing rivers, young bears often learn that boldly approaching nervous anglers results in free meals. Some become so conditioned to bullying fishermen out of their catches that they'll come running when they hear a fish splashing on the line. For this reason, officials at Katmai National Park tell anglers to reel in and move if a bear approaches, or to cut their lines rather than surrender fish to a bear.

Advice to lie down, curl up, and play dead may be the most misunderstood recommendation. Many people misinterpret it to mean, "Be prepared to flop down if you see a bear," Hechtel said, which is what the young woman did in Dawson City. Examples abound in Alaska of people who played dead prematurely or with the wrong kind of bear. An Anchorage hiker who surprised a brown bear feeding on a moose lay down when it charged. The bear stopped, but it then jumped the hiker twice, biting and swatting him before running away. A Juneau woman accompanying a hunter on Admiralty Island instantly dropped into the fetal position after a huffing bear headed her way through thick brush. The brown bear chomped on her ribs and left leg before the hunter found her and scared the bear away with a shot. Years ago, a hiker treed a black bear near Eagle River and then unaccountably lay prone on the trail; the bear descended the tree, bit him, and then bolted when the man screamed. And it was clear that some Alaska kids needed better training after a black bear approached four girls at an Elmendorf Air Force

Base playground in Anchorage in June 2010. Three of them immediately lay down, but the fourth girl talked to the bear and tried to make herself seem bigger before going for help. The bear approached one of the prone girls and mouthed her leg until she screamed. The bear let go but lingered in the area even after adults arrived. The base's wildlife biologist said safety briefings would start clarifying when to play dead.

In another incident—and I'm not advising that anyone try this—a Juneau woman who had been lost in the rain forest for five days lay facedown and closed her eyes when two playful brown bear cubs and their mother approached so closely that she could hear mosquitoes humming around them before they departed. We'd have to score this as another example of the restraint of most bears, because it's hard to imagine an easier target for the alleged man-killer of the North.

One reason not to play dead prematurely is that brown bears are more likely to break off a charge when a person stands fast. Hechtel and others don't believe that bears are bluffing when they launch themselves at a person but stop short of making contact, sometimes repeatedly. Calling such behavior a "bluff" or a "false" charge implies that the bear decides beforehand to fake you out—that it's just screwing with your head. Instead, a bear seems to decide what to do as it's charging, based on your response. The situation is usually different with black bears, Hechtel said. They are a blustery bunch that tend to huff and swat the ground and make little rushes as a way of communicating their agitation. Rarely do they actually attack. More than 90 percent of recorded black bear injuries were minor, according to Herrero in *Bear Attacks*, and most consisted of scratches or bites from habituated and food-conditioned animals. Silent black bears that are intently focused on you as they approach—those are the ones to worry about, Hechtel said.

Even the advice to wait until a bear makes physical contact before playing dead is often misinterpreted. Officials at Denali National Park recommend that people wait for "imminent contact" before curling up and lying still, but everyone's judgment of "imminent" varies, said Pat Own, the park's wildlife biologist. Her definition is "when the bear is breathing on your knees," but in the past, Denali visitors have defined it as anywhere from a dozen to sixty feet away. In two separate incidents in 2004, lone hikers who spotted brown bears immediately hit the ground and curled into a ball. Each bear tried to roll the hiker over with a paw before leaving. (One hiker claimed he then buried his ice axe in the bear's back, after which it growled and left, but skeptical park rangers never found a bear injured in that manner.)

So when is playing dead a good tactic? Many people have heard this simple rule: play dead with a brown bear, fight back with a black bear. The reason is that brown bear attacks are usually defensive (the bear wants to knock you down and eliminate you as a threat). Black bears rarely make physical contact with humans, so an attacking black bear is probably predaceous (it wants to eat you). But bear experts now think that advice is too simplistic. Instead, it's better to take action based on the situation and the bear's behavior, no matter what kind of bear it is. Herrero explains in his book: "The species of bear involved in such attacks offers only a rule of thumb regarding how you should react to try to minimize injury. An additional rule of thumb is this: If an attack cannot be deterred and is defensive, play dead; if predatory, fight back." (For more comprehensive explanations and advice, watch the Safety in Bear Country videos or read Herrero's book.)

What's important is distinguishing between a defensive bear and a nondefensive, aggressive bear. How can someone whose knees are knocking and heart is thumping figure out the best way to respond? Think of encounters as interactions during which you and the bear communicate, Hechtel said. "If you look close, they are sending a bunch of signals." Most episodes unfold over enough time to evaluate the situation and determine the bear's motives. Defensive attacks are usually triggered when a person surprises a bear or otherwise crowds its personal space, such as by trying to get closer to take a picture. In these encounters, the bear usually sees you as a threat to its cubs, its food, or itself, as *Staying Safe in Bear Country* explains. A bear's stress behaviors include a stiffening posture, yawning, teeth popping, moaning, and stamping the ground. More aggressive actions include roaring, chuffing, salivating, swatting at things, and charging.

Because a defensive bear sees the intruder as a threat, Hechtel says the proper message to send is, "Don't worry about me." Ways to do this include stopping immediately, identifying yourself as human by speaking calmly, or perhaps backing up slowly if the bear isn't approaching. Bears that attack in defensive situations often leave once they've neutralized the threat, which is why it makes sense to play dead *after* the bear makes contact. People who have spent time around bears figured this out a long time ago. When Allen Hasselborg was mauled in 1912, he told author John Holzworth, "I knew better'n to move, because Charlie Littlejohn had tried to get away after being mauled by a bear that spring, and it had come back twice and bit him again; the thing to do is to lie quiet and make the animal think you're dead."

In nondefensive situations, a bear that doesn't leave immediately or that approaches you deliberately could be curious, habituated to people, looking for food, or testing its dominance, particularly if it's a subadult. Or it might regard you as prey. Here, your message should be, "Don't mess with me." People can show confidence by standing tall and making themselves look bigger by holding out their jackets, grouping together and raising their arms, or standing on a log or a rock. If a bear seems most interested in grabbing food, you might be able to run it off by making a racket: yell, blow boat horns, fire cracker shells, or bang pots together. If a nondefensive bear does attack, your mission is to fight like hell using whatever's available—sticks, rocks, an axe, your fists and feet. Concentrate on the bear's face, Hechtel advises.

Herrero defines an approach as predatory when it involves stalking, mauling aggressively with the intention to kill, eating a victim's flesh, and dragging, guarding, or caching a body. As an example, he excerpts an account by a young geologist who was working in the field in Interior Alaska in 1977 when a black bear appeared from the brush about ten feet behind her. She clapped, yelled, and made noise to scare it off, but rather than being intimidated, as most bears would be, it approached and then suddenly attacked. She followed advice she'd heard to play dead. Instead of leaving, the bear chewed at her arm and shoulder and bit her skull. When it paused after dragging her into the brush, she reached into her pack for her radio and called nearby colleagues for help. They arrived by helicopter in time to save her, but not her arms. (She eventually returned to her job.) Today, experts would tell her to fight back from the moment the bear attacked.

Such episodes are horrific but extremely rare. Noncaptive black bears in Canada and the United States killed sixty-three people between 1900 and 2009 in fifty-nine incidents, Herrero and his colleagues reported in a 2011 paper. Five fatalities occurred in Alaska, fourteen in the Lower 48, and the rest in Canada. Think about how minuscule that number is compared with the number of times black bears and people cross paths every day on this continent. What's interesting is that black bears behaved as predators in 88 percent of the incidents, the scientists determined, and male bears, both adult and subadult, were involved in 92 percent of these predatory attacks. "That most fatal black bear attacks were predatory and were carried out by 1 bear shows that females with young are not the most dangerous black bears," the researchers noted.

Herrero has documented at least three instances of people using knives or a skull-crushing boulder to successfully fight predaceous black bears. In 1976 a ten-year-old girl defended herself against an approaching black bear by hitting it twice with an axe before running to her house. The bear knocked her down, but she scrambled inside and flung a pot of boiling water in its face when it tried to enter the cabin. "She caused the bear to flee and probably saved her own life," Herrero wrote.

Several people in Alaska have warded off predatory or worrisomely bold black bears by responding aggressively once they recognized the situation. A Forest Service technician who encountered a pair of black bears while hiking on a trail outside of Anchorage found himself in a long standoff with one of the bears when it refused to leave even after he yelled, threw branches, and repeatedly smacked it with a large branch and forced it into a tree. Each time he moved away the bear would climb down and continue to follow him. The bear abandoned the struggle once the hiker reached a main road, according to his account in the *Anchorage Daily News*. A jogger who was charged and bitten by a black bear on a Petersburg trail in 2002 spent ninety minutes slowly retreating and defending herself with a stick until she finally struck it so hard that it left. The same year, a black bear that was trailing a man through the forest near Anchorage wouldn't leave when he yelled and flung a tent stake at it, but it took off when the man charged it. "I got within twenty feet of him, and he decided he was the frightened one," he told the newspaper.

Sometimes defending yourself means being inventive. A seasonal ranger walking on a trail in Denali National Park in 2000 turned around to discover a black bear a few feet behind her. She pelted it with rocks, screamed at it, and even whacked it on the head with her hand, but it wouldn't back off until she cleverly turned up the squelch on her radio and shoved it in the bear's face. Her comments to a reporter about her attitude and the bear's are instructive: "When my voice would falter or get softer he would get closer. When I averted my eyes from him he would get closer. The minute you started acting weak he picked right up on it. I knew I wanted to be aggressive back toward it."

Because both brown and black bears are capable of predatory behavior, experts emphasize responding based on the situation, not the species. In 2000 a brown bear killed a forty-one-year-old man sleeping in a Hyder, Alaska, campground and partially ate him. The bear had been feeding regularly at the tiny community's dump and had become aggressive toward people; in fact, the Forest Service had tried to trap it the night before the man died. The bear that attacked the Huffmans was considered to be predaceous in the absence of other information. Even when there is plenty of information, it may not explain much. In 2010 a female grizzly accompanied by offspring killed and partially ate a camper after attacking two other people in a Forest Service campground a mile from Yellowstone Park. Investigators examined the bear's behavior, body condition, food habits, and known life history. Their detailed report concluded: "In summary, the attack involving an adult female grizzly bear and her 3 yearlings on 3 separate people in the Soda Butte Campground on 28 July 2010 cannot be clearly explained or understood."

Some incidents that seem inexplicable are likely just a matter of not having enough facts, Hechtel notes. For example, he speculates that a young bear fooling around with tents could prompt a frightened reaction from a camper that turns a playful incident into a deadly one. Proving that this is what happened is a different matter, particularly when those involved are dead. One puzzling incident occurred in August 2012 when the remains of a solo backpacker were found partially consumed and cached by a bear in Denali National Park. This was the first time in the park's history that a bear had killed anybody. What's not clear is how an apparently chance encounter turned into a fatal predatory incident. Twenty-six photos in his camera showed that Richard White, age forty-nine, had approached a foraging grizzly within about sixty yards, according to the National Park Service, much closer than the park's quarter-mile limit. The timestamp revealed that he had watched the animal for almost eight minutes as the bear seemingly ignored him, until it fixed its gaze on White in the last few pictures. Attributing the event to the hiker's close approach seems like an obvious explanation, but as Hechtel points out, people violate the park's guidelines all the time without consequence. Until the Park Service completes its investigation, Hechtel says it's difficult to know whether other factors or other bears were involved, or whether there's even enough evidence to explain what happened.

As intimidating and powerful as a brown bear is, it is possible to survive a perilous encounter. In 2012 a North Pole woman vigorously defended herself, her dog, and her two nieces from a young brown bear that followed and repeatedly charged her on a Fairbanks trail, while its sibling loitered nearby. During the prolonged confrontation she blasted it with pepper spray, struck it several times with her walking stick, and squirted it with natural insect repellent as the bear circled and growled. She believed it was testing her, she told the *Fairbanks Daily News-Miner.* The bears continued to intimidate hikers throughout the summer, even ignoring warning shots, although no one was injured. Hechtel points out that this incident likely didn't happen out of the blue, given reports of careless hikers leaving food in the area.

People have occasionally fought brown bears without the help of firearms and survived. The most celebrated contemporary case is that of Gene Moe of Anchorage. He was alone and skinning a deer on Raspberry Island when a female brown bear attacked him during a bad berry and salmon season. Although Moe was sixty-eight years old at the time, he stabbed the bear in the neck several times with his four-inch skinning knife. Moe says the bear dropped after he walloped her and possibly injured a neck vertebra. He thought she was dead but retrieved his rifle and shot her twice, just in case. When Moe appeared with author Marguerite Reiss at an Anchorage book signing for *Bear Attacks of the Century*, he was happy to show people the scars from two skin grafts and 500 stitches. "If you notice, he cut my ear in half with one claw," he told one little boy. The knife was framed with fur and bloodstains intact and accompanied by a plaque that says "Gene Moe's Buck Knife, used to defend himself and to kill a 750-pound brown bear at Kodiak while deer hunting Nov. 1, 1999." When I asked him what went through his mind during the attack, Moe said he was praying for help. "I actually told the bear, 'Man, the Lord's on my side.'" Apparently so, although plenty of victims have discovered prayer isn't always enough.

One incident in which fighting back might have helped occurred in 1996 in the Yukon's Kluane National Park. A pair of backpackers, a husband and wife, saw a young brown bear ahead that didn't seem to notice them, so they left the trail to avoid it. But the bear did notice them and began following. The couple knew they shouldn't run, so they dropped their packs to distract the bear. It didn't work. The bear may have been curious at first, Hechtel says, but what followed was a fairly long period in which the bear apparently tested the hikers as they continued to retreat. That was the time to stand their ground and assert themselves, Hechtel says. Instead, according to a park warden's account in a Whitehorse newspaper, they curled up on the ground and played dead. After sniffing them, the bear pawed at the woman and bit her shoulder. The husband hit it with a stick, but the bear bit him and knocked him down before returning to the woman. Bludgeoning the bear wasn't working, so he ran for reinforcements. Park wardens arrived by helicopter, but it was too late to save the woman. Her husband later said he didn't blame the bear or the park's advice to play dead. "If we'd stood our ground with our packs on, we would have looked big, and it might have been different," he told the *New York Times*. Today, Kluane's bear advice is clear: if a bear is stalking you or attacking at night, "FIGHT BACK!" Hechtel, always reluctant to criticize mauling victims, thinks the episode might have ended differently if the backpackers had carried pepper spray, responded aggressively as soon as the bear began testing them, or fought as hard as possible once it attacked—although there are no guarantees. There never are.

Fortunately, people have other defenses besides prayer, hand-to-hand combat, or firearms. In 1968 Alaska wildlife biologist Frederick Dean suggested that someone should invent a "nonlethal but effective means of stopping a bear dead in its tracks," and biologist Carrie Hunt helped fulfill his wish. Today she's better known for teaching wildlife professionals and others to use trained Karelian bear dogs in aversive conditioning or as protection, but in the early 1980s, as a University of Montana graduate student, she tested prototypes for bear spray she had developed in collaboration with one of the future founders of Counter Assault spray. The Environmental Protection Agency currently registers four commercial bear deterrents.

Bear spray is like weaponized Tabasco blasted in an orange cloud of oily residue. Capsaicin from ground red peppers burns the eyes and swells the mucous membranes in the nose and lungs powerfully enough to cause temporary blindness, coughing, and difficulty breathing. Having accidentally punctured a can by dropping it on a sharp rock, I suspect pepper spray must feel like nasal napalm to the sensitive nostrils of a bear. It's so incapacitating that Alaskan bush pilots duct-tape the canisters to wing struts, store them in pontoons, or insist that passengers bury them deep inside their bags to avoid accidental deployment inside the aircraft. At least one company has started manufacturing storage containers to protect the canisters while being transported in planes and cars.

For a long time, many people doubted whether a harsh spray could actually stop an agitated bear in its tracks. Twenty years after its introduction, Tom Smith, Stephen Herrero, and other researchers analyzed seventy-two incidents between 1985 and 2006 in which people reported defending themselves by spraying curious, aggressive, or food-seeking bears at close range. These incidents involved fifty brown bears, twenty black bears, and two polar bears. Only one person said the spray failed to help at all. "Persons working and recreating in bear habitat should feel confident that they are safe if carrying bear spray," the authors concluded.

The study addressed some common worries about bear spray—the effect of wind, the reliability of the aerosol cans, and the risk of the substance disabling the user. The spray, which is propelled at an average speed of seventy miles an hour, was affected by wind in five instances but still reached the bears. None of the cans failed to work, and nobody was incapacitated by the capsaicin (although people had to leave the area in four cases). Another common fear is that blasting a burning substance into a bear's face could provoke a more serious attack. However, this was not the case; minor injuries occurred in just three of the study's examples, all involving brown bears. Not every bear responds the same, though. In thirteen cases, people had to spray the bear repeatedly to deter it.

Spray can have other useful effects. The hissing sound and the explosive appearance of the orange cloud sometimes frighten bears away. Carrying it can also give people the confidence to stand their ground rather than run, according to Smith. Simply toting a canister isn't enough, though. "A bear running at you at thirty miles per hour is traveling forty-four feet per second," Herrero pointed out at the Fourth International Human-Bear Conflicts Workshop. "A bear that is eighty-eight feet away could be on a person in two seconds. The bear spray use training that I conduct has shown it takes people two to five seconds to deploy bear spray. Bear spray is a great safety tool, but it is not a substitute for avoiding encounters." People should practice using it until they can draw it smoothly, thumb off the safety, and deploy it quickly, he said. (Inert cans are sold for this purpose.)

Bear spray doesn't work if you can't reach it, however. In an unusual incident in 2011, a grizzly injured four of seven teenagers attending the National Outdoor Leadership School (NOLS). During a backcountry trip in the Talkeetna Mountains, one seventeen-year-old was leading a loose line of hikers through a brushy creek drainage. He rounded a bend and surprised the bear, which knocked him down and bit him as he played dead, according to *Alaska Dispatch* writer Craig Medred. The bear might not have noticed the other hikers at first, but it did when they all ran away, despite previous training. In the confusion, the bear attacked three youths who'd scattered from the group. Three of the students carried bear spray in their packs, one in an accessible side pocket and two in a top pocket. But two of them ditched their packs when they started to run, and the third didn't even think about using his spray. Since then, NOLS has stated that students will practice using bear spray, and their training will emphasize mental preparation for such incidents. They'll also carry canisters in holsters or other immediately accessible places. Grouping up as they neared the brushy, obscure turn and making more noise while traveling beside running water could have prevented the episode in the first place.

Some people have mistaken bear spray for a true repellent and have applied it to sheds, planes, tents, and outhouses, only to find their property enthusiastically destroyed by appreciative bears who actually like the stuff. After noticing years ago that bears seemed to be attracted to eau de capsicum, Smith performed an informal experiment by spraying it on the ground. Some bears licked it, rubbed their heads in it, and wriggled their entire bodies in it like a dog—even five days later. He suspects bears like the oil and find spicy pepper tasty for the same reasons we like a shot of Tabasco on our food.

The notion that bear spray works like bug dope has generated at least one urban legend in Alaska. Through the usual friend of a friend, I've heard three different versions of it. The one my brother-in-law told me concerns a charter floatplane pilot who dropped off a fisherman at an Admiralty Island lake. Back in the air, the pilot noticed the man wildly rolling around on the beach. When he returned to find out what was wrong, the fisherman assured him that he was fine—he'd just applied his bear repellent. "Boy, that's some strong stuff!" he (supposedly) exclaimed.

Despite bear spray's successful track record, plenty of Alaskans wouldn't dream of going anywhere in the backcountry without a gun. (Some wouldn't go to the grocery store without one, either.) Skeptical opinions—and outright mockery—flooded online forums and newspaper comments sections in response to coverage of the bear spray study. "Bear spray will help slow down the guy next to you as you run away," someone joked in the *Anchorage Daily News*. Another wrote flatly: "A shot of bear spray will not stop a charging bear. A shot from a high-power gun will."

The bullets versus bear spray debate reignited in 2012 after Smith, Herrero, and their colleagues published a paper titled "Efficacy of Firearms for Bear Deterrence in Alaska." They reported that people carrying guns were injured during aggressive bear encounters at the same rate whether they fired their weapons or not. However, the usefulness of the report's statistical analysis was limited because, as the authors acknowledged, the data set was incomplete: they based their conclusions on 269 incidents, some anecdotal, that had appeared in a variety of sources between 1883 and 2009. There's no way of telling how many people have fired a warning shot at a bear without killing it, though it's fairly safe to say the answer is "a lot." More helpful was information showing why firearms aren't foolproof protection against bears. Among the reasons why guns failed to stop an attack were a lack of time to act, a decision not to shoot, a jammed weapon, a bear too close to shoot, missed shots, an empty gun that couldn't be reloaded, a safety that couldn't be unlocked in time, tripping while trying to fire, and, in a few instances, a shot that triggered the bear into a rush that prevented the person from firing again. "The need for split-second deployment and deadly accuracy make using firearms difficult, even for experts," the authors wrote. "Consequently, we advise people to carefully consider their ability to be accurate under duress before carrying a firearm for protection from bears." They also suggested that all backcountry travelers, both armed and unarmed, should carry bear spray, which, they claimed, has a better success rate than firearms in deterring bear attacks. But one of their most important points was likely overlooked in the fuss: try to avoid dangerous encounters in the first place.

One reason hunters are reluctant to add bear spray to their arsenal is the awkwardness of safely carrying a rifle or shotgun while still keeping a hand free to yank a canister from a holster or front pocket if a bear appears. "As I see it, a person hunting with a long rifle in brown bear habitat and facing a charging brown bear probably needs to have rehearsed in advance whether they will go for their spray or rifle," Herrero said at the conflicts workshop. "Bear spray is easier to use effectively. It is hard to shoot a bear lurching rapidly at you at high speed."

For one thing, spray covers a larger area and doesn't require precise aim. To demonstrate the difference, Gregg Losinski of the Idaho Department of Fish and Game asks people to shoot a Nerf gun at someone playing the role of a charging bear. Then he has them try to stop the "bear" with inert spray. Lesson learned. The choice between bear spray and weapons needn't be an either-or proposition, though. Unquestionably, there are times when a gun has saved someone from injury or death. But bear spray can be useful for hunters when a gun isn't within easy reach, such as when they're in camp, field-dressing game, or hauling meat.

In online discussions, many hunters seem to be either unfamiliar with bear spray or just plain unwilling to depend on a can with a nozzle rather than a gun with a bullet. Some openly ridicule the idea of going outdoors unarmed—ever. You can understand why when you realize how they think about bears. In one hunting forum, an Alaskan who described himself as a realist with common sense sputtered about the improbability of spray stopping a charging bear:

> That SOB is coming right through that can of spray like you know what through a goose! With bullets you can fire multiple times, break bones, tear muscle, sever nerves/spinal column, put him into shock with the force and the noise, cause severe bleeding/trauma, etc., etc., etc. Or . . . you can stand 24′ or less away with a bottle of junk that goes "psssssst." I feel better already just thinking about my canon [sic] going "BOOOOOOOOM!" Consider this . . . an insane, homicidal, murdering, cannabilistic [sic] rapist, that weighs 1,000 pounds and is armed with two long, sharp knives is sprinting at you from 24′ away. Want pepper spray?

In other words, a weapon is what manly men carry on the frontier. Bear spray is what weak-kneed tree-huggers use in the wilderness.

One reason wildlife biologists encourage hunters to consider using spray in some situations is that it can spare bears from unnecessary death. People carrying firearms don't always wait long enough to see what the bear will do or consider what else they can try besides firing (especially if they regard every bear as a cannibalistic, murdering rapist). In Alaska people can legally kill bears "in defense of life or property," as long as they aren't defending themselves because they harassed, provoked, or attracted a bear with food or garbage, or because they unreasonably invaded the animal's habitat (never mind the overall irony of that last clause). Between 1985 and 1996 Alaskans killed 1,024 brown and black bears in reported defense of life or property (DLP) shootings, according to a paper by state biologists Sterling Miller and V. Leigh Tutterrow. That's nearly a hundred bears each year. "It is clear that some people needlessly shot brown bears because they considered the bear to be *immediately dangerous* or *charging*," they wrote (the italics refer to categories on DLP forms). One way to reduce unnecessary killings is to teach people how to recognize a genuinely dangerous situation. "However, such educational efforts are overwhelmed by sensational accounts of bear attacks in popular media, especially shooting magazines," they wrote. "Such accounts tend to leave a more indelible impression on public perceptions than reasonable educational efforts." After news reports of attacks and fatalities, they noticed, DLP kills of both species tended to spike. During their study period, DLP deaths peaked in 1992, when people shot eighty-three brown bears and fifty black bears. Miller and Tutterrow pointed out that this was the same year a food-conditioned bear snatched and killed a six-year-old boy in a village, a predatory black bear killed a woman, and the outdoors editor of the *Anchorage Daily News* wounded a bear that attacked during a surprise encounter. I remember these incidents very well myself.

In the case of the predatory attack, a black bear tried to break into a cabin at Lake Louise, forcing a vacationing couple onto the roof with nothing but a .22-caliber handgun. Reluctant to anger the bear with a potentially ineffective weapon, the husband ran for a skiff to retrieve a better weapon from across the lake. By the time he returned, the bear had climbed a nearby tree, gotten on to the roof, killed his wife, and was feeding on her. Alaskans shot nine bears in DLP incidents over the next three days and a total of seventeen within a month, according to newspaper accounts. These were only the reported shootings; undoubtedly other bears were killed in the guise of hunting season or under the "shoot, shovel, and shut up" ethos.

One condition in the DLP law leaves lots of wiggle room: such shootings are legal as long as "all other practicable means to protect life and property are exhausted before the game is taken." In practice, law enforcement officials are reluctant to second-guess someone's decision to shoot in a threatening situation. State regulations also require shooters in DLP incidents to skin the bear and turn the hide, skull, and claws over to the state. This provision is intended to stop poachers from claiming self-defense, but people who don't want to be bothered or who fear being charged sometimes don't report the shooting.

Sometimes fear can overcome reason, and a gun can overcome fear. This occurred when a Kasilof man left his truck to photograph a brown bear walking along Sterling Highway, a busy road on the Kenai Peninsula. He also took his rifle. A noise frightened the bear, and it stood on its rear legs and made a "barking" sound from thirty-five feet away, the man reported later. Bears typically stand to see or smell better, but the photographer, certain that the bear was charging, shot it and ran back to his truck. He later turned himself in for illegally killing a bear out of season. Without the gun, he probably never would have left the truck.

Hunters in an online forum found it difficult to sympathize with a man who described a DLP shooting that started when a brown bear ran toward his hunting party from 800 yards away. He and his two companions started firing when she was 250 yards away and killed her in a fusillade of fourteen shots, he bragged. Among the criticisms that followed was this observation: "Normally I dont like to second guess but starting to shoot at a charging bear at 250 yards doesnt make a lot of sence [sic] to me. I have had several charge only to stop short at 20 yards or so." Whether the bear intended harm is a big assumption, too. "You know, if you're out on the tundra and there's a lone caribou, a lot of times that caribou will run over toward you, kind of look at you, see what you are and then trot away," Hechtel said. "If a bear does the exact same thing, with the exact same motivation, people freak out because they assume the bear is coming after them."

People who venture outdoors to hunt bears and other animals may unwittingly react differently from people who live in the wilds and have a better understanding of bear behavior, suggested researcher Kathryn Johnson in her master's thesis. She interviewed two dozen Sugpiaq (also known as Alutiiq) people from five communities in the Kodiak archipelago to investigate how they avoid conflicts with bears in or near the villages. She found that between 1901 and 2000, there were only two reported incidents in which bears caused minor injuries to people in the villages. One person was cleaning fish when a female with cubs charged, and the other person surprised a bear while walking at night. The elders she interviewed couldn't recall hearing about other incidents from their parents or grandparents. Outside of the villages, sixteen people were injured and three killed during the same time span, most while hunting.

Johnson speculated that local knowledge of bear behavior and activities, lingering cultural practices that predated contemporary safety advice, and the bears' familiarity with village patterns fostered coexistence. "They never bother people in the village," one person told her. "Leave him alone and he'll leave you alone." Another villager said, "Kodiak bears are one of the most timid animals. They pick up your scent and they're gone." Of course, not everyone shared these ideas about bears, and there have been some DLP shootings in the villages, but the use of electric fences around dumps has reduced many problems. Most people who talked with Johnson described bears as intelligent animals that understand different tones of voice, avoid people, and deserve respect. Johnson suggested that the villagers' mind-set matters because, ever aware that they share the landscape with bears, they remain vigilant and thus avoid trouble. "For the urban dweller (from Alaska or elsewhere) a transition is usually necessary as one puts off suit coat and dons hunting gear," she wrote. "The mental transition follows, from concrete to wilderness, from traffic to bears." It's not a shift most of us make easily, whether we're hunting or not.

Because urban and suburban dwellers tend to think of bears as living somewhere other than where people do, they're often surprised—and ill prepared—when a bear suddenly materializes. That's happened to me even when I thought I knew better. On a kayak trip in Glacier Bay, my husband and I paid close attention to the mandatory orientation lecture, stored our provisions in the required bear-resistant food container (BRFC), and, on our first night, decided to eat dinner on the beach before making camp elsewhere. We thought we were doing everything right. When an agitated brown bear suddenly emerged from the tall grass and walked past where I'd just been sitting, it took me a moment to absorb this new reality.

The bear stopped several yards away and paced in front of us as it yawned, popped its jaws, drooled. We were smart enough to recognize its distress, speak calmly to it, and stand together to appear larger. We weren't, however, smart enough to have extracted the bear spray from the kayak's innards beforehand or to replace the locking lid on the BRFC. First we felt grateful when the bear turned away after a few minutes and walked up the beach. Then we felt worried when it poked its snout into the open BRFC, followed by relief when it kept walking without eating anything, and finally puzzlement when it reared up to batter some alder branches before dropping to graze peacefully. We felt just plain lucky when it ignored us as we scurried around gathering our stuff to leave. Another lesson learned: keep your belongings together.

When the bear reappeared the next morning at our camp a mile away (too close, yes, but tent sites are scarce in Glacier Bay), I had the bear spray with me—not that you could have pried it from my hands whenever I wasn't paddling. After a repeat encounter, bear and kayakers parted ways intact, but rangers later closed the inlet after the same animal tried to bully a solo camper out of his dinner. When we returned the BRFC to park headquarters, the ranger rolled her eyes when I confessed my lapse. "The cans don't do any good if the lids aren't on them," she said. It was excruciating to know that we'd broken a fundamental rule out of simple carelessness, and we felt nothing but fortunate that the bear hadn't taken advantage of our mistake. The ranger's reprimand became a hard little stone I've carried into the backcountry ever since—a reminder that a moment's inattention can provoke a chain of events that often leads to dead bears and sometimes to dead people.

This episode also exposed my own preconceptions about bear behavior. During both encounters, the brown bear had turned sideways, which some people say is a show of dominance, a "Look how big I am" gesture. But Hechtel doesn't think that's the case because, among themselves, bears typically display dominance with a direct frontal approach while making eye contact with their adversary, a behavior I later saw at McNeil River. It's quite possible that the yawning, posturing bear in Glacier Bay was more nervous than anything else—maybe brash enough to challenge us, but insecure enough to back down when we didn't bolt.

What I also overlooked was our own role in making life more difficult for the bears in Glacier Bay. During another encounter, a pair of young brown bears gamboled along the beach toward our tent, oblivious to our presence. We shouted a friendly hello to let them know we were there, and they instantly wheeled and galloped up a rocky slope, their rumps jogging along. Now and then they looked back, to see if we were chasing them, I suppose. You could say this meeting ended well, but too late I understood that we and every other kayaker in the park had pitched our tents on the narrow shorelines where bears travel and forage for roots, grasses, sea creatures. Every bear is forced to make choices when it encounters tents and kayaks and people cluttering the beaches, and sometimes those choices are awfully limited in a place composed of great swatches of rock and ice. Considering the bear's perspective made me stop wondering what a bear might do to me and start wondering what I might be doing to a bear.

Partly, my stunted vision came from an unconscious assumption that humans are always in control, that nature doesn't happen to us without our consent. "Backcountry users should realize that bears may appear anywhere at any time, including islands," Tom Smith and colleagues wrote in a study about human-bear conflicts in the park. "Indeed the saying 'bears are where they find you' is particularly true at Glacier Bay." This seems so obvious now, but never before had I understood how quickly a bear can step into your life, how intensely the blood surges through your heart as your breath quickens and your mind recognizes anew how tender and vulnerable the human body is. There's a visceral irony in this: the moment you're most aware of the possibility of such an ancient form of death is the moment you feel most alive.

Eventually, I came to see how being jolted into that state of primal intensity could become almost addictive, yet also mask the risk that provokes such emotions. Every engagement that ends peacefully builds a sense of intimacy with that other, mysteriously alive world. For some people, that feeling overshadows caution. "I think you can start to believe that you have some special insight that you may or may not have," Hechtel said. When people known for their affinity with bears are injured or killed, others can learn the wrong lessons about both human and bear behavior. It's easy to mistake familiarity with acceptance and to forget that not every bear is alike.

Alaska photographer Michio Hoshino understood that bears have the power to remind us of something we've lost. "People continue to tame and subjugate nature," he wrote in The Grizzly Bear Family Book. "But when we visit the few remaining scraps of wilderness where bears roam free, we can still feel an instinctive fear. How precious that feeling is." A brilliant nature photographer who was experienced in bear country, Hoshino was beloved in Alaska for his humility and good humor and famous in Japan for his ability to capture what a friend called "a different kind of life, a different kind of space, a different kind of time." In 1996, when he was forty-three, he visited a remote refuge in Kamchatka, Russia, to photograph brown bears feeding on salmon and to help a Japanese film crew. Though everyone else slept in a crowded hut or off the ground, Hoshino apparently preferred his tent, despite the presence of an aggressive food-conditioned bear that had resisted numerous attempts to haze it with loud noises and pepper spray. Kamchatka's chief hunting manager had warned Hoshino that the bear had been following him and suggested that he sleep in the hut. Hoshino "refused to believe there was any danger," according to Leonid Baskin, who interviewed witnesses. That night the bear dragged Hoshino into the trees and killed him.

Russian researcher Vitaly Nikolaenko was known for his work on behalf of the Kamchatka Peninsula's brown bears. "He always tested life by either fighting with officials, spooking poachers, standing his ground to strengthen bear hunting rules, arguing with official science or by bothering bears," wrote his friend and colleague Igor Revenko in the International Bear Association's newsletter. (Revenko also had been present at the refuge when Hoshino died). Nikolaenko's years of studying individual bears produced some extraordinary photographs. My favorite is a character study of a serene bear he called Dobrynya, sometimes translated as "Kind Bear" or "Good Guy."

During Nikolaenko's thirty-third field season at Kronotsky State Reserve, he followed and photographed an unfamiliar male bear that clearly signaled it found his presence stressful, according to colleagues Vladimir Mosolov and Tatiana Gordienko. The bear responded so aggressively on two occasions that Nikolaenko began to carry a shotgun. Despite calling the bear "vicious and dangerous" in his field notes, Nikolaenko continued to follow it, pursuing it into an alder thicket one day. Searchers found his body near an unfired flare gun and a patch of snow stained orange by bear spray. The bear had killed him with two blows to the head and chest before heading straight for the mountains. His colleagues speculated that perhaps the pepper spray gave Nikolaenko a false sense of security. "Everything looks as if Vitaly lost his good sense and believed that nothing bad could happen to him, even though he said in his notes that he knew the bear was dangerous," they wrote. When I commented to an Alaska bear biologist that he must have been shocked by Nikolaenko's death, he replied, "Not really."

And what are we to make of Timothy Treadwell? A complex and conflicted person, he spent thirteen seasons camping on the coast of Katmai National Park, fashioning an image in the popular media as someone with a reciprocal relationship with bears, someone who protected bears that didn't need protecting. He routinely violated park regulations by filming himself near bears, sometimes within a few feet. In one scene he touched a bear on the nose after it edged up to him. Pilots once reported seeing him "straddle" a bear. Treadwell's footage includes mesmerizing scenes of bears, but most viewers won't recognize that the credit belongs to the bears, not to Treadwell. "He did things that anyone with a good understanding of animals, and time to do it, could do," Katmai bear-viewing guide Chris Day told me. "It's just that anyone with any sense has chosen not to do this." Treadwell wanted to prove that bears aren't bloodthirsty and vicious, but he also lauded his own bravery in living among animals that could, as he once told the camera, kill him *just like that*. He warned that what he did was dangerous and inappropriate. He also believed that no bear would kill him because of his special insight, his love.

The deaths of Treadwell and his companion, Amie Huguenard, in October 2003 are well documented in Werner Herzog's film *Grizzly Man* and in at least two books, including *The Grizzly Maze*, an evenhanded account by Alaska writer Nick Jans. Treadwell also inadvertently recorded the attack on a six-minutes audio track found on his video camera. I know two people who have heard this recording, and both sincerely wish they hadn't. Even the written account is harrowing. The man who once wrote to biologist Sterling Miller, "I'd be honored to end up as bear shit," discovered in the most terrible way possible that it is not a good way to die.

The recording doesn't explain what initially transpired between the bear and Treadwell or whether this was a wholly predatory incident. As Hechtel points out, the bear didn't drag Treadwell from the tent during the night in an unprovoked attack. Perhaps he left the tent during the heavy rain that afternoon to confront the bear after he heard it moving around—his usual practice, according to a friend. Maybe behavior that Treadwell had found successful in deterring other bears didn't work in this instance, Hechtel says. In any case, the federal Technical Board of Investigation decided that the camp's location in the brush and among a network of bear trails was a primary factor. The board also mentioned Treadwell's decision to stay at Kaflia Bay when bears were in high-powered feeding mode, as well as his habit of approaching bears and allowing them to come within a few feet. "The pattern of behavior exhibited by Treadwell appeared to be a result of his opinion that he had established a special relationship with bears in the area of the camp," the report stated.

The urge to reach across the gulf between human and bear, to transcend the tedious condition of being human, is irresistible for some of us, but such impulses risk distorting the nature of bears. "I think that's where Mr. Treadwell fell apart," Larry Van Daele told me. "He thought that bears felt the same way people do—they felt love, they view the world [the same way]. And they don't. Their whole physiology is different, much less their mental capacity. They have a different perspective of the world and what's right and what's wrong. So we want to make sure we don't disrespect them by putting human virtues on them." Nor can we ask bears to repair whatever emptiness we bring with us into the wilderness.

Treadwell's story offers many examples of purposeful rule-breaking that didn't matter—until the moment it did. "I think the reason he died is that playing the odds eventually caught up with him," Sterling Miller commented. "The fact that he survived for so long misbehaving as badly as he did is a testament to the tolerance bears have for humans." Luck—that's the other intangible. Sometimes you're just plain lucky that the bear you encounter is willing to overlook your mistakes, and sometimes you do everything right and the bear eats your rule book.

Like bears, people can learn. Several years after our Glacier Bay experience, my husband and I were hiking with our blue heeler on a forested trail in Far North Bicentennial Park. When a black bear thrust its head through the bushes lining the path, I was too busy yakking to see it. "Stop," Scott said. "There's a bear." He pointed toward the knoll rising above us. "Grab the dog," I said, and he bent to pick up the leash dragging behind Bix, who didn't notice the bear even when it stepped onto the trail and turned toward us. It was maybe a couple of hundred pounds and about twenty yards away. It made no sound.

"Hey, bear," Scott said. "We don't want to be in your way." You might think it would be wary of us, but people have fed black bears in the nearby parking lots. And the park's wooded trails are popular with mountain bikers, hikers, horse riders, moose, and bears both brown and black. This animal had probably seen many people before. The bear took a few steps toward us. "Stand together," I said. Scott continued grappling with the leash and the dog, who was still, unbelievably, oblivious. The bear took several steady, lumbering paces toward us. "Stand together!" I said more sharply. By now the bear should have run off, yet there it was, walking our way, still looking right at us. "Let's raise our arms," I suggested, and we did.

Quick as a shadow, the bear turned and disappeared into the brush. We returned the way we had come, looking back now and then to make sure we weren't being followed, enjoying the cool morning just a little bit more. "Good dog!" we said as we walked. "Good bear!" But what we also meant was, "Good people!"

the hunted bear

Edward Harriman wanted to kill an Alaskan bear, and why not? He was a railroad magnate who was conquering the continent train by train and dollar by dollar, a nineteenth-century man with a twentieth-century future, a "great maker and harvester of crops of wealth," John Muir said. Being rich and powerful is exhausting work, so Harriman's doctor sent him on vacation. But tycoons don't become tycoons by relaxing. They look around to see what other famous, powerful people are doing, and then they do the same thing, only more so. Inspired by Theodore Roosevelt's grand outdoor adventures and intrigued by a friend's description of Alaska's enormous bruins, Harriman decided to sail north and kill a bear.

He turned a private family cruise into a public act of scientific philanthropy by renovating a steamer into a luxury craft and announcing the Harriman Alaska Expedition of 1899. This "floating university" was a Victorian promenade up the northern coast with twenty-three of the nation's finest scientists, writers, and artists—luminaries such as Muir; nature essayist William Burroughs; George Bird Grinnell, a cofounder of the Boone and Crockett Club; and C. Hart Merriam, chief of the US Biological Survey. Eventually, they produced a thirteen-volume compendium of narrative, research, and illustrations. Most important to Harriman, the sixty-five crew members included two taxidermists and eleven hunters and packers.

The steamer bumped along Alaska's coast that summer, pausing to disgorge the curious and the purposeful to collect samples, draw illustrations, and take photographs. Meanwhile, Harriman and his hunting party tramped about on unsuccessful sorties for bears, inspiring Burroughs to write, "It is much easier in Alaska to bag a glacier than a bear." Finally, an experienced hunter in Seldovia told Harriman to try Kodiak Island, and he immediately diverted the ship. Harriman didn't explain his pressing desire to kill a bear (if he even understood it himself), but really, he didn't have to. He was the kind of man who, when charged by a massive Steller sea lion, charged it right back.

On July 3 a Russian guide named Stepan Kandarkof found Harriman his Kodiak bear. The faded brown female and her cub were "grazing in true bovine fashion" on a green slope in Uyak Bay, wrote Burroughs. Men drove the pair toward the waiting Harriman, and "lest the bear behave in an unpleasant manner a group of hunters were grouped about [Harriman] with enough firepower to tear the bear to pieces," entomologist Trevor Kincaid reported. But the bear remained well behaved, and Harriman killed her with a single bullet from his Winchester. The ship's captain shot the male cub. The tycoon photographed the scruffy female sprawled near a patch of snow for his souvenir album. Then he returned to the ship, leaving others to handle the carcasses, as if he had just signed a business deal that his underlings would complete.

Expedition members cheered when the taxidermist delivered the pelts and skulls to the ship the next afternoon, though no one specified whether they were celebrating the dead animals or merely grateful that Harriman had finally killed his blasted bear. John Muir tsk-tsked in his journal, pointedly referring to the "mother and child," and a small mother at that. Scientist William Dall rewrote a nursery rhyme for the expedition's souvenir album: "And when the eager hunters came / to follow up the track, / the bear withdrew into the brush / And never answered back." Harriman hoped to kill more bears, particularly a polar bear, but he did not loiter around Kodiak seeking ever-larger animals. Onward the expedition sailed in pursuit of knowledge.

Harriman apparently didn't bother to pose for a photograph with his trophy, so we can't study his expression for clues to his mood. Across time and history, all I can make out is the determination of a self-made man who dropped out of school at age fourteen and worked his way into the American brand of aristocracy, which rises from affluence and power rather than bloodline. From this distance, it's easy to see how his act mimicked the traditions that made recreational hunting the exclusive pastime of monarchs and the stylized privilege of medieval nobles. Notice, too, an uncomfortable resemblance to the European habit of turning exotic lands where wild animals thrive into colonial game reserves for wealthy sportsmen. There is no better demonstration of Harriman's tremendous reach than his ability to mount a major expedition based on the impulse to shoot a bear.

More meaningful than the bear hides was the act of killing, a moment so vital that he journeyed 9,000 miles there and back to pull the trigger. He did not find the bear, stalk the bear, study the bear, pack the bear, skin the bear, or eat the bear. He merely shot the bear. In this manner, Edward Harriman became the first big-game hunter who traveled to Kodiak to kill a bear whose only use was metaphorical. He wasn't the last. Did Harriman admire bears? Did he fear them? Can we apply the contemporary cliché and assume he respected them? The accounts of the expedition don't say, and this stubborn opacity, this historical indifference to what I most want to know intrigues and annoys me. Only imagination can describe what Harriman thought as his men herded the bear and her cub toward him, as he aimed his rifle and steadied his breath. Did he feel joy? Did he shake off fear? For even a second, did he think, *This isn't what I wanted?* And when the bears lay dead before him, did that moment satisfy the strange longing that had seized him and sent him north to kill a wild bear?

Every year in Alaska, hunters kill an average of 1,400 to 1,500 brown bears, about the same number estimated to live in all of the Lower 48. Between 1970 and 1996 hunters killed 26,489 brown bears and at least 30,985 black bears in Alaska. Hunters are not usually required to salvage meat from brown bears, and not many people eat it anyway, so most of those bears likely ended up carpeting a floor, draping a wall, or silently posing in someone's house. In 2007 hunters killed 3,250 black bears, a species that more people find edible and even delicious, but salvaging the meat is not required everywhere. The point is, most people who kill a bear in Alaska aren't defending or feeding themselves. Like Harriman, they're satisfying some other need.

I'm no hunter, so how would I know what hunters need? Although I use my guns only for target shooting, my father and grandfather hunted for meat, as do many of my friends. I'm glad Alaskans can still feed themselves by fishing and hunting. Hunting for your own meat is as admirable as growing your own vegetables and far more honest and humane than the factory farming that feeds most Americans today. Given a choice between commercially raised beef and a free-ranging moose untainted by antibiotics or hormones, give me moose meat every time. But learning to be a decent hunter is hard work. My husband and I don't eat nearly enough meat to justify buying better rifles, flying to some remote camp, and acquiring a freezer to store heaps of white-wrapped packages we couldn't finish in ten years.

There's also this: I don't like to kill things. I make my husband take spiders outside. I've shot only paper targets and innocent cans. So yes, killing bears for sport or trophies—whatever you prefer to call hunting that doesn't involve eating what you kill—perplexes me. Maybe I'd think differently if I endured several days of crummy weather before I saw tawny fur rippling through the scope and glimpsed the bear's hard, glinting eye or its magnificent, knowing eye or whatever kind of eye a bear should have. Maybe I'd be thrilled to caress the trigger and witness how that tiny gesture can knock a bear ass over teakettle. Maybe I'd see why some people dream of approaching the great beast that was heaving with life just minutes before, knowing that the animal now belongs only to them. Maybe I'd understand the three or four men who've told me some version of this statement: "I killed a bear once and I don't care to do it again." They don't care to do it again, and they can't remember why they wanted to in the first place.

For 99 percent of our time on earth, humans hunted for survival, not recreation. Now that so many of us mass-produce our food instead of growing or slaying it ourselves, the desire to hunt bears is often earnestly framed as an atavistic salute to our origins. "Bears speak to something primal in the recesses of the human brain, the same quarter of our instinct that makes us hunt in the first place," wrote E. Donnall Thomas Jr. in *Longbows in the Far North*. Let's not patronize hunting as a vestigial impulse, argued the neo-Pleistocene warrior Paul Shepard in *The Others*. Let's remember that hunting made us human—that animals made us human. "The Game" is Shepard's term for the mental and physical tug-of-war between the eaters and the eaten, the escalating strategies of pursuit and evasion, camouflage and threat, adaptation and defense. Animals taught us what to eat, how to predict their movements, how to plan our responses. We learned to compensate for our weaker senses by developing social skills and fashioning tools to harvest, capture, kill, butcher, store, and preserve food. Imagine yourself suddenly transported naked into the wilderness, and you begin to grasp the immensity and importance of what animals gave us and how little of that practical knowledge remains.

From animals, we also learned how to think about the world and our place in it, an evolution of mind that occurred in tandem with the development of spiritual awareness. The Game, Shepard believed, "places animals at the heart of human symbolism." Early cultures recognized as sacred the flux of energy that courses through the reciprocity of eating and being eaten. The Game is particularly intimate between bears and humans because we are predator and prey of the other. We are competitors, too, elbowing each other out of the way to dig roots, pick berries, catch fish, fill our bellies with hot, bloody meat. "Our kind has watched the bear watching, and recognized a being like us," Shepard told bear experts.

If you're going to kill an animal that reminds you of yourself, you'd better do it right. After studying bear ceremonialism in North America and Eurasia, anthropologist Irving Hallowell concluded that "of all the game animals hunted in the north, the bear is the most constant recipient of special attention." Bears weren't worshipped like gods or slain like demons but were recognized as entities acting on behalf of a supernatural power. The entire community was responsible for observing taboos and honoring bears before and after death; poor behavior risked the future supply of bears or other animals. Like other boreal cultures, Alaska Natives understood bear hunting as a delicate negotiation between the inspirited and peopled domains. "For Tlingits, successful hunting traditionally involved not only the use of weapons but also the employment of a complex system of knowledge about the relationships between bears and humans," observed contemporary anthropologist Tom Thornton.

The old ways of killing bears required a frightening intimacy. Alaska Natives often hunted in groups, but even so, it was a dangerous undertaking. Before the introduction of firearms and steel traps in the late nineteenth century, Native hunters devised numerous ways to kill bears. They crippled them with wooden spikes embedded in the trail, strangled them with snares, pierced them with arrow points carved from rock or bone. In the Kantishna drainage in Interior Alaska, Athabascan hunters used trickery: They would release a captured ground squirrel near a bear, which would gobble the squirrel and then follow its tracks to find its nest. Hunters would kill the distracted bear with lances while it was digging up the nest. Tlingit hunters developed a large repertoire of methods, including hunting with dogs and rigging elaborate deadfalls that, when tripped by an unsuspecting bear, released a bone-crushing log. My imagination fails when I try to picture the fortitude required to lie in a deep hollow scraped from a trail's damp earth, waiting to spear a bear when it passed overhead.

Long, sturdy spears also allowed hunters to ambush bears or stab them in their dens. Sometimes a hunter would brace the spear's butt against the ground as a bear charged, jumping aside as it impaled itself. On the Alaska Peninsula, pairs of Sugpiaq hunters hid beside a bear trail until an animal approached. Then one partner leaped out to distract it, while the other speared it, each undoubtedly certain that he was the braver one. One spear from the Brooks Range is a ten-inch-long sharpened grizzly tibia lashed with rawhide to an eight-foot shaft stained with ochre or willow bark. These weapons were used by Athabascan elders like traditional chief David Salmon, an Episcopal priest who at age ninety-four enthralled Fairbanks youngsters with stories of making bear spears tipped with moose bone.

Almost every indigenous group took special care with a slain bear's head or skull. Some northern Athabascans, Eyak, and northern Tlingits buried the heads facing toward the mountains. Other Tlingits dabbed bear heads with red paint and eagle down. A contemporary Tlingit hunter learned from his father to place the bear's skull under a dead tree "so the bear's spirit . . . would have a dry place where it could stay before it started the journey." While living in the northwestern village of Noatak, writer Nick Jans was scolded by a neighbor when he brought home a grizzly with its head still attached. Inupiaq hunters buried the heads or left them in trees. Even now, some Sugpiaq hunters leave the skull facing southward at the site of the bear's death, or they return the hide and bones to that place after a ceremonial feast. "What my grandma told me [was] that the brown bear was our ancestor," a Sugpiaq man on the Alaska Peninsula told interviewers. "That when you did take one, it was a prayer." Claws, teeth, bits of bones, and hides were not trophies so much as tools of divination, shamanistic talismans. The taboos and rites differed, but they all meant the same thing: *It is no small thing to kill a bear. Do it right.*

Necessity demanded this reciprocity, a communal give-and-take, but modern sport hunting lapses too easily into all take and little give. Trophy hunters usually spurn the hard-won meat, the flesh and blood that represent an old covenant with the world: *I will eat you, and you will eat me.* They spirit away the head and hide as a tribute not to the animal but to themselves and to the awesome power of the opposable thumb, the digit that changed the world. For some, the Game is only a game, and one in which the miracles of technology tilt the odds so heavily that the animals themselves are known as game.

"Perhaps the 'down side' to hunting becoming 'too' easy is the failure to generate respect for the animals harvested," a longtime Alaskan bear guide wrote in an online forum. "That may well explain, at least in part, the 'ho hum' attitudes by some about the seriousness of wounding game or even in some cases harvesting animals under at best questionable circumstances. The 'wham bam thank you ma'am' attitude of some does little to engender that time a hunter quietly looks at the animal just harvested and contemplates the gravity of the action just taken."

Paul Shepard was not sentimental about either animals or people, and he abhorred a facile regard for animal rights or a knee-jerk reaction against all hunting. But in a world that's been plowed, fenced, and paved and all its animals managed and allocated, the once sacred hunt has become little more than a hobby. "We are space-needing, wild-country, Pleistocene beings," Shepard wrote in *The Others*, "trapped in overdense numbers in devastated, simplified ecosystems. . . . Our ethics and morality deny the sacredness of the human connection with other life as it is played out in metabolic chains and the numinous presence of animals at the heart of religious experience. When we try to extend our ethics to that with which it is incompatible, we get pictorial and esthetic images of nature, the Renaissance spectator, museum patronage, the culture of abstract appearances and dissociation."

And we get trophy hunting—the act of killing an animal, dismantling it, and hiring someone to compose its remains into a simulacrum of life with a glassy-eyed stare that reveals only the hunter's reflection.

There's a lexicon of hunting, a proper way of naming what happens, how it happens, and why it happens. I'm violating decorum by slinging about the phrase *killing bears*, which some will regard as a tactless or unnecessarily incendiary term. Though I use the word *shooting* to describe the act of discharging a weapon, self-respecting hunters distinguish themselves from shooters. Nobody hunts garbage bears or calf-killing predators, for example; they shoot them. The term *harvesting* is management-speak, a husbandry term meant to convey a planned and sustainable approach to removing surplus animals from a population. Another implication is that wild animals can be reaped like wheat.

Different kinds of hunting have different goals. Subsistence hunting is a legal category in Alaska that describes killing wild game to feed yourself and your family, but if you want to start a bar fight in a hurry, announce your opinion about who really *needs* to kill their food and who merely *wants* to. Sport or recreational hunting is hunting for pleasure—pleasure in the chase, in being outdoors, in participating in a cultural tradition or social pastime. Many hunters dislike the term *sport hunting* because it suggests the whole enterprise is a lark, an exercise in killing animals for fun. Not that hunting *isn't* fun—but it's supposed to be about more than killing. Trophy hunters—call them big-game hunters to evoke a Hemingwayesque aura—seek particular animals based on a fixed aesthetic standard, such as body size or antler shape; rarity and charisma are pluses. Although a sport hunter may not care whether his bear enters the revered lists of Boone and Crockett or Pope and Young, game laws nearly always require him to retrieve the skull and hide because our culture considers trophies the main point of bear hunting. (I refer to bear hunters as males because most are.)

How do bear hunters describe themselves? They're dreamers and frontier seekers, judging from the features and advertisements in hook-and-bullet publications:

> "Like most red blooded American males that hunt, I had a dream of going to Alaska for grizzly bear and moose since childhood."
> "I know I am not alone when I say that hunting Alaskan Brown Bear has been a life-long dream."
> "I have been bow hunting for 26 years with several nice deer to my credit, but I had always dreamed of hunting black bears."
> "For a big-game hunter, an Alaska brown bear hunt has to be a kind of ultimate dream—a fantasy of high adventure set in a wild and rugged landscape untouched by time."
> "A successful Alaskan bear hunt has been a dream of a lifetime come true."

This shared aspiration emerges not from the Game but from the Story, and not from anecdotal tales of "How I Got My Bear" but from the grander narrative that inspires an ordinary person to go into the wilds, find a bear, and kill it because something in that act is essential to his identity. The Game is about the relationship between the hunter and the hunted. The Story is all about the hunter, told often and best by

Theodore Roosevelt, the consummate big-game guy whose ideas still inform modern notions of the fair chase, hunters as conservationists, and the American spirit.

Roosevelt regarded hunting as a "sport for a vigorous and masterful people," a way to mold and express character. He wrote in The Wilderness Hunter (1893):

> In hunting, the finding and killing of the game is after all but a part of the whole. The free, self-reliant, adventurous life, with its rugged and stalwart democracy; the wild surroundings, the grand beauty of the scenery, the chance to study the ways and habits of the wood-land creatures—all these unite to give to the career of the wilderness hunter its peculiar charm. The chase is among the best of all national pastimes; it cultivates that vigorous manliness for the lack of which in a nation, as in an individual, the possession of no other qualities can possibly atone.

Roosevelt's book appeared the same year historian Frederick Jackson Turner famously described how the frontier had forged distinctly American traits, particularly "dominant individualism." Freedom, democracy, self-reliance, wilderness, and manliness were all potent qualities invoked by the frontier, which, by the way, was closed, Turner announced, now that Euro-Americans had settled the continent from sea to shining sea. But sport hunting reanimated the frontier, and its most powerful totem was the grizzly bear—or, rather, the hunter brave and skilled enough to slay a grizzly bear. The cover of The Wilderness Hunter depicts a mustachioed fellow approaching a dead bear. Presumably this was Roosevelt, who devoted two chapters to describing hunts for "Old Ephraim, the grisly." Even as he insisted that the animal's ferocity was overstated, he celebrated bear hunting as the sport's apex: "The most thrilling moments of an American hunter's life are those in which, with every sense on the alert, and with nerves strung to the highest point, he is following alone into the heart of its forest fastness the fresh and bloody footprints of an angered grisly; and no other triumph of American hunting can compare with the victory to be thus gained." No bear, no triumph.

Roosevelt recognized that the West he beatified had been trampled from existence by the very pioneers who had pushed the frontier into the Pacific Ocean. He opened his book by intoning a litany of dwindling game species: bison, elk, pronghorn antelope, grizzlies. He closed it by noting without irony that "settlers and miners have invaded the ground where I killed moose and bear." He and Audubon Society founder George Bird Grinnell had formed the Boone and Crockett Club in 1887 to celebrate the "manly sport" and end the wanton slaughter that had eradicated buffalo and thinned big game throughout the West. They recruited a hundred gentlemen hunters who had each killed at least three big-game animals. Over time, club members ratcheted back the worst hunting excesses, introduced the code of fair chase, and helped create Alaska's first game laws (to the annoyance of many Alaskans). But their original reform efforts were motivated by the hard truth that without big game, there can be no big-game hunters.

Roosevelt's famous refusal to kill a black bear tied to a tree is one reason he's regarded as the patron saint of fair chase. "It was the beginning of a modern hunting ethic that elevated sportsmen to that of hunter-conservationists by promoting taking game only in a respectful manner that did not give unfair advantage to the hunter," explained a 2008 press release announcing the establishment of the Theodore Roosevelt National Wildlife Refuge in Mississippi. The circumstances surrounding Roosevelt's refusal weren't quite as inspirational. The president had been invited to go black bear hunting in the Mississippi Delta in 1902, as described in Douglas Brinkley's history The Wilderness Warrior and Minor Ferris Buchanan's biography Holt Collier. Mindful of his reputation, Roosevelt asked a favor of his hosts: "do see I get the first bear without fail."

Legendary bear hunter Holt Collier agreed to drive a bear past Roosevelt's stand with his forty hunting hounds, "same as anybody would drive a cow," he later explained. Collier was a former slave and a professional hunter credited with killing more than 3,000 bears in his lifetime. By the time his dogs finally harassed an exhausted bear into the president's vicinity, Roosevelt and his companion had left to eat lunch. During the frenzy, the bear killed the guide's favorite dog. Collier couldn't possibly slay the president's bear, so to prevent it from injuring more dogs, he smacked his gun barrel against the bear's head, knocked the animal into a nearby lake, roped it, and lashed it by the neck to a tree. Collier's horn then summoned the president. But with newsmen in camp, Roosevelt could hardly violate the sportsmen's creed he extolled. He handed a knife to a companion, said, "Put it out of its misery," and walked away. Rather than bloody the presidential weapon, the hunter made a poor job of stabbing the bear with a lesser knife, forcing Collier to finish the nasty work. All told, the hunting party killed three bears, but the story that dominated newspaper headlines was the president's refusal to shoot the roped bear. A cartoon that showed Roosevelt turning away from a big-eared cub inspired a Brooklyn toymaker's marketing genius: "Teddy's bear." Nobody seemed to notice that the original bear died rather gruesomely, despite Roosevelt's honorable act.

A century later, we're still putting teddy bears into children's arms, and hunters still invoke this episode—the sanitized version—as the epitome of hunting integrity. Almost never do we hear the disturbing details of what often passes for a fair chase even now—running bears into exhaustion with hounds that are sometimes injured in the fray, shooting bears over bait stations, trapping or snaring bears—inflicting such casual brutality on an animal whose very capacity to resist death makes it an irresistible trophy.

The hunter would say, *We're America's true conservationists, and if it weren't for us, we'd have no wildlife at all.* This role was defined, codified, and championed in 2001 as the North American Model of Wildlife Conservation by Canadian wildlife biologist Valerius Geist and others. They identified seven principles underlying what they describe as an unparalleled example of sustainable resource development: (1) wildlife belongs to everybody, (2) game should be allocated by law, (3) everyone should have the opportunity to hunt, (4) game should not be killed for commercial markets, (5) wildlife policy should be based in science, (6) wildlife are an international resource, and (7) wildlife should be killed only for legitimate purposes.

Environmental ethics scholar Michael Nelson and colleagues pointed out an obvious problem with the final standard: "This principle is as basic and appropriate as it is void of useful insight about defining a legitimate purpose," they wrote in a 2011 critique of the model. Geist and his coauthors identified legitimate purposes as "food, fur, self defense or property protection." That sounds reasonable, but where does trophy hunting fit into this philosophy? Nelson's group mentioned rather delicately that perhaps hunters aren't the only people responsible for wildlife and habitat protection. Geist is refreshingly straightforward about the relationship between hunters and conservation. "Hunters support wildlife conservation because there is something in it for them: a payoff in their annual allocation of wildlife," he wrote in a 2006 paper. "The motive is selfish, not idealistic. As a profit motive drives a capitalistic economy, so a profit motive drives the North American system of wildlife conservation: the hope for a richer harvest and a richer experience in hunting." Roosevelt couldn't have said it better himself.

After the West was tamed, where else but Alaska could a twentieth-century frontiersman cultivate vigorous manliness and hunt for food and sport? George Folta was nineteen years old and fevered by childhood tales of settlers, trappers, and hunters when he headed north in 1916 to live the dream. He couldn't wait to kill a bear. He shot three on his second trip to Kodiak and never stopped after that. Folta later worked as a clerk to the territorial governor, a prosecutor, and a judge, but at heart he was always a bear hunter, famous in the territory for killing perhaps 200 bears in his lifetime. (Some say it was 142, but after the first hundred, who's counting?) "Why did Dad hunt bears?" asked his son, Richard. "Dad believed that he was re-enacting the last tableau of the wilderness frontier tradition embodied by the likes of Kit Carson, Davy Crockett, Daniel Boone and others known for their hunting prowess."

For Allen Hasselborg, Alaska was a wilderness where a man with wits and know-how could thrive. In Minnesota he'd hunted from boyhood, spent his first earnings on a natural history book, and read *The Swiss Family Robinson* ragged. He was shanghaied north on a codfishing boat in 1899, but he was Alaska-bound anyway. He fished, prospected, trapped, and hunted bears on Admiralty Island for cash. He killed a dozen bears in 1907 alone to supply hides and skulls to the insatiable mammalogist C. H. Merriam. ("This year will probably see the finish of the bears as the Indians and everybody are getting excited over Dr. Merriam's $40 bounty on bear skulls," he wrote to a friend.) When a brown bear mauled him in 1912 and damaged his right arm, he blamed himself. Hasselborg built a cabin, grew a garden, guided hunters, and made the island's wilderness his own. "I knew every bear on some of these watersheds and every one of those bears knew me, too," he said, according to biographer John Howe in *Bear Man of Admiralty Island.*

One night Hasselborg killed a bear trying to break into his cabin and then regretted it. He quit hunting bears. By then, he had killed about a hundred bears and figured clients had taken another forty. He continued to guide hunters and photographers but was too ornery and independent to help conservationists' "Save the Bears of Admiralty" campaign in the 1930s. He didn't allow other people to kill bears around his homestead, though, and he learned to be more neighborly toward bruins himself. Once another hunting guide watched Hasselborg scold a large sow and her two cubs for busting through his garden. The bears merely stood on their hind legs before him and listened, the guide reported.

Stories about men like Folta and Hasselborg invoked an intoxicating vision of living fearless and free in a wilderness that seemed remote yet was accessible to anyone willing to pay for steamship fare or a plane ride. For decades, the *Alaska Sportsman* was the keeper of these frontier dreams. Between 1935 and 1972, when it was renamed *Alaska*, the magazine published at least 129 bear-hunting tales, not including the ever-popular mauling stories. Many contributors convinced themselves that they were living the Game in this hunting paradise, even as they watched themselves reenact the fate of the West. Here is Harold Bartlett Scott in 1937, describing a monthlong yacht cruise through Southeast Alaska: "It is just about the last frontier left in the world. I dare say it will not be many years before this great, vast tract of country is opened and will no longer be a frontier. To all who love the out-of-doors, who love Nature in the raw, my advice is: 'Go to Alaska!'" He also recommended that the government encourage more clear-cutting, mining, and oil drilling. Evidently, he was a believer in getting some while the getting was good, as he and his two teenage sons loved "Nature in the raw" by killing three brown bears, three black bears, two mountain goats, and three Sitka deer.

Popular culture made sure Alaska inherited America's waning frontier identity when the territory achieved statehood in 1959. *Life* magazine insisted that Americans' "hybrid vigor" and boundless optimism had a new staging ground: "Already some 'Fifty-Niners' are prodding into the Alaskan spaces. But even when all new land is gone, the pioneer spirit will continue to uphold what the new land offered: freedom, equality, justice and the dignity of man." *Popular Mechanics* hailed the new state as a place where "you can hunt bear in the morning, attend a symphony concert in the evening and play a round of golf at midnight. It's 20th century technology and Wild West frontier in a large economy package."

Even now we use bears to force the frontier spirit into Alaska, as if the state were a Resusci-Anne at risk of expiring without constant reminders that without bears there is no Last Frontier, and there is no Last Frontier without bears. "Black, brown, grizzly and polar bears all share the land referred to as the 'Last Frontier,' rendering Alaska a hunting destination second-to-none," wrote Marc Taylor for the *Sportsman's News*. In an article about father-son bonding, Dick Scorzafava explained, "I'd wanted to take my son Tony bear hunting in Alaska for a long time. I chose Alaska because it's truly the last frontier, and without a doubt one of the most spectacular places on the planet."

If Alaska is a refugium for bears, then it is also a refugium for bear hunters who, intentionally or not, reenact one of our dearest myths, reanimate the stirring vision of Theodore Roosevelt's wilderness hunter, perhaps even reexperience the Game for a few days. They have helped enshrine the idea of Alaska as a perpetual frontier, the last place where a particular kind of man can create a particular identity. Outdoor writer Christopher Batin described that man this way: "The successful Alaska brown bear hunter is a special breed whose skills are honed to razor sharpness on the whetstone of wilderness adversity. Success—and often your very survival—means overcoming fear and fusing a hunter's skills with a warrior's strength of mind and body. You don't just train for a wilderness bear hunt; you survive it. The victors become part of the elite, hunting's best of the best—a brotherhood of hunter-warriors." According to scholar Susan Kollin in *Nature's State: Imagining Alaska as the Last Frontier*, "Alaska is largely defined and understood as male space, a playground where white adventurers may flirt with the primitive. . . ." There's no faster shortcut to the primitive than killing a bear.

I once asked retired bear-hunting guide Pete Buist why people hunt bears for sport. Buist is a former member of the Alaska Board of Game, frequent president and board member of the Alaska Trappers Association, and the 1999 Trapper of the Year. He lives in Fairbanks and remains active in wildlife politics. The army sent him to Alaska to type his way through the Vietnam War, and he stayed to experience his share of the frontier dream on his trapline and with his gun. He's participated in many bear hunts but has killed only one grizzly himself. He doesn't know what motivates other hunters, but "I can tell you why I enjoyed it," he told me. "That is, to do it right takes a fair amount of skill. It's not something like walking out in the back forty and hunting rabbits and pheasants or something. And quite frankly, the idea that you're hunting something that's bigger and badder than you are is appealing."

Few better tools exist to measure your bigness and badness than the bear. "I hunt for the pure combative spirit," a Juneau guide told interviewer Merry Ellefson. "Brown bear is the only one who can fight back, see, he can soak up a lot of lead." Only a trophy-class bear mattered to this hunter; otherwise, he said, it's like shooting women and children: "Well, the thing is, it's kind of a macho thing, there's no question about it, but these big guys you see, these dominant male bears, they are macho. I mean, they're walking around kickin' ass all the time, you know, and so once in a while, they're gonna meet up with someone that's going to kick their ass, that's the way I look at it."

Killing bears also draws some people closer to life's essential mysteries. As a young man, big-game guide Dick Petersen left Wyoming for Alaska, where he learned to live in the lonely winter wilds of the Wrangell Mountains, run dogs, and hunt the way the old-timers did. For him, hunting bears was more about the places it took him—the raw wildness of the Alaska Peninsula, the open country of the coastal Arctic, the rolling hills near Unalakleet. He worked for other guides for years before he bought the hunting concession in Wrangell–St. Elias National Preserve and, with his wife, Gretchen, established an outfitting and horse-trekking business at the historic camp of Horsfeld.

Maybe bear hunting attunes people to one of the biggest human emotions, Petersen told me, which is the fear of death, the fundamental ingredient of a survival instinct too easily lost "on the pavement." He struggled to explain how hunting bears gave him an awareness of being human: "After looking into the dying eyes of a big bear like that . . . there's no way. I mean, when I was young, sure you can look at it in a macho way. But as you get older and you start dealing with the issues of life and death and you have friends and family die, it's different. I think it gives you a real realistic idea of . . . it gives you a different kind of respect, I think. The only way that I can deal with that is a couple of ways: Having humility in the act and salvaging everything as best as possible. And not having a bunch of bravado about it."

Killing a bear must be like riding an emotional teeter-totter between fearing death and delivering it. Ordinary life doesn't present many opportunities to kill something big enough to kill you back. War, murder, law enforcement, self-defense—that about covers it. Some people think killing a bear holds a dark attraction because it's almost like killing a person. Others discover that their bear-hunting dream requires slaying what they profess to love. And what *do* hunters love more—the bear or the dream?

One man began his bear-hunting tale on the Alaska Outdoors Forum by announcing that he had just killed a dream he'd nurtured for thirty-three years. He'd been "smitten" with the idea of grizzly hunting since reading the August 1976 edition of *Outdoor Life* as a ten-year-old, he wrote. On the first day of his guided hunt in the Talkeetna Mountains, he made a careful stalk to within 185 yards of a bear grazing on fall berries.

One shot later, he sat in the tundra cradling the bear's massive head in his lap. "There's almost a sadness in that, a feeling of mortality that furthers the bond I'll forever share with this animal," he wrote. "The big dream, the really Big Dream, is over. Perhaps I'll have the chance to hunt a grizzly again, but it will never be this bear. It will never be those final yards of stalking uphill towards a lifetime of destiny." He concluded his story: "Sitting on the side of that mountain, looking at the bear and the enormous space beyond, I found myself being filled with a mix of faith and humility and felt more genuinely alive than I have in a very long time." This is both the purpose and the paradox of sport hunting: for him to feel genuinely alive, the bear had to genuinely die.

Without death, hunting cannot be authentic, explained Spanish philosopher José Ortega y Gasset. His short treatise *Meditations on Hunting* has made him the thinking person's go-to guy on the hunting ethos. Ortega y Gasset was all about the Game (Shepard was an admirer). Only through hunting can humans reenter the ancient state of being animal, he reasoned, erasing the uneasy gap between humanity and nature. "Hunting submerges man deliberately in that formidable mystery and therefore contains something of religious rite and emotion in which homage is paid to what is divine, transcendent, in the laws of Nature," he wrote. His most quoted statement: "To sum up, one does not hunt in order to kill; on the contrary one kills in order to have hunted."

Most nonhunters don't understand the spiritual dimensions of hunting because most hunting literature focuses on "stalk, kill, and jubilation," argued the late Sarkis Atamian, a psychology and sociology professor who wrote *The Bears of Manley: Adventures of an Alaskan Trophy Hunter in Search of the Ultimate Symbol*. It was better to describe the awe, the mystery of the wilderness, the sense of spirituality that all good hunters experience, he believed. "Killing is not the goal," he wrote. "It is only the means by which he can attain a symbol of paramount importance in his life—his search for the meaning of life." Coincidentally, the meaning of life was best symbolized by the largest animals. "If the trophy does not go above the average, it is hardly a trophy, is it?"

Avoiding cruelty is one of the hunter's main objectives, Atamian explained. Yet his own grizzly hunt was one long chain of bad decisions that prolonged the animal's death. His fear that political pressure would soon end all grizzly hunting prompted a risky 300-yard shot that merely wounded the bear. When he and his guide caught up with the fleeing animal, the guide shot it again. The bear whirled, lunging at its own wounds, and then moved toward the men. "Since my boyhood and throughout the years in Alaska, this had been my dream—the charging grizzly," Atamian wrote. Alas, the bear foiled him by turning away, and Atamian shot it in the hump. Unbelievably, the bear struggled to its feet. "Never had I seen any animal take it so tenaciously, courageously, so defiantly," Atamian wrote. "Yes, he was magnificent, and the way he looked at me, I swear he was begging me to give him back his life or hasten the end." Another bullet, and the struggle ended with another bear ennobled through death. After all, everything dies, Atamian mused after shooting a polar bear herded toward him by an airplane: "It was the manner of dying that mattered."

Atamian does a fine job of explaining his internal reactions (gratitude, humility, awe, spirituality) as well as his external motives (the outdoors, excellent trophies). What's missing is some recognition of a bear's existence as more than a conduit for satisfying his own dreams, reflecting on life and death, discovering his own character. For him, bears operated only as symbols—rewarding for Atamian, not so much for the bears.

Many hunters and guides describe bears as animals that merit a good death from a person worthy in spirit and character. In *All about Bears*, guide Don DeHart described a client who arrived drunk and stayed drunk until he was done dousing his liver with a case of scotch. The hungover hunter wounded a brown bear with an impulsive 300-yard shot but felt too ill to follow it. The bear died before DeHart found it. "I felt sorry for the noble Old Kodiak to be killed by a lucky shot by a drunk like Joe," DeHart wrote. "In my opinion this type of hunter did not deserve such a trophy. . . . My sympathy is all with the bear with this kind of sportsman."

As a packer for famous Kodiak guides Bill Pinnell and Morris Talifson, Marvin Clark once encountered a client who was too impatient to appreciate hunting's true spirit. "Even with as little knowledge as I had about bear hunting at the time, I felt that his attitude was a bit degrading to the manor-born animal he wanted to kill," Clark wrote. "Seemingly Pierre wanted to plunk a quarter into a soda-pop machine to get his trophy rather than patiently hunt. For such a magnificent animal, this seemed like an appalling, even shameful hunt."

Dick Petersen told his clients it was a privilege and a rare experience to kill a bear, a species that has occupied this landscape since the

Pleistocene. "I think, like a lot of old brown bear guides, there comes a point when you feel like, this insurance salesman—from wherever he's from—doesn't deserve to kill this big beautiful carnivore," he said. "All of a sudden at some point, you're not sure the sacrifice is worth it. [There's] the money, the freedom, the seeing the place—and all of a sudden you feel whorish." Still, nobody has ever been denied a hunting license or cheated from a trophy simply because he had an undeserving character.

The true hunt requires certain qualities to achieve authenticity, Ortega y Gasset believed. These include "the harsh confrontation with the animal's fierceness, the struggle with its energetic defenses, the point of orgiastic intoxication aroused by the sight of blood, even the hint of criminal suspicion which claws the hunter's conscience." I'll leave the psychological tangle suggested by the phrase "orgiastic intoxication" to scholars intent on hashing out connections between sex and hunting. Instead, let's focus on fierceness. Ortega y Gasset does not explain whether hunting a rabbit generates the same authentic sensation as hunting a bear—I'm guessing it doesn't—but I wonder about his criteria when I read account after account, both historical and modern, in which a bear is shot while sleeping, eating fish, grazing on berries, mating, emerging from its den, or otherwise going about its business. Often the killing takes place from a distance of more than 100 yards, the length of a football field from goalpost to goalpost. One of Pinnell's clients once shot a sleeping bear that was lying next to a salmon. The guide later said he felt sorry for the bear as he turned it over. "There he had his breakfast all ready, and then man came along and messed up everything. If it had gotten up and had a chance to run or something, that would have been a lot different." Later he added, "They figure a guy, I guess, is hard-hearted when he does some of these things. But after it's over, he sometimes wonders if he's done the right thing."

Boone and Crockett Club's 26th Big Game Awards, 2004–2006 lists the biggest Alaska brown bears, grizzlies, and black bears killed using fair-chase tactics. When shot, the second-place brown bear "was lying in the brush and had no clue the two hunters were anywhere in the area." The third-place brown bear was shot within eight yards as it slept beside a gut pile. The hunter who killed the first-place grizzly tracked his spring bear through the snow (with his guide's help) to an alder thicket, where he shot the resting bear after it caught their scent and charged.

The bow hunter who killed the second-place grizzly on the Bering Sea coast was more daring because he used a barebow, which lacks sighting, aiming, or release devices and requires being near the prey. He used binoculars to search for bears from his guide's boat and then went ashore to ambush approaching animals. He wounded the first bear with a shot he was so sure was fatal that he and his guide recorded "celebration footage" on their video cameras before tracking the blood trail. The wounded animal escaped. He missed the next bear as it stood seven or eight feet away because he didn't account for the strange angle. The animal ran off. The following year his arrow struck a bear that approached within eight yards of his hiding spot. He had to wait four hours until it was light enough to track the bear's blood along the beach. Luckily, it had died just 175 yards away. With this bear, which also qualified as a Pope and Young world record, and with a brown bear he killed that fall in Southeast Alaska, he finally completed his North American Super Slam. At the time, this archery feat required killing one each of twenty-eight native big-game species, four of them bears. He'd had to borrow against his home equity to finance hunts in recent years, he told a reporter, but jazzed by his success, he planned to rehunt the eleven animals that weren't Pope and Young records.

Hunting lore cannot subsist on tales of oblivious bears shot at great distances or while sleeping, so the stories are often riddled with reminders that something bad could happen. A Wisconsin man two animals shy of a North American Super Slam found his four bear hunts fulfilling for this reason. "As far as excitement, the bears are the blood-curdling, adrenaline-high animals because they can kill you," he told a reporter. We can assume they never tried, or he would have told that story.

Some accounts suggest that hunting settles something personal between hunter and hunted. A blurb for the show Dangerous Game previewed an episode this way: "The grizzly bear is one of the world's most formidable predators and for this reason, Doug Painter travels to Alaska to even the score." Apparently, merely being a formidable predator was the bear's offense. An episode of Natural Gear's Wildlife Quest focused on host Shane Jones's second attempt to bag an Alaska Peninsula brown bear, which he described as "the ultimate Northern American carnivore; it's an animal that can turn the tables on you at any time." On day thirteen of a two-week hunt, he and his outfitter finally spotted a suitable bear and watched it kill a caribou calf. After a three-mile stalk, the pair stopped 220 yards away to avoid alerting the feeding animal. "It's sad, but this is Mother Nature, this is how it works out here," Jones said to the camera. "It's the real deal." Then he turned the tables on the bear and shot it, because that's how it works out there.

Like Sarkis Atamian, many hunters imagine themselves slaying a snarling, rushing beast. "One misconception that hunters often bring north with them, is that any brown bruin that sees, smells or hears you in the bush is necessarily going to charge," wrote Marvin Clark Jr. But as guide Bill Pinnell told him, many bears never did; they "just stood there looking at him and the hunter as if to say, 'What are you doing here? This is my territory.'" Dick Petersen described bear hunting as 80 percent glassing—searching a vast landscape from a high point and then trying to intercept a bear. "The whole danger part is overplayed," he said. "They're very timid, actually."

This isn't to say that danger doesn't exist. There are plenty of examples of bears attacking hunters who wounded them or surprised them or attracted them by dragging bloody carcasses through the wilderness. But statistics do not support the fearsome reputation of Kodiak bears, for example. They have been responsible for one death in the past seventy-five years and cause injuries about every other year, according to wildlife biologist Larry Van Daele. As a result, accounts of modern bear hunts are often prosaic affairs emphasizing numbers more than narrative thrills, such as this description of a Kodiak hunt posted on the Big Game Hunting Forums by "Txhornhunter":

> I was very fortunate to take a boar that went 10'- 0" with a 26-14/16" skull. The boar had a truly exceptional hide, very thick and chocolate brown with zero rubs. I spotted the boar courting a sow on the second day of a scheduled ten day hunt. Due to unfavorable wind direction, our stalk ended at 500 yards with the pair topping a ridge looking over their shoulder at us. On Day 3, we hiked back to the area that we thought the pair might be holding up. As sometimes luck goes, the pair came out of the brush at 1:30 pm and at 6 pm after the bears finished their nap and we closed in to 200 yards the boar took 2 shots from my 300 win mag (200 gr. noz. part.).

The end.

What about the hunter's conscience that Ortega y Gasset mentioned? After all, as Thoreau pointed out, "The squirrel that you kill in jest dies in earnest." Some hunters do express regret or at least ambivalence about a bear's death. "Somehow, my reactions always go into reverse after I have killed a large animal," wrote Brien King in a 1937 *Alaska Sportsman* article about a hunting trip. "That night I lay awake a long time wondering why I had gone to so much trouble to murder a fine animal that showed no ill will toward me. Even now there seems to be no justification for it." Nonetheless, he and his guide later killed two bears from a trio they encountered on a river. The survivor returned to sniff the corpses, gave the hunters a bewildered look, and lingered in the nearby forest, moaning and crying. "In that instant, I realized I had shot the last bear I would ever shoot, unless in self defense," King declared. Perhaps he really meant it that time.

Writer Nick Jans described a similar change of heart after killing his second grizzly. "I think that in the end, my story is that of many hunters, who as they went along, discovered that the trail of the quest—the hours and years of moving across the country, watching and listening, waiting and hoping—inevitably leads toward love," he wrote in *The Grizzly Maze*. "Or maybe a hunter one day finds the cumulative weight of souls too heavy. For me, I think it was both."

A Tlingit hunter from the village of Hoonah in Southeast Alaska estimated that he'd killed 300 to 400 brown and black bears. "We never shot a bear just to shoot 'em," he told interviewer Merry Ellefson. "There was always a reason to do it. We used all the meat for food." But, he added, "What always haunted me the most was whenever you'd made a bad shot on a bear, it would start moaning in pain and sounded exactly like a human being that had got shot." Sometimes guides weary of death, too. "I'm tired of killing bears," Dick Petersen told me. "The more you hunt brown bears, the more you do it, the harder it becomes to hunt bears."

Between them, Bill Pinnell and Morris Talifson guided more than a thousand sportsmen. That's a lot of dead bears, so it's no wonder that late in their lives they "ever more readily affirm that they really have no pleasure even in watching a charging brown bruin die." Other longtime guides feel similarly, according to Harry Dodge's history, *Kodiak Island and Its Bears*. After retiring, Bill Poland told the local paper, "I've had about enough of killing. I get so tired of seeing people kill big animals. You get turned off by the overly enthusiastic attitude of some hunters." Park Munsey, among the first to guide photographers and bear viewers, enjoyed hunting and guiding, but not killing. "If I had my preference, the hunters would take a picture of the bear when he gets up close to him and let it go at that," he said.

Sometimes people reckon with their own approaching fates. A Juneau guide once described approaching a bear that his client had paralyzed with a poor shot. Despite its grievous injury, the bear struggled to come after him. "Now I'm saying, geez, those devils, they don't give a quarter and they don't expect it," he said. "But you know, I'm getting older, and I see them and I think, 'They got a life,' and I don't want to kill 'em."

Wildlife biologist Larry Van Daele of Kodiak has probably seen more dead bears and talked to more bear hunters than anybody on the planet. He and his colleague John Crye see an average of 180 brown bears a year because successful hunters (or their guides or taxidermists) must bring the hides and skulls to the Alaska Department of Fish and Game for sealing, a process that allows biologists to measure the animals and tag the trophies as legal. "I don't run into very many people that feel remorse for killing the critter," Van Daele told me. "Once in awhile someone will say, 'Boy, I'm not going to do this again,' but for a guy to 'fess up to something like that to someone they don't know is awful tough. I can't help but think that there are more people that feel that way than want to admit to it."

Van Daele himself was a lifelong hunter when he arrived in Kodiak in 1982, excited about bear research and the opportunity to hunt one of those monster bears he'd grown up reading about. But after a few months of collaring bears and watching them in the wild, he realized he wouldn't be hunting Kodiak's bears after all. "I manage bear hunts, I have for the last twenty-some years, I deal with bear hunters every single day," he told me in his office. "In my professional life I view them as a population, but in my personal life, I could never shoot one. And I don't see why anybody else would want to." But he also understands that interest in hunting the fabled Kodiak bear sustains their conservation. Hunters have to pay for the opportunity, he said, and not many bear viewers will fork over up to $23,000 just to look at a bear.

Trophy hunting in general has far fewer supporters among Alaskans than meat hunting does, according to a 1992 survey conducted by the Alaska Department of Fish and Game. Almost 90 percent of participating Alaskans approved of hunting for food; only 23 percent regarded trophy hunting favorably, and more than half strongly disapproved of it. Even Alaskan hunters weren't that enthusiastic about trophy hunting: half approved, but 27 percent strongly disapproved. Wary of balkanizing their numbers in the face of a disapproving populace, hunters tend to speak carefully on the subject of trophy versus meat hunting. "To each his own" was the prevailing opinion during one long online discussion. Most participants said they hunted because eating wild game was part of their family's lifestyle. Only one hunter acknowledged owning trophies, and even he claimed he always ate the meat. "I consider wildlife and nature the world's highest form of art," he wrote. "Highly skilled taxidermists bring this beauty back to life in my home. Selfish? Most likely. As long as a hunter adheres to the letter of the law and conducts himself ethically, he should be able to do whatever the Hell he wants to with his animal." By the end of the conversation, the hunters had hashed out the definition of "trophy hunter" as someone who hunts only to collect mounts or who kills for the sake of killing. "All of us to a man/woman felt that utilizing the meat from our game is the only ethical thing to do and I am very happy to see that pure trophy hunting has gone the way of the dinosaur," summarized one commenter.

Note, however, that the number of trophies accepted into Boone and Crockett's award program in 2004–2006 increased by 16 percent. In Alaska a guided hunt costs $10,500 for an inland grizzly, but you'll pay double that or more for a Kodiak or an Alaska Peninsula trophy, depending on the length of the excursion, the luxuriousness of the accommodations, and the guide's reputation. Black bear hunts can be as cheap as a few thousand dollars; in predator control areas, some guides will let you kill them for free while you're hunting for other species. Add in hefty transportation costs, licenses and fees, gear, and the expense of shipping heavy hides, and you can see why Alaskans joke about the number of trophy hunters who are doctors and dentists.

No sport hunter kills a bear and walks away full-hearted and empty-handed. Collecting and displaying artifacts of the hunt can seem more ritualized than the hunt itself. It's hard to imagine a more definitive way to represent the gap between culture and nature than trophy hunting. Only human animals want proof, spoils, souvenirs, symbols, reenactments. So there will be photographs, though rarely of the animal slumped or twisted in its original death pose. Big-game hunters intuitively understand the importance of emphasizing the human's smallness against the animal's largeness. Most hunters today pose with their weapons behind or beside the three-dimensional carcass to exploit the exaggerated perspective of the foreground: *See how humble I am, and yet I slew the mighty beast.*

Bear hunters sometimes videotape their experience as if it were a reality show. They document the camp, the stalk, the shot, the death, the celebration. Some footage sold on DVD is described like a snuff film. A promoter of *Secrets of an Alaskan Master Guide* promises "tons of graphic kill footage guaranteed to delight and shock the hell out of you. See breath-taking 'over-the-shoulder' harvest shots of giant grizzlies and black bears that don't go down without a fight. . . . You'll agree that this 'whack-n-stack' footage is Spine-Tingling Stuff."

Naturally, there will be measurements. The accumulated weight of bone, fur, and flesh never fails to impress, and fortunate is the hunter who kills his bear in the fatted days of fall. Most can only estimate the animal's size in the field before they must separate the enormous carcass into parts. Hunters informally "square" hides by measuring the distance between the longest claw on the left foot and the longest claw on the right foot, and the distance from the tip of the bear's nose to the base of its tail. Adding these numbers and dividing by two determines whether a bear is an eight-footer, a nine-and-a-half-footer, or the coveted ten-footer or larger. Hunters so often misjudge a bear's size that some Alaska biologists call the skull calipers they use to collect sealing data the "truthifier."

Major hunting organizations rank record bears by adding the skull length and width to produce a score calculated to the sixteenth of an inch. Skulls must meet a minimum score to qualify for each club's record book, which, as Pope and Young explains, "provides a poignant opportunity to honor each individual outstanding big game animal, for posterity and throughout all of time." The truly ambitious can achieve eternal posterity in the Safari Club by killing a certain number of animals from categories such as "Predators of the World" or "Dangerous Game of Africa." The more species you kill, the more posterity you earn. Alaska holds the Boone and Crockett world records for grizzly, brown, and polar bears ranked by skull size (although the giant grizzly skull was plucked from the tundra). The Alaska Peninsula alone has produced about 40 percent of the top 350 Boone and Crockett brown bears, according to Fish and Game biologist Lem Butler.

Turning real brown bears into realistic-looking brown bears can cost between $3,500 and $8,500—a little extra if the mouth is open. A nice rug is only $125 to $200 per square foot. These are not just trophies but tributes to a fondly remembered moment, souvenirs of the dream. When Pete Buist looks at his bear's tanned hide on the wall, he thinks of himself sleeping in a small, damp tent with the wind blowing outside, climbing through butt-deep snow, having a great time. "I'll be honest with you," he said, "I have a lot of furry things peering down on me from the wall. I can just sit, as I often do in the living room, with no TV and no radio on, and I can see scenes from those adventures."

The story of the adventure may be the most important trophy, one worth sharing around campfires, in bars, on the Web, and in magazines and books. Anyone who thinks nonhunters or antihunters anthropomorphize bears should read some of these tales. Bears become Old Ephraim, Mr. Griz, or Madam Bear, monsters, gluttons, devils, and vermin. They are crafty, cunning, vicious, and saddled with mean dispositions, unless they are kings, monarchs, and noble lords of the wilderness. Sometimes they are shot in their boilermakers or furnaces. Sometimes they wander into a war zone. "I nailed him this morning at 1:58 am!" wrote a man who killed his bear as it stood over marshmallows and honey. "Oh yeah I used the Glock 20! Smoked him good!" For the record, plenty of hunters find such comments distasteful.

In an *Outdoor Life* piece, Alaska writer Christopher Batin described the high emotion generated when one of his bear-hunting companions saw a boar kill a cub, "just a little guy, a milk bear who didn't have a chance." The group examined the small carcass and pictured its dying agony. "We all vowed to kill the killer," Batin wrote. They waited fruitlessly for the bear to return, "stewing in an emotional soup of anger and impatience and empathy for the dead cub." Eventually, one of the group stalked and killed the enormous male (an ex-cub, by the way). After the whooping and hollering, Batin regained his emotional equilibrium. "I couldn't help but admire the cub killer for what he was: a magnificent animal acting on the instincts Nature had given him," he wrote. "And I apologized to him for initially seeing with only the eyes in my head, rather than the eyes of my soul."

An Alaska hunter provoked an online discussion about the casual conventions of describing bears by asking, "Why 'calf killer'? I mean geez, what an ignoble name for a grand beast and a fine trophy. Why not 'berry eater' or 'ground squirrel grinder' or maybe even just (heaven forbid) 'handsome grizzly bear.' This hype that bears are just 'calf killers' disrespects the animal and perpetuates an ignorant approach to an admirable big game quarry." Much joking followed about "blueberry butcher" and "mole muncher," as well as some earnest discussion about the inclination to anthropomorphize animals in the service of killing or saving them. But as ignoble as "calf killer" may sound, what trophy hunter wants to think of himself as the slayer of a blueberry grazer or a root digger? One pragmatic fellow responded, "There are many names used for bears. All of them well deserved. Mostly depends on what he was doing the day he was observed and got hisself shot. I have heard Cub Killer, Calf Killer, Moose Killer, Sheep Killer, Caribou Killer, Man Killer, Marauder, etc., the list is as endless as the number of bears killed. Don't really matter what some want to call them, as long as they get them killed."

The photographs, videos, measurements, trophy mounts, and hunting tales sometimes obscure the living being that existed before a hunter's good fortune became the bear's bad luck. Kodiak biologists try to help hunters understand that a bear is more than a trophy by making a point of saying something complimentary about every carcass they seal. "It may be the scrawniest-looking three-year-old with no hair on it, but you say, 'Boy, look at those teeth. Those are nice, they're not even worn. That's beautiful teeth,'" Van Daele said. "The bear is dead. You want to make sure the guy is proud of what he got, and he can feel good about the whole thing." This empathy has less to do with the hunter's ego than with Van Daele's desire to ensure that the bear is recognized as an individual rather than a mere object or an assortment of measurements. "You need to do something other than just disrespect the critter after it's been killed or wonder what it scores, like some high school kid in the locker room," he said.

Van Daele also encourages hunters to consider what kind of trophy they seek before they head into the field. "Is a trophy something that will go in the trophy book—like a twenty-eight-inch or better skull? If that's what you're after, hide quality doesn't matter," he said. "Or is a trophy the best of everything—a beautiful hide and a huge head? Or is a trophy just a really nice hide—something you're going to be looking at and be proud of, so the skull isn't that important? Or is a trophy just coming home with something because the wife will be pissed off that you spent all this money and didn't get anything? Or finally, is a trophy just going out there and being with this critter? Having the experience of it—and you may not shoot anything, but you have had the experience."

In the end, the bear doesn't much care what kind of trophy it is. Anyway, it's really not about the bear. It's always, always about us.

People say they hunt for many reasons: love of the outdoors, a sense of camaraderie, pride in their skills, respect for family tradition, the desire to eat natural meat taken cleanly and honestly. Some trophy hunters see their pursuit as a way to share the bear's experience. Bear guide Rod Arno, executive director of the Alaska Outdoor Council, was objecting to the practice of bear viewing when he told a reporter: "When I think of wildlife, I don't think of them in my anthropomorphic views of how they relate to my world. When I hunt, I think of relating to their world." I have always wondered how hunters relate to a bear's world through a rifle sight. Former McNeil River sanctuary manager Larry Aumiller explained it to me like this: "Hunters don't really observe bear behavior. They observe opportunities to shoot a bear."

One guide who advocated the close stalk seemed to enjoy this intimacy with the bear's world. "When you are that close you instantly develop a closer bond with that bear," he explained to his fellow hunters. "At that distance you can actually see a bear's lips as its eats berries. You can see its claws as it moves a log. You can see its eyes if it looks at you. You can see its nose moving as it tests the wind." Then he added: "And at that short distance it is hard to miss the vital area, and your big bullet is still packing near max killing potential. And you can see the bullet strike, and hear the bullet impact. Yeah, that's exciting!"

When I asked Van Daele what motivates bear hunters, he supplied two examples at opposite extremes. First, there was the multimillionaire who abandoned a spring hunt with his sons after a couple of cold, luckless days. Instead of jetting home on his private plane, he bought a camper truck in Anchorage to satisfy his curiosity about the Alaska Highway. Partway through the journey he grew bored, sold the truck, called his pilot, and flew home. "Now what is a hunt to that guy?" Van Daele asked. "It's a recreation. It's really no big deal to him." Then there was the man who asked a passel of questions about bear gallbladders. Van Daele told the man he didn't know many details. "And he very seriously said, 'Well, I need to know because my dad is dying of liver cancer and I've been told it's terminal, but I found this Chinese doctor that told me if I can find the gall of a grizzly bear, he can save my dad's life.'"

Most people fall somewhere between the bored and the desperate. Maybe they want a shortcut to feeling alive, the challenge of overcoming the terrain, the pride of status, a brush with death. Some may want to prove their manhood or their superiority, Van Daele allowed, but "I can't put that kind of judgment on them," he said. Some people are simply plunderers. The day before my visit, an embarrassed guide had brought in his client's smallish three-year-old male bear (nobody hires guides to kill small bears, after all). The guide was convinced the hunter had bad bear karma, because every bear they'd spotted had simply disappeared. Weirder still, the guide was positive the dead bear had looked twice as big alive as it was dead. In camp, the hunter reassured the guide, "Oh, it's no big deal because I've already shot four bears"— all of them from helicopters in Russia.

How many bears does a hunter need to kill? "Well, is it really a need?" Van Daele asked. "Is it just that he likes that experience? The adrenaline rush?" I wondered the same thing when I read a 2003 story in *American Hunter* by a man who had come to Alaska vowing to kill only an exceptionally big black bear, because he planned to make this trophy—his ninth—his last. "It was greed, pure and simple, with a splash of hubris," he wrote. "I want a bear as spectacular as this land and ocean where I was hunting, and equal to the grand style of the hunt." After he killed a bear big enough to represent all of Alaska, he was relieved to realize he'd miscounted. This was only his eighth bear, so he could honorably kill one more, he wrote.

Let's be honest, though. Some people just like killing animals. Two hunters once told Van Daele a long anecdote about watching a pair of young bears toy with a shank of rope they'd discovered on the beach. For a couple of hours the bears played tug-of-war, raced back and forth, swung the rope at each other. "Just a wonderful story," Van Daele said, which the hunters concluded by saying, wistfully, if only they'd had a gun with them to shoot those two bears. "You know that they were small, you know that they didn't have much of a hide, you enjoyed watching them, and you were mad because you couldn't go over and kill them?" Van Daele marveled. "How do you get that way?"

Of all the challenges facing hunters—disappearing habitat, diminished opportunities, public controversy—people who think that way may pose the most immediate threat to decent, ethical hunters and guides. "That's what will be the ultimate demise of hunting is that folks continually lose that [respect], and it plays right into the hands of the antihunters," Van Daele said. "You make nonhunters antihunters with that kind of attitude. And the trophy hunter is the one who's most in danger of doing that kind of thing. Very, very few nonhunters have a problem with people who kill something to eat it. But a lot of people have problems with killing something as majestic as a bear just to throw its flat hide on the wall and leave the meat there for the maggots and eagles to eat."

Does it matter to the bear who eats it, what killed it, how it died, or why? Some hunters think about such matters. Thoughtful people mull over what it means to be an ethical hunter on a handful of sport hunting blogs and in the scrum of chat rooms. Among scores of hunting magazines and innumerable books, there are insightful inquiries into fair-chase principles by writers such as Jim Posewitz and Ted Kerasote. Ethicists chew over whether animals have "interests" and conclude, why yes, they do have an interest in staying alive. Some hunters I know proudly abide by a personal and cultural code of ethics. Others say forthrightly that as long as they follow the law, nobody else can tell them what's ethical.

I've made much here of slob hunters, avaricious hunters, cruel hunters, regretful hunters, oblivious hunters. It's unfair to ascribe poor motives and weak character to everyone who kills a bear for sport. There's no way to detect whether individual hunters find their experiences spiritually enlarging or simply fun, and there's no law that says how they should feel. Yet it is undeniable that even the most skilled hunters sometimes fail, and as a result, animals will suffer needlessly (because there's no such thing as necessary suffering), and even a good hunter may turn away from what he's done. How fervently I want to believe that most sport hunters are every bit as ethical and skillful as they claim, that they're conscientious in their actions and conscious of their intentions. Still, wildlife managers estimate that in some rural parts of Alaska, fewer than half the bears killed by subsistence or sport hunters are reported. In Alberta, an estimated one-third of grizzly kills are illegal. On the Kenai Peninsula, biologists believe that black bear losses due to wounding are as high as 16 percent of reported kills. Read the hunting forums: decent hunters and guides chastise those who shoot at bears from their trucks and then discover they've killed a cub, those who wound bears and fail to find them, those who favor the "shoot, shovel, and shut up" school of hunting. But that doesn't make those bears any less dead.

I asked a young friend to describe her experience bear hunting to help me understand. She wrote me a long and eloquent e-mail, although she asked me not to use her real name because she was worried that her college friends wouldn't understand. Jessica was raised in a village on the Bering coast by a father who makes his living as a bear-hunting guide. She's a lovely and gifted person—a talented writer, photographer, and designer. By all accounts, her father is a skilled and ethical guide who has a biology background and hunts judiciously to protect the local bear population. He gave Jessica a .22 when she was ten; she killed her first caribou at eleven. She grew up around bear hunters and watched them perform the time-honored rituals of sharpening knives, cleaning hides, spreading salt, telling stories. "It was almost like a man's version of a sewing circle," she wrote. "The smell too, our garage always smelled like wild game and it's a familiar enough smell that it can carry me back 20 years to the wooden steps I'd sit on and watch . . . waiting to be asked to help in some way."

Jessica started bear hunting with her father as a teenager. She wanted a blonde bear and passed up several opportunities, waiting for the right animal. What she really loved was being outdoors as they snowmachined in the spring, boated along the coast, drifted downriver, scanned the terrain from four-wheelers on the beach. On prom day she hunted with her father and returned home an hour before the dance so her mother could fix her hair.

The spring after her freshman year in college, she went hunting with her father and a family friend one night at about 9:00 p.m., when the Alaska light is clear and golden. She recalled a calm sea dimpled by schools of herring, seals popping up and disappearing, the dorsal fin of an orca that emerged alongside their small aluminum boat as a pod fed on seals. "It was a circle of consumption and nature at work," she wrote. "It was that incredible feeling that comes when you realize you're alive in a place far removed from the securities we try to build for ourselves in modern societies." During their three-hour hunt, they saw minke whales, a beached beluga, and a dozen bears roaming the tundra.

They anchored the boat and went ashore when they spotted a blonde bear headed for the beluga carcass. They stalked the bear in a low crouch that became a crawl. "I could feel my pulse bouncing off my eardrums. The tundra was spongy beneath my hands and knees, its damp, tea-like scent reminding me how very real it all was. It's like the faster your heart beats the more time slows," Jessica remembered. When they were close enough, she fixed on the bear's silhouetted ears and steadied the heavy gun, waiting for the bear to rise. When it did, she fired behind its shoulder. The struck bear began a slow trot, and she fired again. The hunting party approached the fallen bear cautiously, in case it still lived.

"The bear was dead, though. It was all over so quickly," she wrote. Under a tangerine sun in the dimming sky, she and her father hugged several times. I've seen the large framed photograph of them and the bear; Jessie is smiling, but her father is radiant.

They didn't take the meat, because bears that have been scavenging on whale and walrus carcasses are often inedible or riddled with trichinosis and other parasites. "The grizzly was the first animal I'd killed and not eaten . . . and that didn't sit right with me from the moment I saw it lying there in a heap of shiny fur on the tundra . . . and I still feel uncomfortable with it," she wrote. She and her mother and a friend tanned the hide into a thick, honey-colored rug. "I feel connected to that bear in some ways, and I hope that doesn't sound cornball . . . but it's true," she said.

Jessica doesn't think she'll ever kill a grizzly again, other than for survival or defense. Her father doesn't quite understand. "It's just awkward because I know it disappoints him. He jokingly says I'm turning into a tree-hugger," she wrote, adding a smiley emoticon. But she would never tell others not to hunt bears, as long as the kill is legal and quick. "I've seen so many men, and some women, leave our home happy after a trip of a lifetime and a grizzly hunt they imagined for years, saved money for, and set aside some time in their lives for," she wrote. She still loves being in the field with her father, and she has since hunted other animals for the freezer. What has changed is her perspective on hunting. Guns feel obtrusive, somehow separating her from the experience. Maybe bow hunting is the answer, she thinks. All she knows for sure is how much she misses the hunting life, there in her big-city college, too far away from an unpeopled landscape where a person can feel free.

"Hunting has a way of making you seek answers in the questions themselves when science and spirituality mingle so frankly in your mind. I guess it's all a work of nature, humans hunting, orcas hunting, bears hunting . . . maybe it's just part of our nature," she wrote. Jessica still thinks about the moment when she and her father were packing the hide of the bear she had killed, and two older cubs and a female (endearingly, she wrote "a mom bear") appeared above the tree line and lingered. "I sometimes wonder why they watched the way they did," she wrote. "Maybe they had bear-conversation and talked about us, about the killing of this bear, about the things humans do to nature. I told myself they probably waited until we left and then came to the carcass to feed. My dad said that was likely what happened . . . nothing in nature goes to waste." But secretly she wonders if her unsettled feeling about her bear's death will spread to other bears, somehow, "and so I worry that . . . I don't even want to write what I'm thinking, but I think it every time I sleep in a tent or at the river cabin." That is an old and familiar human response, too.

After reading Jessica's candid and insightful account, I could see that she understood the Game. For her, the episode felt like a rite of passage. These days, the community that celebrates such journeys into mystery continues to dwindle. Some Alaska Native hunters feel a similar loss. Modern hunting laws require them to do things that make the proper treatment of living and dead bears impossible. To a Native hunter, wrote anthropologist Tom Thornton, buying licenses, permits, and tags is tantamount to shouting his intentions aloud to bears that will never appear. Christianity and Western science have helped erode vital beliefs, leaving young people with the sense that they should treat bears with respect but with little specific knowledge about how to conduct themselves. Researchers interviewing Alaska Peninsula villagers about the subsistence use of brown bears talked with several people who were worried about the disappearance of elders and therefore of traditional knowledge. One young man said others his age sometimes mocked dead bears or bragged about killing them. "They don't care what happens to the bear after it's dead," he said. "I don't know how come but I guess times are changing. But me and my brothers still do the things to the animals that we were taught to do. I don't see no other way. I know we got to respect the animals."

In all of human history, the number of people who have never hunted far outstrips those who have. Perhaps we've moved too far beyond the time in our history when killing animals could make us human in the ways Shepard and Ortega y Gasset described, so that now the act seems empty, a self-indulgent gesture. Maybe, as Matt Cartmill argued so beautifully in his book A View to Death in the Morning, "We should recognize it as an origin myth, dreamt up to justify the dubious distinction we draw between the human domain and the wild kingdom of nature." Yes, humans eat meat, and a few of us even kill our own. But truthfully, no person who deliberately kills a bear in this world does it because his survival depends on eating that bear. He does it for reasons conjured to suit his own purposes, whether he knows what they are or not.

What Edward Harriman did with the mother and cub he had traveled so far to kill is not clear. Perhaps their pelts weren't fine enough for a rug or a mount. Maybe he just lost interest once they were dead. Eventually, the bear skulls joined the hollow-eyed ranks of former living animals in the National Museum of Natural History. Today, stripped of narrative, they are known simply as specimen 98062, the mother of

98138, two bears killed on Kodiak Island on the third day of July in 1899 and collected by C. Hart Merriam.

When I think of Harriman and his metaphorical bears, I imagine that trembling moment when the hunter hears his own heart pounding, before the gun leaps or the bow thrums, before the bear bites at its flank or bawls in pain or runs as its blood rains upon the earth or falls dead. I wonder if what the hunter wants most of all is to make himself as large in this world as the bear is—yes, even larger—and whether that yearning is so blinding that he really can't see the bear at all. And once he does the killing, it's too late, because all he will ever see is himself posing beside a blank spot in the world where a bear used to be.

the disappearing ice bear

The three polar bears swam ashore at sunset, rising from a cold red sea with such fluid grace that it seemed as if water itself had taken form. My mind had translated the black wedge of their muzzles cutting through the channel into something familiar, like ducks. But these were sea bears, creatures that dwell in oppositions: land and ocean, flesh and ice, light and dark.

The mother and her yearlings shuffled single file along the gravel beach, mirrored by the still pane of water. She swung her head sinuously to sniff the air as they neared the dismantled hulks of three bowhead whales. Villagers from the small Inupiat community of Kaktovik on Barter Island haul the remains of each fall's whale hunt to the "bone pile" on a spit not quite two miles from the outskirts of town. The bear family bypassed curved jawbones picked clean long ago and headed for a massive black wedge of whale surrounded by slabs of ribs and jaws still bloody with shredded meat. They ignored a few trucks parked a couple of hundred feet away as they gnawed and tore at hunks of flesh. One by one, several bears swam the half mile from the narrow barrier island of Bernard Spit and joined them.

As the light failed, the bears glowed briefly in the headlights of arriving vehicles as they climbed the broken scaffolding of the great ribs and jaws to tug at the remains like cats plundering a leftover Thanksgiving turkey. The raw smell of meat rolled in with the chill September air whenever I cracked the window of the old blue pickup I'd rented for $150 a day from the proprietor of the quirky lodgings known as Waldo Arms. Occasionally I started the engine to run the heater and make sure the truck still worked. The innkeeper's partner had warned me about foundering in soft sand or puncturing a tire on the rusty military junk littering the gravel. "You don't want to be out there working on the truck . . . ," she said, pausing, and I finished her sentence mentally: " . . . if a polar bear comes by."

Earlier that day, as a few hundred gulls and I loitered at the spit, villagers had occasionally driven out to see if anything interesting was happening. One van carried several hopeful sightseers who had arrived in Kaktovik on the same flight I'd taken from Fairbanks. Like me, they hadn't realized that the polar bears mostly spend their days resting on Bernard Spit, where a white shape occasionally shimmered like a mirage on the distant shore. As many as fifty-six bears had been counted recently, but these visitors left the island late that afternoon without a single bear photograph to show for their $800 airfare from Fairbanks.

Kaktovik was becoming known as one of very few places in North America where people could count on seeing polar bears gathered so near a settlement. These fall gatherings of bears were a fairly recent phenomenon along the Beaufort Sea coast, and they had attracted the attention of wildlife biologists, too. One of the idling trucks held Tom Evans and Jonathan Snyder from the US Fish and Wildlife Service (USFWS), the agency in charge of managing polar bears, sea otters, and walrus. This was the last field season in a three-year study of these bears and another smaller group that scavenged bowhead carcasses on Cross Island, a small barrier island about 103 miles west where subsistence whalers from Nuiqsut based their hunts. The agency was gathering information that could help buffer bears from the effects of oil and gas development and other human activities on the Arctic coast.

The biologists worked in three-hour sessions scheduled around dawn, day, dusk, and night, compiling data on population demographics and behavior. Every fifteen or thirty minutes they scanned the area and noted the age and sex of all bears present, including those visible on Bernard Spit. To gather focal sampling data, they randomly picked a bear and recorded its actions for twenty minutes, noting whether it was sitting, feeding, playing, interacting with other bears, swimming, or defecating. My version of focal sampling was less thorough: I watched a roly-poly yearling tossing a flap of whale meat in the air again and again, a flotilla of polar bears submarining their way across the channel, a cub licking its mother's bloodied face after she'd filled her belly.

For the wildlife biologists, studying polar bears from pickup trucks was a departure from usual field methods. Most bears inhabit the empire of ice year-round or make only brief forays onto land, a notable exception being the bears of Canada's Hudson Bay. A polar bear's life is mostly one long locomotion through a habitat that is itself adrift. Generally, researchers are an aerial bunch, buzzing in helicopters and airplanes above vast arctic plains to locate bears that can walk as much as 3,800 miles in a year.

"So much is about capturing the animal or implementing them with this or that, or seeing them from an airplane, when some of them are disturbed and they're running away," USFWS wildlife biologist Susanne Miller had told me back in Anchorage. The hours Miller had logged watching polar bears at Cross Island and Barter Island were the highlight of her career, she said. "It just makes you know the animal," she explained. "It's not just a dot on the landscape. It makes you see how they interact with each other and how they work out their problems and how they coexist and how dangerous they are. What ticks them off and what doesn't. It's like the difference between going to the mall and seeing a sea of strangers, or coming into this building and not knowing anyone, versus spending the time to talk to an individual and saying, 'Oh, well, that's what it means to be a Fish and Wildlife Service employee.'"

After lurking for a few days at the bone pile, I couldn't claim to understand what it means to be a polar bear (or a Fish and Wildlife employee, or a Kaktovik resident), but I was forced to recalibrate many hazy notions. The noble monarch traversing prairies of ice in solitary splendor was nowhere in sight. Instead, a temporary society of bears had assembled peaceably at the end of a dirt road in an Inupiat village of fewer than 300 residents. Black streaks smeared their dingy pelts as they grubbed through the oily, bloody residue of whales. Big males fed alongside subadults and mothers with cubs, a tolerance that surprised the researchers, because adult males can easily displace other bears from prime feeding sites on the ice. I wasn't skilled enough to observe and interpret whatever behavioral signals the animals employed to negotiate the terms of their shared meals. Mostly, it seemed they wanted to eat, rest, maybe play a little.

For a dedicated carnivore that regularly appears on lists of the Top Ten Deadliest Animals ("A smack from one of their paws can rip your head clean off," exclaims one website), these polar bears were awfully uninterested in those of us watching them. Most interactions with people came from curious subadults and cubs, the researchers later found. Still, it was hard not to feel a bit like a canned ham when a bear casually padded around the truck's rear bumper and past my window, especially after Tom Evans mentioned that vehicles offer a false sense of security.

"I mean, a polar bear could get into a car just like that," he said, perhaps a bit too enthusiastically. "It would have no problem pushing in any window, and it could rip a door off." Yet most of the time, he added, they don't care about people. His advice was to honk the horn or turn on the engine if an inquisitive bear approached.

These polar bears weren't loafing by day and gorging at night because they prefer rotting whale meat and life in the suburbs (relatively speaking). Bears are pagophilic, that is, ice loving. That's another way of saying they can't survive without ice. They hunt their primary food, seals, from the platform that ice provides. They travel on ice, find their mates on ice, and sometimes build maternity dens and birth their cubs on ice—and not just any ice, either. Most southern Beaufort Sea bears spend their time out on the pack ice where ringed seals live, above the shallow waters and richer biome of the continental shelf. The ice canopy is not a static pane but a shifting ruckus of floes and slabs jostled around by wind and sea currents. Bears lurk at breathing holes and prowl beside canals and pools of open water, trying to snatch unwary seals. In spring they search on land-fast ice for seal pups tucked inside lairs like meals ready to eat.

As the ice cover melts and shrinks through summer, bears enter a hungry season. They can stay with the drift pack as it retreats north into regions where seals and other food are scarce, or they can strike out for shore where perhaps they can scavenge washed-up carcasses. Sometimes this choice means swimming great distances between the edge of the pack ice and the edge of the continent. For bears stranded onshore until the ice returns in winter, the whalers' practice of hauling the meaty remains of bowhead whales away from settlements is providential.

Usually the ice cover shrinks to its minimum extent in September, before the freeze-up begins and the ice starts expanding again. In the 1980s, at minimum extent, the ice edge lay only 30 to 50 miles from Alaska's coast. When I visited during the third week of September two decades later, the pack hovered some 125 miles from Kaktovik in what proved to be the third consecutive year of extreme summer melting. Several years would pass and more sea ice records would collapse before scientists could more clearly yoke a warming climate to dwindling ice and its effect on the survival of hungry polar bears in the Beaufort Sea.

Watching bears at the bone pile was mesmerizing, but sometimes I felt as if I were witnessing something as fantastical and melancholy as the last unicorn. Polar bears inhabit a realm that seems two parts wilderness and one part imagination—a place untouchable and far from the ordinary, anyway. This is mere fancy, of course. Not even the northernmost provinces of the globe lie beyond the reach of explorers and icebreakers, commercial whalers and hide hunters, radiation and soot, chemical pollutants and greenhouse gases. Meanwhile, as the Arctic changed all around us, we visitors, villagers, and researchers sat in our idling vehicles and watched faintly luminous bears stripping the dark and bloody ruins of whales as if we were at a drive-in theater.

The presence of so many polar bears on land was one more strangeness in a place where nobody argues that the climate isn't changing. Rafts of statistics, charts, and graphs tell the story one way. The period from 2005 to 2010 was the warmest on record since measurements began in 1880, according to the Arctic Monitoring and Assessment Programme. The increase in the Arctic's annual average temperature is double that of anywhere else, and the North has experienced a multitude of effects sooner and more dramatically. People who live here tell the story in other ways. Ice breakup comes earlier and freeze-up later. Thawing permafrost—permanently frozen ground that's not so frozen anymore—causes the earth to slump and shorelines to collapse. Villagers no longer rely on underground ice cellars to chill their food. Tundra yields to advancing white spruce and deciduous trees. Robins, blue jays, salmon, humpback whales, beaver, and other rarities appear in places where they've never lived before. Gray whales overwinter rather than migrate to southerly waters. Walrus by the tens of thousands haul out on Alaskan and Russian coasts in the fall, stranded as the Chukchi Sea ice they need as a foraging platform recedes far beyond their feeding grounds. Worsening storms chew off great hunks of coastline, imperiling villagers who are desperate to move before the sea swallows their homes. In hundreds of ways, life in the North is irrevocably changing, say the people who best know this land, ocean, and ice.

The disappearance of arctic sea ice inevitably makes the local global, as science confirms what the Inupiat and other circumpolar inhabitants have been noticing for years. In 1979 satellites began crisscrossing the planet's crown like the shuttle of a loom, accumulating data with every pass. Today, when scientists stand back to scrutinize the big picture, this is what they see: the Arctic is losing ice each summer, lots of ice, and far more quickly than the best climate models predicted. "The current reduction in Arctic ice cover started in the late 19th century, consistent with the rapidly warming climate, and became very pronounced over the last three decades," according to researcher Leonid Polyak and his colleagues. "This ice loss appears to be unmatched over at least the last few thousand years and unexplainable by any of the known natural variabilities." What distinguishes current melting is the magnitude, distribution, and abruptness of these changes, they noted.

Arctic sea ice is a dynamic, three-dimensional jigsaw puzzle constantly reconfigured by the complex interplay among currents, wind, temperature, atmospheric pressure, water vapor, weather, seasons, and more. From year to year, the extent and volume of sea ice fluctuate naturally as the ice cover waxes and wanes with the seasons, explains Julienne Stroeve of the National Snow and Ice Data Center. A canopy of stable, multiyear ice caps the polar basin and remains throughout the year. As freeze-up progresses through the winter, the ice cover reaches its maximum extent in March, before dwindling to its minimum in September.

The ice extent has been declining for decades, but the rate of decline accelerated sharply after 2002. One factor is the albedo effect. Snow and ice reflect sunlight, but the darkness of open water absorbs solar radiation. Before freeze-up, the sea unloads heat into the atmosphere. In an elegantly destructive feedback loop, the warmer air leads to more melting, which creates a bigger expanse of open water, which soaks up and releases more heat, and so on. "The major point is that with rising air temperatures in all seasons, prospects for the ice to substantially recover have dimmed," Stroeve and her colleagues noted in 2012.

The quality of ice is diminishing too, as multiyear ice continues to thin. Patterns of atmospheric pressure have flushed massive amounts of thick ice into the Atlantic Ocean. It is replaced by new, thin ice that is more vulnerable to melting. Less than 2 percent of the ice cover in 2011 was older than six years, compared with 20 percent in 1988, according to a 2011 report on the cryosphere. "The reduction of the age and amount of old sea ice may be one of the most fundamental changes in the Arctic Ocean," wrote the report's authors.

In 2012 scientists reported the greatest seasonal loss of ice ever documented during the satellite era. Between March and September, 4.57 million square miles of ice disappeared. Ice cloaked half as much area as it did between 1979 and 2000 on average. More significantly, the volume was 72 percent below the mean, the Polar Science Center reported. That same year, eighty polar bears swarmed Kaktovik's bone pile one day in

September, surpassing the 2004 high of sixty-five bears. Whether or not there's a direct connection between the loss of summer ice and the number of polar bears onshore, it was impossible to look at photographs of bears lolling on the tundra without seeing their presence as evidence that we're in big, big trouble.

The fate of ice algae and arctic cod is worth fretting about too, but it's the polar bear that grabs our attention and animates the abstractions of graphs and statistics. "Polar bears are the original beauty and the beast all in one," commented Canadian expert Andrew Derocher in his book *Polar Bears.* As the most charming and imposing representatives of a disrupted ecosystem, ice bears provide a sympathetic focus for our worries. And we should worry. In 1993 Derocher and his former professor, Ian Stirling, published the first paper to consider what might lie ahead for polar bears in a changing climate. The abstract began: "If climatic warming occurs. . . ." By 2004, when they published a new overview titled "Polar Bears in a Warming Climate," there was no longer any "if." They concluded that declining ice will trigger cascading effects on denning, bear movements, and the availability of prey—the future of polar bears, really. "All ursids show behavioral plasticity," they wrote, "but given the rapid pace of ecological change in the Arctic, the [bears'] long generation time, and the highly specialised nature of polar bears, it is unlikely that polar bears will survive as a species if the sea ice disappears completely as has been predicted by some."

I asked Derocher about the eerie prescience of their 1993 paper, when the terms *global warming* and *climate change* had hardly penetrated the public discourse. "I thought that climate change was going to be something for the next generation of biologists," he said. "It's become such an all-consuming component of what I do. I had not predicted that. I thought we were talking about a long time ahead. Now most of the research is setting up monitoring points with the idea that we can actually document the demise of a species." He calls it an unnatural history of polar bears, but it's really our unnatural history unfolding before our eyes.

Not many bears made landfall along the Beaufort coast until the late 1990s. Observers surveying bowhead whales from the air spotted most bears offshore near Barrow between 1979 and 1987. Just 12 percent of sightings occurred on land or in open water, according to federal biologists Jeffrey Gleason and Karyn Rode. The situation had flipped by

1997–2005, when 90 percent of September sightings occurred on barrier islands just offshore, on the mainland, or in open water near Kaktovik. Changing ice conditions probably prompted this eastward habitat shift, the researchers wrote.

An increasing proportion of bears could come ashore for even longer periods if sea ice losses continue, suggested now-retired USFWS biologist Scott Schliebe and his colleagues. This could lead to more encounters with people. They estimated that between 4 and 8 percent of the region's 1,500 polar bears roamed the Beaufort Sea coast during September and October in 2000–2005. The farther away the sea ice, the higher the density of bears on land. Most were counted within several miles of Kaktovik, probably attracted by the bone pile and quicker access to ringed seal habitat after shore-fast ice forms. Researchers are now comparing the movements and body conditions of bears that head for shore with those that remain with the ice.

On land or at sea, polar bears are maybe two or three generations from inhabiting mostly zoos. "Because Polar Bears depend on sea-ice habitat that literally 'melts' as temperatures warm, there is an unambiguous relationship between [greenhouse gases], temperature, habitat availability, and persistence of the species," wrote Steven Amstrup, former US Geological Survey (USGS) project leader for polar bear research. If greenhouse gas emissions aren't reduced, "we simply will become Polar Bear historians," he warned.

What often confuses people is that despite gloomy predictions and plaintive photographs of polar bears, not every subpopulation is in trouble—yet. People who believe that climate change is bunk often claim that there are more polar bears than ever—which is true only because hunting bans, international treaties, and intensive conservation measures halted severe overharvesting decades ago. Five countries manage the world's estimated population of 20,000 to 25,000 polar bears: the United States, Canada, Russia, Greenland/Denmark, and Norway. These bears are loosely grouped by location and habitat into nineteen subpopulations identified by the Polar Bear Specialist Group of the International Union for Conservation of Nature. The United States manages two subpopulations: the southern Beaufort Sea stock extends east into Canada and overlaps the Chukchi/Bering Sea bears to the west, a population shared with Russia. Little is known about this second group, so scientists are focusing more attention on those bears to better estimate their numbers and understand their movements.

In 2009 the Polar Bear Specialist Group reviewed everything that is known and agreed that at least eight subpopulations are declining, three are stable, a recovering population in M'Clintock Channel is increasing, and too little is known about seven groups to even hazard a guess. They classify the entire species as "vulnerable." If you divide polar bear habitat into four sea ice ecoregions, as USGS scientists did, then it's easier to see how disappearing habitat affects subpopulations in similar regions and how this loss of habitat will likely progress throughout their range.

At the southern limits, Hudson Bay bears and other subpopulations occupy the Seasonal Ice Ecoregion. If polar bears are the planet's canary in the coal mine, then these bears are the canary's canary. Seasonal ice retreat forces bears ashore in western Hudson Bay for four or five months—even longer for pregnant females—where they burn their own body fat awaiting the ice's return. The warming Arctic increased this endurance test by three weeks on average over thirty years. Between 1987 and 2004, declining body conditions and survival rates led to a 22 percent drop in the population, reported Eric Regehr and coauthors. (The Polar Bear Specialist Group disagrees with the government of Nunavut's claim that this population is doing well.)

Now Alaska's subpopulations may have joined the canary choir. They inhabit the Polar Basin Divergent Ecoregion, where retreating summer ice now carries bears far beyond prime ringed seal habitat. Climate projections predicting the loss of ice—and therefore bear habitat—convinced the US Department of the Interior to list polar bears as threatened in 2008 under the Endangered Species Act. "Future reduction of sea ice in the Arctic could result in a loss of 2/3 of the world's polar bear population within 50 years," the agency concluded, based on nine studies produced by the USGS team. Bears that have less time to hunt seals in summer and fall may not enter winter with enough fat to carry them through. Scientists have since linked longer ice-free periods to declines in adult female survival, breeding rates, and cub litter survival in the southern Beaufort Sea subpopulation. Other studies have reported smaller bears, fewer cubs living to become yearlings, more females denning on land, and a higher proportion of bears fasting.

That sounds a bit abstract until you read some of the specific situations researchers have encountered, including bears clawing through thick slabs of rafted ice in pursuit of ringed seals and radio-collared bears starving to death. Several episodes of cannibalism elicited this response from Amstrup, Stirling, and their coauthors: "During 24 years of research on polar bears in the southern Beaufort Sea region of northern Alaska and 34 years in northwestern Canada, we have not seen other incidents of polar bears stalking, killing, and eating other polar bears." Occasional incidents of infanticide and cannibalism have long been reported, but the timing and number of recent episodes suggest the animals were motivated by hunger, Stirling told a newspaper in 2009.

Such problems will be delayed for bears living in the more northerly Polar Basin Convergent Ecoregion, where ice conditions should provide regular access to seals for a longer period. And the northernmost bears living in Greenland and the islands of the Canadian High Arctic occupy what Amstrup and colleagues described as the "last stronghold," the Archipelago Ecoregion. Even so, geography won't protect them forever if greenhouse gases continue to drive climate change.

Predicting what's likely to happen is easier than pinning down when it will happen. Researchers Stirling and Derocher reviewed the evidence in a 2012 paper focused on southern Beaufort Sea and western Hudson Bay polar bear populations, the best researched groups. "If the climate continues to warm, and eliminate sea ice, polar bears will likely disappear from the southern portions of their range within 30–40 years," they concluded. Save for that sliver of stronghold in the polar basin, arctic summers could be ice free by the late 2020s, according to projections generated by the most reliable climate models. Especially disturbing, however, is that these climate models used the minimum ice extent in 2007 as a baseline, a record that was crushed in 2012. And even the best simulations lag behind actual losses of sea ice observed by scientists, Inupiat, and polar bears, for that matter.

Given all this bad news, it's no wonder some people think all we can do is shrug and accept the inevitable. "The perception that nothing can be done to avoid catastrophic losses and ultimate disappearance of polar bears was exemplified in 2007 when the general media proclaimed polar bears were irreversibly doomed," wrote Amstrup and associates. Amstrup led the USGS team that gathered information for the Endangered Species Act decision in 2008, became the chief scientist for Polar Bears International after he retired, and won the 2012 Indianapolis Prize for extraordinary contributions to animal conservation. He and his colleagues wondered what would happen if we could slow or stop temperature increases. Their model didn't find a critical temperature that triggers a catastrophic point of no return. Instead, it showed that we can control rising temperatures and preserve sea ice habitat if we reduce greenhouse gas emissions—and soon.

Even then, bears in the two southernmost ecoregions would face a hefty risk of local extinction. Still, cutting emissions would improve the probability that more polar bears would persist longer throughout their habitat, Amstrup's group reported. If we control harvests, limit human interactions, and protect them from oil and gas development, they said, the bears may do even better. That's a cheering scenario, tempered by the fact that during the 2012 presidential election, the topic of climate change was conspicuous by its absence. During economic gloom, it seemed, the last thing people wanted to discuss was the planet's future.

Ice bears are especially vulnerable to changes in their habitat because they are so exquisitely shaped by the Arctic. They are the biggest bears on the planet, outsized only by extinct giants. Mature females typically weigh 350 to 550 pounds; males tip the scales at around 900 to 1,300 pounds, although they can top 1,400 pounds. Try to imagine standing beside a polite polar bear on all fours that's taller than five feet at the shoulder (his, not yours). Some Alaska bears too large to be weighed by helicopters may have topped 1,700 pounds, Amstrup noted in an overview of their life history. A Kotzebue Sound trophy displayed at the 1962 World's Fair weighed 2,210 pounds, according to *Outdoor Life* magazine.

Those great furred paws are platters that can float bears over thin ice or scull them across leads and bays. Short claws provide grip, and tiny papillae and suction-like dents on the soles create friction. Even their pads can grow winter fur, which probably provides better traction. Glands in their paws may deposit scents that help bears find each other during breeding season. The pelt so coveted by lovers and kings is an ideal buffer from arctic conditions. Water-repellent guard hairs layer thick, warm underfur, all of it sprouting from black skin that sheaths blubber four inches thick or more. True northerners know that snow and ice are not always white, and neither are polar bears. Their unpigmented hair easily stains to an ivory or yellowish hue, though an annual molt in late spring through summer refurbishes pelts to a pleasing whiteness.

Radio-collaring, tracking, and recapturing bears has eliminated the stirring notion of polar bears as "the cosmopolitan arctic citizen randomly visiting any or all of the polar countries at will through its lifetime," wrote Ian Stirling. Instead of circulating with the grand drift of ice like one herd of giant carnivores, they've eddied out into subpopulations adapted to the geographic and ecological nuances of each region. Bears don't defend territories, but they do exhibit seasonal fidelity, the tendency to return to the same area in the same season. Sometimes they work hard to do so. In the Beaufort Sea, where the ice pack revolves in a clockwise movement known as the Beaufort Gyre, bears compensate for this rotation like kids trotting in place on a merry-go-round.

How far a bear travels in search of food or mates or dens depends on the movement of ice, the availability of food, and the individual animal. A typical female bear in the Beaufort Sea might trek through an annual activity area of about 58,000 square miles, but not all bears are typical. Scientists monitored one bear that roamed an area measuring about 230,000 square miles in a year. Others, says Amstrup, are "homebodies," sticking to smaller areas when everything they need is right there. It's hard to demonstrate whether males' and females' ranges differ, because the shape of the male head—like a traffic cone, Tom Evans told me—rules out radio collars. However, one study of a small number of males didn't reveal significant differences.

The bear's life history is bound to that of ringed seals, the most common and widespread of arctic seals and so dependent on ice that they have joined polar bears on the list of threatened species. Adults are gray with black spots, usually no more than five feet long and somewhere between 110 and 150 pounds. In winter through early summer they prefer stable ice over the continental shelf, where they can haul out to pup, rest, and molt. Unlike other seals, ringed seals scrape open three or four breathing holes in hard ice with their clawed flippers, sometimes maintaining these openings through canopies six feet thick. They also excavate snow dens to rear their pups and take shelter from predators or extreme weather. "There's been a sort of evolutionary war going on between polar bears and ringed seals, where polar bears try every way they can to become more effective hunters of ringed seals, and ringed seals meanwhile are trying not to be polar bear food," Amstrup explained to a group of zookeepers.

Seals basking or molting on the ice are an antsy bunch, constantly raising their heads to scan for predators. Seals that are rarely targeted by bears haven't developed the same wariness. In *Polar Bears*, Stirling described watching many bears stalking seals from his observation post on a rock bluff on Canada's Devon Island. A bear that spots a seal's dark shape in the distance shifts into a slow-motion stealth, with head lowered, before exploding into a charge to beat the seal to its breathing hole. In summer some bears dive beneath the water, surfacing for quiet gulps of air until they can burst onto the ice beside a seal. Others flatten themselves in channels of water running across the ice and slide themselves along with their paws, periodically raising their heads barely enough to check their progress. Still-hunting requires tremendous patience as they lie, sit, or stand beside leads or breathing holes for long, silent minutes—sometimes hours—waiting for an unsuspecting seal to surface so they can yank it from the water with their mouths.

Their sensitive noses also lead them to breathing holes and seal lairs, often from miles away. Their massive forearms jackhammer through the surface, their bullet-shaped heads slide easily into lairs, their enormous canines grasp a wriggling seal firmly and unzip its skin. Newly weaned ringed seals are vulnerable because they're naïve, and their inexperience, combined with 40 to 50 percent body fat, makes them ideal prey. Even a 450-pound polar bear has a minimum daily requirement of about 4.5 pounds of blubber, so bears usually strip the fat layer between skin and muscle, which caches more than half of a seal's caloric bounty. In good times, bears ignore the metabolically inefficient meat, which requires water to digest. Burning fat releases water and spares bears the energy required to warm snow into water. Several studies suggest that the polar bears' regimen of feasting and fasting has fine-tuned their metabolism so they can downshift into a hibernation-like mode when resources are scarce. "This ability could make polar bears the most advanced of all mammals when it comes to dealing with food and water deprivation," Amstrup wrote.

Polar bears are metabolic geniuses in other ways. They mate from March to June, but delayed implantation prevents fetuses from developing until fall. Unlike brown and black bears, which hibernate largely because food is scarce, only pregnant polar bears retire to dens as a way of protecting their tiny, undeveloped cubs until they're ready for the world. Meanwhile, they don't eat, drink, urinate, or defecate for months. Throughout the North, most bears denning ashore settle within several miles of the coast. Hudson Bay bears move to traditional areas anywhere from eighteen to seventy-three miles inland.

Until recently, more than half the collared Beaufort Sea females denned on pack ice, which can whisk a bear several hundred miles from where she started, according to Amstrup. But as the sea ice continues to shrink, trekking from the summer ice pack to shore in the fall could require a journey of 900 miles or more, based on USGS projections, much of it across large expanses of open water. Expending so much energy could mean thinner bears, poorer reproductive success, further population declines. Meanwhile, warming conditions will likely make onshore dens more vulnerable to melting snow or rain; researchers have found one such den that collapsed and killed its three occupants.

Though the chronology varies among regions, females typically give birth in January to blind, lightly haired cubs that, at 1.5 pounds, are Lilliputians to their maternal Gullivers. ("Like a big white rat" is the unflattering description provided by Polar Bears International.) Milk with 31 percent fat ensures that when cubs emerge in March or April, they'll be 22 to 26 pounds of pure adorableness. Mothers usually produce twins, but singletons are common and triplets are possible. A typical female produces only five litters in her lifetime; this slow rate of reproduction is one reason their future is so tenuous. In the past, cubs born in the Beaufort Sea had survival rates of 65 percent from the time they left the den through their first year, and yearlings did even better. One concern now is how young bears will cope with the longer distances they and their mothers will need to travel, especially if food is scarce.

Bears can locomote terrific distances when they want to. In 1992 a female bear traversed the polar basin between Prudhoe Bay, Alaska, and northern Greenland in a four-month plod that swung within two degrees of the North Pole. Satellite telemetry revealed that she traveled almost 3,300 miles in the year after she was collared—despite having denned for four months. Tourists aboard the Russian icebreaker Yamal in August 2001 were surprised to see a polar bear padding across the ice just 13 nautical miles from the geographic North Pole. At the time, this was thought to be the northernmost sighting of a polar bear; they rarely wander above 82 degrees north.

Bears are strong swimmers, too. One radio-collared bear clocked almost 50 miles in a twenty-four-hour swim between Spitsbergen and another island in 2005. Widening gaps between ice and land in summer have raised questions about how far they can or will paddle, though. A long way, reported a 2012 study by USGS researcher Anthony Pagano and others. Twenty female bears outfitted with GPS collars made fifty swims longer than 30 miles in the Chukchi and southern Beaufort Seas between 2004 and 2009. The mean distance was 96 miles, but one bear swam 426 miles in about nine days. It's impossible to say whether bears have always taken such long swims, but they haven't needed to until recently, a USGS news release explained. While the physical costs of such efforts aren't known, the data suggest the bears didn't stop to rest or eat. Researchers recaptured ten of twelve bears originally accompanied by yearlings or new cubs and found that six had kept their offspring, although there was no way to tell when or why the others lost their cubs.

The epic journey of the bear with the longest recorded swim suggests that some will make extraordinary efforts to reach sea ice. Researchers captured and collared bear 20741 on August 23, 2008, not far from Barrow. The satellite record indicates that she swam north for nine days through open water and hauled out on ice. In subsequent days she swam for brief periods, rested, and walked across 878 miles of ice. When captured again on October 26 near the Canadian border, she'd lost her yearling cub and 22 percent of her mass. "Their ability to engage in long-distance swimming may help polar bears in a future of reduced Arctic sea ice," the researchers stated. "The high energetic and reproductive costs experienced by polar bear 20741, however, highlight the potential risks associated with long-distance swimming."

Drowning comes to mind, thanks to widely publicized reports that four bears swimming through open water apparently succumbed to heavy seas near Kaktovik in September 2004. Anecdotal evidence suggest that long swims do exact a price. Four bears that swam 70 miles from the pack ice to Barrow in 2004 arrived so exhausted that a mother and cub rested for hours on the beach before they could continue, the local paper reported. Another slept for two days behind the Naval Arctic Research Laboratory.

Sometimes polar bears take walkabouts on land. One traveled more than 100 miles south along Alaska's Dalton Highway in 2002, startling truckers, chasing musk oxen, and feeding on a caribou carcass during its two-week trek, a hint that its journey may have been related to that year's distant sea ice and hunger. The USFWS called this the longest inland journey by a polar bear ever documented—until 2008, when a young polar bear was shot eating lynx carcasses at the dump in Fort Yukon, an Athabascan Indian village 250 miles south of the Beaufort Sea. Inupiaq hunters from Bering Sea communities have reported seeing polar bears traveling overland along creek drainages near Shishmaref between April and June, or moving 20 miles inland near Kivalina to raid fish caches and eat moose or caribou carcasses. In 2008 three polar bears appeared 45 miles inland near Noorvik. One that was found eating trash in town was killed. A polar bear excited residents of Emmonak in 2010 when it appeared a dozen miles above the mouth of the Yukon River in Southwest Alaska. Many of the 800 villagers watched the bear floating in the river from their boats before it disappeared into the brush. Tom Evans of the US Fish and Wildlife Service told reporters that polar bears stranded onshore by retreating Bering Sea ice appear every three to five years near the Yukon-Kuskokwim Delta.

Despite such occasional forays on land, the biggest concern for bears is how they will survive when the changing ice conditions also profoundly affect the ringed seal population. Ringed seals accounted for more than half of all prey consumed by bears across the Canadian Arctic in a study by Gregory Thiemann and colleagues. When ringed seals aren't available, polar bears eat bearded, harp, hooded, and harbor seals, as well as beluga whales and narwhals. Beaufort Sea bears may be more vulnerable than bears elsewhere because their diet is the least diverse, consisting mostly of ringed seals, with some beluga and bearded seal meat for variety.

To eat whales, bears still need a platform of ice to kill them, just as they do for seals. In 1999 a Canadian researcher tracking polar bears discovered more than two dozen bears surrounding seventy-five belugas and a bowhead whale in an ice opening known as a sassat—rather like diners ogling the lobsters in a restaurant aquarium. Many of the whales were injured or dead. From a helicopter, Canadian biologists once spotted eight polar bears in the midst of five dead belugas and four narwhals, two of which had been dragged several hundred feet from the water and remained alive despite being stripped of blubber. They also saw a male polar bear hauling a beluga calf from the open ocean onto an ice floe. The bear had previously killed another calf, which a female and her cub were feeding on nearby.

Given their dazzling life history, polar bears don't need the burnish of legend and myth to seem interesting. But some ideas persist, making it hard to sieve fact from fable. Oral and written accounts have described polar bears as left-handed animals that hide their black noses while hunting to avoid detection and sometimes hurl rocks and ice blocks at their prey. Scientists say there's no evidence for left-handedness, but many Inupiat know perfectly well that polar bears prefer to strike with their left paws. "When polar bears are hunting seals, they cover their nose with their right hand and have their left hand ready to kill a seal," a Shishmaref elder explained in a subsistence study. Wainwright hunters advised anthropologist Richard Nelson that moving to the right of a charging bear improves one's chances of dodging a blow. Watching the particular genius of arctic hunters convinced Nelson that if a bear ever charged him, he would do the same. (Brown bears are more skilled with their sinistral paws, too, say villagers in Northwest and Southeast Alaska.)

Wainwright hunters also reported that polar bears conceal their noses with a paw or tongue, behavior reportedly observed by Danish explorer Peter Freuchen as well. Stirling has heard stories of such trickery from Native hunters who have never witnessed it personally. "All I can say is that in several thousand hours of watching polar bears hunt, none of us has ever seen a polar bear cover its nose," Stirling noted. "If it does happen, it certainly is not very common." One Inupiaq hunter told Nelson that he had watched a bear grasp a piece of ice, stand upright, and throw it at a group of walrus to isolate a young one. (It didn't work, he said.) Perhaps temper tantrums are the source of the bear's alleged dexterity with ice, Stirling speculated, citing another researcher's experience of seeing a bear furiously tossing ice around after it had flubbed an attack on a seal. Having watched annoyed bears whack at snow, cubs, and oil drums, Stirling doubts only the frequency of such fits.

The hard gaze of Western science may never prove whether bears are southpaws, ice tossers, or nose hiders, but it has dismantled the misconception that polar bears are living solar panels. This idea began with scientists trying to explain why polar bear fur doesn't absorb ultraviolet light. They hypothesized that the hollow, transparent hairs conduct radiation to the bear's black skin, helping it stay warm. The possibility that polar bear hair acts like a fiber-optic cable spread to the popular press, including a *Washington Post* story that reported, "The bears' white fur may be the most efficient solar collector there is." Finally, physics professor Daniel Koon hauled this long-standing assertion into the lab and emerged with data showing that very little light enters or travels the length of the hair. Instead, he reported, the keratin that forms the unpigmented hair likely absorbs light—though not enough to make any thermal difference. So much for the subspecies of bear he named *Ursus fiberopticus*.

When the future of polar bears comes up in public conversations, someone usually insists that the bears will adapt to their circumstances by moving to land and learning to graze on berries, catch birds, hunt musk oxen, harvest eggs, eat fish, and develop other creative diet strategies. It's true that polar bears have sometimes been seen eating novel foods such as crabs, clams, old-squaw ducks, goose eggs, and seaweed. Researchers and others have occasionally witnessed polar bears chasing and sometimes killing musk oxen and reindeer. But what people are suggesting, basically, is that carnivorous polar bears will suddenly turn into omnivorous grizzly bears—even though arctic grizzlies are among the smallest and least populous of their kind because food is so limited in the North.

Experts valiantly try to correct such misconceptions. "Polar bears are large animals and they got that way by eating seals, not berries," Stirling and Derocher wrote in 2007. Bears maintain their size with fat, and lots of it, which is why they specialize in eating what Amstrup calls "giant fat pills." Stirling and another researcher once estimated that, on average, it takes forty-five ringed seals or their equivalent to sustain a polar bear for a year. To survive as a vegetarian, it would need to eat about a third of its body weight in berries each day, estimated ursine nutrition expert Charles Robbins—that's 330 pounds of blueberries for a 1,000-pound animal (not to mention, where would all these hypothetical berries grow year-round?). Physiologically, polar bears simply are not built to thrive on land. Their thermoregulation systems can't sustain the serious chase necessary to run down an ungulate. Nor can they adapt or evolve quickly enough to survive radical changes to their habitat.

And, scientists point out, the terrestrial ursine niche is already occupied by the eminently successful grizzly bear—a species perfectly capable of bossing around polar bears, as they proved in Kaktovik. I witnessed that myself when a grizzly and her two yearlings appeared at the bone pile one evening. She was much smaller than the five polar bears feeding on the whales, but when she sauntered along the beach, every polar bear abandoned the carcasses. One, it must be said, ran away like a little girl and leaped into the ocean. After about ten minutes, the white bears edged back to the buffet. Later the grizzly chased off a female and her cubs. The scene reminded me of something that had occurred at the Alaska Zoo: a polar bear and a brown bear had been raised together as orphans but had to be separated as five-year-olds when Oreo the brown bear attacked Ahpun the polar bear.

At least a dozen different grizzlies scavenged the bone pile in 2004. Eight grizzlies and twenty-four polar bears feasted during one three-hour period, the USFWS reported. Only four or five grizzlies appeared in subsequent falls, but it's not a trend that's appreciated by either the villagers or the polar bears. Usually U. arctos ousted all but the biggest of U. maritimus through sheer attitude, until eventually everyone settled into some amicable arrangement. Overall, grizzlies triggered aggressive encounters in Kaktovik more often than polar bears did, most often with each other, the USFWS researchers reported. (Predictably, news that grizzlies were shouldering aside polar bears incited raging online debates among the "sharks vs. bears vs. alligators vs. lions" crowd.)

Some interspecies encounters are obviously friendlier, given reports of grizzly–polar bear hybrids spotted or shot in recent years. Until grizzlies started ranging farther north, geographic rather than genetic distance prevented successful pairings, except in zoos. Then an Idaho man who paid $45,000 to hunt polar bears in the Northwest Territories in 2006 killed the first confirmed wild hybrid, an animal with the creamy fur of its mother and the brown patches, long claws, dish face, and hump of its grizzly father. An Inuvialuit hunter on Victoria Island shot a bear whose DNA identified its mother as a grizzly-polar hybrid and its father as a grizzly, making it perhaps the first wild second-generation hybrid recorded, according to the province's Department of Environment and Natural Resources. In 2012 two Northwest Territories biologists spotted a hybrid traveling with a grizzly in Viscount Melville Sound, and they suspected they had photographed another hybrid. Hunters on Victoria Island also killed a polar bear with two hybrid cubs that spring. The way things are going, Boone and Crockett will need to invent a new trophy category. Nobody seems to have settled on either pizzly or grolar bear for a name, but we'd better hurry. (Try nanulak, suggested Canadian wildlife officials, who merged the Inuit bear names nanuk and aklak.)

Research that pegged the divergence of polar bears from the brown bear lineage to between 111,000 and 166,000 years ago excited people who were eager to believe that polar bears had adapted speedily to survive a warm period known as the Eemian, so obviously they could do so again. Then a research team that used more accurate nuclear genome sequencing dated this separation to between 4 million and 5 million years ago, suggesting a much slower adaptation by an animal that may have been quite different from today's U. maritimus. The researchers also deciphered the population's response to past climate fluctuations based on genetic evidence. Polar bears apparently thrived in the chilly Early Pleistocene and diminished in warmer periods, when some may have toughed it out in High Arctic refugia. The population has been declining for the past 500,000 years, however. "We also found, perhaps unsurprisingly, that polar bears occur in much smaller numbers today than during prehistory," senior author Charlotte Lindqvist commented in a press release. "They have indeed lost a lot of their past genetic diversity, and because of this, they are very likely more sensitive to climate change threats today."

Past performance is no guarantee of future results, scientists note. Even if a few bears managed to survive at the tippy-top of the globe, what would they eat? The future isn't too promising for ice seals, either. Derocher points out that killer whales moving into arctic waters already pose major competition as fellow carnivores. Nor did ancient polar bears have to contend with organic pollutants, hunters, oil drilling, or the ship traffic now pulsing through open channels. Well, who wouldn't wish for some solution easier than changing the way we live? Carting polar bears to Antarctica sounds simple compared to limiting greenhouse gas emissions, as long as nobody minds inflicting hungry bears on defenseless penguins. I once heard a caller to a late-night talk show ask why we can't provide Styrofoam floes for polar bears. Apparently, that's a suggestion Steven Amstrup frequently receives. The Arctic lost an expanse of sea ice thirty-five times larger than Indiana in 2012, he told a *Christian Science Monitor* reporter. "How much Styrofoam can we make?"

Around the world, at least 650 species and counting have responded in some major way to environmental shifts. "The direct impacts of anthropogenic climate change have been documented on every continent, in every ocean, and in most major taxonomic groups," concluded biologist Camille Parmesan in 2006 after reviewing hundreds of long-term or substantial studies. Some species responded by shifting to colder waters, higher elevations, more northerly climes. Some adapted by breeding earlier or by becoming more tolerant of temperature changes. Some species disappeared. In the past few decades, two-thirds of harlequin frog species have vanished from the cloud forests of Central and South America.

Yet a polar bear, not a harlequin frog, made the cover of *Time* magazine's special report on global warming in April 2006. The poignant photograph shows a lone bear sailing a floe the size of a dining table. (This is not an unusual way for polar bears to travel, according to Derocher.) The polar bear, the magazine wrote, is "one of those iconic animals that almost everyone agrees the world would be far poorer without." The word *icon* is now officially iconic with regard to polar bears. US Congressman Jay Inslee called them a "beloved American icon" at risk from global warming. "Polar Bear: Arctic Icon at Risk," announced the Environmental Defense Fund. A Facebook page named "People for the Protection of Drowning Polar Bears" begins, "Unfortunately, polar bears are fast becoming an icon of global warming." But icons aren't at risk. Real bears are.

Why fixate on the polar bear and not the frog? Perhaps because the polar bear makes such big tracks through Western cultural history. Few people have seen a wild polar bear, yet they roam freely through our imaginations. They speak in scores of children's books, gaze from calendars and desktop computers, snuggle babies in cribs. They frolic through animated movies, play the comic foil in live-action adventure flicks, illustrate nature's wonder and cruelty in a hundred documentaries. A mysterious polar bear improbably menaced tropical castaways in the cult TV series *Lost*.

The animal's size, its fierce grace, its mastery over a harsh landscape, its very whiteness fascinated early explorers and traders, who usually likened them to what was already familiar. Norsemen called them the "white sea deer" and the "sailor of the floe," but nineteenth-century whalers saw the farmer in its plodding steps. Lapps avoided speaking their real name and instead referred to "God's dog" and the "old man in the fur cloak." Scientists couldn't make up their minds, mixing Greek and Latin to experiment with the genus *Thalarctos*, "sea bear of the North." In 1971 they returned to the original *Ursus maritimus.*

A curious tension between discovery and destruction attended those early encounters. Perhaps it was too hard to reconcile an animal the color of goodness and purity with its role as the greatest predator in a place that could so easily kill the naïve and the unwary. Cruelty competed with pity, admiration battled fear. When the Dutch navigator William Barents and his sailors saw their first white bear in 1594, their immediate response was to shoot it, follow it in a rowboat as it swam away, and then lasso the creature, thinking to catch and display it as a "strange wonder" in Holland, wrote officer Gerrit De Veer. But, he added, "she used such force, that they were glad that they were rid of her, and contented themselves with her skin only, for she made such a noyse, and stroue [strove] in such sort, that it was admirable."

Engraver Thomas Bewick gave the polar bear a shyly doggish aspect in his eighteenth-century work *A General History of the Quadrupeds*. He even remarked on their affection for their young, which was "so great that they embrace their cubs to the last, and bemoan them with the most piteous cries." Perhaps he drew from an account published about the otherwise undistinguished 1773 arctic expedition of Captain John Phipps, who bestowed the name *Ursus maritimus* on the sea bear. His crewmen entertained themselves by tossing walrus meat to a polar bear and her nearly grown cubs. The chronicler of this episode marveled first at how she carried bits of walrus to each cub before returning for another share, and then at the touching way she tried to rouse them after the sailors "leveled their muskets at the cubbs and shot them dead." They killed her when she returned, moaning and crying, to lick the cubs' wounds.

Piteous cries notwithstanding, arctic explorers and whalers often shot every bear they saw, sometimes killing mothers to capture their cubs. This is how polar bears came to live in such bizarre settings over the centuries, usually as status symbols for the powerful and wealthy. A white bear was said to be among Alexandria's many wonders in the third century BC, although some academics suspect it was actually an albino brown bear. But those were definitely polar bears romping in a Roman emperor's pool, in the first king of Prussia's hunting arena, and in the maharaja's personal zoo in Mysore, India. Holy Roman Emperor Frederick II traded a polar bear for a Cairo giraffe. This vigorous market in bears dead and alive helped advance the cartography of Greenland and the eastern Canadian archipelago in the Middle Ages. Even priests coveted the thick pelts to drape on altars and pulpits and around their cold feet. Long before oil, the Arctic's wealth was counted in narwhals, gyrfalcons, and polar bears.

Such a debased treasure, though. King Henry III muzzled and chained his white bear in the Tower Menagerie, along with his other living jewels. Two polar bear cubs presented to King James in 1609 became slightly favored residents of the infamous Bear Garden, where the public enjoyed the bloody baiting spectacles between hounds and bears. James could not resist an act of royal one-upsmanship with the special envoy from Spain: he turned "a white bear into the Thames where the dogs baited him swimming, which was the best sport of all." Almost all the garden's bears were killed in 1656 after several attacks on spectators. "One white cub was spared, saved by its youth and rare color, and the association with innocence," wrote literary scholar Barbara Ravelhofer.

In an era fraught with environmental anxieties, youth and innocence made the polar bear cub named Knut a modern pop star after he was rejected by his mother at the Berlin Zoo in 2006. Photographs and videos swarmed the Internet showing him being brushed, bottle-fed, cuddled, tickled, weighed, dandled, and put to bed with stuffed animals. About 400 journalists attended his public introduction, and for a time, 10,000 people a day visited his exhibit. No wonder the zoo registered him as a trademark. "Knutmania" celebrated him in songs, a book, and a film and on a weekly television show, posters, magazine covers, a commemorative coin, and a special stamp. People needed no help making an emotional connection between Knut and a barrage of sobering headlines about the threat of climate change. "Its soooo cute and its horrible to think that in 15 years polar bears could not exist anymore," wrote someone who attached an obligatory sad-face emoticon to her comment.

Knut drowned in 2011 when he pitched into his pool after suffering a seizure caused by encephalitis. Mourning fans protested plans to stuff him for display. They wanted to remember him as he was—a symbol not just for bears or even for the Arctic, but for doing something about climate change. Anything.

The deepest, truest relationship between people and polar bears exists among the indigenous cultures of the circumpolar north. Traditional knowledge of the behavior and life history of polar bears developed through generations of experience in an environment that demands sophisticated survival strategies from people and bears alike. Grounding this practical knowledge was a worldview that understood how *inua*— the indwelling spirit—infused everything, even rocks, snow, wind. People whose existence depended on eating mostly animals understood the importance of *ella*, a concept that anthropologist Anne Fienup-Riordan explained as an "awareness" of animals. This awareness requires reciprocity and respect, which are expressed through cultural beliefs, bear ceremonialism, and rituals.

Some of these beliefs and practices are particular to Alaska's Inupiat and Siberian Yup'ik people, or even to certain villages, and some reflect a broader understanding shared among circumpolar peoples. A common theme is a regard for bears as a special kind of animal similar to people, a creature helpful as well as threatening, according to research gathered by the Alaska Nanuuq Commission: "This paradox appears to characterize some ambivalence in Eskimo tales, mythology, and other cultural expressions about Nanuq." (Different spellings of the traditional name for polar bears appear in writings and storytellings, although *nanuq* is most common, according to the report.) The written record, however, is filtered through Western eyes and seems thin compared with centuries of knowledge transmitted by an oral culture.

In northern societies the *nanuq* inhabited domains that were natural and supernatural, practical and spiritual. A bear's carcass could be parceled into meat, fur, and tools to help a person survive the Arctic. Its fat burned better than seal and walrus oil. Durable bones became the iron of the North for implements such as needles, picks, and scrapers. Even ribs could make a set of armor. A hunter clad in bearskin pants could kneel on the ice more comfortably and patiently while waiting by a seal hole, as a bear does. The luxurious expanse of a hide padded boats or tents. A bit of fur used to swipe water across sled runners helped form a frozen, slick surface. Polar bear fur is still used for hoods, overmitts, and mukluks and in crafts. The polar bear can heal, too. Contemporary Uqqurmiut elders from South Baffin Island recall using one or two drops of melted fat from around the bear's stomach as an earache cure. Massaging boiled bear oil on the shoulders like Vapo-Rub is good for colds. Russia's Chukotka natives consider fat a good remedy for chilblains and use it as a protective facial cream in the coldest weather.

Bears walked in many forms in the stories from that distant time, when ten-legged bears and other fantastic creatures livened up the world and animals conversed with one another and with people. The boundary between person and animal was not so rigid then. Arctic adventurer Knud Rasmussen learned about this relationship from an Iglulik shaman named Aua, who told him, "Men and the beasts are much alike. And so it was our fathers believed that men could be animals for a time, then men again." How useful this must have been, to know the world as a bear by swimming through that cold, dark ocean or padding for miles across the ice without wearying.

Navigating this complicated cosmos required amulets, songs, taboos, and shamans to intercede with the supernatural, assisted by one or more helping spirits. These spirits might be a ball of fire, an ogress, a deceased relative, or an animal, but many people considered bears in human form the most powerful spirits—creatures so potent that they could fly shamans to the moon, to the bottom of lakes, across the countryside, to the underworld, and to the world beyond. These ideas have reached across a thousand years from ancient Dorset to contemporary artists, who still think and dream their carvings into flying bears, flying men, men flying on bears, bears flying on narwhals—all of them crossing time and space together.

Bears living in this world taught hunters such tactics as camouflaging themselves in white parkas and learning the art of stalking and stillness. "The fact that Eskimos and polar bears use almost identical methods for hunting seals atop the ice, and to some extent, at breathing holes is more than a coincidence," observed ethnographer Richard Nelson, who spent a winter with hunters from Wainwright. Before snowmachines and firearms, Inupiaq people wielded lances and hunted on foot or with dog teams. Sometimes they delivered death by means of frozen balls of fat that released coils of sharp whale baleen as the bear digested the bait. One great hunter named Takumik knifed a bear as it stood on its hind legs, Nelson reported.

Knowing where and how to kill bears meant understanding the animal's physiology as well as its behavior. For example, bears that have just emerged from water are virtually impervious to bullets, hunters told Nelson, because ammunition hardly penetrates wet fur. (An experienced non-Native hunter on the Alaska Peninsula once wrote that high-speed bullets striking a wet brown bear usually explode on impact, ringing as if they'd hit metal and rarely killing the bear.) Killing bears also meant understanding how to behave before the hunt and after death so as to convey respect and ensure future kills.

Bears offered a different kind of livelihood when trophy hunting created its own economy in communities such as Kotzebue, Teller, Point Hope, and Barrow. Inupiaq men who worked as guides earned between $500 and $2,000, and women fleshed hides for $25 or more apiece. Selling or bartering hides was also legal then. The late Harry Brower Sr., a highly respected whaling captain and elder in Barrow, killed his first of many bears at age fifteen, but he also felt great affection for them. When he was younger he reared a pair of orphaned polar bear cubs, bottle-feeding them with Carnation milk, napping with them on the tundra, playing with them, leaving them in the house when he went to school. "That's how come the polar bears don't like to eat me," he told oral historian Karen Brewster. Once Brower gave the cubs a mouse to play with; they never harmed it. At three, they were too big to keep and traveled by boat to a San Francisco zoo. "And that was the end of those two cubs," he said. "I missed them a lot."

Sport hunting became a critical conservation issue in Alaska when non-Native hunters began using airplanes to find bears in the 1950s and 1960s. Typically, pilots flew in tandem, using two ski-equipped Super Cubs, during March and April. One plane carrying the hunter followed bear tracks until the animal came into sight. After landing, the hunter "stalked" the bear. "If an ordinary stalk is impossible, it is commonly reported to us that the cover plane will herd or attempt to herd the bear back within range of the hunter," reported Alaskan wildlife managers. The annual harvest quickly escalated. In the 1967–1968 season, two-thirds of the 351 bears killed were taken by sport hunters—most by plane, and most by nonresidents.

The Marine Mammal Protection Act of 1972 banned sport hunting for polar bears in Alaska, but it left intact the hunting rights of coastal Native Alaskans who used bears for subsistence or to make handicrafts, as long as they were not wasteful. The USFWS now comanages subsistence hunting with the Alaska Nanuuq Commission, the Inupiat-Inuvialuit Game Commission, and the US-Russia Joint Commission. The commercial sale of hides remains illegal in Alaska, but it occasionally occurs. In 2006 a Barrow man was convicted of mailing a polar bear hide to an undercover federal agent who had paid $2,500.

Today, polar bears are not deliberately hunted by Inupiat so much as shot when the opportunity arises, usually while whaling or hunting seals and walrus, said Charlie Johnson, a founder and executive director of the Alaska Nanuuq Commission (Johnson died in 2012). The Alaska harvest of thirty-four bears in 2009–2010 was the lowest since the first reliable records in 1980–1981, according to the USFWS. "Our taking of polar bears has diminished for several reasons," Johnson told me. "One, the old hunters are dying off and the young people aren't taking up the hunt. Secondly, alternative clothing, like from Eddie Bauer's, is available. And thirdly, and probably most importantly, it's the lack of ice. The loss of habitat."

The Alaska Nanuuq Commission represents fifteen Alaskan villages in treaties and agreements with counterparts in Russia and Canada. The 2011 agreement with Canada's Inuvialuit Game Council reduced the annual quota for the southern Beaufort population to thirty-five bears from Alaska and thirty-five from Canada. "That quota, which is voluntary, has never been exceeded, so it's a very well-run, well-thought-out document that's been very successful," said Johnson in his Nome office. Russia recently lifted a 1956 hunting ban, based on the premise that allowing sustainable subsistence harvests would help curb poaching. The US-Russia Joint Commission agreed that Natives in Alaska and Chukotka would share an annual harvest of fifty-eight polar bears from the Bering and Chukchi Seas.

The Alaska Nanuuq Commission also gathers traditional knowledge, collects biological samples, develops research projects, and conducts workshops in villages to encourage people to submit harvest information and avoid hunting females and cubs. "Although cubs are much more tasty," Johnson noted with a smile.

For Alaska Natives, hunting, fishing, and gathering are not merely ways to fill the belly or sell crafts; they mean kinship, purpose, and heritage—everything that makes the Inupiat and other cultures the "real people." At the turn of the twenty-first century, 63 percent of arctic households harvested game, and 92 percent of them "used" it. Again and again, in testimony and in conversations about climate change and oil development, coastal people referred to the ocean as their garden, the source of bowhead and beluga whales; walrus; bearded, ringed, and spotted seals; and occasionally polar bears.

"'Is it Fat?' is a commonly asked question by 'polar bear eaters,' when one is brought back to town," reported a study on land use in Shishmaref. "Polar bear paws are a special delicacy." A transplanted Bostonian who moved to Point Hope in 1980 described the taste in his blog: "The most delicious meat I have ever tasted in all my life has been polar bear meat. It is jet black, grainy like an old piece of gnarled wood but it is so sweet and tender, better than the best prime rib I have ever eaten. It was the only time I have ever asked for seconds and everyone all at once said NO!"

A polar bear's true value can't be measured exclusively in meals or cash, though. For Native people, subsistence is a human right, explained Barrow community leader Ronald Brower Sr. at a science conference in 1978. "We don't separate ourselves as a species from our food chain since we are on the top bracket of the predator/prey system of hunting," he said. After the ban on trophy hunting, he noted, more polar bears entered communities, offering cultural and artistic inspiration as well as an additional source of food. "We consider the polar bear to be one of our more fantastic wild creatures of the sea," he said. "The bear, especially the polar bear, is important in the area of religion in the Arctic regions. It has developed its own cult; it's a secret society, a cult which is not openly expressed and has [led] to different forms of traditional cultural relationships."

Indigenous scholars have been documenting and preserving polar bear songs and dances from the original village on King Island, or Uki-vok, an isolated rock forty miles from the Seward Peninsula. Villagers migrated to the mainland in the 1960s in a forced relocation, but they've resisted cultural erosion through a renaissance in art, language, history, dance, and song. Ethnomusicologist Maria Williams helped King Island culture bearers organize the project. She wrote that the islanders regard their polar bear songs as their "most sacred repertoire." The songs, which describe what took place between hunter and bear, are composed for village gatherings hosted by the successful hunter. Killing the bear becomes a gesture made on behalf of the community. In Shishmaref, dances still honor young hunters, Charlie Johnson said. "The dancer's experience is a return, not to another time, but to places in one's self," suggested Paul Shepard in The Others. "Dancing the animal transports the dancer toward what animals have not forgotten."

I felt as if I had stepped into a different world of knowing when Perry Matumeak beckoned me inside the artisans' workshop at Barrow's Inu-piat Heritage Center. He brought me a stool so I could sit and watch as he etched scenes on glossy black disks cut from slabs of bowhead whale baleen. Other men labored at their own projects in the large room. When I asked if polar bears had been hanging around town re-cently, Perry described looking out his window one day to see a large white figure pacing across the distant tundra. "Polar bears—they're so pretty," he said. "They're just like horses. They're beautiful, beautiful animals. Their beauty makes people forget how dangerous the polar bear can be." He didn't like shooting them, though. "I let others do the killing."

On the engraving I bought, Perry had etched a sun radiating long, thin rays above a tableau of three figures: a man in a parka wields a spear taller than he is, readying it and himself for what might come as a big polar bear steps forward, seemingly without threat; a husky stands be-tween them. This moment before confrontation seems almost peaceful. Perhaps the bear will run away. But probably not.

It's a romantic souvenir, intended for tourists like me. Yet somehow, through a few artful lines, Perry has given his scene motion and dimen-sion, invoking the tension and inevitability that, before long, may never happen again between human and polar bear. Dancing the animal, drawing the animal, eating the animal—all are ways of recalling what it was like to be the animal, from that fluid time when bears and people understood each other, flew with each other, became each other.

One morning in Kaktovik I peered at Bernard Spit through the telescope in the dining room at Waldo Arms. At least twenty polar bears were visible on the flat barrier island. A few wandered about, but most lazed on the ground like a pack of bored dogs. Behind me a helicopter pilot and a filmmaker argued about definitions of wilderness and the consequences of oil drilling. The pilot insisted that since only wealthy people and elitists could visit the Arctic National Wildlife Refuge, which encompasses Kaktovik and Barter Island, preserving it from development was silly. The filmmaker had recently spent a year in the refuge. Humans need wilderness, he said passionately, almost angrily. The pilot remarked to a man reading a magazine, "You're awful quiet." The reader said, "That's because I've heard all the arguments on both sides before."

I tuned out the debate when I realized that three people were walking around on Bernard Spit. The nearest bears edged away slowly, but a single bear ambled toward the visitors—perhaps a guide and tourists, a local told me later. When the trio stopped and formed a tight group, the bear veered away. A pair of yearlings crept closer before bolting. Then, after retreating a few yards, they paused and turned back. Their mother joined them, and shoulder to shoulder the bears walked with swaying heads toward the people. One man waved his arms and then seemed to pound the ground with a stick. The bears halted. Moments later a puff of smoke drifted between the two groups, and the bears half-trotted away. Had he tossed a noisemaker or a rock?

A message scrolling regularly on the local cable channel warned, "Beware of the Polar Bears! Do not leave children unattended outdoors. Store meat products properly. These bears are extremely dangerous. Thank you from the North Slope Borough Wildlife Department." Villagers had recently killed four bears that ventured into town even before the whalers brought in the bowheads, a resident told me: "one big old bear getting into stuff, and a sow and cubs that shouldn't have been shot." Apparently, a pair of teenagers had killed the two-and-a-half-year-old cubs and were skinning them when the mother approached, and they killed her too. The filmmaker had recorded some of the scene. "It was bad," was all he would say.

One year, whalers dragged bowhead carcasses to the dump on the village's south side, drawing brown bears north from the coastal plain. But hauling bones to the spit didn't always prevent polar bears from wandering into town either. Just after dawn one foggy morning, I was driving toward the bone pile when I saw a bear and her two spring cubs top a gravel rise and walk along the beach. Their heads moved constantly as they smelled the air and the ground. They walked over to the blue cook shack where the community gathers to butcher whales, and the female stood on her hind legs to peer into an empty metal Dumpster. Alluring cooking smells, meat left to freeze in entryways, children playing outside—these were everyday situations that people had to consider when an average of twenty-five polar bears a day visited the island in September.

"The first year I saw some crazy stuff, with kids on four-wheelers approaching bears to within twenty feet, throwing rocks at them, stuff like that," wildlife biologist Susanne Miller told me. "I thought, 'Aggh, we've got to do something here, we've got to put up some signs or get the community council to write up a brochure or put up a poster or get some guidance.'" The villagers didn't care for these ideas. "They were like, 'Hey, we've been living up here with these bears for a long time safely, we really don't need anyone telling us what we can do and cannot do, so back off.' And I did." What did work was a mother who gave her kids hell for throwing rocks at bears. "That's better," Miller said. "That's them managing themselves."

Sensitive researchers have learned to run their ideas by Native communities, explain what they hope to accomplish, and incorporate community ideas. Miller and her colleagues have worked especially hard to communicate with villagers about research and management projects. After residents objected, for example, USFWS scientists ditched a proposal to mark bears with paint so they could track individuals and their feeding habits. Tagging, marking, anesthetizing, or otherwise tampering with bears is often regarded by Native people as disrespectful or even dangerous to the bears; they also worried that the paint would taint the meat and destroy hides.

Not every Inupiat community shares the same ideas about how to handle polar bears, said Geoff Carroll, a state wildlife biologist who has lived in Barrow for nearly four decades. He's studied everything from bowhead whales to caribou to a vole that someone brought to his office during our conversation. "They have a real casual attitude in Kaktovik," he said. "People here [in Barrow] are more afraid of them [polar bears] and more reactive—they're more likely to shoot them." Partly that's because aggregations are less common in Barrow.

However, Carroll said, the town was nearly overrun with polar bears in 1992, after whalers were allowed to resume fall hunting. They butchered the whales on the community's beachfront, "blowing good whale smells out for a hundred miles," Carroll said. In the past, whale remains had been returned to the sea (often resulting in their redistribution along the shore) or dumped at the landfill. Then villagers moved butchering outside of town and hauled the carcasses to Point Barrow, about twelve miles from the community. Local tour guides began driving visitors out there to look for any of the half dozen bears that might be hanging around. I had once seen a bear there myself, but it loped away as soon as it heard our vehicle, presenting the rapidly shrinking view of the south end of a northbound polar bear.

An aggregation of almost sixty polar bears appeared at the Point Barrow bone pile in 2002 (later reports tallied eighty to a hundred animals). "They behaved surprisingly well," Carroll said. Nobody was quite sure why they had come, because they didn't appear unhealthy or hungry. When bears started drifting into town—some residents believed tour groups were pushing them away from the bone pile—the borough reinstituted patrols to haze bears from town and shot an aging 1,100-pound bear that had violated a "three strikes and you're out" policy. More recently, the North Slope Borough and USGS set up barbed wire around the Barrow bone pile to collect hair samples for DNA analysis. Preliminary results showed that ninety-seven different bears visited the carcasses between October 2010 and late May 2011, according to Jason Herreman of the borough's wildlife department.

Such gatherings have yet to cause any maulings in Alaska, which are extremely rare and usually involve starving animals. (There have been recent maulings and fatalities in Canada, Svalbard, and Russia, however.) Pete Sovalik, an animal caretaker for twenty years at the Naval Arctic Research Laboratory, once told an interviewer that bears feared people and normally wouldn't even bother dogs unless they were hungry. "Only [when] they hungry they try to get something to eat—they don't care what it is," he said. Chukotka sea hunters in Siberia agreed. "The polar bear is cowardly by nature," they advised interviewers. "When it meets a human and there is an opportunity, it tries to escape." A list of thirteen precautions from Chukotka elders included these two: "Do not approach a feeding, hungry, skinny, exhausted bear" and "Do not approach an ill, skinny, and hungry polar bear."

Starvation was responsible for the only recent fatality caused by a polar bear in Alaska. In 1990 a bear attacked twenty-eight-year-old Carl Stalker fifteen yards from his door in the tiny coastal village of Point Lay. Stalker distracted the bear from his pregnant wife and fought it with an eight-inch pocketknife. She escaped, but he was nearly consumed by the time the search party located the bear on the sea ice two hours later. The necropsy revealed a bear so malnourished that it didn't even have fat surrounding its heart, usually the last place it disappears. Similarly, a 305-pound male bear with almost no fat reserves lunged through a window at the Oliktok Point Air Force Radar Station in December 1993 and badly mauled a mechanic before his coworkers returned with a shotgun. The bear had stood on its hind legs and shoved its paws against the glass. "If you've ever seen pictures of a polar bear pushing at the ice trying to dig through, that's what they said it was like," reported the station chief.

In almost 500 hours of close observation during the Kaktovik and Cross Island study, Susanne Miller said, only one bear behaved aggressively toward them: a mother bear rushed a truck after apparently being startled by an engine turning over, but she broke off her charge. Yet the Royal Geographical Society's 2003 manual on polar expeditions dispensed this advice to would-be explorers: "Polar bears are one of the world's most dangerous animals to man. They are hunters and will not distinguish between you and a seal." Like brown and black bears, polar bears usually approach people because they're curious; their success on the ice depends on investigating creatures that move and therefore could be food. This trait has often betrayed them; explorers often commented that they didn't need to hunt bears because bears would come to them.

Hunters and researchers recognize the importance of around-the-clock wariness out on the ice, though. When Geoff Carroll and his crew of three began counting bowhead whales from ice camps in 1976, they set up a wire alarm system around the perimeter. "All those years it was probably never set off by a bear but about eighty times it was set off by someone stumbling out of the tent to take a leak," he recalled. They also posted a twenty-four-hour guard in the cook tent. Carroll emphasized the importance of placing a gun in every tent and lectured the crew about knowing how each weapon worked. One night the guard felt a presence and looked up to see a bear poking its head through the door—right beside the gun. He yelled at the bear and smacked its skull with a frying pan. Carroll awoke in a stupor and left his tent in time to see the bear backpedaling from the cook tent, "pissed off at the world." The bear rushed Carroll, who fumbled with his weapon's safety ("I hadn't followed my own instructions") before giving up and swinging the rifle at the bear. This knocked the bear over but shattered the gunstock. "It was kind of a draw at that point," he said. The animal leaped up, someone else shot it, it ran off, and another shot dropped it. They donated the carcass to a family.

Wildlife managers fear that conflicts will increase as diminishing sea ice strands increasing numbers of bears on land. The USFWS trains oil-field workers to haze bears safely and has helped the North Slope Borough fund community bear patrols that use nonlethal techniques to protect people and bears from each other. The Kaktovik Polar Bear Committee erected a barrier at the bone pile and has tried to reduce attractants that might draw bears into the village; it also educates villagers about safety. In Alaska the number of polar bears killed for safety reasons (usually animals that won't leave an area) is about ten per year, up from three per year a decade ago. Under the Marine Mammal Protection Act, it is legal to kill polar bears in defense of life but not property. Bears killed by Alaska Natives for any reason count toward the annual subsistence quota.

A different sort of invasion has created other problems for Kaktovik: bear watchers. The Kaktovik Polar Bear Committee has collaborated with the USFWS to produce brochures on viewing, safety, and community facilities so that visitors know what to expect in a town with only two inns and almost no services. The committee also recruited four teenagers as youth ambassadors to give safety talks and act as community role models. The Arctic National Wildlife Refuge now requires permits for commercial polar bear viewing on refuge lands and waters around Kaktovik and holds training workshops for guides. It's a melancholy sort of ecotourism that is probably limited only by the exorbitant cost of traveling to Kaktovik. Those who come understand that they are likely among the last people who will see polar bears in the wild. "This is something our grandchildren might not have a chance to do," one tourist told *Alaska* magazine writer Rebecca Luczycki. "So it was worth every penny."

When I talked with Andrew Derocher about his early studies, I secretly hoped for enough scientific hedging to cast doubt on the projected fate of polar bears. Mind you, our conversation occurred before accelerating ice losses prompted even more dismal predictions. Derocher said he tried to remain optimistic, but he thought the solutions would probably have to come from industry. "There is no easy conservation fix," he told me. "Without stabilizing the climate by taking serious and urgent action on climate change, I don't see a future for polar bears at all." The North will have an ecosystem, he said, but it will probably look more like the Atlantic Ocean and nothing like the Arctic Ocean.

You'd think that officially recognizing the polar bear as a threatened species would be a good start. In fact, the federal government's decision was a call to action, but so far, there hasn't been much action—except by lawyers. The Department of the Interior said the polar bear listing couldn't be used to set climate policy, limit greenhouse gas emissions, or prevent oil and gas development permitted under the Marine Mammals Protection Act, rules continued by the Obama administration. Governor Sarah Palin and her successor, Sean Parnell, sued over the listing (as have other pro-development and environmental groups), arguing that the science was flawed and polar bear populations are at their all-time high. They lost their appeal in March 2013.

Following the decision to list polar bears as threatened, the Fish and Wildlife Service designated 187,000 square miles as critical habitat to help protect the bears; most of it was sea ice, but it also included terrestrial denning and barrier island habitats. This designation would require federal officials to consider whether any proposed activities in the habitat would harm bears. In January 2013 a federal district court judge in Alaska ruled that protecting polar bears is important, but the habitat designation was too extensive and violated some technical procedures. The USFWS was ordered to revise the habitat plan and correct its deficiencies. With or without an appeal, doing so will take years.

The terrible irony that escapes no one is that burning fossil fuels caused the ice to disappear, and now that the ice is disappearing, the oil and gas industry is rushing north to exploit newly accessible resources. Even as 5 million gallons of oil flooded the Gulf of Mexico during the Deepwater Horizon disaster, Alaska's leaders pressured the Obama administration to continue to allow arctic offshore oil and gas exploration. Eventually, it did. Royal Dutch Shell began preliminary exploratory drilling in both the Chukchi and Beaufort Seas in the fall of 2012, the first time in more than two decades that two rigs drilled simultaneously in Alaska's coastal waters, the company said. If Shell taps into the

the watched bear

The path to Brooks Falls cut through a shadowy spruce forest hushed by soft moss and made dreamy by veiled green light. Nobody in the small group of strangers walking ahead of me paused to absorb the scenery as we passed numerous trails furrowing the plush vegetation and intersecting the path. I stepped around piles of dense scat that illustrated how convenient the area's bears found this human route and quickened my pace to catch up to the others. Still, how risky could this excursion to Katmai National Park be if day-trippers were permitted to wander unescorted in a place inhabited by scores of the world's largest brown bears?

The ranger who delivered the mandatory bear etiquette talk for visitors emphasized that brown bears could appear anywhere and at any moment: along the path, beside the river, in the river, near the Brooks Camp lodge, around the campground, on the beaches of Naknek Lake and Lake Brooks. Bears own the right-of-way by virtue of park policy and plain pragmatism, so if a bear commandeered the path, he said, we should step off and let it pass. If we encountered a bear napping on or near the trail, we should either stop and wait or turn back to avoid disturbing it. A bear jam might cause us to miss our return charter to Homer, but that would be our problem, not the bear's. No loitering once we reached the elevated boardwalk, advised the ranger. Instead, we should walk directly to one of the two viewing platforms overlooking the upper river. "And don't rest things on the ledge," he cautioned. "If it falls, we won't go and get it."

Before setting out, most people lingered to read a handwritten sign warning that a bear with a trio of two-and-a-half-year-old cubs had charged an angler and stolen his fish recently. I wondered how many folks fly to Brooks Camp to watch bears, undergo the orientation, and then decide to wait quietly at the lakeside shelter until their plane leaves.

Each of us had paid more than $500 for the privilege of watching bears at close range, forgetting that here the bears can watch us right back, for free.

Once on the boardwalk, I left my new best friends to investigate the Riffles Platform on the river's midsection. No one else occupied the deck. A breeze rustled through the tall grass, and sunlight rippled across the clear, shallow water sliding toward Naknek Lake. I opened a small notebook to record lyrical thoughts about this bucolic scene and immediately fumbled it through the grate and into the grass ten feet below. As I eyed the emergency staircase—in a jiffy, I could duck under the rope and retrieve the pad—a young bear sauntered from the trees and settled its rump on the riverbank to watch the water. Hello, bear. So long, notebook.

As quietly as a teenager past curfew, I crept toward the railing, but my boot clanged against the grate and the bear jumped exactly as if I had hollered "Boo!" It whipped its head around, then visibly relaxed when it saw me and returned to contemplating the river. My hand stole into my jacket to retrieve my crummy digital camera so I could photograph the russet pelt, the velveteen ears, the casual slouch. The camera beeped and fussed before flashing the low-battery warning and shutting down. Fine. I'd promised myself that I wouldn't spend the day with a camera mashed to my face anyway. The world would survive without one more photograph of a bear snatching a salmon in midair.

A dramatic splashing downriver jolted the bear into a scramble for the alders. I strained to see what could frighten a bear. A bigger bear, of course, wading toward the falls. It dawned on me that young bears live with a certain amount of anxiety and tension, knowing that there are always other bears willing to deliver a vigorous thrashing. I followed the big bear to the Falls Platform, where it slumped in a whirlpool of cascading water, apparently more interested in cooling off than fishing. A couple of subadults orbited between the falls and the riffles. During July, an average of sixty-eight bears regularly visit the river at different times to feed on sockeye salmon, park researchers say (the number varies each season), but on this sunny, windy day, most seemed to prefer the trees.

People arrived throughout the afternoon, negotiated a viewing spot, waited for something fantastic to happen, and left after a few minutes. Thousands of photographs depict an iconic salmon hurtling into the gaping maw of an iconic bear at Brooks Falls, probably heightening expectations in the same way wildlife documentaries convince us that nature is an on-demand, close-up experience jam-packed with action. Not every visitor wielded a camera. One young woman sat cross-legged on a bench and watched quietly without any lens between her and the bears. Another woman read a Dean Koontz novel, ignoring bears and people alike. The serious photographers stationed tripods beside the railing and refused to budge for fear of missing that once-in-a-lifetime shot. Sometimes luck favors the patient and the pushy. Viewers in 2006 saw a wolf slip from the trees, ignore a preoccupied bear, and pluck a salmon from the river.

After a restful hour soaking in the roiling water, the big bear heaved itself to its feet and plodded downriver. Moments later a female with three yearlings ventured from the dense trees on the opposite shore. She scanned the river to make sure the coast was clear as the cubs clustered behind her, one resting its head on her back. Shutters clattered and beeped, people elbowed one another for more real estate at the railing, and I couldn't resist flogging my failing camera into recording a few final images. The family waded into the current, and the mother dipped her head beneath the surface. The yearlings ignored us but peered around, presumably on the lookout for other bears. A few fishless minutes later, the group climbed the bank and padded single file below the platform. Dark bands marked the pelt of one cub; another had a gashed shoulder. The last cub glanced up at the onlookers—click click click—before greenery swallowed the family.

The thrill lasted all afternoon until a man told me how he'd photographed the most amazing event ever. A female with three spring cubs started to cross the river near Brooks Camp, the site of park headquarters and a private lodge. Two cubs followed her into the water, he said, but the third refused and bawled from shore. In midriver the mother turned back, prompting bleats and moans from the accompanying cubs. She let the two of them climb onto her back and ferried them across before piggybacking the third cub. "Wow, that's great!" I said, feigning happiness at his good fortune while envy chewed on my heart. Surely I deserved to see baby bears riding their mother's back, too.

The afternoon might have been entirely lost to bitter thoughts if I hadn't just read *The Lost Grizzlies* by Rick Bass. The book describes how scientists and Doug Peacock, a fierce lover of bears, investigated rumors of grizzlies in Colorado's San Juan Mountains. The last known bear in the range had died in 1979. The expedition searched unsuccessfully for bear scat, a track, a tuft of fur—any proof that a single grizzly still ghosted through the mountains. They hoped, Bass wrote, to fill "that empty place in our hearts." At Brooks River, nobody searches for bears. You stand in place and wait for bears to walk past you, and they do.

I was glad to have the Riffles Platform to myself again in late afternoon. Losing the notebook and camera allowed me to ease into the wordless animal pleasures of sun and wind and river. Now and then a bear's broad back parted the silky grass as it passed by. I could read the past on the scarred pelts and see the future embedded in the fat and muscle and bone that animates a bear from one winter to the next. One rangy bear lunged after a silver streak and brought the struggling fish ashore in its jaws, its ravenous hunger palpable in the way it stripped glittering skin from coral meat, chewed hunks of flesh, licked the blood-smeared grass. These hours were a great lesson in the necessary patience of bears.

The appeal of watching bears being bears has nearly overshadowed the park's other big draws—the volcanic landscape of the Valley of Ten Thousand Smokes and the spectacular sport fishing that attracted the area's first recreationists. About 2,200 brown bears live in Katmai National Park and Preserve, which was expanded in 1980 to protect fish and wildlife habitats, particularly the "high concentrations of brown/grizzly bears and their denning areas." It is these concentrations that draw viewers to about a dozen places throughout the park and preserve.

Because the bears at Brooks River hardly acknowledge the people gawking from the platforms, because none of the viewers carry guns, because remarkably few incidents occur where people and bears gather, it is easy to assume that the innocent act of watching is harmless, that somehow human and beast have made an agreement: we'll watch you, and you'll amuse us, surprise us, teach us, inspire us. But (there's always a but) bringing people and bears together, even with good intentions, and even with the bears' welfare in mind, undoubtedly costs bears more than it costs people.

The bear-viewing industry—and the fact that it's called an industry should tell you something—has prompted researchers, wildlife managers, bear advocates, and hunters to consider the ethical and biological consequences of watching bears. Can the practice of bear viewing alter the animals' behavior, disrupt their activities, pressure bears away from their feeding grounds? How would we know? Does bear viewing somehow "corrupt" bears by making them less wild? If we believe that an instinctive fear of humans is the thin shield protecting us from a potential predator, what happens when that fear subsides? What do bears risk when frequent exposure to people diminishes their own wariness? Who's responsible if a hunter legally kills a bear that's unafraid of people after it leaves a protected wilderness area? How do we weigh the value of a bear as one person's trophy against the value of a living animal seen by many?

Beneath a multitude of philosophical and practical questions lie two fundamental mysteries: Why do so many bears allow their only true predator to approach so closely? And why do so many people want to share the company of bears?

Among the first people to spend day after day in the company of a gathering of bears were photographer Cecil Rhode and his partner Dick Chace. For two weeks in 1952 they photographed and filmed bears at the falls of McNeil River, about seventy-five miles north of Brooks River. Once they counted thirty-two bears in sight. "As we sat and watched, a feeling of awe came over us," Rhode wrote in *National Geographic*. "It was as if this fishing had been going on unchanged for centuries." He identified the location only as somewhere near the base of the Alaska Peninsula. The US Fish and Wildlife Service (USFWS) agent who had told him about the concentration of bears had asked him not to name the river. "He quite rightly wanted to keep the location from becoming common knowledge among hunters," Rhode wrote. "For though the Territory reaps an average of $2,000 on every brownie felled by a trophy hunter— in license and guide fees, transportation, and lodging expenses—the bear alive is worth infinitely more to the photographer and Nature enthusiast." This was a new way of assigning value to bears. The territorial Alaska Game Commission and the USFWS agreed and banned hunting at McNeil River in 1955. Twelve years later, commercial fisherman and legislator Clem Tillion persuaded the Alaska state legislature to create the McNeil River State Game Sanctuary. "I wanted a place where bears weren't afraid of us," Tillion later told writer Tom Walker.

This idyllic vision soon eroded as campers, fishermen, and photographers discovered the river just an hour's flight from the Kenai Peninsula. They crowded bears from fishing spots and stalked them for close-ups. Bears learned to steal food and bully anglers. "There were no controls," wildlife biologist Jim Faro recalled in 2003. "People were going on both sides of the falls, basically harassing the bears, and we saw the bears starting to abandon the falls." Faro took charge of the sanctuary in

1969, the same year a photography guide killed a bear and orphaned two spring cubs. The following year a photographer creeping through the grass surprised a bear fishing on Mikfik Creek and shot her when she charged, an incident that Faro called "totally avoidable." Wildlife officials later killed her yearling. By the early 1970s, the number of bears gathering at the river had dropped into the teens, a trend blamed variously on poor salmon runs, record bear harvests outside the sanctuary, deteriorating relations between people and bears, and a tagging project that inadvertently killed nine bears.

Similar problems plagued Brooks River in what was then Katmai National Monument. In 1950 a tourist enterprise began catering to anglers who didn't mind sleeping in wall tents. Concessioner Ray Petersen peered into the future and foresaw floods of visitors because "tourists are the biggest thing that Alaska can develop," he said, according to *Tourism in Katmai Country*. Before long, a cozy private lodge appeared, and the one-man ranger station expanded into a serious outpost that included a public campground. Far fewer bears gathered at Brooks than at McNeil, but despite efforts to separate garbage and bears, the camp inevitably attracted animals that raided burn barrels and trash cans, broke into supplies left on the beach, tore up tents, and scavenged fish entrails left by anglers. For a time, in the great tradition of parks elsewhere, lodge staff took clients to watch bears feeding at the local dump.

The danger of food-conditioning bears became clear in 1966 when a camper cooked fish for dinner, left his dirty dishes out, and nearly became an entree himself when a bear grabbed him by the butt as he slept and tried to haul him away. Another camper ran the bear off. The next year the chief ranger sent an SOS to University of Alaska professor Frederick Dean, one of the state's first professional bear biologists. Dean had come north in 1954, when "there were lots of bear stories but very little bear science," he told me.

Three reconnaissance trips to Brooks Camp uncovered poor garbage handling and lax boundaries between people and animals, the same kind of trouble that led to the mauling deaths of two young women in Montana's Glacier National Park that summer. Dean and his wife, Sue, learned firsthand how bold food-conditioned bears could be when a bear shredded their tent while they ate at the lodge. In another incident, a man said he'd shared the public campground with a bear for most of the night. "The camper was sleeping on a table under a tarp when he awoke to see a large bear . . . under the tarp with him," a ranger reported. "The bear dragged the camper's pack out into the rain, and evidently left it there, as the camper reached out and dragged it back under the tarp." Some bears weren't intimidated by people at all. "They are matter-of-fact to the point of creating an illusion of complete safety," the ranger wrote. "In fact, they sometimes appear to view human beings with the same type of attitude they exhibit toward the scavengers that hover about them while they are feeding."

The human response to these bears was often obliviousness, Dean wrote. "The visitor takes the role of photographer and attempts to get pictures that will record the fact that he was close to a bear. In trying to fill the frame, he may pursue the bear rather closely. . . . Some of the visitors demonstrate astounding foolishness in this respect." Ranger Clifford Estabrook described trying to overcome this cavalier attitude during one episode: "Some of the older and less active visitors showed a reckless tendency to get between the yearling and the sow and I was hard put to keep people in the lodge or on the porch without a great deal of fuss." Among those who took bears seriously were four archaeologists whose previous encounters had left them "in a wary mood." After two of them heard growling in the brush, all four bolted up nearby spruce trees in a panic. "Three trees had been prepared for such purpose, but only one person chose a prepared tree," the ranger noted. His memo concluded: "Overall reactions: Fear, warn others, climb trees."

It is a scientific fact that some people are not terribly bright when it comes to bears, so it's no surprise that astounding foolishness still continues. Of three bear charges reported at Brooks Camp in 2003, for example, two involved photographers pestering a sow with four cubs-of-the-year. In one incident, a photographer snapped flash photos of the cubs from ninety feet away as their mother fished in Naknek Lake. She did not approve. When a bear technician tried to usher away four paparazzi hovering within twenty-five feet of the entire family, the mother charged but halted a few yards short of the group—an act that speaks well of the general character of bears, in my opinion.

The original source of the trouble, Dean explained in his report, was the terrible location of Brooks Camp, which might as well have been named "Bear Town," given its position on a narrow isthmus between Brooks and Naknek lakes. The sockeye salmon run in late June and July regularly drew about twenty bears, and others wandered through. Bear boulevards paralleled the lakes and the river, lesser trails threaded between buildings, and day beds pocked the forest and grasslands. In

September drifting fish carcasses draw bears back for a buffet along the shore of Naknek Lake. National Park Service (NPS) biologist Terry De-Bruyn inventoried other flaws in a 1999 report: A trail from Dumpling Mountain acted as a conveyor belt that delivered bears directly into the campground. Tent sites snuggled against bears' mark trees. Visitors walking to the falls "must run a gauntlet of bear activity" as bears shifted between fishing the river and traveling the Naknek Lake shoreline. High-bush cranberries lured bears into the compound. In other words, people had colonized important bear habitat and then wondered, *Why all the trouble?*

Dean urged a philosophical shift in his advice to the National Park Service. He distinguished between *bear country* and *human country*, terms first used by ranger Darrell Coe and other park staff. Places that people inhabit are human country. Wild places dominated by bears and merely visited by people are bear country. The boundaries between the two realms could not be marked by maps or fences, Dean wrote; they existed solely in the minds and behavior of people and bears. "When the bear begins to consider that he is the trespasser as he comes into human country, then humans have established human country," he wrote. "Until the concept is a part of the bear's reaction, then the human is still operating in bear country for all practical purposes." Most interactions in bear country occur when people accidentally or purposefully interrupt animals minding their own business, he said. Bears that enter human country are passing through, curious, or attracted to something delicious. The boundaries fluctuate, depending on the terrain, the plant cover, the distance from buildings, and how well bears and people know the area, he explained. At Brooks Camp these borders shifted every season when visitors left and bears reclaimed the entire area to gorge on spawned and dead salmon.

Encounters became inevitable as the number of bears and people frequenting the camp increased and each group crossed through the other's country largely at will. In 1967 only about 1,200 people visited the entire Katmai National Monument. In the 2000s about 12,000 to 14,000 people arrived at Brooks Camp each summer, with around 300 visitors a day during peak tourist season in July, according to park documents. Between 1993 and 2000 park staff documented at least forty-two bear-human conflicts on the Brooks Falls trail alone, reported DeBruyn and coauthors in a 2004 paper. In one episode a running bear bowled a boy over, injuring him slightly. Bears "trespassed" (or tried to) in just over a thousand incidents recorded at Brooks Camp between 2003 and 2006, according to a management report by park biologist Tamara Olson and colleagues. Rangers also documented forty-nine incidents of bears "directly or aggressively approaching people." Almost half involved fly fishermen who usually attracted a bear's attention by catching a rainbow trout. Eight people reinforced bad behavior by surrendering their catches, although fish-stealing incidents have diminished greatly since the introduction of stricter fishing regulations.

Park managers tried to address obvious problems in the 1990s with a plan to move Brooks Camp about a mile away and limit the number of daily visitors to eight-five, but US Senator Ted Stevens obstructed funds for such efforts because he considered them antidevelopment. After he was voted out of office in 2008, planners got busy again, and in 2012 the NPS asked for public comments on proposals to move the camp, replace the floating bridge with a permanent overhead structure, and make other changes to reduce bear-human conflicts.

Several of Dean's suggestions have diminished problems at Brooks Camp. Bears are considered trespassers in the camp, but the park has also helped protect bear country (and visitors) by building about 900 feet of elevated boardwalk and three viewing platforms beside the river. Electric fences installed around the campground and other irresistible spots have hardened the boundaries. Strict rules about handling food and garbage mean that few bears enjoy illicit gains. Defining human country often involves hazing bears with air horns, rubber slugs, and cracker shells to make them leave camp, stop destroying property, or relinquish custody of the floating bridge over Brooks River so crowds of pedestrians can cross.

Perhaps the most surprising development over time has been the number of bears feeding at Brooks River in midsummer and fall. Dean estimated that about twenty bears frequented the river, and it seemed reasonable to expect that increasing numbers of visitors would drive bears away. Instead, about seventy identifiable bears now appear in July and fifty in September. Larger protected areas, strong salmon runs, more habituated bears, and a growing population throughout the Alaska Peninsula probably explain this trend, according to Olson and others. Similarly, several bear experts have warned over the years that more bears plus more people inevitably equals injuries or deaths. Yet in the past fifty years, bears at Brooks River have hurt only two people: the careless camper in 1966, and a seasonal ranger bitten on the arm while running from a bear in 1991. How can this extraordinary record be possible?

Fred Dean presciently suggested one answer when he identified Katmai's greatest research need: bear and human ethology. "Exactly what is the behavior of both types of animals during an encounter, what are the reasons for the various outcomes of encounters, exactly what is the level of risk to man during the course of different activities in bear country under different situations, and what is the proper behavior for man under different circumstances?" he asked. "These are problems that will require extended work by rather special individuals before the answers will become apparent."

Enter the "rather special individuals." First there was Jim Faro, who recognized that the best way to manage bears at McNeil River was to manage people. In 1973 he limited public access with a permit system. Three years later he hired Larry Aumiller to supervise the sanctuary in the summers. Aumiller had always intended to teach art to high school students and didn't have a biology or wildlife degree, but his fieldwork with bears at nearby King Salmon had impressed Faro. "I'd seen how he handled himself—he's got very good people skills, he's a sensitive type who would recognize the needs of the bears," Faro said in 2003. "The program is built around people adjusting their behavior to the bears. That's a foreign concept to some. A lot of people have a problem with the idea that bears tell us how to run the sanctuary. Larry is the interpreter. It works, and he's improved on it. When it comes to reading and understanding how bears behave, there is nobody in the world that has his finesse."

Operating on instinct and observation, Aumiller learned how to encourage habituation, a behavior long recognized in animals. Many people mistake habituated bears for "tame" or food-conditioned bears. But bear expert Tom Smith described it as "an adaptive behavior allowing an animal to ignore disturbances that have proven benign." Over time, as nothing particularly bad happens, many bears respond neutrally to what might otherwise disturb them—people, roads, buildings, tour buses. Not every bear becomes habituated or habituates to the same degree. Researchers regard habituation as a continuum influenced by season, location, and individual temperament. Highly habituated bears ignore people at the McNeil River falls and elsewhere in the sanctuary, according to a 1994 paper by Aumiller and former sanctuary staff biologist

Colleen Matt. These bears nurse cubs, nap, and sometimes even mate within several yards of people. By unwittingly drawing their wary companions or offspring closer to people, they foster new generations of habituated animals. Partially habituated bears stick to the opposite riverbank when people are present and may flee when encountering a human elsewhere. Wary bears avoid people altogether, often fishing only at night.

The differences between bear watching at McNeil River and at Brooks River presented researchers with intriguing questions about the process of habituation, however. For example, one afternoon at Brooks made four days at McNeil seem like entering a Zen garden after attending the county fair. Both places are dedicated to protecting bears and keeping people safe, but the national park endures far more pressure to accommodate herds of visitors. At McNeil, the highest daily number of visitors for an entire summer was 304, but in recent years that total has fallen below 200. At least one staff member escorts viewers in groups of ten or fewer to the river, where they spend hours sitting on two viewing pads as the bears move around them freely. Brooks visitors are told to stay at least fifty yards from bears, but the staff can't possibly supervise a couple hundred people a day who are fishing, camping, walking, or bear watching in a widespread area. Protocols differ, too. Brooks visitors are advised to give way to bears unless they are being followed, whereas McNeil visitors are coached to stand their ground if approached. Two Katmai employees visiting McNeil on a busman's holiday were surprised to hear we could keep toothpaste and toiletries in our tents, as was I. None of us understood yet how clearly Aumiller and his staff had established the boundaries between human country and bear country.

Undoubtedly McNeil's strict and consistent practices have contributed to its stellar safety record. No bears or people have been injured, and no staff member has ever fired a gun at a bear, even in warning. Only thirteen serious charges occurred between 1976 and 2004, with two bears responsible for five incidents between them, according to the sanctuary's 2004 report. All were either partially habituated or nonhabituated. This buttresses an early observation by Aumiller and Matt: "We found that, in the absence of a food reward, habituated bears were safer than wary bears."

Here's the big question, though: why have so few people been injured at Brooks Camp, despite its looser structure, greater number of visitors, more frequent negative conflicts, and less focused management?

Compounding that puzzle is the example of Cecil Rhode and his partner planting themselves amid McNeil's presumably nonhabituated bears. You'd think the sudden appearance of humans would have caused the bears to run away or perhaps respond aggressively. Instead, Rhode reported that most bears quickly accepted their presence or kept to the opposite bank. One bear that inadvertently approached within eight feet "simply did an about-face and lumbered back down the trail, the fish still firm in his mouth."

Enlisting wild bears in habituation experiments is not something scientists seem eager to try. However, seasoned bear researchers interested in the mechanisms of habituation produced two important papers in 2005 that offer insights. They identified the innate social flexibility of bears as a major factor in habituation. This adaptability becomes especially apparent in coastal areas such as Katmai National Park, where abundant fish, berries, and other food support a dense bear population. Accommodating other bears takes less energy than fighting or fleeing. In other words, they've developed bear-bear habituation, according to Tom Smith, Stephen Herrero, and Terry DeBruyn, coauthors of both studies. Because bears can habituate to each other in these conditions, the hypothesis goes, they more easily habituate to people—even people who aren't as polite as the McNeil staff. This may explain why bears gathering in remote coastal areas tolerate viewers, despite the absence of a structured setting.

What we casual observers call a bear's personal space, these researchers and others refer to as overt reaction distance, or ORD: the distance at which a bear displays an obvious response, such as huffing, yawning, fleeing, or charging. *Overt* emphasizes that we may not recognize a bear's internal response to stress, such as an increased heart rate. In high-density coastal populations, habituated bears have extremely short ORDs, "occasionally as short as the reach of their paws," Smith observed. People and other bears can approach quite closely before the animal reacts by moving or trying to force the intruder to back off. Out on the lonely tundra, bears exhibit ORDs up to 150 yards and are more likely to respond aggressively to interlopers. "We maintain that bear-to-bear habituation is the single most important factor that influences brown bear aggressiveness toward humans on a regional scale," the researchers stated.

Bears can habituate in low-density habitats if they encounter people frequently. Denali National Park is a good example. "There's no doubt about it, we have habituated bears along the road," said wildlife biologist Pat Owen. "They can be eating berries, and a bus with fifty people arrives, and the bears keep eating." Park managers must be aware of the differences in ORDs, because bear-viewing guidelines differ considerably among the various parks. For example, Denali regulations require a 300-yard buffer—far greater than elsewhere. "Fifty yards, in my opinion, is not enough [in Denali]," Owen said. "You can easily get away with that in places like McNeil, but bears definitely react at much greater distances here. And any distance that changes an animal's behavior is too close."

The true difference between Brooks Camp and McNeil River is not how bears treat people but how people treat bears. Humans make most of the compromises at McNeil, while Brooks bears are like long-suffering hosts enduring tedious guests. Locating the ambiguous line between bear country and human country also means recognizing the mental barriers that can prevent us from respecting each other's personal space. Often we don't see that line until we cross it, and perhaps that's true for bears as well. The trouble is that human country tends to be voracious, intrusive, and nearly unstoppable, even in the places we label "wilderness." Some people don't even believe in bear country. For them, the whole world is human country, with a few bits loaned to wildlife—bits being the operative word.

Bears can habituate to each other, and bears can habituate to people, but researchers identify a third dynamic at work: human-to-bear habituation. Smith and his colleagues described this phenomenon as "when a person's initial response to caution and wariness to brown bears gives way to a careless casualness"—or an astounding foolishness, as Fred Dean would say. I saw how easily this could happen during a bear-viewing outing in Geographic Harbor, a sheltered lobe of Amalik Bay on the Katmai coast.

As our de Havilland Otter circled the harbor before splash-landing in the turquoise water, I turned my attention from the rust-colored volcanic slopes to the dark shapes moving along the beach. Another pilot radioed that he had counted fifteen bears. "Only half are mechanical—the rest are real," joked our pilot and guide, Gary Porter. As we skiffed from the floatplane dock to shore, clients tried to remember the collective noun for a group of bears. A covey? A pod? "A tribe," someone said. (It's a sleuth.) What, then, would we call sixteen bear watchers? A gaggle? A goggle? A galumph, I decided, as we trudged in hip boots to Geographic Creek.

The clean smell of grass cut the stink of dead salmon littering the banks. Porter directed us to the "grassy knoll," a slight rise near the creek mouth. We awkwardly maneuvered ourselves into trail chairs lining the ground and tried not to tip over as we leaned back. Because I have a short ORD to people, I chose the end closest to the harbor, a spot that seemed awfully exposed when I recognized a bear trail several feet away.

Behind us, a brown lump napped in the grass. Downstream, three bears crashed through shallow water while another tossed around a dead salmon. A female leading a cub of the year meandered through the meadow across the stream and paused to lift her twitching snout. Shutters clickety-clicked, cameras beeped, amateur videographers narrated the scene. We'd all become directors of our own private nature films as the urgency of documenting the experience overwhelmed the thrill of experiencing the experience. We needed solid proof that we'd come this close to Katmai's famous bears.

In July I'd flown to Brooks Camp with Porter's outfit, Bald Mountain Air Service. When he discovered my interest in bears, he offered me a free seat in August on one of his daily trips from Homer to the Katmai coast. Gary Porter is the archetypal Alaskan bush pilot: he's been flying since he was a teenager, his ancestors were Gold Rush pioneers, his father was a hunting guide, and he has a substantial mustache. "My dad said a long time ago that one of these days, people will come just with a camera," Porter told me. In the mid-2000s he flew 1,200 to 1,300 people with cameras to Katmai each season, as did many other operators.

Before leaving for Geographic Harbor, Porter had described how warm Japanese ocean currents produce a moderate climate that, combined with volcanic ash, nurtures the "super-rich" environment that supports so many bears. This was all very interesting, but everyone burned to know one thing above all: "How close will we be to the bears?" a woman in gold earrings and red lipstick finally asked.

"I can't answer that one," Porter said. "I haven't ever been touched by a bear, but I've been so close I thought they could touch me."

"Oh my God!" a man said, voicing the reaction of those who suddenly looked as if they'd rather go halibut fishing after all.

"The thing is," Porter said, "and it becomes real apparent, there isn't any real danger, mostly because bears don't pay any attention to you. If anything, they're a little afraid of you." And a little curious, he allowed. "They have teeth and claws. But mostly they like to fish. They don't like people. We're stringy and we're covered in bug dope."

After thousands of years living around Alaska Natives, he explained, bears have developed a good understanding of people. "Bears, pretty much at a glance, can tell what your intentions are. They probably know what your intentions are better than you do," he said. His easy manner helped him navigate the tricky problem of convincing nervous clients they had little to worry about while conveying the equally important message that their own actions mattered. He explained that we'd sit in a row as bears fished in the river about thirty feet away. "They're used to us being there," he said. "We've been in the exact same spot for thirteen years."

The bear-watching business must have honed Gary's ability to read human behavior, too. He predicted that most of us would follow directions, but one person would edge slightly beyond everyone else. "For bears, that's a big warning sign," he said. "We watch that. They'll walk by and they don't look at anybody else that's lined up except for that one person." That kind of rude boldness can convince bears not to take a chance on fishing, he said. "Most of the time they just say, 'Nope, too much for me,' and they're off."

I thought he'd explained all this quite clearly, yet soon after we arrived at Geographic Creek, a woman stood and wandered along the row of watchers. "Sit down, have a seat," Porter said, looking up at her. Back problems made her uncomfortable, she insisted. "Can you sit with this chair?" he asked in a friendly tone that nonetheless suggested it wasn't really a question. She did. "Sometimes I don't think that people have any idea," he said to me in a lowered voice before shrugging. "People are people. If we didn't make an attempt to make everybody sit, everybody'd be standing within ten minutes." "Maybe you should use pepper spray on poor listeners," I suggested. "Yeah, there's a lot of selective hearing," he said.

Later, two women decided they needed photographs of themselves posing near the napping bear behind us. They half-crouched as they crept toward the bear. Porter was occupied with clients at the row's far end, but a guide from another group spotted them and said firmly, "Ma'am, not today. We're not going to be over there today." And she shepherded them back to the line.

When Gary returned, he said, "A little different than Brooks Camp, isn't it?" Well, yes. A bear's approach feels more immediate, more intimate, when you're sitting on the ground rather than standing ten feet above them on a platform. Even a railing can foil the sense of vulnerability, intimacy, and trust required at places like Geographic Harbor. The grassy knoll was far less crowded than Brooks Camp, too, although other groups regularly visit the harbor. Shortly after we arrived, a group of photographers left for their bear-viewing yacht anchored offshore, but another half dozen people arrived on what Gary called a "splash and dash" tour. Our galumph was growing.

For most wild creatures, survival means escaping from people as fast as they can. Bear viewing allows us to believe that, for once, we're not the boogeymen of the wilderness. The guides' mellow attitudes and quiet coaching calm us as much as the bears. With every encounter that doesn't result in mayhem or terror, our anxiety subsides little bit more, until we're no longer dizzy with adrenaline every time a bear approaches. We are habituated.

The risk lies in forgetting that every animal is different, that you haven't been awarded blanket immunity just because you like bears and some bears will let you hang around. The exemplar for the worst kind of human-to-bear habituation was the late Timothy Treadwell, whose footage included scenes of him touching bears and bears pressing their snouts to his camera. The book he coauthored with Jewel Palovak, *Among Grizzlies: Living with Wild Bears in Alaska*, described behavior that even he repudiated in the epilogue: "It is my greatest fear that some people might attempt to copy my past dangerous style of study and become injured or killed."

Years after a bear killed him and his friend Amie Huguenard on the Katmai coast, Treadwell continues to demonstrate how not to behave around bears in reruns of *Grizzly Man Diaries*, still airing on Animal Planet. His dramatic display of human-to-bear habituation modeled a flawed understanding of bear behavior, Smith and his colleagues observed. The conditions that allow bear-to-human habituation to develop do not automatically exist wherever bears do. "Failure to make that distinction may lead others to assume that close approaches to wild bears are possible if one only fosters the attitude and behaviors set forth by Treadwell and Palovak," they wrote.

Viewing guides Ken and Chris Day often encountered Treadwell in action and didn't like what they saw. "He was a perfect example of what bears will tolerate," Chris said. "And Timothy did things that Ken could do, I could do, anybody that has some experience could do. There are bears that will let you just scratch them. There's bears that will let you kiss them on the nose. They're just things that we have chosen not to do." Because of people like Timothy—and "probably people like us," she said—people assume that bear watching is easy and 100 percent safe. "Prior to Timothy dying, it was to the point where people were buying bear-viewing trips like it was a trip to the park or the zoo—no safety questions, arguing with you that they wanted to bring a year-old child because they didn't understand why that was an issue," she said. Some pilots just dropped off unescorted viewers, and unprepared campers pitched their tents willy-nilly in Hallo Bay, sometimes in important bear grazing areas. "That dried up after Timothy died," Chris said. "You very seldom see a camper down there anymore, and when they do [camp], they have electric fences and they're properly outfitted. They've got some understanding." The park also changed its regulations to allow camping only on the fringes of favored bear foraging grounds.

Like the occasional photographer, biologist, and animal trainer, Treadwell grew complacent about his ability to understand and influence wild animals. Perhaps he succumbed to what Loren Eiesely called "the long loneliness" that separates humans from most other creatures. Treadwell must have emotionally closed that distance and then confused his desire to be part of the bear hierarchy with actually belonging to it. Some people called him a "bear whisperer," a label often applied to the Days and to Larry Aumiller. The difference is that they don't see themselves that way.

"It's not about whispering to a bear," Chris Day said. "It's about listening to an animal."

The notion of ordinary people sitting beside a salmon stream as bears walk past seemed daft not long ago, and it probably still strikes many that way. Places like McNeil River, Brooks Camp, and Pack Creek on Admiralty Island proved as early as the 1970s that humans and bears can get along in close quarters, but the industry boomed in the 1990s. Homer businesses estimated that 25,000 people made bear-watching trips in 2004 to McNeil River, Katmai National Park and Preserve, Wolverine Creek, Lake Clark National Park, and Pack Creek and Anan Creek in Southeast Alaska. And that didn't include visitors to lesser-known areas on the Alaska Peninsula, on Kodiak Island, and in Southeast Alaska. About thirty people visited a coastal salt marsh frequented by bears in

Lake Clark National Park in 1995, but annual visitation has ballooned to more than 550 since the establishment of a nearby bear-viewing lodge, according to the NPS. The superintendent reported giving permits to fifty-one bear-viewing companies in 2010.

People pay lots of money to see lots of bears—several hundred dollars for day trips, and thousands of dollars for stays in deluxe lodges and boat trips. Economics has become an important part of the argument for those who support wildlife watching and want it to be treated with as much consideration as hunting. People who visit Alaska primarily to aim their eyeballs at wild bears spend 2.6 times more than tourists with other interests, according to a 2005 study by the Institute of Social and Economic Research. The Alaska Department of Fish and Game estimated that bear hunters contribute about $8 million to the peninsula's economy. In contrast, one economic analysis calculated that visitors to Katmai National Park and Preserve alone spent almost $50 million in 2007, money that trickles down to flight services, lodgings, restaurants, and retail stores. But bear viewing has one unassailable advantage over hunting: "You're never going to photograph the hides off those bears," Chris Day said.

The enthusiasm for bear viewing raises an important question: who watches the watchers? Ken and Chris Day offered guided bear-viewing trips in the early 1990s but nearly left the field when unskilled operators appeared. "Yahoos," Chris called them. "Number one, they didn't know how to view bears, and so we worried about safety," she said. "We worried mostly about the bears because it is a tremendous testament to the tolerance of the bears, what they've put up with over the years. But we almost quit because we thought, we don't even want to be part of this anymore. Then we decided that if we're not out there, there won't be anybody out there doing it right. And most of them want to do it right."

Several people recommended the Days to me because of their extensive knowledge of natural history and bear behavior. (They have since retired.) They could have filled three planes with tourists every day, but they limited their groups to nine to avoid overwhelming the habitat. They were almost evangelical about focusing on education; Chris didn't allow people to yammer about dinner plans while watching bears, for example. "We want them to come away with good pictures, but we want them to come away with an understanding about bears and where they live," she said. "And you hope that as you do that, every one of those people leaves as an ambassador for the bears in their country."

Rangers, wildlife biologists, and other staff encourage the best behavior from people and bears in managed sites such as Brooks Camp, McNeil River, and Pack Creek, but no agency can afford to station a playground monitor everywhere people and bears meet, particularly when budgets are tight. The National Park Service and the Alaska Department of Fish and Game collaborated with bear-viewing businesses to create a best-practices document for the Katmai coast and west side of Cook Inlet in 2003. The guidelines recommended using regular viewing areas and routes, maintaining a proper distance from bears, moving in groups, and keeping human food from bears, among other principles. More than 80 percent of groups visiting Geographic Bay in 2011 consistently followed these guidelines, according to Katmai coastal biologist Carissa Turner, who evaluated visitors over eleven days. Only one group of unguided visitors scored poorly.

Bear-viewing guides know how much their reputations depend on one another. The Kodiak Unified Bear Subcommittee began offering a three-day training course for bear-viewing operations at the local college campus, the brainstorm of guides Harry and Brigid Dodge of Kodiak Treks. Peer pressure and annual meetings of the Katmai Service Providers and other groups also encourage self-regulation, Gary Porter said. "We all kind of depend on each other to operate this way," he said. "You can imagine without something like that, without good cooperation between all the members, all the operators, what if we were to all stand up here on this [bank], running back and forth? Shoot. It wouldn't work at all." If the bears disappear, after all, so will the clients.

In some places, agencies rely on stakeholders to work things out. At Wolverine Creek and Cove, bear viewers, sport fishermen, and bears compete for the same 1,700 square yards of fishing habitat, eighty miles south of Anchorage on the Alaska Peninsula. About 500 people visited the cove annually in the 1980s, mostly to fish. Two decades later, 9,000 people descended each year. Anglers and viewers drifted through the inner cove in skiffs, jostling for prime spots. A cadre of food-conditioned bears developed, thanks to careless visitors and to irresponsible guides who deliberately fed the bears so their clients could take better pictures. This probably didn't seem like such a bright idea when some bears tried to climb into the skiffs, forcing people to whack them with paddles.

For a few years, Alaska Fish and Game used a federal grant to establish and run a field camp, according Joe Meehan, state lands and refuge program coordinator. The agency also formed a steering committee with representatives from tourism-related businesses, anglers, and the public. The committee developed guidelines to reduce user conflicts and make room for bears. By the time the grant ran out, Meehan wrote in an e-mail, the agency and the committee felt that things were working well—"or as well as can be expected when 10,000 people, a dozen bears, and thousands of salmon are crammed into a small cove." The department now manages the area by making a couple of visits each summer and having regular discussions with the committee and users. The current situation satisfies the department's major concerns, he said: bears can fish without being harassed or food-conditioned, people can still visit, salmon runs remain strong. What's harder to address, Meehan said, is the quality of the experience. "Comparing bear viewing to dining," he wrote, "I consider Wolverine Creek a fast food joint (while McNeil is a gourmet restaurant): lots of people, lots of activity (bears, fish, boats, planes, fishing lines, etc.) but it fills the gut and gives you what you want (beautiful scenery, wild bears, catching Alaskan salmon, easy logistics and relatively cheap)." Most people tell him that they had a great time, despite the crowds.

Bear viewers cannot overlook their own obligations, either. The act of watching can exploit the tolerance of wild animals and devolve into self-absorption. Photographers can pursue images at the expense of their subjects. Enthusiasts can mistake a bear's nonchalance for a spiritual connection. Adventure lovers can substitute thrills for insight. If you're not careful, you won't even see the bear filling the lens.

"It's a privilege," Chris Day said. "It's not Disneyland, it's not a theme park. It's real, it's wild and it's fragile."

Just how fragile is bear country when it's invaded by galumphs of people loaded with cameras, binoculars, and benign intentions? Like other animals, bears balance risk against need. If good food is available nearby, then wary bears have little reason to stick around. If resources are scarce, or if fleeing takes more energy than staying, then some bears will adapt. They may fish less but fish harder, forage at night or in the early morning when people are absent, or shift to marginal habitat where they feel more comfortable (possibly displacing other bears). Without experimental studies, most research can describe only correlations between human and bear behavior, not causal links. The absence of adult male bears at Wolverine Cove, for example, could be related to their tendency to avoid people, a lack of sufficient salmon to make fishing worthwhile, or better fishing elsewhere. It's tough to disentangle factors in a bear's fishing success when the depth of the river, the strength of the salmon run, and the time of year all matter.

Research to date shows that the presence of people does affect the way bears conduct their lives, in subtle and not-so-subtle ways. Fishing activity at Wolverine Creek dropped when boat and plane traffic was heaviest. Nonhabituated bears delayed their arrival at Brooks River when the lodge closed later than usual one fall. Bears avoided sections of Kulik River where boats often zipped through and planes landed frequently. On the Chilkoot River near Haines, bears caught almost three times as many salmon, and at a faster rate, when people were absent or at least 300 feet away. (Think how your meals would be disrupted if bears were standing in the room watching you.) A long-term study at O'Malley River on Kodiak Island found that structured bear viewing disturbed bears much less than when people were permitted to come and go freely. Time-lapse cameras stationed at Geographic Bay in 2007–2009 revealed that maximum bear numbers decreased as human visitors increased, according to park researchers Carissa Turner and Troy Hamon. However, the number of bears increased when a ranger was present, perhaps because viewers distributed themselves differently, Turner speculated at a 2011 symposium.

Maybe what happens isn't always about us; maybe it's sometimes about them. Let's not forget that bears are individuals with their own histories, genetic predispositions, and learned behaviors, noted Terry DeBruyn in a 1999 review of bear-human interactions at Brooks River. Some nonhabituated bears might be avoiding dominant bears rather than, or in addition to, people, he wrote. If a bear pops from the brush at McNeil River and spots ten people and one enormous alpha bear, who can say exactly why it chooses to go elsewhere to feed?

Not all bears regard people as nuisances. Males generally dominate foraging areas but tend to be the most leery of people, and females sometimes exploit this wariness to diminish the chance of a male killing their cubs. At Geographic Harbor we saw a female deposit her cub a few yards away from a group of delighted photographers while she fished downstream. Bears that treat viewers like babysitters are said to be "caching cubs." During an experiment conducted by Karyn Rode and colleagues, male bears shifted to grazing at salt marshes free of people when viewers showed up at Douglas River, but females, both with and without cubs, increased their use of salt marshes where people were present. At a British Columbia site, females with cubs preferred fishing after people arrived, apparently because the males disappeared from the salmon stream just before the commercial tours arrived every day at 7:00 a.m. The viewers provided bear families with a "temporal refuge," according to researchers Owen Nevin and Barrie Gilbert.

Good management can belay most of the negative effects of bear watching, the research suggests. "An over-arching principle that should guide the planning process is that 'bears come first,'" wrote Terry De-Bruyn and Tom Smith in a review of viewing practices. Several sites already provide bears with predictable periods when they can eat without being ogled, and managers should consider leaving bears entirely alone in particularly important foraging areas, they suggested. Most managed areas require buffers of 90 to 150 feet between bears and people, but expanding the buffer could improve ursine well-being. Allowing bears to define how closely they want to approach people is more respectful, according to DeBruyn and Smith. The researchers also recommended limiting the size and number of bear-watching groups, training guides through certified programs, paying agency guides well enough to diminish turnover, and including interpretation that emphasizes ecological and cultural contexts.

Still, bear-human habituation is generally better for people than it is for bears, according to a list of costs and benefits identified by Herrero and others. By allowing people to watch them safely in a natural setting, habituated bears provide aesthetic pleasure, promote education about wildlife ecology, encourage conservation, and contribute significantly to local economies dependent on ecotourism. Habituated bears are also less likely to threaten or harm hikers and viewers. In return, habituated bears can use resources along roads or popular rivers that might otherwise be inaccessible. Individual animals benefit when they exploit viewers to avoid unpleasant encounters with other bears.

However, habituation can also lead to food-conditioning when people are careless, the researchers noted. It can encourage people to approach too closely, risking injury for them and harassment or death for the bear. People who respond poorly when a bear approaches them (by running away, say) risk provoking a dangerous reaction. Park managers in Canada's Banff National Park discourage habituation because bears that become comfortable around roads or railways are more likely to be killed or injured by traffic. Similarly, bear jams can create hazardous situations for motorists.

Roadside poachers and unscrupulous hunters can also take unfair advantage of habituated bears. In 2009 a young brown bear grazing beside the busy Sterling Highway in Alaska's Kenai Wildlife Refuge provided an irresistible—but legal—target for a pair of hunters, who shot it several times in front of a crowd of motorists watching the animal. A longtime hunter who witnessed the shooting described it as dangerous to bystanders, not to mention unsportsmanlike. "If that was hunting, I'm a jet pilot," he told the *Redoubt Reporter*. One of the hunters later apologized publicly, claiming he had killed the bear because he thought it was endangering viewers.

As the gold standard in bear watching, McNeil River makes it pretty clear what works and what doesn't. Yet land management agencies lack a "unifying philosophy" to guide such activities regionally, DeBruyn and Smith observed, adding that "viewer safety and bear management operates more by default than design" in some places. Bear habitat, behavior, and needs vary too much for a one-size-fits-all mentality, they said. Only more research can illuminate the process of habituation and the full effects of bear viewing. Their basic point distills to this: bears and people may have shared Alaska's landscape for several millennia, but that can't possibly prepare bears for what happens when hundreds of people suddenly materialize in the very places bears most need to survive.

Habituated bears offer us great photographs, one-of-a-kind experiences, and a more intimate understanding of the natural world. But in places like Katmai National Preserve, habituation can seem like a cruel trick when hunters suddenly replace watchers, and the bears can't tell the difference. Lines on maps don't prevent bears in protected areas from searching elsewhere for food or mates. Most bears spend perhaps a month fishing in the preserve and the rest of their time making the rounds of salt marshes, tidelands, berry patches, and other salmon runs. Sometimes their stomachs lead them to places where people await them with rifles rather than cameras.

Hunters killed ten of about sixty bears tagged at McNeil River in its early years, Derek Stonorov concluded in a research paper for the National Parks Conservation Association. Later, when the state opened hunting in the McNeil River State Game Refuge adjoining the sanctuary, bear advocates flooded the first drawing for hunting permits in 1995 and won six of eight permits. Only one bear was killed, and the state Board of Game closed hunting at the request of Governor Tony Knowles.

However, Governor Frank Murkowski appointed board members who were more sympathetic to hunters and guides than to wildlife watchers. In 2005, against the recommendation of Fish and Game biologists, the board voted to allow bear hunting in the refuge and on other state lands surrounding McNeil River, as well as near the bear-viewing sanctuary at Pack Creek on Admiralty Island.

The decision was a classic example of frontier thinking. Many Alaskans are still unhappy that the Alaska National Interest Lands Conservation Act of 1980 (ANILCA) turned 43 million acres of land into ten national parks and expanded three others, including Katmai. Depending on one's outlook, ANILCA either created the century's greatest conservation legacy by protecting the wilderness or it "locked up" natural resources and crushed Alaskans' freedom. The last thing many Alaskans want is more protection for bears on state lands. This is how Pete Buist, a board member at the time, explained it: "When you get right down to it, you have millions and millions of acres in Alaska where only nonconsumptive use is allowed," he told me. (By "nonconsumptive," he meant photography and bear viewing.) "There are very few places where nonconsumptive uses are limited or even regulated in any way. And I think it's selfish of those people to demand even more places to be closed when they're not utilizing the places that are already closed and set aside for them."

Bear-wise, this argument works both ways. Since 2005, the Board of Game has made it easier to kill *Ursus arctos* than at any time since the early territorial days. Liberal regulations and predator control programs encourage hunters to reduce bear populations in much of the state. In 1970 the brown bear harvest totaled 632; now it's 1,400 to 1,500 bears annually—sometimes more. The state manages bears for trophy hunting on the Alaska Peninsula, where harvests averaged 331 bears a year between 2001 and 2007, according to Fish and Game reports.

Buist, a trapper and former bear-hunting guide, didn't think hunters would be much interested in killing habituated bears anyway. "A hunter who wants to hunt a wild brown bear, he has no interest in hunting a bear who's been used to fishing next to tourists all summer," he said. "Now that's not to say every hunter, because there are hunters who just want a three-dimensional bear to be two-dimensional and live in their house." Fearing the bad publicity that two-dimensional McNeil bears could inflict on them, a few hunting organizations opposed opening the season. But board member and chair Ron Somerville saw the McNeil vote as a "major management philosophical crossroads" between hunting bears and watching them. Somerville is a former state biologist and a past executive director of the pro-hunting Alaska Outdoor Council. "There is no mutually exclusive conflict between viewing of bears and hunting if you consider them as a population," he said during a board meeting. "That's been brought up in the testimony here. There is no conflict until you start identifying that the loss of one viewable bear at McNeil River is some mortal sin."

Sanctuary manager Larry Aumiller's vision of McNeil River's purpose was entirely different. "We're not dealing with a population at all," Larry told me. "We're dealing with an experience. It's a wildlife viewing experience. And there's several parts of it you want to nurture and enhance. If you're that kind of a person." From experience, he knew that once they ventured outside the sanctuary, some habituated bears would avoid people and some wouldn't. And at the wrong time of year, a bear that hesitates for a moment or two at the sight of a human is probably a dead bear.

The board's stance contributed to Aumiller's decision to retire from "the world's greatest job" in 2005, after thirty years as sanctuary manager. "To purposely and knowingly kill these habituated animals for trophies is beyond any definition of reasonable ethics or fair chase and, I believe, is morally wrong," Larry wrote in an op-ed piece for the *Anchorage Daily News*. "I've always envisioned that I'd be at McNeil River until I couldn't physically do it anymore. But I can't continue to remove the bears' only protection—their natural wariness—knowing that even more of them will soon be exposed to hunting."

Two years of negative publicity and 40,000 public comments later, the board reversed itself and announced a ten-year moratorium on further hunting proposals at McNeil and Pack Creek. Aumiller's retirement might have seemed premature, given this decision, but Ken and Chris Day knew better. "The bears simply dodged a bullet," Chris told the *Homer Tribune*. "They are no better off now than they were before. They still have incredible hunting pressure in the Katmai Preserve." As part of ANILCA, hunting is allowed in Katmai National Preserve, which borders Katmai National Park and lies kitty-corner to McNeil sanctuary. The state regulates hunting seasons and bag limits, but as with commercial bear viewing, the NPS controls the guide concessions. About 75 percent of bears harvested in the preserve are killed on guided hunts, the state says. Most hunters are nonresidents, who are required to hire guides or accompany close relatives.

Since 1995 the Days had logged observations of trips they'd made to Funnel, Moraine, and Battle Creek drainages in the preserve, often counting thirty-five to sixty bears per trip in the early years. By 2006 those numbers had decreased by about two-thirds. "We used to see seven to ten big male bears, and I mean 900- to 1,000-pound bears, every day," Ken said in late 2005. "We've seen two this year. Last year we saw one." Other viewing guides and photographers, including Derek Stonorov, have noticed the same trend, and they all blame overhunting. Between 2001 and 2010 hunters harvested 257 brown bears in the entire subunit, far more than the department's original report of 108. But the National Park Service argued that this wasn't affecting the park's mandate to protect "high concentrations," particularly since the park's bear population had apparently increased since 1980. The state considers recent harvest percentages to represent "moderate pressure" and to be within the acceptable range for a stable and healthy population, according to Fish and Game management reports.

In 2007 the Days and several others asked the Board of Game to at least shift opening day of hunting season in the preserve from October 1 to mid-October, to give habituated bears more time to disperse from salmon streams and offer hunters more of a challenge. Opening day had been October 7 until 1999, they pointed out. The board rejected this and similar proposals, as it had before and has since.

The ethics of hunting habituated bears was a lively but abstract debate for most people until the fall of 2007, when the Days flew an Anchorage TV news crew and a few photographer-naturalists to Kukaklek Lake in Katmai Preserve, about twenty-five miles from McNeil River falls. The group's videos showed habituated bears swimming, fishing, and grazing on berry slopes on September 30. The next morning they filmed two camouflage-wearing bow hunters and their guide waiting in the open tundra about a hundred yards from their lakeside camp. A young female bear that had strolled past their tents the previous evening approached them without any wariness, and a hunter loosed an arrow from about forty feet away. The wounded bear ran into the nearby alders, and guide Jim Hamilton shot her with his rifle.

The footage appeared on television, in newspapers, and across the Web, provoking outrage from all quarters. The hunters complained to the Alaska state troopers that the group had illegally interfered with their hunt, but the troopers took no action. Hunter Willis Paul called the news video misleading in a piece published on the National Rifle Association's website. "This was a once-in-a-lifetime experience, and I feel that the crew definitely robbed me of my enjoyment," he said. He charged that Ken Day "did not take credit for causing the bears to possibly lose fear of humans as he frequently guides wildlife-watching clients to the site for close encounters with the bears." Guide Jim Hamilton defended the hunt in a written statement to the press. "I have my own love for the natural world that I choose to express in a different way," he wrote. "I cannot agree with the argument that habituating bears is a good idea and that hunting them is neither fair chase nor unethical." His experience had taught him that bears from protected areas don't behave any differently from other coastal bears, perhaps not realizing that he wasn't making much of a case for the rigors of trophy hunting on the Alaska Peninsula. He called the Days "self-serving" and motivated by the economic benefits of bear viewing. He didn't mention that his business, True North Adventures, advertised bear-viewing tours on Kodiak Island. Nor did he mention that a dozen of his hunting clients had bagged trophies in the Katmai preserve in 2005, according to his website. At $15,900 per bear, he'd earned $190,800 in less than a week.

The National Park Service and the Alaska Department of Fish and Game avoided treading through the treacherous territory of hunter ethics. Fair chase is a concept, not a law, each agency noted in press releases. Not even the national Association of Fish and Wildlife Agencies could define fair chase, and it ultimately gave up trying because the issue was too divisive, the state argued. It was the Board of Game's job to consider ethics, fair chase, and differing viewpoints when making regulations, the state asserted (which surely caused some chortling among people familiar with board meetings). Besides, the preserve's bear population was healthy and stable. People who didn't like the hunt should talk to Congress or the Alaska state legislature about changing the laws, said NPS regional director Marcia Blaszak, declining to get involved in state regulations.

The agencies were unwilling to criticize hunters but happy to fault bear viewers. The state's press release asked, "Is it ethical to view bears at close distances in areas open to hunting?" Park superintendent Ralph Moore blamed bear viewers for habituating the animals in the first place in an *Anchorage Press* article. Even a website devoted to Katmai's bears posted the Kukaklek Lake video to warn people against visiting the preserve and other areas where "hunted bears are habituated by bear viewers." Nobody mentioned the role of sport fishermen, who accounted for more than 80 percent of visitors to the Katmai preserve, according to the NPS. In fact, the average daily number of bear viewers at Moraine Creek was usually substantially lower than the number of fishermen until 2011, when bear viewers (twenty-eight per day) outnumbered fishermen (twenty-three per day) for the first time.

However, the ethical implications of hunting habituated bears would shift mightily if bear-to-bear habituation leads to bear-to-human habituation, as Smith and his colleagues hypothesized. In other words, the bears are behaving naturally, not being "tamed" by bear viewing. "Because some claim that bear viewing habituates bears to humans and that hunting those same bears is unethical, specific research addressing this issue is needed," the researchers acknowledged.

The National Park Service later terminated Hamilton's contract for material breach, without announcing why. Alaska state troopers reported that in January 2010 Hamilton had "voluntarily surrendered his Registered Guide-Outfitter License with the understanding that the Alaska Big Game Commercial Services Board had an active investigation against him regarding his failure to have client's big game animals sealed by ADF&G and failure to submit hunt records." (The board's investigations are confidential, and an investigator did not respond to my inquiry.)

Following the controversy over the Kukaklek Lake incident, the NPS took the unusual step of releasing an environmental assessment before offering two new hunting concessions in the preserve. (Hunters represent about 1 percent of all preserve visitors.) Although the agency could have ended guided hunts in the preserve, it didn't. The total number of clients allowed in the preserve each year would remain at twenty-eight, although park managers readjusted the guiding areas so that nine fewer clients would be permitted to kill bears around Moraine Creek. In Derek Stonorov's opinion, park managers weren't conservative enough, since the park doesn't limit the number of nonguided bear hunters in the preserve. He also thought it was misleading for the park to suggest that the state would remedy any overharvesting. "Does the NPS really think the Board of Game—[which] embraces predator control, bear snaring, bear baiting, and seeks to curtail bear populations in many areas—is going to respond to what the NPS thinks is an overharvest in the Preserve?" he asked in comments to the agency.

The NPS avoided discussing the conflicting values of bear viewers and bear hunters except to say, "The NPS is not aware of any studies that have shown a formal link between habituation to humans and vulnerability to harvest." Besides, the environmental assessment asserted, viewers don't visit the preserve at the same time as hunters. Derek's response was a politer version of "Duh." He wrote, "Bear viewers avoid the Preserve during fall hunting seasons expressly to avoid conflict and what can amount to a negative experience."

If nothing else, the video of the Kukaklek Lake incident exposed what Derek and others consider the big lie of bear hunting on the Alaska Peninsula. There was no dangerous battle of wits between the hunter and the hunted, no vicious beast stalking the stalker, no great personal risk. The bear had simply strolled without fear past the hunters, who had rolled out of their sleeping bags and walked a hundred yards to kill her. Ken Day has long said that hunting in the preserve is no challenge at all. "To me, the people that hunt the Katmai Preserve, they're unskilled hunters and they want it easy," he told me. The video depicted the reality of bear hunting in the region as it has always been, bear biologist Tom Smith commented in the *Anchorage Press*: "It's not much of a hunt when bears are so tolerant—much like shooting cattle in a pen, an unarguable point." Larry Aumiller explained hunting on the Alaska Peninsula like this: "It's not about the reality, it's about the perception. It is the most ridiculous thing. And you don't even have to get within a hundred yards. This is how hard it is. Watch carefully." He crooked his trigger finger as if firing a rifle, and then he laughed as if it weren't funny at all.

Ron Somerville and other board members saw no reason at all to separate viewing and hunting, because one bear in a population is the same as another. They didn't oppose the existence of the McNeil River sanctuary; they just didn't understand why those particular animals deserved special treatment. Wildlife biologist Fred Dean, no sentimentalist, thinks it's worth recognizing the kind of collaboration it takes to create a place like McNeil. "This is a construct that has been built by people and bears that is extremely special," he told me. "And the notion that we can't afford as a society to forgo some of our activities in certain areas— I think it boils down a lot to the [opinion]: 'I don't like to be told what and where and when I can do things.' And I think Alaska's got a bigger case of that than a lot of other places."

State wildlife biologist Larry Van Daele manages Kodiak bears, one of the world's prized hunting trophies, but he has no qualms about treating bears differently in some places. "Quite honestly, the bears of Mc-Neil are more important than the bears that live in the middle of Katmai Park," he told me. "They are more important than the bears that live someplace else that's open to hunting. . . . And we need to accept that fact. By accepting that, it doesn't belittle you as a person. It also doesn't precipitate this domino effect that folks say will shut down hunting for the whole state. What it does is show you as a rational person that's willing to work with other folks."

Most wildlife population studies don't acknowledge that animals are individuals, noted Terry DeBruyn in *Walking with Bears*. Before coming to Alaska to work for the NPS and later the USFWS, he spent six years shadowing a tolerant black bear named Carmen and five of her litters through the forests of Michigan's Upper Peninsula as part of his master's research. His book recounts close observations of their daily activities, foraging techniques, life histories, and behavior framed through a scientist's sensibility. Wildlife managers usually decide what happens to animal populations using small samples and large extrapolations, DeBruyn noted. "How much more informative and accurate it would be to make predictions about a population based on an intimate knowledge of all its individuals," he wrote. He and Tom Smith elaborated on this point in their bear-watching review: "Because populations are comprised of individuals, and because individuals, particularly in highly intelligent species like bears, have variable behaviour, predicting the population-level consequences of wildlife viewing based on mean responses can be misleading and therefore ultimately uninformative." What's needed, they wrote, is long-term research on the behavior, habitat use, and energetics of individuals, a task made far easier by the ability to observe habituated bears.

Some individual bears may be particularly valuable to a population, DeBruyn pointed out. For example, certain females tracked in one Kenai study were responsible for much of the local population's growth because they were more successful at raising cubs than other females. State biologist Harry Reynolds mentioned a male bear in Northwest Alaska that he and his colleagues collared as a seventeen-year-old. They recaptured and recollared him for the last time when he was thirty-two, and he lived a couple more years before a Noatak villager found his collar on the tundra. That bear was one of two males that had each sired 11 percent of the 120 cubs the researchers genotyped, a significant genetic contribution from an animal that had clearly mastered life in a difficult environment.

Some bears make outsized contributions to human understanding, too. To Larry Aumiller, the highly habituated bear named Teddy was a rather special individual who disproportionately influenced people because she was so easygoing around humans. In 2004 alone, Teddy and her pair of two-and-a-half-year-olds accounted for more than 10 percent of all bear use days at McNeil River. The loss of such a bear to a hunter would be "catastrophic," Aumiller wrote in his annual report.

There is a price to pay when researchers—and photographers and naturalists and viewers—come to know individual animals. I heard the pain in Larry Aumiller's voice as he fretted about quitting his job, knowing that hunters were killing bears he had encouraged to trust people. I sensed it in Terry DeBruyn's afterword, where he reported that a hunter had killed the bear he knew as Carmen over a bait station. A year later DeBruyn found her daughter Nettie dead from a poorly placed arrow that had prolonged her suffering. Both bears had cubs when they died, though it's illegal to kill females accompanied by offspring in Michigan. The four orphaned cubs probably did not survive long. "It seems a bitter irony that the bears which contributed so much to increase our knowledge and understanding of their kind would, in the end, be killed by those who obviously knew and cared so little," DeBruyn wrote.

It wasn't knowing the names of these bears that gave me such a pang as I read this; it was the sense of loss that comes from understanding, however slightly, that individual bears live complicated, interesting lives. But that's not a concept wildlife managers can explain to game boards, and it's not what most game boards want to hear anyway.

What worried me about bear viewing—as thrilling as I found every second—was the risk of bears becoming just another commodity, not for businesses but for viewers. We didn't collect claws and hides; our trophies were close-up photographs and exciting stories. Once an animal becomes reduced to a collectible, it flattens into mere diversion. In a passionate rant against "media crimes against wildlife," veteran bear biologist Charles Jonkel argued that too many films, books, and television shows promote amusement at the expense of information. "We have all forms of people out making fools of wildlife, distorting science and biology for money, creating huge audiences based on personalities and egos, and packaged as entertainment with high-profit goals," he wrote. Just because bears will share their space with us doesn't mean they want people walking around with them or treating them like pets, he added. "If the hunter can live with a 40-page book of rules and laws, bag limits, shooting hours, closed areas, etc., so can those who profit from exploiting wildlife with cameras, pens, TV shows, field glasses, and harmonicas."

How can we recognize, understand, deepen the connections between ourselves and wild animals unless we somehow close that distance between secondhand knowledge and firsthand experience? Paul Shepard wondered about reducing our relationship with the natural world to spectatorship or untouchability—"the peculiar sentiment that animals and I should be friends at a tidy remove rather than interacting in each other's physical and psychic domains, used and user." Without spending time in their presence, how can we understand that bears are not merely harvest statistics or generic photo models or demographic categories, that bears not only look different from one another but also have different histories and personalities and behaviors?

All we can do, I suppose, is interrogate our intentions and actions, as individuals and as a species. The people I most admire did this by reading research, comparing experiences, questioning when and where and why they led other people, almost literally by the hand, to gatherings of bears. They made choices about those they guided. They spoke publicly on behalf of bears, not for any cynical business reasons but because they believed that bears matter. To them, respect wasn't a synonym for fear but a way of responding with gratitude and humility to the world's great gifts. They asked us to do more than photograph or watch or view bears. They wanted us to really see bears, if only for one afternoon in our entire lives.

the predatory bear

Mark Richards and his wife, Lori, live in a log cabin just below the Arctic Circle and not too far from Canada. The former high school sweethearts were newly married when they canoed down the Yukon River in 1980, bound for a different kind of life than the one they knew in Los Angeles. People in the tiny village of Eagle told them that if they wanted to survive in the Bush, they should first spend a winter in Fairbanks to build up their grubstake and see if they could tolerate the cold. They passed the test, and the next summer they lined their canoe up the Kandik River, built their cabin with an axe and a bow saw, and named their new home Beaver Bend. The nearest town is 130 miles away by water; the closest person is 40 miles away by air. They raised and homeschooled three children at Beaver Bend and sent them off to college. They burn wood for heat and haul water from the creek. Their staples come by bush plane, but everything else they work for—hard. They net whitefish and grayling, pick berries, dig roots, grow vegetables, gather wild plants, hunt, and trap.

"Occasionally, the meat from a wandering black bear makes its way to our summer table, its fat rendered into much-needed lard, its hide tanned and sewed into mukluks or overmitts," Richards wrote in an essay titled "Transcending the Place of Food." Moose and caribou provide meat for the winter and hides for leather, parkas, sleeping pads, and other gear. In the spring they eat beavers. Mark Richards may be one of the few people in Alaska who can recommend the flesh of a fat wolf or casually mention breakfasting on leftover hare. "This circumpolar place where we live defines us and is in effect our menu," he wrote.

Richards calls himself a "techno-primitive." Moss and solar panels cover his roof. He runs his trapline with a dog team and snowshoes, and he uses a satellite link and a laptop to beam his thoughts onto glowing computer screens all over Alaska. When he posts photographs and descriptions of his latest moose hunting expedition or a wintry circuit of his trapline, someone usually says something like, "You're living the life many dream of yet never do."

This is the Alaska dream, with something for everyone who longs for a simpler existence: self-reliance, intimacy with nature, solitude, a place where you can live the way you want with nobody to tell you any different. Today, few people have the will, ability, or opportunity to make such a fully rounded life so far from civilization, to become "hunters-and-gatherers of the 21st century," as Richards says. Even Alaska Natives—hunter-gatherers in this century and all the ones before it—rarely live in this kind of isolation, this far off the grid.

But elements of the dream lie within the reach of most Alaskans, even the 83 percent of residents who live in urban communities. The most potent and constant reminder of this yearning may be the presence of wild animals. Alaska is one of the few places where people inhabit a landscape still enlivened by wolves, bears, moose, caribou, lynx, wolverines, eagles, and many other rare and wondrous creatures of water, land, and air. Even if you don't see them or hunt them or eat them or wear them, you know they're out there. How you think about wild animals is one measure of how you see yourself, your culture, and your place in life. Perhaps this is why wildlife issues in Alaska are so passionately, sometimes virulently, debated.

Because his family lives intimately with animals and depends on them to survive, Richards has lots to say about wildlife management to fellow hunters and others interested in the outdoors. He's the cochair of the Alaska chapter of Backcountry Hunters and Anglers, an organization that focuses on hunting ethics, natural resource issues, and conservation. He writes newspaper commentaries and position papers, reads reports from the Alaska Department of Fish and Game, talks to biologists, comments on legislation, testifies at meetings. He is thoughtful and respectful on topics that often incite apoplexy. On the Alaska Outdoors Forum website, he goes by "Bushrat," but he always uses his real name and usually signs off with a friendly gesture, like "All the best to you," no matter how cranky the discussion. At the end of one long, contentious thread, an anonymous wildlife biologist wrote: "Bushrat, Mark Richards, is the single most educated and aware participant in this thread, and I hope everyone acknowledges and understands the vast amount of time he has committed to not only living in the wilderness, but learning about it through others' eyes."

No hunter has been as outspoken as Richards about the Alaska Board of Game's ever-expanding use of predator control to eliminate wolves and bears in an effort to produce more moose, caribou, and deer for hunters. By early 2013, the board had approved eighteen predator control plans throughout the state (six are considered "inactive"). Like many Alaskans, Richards doesn't oppose short-term predator control in certain conditions. For example, he approves of a state project using aerial shooting to eliminate specific grizzlies that are superefficient at killing musk oxen in a severely declining herd on the North Slope. He's not a fan of "ballot-box biology." But, like many Alaskans, he questions the board's apparent zeal for expanding lethal control to satisfy unrealistic demands for a moose or a caribou in every pot, regardless of what wildlife biologists recommend or whether there's any evidence that such tactics work. "The role of the hunter is grounded in conservation and stewardship and respect for the land and animals," Richards wrote in one opinion piece, "not in extreme plans to 'grow more caribou' at any and all costs."

At first, the game board's plans focused on allowing private pilot and shooter teams to cull most of the wolves from specific predation control areas (PCAs), either from planes or by landing and shooting—practices that Alaskan voters have twice banned only to be overruled by the legislature. Then the board began mulling ways to reduce bear populations in a few areas to improve the survival of newborn moose and caribou. Some studies show that reducing calf mortality would require the elimination of at least 60 percent of brown bear populations and 80 percent of black bears, but finding and killing that many bears isn't as easy as shooting wolves from the air. So step by step, year by year, the board has approved methods that are rarely used anymore in modern wildlife management. They include snaring bears, shooting bears over bait, spotting bears from planes and then landing to shoot them, killing cubs and females with cubs, and killing unlimited numbers of bears year-round. To encourage more people to kill more bears, the board has legalized the sale of hides and skulls from PCAs. In some places it has dropped the requirement to salvage black bear meat. In less than a decade, bears have turned from icons of wilderness into frontier vermin.

The International Association for Bear Research and Management called these control methods "highly controversial" when they were first proposed. "Most represent practices that wildlife agencies have specifically culled from their allowable hunting practices in recent decades," wrote vice president Karen Noyce, "either because of their potential for major impact on populations or because a growing proportion of both the hunting and non-hunting public felt them to be unethical." The bear's life history is one reason biologists worry about wholesale removal. In Alaska, female grizzlies often don't start producing young until they're several years old. The survival rate of cubs can be dismal in some places, and those that do live may stay with their mothers for two, three, even four years. The result is one of the slowest reproductive rates of any North American mammal.

Though it's easier than ever to kill bears in Alaska, people wielding predator control permits have so far failed to eliminate enough of them to meet the board's goals. Fuel is expensive, time is short, and killing bears is hard work. To speed things along, board members approved sending state biologists or contractors up in helicopters in 2013 and 2014 to shoot as many brown and black bears as possible within a 540-square-mile area in Southwest Alaska. The board has also moved steadily toward allowing the general public to use some particularly controversial methods, not as a formal means of predator control but to increase hunting opportunities. Classifying black bears as "furbearers" was a prelude to opening general trapping seasons, and it's legal to shoot grizzlies at bait stations in several places. There's a new normal when it comes to killing bears in Alaska.

"The entire aspect of bear control is extreme and ridiculous and it saddens me as a hunter and a conservationist," Richards wrote in an e-mail. Although the Board of Game and the Alaska Department of Fish and Game insist that fair-chase ethics don't apply because predator control is not hunting, he fears that many people will assume that all hunters approve of such distasteful practices as shooting or snaring cubs. As a minority of the populace, he says, hunters can't afford to lose support from nonhunters, most of whom don't oppose killing animals for meat. "It's bad not just for hunters but bad for the state of Alaska," he told me. "And we are taking a black eye for a lot of these things, for how we're managing our bears."

The current catchphrase for the state's approach to manipulating populations of predators and prey is "abundance management." That sounds gentler than its original name, "intensive management," and more determined than the vague "active management." No matter what you call it, intensive management (IM) is not a philosophy or a policy.

It's a legal mandate based on a 1994 statute that established human consumption as the highest and best use of moose, caribou, and deer in most of Alaska. Thus, whenever the game board decides that predators are suppressing particular game populations at the expense of people, it must use intensive management to create a harvestable surplus for hunters. "Predators have to bear their responsibility for restoration of abundance in a declining situation" is how the law's sponsor explained it. Intensive management can include benign methods such as improving habitat with controlled fires. But so far, it mostly means killing wolves and bears.

The IM law, as people call it, was a dream come true for hunter advocacy organizations such as the Alaska Outdoor Council (AOC), which has been pressuring state officials for aggressive predator control for decades. More recently, two former state senators founded the Alaska chapter of Sportsmen for Fish and Wildlife (SFW), a controversial group heavily involved in wildlife management in several western states. Former officers and board members of the AOC and SFW have served on the Board of Game and in important Fish and Game positions, where they've had influential roles in advancing predator control policies. The dynamics of these politics are nicely distilled in a Canadian review of northern predator control programs: "Since Statehood, the controversy surrounding predator control in Alaska has been a roller coaster ride driven by the sentiments of elected Governors who have the authority to appoint members to the powerful Board of Game (BOG). The BOG has been accused of being hijacked by hunters' and trappers' interests, often in opposition to the majority of Alaskans."

In territorial days, bears served as both target and pawn in political battles that pitched Alaskans against Outsiders. Historian Morgan Sherwood called those early episodes the "Bear Wars." These days, some people call the state's approach to wildlife management the "War on Bears," and it's one that sets Alaskan against Alaskan. "Like it or not," Mark Richards tells fellow hunters, "this predator control thing is very much about politics, about perception, about the appearance of respect for all views." It's also about identity. A prominent supporter of abundance management, former state senator and SFW founder Ralph Seekins, has described people who oppose predator control as "parasitical" preservationists intent on forcing their "'no-use' religion" on others. Hunters and trappers, he insists, are the true conservationists, the stewards of our God-given resources. "This isn't about wolves," he once said in a televised debate about predator control. "This is about who gets to control Alaska."

Not only about who controls Alaska but about who controls the idea of Alaska, who defines what it means to be an Alaskan, and who decides what wild animals are good for, anyway.

Predator control has long burned through Alaska's history like an underground peat fire, occasionally erupting into national view. We argue about the proper use of wild animals, but what we're really arguing about is how people fit into the natural world. To generalize: Opponents of predator control often say that wildlife and Alaska Natives worked out matters long before Euro-American settlers arrived; that natural cycles swing up and down and should be allowed to do so; that messing with the balance of prey and predator to favor a minority of residents is shortsighted, unnecessary, unrealistic, and often unsuccessful. They believe that predator control is intended to benefit urban hunters far more than subsistence hunters and trappers like Mark Richards, who actually do make a living off the land. Furthermore, they argue, the Board of Game caters to people with whom it agrees and ignores everyone else—even Alaskans who aren't allied with environmental and animal rights groups, even Alaskans who hunt but dislike predator control. They also criticize the board's reliance on thin data, minimal research, skimpy monitoring, and sweeping assumptions that widespread predator control can effectively manage wildlife populations.

Advocates of predator control say it's precisely because people belong in the natural world, because we've already interfered with natural mechanisms, that we have a right—even an obligation—to adjust the balance when it favors too many predators at the expense of humans. Nobody wants to eradicate all predators, they say, but they point to Fish and Game assertions that predators eat 70 or 80 percent of the moose and caribou that die annually—moose and caribou that technically belong to people. Remove enough predators to help ungulate populations, they believe, and the habitat will reach its full potential and produce enough surplus game to satisfy hunters. "We know this land will carry a lot more animals than it does on its own natural level," former board chair Mike Fleagle once said. They resent what they see as meddling Outsiders or antihunting extremists (often called "antis") who have no real conception of how Alaska or nature works. They derive moral and legal authority from the Alaska Constitution, which says that fish and wildlife shall be "utilized, developed, and maintained on the sustained yield principle, subject to preferences among beneficial uses" (that last clause is the tricky part). In other words, this isn't the wilderness; this is the frontier, where the whole idea is to make the most of natural resources.

Since statehood, people have hashed out these arguments through lawsuits, ballot initiatives, tourism boycotts, failed summits, and public relations campaigns. What both unites and divides many Alaskans is a deep connection with the idea and the practice of subsistence: the customary and traditional use of wild foods to feed yourself and your family. Subsistence practically defines what it means to be Alaskan—to hunt, fish, dig for clams, pick berries, gather mushrooms, harvest herring roe, go whaling for bowheads or belugas if you're Native, and much more. What happens when there are only so many resources to go around, though? Do families who live in rural Alaska and depend heavily on wild game for food have more right to the moose near their village than someone who flew in from Anchorage or Tennessee? Do a Native person's cultural traditions outweigh those of someone who grew up hunting for deer in the Midwest with his grandfather?

Advocates of predator control believe that everyone deserves a crack at that moose. If you can't put a moose in every pot, the answer isn't fewer pots but fewer predators, and therefore more moose for everybody. Villagers usually support predator control, but they generally want more moose, fewer predators, and fewer nonresident and nonlocal hunters. Others object to killing multitudes of wolves and bears to satisfy urban hunters with access to Costcos just around the corner. Complicating matters is a major legal conflict between the state and federal governments. The Alaska National Interest Lands Conservation Act gives rural residents—most of whom are Native—a subsistence priority on federal public lands. That includes about 60 percent of the state. The Alaska Supreme Court ruled in 1989 that this rural priority violates the state constitution. Alaska's inability to resolve the conflict means that each government manages subsistence uses on its own lands and waters. The resulting pile of hunting regulations is about as much fun to figure out as a quadratic equation.

Meanwhile, state wildlife biologists must try to navigate a political ecosystem infused with the values of those in charge. The system was engineered this way. The governor appoints citizens to the seven-member Board of Game but has no legal requirement to balance constituencies. The legislature confirms or rejects these appointments, writes laws, and controls the budget of the Alaska Department of Fish and Game. The Board of Game adopts hunting regulations and allocates game in periodic meetings held around the state. Residents can propose changes to regulations, testify at board meetings, or seek seats on their local Fish and Game advisory committees, which offer their opinions to the board. State wildlife biologists manage hunts and monitor wildlife populations, conduct research, carry out the board's directives, gather information, and offer recommendations.

Under three consecutive governors who pushed for predator control, the board's preoccupation with intensive management has noticeably changed how the Division of Wildlife Conservation operates and where it focuses its attention. The amount of work the department invests in predator control programs is a "significant increase from what we have had in the past," the interim director of the Division of Wildlife Conservation told the board in 2012. Regional supervisor Grant Hilderbrand, who has since left the department, told me that the increased legal and scientific demands of intensive management forced his office to significantly restructure its programs.

"At one time the constituency of the Alaska Department of Fish and Game was the well-being of wildlife populations," Fairbanks bear biologist Harry Reynolds told me after he retired. "And now it seems like it's the well-being and feeding and care of the Board of Game and intensive management. It's almost like the rationale for various programs comes down to the mantra of intensive management: 'It's the law, we've got to do it.'"

That rationale is embedded in the IM process. The board sets population and harvest objectives wherever moose, caribou, or Sitka black-tailed deer are important for human "consumptive use." To date, that covers 97.5 percent of the state's land area. If population estimates or harvest numbers don't meet those objectives, the board must consider using intensive management before reducing harvests. A persistent criticism is that many population objectives are based on misty-eyed notions of how many moose and caribou inhabited the state during what one hunting group calls "the glory days of the 1950s, 60s, and 70s," when Alaska was the "great Serengeti of the North." To many wildlife biologists, this was the era when herds swelled to artificial highs after decades of widespread trapping, shooting, and poisoning of predators, followed by some spectacular population crashes triggered by overgrazing, overhunting, bad winters, and predation.

Moose biologist Vic Van Ballenberghe says these population objectives reflect wishful thinking and WAGs (wild-ass guesses) that ignore reality: those peak populations were clearly unsustainable. Van Ballenberghe is to wildlife science what Mark Richards is to hunting. He worked for state and federal wildlife agencies for almost thirty years before retiring, and he's written more than a hundred scientific papers about moose and predator-prey relationships, as well as a book about moose based on his long-running research in Denali National Park. Van Ballenberghe also served on the Board of Game in the 1980s and was twice reappointed but not confirmed for political reasons. He's been one of Alaska's most public and persistent critics of intensive management in the mainstream press and in professional journals.

Like Richards, he doesn't oppose predator control as part of a clearly defined and scientifically based program. He objects to predator control as it is practiced now. He considers the IM statute the core problem. "First of all, it commits you to never-ending predator control because you're chasing this unattainable objective," he said. "Secondly, it gives hunters false expectations that we can get back there. So if we're not going to get there, they're going to be unhappy and they're going to be pushing for more and more wolf control. The truth of the matter is we have an unlimited demand for moose and caribou and sheep here, and even if we tripled or quadrupled a lot of these populations, there would still be more demand." Because Van Ballenberghe is a hunter, he understands the psychology that drives people to want more, more, more. "People have known this since I was a grad student many years ago—that hunters, no matter if game is at high density, they don't think there's as many as there were at one time," he said.

That phenomenon is suggested by a Fish and Game graph titled "Historical perspective on the 'good old days.'" Moose harvests were poorest from 1974 to 1982, after those epic herds crashed. But since then, the caption notes, "a steady average of about 29,000 moose hunters (including non-residents) have had a reported success rate of 23 percent to 30 percent." That's in the same ballpark as pre-1974 harvests.

In other words, moose hunting is about as good as it ever was. Though moose hunters take between 7,000 and 8,000 moose annually, the board hopes to raise that annual harvest to well above 10,000. Even if moose and caribou herds expand, they'll be paced by a human population likely to add another 200,000 residents by 2035, further pressuring habitat and crowding hunting grounds,

Nevertheless, many hunters and rural residents are convinced that there's an obvious solution to what they see as a grievous lack of game: Kill a bear, save a moose. Or, kill a bear, save a lot of moose, if you're former game board chairman Cliff Judkins. "When I look at the bear out there, I see nine moose that are going to live if I kill it. Some of us are thinking of a different reason for shooting them than we were some years ago," he said at a 2007 meeting. The simplistic notion that every dead bear (or wolf) spares a moose is common among predator control supporters. This may be true "on a very, very small, very, very localized scale," Grant Hilderbrand told me. But on a population scale, he said, removing bears creates a gap that other bears will fill, so over time, little dramatic change occurs.

Furthermore, not every bear kills calves. Some prefer salmon, vegetation, ground squirrels, carrion. Some are simply better hunters than others. Researchers Rod Boertje and colleagues once observed nine radio-collared bears killing twenty-nine moose calves, but four of those bears killed twenty-one of the calves. Van Ballenberghe saw the same patterns in his moose research. "There were some bears at Denali that were specialists at killing calves," he said. "There were some that were afraid of moose cows and would run away from moose cows with calves." Confounding matters further, individual bears can shift their own feeding habits during their lives. "The same individual bear may behave differently if she has a cub of the year versus if she's alone versus if she has a two-year-old," Hilderbrand said.

Wildlife managers face major challenges in figuring out who's killing what and how many in multipredator systems. Brown bears, black bears, and wolves prey on moose, caribou, and each other to different degrees in different areas, Harry Reynolds said. Add the vagaries of severe winters, wildfires, disease, habitat changes, and alternative food sources like salmon, and the web of life seems more like an impossible snarl, even without the confounding effects of hunting and other human influences. The result is that widespread lethal control inevitably kills bears that don't eat calves and misses bears that do. This, however, is not a problem for those who have adopted the "kill them all and let God sort them out" philosophy of wildlife management.

So does predator control work? The short answer is, "it's complicated"; the long (very long) answer depends in part on what you're measuring and how, whether those measurements are accurate, and for how long you've studied the situation. From a scientific standpoint, manipulating predator and prey populations in Alaska is largely based on a theory called low-density dynamic equilibrium (LDDE). This concept holds that lightly hunted populations of wolves and bears, together with weather events, can suppress lightly hunted ungulate populations in what's commonly known as a "predator pit." Without reducing predators to improve calf survival, the moose and caribou can't escape the pit. That's one theory, anyway. How the state's wildlife managers apply it is a different issue. Not even the professionals can agree on the use of intensive management to manipulate prey and predator populations. Members of the Alaska chapter of the Wildlife Society spent three years updating the organization's position statement on IM before circulating it for review in 2011. "Comments ranged from very positive to very negative, as you would expect for a topic that was bound to be controversial," wrote president Kris Hundertmark. The board decided to keep working on the revision.

The Alaska Department of Fish and Game explains why it's not easy to make blanket statements about what works and what doesn't: "The relative importance of predation by wolves and bears varies among areas, and the relative effectiveness of reducing primarily one predator to increase moose harvest where one or more predators exist is not well documented." That's because tracking the results of different strategies is expensive, time-consuming, and logistically difficult in a vast and varied landscape. As a result, reviews of such studies (and there aren't very many for bears) often compare apples, oranges, pears, and pineapples, making it easy to pluck out supporting evidence and difficult to determine clear cause and effect. Difficult, that is, unless you're on the Board of Game, which seems to assume that predator control works all the time, everywhere, as long as you do enough of it.

Boertje and colleagues reviewed numerous case histories and studies and concluded in a 2010 paper, "Substantially reducing predation for several years can result in more moose and elevated yields of moose in inland Alaska's moose-bear-wolf systems," particularly in settled areas.

But, they added, "in more remote areas, where bear habitat is contiguous and access is poor, no data are available to evaluate whether private take of bears can be a successful, long-term management tool to decrease bear numbers and to elevate sustained yield of moose."

In one of the lengthier research projects, department biologists captured and translocated nearly all the bears—109 black bears and 9 brown bears—away from one control area near McGrath, where wolves had been partially eliminated and hunting was restricted. Within six years, the black bear population rebounded to 111. Summer and autumn survival rates of moose calves improved, but deep snow in 2004 and 2008 meant that predator removal improved calf survival by an average of only 13 percent, biologist Mark Keech reported to the board in 2012. "Predator control really didn't gain us much in winter survival," he said. "What really affects survival is snow depth." More than three feet of snow, combined with deep cold, resulted in the deaths of half or more of the calves entering winter. "In the short term, reducing a substantial number of predators in a small area did increase overall survival and population size, with moose density increasing by 45 percent," Keech and coauthors wrote in a 2011 paper. "However, our experimental program was too costly to routinely utilize," they added. The department spent more than $2 million on research for this project alone. Returns may already be diminishing; in 2010–2011 the trend of increasing moose abundance stalled and then declined slightly during the next two years, according to a Fish and Game performance report.

Four veteran wildlife biologists—Sterling Miller, John Schoen, Jim Faro, and David Klein—reviewed these studies and others in a 2011 analysis of trends in intensive management for grizzly bears in Alaska. They acknowledged that under some circumstances, bears may limit the growth of moose populations by preying heavily on calves. "However, there are no studies demonstrating that increased grizzly bear hunting or reduced grizzly bear abundance resulted in more harvestable moose," they wrote.

Van Ballenberghe has never disputed research showing that predator control can work in some places for at least a short time—he conducted some of it himself. "What's really the nub of the matter to me is that there is no requirement in the regs or in the statutes that we have any kind of a scientific basis for what the board does," he told me. "There's a legal issue in that they can't be arbitrary or capricious. And they certainly go through the motions. But nothing requires them to do things with sound science standards." That would include, among other things, collecting accurate information about predator and prey numbers beforehand, determining mortality causes and rates, and closely monitoring the effects of predator removal—none of which is done consistently or comprehensively under state predator plans. "Such programs can lead to ecological damage by triggering ungulate eruptions, habitat destruction, and crashes in prey populations, and they may threaten predator population viability," Van Ballenberghe wrote in a 2011 commentary in The Wildlife Professional. "By any standard, that is mismanagement." He considers the situation in Tanana Flats south of Fairbanks a prime example of unintended consequences of intensive management. After decades of wolf control and liberal bear hunting, the moose population grew so much that management biologists have struggled for years to keep the herd from overwhelming the habitat. Biologists succeeded largely by persuading reluctant hunters that killing calves, cow moose, and antlerless bulls was the only way to avoid an eventual population crash.

Since 2011, Fish and Game staff have produced feasibility plans to help the game board decide whether IM is likely to succeed in certain areas. The board is not obligated to use this information, however. The plans describe such factors as landownership patterns, habitat quality, local support, and the frequency of deep-snow winters. For example, under one plan, department staff using helicopters and planes would remove about 90 percent of the wolves in a PCA near the villages of Allakaket and Alatna and then suppress the population for five years. The estimated cost: $548,000, not including personnel. (Although brown and black bears are the area's main moose eaters, villagers oppose bear control for cultural reasons.) But in nine of twenty winters, snow depths in the area exceeded three feet, usually for months at a time—the same conditions that virtually erased gains in calf survival near McGrath. Some department biologists have suggested that predator control might not be worth the effort where deep snow occurs in at least half the winters because moose—especially calves—will inevitably perish in high numbers. Despite the toll this new plan would take on budgets and wolves, the substantial risk of losing calves to natural causes did not trouble the game board. The plan isn't really intended to meet IM objectives anyway. Instead, the idea is to produce an additional 300 to 350 moose over a decade and "reallocate" them from wolves to humans. Those will be some mighty expensive moose.

Although board and department leadership insists the state's programs are scientifically grounded, hundreds of scientists have disagreed in periodic letters and resolutions. The American Society of Mammalogists, for example, wrote three letters of concern and in 2006 approved a resolution with a chain of whereases noting things such as the importance of obtaining reliable population estimates instead of relying on historical estimates that are probably inaccurate. Governors, department administrators, and the Board of Game have shown no sign of taking these letters, resolutions, and presentations seriously, aside from the occasional defensive remark or dismissive response.

"I would have thought we gained a lot of ground in the '60s and '70s in terms of ecological literacy," wildlife biologist Terry DeBruyn told me. "And you turn around and, oh boy, it all disappeared." DeBruyn has studied black and brown bears and is now the polar bear project leader for the US Fish and Wildlife Service. When I asked him about predator control, he shrugged and said, "There's no doubt about it, it works. If you kill the predators, you'll probably have some more caribou or whatever you're after." But, as bear biologists have repeatedly noted, the slow reproductive rate of bears is a major conservation concern, particularly for brown bears. Only long-term, ongoing research examining how predators and prey regulate each other can offer insights into population dynamics and explore the effects of weather and other variables, DeBruyn said. One example is the moose and wolf population on Isle Royale in Lake Superior, which has been studied since 1958 and demonstrates that even a "simple" one predator–one prey system experiences major fluctuations and unpredictable events. But people who want a guarantee that they'll get their caribou next year usually aren't interested in the long-term subtleties of wildlife science.

The Board of Game and the Department of Fish and Game have long ignored most of the recommendations and guidance offered by the National Research Council committee that published *Wolves, Bears, and Their Prey in Alaska: Biological and Social Challenges in Wildlife Management* in 1997, at the request of Governor Tony Knowles. The panel of scientists found evidence that wolves and bears can suppress game populations in certain circumstances and that removing predators can hasten recovery "under appropriate conditions." However, in northern ecosystems, they wrote, it's unrealistic to expect that game populations can be managed into permanent stability. Complicating matters was that a dozen wolf or bear control cases in Alaska were "less informative than might have been hoped," the reviewers said. The design, execution, and monitoring of results had serious deficiencies because Fish and Game biologists usually didn't have proper resources. "Differences in interpretation are possible because the supporting data are sparse," the authors found.

With so many approaches tried, teasing out which factors mattered became more difficult. For example, the panel said, twenty-five years of caribou data provided by Patrick Valkenburg showed that calf survival declined as wolf numbers increased, but the amount of summer rainfall also showed a positive correlation. So which had a greater effect, weather or wolves? "Variations in weather, habitat conditions, and behavior of predators and prey guarantee that outcomes will be varied, difficult to predict, and difficult to interpret," the reviewers concluded. This lengthy report suggested, among other measures, that wildlife managers establish better standards and guidelines and abandon the "why not try snaring bears?"style of the game board. Instead, they should conduct predator control programs as scientific experiments, using a study design that compares results in a PCA with results in a similar area where the population isn't manipulated.

The council's original chair, Gordon Orians, reviewed current predator control plans at the request of Sterling Miller and his colleagues. Orians determined that the state's plans still don't include adequate predator or socioeconomic research, experimental design, or monitoring before and after predator control. "Indeed, recent predator control efforts have not been designed to test whether predators are actually controlling prey populations," he concluded. "Rather, control efforts have been initiated under the assumption (or conviction) that predators are the cause and that the solution to the 'problem' is intensive predator control."

One reason definitive answers remain elusive is that most control programs are designed to reduce predators to produce more ungulates for humans (management) rather than to provide insights into predator-prey dynamics (science), according to the Wildlife Society's technical review of carnivores. In Alaska the board's decisions force biologists to mingle science and management, which is a bit like mixing vinegar and baking soda and then, after the foam erupts, trying to separate the two. The pilot-gunner teams take to the air, hunters set up bait stations, trappers lay out snares, and then wildlife biologists count, analyze, track, model, and theorize, based on what happened. They don't have the luxury of conducting tests or experiments.

Research for the sake of research is the work of universities, Fish and Game spokesperson Cathie Harms explained to me when the department was beginning bear control. "Having never had a state program to reduce a number of bears for management purposes, we're really, literally kind of learning as we go because we don't have any history of what works really well and what doesn't," she said. "So we're really experimenting and documenting and determining what the tools are. If it turns out that what we tried doesn't work, we're not going to try it again." By "experimenting," she meant trying things out, not experimenting in the scientific sense. The method of "learning by doing" is known as adaptive management. Wildlife managers undertake actions even if they are uncertain about the outcome, according to ecologist Caryl Elzinga, but they measure and evaluate the effects and apply their insights to future actions. But as Harry Reynolds once told me, "adaptive management" may roll off the tongue nicely, but it isn't "trying things and picking and choosing and seeing what works. It means clear measures of success or failure." For the board, though, there are really only two clear measures of success or failure: population objectives and harvest objectives.

"I truly don't see that the debate on this issue lies with the biology," Grant Hilderbrand told me. "The debate lies with whether or not it is socially acceptable to prioritize one species over another and, in doing so, conduct biological control activities on one species to benefit another." The IM statute answered this question years ago, he said. Board of Game member Teresa Sager Albaugh, a reliable pro–predator control vote, understands this. "While social considerations and values are important to this process, I think we need to be careful about presenting to the public the concept that they're going to be the factor upon which a program is adopted or not," she said in a 2012 discussion of the department's new IM protocol. She wasn't implying that the board has no interest in public opinion, she said, but the IM statute had already established the fundamental criterion: the highest and best use of game is human consumption. Thus, the Board of Game's mission isn't uncovering the nuances of predator-prey dynamics or understanding Alaska's ecosystems (science). It's deciding who gets what (management).

What frustrates many Alaskans is that so much of the money and effort expended on predator control largely benefits the 15 percent of residents with hunting licenses, as well as some commercial guides and nonresident hunters. Periodically, some starry-eyed dreamer tries to convince the legislature to rechristen the Board of Game as the Board of Wildlife to better represent so-called nonconsumptive users. (Board members often point out that they like to watch and photograph wildlife, too). So far, these efforts have failed. Rod Arno of the Alaska Outdoor Council e-mailed me this response to recurring complaints about the board's balance: "The critics are unbalanced if they believe there are enough anti-hunters in Alaska to warrant a seat on a board that regulates hunting and trapping. Predator Worshipers should start their own faith, not try and participate on a regulatory board that is bound by the Alaska Constitution's Article VIII."

Hunters feel a deep sense of entitlement partly because of the way wildlife agencies are funded. The Pittman-Robertson Act collects excise taxes from the sale of ammunition, guns, bows and arrows, and other equipment and redistributes the money to states for fish and wildlife restoration. As a target shooter, I like to think I contribute, too, but a former board member told me that doesn't count. Ironically, fears that President Barack Obama would restrict gun rights have spiked weapon and ammunition sales since early in his first term, creating windfalls that added $34 million to Alaska's coffers in 2011 alone, according to the Department of the Interior. Paranoia may be conservation's best friend.

Nonhunters would happily pay their way if anybody would let them. A 2003 bill to tax wildlife-viewing activities in Alaska could have raised an estimated $11 million to manage nongame animals, but it died in the legislature. One obstacle was opposition from hunter groups unwilling to relinquish any say in wildlife management to others, according to the director of the Division of Wildlife Conservation at the time.

In the meantime, nonresidents contribute more than anybody. Ten percent of hunters in Alaska are nonresidents, but because they pay more for licenses and fees, they contribute 85 percent of the Division of Wildlife Conservation's budget outside of federal funds, Cathie Harms said. A nonresident hunter pursuing a moose pays $85 for the license and $400 for the tag, for example. In contrast, "for $25 a resident can take home a thousand pounds of meat," Harms said. Even so, Alaska is a bargain for nonresident hunters compared with most western states. Attempts to raise fees for everyone have failed repeatedly, and the department can't afford to alienate nonresidents who might head to Canada instead, she said. Meanwhile, the game board routinely waives the $25 tag fee for brown bears throughout much of Alaska to encourage more hunters to kill more bears.

You can't say nobody warned Alaskans. In 1955 conservationist and biologist Ira Gabrielson came north to offer advice to the good citizens writing the state constitution. Gabrielson had been the first director of the US Fish Wildlife Service and had recently studied state wildlife agencies. "Wildlife management, if you could deal only with the wild populations and their problems, would be relatively simple," he told them, "but in my opinion most wildlife management consists of five percent dealing with wildlife things and 95 percent dealing with wild people, and most of the problems and most of the headaches in wildlife administration come from human attitudes and human problems, not from the wildlife problems."

Bears didn't suddenly wake up one day and decide to start eating defenseless calves. Although wolves long took most of the blame and suffered most of the consequences of predator control, studies in the late 1970s and early 1980s began to show that brown and black bears can be significant predators of newborn moose and caribou. In some places, bears consume up to half of all calves, occasionally more. A few studies concluded that this predation was the biggest reason moose populations diminished by severe winters weren't recovering well. "In response to these findings, grizzly bear management in most of Alaska shifted from conservative management toward management designed to reduce grizzly bear abundance even though a causal link between bear predation and ungulate abundance remained unestablished," wrote Sterling Miller and colleagues in a *Journal of Wildlife Management* paper.

Starting in about 1980, their analysis showed, the state embarked on a kind of slow-motion predator control program for bears. By waiving tag fees, lengthening seasons, and raising bag limits, the Board of Game hoped hunters would reduce bear populations and thus improve prey populations. These liberalized regulations eventually applied to more than three-quarters of the state, the researchers calculated. During the same period, grizzly harvests increased sharply. The mean annual harvest in this "liberal hunt area" was 387 bears in the late 1970s. By the mid-2000s, it was 827 bears.

In 2001 McGrath biologist Toby Boudreau told a reporter that state-sponsored bear control seemed unimaginable. "That's a place I don't think anyone wants to go," he said. "People have a lot of respect for brown bears." That taboo disappeared with the election of Governor Frank Murkowski in 2002. His predecessor, Tony Knowles, had made himself very unpopular among hunters by suspending wolf control programs unless they were cost-effective, based on sound science, and publicly supported. Many still blame Knowles for what they consider to be a state overrun by carnivores. Murkowski shifted direction fast enough to cause whiplash, immediately appointing six predator control advocates to the seven-member game board. "My directive to them is to manage our wildlife for abundance, which is a higher standard than even the sustained yield principle required by the state constitution," he announced. Departing board member Joel Bennett told the *Anchorage Daily News*, "[The appointments] are a step back in time, to say the least. To an older day when wildlife in the state was purely at the beck and call of hunters."

Pro–predator control groups were finally happy. As the new board revved up a conveyor belt of control plans, it seized on complaints from hunters and rural residents that bears were gobbling more than their share of ungulates. Here's an example from someone who submitted the standard proposal form in 2004, asking the board to legalize the killing of bear cubs and mothers:

ISSUE: *Declining moose populations. Bears are eating calves.*
WHO IS LIKELY TO BENEFIT? *Moose and their calf [sic].*
WHO IS LIKELY TO SUFFER? *Animal cultists (animal rights people who worship animals and put them before people).*
OTHER SOLUTIONS CONSIDERED: *The department could shoot bears from the air, but this would be too politically incorrect.*

Not anymore.

A prime example of how politics and special interests have trumped wildlife science occurred in Game Management Unit 16, an area across Cook Inlet from Anchorage that's roughly the size of Maryland. Moose were uncommon there before the 1940s, according to the Alaska Department of Fish and Game, but by the 1960s, they numbered about 10,000. When the moose population in Unit 16 shrank to an estimated 3,200 to 3,900 animals, biologists blamed wolves and numerous bad winters. Opening a hunt in the 1980s that harvested at least 100 cows per winter probably didn't help. Eventually, hunting was severely restricted, but the board has given Unit 16 a lot of attention since 2004 because the state's largest population of urban hunters lives in nearby Anchorage and the Matanuska-Susitna Valley. The board established a PCA that covered much of the unit and approved aerial wolf control to help reduce their numbers by 80 percent. A few years later, it added black bears to the control program.

At the time, department biologists told the board they didn't really know how many wolves, brown bears, and black bears inhabited the PCA. Estimates varied widely. They pegged the brown bear population at 625 to 1,250, for example. Black bear population estimates started with 1,376 to 1,574 animals and kept changing until the department settled on 3,200 to 3,800 following a 2007 survey. The lack of more precise population data is a chronic criticism of predator control plans. The department does the best it can with an insufficient budget, but it often relies on harvest reports, sightings, density extrapolations from similar habitats, and trend surveys rather than expensive and time-consuming censuses, which, according to Van Ballenberghe, most professionals consider more reliable. Fish and Game had demonstrated how inaccurate surveys could be when a 2001 census of the McGrath PCA counted 3,660 moose, far more than the original estimate of 869. (The board readjusted the predator control plan so it could continue to remove wolves and bears anyway.)

Unit 16 presented an even more complicated problem, though. "Biologists also don't know which predator—bears or wolves—is most responsible for killing moose calves," a department newsletter reported—*after* the bear control program had started. Nor did they know which species of bears was the culprit. Without studies or surveys, I asked Hilderbrand, how did the department identify black bears as responsible for most moose calf deaths? Anecdotal reports from the public and field observations from biologists monitoring moose, he said.

Hilderbrand had shown the board a population model demonstrating that if it wanted to reach its moose population and harvest objectives in Unit 16's PCA, it would probably have to eliminate at least 60 percent of the black bears, most of them females (assuming black bears were actually the biggest calf predators). "Obviously I'm not advocating for this, but when we talk about . . . times that different predator populations were actually held in check for a long time, you [have to] go back to territorial days when they were using broadcast poison," Hilderbrand told me. "Obviously that's something that's not legal, nor do I think it's tenable. But that's what it would probably take to get to where they [board members] want to go." Department biologists scrambled to convince the board to hold off on adding brown bears to the predator control plan until they could evaluate the results of removing wolves and black bears.

The board chose the next best alternative to broadcast poison—unlimited killing. Residents with free predator control permits could take as many black bears as they liked—yearlings, adults, cubs, mothers—and the more the better, as far as the board was concerned. "It's really true we're not going to control this population or have much effect unless females are taken," said member Ron Somerville (he has since left the board). "This is just a reality of this type of predator management program." Some hunters felt queasy about the new "any bear" provision, which also applied to grizzly bears and their offspring near Mc-Grath. "Allowing the harvest of sows and cubs or cubs alone is crossing a moral and ethical boundary that I would be ashamed to see the state of Alaska cross," guide Jake Jefferson wrote in a letter to the board. Killing every bear possible would undoubtedly boost moose numbers, but it would also degrade the image of Alaska hunters, he wrote: "At what point do we decide that predator control is about management and not eradication?" But any method was okay with Duane Goodrich of Palmer, who served on the Matanuska Valley Fish and Game Advisory Committee. "I don't believe in fair chase for vermin," he told the *Anchorage Daily News*. "If you're trying to get rid of them, why worry about it?"

I asked the executive director of the Alaska Outdoor Council, Rod Arno, whether he thought shooting cubs would cause a public backlash, something that Mark Richards and other hunters worried about. "If hunters could help manage one of Alaska's renewable resources on a sustained-yield basis for the benefit of themselves, in the form of wild food to eat, and income to the State where would the backlash come from?" Arno asked in an e-mail. "The backlash would come," he wrote, "from 'wildlife worshippers' who oppose the killing of wildlife by humans for any reason; nothing hunters do to try and make themselves socially acceptable other than quit hunting will ever appease them. It's naive and shows a lack of experience for anyone to say capitulating to anti-hunters will ever gain their support to manage wildlife for human consumption."

Retired state biologist Patrick Valkenburg, then a vice president of the Alaska Outdoor Council, used a more pragmatic tone. "There are certainly many hunters who don't like the idea of bear control, especially killing sows and cubs. This is a real dilemma for wildlife managers," he e-mailed. "Unfortunately, I think it is becoming clear that bear numbers can't be reduced without removing the protection from sows and cubs." Besides, bear populations are far more resilient than once thought, he said. Look how rapidly they recovered from the widespread poisoning of the 1950s.

Killing more than 2,600 black bears seemed daunting, but Sportsmen for Fish and Wildlife and its nonprofit arm, Sportsmen for Habitat, announced that they were eager to help in this grand cause by sponsoring bear-baiting camps for their members in Unit 16. But despite regulations passed specifically to benefit these efforts (more about that later), the board was unsatisfied with the 300 or so black bears being killed annually in the unit.

Let's try something new, suggested board members, who were encouraged by the enthusiasm of newly appointed Fish and Game officials with strong ties to the AOC and SFW. They approved a snaring "experiment" using qualified trappers to catch black bears using foot snares placed on the ground or in baited five-gallon buckets attached to tree trunks at shoulder height. Bears that reach into the pails trigger a cable that holds them by the paw until the trapper arrives to dispatch them. Mark Richards was among those who opposed this plan. Aside from the ethical considerations, he asked, how would trappers avoid catching young brown bears—and how would they handle a nightmare scenario like a snared cub being defended by its agitated mother? The board solved the problem by allowing trappers to kill up to ten "incidental" brown bears in case department biologists couldn't fly out with tranquilizers to release them safely. After all, brown bears are predators too, they reasoned. Sure enough, in the experiment's first year, trappers snared eighty-one black bears and eight brown bears, three of which were euthanized when they couldn't be freed safely. Between 2009 and 2012, trappers released at least seventeen brown bears caught in black bear snares—a sign that the bucket design needs more work if the board is going to allow widespread black bear trapping.

Did clearing out predators help moose calves survive their first wobbly weeks? In 2010 the department tracked the fates of radio-tagged calves born in an area with the highest reduction in black bears. By then, hunters and people with predator control permits had killed at least 2,500 black bears and 645 brown bears in Unit 16 since 2005. The study confirmed what every Alaskan knows: most baby moose die before autumn. About half the monitored calves perished in their first two and a half weeks; by six months, 80 percent were gone. As research biologist Lou Bender later explained to the board, "If you're a moose calf, the first three weeks of life pretty much suck, and the first five weeks aren't all that better, but once you get through five weeks, you're doing pretty good." Black bears did not top the list of calf predators, however. They were responsible for about 21 percent of known mortalities, while 53 percent ended up in the bellies of brown bears. Biologists couldn't determine which predator killed 15 percent of the calves. More cows, calves, and yearlings were surviving the winter—partly due to low wolf populations, the department believed—but so far, predator control wasn't improving calf survival.

This is one of the difficult puzzles in predator-prey management: does removing bears to improve calf survival actually lead to more harvestable moose later? Harry Reynolds thought the board should focus less on calf survival and more on yearling survival. "The figures for calves are always more dramatic because one of their jobs is to die," he explained. "One of the bear's jobs is to be predators and eat vegetation, and one of the calves' job is to do their part for the ecosystem." This point was repeated in a technical review of predator management programs released in 2012 by the Wildlife Society, a professional organization. Agencies usually rely on short-term, indirect methods such as measuring calf mortality rather than gathering information about the direct, long-term effects of predator control on ungulate populations, the review noted. "Almost without exception, these investigations reveal that most mortality is attributable to predation," the review concluded. "The connection between predator and prey is oversimplified through this approach, however, especially when it only lasts a few years. Predation on ungulates is an expected major cause of mortality, outside of human harvest." In other words, that's what happens in nature: predators eat prey.

However, upon learning that brown bears were eating the biggest share of calves in Unit 16, board members didn't throttle back on killing wolves or black bears. Instead, they doubled down on brown bears by opening a year-round season in most of the unit and creating an "experimental" 900-square-mile brown bear control area where people with permits could snare brown bears or shoot them over bait. "We're really changing the way this board operates," vice chair Ted Spraker said. "I think this is justified in this case." Mark Richards couldn't believe it: "Well, duh, you just killed all the black bears around there, and now you're saying you want to trap grizzly bears because grizzly bears are killing more than black bears are? I mean, come on, give me a break." Department biologists had suggested from the beginning that black bears thrived in Unit 16 because wolf control and increased grizzly harvests had helpfully removed two of their main predators and competitors. Board member Ben Grussendorf thought that eliminating more brown bears seemed like a dandy way to produce even more black bears. "Probably the greatest takers of black bears are brown bears," he said. "That's a main part of their diet. They know what subsistence is, too."

But other board members figured they might as well try snaring brown bears, since nothing else seemed to make much of a difference. "I think we ought to do this for awhile and see if there's any impact, see what happens," said chair Cliff Judkins. "If it's not doing anything, two or three years from now we need to change the damn plan and do something that works." What that might be, no one suggested.

In the meantime, the board added another predator to the mix: nonresident moose hunters. "So really, who are we doing this for?" Mark Richards asked. "It's not just for the resident hunters. It's for the trophy hunters as well, and for the guides." Allowing out-of-state hunters to harvest game in PCAs is a touchy subject for many hunters and for people opposed to predator control. The game board and predator control advocates have insisted for years that intensive management is all about feeding Alaskans, yet in 2010 the board voted down proposals to eliminate nonresident hunting for caribou and moose in several PCAs. "Everybody loves to beat up on the ugly, old nonresident but the fact is they pay a lot of the game management bills in Alaska," said Fish and Game spokesman Bruce Bartley after the board approved fifty bull moose permits issued to nonresidents in the Nelchina region for the first time in a decade. To many people, the decision only reinforced the perception that intensive management is little more than expensive game farming. The AOC's Rod Arno took on the "antis" in a letter to the editor: "Alaska hunters and nonresident hunters will benefit from predator/prey management; why not trophy hunters too?"

Why not indeed? There's no sense in letting nature waste perfectly good bull moose when out-of-state trophy hunters could help, figured assistant guide David McHoes. "Much of the available surplus of bull moose is being managed for the benefit of scavengers and maggots," he wrote in his proposal to allow nonresident moose hunters into Unit 16, even though the population hadn't reached the game board's objectives yet. McHoes also happened to be one of the unit's bear trappers. During the snaring project's first summer, he caught twenty-seven black bears, he wrote in *Alaska Trapper* magazine. By his reckoning, 2,000 resident hunters would generate $50,000 in revenue, but 50 guided nonresidents could add more than $500,000 to the economy, what with airfare, lodging, taxidermy, and fees of $5,000 to $10,000 for guides like him. The only people who stood to lose anything were resident hunters, he wrote: "These individuals would rather see surplus moose end up as scavenger and maggot food then [*sic*] to allow non-resident hunters to harvest some of them." Out-of-state hunters usually take the antlers and leave the meat for Alaskans anyway, he argued. The board approved his proposal as a way to reduce the number of bulls, which would otherwise compete with productive cows for food and habitat. Nonresident trophy hunters using guides would be most successful at harvesting these bulls, the board reasoned.

Two years later, department staff spent a few hours at a board meeting essentially conducting a postmortem on the problem that had vexed so many people for so long. What happens to moose calf survival rates if you kill about 3,000 black bears and 800 brown bears in the neighborhood? Long story short: Nothing. Zero. Zip. Researchers had repeated the calf mortality study in 2012 and found that after eleven years of wolf control, five years of black bear control, and two years of brown bear control, only about 14 percent of tagged moose calves survived until late fall. Bender told the board that he could detect no relationship between calf survival and bear removal at any scale: "Even the most intensive level of treatment . . . [in] the Brown Bear Control Area, where basically everything was wide open for brown bears—any way you can think of to kill them and take them, that's fine, as many as you want, just rack 'em and stack 'em and get 'em out of there—even that . . . was ineffective in terms of getting either near the desired reduction of bears and/or having any influence whatsoever on calf survival." The most likely reason that calf survival rates hadn't budged was that the public simply hadn't killed nearly enough bears to make a difference, he said. Despite the startling number of bears removed from the PCA, harvest percentages never approached the original goal of reducing the black bear population by 80 percent and the brown bear population by 60 percent. In fact, public interest in killing as many bears as possible had dwindled significantly after the first thrilling seasons of unlimited bags, baiting camps, and snaring. Trappers had snared twenty-one brown bears during the experiment's first year, for example, but only two the following season.

The principle had seemed so straightforward: kill some bears, save some calves, grow some moose. Spraker and other board members couldn't quite believe the department's conclusions. Even more puzzling was the news that the unit's moose population had surpassed the low end of the population objective. If hard-core predator control didn't deserve the credit, what accounted for the area's increased moose numbers? Good weather and habitat conditions might have helped, speculated regional supervisor Bruce Dale. Maybe severe reductions in the unit's wolf population had contributed to cow survival, Bender suggested. Unfortunately, he said, nobody could say for sure because the department hadn't started monitoring the moose population until 2005—after predator control had began. Board member Pete Probasco asked whether more bears could inhabit Unit 16 than anyone had suspected. "I'm extremely unconfident of our bear population [estimates] in GMU 16 or virtually anywhere," Bender replied (a statement that should prompt a hard look at all bear control plans). Bears are especially tricky to spot in brushy or forested regions like Unit 16, he explained, so counting them accurately in a small geographic area is "very, very, very hard to do."

In light of these disappointing results, the board approved the department's request to suspend—but not eliminate—bear control in Unit 16. "We don't want to take this off the books," Dale assured board members. "We want to leave the tools in place." But rather than continue the unsuccessful and controversial control methods, Dale said, the department preferred to focus on developing a better way to estimate bear populations quickly and accurately. Another project would experiment with the use of camera-equipped collars to identify and perhaps remove individual bears that are especially skilled predators.

Nobody said, "We told you so," but perhaps they should have. Before bear control began, Hilderbrand and other biologists had mentioned the iffy nature of wildlife population estimates, the dearth of solid information about interactions among multiple predators, and the lack of baseline data that could make before-and-after comparisons more useful. But delaying the IM plan long enough to conduct proper wildlife censuses would have wasted time and moose, as far as the board was concerned. As a result, nobody could explain with any certainty—scientifically, anyway—why the moose population had increased. The grand "experiment" in Unit 16 had cost a lot of money (at least $436,000) and reaped a lot of controversy. Those who had once been enthusiastic about participating in public bear control had faded away, but those who had always opposed it were still mad.

Some board members couldn't understand why Unit 16's plan had failed when predator control had been so successful near McGrath. Bender reminded them that department staff, not volunteers, had used helicopters to transport half the brown bears and all but a few of the black bears at least 150 miles away from McGrath. Private pilot-gunner teams had also eliminated 75 percent of the wolves. In response, moose calf survival had improved from an annual average of 30 percent before predator control to 46 percent. "Now, that's not a small increase, either biologically or statistically," Bender said. Nevertheless, he noted, about 55 percent of calves born in the study area didn't survive to weaning, much less adulthood.

He failed to point out another important fact: three years after giving all those bears free helicopter rides, the black bear population around McGrath PCA had rebounded to almost 75 percent of its earlier total. One implication is that black bear populations can recover faster than previously thought. Another is that even small improvements in calf survival would require Fish and Game staff to cull predators thoroughly and regularly—an approach that seems uncomfortably close to state-sponsored game farming, no matter what you call it. Some people might question whether spending $2 million and years of effort is worth such temporary gains, but Spraker immediately grasped the possibilities. "The take-home message to me is that you've shown that . . . the tools that we've authorized so far . . . haven't been successful. But in McGrath, they were," he said to Bender. "So it looks like what you've clearly shown is that 16B needs to be . . . ramped up, the department [needs to] get involved in it or hire people to do it, if . . . what you really want to do [is] increase the moose population." In other words, if the public doesn't share the Board of Game's commitment to eliminating most of the bears from Subunit 16B, the board will delegate bear-killing duties to the Fish and Game Department.

That decision likely depends on how well aerial bear shooting works in Subunit 19A, not far from McGrath. Eight years of wolf control, hunting closures, and liberal bear seasons have done nothing to improve a sparse moose population that is an important food source for several Native communities, but local interest in eliminating the four-legged competition has been dampened by the low price of wolf pelts and the high cost of fuel. So the board has approved a strategy that Spraker described as "surgical and efficient." In the spring of 2013 and 2014, department staff in helicopters will shoot every brown and black bear possible (including cubs and females) in a 540-square-mile area that straddles the middle Kuskokwim River. In effect, the state will subsidize the creation of a temporary, nearly predator-free zone. Biologists estimate that 10 to 15 brown bears and 135 to 160 black bears inhabit this "bear control focus area." The department ruled out relocating the bears because that would cost an additional $25,000 to $30,000 and because residents living elsewhere don't want bears dropped off in their neighborhoods. Nobody explained how the program would prevent wandering bears from quickly occupying the newly emptied habitat, however. As the Wildlife Society's carnivore review noted, it's difficult to understand how predator populations respond to lethal control without documenting whether the remaining bears are survivors or immigrants.

In the early 1960s the new Alaska Department of Fish and Game conducted a secret campaign to shoot brown bears from airplanes on behalf of Kodiak Island cattle ranchers. Local hunting guides tipped off *Outdoor Life* magazine, which ran a story in August 1964 titled "The Kodiak Bear War" by well-known Alaska writer Jim Reardon. The spectacular cover depicted a Piper Super-Cub strafing a snarling brown bear. Public outrage embarrassed the department into trading airplanes for hunting dogs for a few years, before it eventually dropped bear control altogether. A half century later, shooting bears from planes for the exclusive benefit of a few people has once again become the most innovative solution for managing bears on the Last Frontier. The paradox is that such blunt methods are a quick and dirty way to unwild what supposedly makes Alaska so meaningful to sport, trophy, and subsistence hunters. Finessing the vocabulary is merely part of the process of making these techniques seem ordinary. "I really look forward to the day that we don't use the term 'intensive management' any longer," Spraker said. "It's not intensive management, it's just something that the department does, recognizing and identifying wise use of the resource. . . . 'Intensive management' is almost like 'sport hunting' to me, one of those terms we hope we will not use in the future." The practice, yes. The term, no.

The push to legalize bear trapping outside of PCAs wasn't Sarah Palin's idea. Nor did she introduce politics to wildlife management for the first time in history. However, she bludgeoned the Department of Fish and Game with such blunt political force that the aftermath persisted long after she quit her job to become the self-declared Mama Grizzly of the Tea Party.

The Alaska Outdoor Council's political action committee endorsed Palin when she ran for governor, and she signaled her allegiance to abundance management by appointing AOC executive director Rod Arno and other predator control supporters to her transition team. She not only continued her predecessor's enthusiasm for predator control; she also proved herself a little too gung-ho when her plan to pay volunteer pilot-gunner teams $150 for each wolf they collected was ruled an illegal bounty in court. In addition, she spoke out against a citizens' ballot initiative to restrict aerial predator control to department employees during biological emergencies only.

Two weeks before the election in which voters would decide on this initiative, the Alaska Department of Fish and Game distributed thousands of glossy booklets titled *Understanding Predator Management in Alaska*, produced with $400,000 that the department had never officially requested. Total coincidence, everyone insisted. A record 56,000 people had signed the petition placing the initiative on the ballot, but misleading advertising and a confusing "vote 'yes' if you mean 'no' " phrasing from the state's election office helped sink it. Palin also introduced a bill to legalize the airborne shooting of wolves, wolverines, and bears by citizens. This bill would have relieved the game board from the tedious burden of considering recommendations from Fish and Game or even following pesky intensive management rules. The bill passed in the Alaska house but died in committee when the session ended.

Palin outsourced the direction of wildlife management to special-interest groups to an unprecedented degree. Fish and Game's new deputy commissioner was Patrick Valkenburg, former state caribou biologist and vice president of the AOC. Former AOC executive director Jennifer Yuhas served as the department's legislative liaison and public information officer. And Palin invented a position—assistant commissioner of abundance management—for Corey Rossi, the predator management adviser for Sportsmen for Habitat. She had originally submitted his name as a possible commissioner of the Department of Fish and Game, but the joint Boards of Fish and Game nominated someone else. Rossi didn't have a college degree, and his only training in wildlife management stemmed from a federal job supervising pest control projects such as removing birds from airport runways and rats from the Aleutian Islands. (Critics called him a "gopher choker.") More important, he had employed Palin's parents, who led his list of references.

Rossi took the lead in proselytizing for the administration's predator policies. When actress Ashley Judd appeared in a Defenders of Wildlife television ad criticizing Alaska's aerial wolf control program, Palin's chief of staff dispatched Rossi to wangle invitations to appear on local talk shows and write an op-ed piece in defense of the program. "Perfect! Thanks!" Palin e-mailed. "It'll be our opportunity to explain to the rest of the world why we do this. Sort of like them killing snakes, rats, coyotes, etc. to protect their crops and livestock—I don't hear anyone griping about the practice." As the bad publicity continued, she blasted an SOS to her staff, asking them to urge Rossi's people to start pushing back. "I'm honestly getting my ass kicked on this one and have no idea why people aren't standing up to defend the practice they ask me to enact and support," she wrote.

Rossi and Valkenburg acted as an instant response team, ever prepared to push back against persistent criticism from wildlife professionals—some of whom had resigned or retired from Fish and Game to escape an agency inexorably sinking into political quicksand. In a rebuttal to a commentary describing the flaws in intensive management by Van Ballenberghe, they accused "well-meaning" scientists of blurring the line between science and policy. "In our view, it is unlikely that these scientists would be criticizing the science if they did not disagree with the policy," they wrote, apparently oblivious to the amusing irony of this statement. (Board of Game member Ted Spraker was a coauthor.)

Rossi and Valkenburg also shepherded several controversial proposals through the game board approval process. One was the decision to snare black bears. Another was assisting Sportsmen for Habitat set up bear-baiting camps in Unit 16, a project Rossi had helped organize before his appointment. The board approved Rossi's proposal to allow Sportsmen for Habitat to ferry its members and their gear to these camps in helicopters, a scheme that dissenting board member Ben Grussendorf called a "jihad against black bears by paramilitary groups." Mark Richards pointed out that the board had waived the requirement to salvage perfectly good black bear meat in Unit 16 while manipulating the ecosystem to produce more moose meat. Why not encourage people to eat black bears instead? he asked. SFW president Ralph Seekins assured the host of an outdoors program that of course his group would salvage black bear meat—except for him, of course. "A lot of people eat black bear," Seekins said. "I don't. If you've seen a black bear skinned it looks an awful lot like a human, and when I look at that, I would just rather not eat someone's triceps."

Valkenburg had long supported trapping as a method of predator control and as a source of income for trappers—by letting paying clients shoot snared bears, as they do in Maine. In 2010, with no public notice, the board gave black bears furbearer status, making it legal to sell their hides and parts (except gallbladders). Valkenburg also discussed plans to classify grizzly bears as furbearers so they could be trapped in the state's interior, while coastal brown bears retained big-game protection—exactly how the territory had managed them a century earlier. "The idea behind that is that brown bears are economically a very valuable animal, much more valuable than Interior grizzlies," he explained to the board. As trophies, he meant.

Palin had resigned by then, but her successor, Sean Parnell, continued her wildlife policies. These often led to skirmishes with federal agencies and lawsuits over such matters as the listing of polar bears as a threatened species, recovery plans for an endangered population of beluga whales in Cook Inlet, and refusals to let the state conduct predator control in national parks, refuges, and preserves. Surprisingly, the legislature responded to public pressure and refused to confirm Parnell's first two appointments to the Board of Game—a trapper with a biblically inspired philosophy of wildlife management and a hunting guide with a history of civil infractions. The AOC tried to strong-arm the legislature into approving this second appointment by relaying a threat Rod Arno had e-mailed to the head of the state Republican Party: "Let legislators know we'll go after everyone of them who votes against Keogh next November." The executive director of SFW, Dane Crowley, attempted to browbeat Fish and Game commissioner Denby Lloyd into reprimanding several "renegade" employees for criticizing the department's focus on predator control in an *Audubon* article. Crowley was also offended by their lackluster enthusiasm for intensive management. "I think it high time to remind these folks in region II who it is giving the marching orders," he e-mailed.

The public started wondering the same thing when Lloyd abruptly appointed Rossi as director of the Division of Wildlife Conservation in 2010, replacing a career biologist. More than fifty former state wildlife professionals signed a letter to Parnell protesting the political appointment of such an unqualified person to one of the state's most important jobs. "We are concerned that this high-profile leadership change is a signal that professional management will be replaced by a simplistic abundance management model where maximum production of wild game meat is the state of Alaska's single, overriding objective," they wrote, stating what seemed obvious to almost everyone else. Signers included Vic Van Ballenberghe, Grant Hilderbrand, Harry Reynolds, John Schoen, Sterling Miller, and other well-known bear experts. SFW claimed credit for Rossi's appointment in a press release, but Lloyd denied that the organization had influenced his decision. He said he'd come to appreciate Rossi's "can-do attitude."

That can-do attitude seemed less admirable when Alaska state troopers announced in January 2012 that they had charged Rossi with twelve counts of illegal hunting in Unit 16B, including guiding two nonresident hunters on a bear-baiting hunt and then falsely claiming that he'd killed all four black bears taken. Troopers dated the alleged violations to several months before Rossi's recruitment by Palin. He resigned immediately and later pleaded guilty on two counts, according to the *Alaska Dispatch*.

Many Fish and Game employees cheered his departure, reported retired state biologist Rick Sinnott in his *Alaska Dispatch* column. Rossi was a "single-minded zealot," he wrote. "He wielded his political support like a big stick. I worked under Rossi for several years, and I've never worked for a person with worse supervisory skills. He continued to guide clients, at least once in exchange for a free hunt outside of Alaska, after he was appointed as director of wildlife conservation. He was not committed to wildlife conservation; he was committed to hunting, trapping and guiding."

After Rossi's resignation, reports of other unethical practices emerged, including an attempt to pressure a Nome biologist into bending hunting regulations on behalf of Board of Game chair Cliff Judkins and a former board member. Rossi was also criticized for exploiting his position to award three valuable big-game tags known as "governor's permits" to Sportsmen for Habitat, the organization he had helped found. Another tag went to SFW's national office. Each year, the state gives fewer than a dozen of these tags to conservation groups to auction or raffle off as fund-raisers, which can bring in tens of thousands of dollars (the state receives a small cut). Most damaging were revelations published in the *Anchorage Daily News* detailing Rossi's behind-the-scene efforts to essentially create private game reserves for wealthy hunters, a scheme similar to controversial SFW operations in other states. The state would give large landowners special game permits in exchange for performing "public-interest benefits," such as improving moose habitat, creating hunting access, or killing predators. Hunters would then buy these permits from the landowners. So much for the principle of common ownership of wildlife touted so piously by believers in abundance management.

Rossi's misdeeds were still fresh and Valkenburg had retired by the time the board took up the issue of black bear trapping as a general hunting method in 2012. Fish and Game biologists had routinely recommended against the practice until the Rossi and Valkenburg era. Mark Richards, many wildlife biologists, a few thousand members of the public, and even former governor Tony Knowles testified against the proposal or registered their opposition. Eventually, the board voted against legalizing bear trapping in three areas, based largely on safety concerns for people who might be wandering through the woods where angry grizzlies were tethered to snares. "I don't think anyone on this board is opposed to using this method," Spraker said. "And speaking just for myself, I do not think this is inhumane or barbaric or any other term which have been associated with snaring of bears." The board asked the department to test prototypes that could catch black bears but not young grizzlies, and report back.

The steady march toward legalizing bear trapping throughout Alaska is only one way the board continues to refashion the unthinkable into the routine. Baiting grizzlies and brown bears is another. Shooting black bears over bait has long been popular in several states and Canadian provinces. Hunters lure bears into established sites by setting out barrels of dog kibble, honey, bacon grease, popcorn, doughnuts, grain, rotting meat, and the like. From a nearby tree stand, a discerning hunter can be choosy about which bear he kills. Why anyone is surprised that grizzlies are drawn to free chow lying around in the great outdoors is baffling, but some Alaskan hunters have been complaining in recent years that brown bears are muscling black bears out of the way, destroying bait stations, and making it dangerous for them to leave their tree stands.

Mindful of the bitter controversy over a failed citizens' initiative to ban black bear baiting in 2004, the Board of Game has always rejected requests to legalize the baiting of grizzlies as a general hunting method. Board members have often claimed they would sanction such extreme measures as snaring, cub killing, unlimited bags, and grizzly baiting only as temporary remedies exclusive to PCAs. But in 2012 the game board narrowly approved the baiting of grizzlies in a few areas of Interior Alaska solely to provide hunting opportunities. Spraker was among those who spoke against the method: "The way I see it, I believe that brown bears are certainly of a different status than black bears." A year later he changed his mind. Right after suspending bear control in Unit 16B, the game board legalized the killing of brown bears over bait throughout the entire unit, as well as in the Nelchina region—not as predator control but as hunting. "If you can bait a black bear you should be able to bait a brown bear," Spraker said. The Unit 16 intensive management "experiment" had demonstrated that baiting bears was unlikely to reduce calf predation, he acknowledged, but that was no longer the point. Baiting was now just another opportunity for hunters—including nonresidents and guides—to kill more brown bears. Retired Fish and Wildlife trooper Bob Mumford was the only member who protested. "I do believe this devalues them as a trophy when you're taking them over bait," he said.

A month later the board completed its philosophical evolution by approving brown bear baiting in two more units on the Kenai Peninsula, making the method legal in eight areas throughout the state. Requiring baiters to salvage all edible meat in the spring was a gesture toward treating baiting like subsistence hunting. Few people like the taste of brown bear, but there's no law that says you have to eat it once you take it home. Mumford was still not keen on treating brown bears like black bears. "It's not a different-colored bear," he said, "it's a different species of bear." And he feared that grizzly baiting would give nonhunters another reason to think badly of hunters. But in the end, even he supported the new regulations.

A few weeks after the Kenai decision, a "professional bow-hunting consultant" in California announced in a hunting forum that for the first time, nonresidents accompanied by a licensed outfitter could hunt brown bears over bait in Alaska. Within days, his outfitter had fully booked the 2014 season with six bow hunters who would seek their dream bears in Unit 16B. He'd already started a waiting list for 2015, and other guides were busy recruiting clients, too. Apparently, plenty of hunters are perfectly happy to harvest their trophy while it's eating doughnuts.

In the old days, Natives practiced predator control naturally; it was part of how they lived, a means of survival. They hunted and trapped carnivores for meat and hides, embedded sharpened bone in balls of fat, killed bears and wolf pups in the den. These days, the popularity of trapping wolves for money has fallen off, even as villages compete with sport hunters for moose and caribou. McGrath resident Ray Collins told the board in 2006 that many villagers don't like to kill bears if they don't need the hide or the meat. At one time, people fed bear meat to dogs, but villagers don't keep dog teams anymore, he said. They harvested black bears that wandered into fish camps, but few people have fish camps now. Lately, the price of fuel for snowmachines and all-terrain vehicles has discouraged people from actively seeking animals if there's no immediate reason to kill them. In other communities, villagers regard bear control as disrespectful. To encourage villagers to take more bears and wolves on the Yukon Flats, the community of Beaver and the Council of Athabascan Tribal Governments used grants to sponsor bear derbies, present trapping clinics, and contribute gas to trappers. As the old ways of life fade, it has fallen to governments to keep the frontier going.

Talk all you want about calf mortality and population objectives and density and sustainability, but just like those bait balls, there's an opinion inside waiting to uncoil. Yet opinions do change, as evidenced by a new management philosophy in neighboring Yukon Territory. In his book *Wolves of the Yukon*, Canadian wolf biologist Bob Hayes described a slow transformation in how Yukoners think about wolves since aerial control started in 1982. "Environmental groups did their part to help shift public policy, but the real change came from ordinary Yukoners," he wrote. "The common thread in all voices was questioning wolf control as the only solution for increasing big game populations." Hayes himself had conducted aerial wolf control, but he lobbied to end it because he thinks science has answered the question of whether periodic, broad-scale wolf control works: "It has limited benefit to prey populations, it does not last, and should be relegated to the past along with poison and bounties."

Recently, three members from each political party in the Yukon Territory served on a committee that held community hearings, reviewed research, and evaluated the results of aerial control. Hayes was amazed at the calm nature of these meetings, compared with the high emotion and anger of the 1980s. Ultimately, the committee decided not to recommend aerial wolf control as a management tool. "Strong concerns from the public who did not support intensive aerial control as a form of management were heard throughout the review," the 2012 wolf management plan stated. "It does not engage communities, it is extremely costly to implement, and must be ongoing to be successful." Instead, hunting and trapping regulations will be liberalized (although Hayes doesn't think this will work either), local people will take care of local issues, and the provincial minister can still consider control methods if necessary. "Although attempts may be made to reduce wolves in some parts of the Yukon, it is understood that in most of the territory no management intervention is desired and the system is naturally self-regulating," the plan stated.

Reading this reminded me of another bit of advice Ira Gabrielson offered to the framers of Alaska's constitution. During his study of state wildlife agencies, he was surprised to discover that the best management system was a small bipartisan committee. The threat of deadlock persuaded the members to buckle down and protect resources rather than waste time politicking.

In Alaska, us-versus-them debates are easiest to resolve when the Board of Game is composed mostly of us or them. What flummoxes the political ecosystem is when the two groups overlap. Not all hunters agree that expanded predator control is wise or that extreme methods are ethical. Not every nonhunter is an antihunter. Plenty of hunters consider themselves environmentalists, and many environmentalists hunt. I can dislike the idea of shooting bears over bait and still understand why some hunters think bear baiting helps them choose the right animal, for example. I can disagree with the purpose or scale of bear baiting without believing that all hunters are bad. I've never shot a moose or a bear or a wolf, but that doesn't mean I think nobody else should. I'm glad that Mark Richards lives a life in which killing an animal is an honest transaction, and gladder still that there are people like him who know the difference between killing a bear to feed yourself and killing a bear to feed your ego. Yet there's little opportunity to discuss predator control rationally when special-interest groups run wildlife agencies, when anyone who questions the wholesale use of predator control— even wildlife professionals—is branded an "anti" and ignored. Ralph

Seekins was right: this really is about who controls Alaska—or, rather, who doesn't.

One feat predator control has accomplished is turning bears from charismatic megafauna into land sharks. In the imagined landscape conjured by the most fervid control supporters, bears function as nothing but calf killers, single-minded slaughtering machines that, along with wolves, have driven Alaska's innocent ungulates to the brink of extinction. Certainly many ethical, concerned hunters don't fit that caricature, but online comments like these aren't uncommon, either:

> "Predators are just that. They need to be eradicated to the fullest extent possible. Knowing full well we will never be able to fully rid ourselves of them. They are just [too] cunning and have too many places to hide."
>
> "Bears are brutal, mean, dangerous, and dirty animals. Nobody has been able to point out a single valid use for bears that I agree with."
>
> "I guess my perception of a majestic animal doesn't really include grizzly bears. I view grizzly bears as troublesome overgrown predators that look beautiful from the comfort of your couch or from a safe distance. How much do people really respect the majesty of grizzly bears? Most people respect grizzly bears because they are huge, mean, and nasty."
>
> "Perhaps F&G needs a newer classification, something like PREDATOR. Perhaps all that is really needed is two classifications: Predator and Prey. P.S. Wolves are big game species. How are bears special?"

Good question. Why did Alaska wait so long to go after bears?

Van Ballenberghe told me in the 1990s, "Bears have a higher perceived status than wolves. No one would suggest shooting sows with cubs." Fifteen years later, he said, "For years, the focus was on wolves. And I'm damn glad that now bears are sharing some of the burden. I'm ashamed to say that as a biologist. We've known for years that in many places bears are at least as important as predators on moose and caribou as wolves are, but it's just recently come to the attention of the predator controllers that maybe they can produce a few more moose if they kill some bears."

Mark Richards's theory is that the contentious reintroduction of wolves in the Lower 48 has spread derisive attitudes. "It's really influenced hunters here in Alaska to view predators in a different way," he told me. "That's really unfortunate. It's unfortunate that hunters have moved away from the old school, Aldo Leopold–type conservationism, and how that happened, I don't know. Especially with grizzly bears."

People often see black bears as less valuable than brown bears (I've inadvertently done this myself by writing more about brown bears than black bears). Richards has heard that sentiment from guides. "I don't want to make an emotional argument—nobody does when we're talking science—but the fact is that emotionally we feel differently about grizzly bears," he said. "We have a special view of them, as a special apex predator, but also as an omnivore. We've seen them extirpated in the Lower 48 and we don't want to see that happen here." Brown bears are more valuable socially to wildlife viewers and more valuable economically to the guide industry and nonresident hunters, he added. Terry DeBruyn said wildlife professionals also unconsciously adopt a ranking system based on the species they research: "Brown bears for a lot of biologists are a step above black bears. And polar bear biologists think they're the cat's meow."

Alaska's policies create a curious compartmentalization in which bears are assigned value in sport or subsistence hunts, but not if they're being "removed." A proposal to eliminate bag limits statewide for black bears elicited this response from Spraker (whom I quote so often because he's the most talkative and long-lasting board member): "I think in a way it's disrespectful to black bears when you start putting this no limits on black bears. You know, it's a big game animal, it's a highly sought-after trophy animal for a lot of people. . . . I hate to see us go in the direction of no limit on a species like this." Yet more than 3,000 black bears were killed in the first decade of the twenty-first century in Unit 16—just one corner of Alaska. "We treat 'em like varmints," DeBruyn told me. "Really, we do. Some places you can kill five, you can kill bears all year-round, and it doesn't matter. There's not even a limit on it. That's an ignorant thing, I think, to just say you can do that without even knowing how many you've got. There's a certain amount of arrogance that goes along with that."

Returning to the old methods of killing bears also damages our ideas about them, some people believe. "Permitting the baiting and snaring of bears would challenge the ethical and cultural standards that have guided wildlife management in Alaska since statehood in 1959," wrote wildlife biologist and professor emeritus David Klein in a newspaper commentary. "Such permission would degrade the bear in the eyes of both the hunting and non-hunting public." Harry Reynolds once made a similar comment to the board: "I think that it reduces the status of black bears as a valued game animal for residents and nonresidents alike. An animal that can be snared is not looked upon as a valued or big game animal."

For some guides, the reversion to regulations reminiscent of territorial days diminishes the economic and psychological value of bears. When the board approved the selling of grizzly hides with the claws attached as an incentive to hunt the bears, the Alaska Professional Hunters Association wrote in its newsletter: "This was a sad loss for the integrity of all brown and grizzly bear hunts as it lowered the status of this species which will ultimately be utilized against us by those opposed to all bear hunting." In a passionate newspaper commentary celebrating the attributes of bears, big-game guide Karl Braendel called on other guides to speak out against the state's new attitudes: "Predator control leads us into that endless twilight zone of killing that cheapens a whole species in people's eyes, and by depreciating their lives we demean our own." He added, "You don't snare the King, or shoot her from an airplane, and you don't kill her cubs." Board of Game member Teresa Sager Albaugh has argued that sparing brown bears from baiting encourages the notion that the board devalues black bears. To her, using the same methods to kill both species is a way of establishing equal worth.

One hunter pointed out that by declaring "war" on bears and wolves, the Alaska Department of Fish and Game had made the derisive term "calf-killer" not only popular but also defensible. "I am NOT comparing bears to humans, but I am comparing propaganda methods," he posted on the Alaska Outdoors Forum. "The 'right' (calf-killers) and the 'left' (warm fuzzy teddy bears) are both guilty. All we are talking about is bears, doing what bears do."

If only we were. Nobody's really talking about bears in those cheerless hotel conference rooms and convention centers where the Board of Game meets for ten days at a time. They're talking about numbers jammed into pie charts, tables, tallies, and graphs to describe harvest, survival, mortality, productivity. They don't talk about bears; they talk about meat and claws, skulls and hides, cannibal bears, baited bears, snared bears, nuisance bears, predatory bears, dead bears. They decide what should be salvaged and what can be discarded, who deserves more and who deserves nothing. The point is not to manage wild animals, because being unmanageable is the essence of being wild. What they manage is the abundance of animals, the reduction of animals, the production of animals, the reallocation of animals, the idea of animals. There's no talk of ecosystems, biodiversity, or other newfangled ideas in these rooms; nor is there much discussion of the old-fashioned conservation ethos that's been surrendered so easily. Instead, they speak of units, regulatory seasons, control areas, objectives, harvests, populations. Nobody talks much about how bears live out there in the Last Great Wilderness, or how they die here on the Last Frontier. Nobody really talks about bears at all.

the story of bears

You may have never seen a bear in your life. You may never wish to. But somewhere in your mind, your dreams, or your experience, a bear lives through story, whether that bear is divine or demonic, gentled or wild, teacher or punisher. The collective noun for bears is "sleuth," as in "a sleuth of bears," but I propose we change that noun to "story": a story of bears. Bears travel in stories, after all, and rarely alone.

If you lack a bear story of your own, you can borrow someone else's. My head is stuffed with stories on loan from others: bears that steal coffee beans from campers, bears that break into mercantiles and sleep in nests of T-shirts, bears that press their faces against kitchen windows to spy on cooling blueberry pies, bears that chase people biking beside the Trans-Alaska Pipeline, bears that run away not from bear spray but from people coughing because of bear spray. Possibly my favorite story comes from Ginny Wood, a conservationist hero from Fairbanks and one of the founders of Camp Denali. In the winter of 1961, when the camp was closed for the season, a grizzly busted into the storehouse and devoured everything in reach. Unfortunately, the jam jars were shelved beside the matches, which the bear somehow managed to ignite. The building burned, but the bear escaped. That spring, as Ginny and her business partner, Celia Hunter, sifted through the wreckage, they discovered their kitchen curtains embedded in a pile of scat, having journeyed intact through the bear's alimentary canal. So Ginny and Celia washed the curtains and hung them up again.

Well, there are plenty of other bear stories in the world, stories that are silly, epic, scary, sad. I like those with a happy ending, myself. Sometimes, though, it feels as if we tell one kind of bear story over and over, perhaps because it's the one we all know best. Here is a version of it, though I'll warn you that it begins in the Old World and takes the long way around to the New: Several years ago I was in Italy for the Sixteenth

International Conference on Bear Research and Management, which was held in the Trentino Province in the foothills of the Alps. Perhaps you weren't aware (as I wasn't, until recently) that a few native brown bears live in Italy (and Greece, Turkey, Romania, Croatia, Austria, Japan, Iran . . . but I digress). One day the bear experts made a field trip to Adamello-Brenta Natural Park, where native brown bears had dwindled to perhaps three individuals until Project Life Ursus released ten Slovenian bears into the alpine forests, starting in 1999. As bears do, they found one another and began making a few more bears, so that by 2011, despite losses and disappearances over the years, at least thirty-three bears inhabited the region.

The chance of seeing a bear during our hike in the park was slight, especially because bear experts tend to travel in chattering packs. But just knowing that brown bears lived in these parts made the foggy beech forest seem more mysterious, the hike a bit more invigorating. As we walked, Filippo Zibordi of the park's wildlife office told me that he and his colleagues knew they could never hope to return the bear population to what it once was. And this truth made him feel "pity for what we have destroyed." They hoped merely to establish some equilibrium, with perhaps forty to sixty bears living in a contiguous area of the Alps in northern Italy, Switzerland, Germany, and Austria. Throughout Europe, conservationists are attempting to rewild natural areas with brown bears, wolves, lynx, and other native carnivores, although not everyone welcomes the idea or the animals. Zibordi estimated a 50–50 split between Italians who feared bears because they were unprepared for their presence and those who would drive a long way to see them. But why would Italians care about bears at all? I wondered, thinking of the pastoral hills of Umbria and the cosmopolitan streets of Rome. Because, Zibordi said, the bear was a symbol of nature's quiet and peace, of nature itself.

Having seen the lovely, lonely forests of northern Italy, I paid attention when the saga of a Trentino bear made international headlines. JJI was the official name of a male born to one of the Slovenian bears. In 2006, as a brash two-year-old, he wandered almost 200 miles from northern Italy through Austria and into Bavaria. There he became the media sensation known as "Bruno," the first wild bear to appear in Germany in 170 years. Bruno's boldness was also his downfall. News outlets delighted in reporting his serial transgressions: he killed more than thirty sheep, ate chickens and pet rabbits, stole honey, snacked on a guinea pig, and was even seen napping outside a police station. A hobby farmer who had lost three prized rams to Bruno didn't think the government's cash compensation could heal his emotional loss, he told *Spiegel International*. The farmer didn't want the bear to die, but he described Bruno as a bloodthirsty animal killing for fun. "There's no room here for such a wild animal," he said. "He should go where he can't do any damage, for example into a wildlife park." The Bavarian minister declared Bruno a problem bear and issued an order to kill him on sight, but the public outcry forced the minister to hire a group of Finnish trackers to attempt a live capture.

After Bruno outwitted the trackers for two weeks, exasperated authorities gave Bavarian hunters permission to shoot Bruno, which someone did the very same day. Protests, memorials, even death threats to the minister followed. *Der Spiegel* eulogized the bear extravagantly: "We share a collective guilt for Bruno's demise, our inability to co-exist with nature has yet again prompted us to reach for the trigger. Bruno is dead and we are all the poorer for it: May his ursine soul rest in peace." Though Italy asked for the return of its dead bear, the German government refused, and today Bruno is displayed in Munich's Museum of Man and Nature in a rather nice glass cube. He is posed as if plundering a domestic beehive, a display of honesty over idealism, I suppose.

Bruno's brief but splashy odyssey and his unfortunate end became the subject of an American diplomatic cable titled "Bruno's Last Stand," which was released by Wikileaks in 2010. The cable eloquently diagnosed the bear's demise. "True wilderness, even in mountainous Bavaria, hasn't really existed in Germany for generations—nature is good, as long as it is controlled, channeled, and subdued," it said. "If the saga of Bavaria's 'Problem Bear' is any indicator, the strategy of reintroducing wild bears to the Alps, at least the German Alps, may be doomed to failure—that is, unless the bears are willing to cooperate by not being too wild."

The cable revealed a peculiarly American stance by pointedly noting that perhaps Germany isn't as "green" as it thinks it is, that the country seems uneasy at the prospect of untamed nature: "The contrast between the massive hunt for the first wild bear in over 170 years and the recent story of a clawless housecat treeing a bear in New Jersey couldn't be much more stark." This seems to suggest that Americans are far more comfortable with wildlife than Germans are, that we have learned to live with bears and see them for the harmless goofballs they are, that even a cat is braver than a German.

The truth is, of course, that efforts to protect or restore black bears in places like Arkansas and Louisiana and grizzly bears in the Greater Yellowstone ecosystem are complicated by the same attitudes and difficulties that confront bears of all species wherever they live. Not everyone wants to be rewilded. Still, a few dedicated organizations and people devote an unbelievable amount of work to returning native carnivores to their former haunts in a few corners and nooks of the world.

I can't help but compare those heroic—and possibly futile—efforts to Alaska's situation. Although we have experienced a few Brunos of our own, we have an extravagance of bears. We have so many bears that every year we kill a Europe's worth of them as nuisance animals. Sometimes I fear that we treat bears as if they were our Permanent Fund, compiling so much interest that we don't bother counting our riches; we simply distribute the proceeds year after year. Many Alaskans scoff or shrug at the suggestion that we could ever run out of bears. Perhaps they're right, but we worriers know that most wildlife populations don't vanish overnight, as in the grand extinguishings of the past. They erode at the edges, become islands unto themselves, retreat to hidden pockets, evaporate quietly.

Complacency is what I fret about. "Wilderness is not a single region, but a condition of being of the natural world," wrote novelist and Idaho native Marilynne Robinson. "If it is no longer to be found in one place, we assume it exists in other places." Substitute the word bear for wilderness: If bears are no longer to be found in one place, we assume they exist in other places. Who needs bears in Juneau, Healy, Anchorage, or Soldotna when so many bears live in other, wilder provinces of Alaska, robbing us blind of our prized livestock, behaving as if the world belongs to them when it so clearly belongs to us? Many people feel like the Bavarians, I suspect, willing to tolerate bears only if they're not too wild. The late governor Walter J. Hickel, a great promoter of Alaska as the ruler of its own resources and its own destiny, said it right out loud: "You can't let nature run wild." So far, we aren't.

I find comfort in the words of Harry Reynolds, who retired as a state bear biologist and immediately began working for the conservation of a handful of brown bears in Mongolia's Gobi Desert. "In Alaska we kind of have the unparalleled opportunity that no other country except for

Russia has—to screw up and recover from it in terms of bear popula-tions," he told me. "If they screw up in the Gobi Desert, the bears are gone. If we screw up in Alaska and we kill a thousand more bears than we should, or they go away some place, we could recover. We shouldn't depend upon that—and I'd never say this is a philosophy that we can squander—but if we do, through well-meaning approaches, screw up, we can still recover." Like Harry, I'd prefer not to screw up at all.

Whether that's possible, I couldn't say, but perhaps part of the prob-lem is that we lack the imagination to conceive of any other outcome but screwing up, sooner or later. In his provocative essay "The Trouble with Wilderness," environmental historian William Cronon challenged the lines we've drawn between nature and civilization, frontier and wil-derness. A romantic ideology of wilderness forces people outside of the natural world, he argued, so that our insistence on a nature purely wild has fostered a prevailing belief: "The place where we are is the place where nature is not." *The place where we are is the place where bears are not.* Maybe we would do better by bears and by ourselves if we stopped in-sisting that they carry the burden of symbolic wilderness, if we stopped mentally exiling them into some hazy notion of a wilderness *out there* and started acknowledging that they have always—physically, mentally, and sometimes, spiritually—been *here*, among us. This is not a call to strip bears of wildness (as if we could) but rather to stop insisting that they represent ideas that are more about us than about them.

Every day I am grateful that so much of Alaska is marked by efforts to protect landscapes, habitats, wilderness, and wildlife, because I have no illusions about what would happen otherwise in this frontier-grasping state. But bears will never remain within the boundaries we draw, not only because of their habits but also because of ours. Long ago we in-vited them into our stories, our myths, our dreams, our nightmares, our lives. We have always sought them out where they live, for their hides, their meat, their beauty, their strength, their knowingness. Human country and bear country can exist side by side, but imagine if we saw these principalities as not entirely distinct or mutually exclusive, if we accepted the porousness of such borders. If we did, we could sit beside a river and, from a companionable distance, watch giant coastal brown bears as they fish, or see a black bear pass through the backyard with-out automatically reaching for the phone or a gun, or understand that we lose nothing and gain everything if we're willing to trade carbon for polar bears. Perhaps if we cede a trail here or there, if we take a share of wild food but don't begrudge so much of it to other creatures, if we bother to learn something about how bears actually live and behave, we will stop reenacting a past that is so ill suited to the future we need.

Derek Stonorov called his own sentiments "huge wishful thinking," and so are these, but if I have any faith, it resides not in humanity but in him and all the other bear people. And I have faith in bears, too. Here, then, is my final story: Late one August I flew in a tin can of a plane to a public cabin in the Wrangell–St. Elias Mountains, where I planned to spend a week alone near the Chitistone River. On my second morning I sat on a bench next to the fire pit, sketching the abraded peaks rising in the distance. No sound, no smell, not even sight alerted me to the shadowy presence beside me. Some vibration at the edge of awareness made me look up. Three feet away, just beyond reach of an outstretched arm, stood a black bear. It was Every Bear. It was Black Place, Dark Thing, Lightfoot. It was Bluetail, it was Broad-foot, it was the Dog of God. The black bear did not look at me as it stood there, facing the same direction I did, and for one long, elastic moment, I wasn't afraid. I wasn't even human. For that one moment, anything was possible.

notes

ABBREVIATIONS

ADF&G	Alaska Department of Fish and Game
ADN	*Anchorage Daily News*
FDNM	*Fairbanks Daily News-Miner*
Int. Conf. Bear Res. Mgmt.	*International Conference on Bear Research and Management*
USFWS	US Fish and Wildlife Service
USGS	US Geological Survey

THE METAPHORICAL BEAR

3 *"The Dipper is"*: India Spartz, *Eight Stars of Gold: The Story of Alaska's Flag* (Juneau: Alaska State Museums, 2001), 9.

3 *More than 70 percent*: Sterling Miller, *Brown Bears in Alaska: A Statewide Management Overview*, Wildlife Technical Bulletin No. 11 (Juneau: ADF&G Division of Wildlife Conservation, December 1993), i; *Polar Bear (Ursus maritimus): Chukchi/Bering Seas Stock* (USFWS Marine Mammals Management, rev. January 2010), 2; *Polar Bear (Ursus maritimus): Southern Beaufort Sea Stock* (USFWS Marine Mammals Management, rev. January 2010), 2.

4 *"It is difficult to envision"*: Morgan Sherwood, *Big Game in Alaska: A History of Wildlife and People* (New Haven, CT: Yale University Press, 1981), 24.

4 *"So many people today"*: Kyle Hopkins, "Reality TV Invades Alaska," ADN, February 2, 2011.

5 *"Bestriding two worlds"*: Merle Colby, *A Guide to Alaska: Last American Frontier* (New York: J. J. Little & Ives, 1939), Google eBook, 15.

5 *Nothing less than challenge*: Merle Colby, *What Has Alaska to Offer Postwar Pioneers?* (Office of War Information, August 1944), introduction, http://www.historians.org/projects/giroundtable/Alaska/Alaska_TOC.htm.

5 *"There is the look"*: Ralph Crane, "Alaska: The Hard Country," *Life*, October 1, 1965, 66.

6 *"Question—Why do we"*: Bryan Hickock, comment on Rick Sinnott, "Educating Bears by Educating People," *Alaska Dispatch*, May 23, 2011, http://www.alaskadispatch.com/article/educating-bears-educating-people.

6 *"From the nineteenth century"*: Patricia Nelson Limerick, *The Legacy of Conquest: The Unbroken Past of the American West* (New York: W. W. Norton, 1988), 316.

6 *"While the sourdough"*: Theodore Catton, *Inhabited Wilderness: Indians, Eskimos and National Parks in Alaska* (Albuquerque: University of New Mexico Press, 1997), 90.

6 *"Animals are stylized"*: Edward Hoagland, "Dogs and the Tug of Life," in *Heart's Desire: The Best of Edward Hoagland* (New York: Simon & Schuster, 1991), 280.

7 *"The conservation associations"*: Thomas Riggs Jr. to H. C. Copeland, June 3, 1920, State of Alaska Archives, Office of the District and Territorial Governor, RG 101, box 178, series 130, file 25, Fish & Game: Alaska Game Commission 1920.

7 *"If Alaska is ever"*: George Wilson, affidavit, July 8, 1920, Alaska State Archives, Office of the District and Territorial Governor, RG 101, box 183-18, series 130, file 49-4, Predatory Animals & Birds & Bounties.

7 *"were it not for the presence"*: L. J. Palmer, "Wildlife Problems on Kodiak Island," 1938, quoted in Harry B. Dodge III, *Kodiak Island and Its Bears: A History of Bear/Human Interactions on Alaska's Kodiak Archipelago* (Anchorage: Great Northwest Publishing, 2004), 151.

7 *"Civilization is moving north"*: Mike Coppock, "The Cowboy Kings of Kodiak," October/November 2008, 60, http://www.Americancowboy.com.

7 *An estimated 700 to 800 bears*: Chris Servheen, "Status and Management of the Grizzly Bear in the Lower 48 United States," in *Bears: Status Survey and Conservation Action Plan*, ed. Christopher Servheen, Stephen Herrero, and Bernard Peyton (IUCN/SSC Bear Specialist Group, 1998), 51.

7 *"The grandest and most powerful"*: David Petersen, "Old Ephraim's Last Stand," *Mother Earth News*, March/April 1985, 2.

8 *"Bears conjure up"*: Jordan Carlton Schaul, "Bears of the Last Frontier: Interview with Chris Morgan (Ecologist, Author, TV Host)," May 5, 2011, http://newswatch.nationalgeographic.com/2011/05/05/bears-of-the-last-frontier-chris-morgan/.

8 *"I think nothing"*: Jeannette J. Lee, "Grizzly to Grace Alaska Quarter," *Juneau Empire*, April 24, 2007.

8 *Two weeks after*: "Governor Palin Introduces Bill to Streamline Predator Management Laws: HB 256/SN 176 Clarify, Clean up Statutes, Encourages Abundance-Based Management," news release 07-14, ADF&G, May 11, 2007.

8 *Protecting polar bears*: E-mail from Sarah Palin to Sharon Leighow, "Re: For Your Review and Approval—Polar Bear Release," August 4, 2008, *Wall Street Journal* online, http://online.wsj.com/public/resources/documents/palin080 42008.pdf.

9 *"The current attitude"*: Sterling Miller, "The Slow Revival of America's Grizzlies," National Wildlife Federation blog *Wildlife Promise*, March 19, 2012, http://blog.nwf.org/2012/03/the-slow-revival-of-americas-grizzlies/.

9 *Hunters kill*: *Managing Alaska's Wildlife* (ADF&G Division of Wildlife

Conservation, 2010), 5; Amy Pinney, "Brown Bear Research in Alaska," *Alaska Fish & Wildlife News* online magazine, April 2012.

9 "*Alaska is being chopped*": Frederick C. Dean, *A Land Use Philosophy Proposal for Bear Management* (Fairbanks: Department of Wildlife and Fisheries and Alaska Cooperative Park Studies Unit, University of Alaska, 1975), 7–9.

10 "*The bottom line*": John Hechtel, "Review of 'On Nature's Terms: Predators and People Co-existing in Harmony,'" *International Bear News* 14, 2 (May 2005): 40.

10 "*It was my ghost grizzly*": Jim Rearden, *Alaska's Wolf Man: The 1915–55 Wilderness Adventures of Frank Glaser* (Missoula, MT: Pictorial Histories Publishing, 1998), 179.

11 "*Why does our fascination*": Todd Smith, "A Bear in the Dark," *Outdoor Life*, April 2004, 11.

11 "*Most folks can never really see*": Colleen Matt, *Summary of 3rd International Bear-People Conflicts Workshop*, Canmore, AB, November 15–17, 2009, 46.

12 "*Argument, it seems to me*": John Livingston, *The John Livingston Reader* (Toronto: McClelland & Stewart, 2007), 128.

THE UNSEEN BEAR

15 "*Among the earliest forms*": David Quammen, *Monster of God* (New York: W. W. Norton, 2003), 3.

16 "*They have a gospel-like value*": Paul Schullery, *Lewis and Clark among the Grizzlies: Legend and Legacy in the American West* (Guilford, CT: Globe Pequot Press, 2002), 6.

16 "*The wonderful power of life*": Elliott Coues, ed., *History of the Expedition under the Command of Lewis and Clark*, vol. 1 (Mineola, NY: Dover Publications, 1979), Google eBook, 307.

16 "*it was a most tremendious looking anamal*": *The Journals of the Lewis and Clark Expedition*, May 5, 1805, University of Nebraska Press/University of Nebraska–Lincoln Libraries Electronic Text Center, http://lewisandclarkjournals.unl.edu.

16 "*he wounded him*": Ibid., October 20, 1804.

16 The more dramatic episodes: Raymond Darwin Burroughs, ed., *The Natural History of the Lewis and Clark Expedition*, 2nd ed. (East Lansing: Michigan State University Press, 1995), 59.

17 The expedition's published journals: Dan Flores, *The Natural West: Environmental History in the Great Plains* (Norman: University of Oklahoma Press/Red River Books, 2003), 76.

17 After reading them: William Henry Wright, *The Grizzly Bear: The Narrative of a Hunter-Naturalist* (New York: Charles Scribner's Sons, 1909), eBook, 26.

17 "*He is the enemy of man*": Henry Marie Brackenridge, *Journal of a Voyage up the Missouri River, in 1811* (Pittsburgh, PA: Cramer, Spear & Eichbaum, 1814), http://user.xmission.com/~drudy/mtman/html/Brackenridge/Brackenridge.html.

17 *Naturalist George Ord:* Samuel N. Rhoads, *A Reprint of the North American Zoology, by George Ord,* 2nd ed. (Haddonfield, NJ: Samuel Rhoads, 1894), 299–300, http://archive.org/details/reprintofnorthamooordg.

17 *Most biologists estimate:* "Grizzly Bear Recovery," USFWS Endangered Species, http://www.fws.gov/mountain-prairie/species/mammals/grizzly/.

17 *Traps, guns, poison:* William T. Hornaday, *Our Vanishing Wild Life: Its Extermination and Preservation* (New York: Charles Scribner's Sons, 1913), 178, http://www.gutenberg.org/dirs/1/3/2/4/13249/13249-h/13249-h.htm.

17 *Four decades of hard work:* "Threatened Grizzly Bear Populations and Their Recovery," USFWS, Interagency Grizzly Bear Committee online, May 2, 2013, http://www.igbconline.org/index.php/population-recovery/current-status-of-grizzly-populations.

17 *In 2005 CBS News sent:* Lesley Stahl, "Bears in the Backyard," *60 Minutes,* June 2005, http://www.cbsnews.com/video/watch/?id=699730n.

18 *"It's one thing to appreciate":* Rebecca Leung, "Not in My Backyard . . . ," *60 Minutes,* February 11, 2009, http://www.cbsnews.com/8301–18560_162–699622.html.

18 *"Humans are the primary agent":* Charles Schwartz, Mark A. Haroldson, and Gary C. White, "Hazards Affecting Grizzly Bear Survival in the Greater Yellowstone Ecosystem," *Journal of Wildlife Management* 74, 4 (2010): 654.

22 *Archaeologists investigating France's:* Paul Pettitt, *The Paleolithic Origins of Human Burial* (New York: Routledge, 2011), eLibrary edition, 114.

22 *"Régourdou constitutes a convincing":* Brian Hayden, *Shamans, Sorcerers, and Saints: A Prehistory of Religion* (Washington, DC: Smithsonian Books, 2003), 134.

23 *Scattered throughout the chambers:* Zach Zorich, "A Chauvet Primer," *Archaeology,* March/April 2011, 39.

23 *Across 5 million years:* John Davison, Simon Y. W. Ho, Sarah C. Bray, Marju Korsten, Egle Tammeleht, Maris Hindrikson, Kjartan Østbye, Eivind Østbye, Stein-Erik Lauritzen, Jeremy Austin, Alan Cooper, and Urmas Saarma, "Late-Quaternary Biogeographic Scenarios for the Brown Bear (*Ursus arctos*), a Wild Mammal Model Species," *Quaternary Science Reviews* 30 (2011): 425.

23 *The parallel passages of bear and human:* For an accessible and thorough review of current research, see Bonnie L. Pitblado, "A Tale of Two Migrations: Reconciling Recent Biological and Geological Evidence for the Pleistocene Peopling of the Americas," *Journal of Archaeological Research* 19, 4 (2011): 327–375.

24 *Even now, a few brown bears:* Bruce N. McLellan, Chris Servheen, and Djuro Huber (IUCN SSC Bear Specialist Group), "*Ursus arctos,*" IUCN Red List of Threatened Species, Version 2012.2 (2008), http://www.iucnredlist.org/details/41687/0.

24 *"Not surprisingly, human societies":* Juha Janhunen, "Tracing the Bear Myth in Northeast Asia," *Acta Slavica Iaponica* 20 (2003): 1.

24 *"Bears do, first of all"*: A. Irving Hallowell, "Bear Ceremonialism in the Northern Hemisphere," *American Anthropologist* 28, 1 (January–March 1926): 148–149.

24 *At a time when:* Lydia Black, "Bear in Human Imagination and in Ritual," *Ursus* 10 (1995): 345.

24 *The Saami people:* Noel D. Broadbent, Jan Storå, Britta Wennstedt Edvinger, and Katherine Rusk, "Ritual Sites," in *The Search for a Past: The Prehistory of the Indigenous Saami in Northern Coastal Sweden* (Arctic Studies Center, National Museum of Natural History, Smithsonian Institution, 2004), http://www.mnh.si.edu/arctic/features/saami/ritualsites.html.

25 *In ancient China:* Janhunen, "Tracing the Bear Myth," 20.

25 *The Ainu of Hokkaido:* Emiko Ohnuki-Tierney, "Ainu Sociality," in *Ainu: Spirit of a Northern People*, ed. W. W. Fitzhugh, and C. O. Dubreuil (Washington, DC: National Museum of Natural History, Smithsonian Institution, 1999), 241.

25 *Hallowell's survey:* Hallowell, "Bear Ceremonialism," 148.

25 *"In short, I think":* Ibid., 161.

25 *"After describing the study":* Hannah Loon and Susan Georgette, *Contemporary Brown Bear Use in Northwest Alaska*, Technical Paper No. 163 (Juneau: ADF&G Division of Subsistence, 1989), 44.

25 *Tlingits sometimes referred to bears:* Thomas F. Thornton, *Subsistence Use of Brown Bear in Southeast Alaska*, Technical Paper No. 214 (Juneau: ADF&G Division of Subsistence, February 1992), 30–31.

26 *Koyukon Athabascans:* Richard K. Nelson, *Make Prayers to the Raven: A Koyukon View of the Northern Forest* (Chicago: University of Chicago Press, 1983), 174.

26 *This practice is nearly as old:* J. P. Mallory and D. Q. Adams, eds., *Encyclopedia of Indo-European Culture* (Chicago: Fitzroy Dearborn, 1997), 55–56.

26 *The bear is brother:* Thornton, *Subsistence Use*, 30, 38.

27 *"Man and animals":* Douglas A. Clark and D. Scott Slocombe, "Respect for Grizzly Bears: An Aboriginal Approach for Co-existence and Resilience," *Ecology and Society* 14, 1 (2009): 4, http://www.ecologyandsociety.org/vol14/iss1/art42/.

28 *"I guess I constantly":* Barrie Gilbert, "Emerging from the Dark Side: A Reinterpretation of Grizzly-Human Relationships Based on Current and Historical Evidence," abstract, 14th International Congress on Bear Research and Management, Steinkjer, Norway, July 28–August 3, 2002.

28 *A 2007 episode:* James Tapper, "Latest TV Fake Scenes: 'Grizzly Attack' on Survival Show Was Man in Fancy-Dress Bear Costume," *Daily Mail* online, July 28, 2007.

29 *Even real bears transmogrify:* See Natalie Phillips, "Legend Brewin'," *ADN*, December 16, 2001; Craig Medred, "Campfire Whopper Balloons to New Dimensions on the Web," *ADN*, November 5, 2006; Peter Porco, "Forest Service

Details Give the Lie to Monster Hunting Myth," ADN, May 7, 2003; and "World Record Grizzly Bear," Urban Legends online, http://urbanlegends .about.com/library/bl-grizzlybear.htm, for e-mail and photographs.

30 *"I have been trying to kill"*: Ray Massey, letter to the *Oklahoma Sun*, July 31, 2006.

30 *"Images of the great bear"*: Paul Shepard, *The Others: How Animals Made Us Human* (Washington, DC: Island Press/Shearwater Books, 1997), 29.

32 *This was nicely illustrated*: Kerry McQueeney, "'It Came so Close It Sniffed His Hoodie': Tourists Reveal the Terrifying Moment a Grizzly Bear Charged at Them. And They Didn't Even Flinch," *Daily Mail* online, February 28, 2012.

33 *"After about twenty minutes"*: Barbara Mikkelson and David P. Mikkelson, "Playground Bears," Snopes.com, April 24, 2010, http://www.snopes.com /photos/animals/playgroundbears.asp.

36 *Z.B. weighed 350 pounds*: Spencer Linderman, *Ground Tracking of Arctic Grizzly Bears* (Juneau: ADF&G Division of Game, 1974), 2.

36 *"Visual ground tracking"*: Ibid., 16.

37 *"Z.B.'s movements"*: Ibid., 11.

37 *"Every habitat has foods"*: John Hechtel, "Activity and Food Habits of Barren-Ground Grizzly Bears in Arctic Alaska" (M.S. thesis, University of Montana, 1985), 66.

37 *"This position also permitted"*: Linderman, *Ground Tracking*, 5.

37 *Himalayan brown bears*: Muhammad Ali Nawaz, "Ecology, Genetics and Conservation of Himalayan Brown Bears" (Ph.D. diss., Norwegian University of Life Sciences, 2008), iii, http://www.bearproject.info/uploads/publications /PhD%20thesis%20Nawaz.pdfNawaz.

38 *In central Sweden*: J. Swenson, A. Jansson, R. Riig, and F. Sandegren, "Bears and Ants: Myrmecophagy by Brown Bears in Central Scandinavia," *Canadian Journal of Zoology* 77, 4 (1999): 551.

38 *Slovakian brown bears*: "Drunk Bears Looking for a Fight," *Croatian Times*, November 14, 2008.

38 *In Yellowstone National Park*: David J. Mattson, Katherine C. Kendall, and Daniel P. Reinhart, "Whitebark Pine, Grizzly Bears, and Red Squirrels," in *Whitebark Pine Communities: Ecology and Restoration*, ed. Diana F. Tomback, Stephen F. Arno, and Robert. E. Keane (Washington, DC: Island Press, 2001), 123–125.

38 *Yellowstone bears slurp earthworms*: David J. Mattson, Marilynn G. French, and Steven P. French, "Consumption of Earthworms by Yellowstone Grizzly Bears," *Ursus* 13 (2002): 110; Don White Jr., Katherine C. Kendall, and Harold Picton, "Potential Energetic Effects of Mountain Climbers on Foraging Grizzly Bears," *Wildlife Society Bulletin* 27, 1 (Spring 1999): 149.

38 *While Z.B. gnawed:* John Schoen and Scott Gende, "Brown Bear (*Ursus arctos*)," in *A Conservation Assessment and Resource Synthesis for the Coastal Forests and Mountains Ecoregion in the Tongass National Forest and Southeast Alaska,* ed. John W. Schoen and Erin Dovichin (Anchorage: Audubon Alaska and Nature Conservancy of Alaska, 2007), eBook, 7–10.

38 *Glacier Bay's black and brown bears:* Steve Partridge, Tom Smith, and Tania Lewis, *Black and Brown Bear Activity at Selected Coastal Sites in Glacier Bay National Park and Preserve, Alaska: A Preliminary Assessment Using Noninvasive Procedures,* Open-File Report 2009-1169 (Reston, VA: USGS, 2009), 14, 60–61.

38 *A "crittercam" attached:* Riley Woodford, "Critter Cam Reveals Bear's Eye View," *Alaska Fish & Wildlife News* online magazine, October 2003.

39 *In the fall:* Ralph A. Nelson, G. Edgar Folk Jr., Egbert W. Pfeiffer, John J. Craighead, Charles J. Jonkel, and Dianne L. Steiger, "Behavior, Biochemistry, and Hibernation in Black, Grizzly, and Polar Bears," *Int. Conf. Bear Res. Mgmt.* 5 (1983): 286.

39 *One of the largest:* John W. Schoen, Sterling Miller, and Harry V. Reynolds III, "Last Stronghold of the Grizzly," *Natural History,* January 1987, 56.

39 *A prime example:* "Whitebark Pine to Be Designated a Candidate for Endangered Species Protection," news release, USFWS, July 18, 2011.

39 *Calculate the hours:* Linderman, *Ground Tracking,* 11, appendix I, 9.

40 *"His travels often lasted":* Ibid., 6.

40 *Over the summer:* James G. Gebhard, "Annual Activities and Behavior of a Grizzly Bear (*Ursus arctos*) Family in Northern Alaska" (M.S. thesis, University of Alaska, 1982), 215.

40 *Brown bears are evolving:* Ian Stirling and Andrew E. Derocher, "Factors Affecting the Evolution and Behavioral Ecology of the Modern Bears," *Int. Conf. Bear Res. Mgmt.* 8 (1990): 191.

41 *Naturalist Adolph Murie:* Adolph Murie, *The Grizzlies of Mount McKinley* (Seattle: University of Washington Press, 1981), 11.

41 *Experiments with captive:* Riley Woodford, "Testing Bears' Color Vision," *Alaska Fish & Wildlife News* online magazine, April 2005.

41 *The researchers who studied:* Ellis S. Bacon and Gordon M. Burghardt, "Learning and Color Discrimination in the American Black Bear," *Int. Conf. Bear Res. Mgmt.* 3 (1974): 35.

41 *The nose is embedded:* Chris Peterson, "Grizzlies Have Great Sniffers," *Hungry Horse News,* August 3, 2005; Michael Jamison, "Neurosurgeon: Griz Are Sniffing Champs of the Wild," *Missoulian,* July 29, 2007.

42 *As a doctoral student:* Barrie Gilbert, "Opportunities for Social Learning in Bears," in *Mammalian Social Learning: Comparative and Ecological Perspectives,* ed. Hilary O. Box and Kathleen Rita Gibson (Cambridge: Cambridge University Press, 1999), 231.

42 *"Now if a rufus [sic] hummingbird":* Fred L. Bunnell, "Rapporteur's Report," in

Bear-People Conflicts: Proceedings of a Symposium on Management Strategies, April 6–10, 1987, ed. Marianne Bromley (Yellowknife: Northwest Territories Department of Natural Resources, 1989), 229.

42 "To live for a long time": Interview with Harry Reynolds.

42 "Although other grizzlies": Linderman, Ground Tracking, 9.

42 A population of grizzlies: Robert J. Gau, Ray Case, David F. Penner, and Philip D. McLoughlin, "Feeding Patterns of Barren-Ground Grizzly Bears in the Central Canadian Arctic," Arctic 55, 4 (December 2002): 341–342.

42 One study of brown bears: Rodney D. Boertje, William C. Gasaway, Daniel V. Grangaard, and David G. Kellyhouse, "Predation on Moose and Caribou by Radio-Collared Grizzly Bears in East Central Alaska (USA)," Canadian Journal of Zoology 66, 11 (1988): 2492.

43 With the doggedness: M. A. Austin, M. E. Obbard, and G. B. Kolensoky, "Evidence for a Black Bear, Ursus americanus, Killing an Adult Moose, Alces alces," Canadian Field-Naturalist 108, 2 (1994): 237.

43 Studies conducted: The ADF&G commonly refers to Warren B. Ballard, "Bear Predation on Moose: A Review of Recent North American Studies and Their Management Implications," Alces Supplement 1 (1992): 167.

43 Not all bears kill calves: Interviews with Harry Reynolds and Vic Van Ballenberghe.

43 US Fish and Wildlife Service biologists: Mark R. Bertram and Michael T. Vivion, "Black Bear Monitoring in Eastern Interior Alaska," Ursus 13 (2002): 75.

43 "From tracks it was apparent": Mitchell Taylor, "Grizzly Bear Sightings in Viscount Melville Sound," in Polar Bears: Proceedings of the Eleventh Working Meeting of the IUCN/SSC Polar Bear Specialist Group, ed. Øystein Wiig, Erik W. Born, and Gerald W. Garner, (Copenhagen, Denmark, January 25–27, 1993), 191.

44 In at least ten: Patricia E. Reynolds, Harry V. Reynolds, and Richard T. Shideler, "Predation and Multiple Kills of Muskoxen by Grizzly Bears," Ursus 13 (2002): 81–82.

44 Bear No. 1086: Hechtel, "Activity and Food Habits," 59.

44 Researchers surveying seabirds: Edgar P. Bailey and Nina H. Faust, "Distribution and Abundance of Marine Birds Breeding between Amber and Kamishak Bays, Alaska, with Notes on Interactions with Bears," Western Birds 15 (1984): 172.

44 After the 1964 earthquake: Bruce H. Campbell, "Activities of Brown Bears on the Copper River Delta, Alaska and Their Impact on Nesting Dusky Canada Geese," Northwestern Naturalist 72 (Winter 1991): 93.

45 Adolph Murie noted: Murie, Grizzlies of Mount McKinley, 216.

45 One survey found: Victor G. Barnes Jr., "Brown Bear–Human Interactions Associated with Deer Hunting on Kodiak Island," Int. Conf. Bear Res. Mgmt. 9, 1 (1994): 70.

45 Before the salmon runs: Tom Smith and Steven Partridge, "Dynamics of

Intertidal Foraging by Coastal Brown Bears in Southwestern Alaska," *Journal of Wildlife Management* 68, 2 (2004): 234–235.

45 *The same way, I suppose:* George Gmelch, *Resource Use in Glacier Bay National Preserve* (US Department of the Interior, National Park Service, 1982), 64.

46 *One term for this effect:* Clive G. Jones, John H. Lawton, and Moshe Shachak, "Organisms as Ecosystem Engineers," *Oikos* 69, 3 (April 1994): 373.

46 *During the high season:* Christy A. Welch, Jeffrey A. Keay, Katherine C. Kendall, and Charles T. Robbins, "Constraints on Frugivory by Bears," *Ecology* 78, 4 (1997): 1112, 1115.

46 *Brown bears on Chichagof Island:* Mary F. Willson, "Mammals as Seed-Dispersal Mutualists in North America," *Oikos* 67, 1 (May 1993): 167.

46 *They're not looking for dessert:* Charles T. Robbins, Jennifer A. Fortin, Karyn D. Rode, Sean D. Farley, Lisa A. Shipley, and Laura A. Felicetti, "Optimizing Protein Intake as a Foraging Strategy to Maximize Mass Gain in an Omnivore," *Oikos* 116, 10 (2007): 1676; Karyn Rode and Charles T. Robbins, "Why Bears Consume Mixed Diets during Fruit Abundance," *Canadian Journal of Zoology* 78, 9 (2000): 1640.

47 *But studies of captive bears:* Robbins et al., "Optimizing Protein Intake," 1681.

47 *"Bears rapidly gained fat":* Bruce N. McLellan, "Implications of a High-Energy and Low-Protein Diet on the Body Composition, Fitness, and Competitive Abilities of Black (*Ursus americanus*) and Grizzly (*Ursus arctos*) Bears," *Canadian Journal of Zoology* 89, 6 (2011): 546.

47 *One female who weighed:* Ibid., 551.

47 *Bears work in bulk, though:* Robbins et al., "Optimizing Protein Intake," 1644.

47 *Thanks to an active digestive system:* Mary F. Willson and Scott M. Gende, "Seed Dispersal by Brown Bears, *Ursus arctos*, in Southeastern Alaska," *Canadian Field-Naturalist* 118, 4 (2004): 501–502.

48 *The other kinds of food:* Anna Traveset, Teresa Bermejo, and Mary F. Willson, "Effect of Manure Composition on Seedling Emergence and Growth of Two Common Shrub Species of Southeast Alaska," *Plant Ecology* 155 (2001): 32.

48 *Lilies overlooked by the bears:* Sandra E. Tardiff and Jack A. Stanford, "Grizzly Bear Digging: Effects on Subalpine Meadow Plants in Relation to Mineral Nitrogen Availability," *Ecology* 79, 7 (1998): 2226.

48 *Bears also made "modest but significant":* Daniel F. Doak and Michael G. Loso, "Effects of Grizzly Bear Digging on Alpine Plant Community Structure," *Arctic, Antarctic, and Alpine Research* 35, 4 (2003): 427.

48 *When bears dig dens:* David R. Butler, "Human-Induced Changes in Animal Populations and Distributions, and the Subsequent Effects on Fluvial Systems," *Geomorphology* 79 (2006): 455.

48 *"It is already too late":* Ibid., 457.

49 *Compare his 350 pounds:* Charles Schwartz, Sterling Miller, and Mark A. Haroldson, "Grizzly Bear," in *Wild Mammals of North America: Biology,*

Management, and Conservation, ed. George A. Feldhamer, Bruce C. Thompson, and Joseph A. Chapman (Baltimore: Johns Hopkins University Press, 2003), 559.

49 *The size differences among brown bears:* Robert L. Rausch, "On the Status of Some Arctic Mammals," *Arctic* 6, 2 (July 1953): 96.

49 *"On such a system twin bear cubs":* Ibid.

49 *Similarly, Dirk Pieter Erdbrink:* Björn Kurtén and Elaine Anderson, *Pleistocene Mammals of North America* (New York: Columbia University Press, 1980), 184.

49 *After studying 357 bear skulls:* Robert L. Rausch, "Geographic Variation in Size in North American Brown Bears, *Ursus arctos* L., as Indicated by Condylobasal Length," *Canadian Journal of Zoology* 41, 1 (1963): 33.

49 *Bear taxonomy has been recomplicated:* A. C. Kitchener, "Taxonomic Issues in Bears: Impacts on Conservation in Zoos and the Wild, and Gaps in Current Knowledge," *International Zoo Yearbook* 44 (2010): 34.

49 *Bear skulls do display:* Stirling and Derocher, "Factors Affecting," 198.

50 *Harry Reynolds and other wildlife biologists:* Schwartz, Miller, and Haroldson, "Grizzly Bear," 560.

50 *"Salmon was the most important source":* Grant V. Hilderbrand, Charles C. Schwartz, Charles T. Robbins, M. E. Jacoby, Thomas A. Hanley, S. M. Arthur, and Christopher Servheen, "The Importance of Meat, Particularly Salmon, to Body Size, Population Productivity, and Conservation of North American Brown Bears," *Canadian Journal of Zoology* 77, 1 (1999): 132.

50 *"It looks more like a hippopotamus":* John Schoen, "Conserving Alaska's Bears: Challenges and Opportunities" (presented at the 7th Alaska Bear Forum, Anchorage Museum of History and Art, April 19, 2005).

50 *In southwestern Alaska:* Craig A. Stricker, Steven D. Kovach, Gail H. Collins, Sean D. Farley, Robert O. Rye, and Michael T. Hinkes, "Inter-annual Variation in the Foraging Ecology of a Brown Bear Population in Southwest Alaska" (poster presented at the American Geophysical Union fall meeting, San Francisco, December 2010).

51 *The average adult female:* Grant Hilderbrand, Stacy G. Jenkins, Charles C. Schwartz, Thomas A. Hanley, and Charles T. Robbins, "Effect of Seasonal Differences in Dietary Meat Intake on Changes in Body Mass and Composition in Wild and Captive Brown Bears," *Canadian Journal of Zoology* 77, 10 (1999): 1626.

51 *"Fat is the essential currency":* Robbins et al., "Optimizing Protein Intake," 1676.

51 *Those living in meat-rich habitats:* Hilderbrand et al., "Importance of Meat," 135.

51 *Fatter mothers also gave birth:* Charles T. Robbins, Merav Ben-David, Jennifer K. Fortin, and O. Lynne Nelson, "Maternal Condition Determines Birth Date and Growth of Newborn Bear Cubs," *Journal of Mammalogy* 93, 2 (2012): 543.

51 *There were between 191 and 551 bears:* Sterling Miller, Gary C. White, Richard A. Sellers, Harry V. Reynolds, John W. Schoen, Kimberly Titus, Victor G. Barnes Jr., Roger B. Smith, Robert R. Nelson, Warren B. Ballard, and Charles C. Schwartz, "Brown and Black Bear Density Estimation in Alaska Using Radiotelemetry and Replicated Mark-Resight Techniques," *Wildlife Monographs* 133 (January 1997): 22.

51 *Salmon are so valuable:* Grant Hilderbrand, Sean D. Farley, Charles C. Schwartz, and Charles T. Robbins, "Importance of Salmon to Wildlife: Implications for Integrated Management," *Ursus* 15, 1 (2004): 6.

51 *On Admiralty Island:* Merav Ben-David, Kimberly Titus, and LaVern R. Beier, "Consumption of Salmon by Alaskan Brown Bears: A Trade-off between Nutritional Requirements and the Risk of Infanticide?" *Oecologia* 138 (February 2004): 471.

51 *This happens on Kodiak Island:* Lawrence J. Van Daele, Victor G. Barnes Jr., and Jerrold L. Belant, "Ecological Flexibility of Brown Bears on Kodiak Island, Alaska," *Ursus* 23, 1 (2012): 25.

52 *Arctic grizzlies living:* Mark A. Edwards, Andrew E. Derocher, Keith A. Hobson, Marsha Branigan, and John A. Nagy, "Fast Carnivores and Slow Herbivores: Differential Foraging Strategies among Grizzly Bears in the Canadian Arctic," *Oecologia* 165, 4 (April 2011): 883.

52 *Females basically stop growing:* Schwartz, Miller, and Haroldson, "Grizzly Bear," 559.

52 *For example, Smith and Partridge:* Smith and Partridge, "Dynamics of Intertidal Foraging," 238.

52 *Some females with spring cubs:* Ben-David, Titus, and Beier, "Consumption of Salmon," 471.

52 *Similarly, Jennifer Fortin and her colleagues:* Jennifer K. Fortin, Sean D. Farley, Karyn D. Rode, and Charles R. Robbins, "Dietary and Spatial Overlap between Sympatric Ursids Relative to Salmon Use," *Ursus* 18, 1 (2007): 26.

53 *On shallow creeks:* Scott M. Gende, Thomas P. Quinn, Mary F. Willson, Ron Heintz, and Thomas M. Scott, "Magnitude and Fate of Salmon-Derived Nutrients and Energy in a Coastal Stream Ecosystem," *Journal of Freshwater Ecology* 19, 1 (March 2004): 155.

53 *"Multiplied over the course":* Scott Gende, Thomas P. Quinn, and Mary F. Willson, "Consumption Choice by Bears Feeding on Salmon," *Oecologia* 127, 3 (2001): 379.

53 *"It is easy for humans":* Ibid., 380.

53 *In shallow channels where it's easier:* Scott M. Gende, Thomas P. Quinn, Ray Hilborn, Andrew P. Hendry, and Bobette Dickerson, "Brown Bears Selectively Kill Salmon with Higher Energy Content but Only in Habitats that Facilitate Choice," *Oikos* 104, 3 (2004): 525–526.

54 *No one understood:* Charles T. Robbins, Charles C. Schwartz, and Laura A.

Felicetti, "Nutritional Ecology of Ursids: A Review of Newer Methods and Management Implications," *Ursus* 15, 2 (2004): 162.

54 *The distribution chain works like this:* Scott M. Gende, Richard T. Edwards, Mary F. Willson, and Mark S. Wipfli, "Pacific Salmon in Aquatic and Terrestrial Ecosystems," *BioScience* 52, 10 (October 2002): 917–918.

54 *Ecologist Tom Reimchen:* Tom Reimchen, "Salmon Nutrients, Nitrogen Isotopes and Coastal Forests," *Ecoforestry* 16, 3 (Fall 2001): 13.

54 *On several streams:* Thomas P. Quinn, Stephanie M. Carlson, Scott M. Gende, and Harry B. Rich Jr., "Transportation of Pacific Salmon Carcasses from Streams to Riparian Forests by Bears," *Canadian Journal of Zoology* 87, 3 (2009): 198–199.

55 *Grant Hilderbrand calculated:* Grant V. Hilderbrand, Thomas A. Hanley, Charles T. Robbins, and Charles C. Schwartz, "Role of Brown Bears (*Ursus arctos*) in the Flow of Marine Nitrogen into a Terrestrial Ecosystem," *Oecologia* 121, 4 (1999): 549.

55 *If salmon-derived nitrogen does help:* James M. Helfield and Robert J. Naiman, "Salmon and Alder as Nitrogen Sources to Riparian Forests in a Boreal Alaskan Watershed," *Oecologia* 133 (2002): 580.

55 *"Southeast Alaska has over 5000":* Gende et al., "Pacific Salmon," 920.

56 *Brown and black bears tend to eat:* Tom Reimchen, "Some Ecological and Evolutionary Aspects of Bear-Salmon Interactions in Coastal British Columbia," *Canadian Journal of Zoology* 78, 3 (2000): 455; Gende, Quinn, and Willson, "Consumption Choice," 380; Gende et al., "Brown Bears Selectively Kill," 526.

56 *In streams where bears:* Stephanie M. Carlson, Ray Hilborn, Andrew P. Hendry, and Thomas P. Quinn, "Predation by Bears Drives Senescence in Natural Populations of Salmon," *PLoS ONE* 2, 12 (2007): e1286.

56 *"Where bear activity was high":* Ned Rozell, "Early Death May Benefit Bear-Pressured Salmon," *Alaska Science Forum*, September 19, 2005, article 1768.

56 *Blowflies laid more eggs:* Erin Meehan, Elizabeth E. Seminet-Reneau, and Thomas P. Quinn, "Bear Predation on Pacific Salmon Facilitates Colonization of Carcasses by Fly Maggots," *American Midland Naturalist* 153, 1 (January 2005): 149.

57 *Caddis flies also strongly prefer:* Monika Winder, Daniel E. Schindler, Jonathan W. Moore, Susan P. Johnson, and Wendy J. Palen, "Do Bears Facilitate Transfer of Salmon Resources to Aquatic Macroinvertebrates?" *Canadian Journal of Fisheries and Aquatic Sciences* 62 (2005): 2289.

57 *Flies, midges, and other invertebrates:* Katie S. Christie and Thomas E. Reimchen, "Presence of Salmon Increases Passerine Density on Pacific Northwest Streams," *Auk* 125, 1 (2008): 55.

57 *Gende suggested one possibility:* Gende et al., "Pacific Salmon," 923.

57 *That many moose:* Joel Berger, Peter B. Stacey, Lori Bellis, and Matthew P.

Johnson, "A Mammalian Predator-Prey Imbalance: Grizzly Bear and Wolf Extinction Affect Avian Neotropical Migrants," *Ecological Applications* 11, 4 (August 2001): 954–955.

58 *Such losses add up:* Gregory S. Butcher and Daniel K. Niven, "Combining Data from the Christmas Bird Count and the Breeding Bird Survey to Determine the Continental Status and Trends of North America Birds" (National Audubon Society, June 14, 2007), http://stateofthebirds.audubon.org/cbid/content/Report.pdf.

58 *Biologist Steeve Côté suspects:* Steeve D. Côté, "Extirpation of a Large Black Bear Population by Introduced White-Tailed Deer," *Conservation Biology* 19, 5 (October 2005): 1669.

58 *An emerging field of study:* Martin Wikelski and Steven J. Cooke, "Conservation Physiology," *Trends in Ecology and Evolution* 21, 1 (January 2006): 38.

58 *"Landscape fragmentation had a large":* Mark A. Ditmer, Karen V. Noyce, Timothy G. Laske, and Paul A. Iaizzo, "Creating a Metabolic Map to Assess Potential for Range Expansion of American Black Bears," *International Bear News* 21, 4 (November 2012): 30.

58 *One bear's heart rate:* Timothy G. Laske, David L. Garshelis, and Paul A. Iaizzo, "Monitoring the Wild Black Bear's Reaction to Human and Environmental Stressors," *BMC Physiology* 11, 1 (2011): 11.

58 *Alaska wildlife biologist John Schoen:* John W. Schoen, "Bear Habitat Management: A Review and Future Perspective," *Int. Conf. Bear Res. Mgmt.* 8 (1990): 143.

59 *Researcher Ralph Nelson:* Linda Witt, "The Bear Facts? Dr. Ralph Nelson of the Mayo Clinic Studies the Miracle of Hibernation," *People*, March 27, 1978, http://www.people.com/people/archive/article/0,,20070479,00.html.

59 *In the circumpolar north:* John D. C. Linnell, Jon E. Swenson, Reidar Andersen, and Brian Barnes, "How Vulnerable Are Denning Bears to Disturbance?" *Wildlife Society Bulletin* 28, 2 (2000): 401.

59 *Some male black bears denned:* Charles Schwartz, Sterling D. Miller, and Albert W. Franzmann, "Denning Ecology of Three Black Bear Populations in Alaska," *Int. Conf. Bear Res. Mgmt.* 7 (1987): 285.

59 *Van Daele recorded lone females:* Larry Van Daele, "Population Dynamics and Management of Brown Bears on Kodiak Island, Alaska" (Ph.D. diss., University of Idaho, 2007), 21.

59 *Almost a quarter of the males:* Ibid., 22.

60 *Inland Nunamiuts believed:* Robert L. Rausch, "Notes on the Nunamiut Eskimo and Mammals of the Anaktuvuk Pass Region, Brooks Range, Alaska," *Arctic* 4, 3 (December 1951): 166.

60 *Kutchin Athabascans told anthropologist:* Richard K. Nelson, *Hunters of the Northern Forest: Designs for Survival among the Alaskan Kutchin* (Chicago: University of Chicago Press, 1986), 125–126.

60 *A Wisconsin black bear*: Margaret Ludwig Heino, "American Black Bear Hibernating in Bald Eagle Nest," *International Bear News* 14, 1 (February 2005): 27.

60 *Black bears living*: Eugene J. DeGayner, Marc G. Kramer, Joseph G. Doerr, and Margaret J. Robertsen, "Windstorm Disturbance Effects on Forest Structure and Black Bear Dens in Southeast Alaska," *Ecological Applications* 15, 4 (August 2005): 1313.

60 *Brown bears on Chichagof*: John W. Schoen, LaVern R. Beier, Jack W. Lentfer, and Loyal J. Johnson, "Denning Ecology of Brown Bears on Admiralty and Chichagof Islands," *Int. Conf. Bear Res. Mgmt.* 7 (1987): 299.

60 *"Some cave dens are rubbed smooth"*: Schoen, Miller, and Reynolds, "Last Stronghold," 57.

60 *Schoen's colleague*: Riley Woodford, "Where Sleeping Bears Lie," *Alaska Fish & Wildlife News* online magazine, January 2010.

60 *On the seemingly featureless*: Richard T. Shideler, "Denning Ecology of Grizzly Bears in the Oilfield Region of Alaska's North Slope" (presented at the Wildlife Society's 13th Annual Conference and Trade Show, Anchorage, September 2006); "Grizzly Bears (*Ursus arctos*)," in *Alaska's North Slope Oilfields* (Technical Brief, BP Exploration, June 2001), 1–2.

61 *On the Kenai Peninsula*: Schwartz, Miller, and Franzmann, "Denning Ecology," 287.

61 *"A lot of times"*: Woodford, "Where Sleeping Bears Lie."

61 *"We've done over a thousand"*: Greg Breining, "The Secret Lives of Bears," *Minnesota* (Fall 2012): 20.

61 *Most Kodiak bears*: Van Daele, "Population Dynamics," 21.

61 *Females in Denali National Park*: Nathan S. Libal, Jerrold L. Belant, Bruce D. Leopold, Guiming Wang, and Patricia A. Owen, "Despotism and Risk of Infanticide Influence Grizzly Bear Den-Site Selection," *PLoS ONE* 6, 9 (September 2011): 8.

62 *"It was a cave"*: Interview with Tom Mills by Merry Ellefson.

62 *"Clearly the bear"*: Paul Shepard and Barry Sanders, *Sacred Paw: The Bear in Nature, Myth, and Literature* (New York: Viking Penguin, 1985), 57.

62 *For part of the year*: Interview with Brian Barnes.

63 *The bears' metabolic rate*: Øivind Tøien, John Blake, Dale M. Edgar, Dennis A. Grahn, H. Craig Heller, and Brian M. Barnes, "Hibernation in Black Bears: Independence of Metabolic Suppression from Body Temperature," *Science* 331, 6019 (February 18, 2011): 906.

64 *During the study of fifteen wild*: Laske, Garshelis, and Iaizzo, "Monitoring the Wild Black," 9.

64 *Oil companies on the Kenai Peninsula*: Craig Medred, "Bear Savaging Swift, Deadly, Unique," ADN, February 10, 1998.

64 *Six years later*: ADF&G news release, March 2004.

64 *During brief missions:* Gilles Clément, "The Musculo-skeletal System in Space," *Fundamentals of Space Medicine* 23 (2011): 181–182.

65 *"Your body will not allow":* Paul A. Iaizzo and Timothy G. Laske, "The Heart of the Hibernating Bear: Medical Possibilities from Bear Den to Hospital Bed" (video presentation to Young Scientist Roundtable, Wayzata Public Schools, February 1, 2011), http://vimeo.com/29373040.

65 *Grizzlies lose between 24 and 43 percent:* Schwartz, Miller, and Haroldson, "Grizzly Bear," 559.

65 *"We find that overwintering":* Henry J. Harlow, Tom Lohuis, Thomas D. I. Beck, and Paul A. Iaizzo, "Muscle Strength in Overwintering Bears," *Nature* 409 (February 22, 2001): 997.

65 *Harlow's later work suggests:* Henry J. Harlow, Tom Lohuis, R. C. Anderson-Sprecher, and Thomas D. I. Beck, "Body Surface Temperature of Hibernating Black Bears May Be Related to Periodic Muscle Activity," *Journal of Mammalogy* 85, 3 (June 2004): 418.

65 *Hibernating bears don't urinate:* Henry J. Harlow, "Climate Change Influence on Hibernation Patterns of Bears" (video presentation at Questioning Greater Yellowstone's Future: Climate, Land Use, and Invasive Species, the 10th Biennial Scientific Conference on the Greater Yellowstone Ecosystem, Yellowstone National Park, Wyoming, October 11–13, 2010), http://vimeo.com/30752553.

65 *As they slept:* Iaizzo and Laske, "Heart of the Hibernating Bear"; Paul A. Iaizzo, Timothy G. Laske, Henry J. Harlow, Carolyn B. McClay, and David L. Garshelis, "Wound Healing during Hibernation by Black Bears (*Ursus americanus*) in the Wild: Elicitation of Reduced Scar Formation," *Integrative Zoology* 7, 1 (2012): 56.

65 *What bears do:* Constanza Villalba, "10 Lessons Medicine Can Learn from Bears," *Scientific American*, January 6, 2009, http://www.scientificamerican.com/slideshow.cfm?id=bear-hibernation-science.

66 *"So if some people think bears":* Daniel Simberloff, "Biodiversity and Bears—A Conservation Paradigm Shift," *Ursus* 11 (1999): 23.

67 *But without more data:* Ibid., 25.

67 *"They're conducting their lives":* Interview with Ernestine Hayes.

67 *Z.B. is, of course, long dead:* William Wilbanks, *Forgotten Heroes: Police Officers Killed in Alaska, 1850–1997* (Paducah, KY: Turner Publishing, 1999), 9.

THE SOCIAL BEAR

72 *Bears are notable:* Mary Jane West-Eberhard, *Developmental Plasticity and Evolution* (New York: Oxford University Press, 2003), 10.

72 *A happy collusion:* Derek Stonorov and Allen W. Stokes, "Social Behavior of the Alaska Brown Bear," *Int. Conf. Bear Res. Mgmt.* 2 (1972): 233–234.

73 A recent theory: Stephen Herrero, Tom Smith, Terry D. DeBruyn, Kerry Gunther, and Colleen A. Matt, "From the Field: Brown Bear Habituation to People—Safety, Risks, and Benefits," *Wildlife Society Bulletin* 33, 1 (2005): 362–373; Tom S. Smith, Stephen Herrero, and Terry D. DeBruyn, "Alaskan Brown Bears, Humans, and Habituation," *Ursus* 16, 1 (2005): 1–10.

73 Aumiller and his staff: See Larry Aumiller and Colleen Matt, "Management of McNeil River State Game Sanctuary for Viewing of Brown Bears," *Int. Conf. Bear Res. Mgmt.* 9 (1994): 51–61.

74 This social architecture: Thomas Griffin and Edward W. Weiss, *McNeil River State Game Sanctuary Annual Management Report*, Special Areas Management Report (ADF&G Division of Wildlife Conservation, 2011), 5.

74 "The ability to recognize": John J. Craighead, Jay S. Sumner, and John A. Mitchell, *The Grizzly Bears of Yellowstone: Their Ecology in the Yellowstone Ecosystem, 1959–1992* (Washington, DC: Island Press, 1995), 154.

74 During the summer of 1970: Stonorov and Stokes, "Social Behavior," 234.

75 After observing twenty-two different bears: Ibid., 235.

75 Bears also communicate: Maria Pasitschniak-Arts, "Ursus arctos," *Mammalian Species* 439 (April 23, 1993): 6–7.

75 Less than 3 percent: Allan L. Egbert, "The Social Behavior of Brown Bears at McNeil River, Alaska" (Ph.D. diss., Utah State University, 1978), 46.

76 In a study by Egbert and Stokes: Allan L. Egbert and Allen W. Stokes, "The Social Behaviour of Brown Bears on an Alaskan Salmon Stream," *Int. Conf. Bear Res. Mgmt.* 3 (1974): 54.

76 Egbert reported: Egbert, "Social Behavior," 47.

78 "Larry knows more": E-mail from Sterling Miller.

80 Staff recorded thirteen charges: Memorandum from Larry Aumiller to Joe Meehan, "2004 McNeil River Field Report," December 20, 2004.

81 "We determined that": Sam Steyært, Anders Endrestøl, Klaus Hackländer, Jon Swenson, and Andreas Zedrosser, "The Mating System of the Brown Bear Ursus arctos," *Mammal Review* 42, 1 (January 2012): 12.

81 For example: Charles Schwartz, Sterling Miller, and Mark A. Haroldson, "Grizzly Bear," in *Wild Mammals of North America: Biology, Management, and Conservation*, ed. George A. Feldhamer, Bruce C. Thompson, and Joseph A. Chapman (Baltimore: Johns Hopkins University Press, 2003), 563.

81 One Yellowstone female mated: Kim R. Barber and Frederick G. Lindzey, "Breeding Behavior of Black Bears," *Int. Conf. Bear Res. Mgmt.* 6 (1987): 129.

81 In Polar Bears: Andrew Derocher, *Polar Bears: A Complete Guide to Their Biology and Behavior* (Baltimore: Johns Hopkins University Press, 2012), 148.

81 Their mate choices favor: Stephen Shuster, "Sexual Selection and Mating Systems," *Proceedings of the National Academy of Sciences* 106, Supplement 1 (June 16, 2009): 10,009.

82 Females stop growing: Schwartz, Miller, and Haroldson, "Grizzly Bear," 558–559.

82   *"The apparent success"*: Steyærtet al., "Mating System," 23.

82   *This seems borne out*: Adrienne I. Kovach and Roger A. Powell, "Effects of Body Size on Male Mating Tactics and Paternity in Black Bears, Ursus americanus," *Canadian Journal of Zoology* 81, 7 (2003): 1264–1265.

82   *That size difference*: Schwartz, Miller, and Haroldson, "Grizzly Bear," 563.

82   *In contrast, William Boone and colleagues*: William R. Boone, M. Elaine Richardson, and Jennifer A. Greer, "Breeding Behavior of the American Black Bear Ursus americanus," *Theriogenology* 60, 2 (July 2003): 293; Stephen Herrero and David Hamer, "Courtship and Copulation of a Pair of Grizzly Bears, with Comments on Reproductive Plasticity and Strategy," *Journal of Mammalogy* 58, 3 (August 1977): 442.

82   *Males that mated frequently*: Eva Bellemain, Andreas Zedrosser, Stéphanie Manel, Lisette P. Waits, Pierre Taberlet, and Jon E. Swenson, "The Dilemma of Female Mate Selection in the Brown Bear, a Species with Sexually Selected Infanticide," *Proceedings of the Royal Society B* 273, 1584 (2006): 288–289.

82   *In the sperm Olympics*: Montserrat Gomendio and Eduardo R. S. Roldan, "Implications of Diversity in Sperm Size and Function for Sperm Competition and Fertility," *International Journal of Developmental Biology* 52, 5 (2008): 439.

82   *Both brown bears*: Kovach and Powell, "Effects of Body Size," 1264; Serge Larivière and Steven H. Ferguson, "Evolution of Induced Ovulation in North American Carnivores," *Journal of Mammalogy* 84, 3 (2003): 944.

83   *In a clever survival strategy*: Schwartz, Miller, and Haroldson, "Grizzly Bear," 564.

83   *In their first two months*: Riley Woodford, "Bear Milk," *Alaska Fish & Wildlife News* online magazine, June 2007.

83   *A brown bear named Red Collar*: Thomas Bledsoe, *Brown Bear Summer: Life among Alaska's Giants* (New York: E. P. Dutton, 1987), 39.

83   *The champion of mothers*: Randall J. Wilk, John W. Solberg, Vernon D. Berns, and Richard A. Sellers, "Brown Bear, Ursus arctos, with Six Young," *Canadian Field-Naturalist* 102, 3 (1988): 541.

84   *One controversial hypothesis*: Eva Bellemain, Jon E. Swenson, and Pierre Taberlet, "Mating Strategies in Relation to Sexually Selected Infanticide in a Non-Social Carnivore: The Brown Bear," *Ethology* 112 (2006): 238–239; Bruce N. McLellan, "Sexually Selected Infanticide in Grizzly Bears: The Effects of Hunting on Cub Survival," *Ursus* 16, 2 (2005): 148.

84   *But wildlife biologist Sterling Miller*: Sterling Miller, "Detection of Differences in Brown Bear Density and Population Composition Caused by Hunting," *Int. Conf. Bear Res. Mgmt.* 8 (1990): 403.

84   *"Convincing evidence"*: Sophie M. Czetwertynski, Mark S. Boyce, and Fiona K. Schmiegelow, "Effects of Hunting on Demographic Parameters of American Black Bears," *Ursus* 18, 1 (2007): 3.

85   *Cub survivorship*: Sterling Miller, Richard A. Sellers, and Jeffrey A. Keay,

"Effects of Hunting on Brown Bear Cub Survival and Litter Size in Alaska," *Ursus* 14, 2 (2003): 148–149.

85 *In a 2005 study:* McLellan, "Sexually Selected Infanticide," 151.

85 *Polly Hessing witnessed:* Pauline Hessing and Larry Aumiller, "Observations of Conspecific Predation by Brown Bears," *Canadian Field-Naturalist* 108, 3 (1994): 333.

85 *At McNeil, several have drowned:* Aumiller to Meehan, "2004 Field Report."

86 *"If you come out":* Sean Farley, Alaska Board of Game meeting, March 15, 2003.

86 *The life histories:* Ibid.

86 *About 31 percent:* Richard A. Sellers and Larry Aumiller, "Brown Bear Population Characteristics at McNeil River, Alaska," *Int. Conf. Bear Res. Mgmt.* 9, 1 (1994): 288.

86 *"They're terrible moms":* Sean Farley, Alaska Board of Game meeting, March 15, 2013.

86 *Steven Kovach and colleagues:* Steven D. Kovach, Gail H. Collins, Michael T. Hinkes, and Jeffrey W. Denton, "Reproduction and Survival of Brown Bears in Southwest Alaska, USA," *Ursus* 17, 1 (2006): 19.

86 *Occasionally, distracted mothers:* Bledsoe, *Brown Bear Summer*, 166–180.

87 *In Denali National Park:* Frederick C. Dean, Rick McIntyre, and Richard A. Sellers, "Additional Mixed-Age Brown Bear, Ursus arctos, Associations in Alaska," *Canadian Field-Naturalist* 106, 2 (1992): 257.

87 *"While the aircraft circled":* Ibid., 258.

87 *Mixed-age litters:* Jon E. Swenson and Mark A. Haroldson, "Observations of Mixed-Age Litters in Brown Bears," *Ursus* 19, 1 (2008): 73.

88 *A long-term study:* Harry V. Reynolds, *Effects of Harvest on Grizzly Bear Population Dynamics in the Northcentral Alaska Range, July 1, 1996–June 30, 1998* (ADF&G Division of Wildlife Conservation, 1999), 5.

88 *Some bears achieve:* Loyal Johnson and Paul LeRoux, "Age of Self-Sufficiency in Brown/Grizzly Bear in Alaska," *Journal of Wildlife Management* 37, 1 (January 1973): 123.

89 *"Apparently taking care":* Jiska van Dijk, "Considerations for the Rehabilitation and Release of Bears into the Wild," in *Rehabilitation and Release of Bears*, ed. Lydia Kolter and Jiska van Dijk (Köln, Germany: Zoologischer Garten Köln, 2005), 11.

89 *"Generally if an animal":* Fred L. Bunnell, "Rapporteur's Report," in *Bear-People Conflicts: Proceedings of a Symposium on Management Strategies, April 6–10, 1987*, ed. Marianne Bromley (Yellowknife: Northwest Territories Department of Natural Resources, 1989), 229.

89 *"While one cannot exclude":* Barrie Gilbert, "Opportunities for Social Learning in Bears," in *Mammalian Social Learning: Comparative and Ecological Perspectives*, ed. Hilary O. Box and Kathleen Rita Gibson (Cambridge: Cambridge University Press, 1999), 232–233.

90 *A young brown bear:* Volker B. Deecke, "Tool-Use in the Brown Bear (*Ursus arctos*)," *Animal Cognition* 15, 4 (July 2012): 725.

90 *"SJ would immediately":* Robert Fagen and Johanna Fagen, "Individual Distinctiveness in Brown Bears, Ursus arctos L," *Ethology* 102, 2 (1996): 221.

91 *In his dissertation:* Michael Luque, "Fishing Behavior of Alaska Brown Bear Ursus arctos" (M.S. thesis, Utah State University, 1978), 15–16.

91 *Some dominant bears:* Ian D. Gill and James M. Helfield, "Alternative Foraging Strategies among Bears Fishing for Salmon: A Test of the Dominance Hypothesis," *Canadian Journal of Zoology* 90, 6 (June 2012): 773.

92 *In his book:* Will Troyer, *Into Brown Bear Country* (Fairbanks: University of Alaska Press, 2005), 67.

92 *"No behavioral concept":* E. O. Wilson, *Sociobiology: The Abridged Edition* (Cambridge, MA: Harvard University Press, 1980), 84–85.

93 *After studying the play:* Robert Fagen and Johanna Fagen, "Juvenile Survival and Benefits of Play Behaviour in Brown Bears, Ursus arctos," *Evolutionary Ecology Research* 6, 1 (2004): 89.

93 *"Play involves both control":* Ibid., 98.

93 *Ethologists have long recognized:* Suzanne D. E. Held and Marek Špinka, "Animal Play and Animal Welfare," *Animal Behaviour* 81 (2011): 891.

93 *Researcher Jaak Panksepp:* Marc Bekoff, *Animal Passions and Beastly Virtues: Reflections on Redecorating Nature* (Philadelphia: Temple University Press, 2006), 126.

93 *Play behavior signals:* Held and Špinka, "Animal Play," 897.

93 *"Scientists have been reluctant":* Samuel D. Gosling and Oliver P. John, "Personality Dimensions in Nonhuman Animals: A Cross-Species Review," *Current Directions in Psychological Science* 8, 3 (June 1999): 69.

94 *"The prevailing view implies":* Donald R. Griffin, *The Question of Animal Awareness: Evolutionary Continuity of Mental Experiences*, rev. ed. (New York: Rockefeller University Press, 1981), 125.

94 *Some researchers have adapted:* Gosling and John, "Personality Dimensions," 70–71.

95 *"There is strong evidence":* Samuel D. Gosling and Simine Vazire, "Are We Barking up the Right Tree? Evaluating a Comparative Approach to Personality," *Journal of Research in Personality* 36, 6 (2002): 612.

95 *One example they cited:* Ibid., 610–611.

95 *After comparing their assessments:* Fagen and Fagen, "Individual Distinctiveness," 225.

95 *Research on creatures:* Niels J. Dingemanse and Denis Réale, "Natural Selection and Animal Personality," *Behaviour* 142, 9–10 (2005): 1169.

96 *For example, in a study:* Daniel Nettle, "The Evolution of Personality Variation in Humans and Other Animals," *American Psychologist* 61, 6 (September 2006): 625.

96 *"In general, biologists"*: Ian Stirling and Andrew E. Derocher, "Factors Affecting the Evolution and Behavioral Ecology of the Modern Bears," *Int. Conf. Bear Res. Mgmt.* 8 (1990): 197.

96 *"By all indications"*: Sterling Eide and Sterling Miller, "Brown Bear," revised by Larry Van Daele, in *Alaska Wildlife Notebook Series* (ADF&G, 2008).

97 *"They are not punched"*: Interview with LaVern Beier by Merry Ellefson.

97 *Bears don't stake out territories*: Schwartz, Miller, and Haroldson, "Grizzly Bear," 565–566.

98 *At least twelve*: Sterling Miller and Warren Ballard, "Homing of Transplanted Alaskan Brown Bears," *Journal of Wildlife Management* 46, 4 (October 1982): 872.

98 *A Yukon grizzly*: Vernon D. Berns, Gerry C. Atwell, and Daniel L. Boone, "Brown Bear Movements and Habitat Use at Karluk Lake, Kodiak Island," *Int. Conf. Bear Res. Mgmt.* 4 (1980): 296.

98 *Two-year-old brown bears*: Bruce N. McLellan and Frederick W. Hovey, "Natal Dispersal of Grizzly Bears," *Canadian Journal of Zoology* 79, 5 (2001): 842.

98 *Half of the eighteen male*: Charles Schwartz and Albert Franzmann, "Dispersal and Survival of Subadult Black Bears from the Kenai Peninsula, Alaska," *Journal of Wildlife Management* 56, 3 (July 1992): 429.

99 *"Our results thus indicate"*: Ole-Gunnar Støen, Eva Bellemain, Solve Sæbø, and Jon E. Swenson, "Kin-Related Spatial Structure in Brown Bears Ursus arctos," *Behavioral Ecology and Sociobiology* 59, 2 (December 2005): 195.

99 *Among Scandinavian bears*: Andrés Ordiz, Ole-Gunnar Støen, Jon E. Swenson, Ilpo Kojola, and Richard Bischof, "Distance-Dependent Effect of the Nearest Neighbor: Spatiotemporal Patterns in Brown Bear Reproduction," *Ecology* 89, 12 (2008): 3333.

100 *Researchers who tracked*: Gordon Stenhouse, John Boulanger, John Lee, Karen Graham, Julie Duval, and Jerome Cranston, "Grizzly Bear Associations along the Eastern Slopes of Alberta," *Ursus* 16, 1 (2005): 35.

THE URBAN BEAR

102 *The Juneau Police Department's weekly log*: Juneau Police Department, "JPD Urban Bear Activity Summary," September 3–9, 2002.

103 *A week later*: Kristan Hutchison, "Bear Shot in Tussle," *Juneau Empire*, September 5, 2000 (correction September 6, 2000).

103 *By year's end*: Memorandum from Neil Barten to Maria Gladziszewski, January 24, 2003.

103 *They served on the mayor's*: Pat Costello, "Garbage Problem Poses Risk to People, Bears," *Juneau Empire*, November 18, 2001.

103 *They also wrote*: Mark Farmer, "We Still Haven't Solved the Bear Problem," *Juneau Empire*, July 30, 2001.

103 *The Juneau Empire published:* Joanna Markell, "Bear Patrol Takes to Street," *Juneau Empire,* August 3, 2001.

104 *The mayor's interest:* Joanna Markell, "City Bear Committee Is Back," *Juneau Empire,* August 15, 2001.

104 *"Great Shootout of 1987":* Neil Barten, "Unit 1C Black Bear Management Report," in *Black Bear Management Report of Survey and Inventory Activities, 1 July 2004–30 June 2007,* ed. Patricia Harper (Juneau: ADF&G Division of Wildlife Conservation, 2008), 37–38.

104 *As a newspaper reporter:* Sherry Simpson, "The Sad Tale of Juneau's Garbage Bears," *Juneau Empire,* August 26, 1991, 15–16.

104 *New ordinances:* City and Borough of Juneau, "An Ordinance Repealing and Reenacting the Urban Bear Ordinance," CBJ 03.30.0353 Ordinance 2004-11.

105 *The ticket giver:* Joanna Markell, "Garbage Law Limited by Privacy Concerns," *Juneau Empire,* August 5, 2002.

105 *The yearling survived:* Tony Carroll, "Glacier Bear Shot in Thunder Mountain Park," *Juneau Empire,* July 17, 2003.

106 *Kermode bears:* H. D. Marshall and K. Ritland, "Genetic Diversity and Differentiation of Kermode Bear Populations," *Molecular Ecology* 11, 4 (2002): 685.

107 *Bears began reclaiming:* Hank Hristienko and John E. McDonald Jr., "Going into the 21st Century: A Perspective on Trends and Controversies in the Management of the American Black Bear," *Ursus* 18, 1 (2007): 72.

107 *Today, an estimated 850,000 to 950,000:* D. L. Garshelis, D. Crider, and F. van Manen, "*Ursus americanus,*" IUCN Red List of Threatened Species, Version 2012.2 (2008), http://www.iucnredlist.org/details/41687/0.

107 *Researchers caution, however:* David L. Garshelis and Hank Hristienko, "State and Provincial Estimates of American Black Bear Numbers versus Assessments of Population Trend," *Ursus* 17, 1 (2006): 6.

108 *In 1992, for example:* "The Price Paid by the Bears," Conservation Officer Service Bear Statistics, http://records.viu.ca/www/discover/rmot/tblbear.htm; Colleen Matt, *Summary of 4th International Human-Bear Conflicts Workshop* (Missoula, MT, March 20–22, 2012), 16.

108 *"Managing bear-human conflict":* Rocky D. Spencer, Richard A. Beausoleil, and Donald A. Martorello, "How Agencies Respond to Human–Black Bear Conflicts: A Survey of Wildlife Agencies in North America," *Ursus* 18, 2 (2007): 217.

108 *Even amusing stories:* Matt Sutkoski, "Bare Gov. Shumlin Barely Bails on Bothersome Bears," *Burlington Free Press,* April 13, 2012.

108 *In Nevada's Lake Tahoe basin:* Jon P. Beckmann and Joel Berger, "Rapid Ecological and Behavioural Changes in Carnivores: The Responses of Black Bears (*Ursus americanus*) to Altered Food," *Journal of Zoology London* 261 (October 2003): 210–211. See also Jon P. Beckmann and Joel Berger, "Using

Black Bears to Test Ideal-Free Distribution Models Experimentally," *Journal of Mammalogy* 84, 2 (2003): 594–606; Jon P. Beckmann and Carl W. Lackey, "Carnivores, Urban Landscapes, and Longitudinal Studies: A Case History of Black Bears," *Human-Wildlife Conflicts* 2, 2 (Fall 2008): 168–174.

109 *Humans killed every one:* Jon P. Beckmann, "Bears Will Be Bears: Conserving Black Bears by Altering Human Behavior," *Wildlife Professional* (Winter 2009): 50.

109 *Researchers investigating the ecology:* S. Baruch-Mordo, S. W. Breck, K. R. Wilson, and J. Broderick, "Urban Black Bear Ecology: Fluctuating Synanthropy and Its Implications for Management" (poster presented at the 20th International Conference on Bear Research and Management, Ottawa, Canada, July 17–23, 2011); Eric J. Howe, Martyn E. Obbard, and Heather Smith, "Literature Review of Factors Affecting Nuisance Bear Activity," in *Nuisance Bear Review Committee Report and Recommendations* (Ontario: Minister of Natural Resources, August 28, 2003), appendix 9.

110 *Instead of avoiding:* Thomas M. McCarthy and Roger Seavoy, "Reducing Nonsport Losses Attributable to Food Conditioning: Human and Bear Behavior Modification in an Urban Environment," *Int. Conf. Bear Res. Mgmt.* 9, 1 (1994): 79.

110 *Minnesota black bears:* Mark A. Ternent and David L. Garshelis, "Taste-Aversion Conditioning to Reduce Nuisance Activity by Black Bears in a Minnesota Military Reservation," *Wildlife Society Bulletin* 27, 3 (Autumn 1999): 727.

110 *Whistler black bears:* Lori Homstol, "Applications of Learning Theory to Human-Bear Conflict: The Efficacy of Aversive Conditioning and Conditioned Taste Aversion" (M.S. thesis, University of Alberta, 2011), 70.

110 *But thiabendazole didn't ruin:* Kari Signor, "Investigating Methods to Reduce Black Bear (Ursus americanus) Visitation to Anthropogenic Food Sources: Conditioned Taste Aversion and Food Removal" (M.S. thesis, Utah State University, 2010), 36.

110 *Ammonia or pepper sauce:* Eileen M. Creel, "Effectiveness of Deterrents on Black Bear (Ursus americanus) to Anthropogenic Attractants in Urban-Wildland Interfaces" (M.S. thesis, Humboldt State University, 2007), 24, 39–46.

110 *"Only 1 bear":* McCarthy and Seavoy, "Reducing Nonsport Losses," 79.

110 *Even the full-on:* Jon P. Beckmann, Carl W. Lackey, and Joel Berger, "Evaluation of Deterrent Techniques and Dogs to Alter Behavior of 'Nuisance' Black Bears," *Wildlife Society Bulletin* 32, 4 (2004): 1145.

111 *After hazing wild and food-conditioned bears:* Rachel L. Mazur, "Does Aversive Conditioning Reduce Human–Black Bear Conflict?" *Journal of Wildlife Management* 74, 1 (2010): 52–53.

111 *Officers and biologists:* Matt, *Summary of 4th International Human-Bear Conflicts Workshop,* 75.

111 *Alaska Department of Fish and Game wildlife technician:* Larry Lewis, "X3W Wild-life Protection and Control Webcast," http://www.taser.com/videos/events /larry-lewis-video; Larry Lewis, Donald Dawes, Andrew Hinz, and Phil Mooney, "Tasers for Wildlife?" *Wildlife Professional* (Spring 2011): 44–46.

112 *Among wildlife agencies:* Spencer et al., "How Agencies Respond," 221.

112 *Between 1986 and 1997:* Barten, "Unit 1C Black Bear Management Report," 38.

112 *"They seemed to have enjoyed":* E. L. Young and Thomas McCarthy, "A Problem of Progress: Bear Conflict in Southeast Alaska," *Alaska Fish & Game* 21, 5 (September–October 1989): 36.

112 *"We are not in the bear-moving business":* Melanie Plenda, "Concern Grows about Official Bear Shootings," *Juneau Empire*, August 23, 2002.

112 *Studies testing the effects:* S. Baruch-Mordo, S. W. Breck, K. R. Wilson, and J. Broderick, "The Carrot or the Stick? Evaluation of Education and Enforcement as Management Tools for Human-Wildlife Conflicts," *PLoS ONE* 6, 1 (2011); J. Michael Campbell, "The Effect of Education in Reducing Bear Attractants on Cottage Properties: Manitoba's 'Bear Smart' Program," *Forest Policy and Economics* 19 (2012): 56–65.

112 *Gauging progress simply:* Meredith L. Gore, Barbara Knuth, Paul Curtis, and James Shanahan, "Education Programs for Reducing American Black Bear–Human Conflict: Indicators of Success?" *Ursus* 17, 1 (2006): 78.

112 *For example, Nevada's Division of Wildlife:* Annie Flanzraich, "Lake Tahoe Bear Season Down, but Maybe Not Out," *Sierra Sun*, September 9, 2009.

113 *Other wildlife managers:* Matt, *Summary of 4th International Human-Bear Conflicts Workshop*, 27–28.

113 *Researchers who analyzed:* Adrian Treves, Kirsten J. Kapp, and David M. MacFarland, "American Black Bear Nuisance Complaints and Hunter Take," *Ursus* 21 (2010): 30.

113 *Several similar studies:* Matt, *Summary of 4th International Human-Bear Conflicts Workshop*, 27, 62.

114 *Within a week:* Riley Woodford, "City Gets out of the Business of Killing Bears," *Juneau Empire*, October 7, 2001.

115 *"Bears are without virtue":* Tom Cunningham, letter to the editor, *Juneau Empire*, June 29, 2001.

115 *"Sure, it's inconvenient":* Jane Roodenburg, letter to the editor, *Juneau Empire*, August 30, 1999.

116 *When anthropologist:* Patricia Partnow, "Ursine Urges and Urban Ungulates: Anchorage Asserts Its Alaskanness," *Western Folklore* 58, 1 (Winter 1999): 54.

116 *"I know that's what bears do":* Megan Holland, "Neighborhood Awakes to Sound of Calf Killing," *ADN*, June 24, 2004.

117 *"You'd think I'd be an expert":* Interview with Rick Sinnott by Nellie Moore.

117 *When someone dumped rotting fish:* Rosemary Shinohara, "State Hogties Bear Expert over Remarks," *ADN*, July 28, 2005.

117 "*unsung hero*": Dave McClannahan, letter to the editor, ADN, August 6, 2005.

117 "*fantastic public servant*": Jeff Lowenfels, letter to the editor, ADN, August 6, 2005.

117 "*stop bad-mouthing*": Charles Howard, letter to the editor, ADN, August 6, 2005.

118 *One spring, he and Coltrane shot:* Megan Holland, "Biologist Shoots Grizzly in Eagle River," ADN, June 27, 2004.

118 *Coltrane later told:* Doug O'Harra, "Biologist Loves Wildlife, Hates Killing Bears," ADN, August 21, 2005.

119 *A woman angry:* Kay Pederson, letter to the editor, ADN, July 2, 2004.

119 *One man blamed:* John Whiting, letter to the editor, ADN, July 2, 2004.

119 *And a reader chastising:* Maria Burstein, letter to the editor, ADN, July 2, 2004.

119 *In the more recent survey:* Responsive Management, Anchorage Residents' Opinions on Bear and Moose Population Levels and Management Strategies, 2010, 28.

120 *Only about one in twenty:* Ibid., iii.

120 *Still, the number of people:* Ibid., 52.

120 *A third of respondents:* Ibid., 116.

120 "*What's the purpose*": Responsive Management, Anchorage Residents' Opinions on and Experiences with Bears and Other Wildlife, Focus Group Report, 2009, 22.

120 "*Maybe I'm simple-minded*": Ibid., 25.

120 *The 1995 incident was:* Tom Bell, "The Primal Fear: If We Are Much More Likely to Be Killed by a Car, Why Are We So Terrified of Bears?" ADN, July 14, 1995.

120 *In 2007 a police officer shot:* Kate Pesznecker, "Curious Holiday Crowd Dooms Young Grizzly," ADN, July 6, 2007; Craig Medred, "Bears of Last Summer Will Be Back Shortly," ADN, January 29, 2009.

121 "*One of the most startling findings*": Sean Farley, Herman Griese, Rick Sinnott, Jessica Coltrane, Chris Garner, and Dave Battle, *Brown Bear (Ursus arctos) Minimum Population Count, Habitat Use, Movement Corridors, and Food Resources across Fort Richardson Army Post, Elmendorf Air Force Base, Campbell Tract Area, and the Municipality of Anchorage, Alaska* (Department of the Army, October 2007), 18.

121 *After gathering hair samples:* Ibid., 15.

121 "*They're not really a wilderness*": Anchorage Waterways Council meeting, January 30, 2009.

121 "*Within any given day*": Farley et al., *Brown Bear*, 12.

121 *Salmon formed:* Ibid., 16.

122 *The dim light of midnight:* Mike Celizic, "Teen Who Survived Bear Attack: 'Mostly It Was Scared,'" *Today Show*, MSNBC, October 20, 2008, http://www.today.com/id/27276527/site/todayshow/ns/today-today_news/t/teen-who-survived-bear-attack-mostly-it-was-scared/#.UPXInYnjmkI.

122 *"We're not going to just"*: George Bryson, "Is 'Rogue Grizzly' on the Loose? Not Likely," ADN, July 3, 2008.

122 *Five weeks later*: Megan Holland, "Mauling Victim Recounts Attack on City Trail," ADN, August 10, 2008.

122 *"This is Alaska"*: Craig Medred and James Halpin, "2nd Woman Mauled in Bicentennial Park," ADN, August 9, 2008.

123 *DNA tests showed*: Craig Medred, "DNA Test IDs Grizzly in Mauling Jogger," ADN, October 23, 2008.

123 *The dead bear's two cubs*: Andrea Hirsch, "Indianapolis Zoo Becomes Haven for Orphaned Bear Cubs," *Hendricks County Flyer*, September 5, 2008.

123 *In response to the park*: Rick Sinnott, "Is Bear Population Growing in Anchorage, Alaska?" *Alaska Dispatch*, August 22, 2012.

124 *Tolerating twenty bears*: "Fatal Car Crashes and Road Traffic Accident Statistics for 2008," http://www.city-data.com/accidents/acc-Anchorage-Alaska.html.

124 *While driving home*: Megan Holland, "Biologist Rick Sinnott Wounded in Drive-by in Anchorage," ADN, October 20, 2006.

124 *"I'll hire biologists"*: Larry Kaniut, "'Los Anchorage' Is Too Soft on Bears," ADN, April 19, 2009.

124 *Sinnott responded by quoting*: Rick Sinnott, "Kaniut Has Changed Advice on Bears," ADN, May 11, 2009.

125 *"Numbers of bears fluctuate"*: Sinnott, "Is Bear Population Growing?"

125 *Since 1908, she found*: Rick Sinnott, "Case Histories: Recounting Some Terrible Alaska Bear Attacks," *Alaska Dispatch*, April 12, 2012.

125 *This pattern continued*: Michelle Theriault Boots, "Bear Mauling Victim Believed 'This Is the End,'" ADN, May 15, 2012; Michelle Theriault Boots, "Grizzly Sow Attacks Woman on Eagle River Trail," ADN, June 16, 2012; Lisa Demer, "Big Bruin Chases Hiker up a Tree on Bird Creek Trail," ADN, June 11, 2012; Lisa Demer, "Victim Startled Sow with Cubs," ADN, July 23, 2012.

126 *Wild black bears killed*: Stephen Herrero, Andrew Higgins, James E. Cardoza, Laura I. Hajduk, and Tom S. Smith, "Fatal Attacks by American Black Bear on People: 1900–2009," *Journal of Wildlife Management* 75, 3 (2011): 596–601.

126 *A Swedish foreign-exchange student*: Associated Press, "Bear Encounter Gives Swedish Exchange Student Tale to Take Home," ADN, May 19, 2004.

126 *A bear that ventured*: Joanna Markell, "Bear Snubs Cheese Pinwheels for Bath," *Juneau Empire*, October 27, 2002.

126 *A twenty-two-year-old Juneau hairdresser*: Jonathan Grass, "Woman Punches Bear to Save Her Dog," *Juneau Empire*, August 30, 2011.

127 *Some of this concern stems*: Outdoor News Bulletin, cited in "Wildlife Damage Management in the News," *Probe* 216 (May/June 2001): 3, http://digitalcommons.unl.edu/icwdmprobe/75/.

127 *More recently, the family*: Francis and Ives v. United States, "Findings of Fact,

Conclusions of Law, and Order," 15–16, Case 2:08CV244 DAK, US District Court, District of Utah, Central Division, May 3, 2011, http://courtweb .pamd.uscourts.gov/courtwebsearch/utdc/FFSS7TXIiH.pdf.

128 *In late 2011:* Roxana Orellana, "Utah Judge Dismisses Bear-Attack Wrongful Death Lawsuit," *Salt Lake Tribune,* October 14, 2011.

128 *The irony is:* "Rabies Risk from Bear Attacks," *State of Alaska Epidemiology Bulletin,* October 17, 2002; "Dog Bites and Human Deaths from Dog Attack in Alaska: A Public Health Tragedy," *State of Alaska Epidemiology Bulletin,* April 17, 1981.

129 *"I can think of few worse places":* Beth Bragg, "Eagle River Trail Would Be Bear Road, Biologist Warns," *ADN,* July 18, 2008.

129 *Planners later decided: Chugach State Park Trail Management Plan, Public Review Draft, Issue Response Summary* (Alaska Department of Natural Resources, August 2011), 44.

129 *As if to underscore:* Mike Campbell, "Risking a Run-in?" *ADN,* September 22, 2009.

129 *Sinnott also took on:* Megan Holland, "Bear Encounters Create Dispute over Trail Status," *ADN,* June 16, 2010.

129 *The following year:* Megan Holland, "Bear Attacks Bicyclist on Anchorage Trail," *ADN,* June 15, 2010.

129 *Sullivan refused to do anything:* Rick Sinnott, "Mayor Sullivan Is Betting Anchorage Bears Will Behave," *Alaska Dispatch,* May 30, 2011.

129 *"Do we want our urban parks":* Holland, "Bear Encounters."

130 *"Sullivan said he would":* Holland, "Bear Attacks Bicyclist."

130 *"Like floods, bears are":* Colleen Matt to Mayor Mark Begich, June 30, 2004.

130 *The plan recommended:* Anchorage Bear Committee, *Guidelines for Maintaining Bear Habitat while Reducing Bear-Human Conflicts in the Municipality of Anchorage and Chugach State Park* (June 2004).

131 *City officials not only ignored:* Michelle Theriault Boots, "Owners of Urban Chickens Battle Predators," *ADN,* July 8, 2012.

131 *Within a couple of months:* Ben Histand, "A Heavy Yoke," *Anchorage Press,* August 17, 2011.

131 *Of the eight bears killed:* Jill Burke, "Are Backyard Chickens Too Dangerous for Urban Bear Country?" *Alaska Dispatch,* October 25, 2012.

131 *"I don't understand people":* Rob Chaney, "Bear Conflicts a Continentwide Challenge," *Missoulian,* March 21, 2012.

131 *"Five years ago":* Felicity Barringer, "Bears' Taste for Chicken Sets up Collision Course," *New York Times,* July 6, 2012.

131 *Rather than require chicken ranchers:* Burke, "Are Backyard Chickens Too Dangerous?"

131 *Perhaps they hadn't bothered:* AR No. 2011-100, "A Resolution of the Anchorage Municipal Assembly to Foster Bear Awareness, Outdoor Safety Practices,

Minimizing Bear Attractants around Homes, Campsites, and Cabins, Building a Sense of Personal Responsibility and Stewardship for Our Bears and All Our Wildlife Resources," March 29, 2011.

132 "*Maybe he came back to live*": Ernestine Hayes, *The Story of the Town Bear and the Forest Bear* (Juneau: Hazy Island Books, 2011), 32.

THE FEARSOME BEAR

134 "*Nine times out of ten*": Larry Mueller and Marguerite Reiss, *Bear Attacks of the Century: True Stories of Courage and Survival* (Guilford, CT: Lyons Press, 2005), 161.

134 *A collective faith*: Thomas Curwen and David Petersen, "The Nature of the Beast," *Los Angeles Times*, August 2, 2005.

134 *The guide suspected*: Shannon Huffman Polson, *North of Hope: A Daughter's Arctic Journey* (Grand Rapids, MI: Zondervan, 2013), 221–224.

135 *A necropsy showed*: Associated Press, "Necropsy Yields No Clues about Why Bear Killed Alaska Couple," *Seattle Post-Intelligencer*, July 6, 2005.

135 "*All indications now*": Tom Kizzia, "Victims of Bear Attack Were Wilderness Vets," ADN, June 28, 2005.

135 *National Geographic Adventure magazine*: Jonathan Waterman, "ANWR Grizzly Attacks: They Did Everything Right," *National Geographic Adventure*, October 2005, 55.

136 *When a wounded brown bear*: John M. Holzworth, *The Wild Grizzlies of Alaska* (New York: G. P. Putnam's Sons, 1930), 18–20.

136 "*We're not just afraid of predators*": E. O. Wilson, "In Praise of Sharks," *Discover*, July 1985, 48.

137 "*Hell's jaws are a picket fence*": Paul Shepard, *The Others: How Animals Made Us Human* (Washington, DC: Island Press/Shearwater Books, 1997), 29.

137 "*For a person who neither*": Stephen Herrero, "Man and the Grizzly Bear (Present, Past, but Future?)," *BioScience* 20, 21 (November 1, 1970): 1152.

139 *In the summer of 1999*: Dan Davidson, "Bear Mauling in Tent City," *Klondike Sun*, July 23, 1999.

141 *About a third of Alaskans surveyed*: Suzanne Miller, Sterling D. Miller, and Daniel W. McCollum, "Attitudes toward and Relative Value of Alaskan Brown and Black Bears to Resident Voters, Resident Hunters, and Nonresident Hunters," *Ursus* 10 (1998): 363.

142 *Tom Smith and Stephen Herrero combed*: Tom S. Smith, *A Century of Bear-Human Conflict in Alaska: Analyses and Implications* (Alaska Science Center, USGS, last reviewed May 31, 2007), http://www.absc.usgs.gov/research/brownbears/attacks/bear-human_conflicts.htm.

142 *Out of curiosity, I looked*: "Statewide Moose-Vehicle Crashes by Severity, 1977–2007," in *Revised Environmental Assessment, Parks Highway: MP 44-52*, "Appendix F: Moose Vehicle Collision Analysis" (Anchorage: Alaska Department of Transportation and Public Facilities, September 2010), 12.

143   Brown bears are more: Stephen Herrero, *Bear Attacks: Their Causes and Avoidance*, rev. ed. (Guilford, CT: Globe Pequot Press, 2002), 199–206.

143   Because coastal bears: Tom S. Smith, Stephen Herrero, and Terry D. DeBruyn, "Alaskan Brown Bears, Humans, and Habituation," *Ursus* 16, 1 (2005): 6.

143   "The shorter the ORD": Ibid., 5.

143   Exhibit A: a hunting magazine: Jim Shockey, "Black Bears—Simple Fools or Cunning Killers," *Outdoor Life* online, September 2007.

143   Given our own thirst: David Quammen, *Monster of God* (New York: W. W. Norton, 2003), 4.

144   If Billy were alive: Riley Woodford, "Fact versus Frenzy Bear Program Burns Biologists," *Alaska Fish & Wildlife News* online magazine, February 2009.

145   "Wilderness was suddenly 'in'": Roderick Frazier Nash, *Wilderness and the American Mind*, 4th ed. (New Haven, CT: Yale University Press, 2001), 316.

145   In 1911, for example: Donald H. Robinson and Maynard C. Bowers, "Visitation Statistics, Appendix D," in *Through the Years in Glacier National Park: An Administrative History* (Glacier Natural History Association, May 1960), http://www.gov/history/history/online_books/glac/.

145   The National Park Service encouraged: Alice Wondrak Biel, *Do (Not) Feed the Bears* (Lawrence: University Press of Kansas, 2006), 20.

145   Expert Stephen Herrero found: Herrero, *Bear Attacks*, 6.

145   Instead of addressing the role: Biel, *Do (Not) Feed*, 41–42, 67.

146   People grasped at explanations: Emmett Watson, "Menace in Our Northern Parks," *Sports Illustrated*, October 30, 1967, 74; Jack Olsen, *Night of the Grizzlies* (New York: G. P. Putnam's Sons/Signet Classics, 1969), 167–168.

146   The investigation hadn't reached a conclusion: Watson, "Menace," 74.

146   In a paper titled: Gairdner B. Moment, "Bears: The Need for a New Sanity in Wildlife Conservation," *BioScience* 18, 12 (December 1968): 1106.

147   In a 1970 forum: Herrero, "Man and Grizzly," 1148.

147   "Probably the most dangerous": Ibid., 1149.

147   "We should preserve grizzly bear": Stephen Herrero, "Conflicts between Man and Grizzly Bears in the National Parks of North America," *Int. Conf. Bear Res. Mgmt.* 3 (1976): 140.

147   "Your best defense in bear country": Herrero, *Bear Attacks*, xii.

148   The result was: *Staying Safe in Bear Country: A Behavioral-Based Approach to Reducing Risk* (Atlin, BC: Wild Eye Productions, Safety in Bear Country Society, 2001, rev. 2008), http://www.bearsmart.com/video/206.

149   An Anchorage hiker who surprised: David Hulen, "Grizzly Mauls Hiker Near Visitor Center," *ADN*, May 17, 1995.

149   A Juneau woman accompanying: "Grizzly Attacks Woman on Admiralty Island," *Juneau Empire*, August 10, 2008.

149   Years ago, a hiker: Craig Medred, "Bear Behavior," *ADN*, May 30, 1993.

149   And it was clear that some Alaska kids: Jack Sanders, "Conservation Officers

Review Base Bear Policy after Incident," Joint Base Elmendorf-Richardson, June 9, 2010; Kyle Hopkins, "Anchorage Bears Lose Frequent Confrontations," ADN, June 5, 2010.

150 *In another incident:* Megan Holland, "Woman Lost for Five Days Braved Bears, Lives on Snow," ADN, July 2, 2005.

150 *In two separate incidents:* Craig Medred, "No Bear, Ax to Back up Hiker's Tale," ADN, August 23, 2004.

151 *"The species of bear involved":* Herrero, Bear Attacks, 107.

152 *"I knew better'n to move":* Holzworth, Wild Grizzlies, 19.

152 *As an example, he excerpts:* Herrero, Bear Attacks, 95–100.

152 *Noncaptive black bears in Canada:* Stephen Herrero, Andrew Higgins, James E. Cardoza, Laura I. Hajduk, and Tom S. Smith, "Fatal Attacks by American Black Bear on People: 1900–2009," *Journal of Wildlife Management* 75, 3 (2011): 598.

153 *"That most fatal black bear attacks":* Ibid., 596.

153 *"She caused the bear to flee":* Herrero, Bear Attacks, 94.

153 *A Forest Service technician:* Craig Medred, "Girdwood Hiker Battles, Races Bears," ADN, July 20, 2003.

153 *A jogger who was charged and bitten:* Katie Pesznecker, "Woman, Bear Trade Blows," ADN, July 12, 2002.

153 *"When my voice would falter":* Tim Mowry, "Denali Park Ranger Gets Creative to Fend off Brazen Bear," FDNM, August 16, 2000.

154 *In 2000 a brown bear killed:* Molly Brown, "Brown Bear Kills, Feeds on Ketchikan Man, State Says," ADN, July 18, 2000.

154 *"In summary, the attack":* Kevin Frey, Sam Shepard, Kerry Gunther, Stephen Herrero, Chris Servheen, Dan Tyers, and Mark Bruscino, *Investigation Team Report: Attacks by a Grizzly Bear in Soda Butte Campground on the Gallatin National Forest on July 28, 2010* (August 13, 2010), 16.

154 *One puzzling incident:* "Investigation Continues in Fatal Bear Attack," news release, Denali National Park and Preserve, National Park Service, August 29, 2012; Casey Grove, "San Diego Man Dies in Denali Grizzly Attack," ADN, August 25, 2012.

155 *During the prolonged confrontation:* Tim Mowry, "North Pole Woman Uses Insect Repellent to Fend off Granite Tors Grizzly," FDNM, July 15, 2012.

155 *He was alone and skinning:* Mueller and Reiss, Bear Attacks, 152–156.

155 *Instead, according to a park:* "Bear Fatally Mauls Hiker," *Whitehorse Daily Star*, July 8, 1996.

156 *"If we'd stood our ground":* Clyde H. Farnsworth, "After Fatal Mauling in Canada: Too Many Bears?" *New York Times*, August 4, 1996.

156 *In 1968 Alaska wildlife biologist:* Frederick C. Dean, *Brown Bear–Human Interrelationship Study*, NPS PO 126–301, unpublished report (National Park Service, 1968), 35.

156 *Today she's better known for:* James Claar and Doug Zimmer, *Bear Spray Report* (Interagency Grizzly Bear Committee, June 2008), 10–11.

157 *Twenty years after its introduction:* Tom S. Smith, Stephen Herrero, Terry D. De-Bruyn, and James M. Wilder, "Efficacy of Bear Deterrent Spray in Alaska," *Journal of Wildlife Management* 72, 3 (2008): 640.

157 *"Persons working and recreating":* Ibid., 644.

157 *"A bear running at you":* Colleen Matt, *Summary of 4th International Human-Bear Conflicts Workshop* (Missoula, MT, March 20–22, 2012), 18.

157 *In an unusual incident:* Craig Medred, "How Could NOLS Students Have Avoided Bear Attack?" *Alaska Dispatch*, March 26, 2012; Craig Medred, "New Report Details 2011 Alaska Grizzly Bear Attack on Outdoors School Students," *Alaska Dispatch*, March 25, 2012.

158 *After noticing years ago:* Tom S. Smith, "Attraction of Brown Bears to Red Pepper Spray Deterrent: Caveats for Use," *Wildlife Society Bulletin* 26, 1 (1998): 93.

159 *They reported that people:* Tom Smith, Stephen Herrero, Cali S. Layton, Randy T. Larsen, and Kathryn R. Johnson, "Efficacy of Firearms for Bear Deterrence in Alaska," *Journal of Wildlife Management* 76, 5 (July 2012): 1023.

159 *"The need for split-second deployment":* Ibid., 1025.

159 *"As I see it":* Matt, *Summary of 4th International Human-Bear Conflicts Workshop*, 19.

160 *To demonstrate the difference:* Ibid., 22.

161 *"It is clear that some people":* Sterling Miller and V. Leigh Tutterrow, "Characteristics of Nonsport Mortalities to Brown and Black Bears and Human Injuries from Bears in Alaska," *Ursus* 11 (1999): 250–251.

161 *In the case of the predatory attack:* Gail Randall, "Killer Bear a Mystery to Experts," *ADN*, July 10, 1992.

161 *Alaskans shot nine bears:* Craig Medred, "When It Comes to Bears, Reason Often Disappears," *ADN*, August 6, 2000.

162 *Outside of the villages:* Kathryn R. Johnson, "Examining the Frequency and Characteristics of Human-Bear Conflicts in the Native Villages of the Kodiak Archipelago" (M.S. thesis, University of Alaska Anchorage, 2008), 21.

163 *"They never bother people":* Ibid., 65–66.

163 *"For the urban dweller":* Ibid., 73.

165 *"Backcountry users should":* Tom Smith, Terry D. DeBruyn, Tania Lewis, Rusty Yerxa, and Steven Partridge, "Bear-Human Interactions at Glacier Bay National Park and Preserve: Conflict Risk Assessment," *Alaska Park Science* (Summer 2003): 25.

165 *Alaska photographer Michio Hoshino:* Sherry Simpson, "A Short, Happy Life," *We Alaskans* magazine, *ADN*, October 13, 1996.

165 *"People continue to tame":* Michio Hoshino, *The Grizzly Bear Family Book* (New York: North-South Books, 1997), 3.

165 *Though everyone else:* George Bryson, "The Final Days of Michio Hoshino," *We Alaskans* magazine, ADN, October 13, 1996.

166 *Hoshino "refused to believe":* Leonid Baskin, "Bear Behaviors Potentially Contributing to the Fatal Mauling of Two Photographers," *International Bear News* 15, 2 (May 2006): 18.

166 *"He always tested life":* Igor Revenko, "Life Devoted to Brown Bears," *International Bear News* 13, 1 (February 2004): 6.

166 *"Everything looks as if":* Vladimir Mosolov and Tatiana Gordienko, "His 33rd Field Season," *International Bear News* 13, 1 (February 2004): 7.

167 *Perhaps he left the tent:* Craig Medred, "Treadwell: 'Get Out Here, I'm Getting Killed,'" ADN, October 9, 2003.

167 *"The pattern of behavior exhibited":* Joe Fowler, Technical Board of Investigation, Case Incident 03-109 (National Park Service, convened November 20, 2003), 4.

THE HUNTED BEAR

170 *He was a railroad magnate:* John Muir, *Edward Henry Harriman* (New York: Doubleday, Page, 1912), 1, http://www.sierraclub.org/john_muir_exhibit/writings/edward_henry_harriman.aspx.

170 *Being rich and powerful:* William H. Goetzmann and Kay Sloan, *Looking Far North: The Harriman Expedition to Alaska, 1899* (Princeton, NJ: Princeton University Press, 1983), 5–6.

170 *Meanwhile, Harriman:* John Burroughs, *The Writings of John Burroughs: Far and Near,* vol. 13. (Boston: Houghton, Mifflin, 1904), Google eBook, 44.

171 *He was the kind of man:* Ken Chowder, "North to Alaska," *Smithsonian,* June 2003, 100.

171 *On July 3:* Goetzmann and Sloan, *Looking Far North,* 120–126.

171 *The faded brown female:* John Burroughs and John Muir, *Alaska: The Harriman Expedition, 1899* (reprint, New York: Dover Publications, 1986), 85.

171 *Men drove the pair:* Goetzmann and Sloan, *Looking Far North,* 120.

171 *John Muir tsk-tsked:* Linnie Marsh Wolfe, *Son of the Wilderness: The Life of John Muir* (reprint, Madison: University of Wisconsin Press, 2003), 284.

171 *Scientist William Dall rewrote:* William H. Dall, "First Lessons in Natural History," in *The Harriman Alaska Expedition: Chronicles and Souvenirs May to August 1899,* 127, W. Averell Harriman Papers, American Memory Digital Collections, Library of Congress, http://memory.loc.gov/mss/amrvm/vmh/vmh.html.

172 *Every year in Alaska:* Amy Pinney, "Brown Bear Research in Alaska," *Alaska Fish & Wildlife News* online magazine, April 2012.

172 *Between 1970 and 1996:* Sterling Miller and V. Leigh Tutterow, "Characteristics of Nonsport Mortalities to Brown and Black Bears and Human Injuries from Bears in Alaska," *Ursus* 11 (1999): 241.

172 In 2007 hunters killed: Riley Woodford, "Who Takes Home Alaska Wildlife?" *Alaska Fish & Wildlife News* online magazine, January 2009.

173 *"Bears speak to something primal"*: E. Donnall Thomas Jr., *Longbows in the Far North: An Archer's Adventures in Alaska and Siberia* (Mechanicsburg, PA: Stackpole Books, 1993), 105.

173 *"The Game" is Shepard's term*: Paul Shepard, *The Others: How Animals Made Us Human* (Washington, DC: Island Press/Shearwater Books, 1997), 19.

174 *The Game, Shepard believed*: Ibid., 25.

174 *"Our kind has watched the bear"*: Paul Shepard, "The Biological Bases of Bear Mythology and Ceremonialism," *Trumpeter* 23, 2 (2007): 76.

174 *After studying bear*: A. Irving Hallowell, "Bear Ceremonialism in the Northern Hemisphere," *American Anthropologist* 28, 1 (January–March 1926): 148.

174 *"For Tlingits, successful hunting"*: Thomas F. Thornton, *Subsistence Use of Brown Bear in Southeast Alaska*, Technical Paper No. 214 (Juneau: ADF&G Division of Subsistence, February 1992), 28.

174 *In the Kantishna drainage*: Caroline L. Brown, *Customary and Traditional Use Worksheet, Brown Bear, Game Management Units 20A, 20B, and 20C*, Special Publication BOG 2012-02 (Fairbanks: ADF&G Division of Subsistence, 2012), 2.

174 *Tlingit hunters developed*: Thornton, *Subsistence Use*, 66.

175 *Then one partner leaped out*: Harry B. Dodge III, *Kodiak Island and Its Bears: A History of Bear/Human Interactions on Alaska's Kodiak Archipelago* (Anchorage: Great Northwest Publishing, 2004), 24.

175 *These weapons were used*: Alex deMarban, "Life and Values Twine in Native Priest's Stories," *ADN*, October 24, 2006.

175 *Other Tlingits dabbed bear heads*: Hallowell, "Bear Ceremonialism," 76.

175 *A contemporary Tlingit*: Unpublished interview by Merry Ellefson.

175 *While living in the northwestern village*: Nick Jans, *The Grizzly Maze: Timothy Treadwell's Fatal Obsession with Alaskan Bears* (New York: Dutton, 2005), 179.

175 *"What my grandma told me"*: James A. Fall and Lisa B. Hutchinson-Scarbrough, *Subsistence Uses of Brown Bears in Communities of Game Management Unit 9E, Alaska Peninsula, Southwest Alaska*, Technical Paper No. 235 (Juneau: ADF&G Division of Subsistence, 1996), 10.

176 *"We are space-needing"*: Shepard, *The Others*, 317.

177 *"Like most red blooded American males"*: Jim Townsend, "The Big Bore Grizzly," *Bear Hunting Magazine*, January/February 2010.

177 *"I know I am not alone"*: Bill Ziupko, "A Brown Bear Hunt to Remember," testimonial, Alaska Wilderness Charters and Guiding, November 25, 2008.

177 *"I have been bow hunting"*: Kendall Helton, "Memories from Alberta," *Bear Hunting Magazine*, January/February 2010, http://www.bear-hunting.com /issue_01_02_2010.cfm.

177 *"For a big-game hunter"*: Dan Sisson, "Bear Hunt at Terror Bay," *Field & Stream*, January 1985, 50.

177 "A successful Alaskan bear hunt": Mike Promisco, 2008 testimonial, Litzen Guide Service, http://www.litzenguideservice.com/testimonials.htm.

178 *Roosevelt regarded hunting:* Theodore Roosevelt and George Bird Grinnell, eds., *American Big-Game Hunting: The Book of the Boone and Crockett Club* (New York: Forest & Stream, 1893), Google eBook, 14.

178 *"In hunting, the finding and killing":* Theodore Roosevelt, *The Wilderness Hunter: An Account of the Big Game of the United States and Its Chase with Horse, Hound and Rifle* (New York: G. P. Putnam's Sons, 1893), Google eBook, xv.

178 *Roosevelt's book appeared:* Frederick Jackson Turner, "The Significance of the Frontier in American History," in *The Annual Report of the American Historical Association* (1893), 199–227, http://www.library.wisc.edu/etext/wireader WER0750.html.

178 *"The most thrilling moments":* Roosevelt, *Wilderness Hunter*, 308.

178 *He closed it by noting:* Ibid., 465.

179 *"It was the beginning":* James L. Cummins, "New Refuge in Mississippi Protects Birthplace of Fair Chase," Boone and Crockett Club, October 24, 2008, http://www.boone-crockett.org/news/featured_story.asp?area=news&ID=31.

179 *Mindful of his reputation:* Douglas Brinkley, *The Wilderness Warrior: Theodore Roosevelt and the Crusade for America* (New York: Harper Perennial, 2010), 432.

179 *Legendary bear hunter:* Minor Ferris Buchanan, *Holt Collier: His Life, His Roosevelt Hunts, and the Origin of the Teddy Bear* (Jackson: Centennial Press of Mississippi, 2002), 166.

179 *By the time his dogs:* See Brinkley, *Wilderness Warrior*, 438–442; Buchanan, *Holt Collier*, 166–174.

180 *They identified seven principles:* Valerius Geist, Shane P. Mahoney, and John F. Organ, "Why Hunting Has Defined the North American Model of Wildlife Conservation," *Transactions of the North American Wildlife and Natural Resources Conference* 66 (2001): 177–178.

180 *Environmental ethics scholar:* Michael P. Nelson, John A. Vucetich, Paul C. Paquet, and Joseph K. Bump, "An Inadequate Construct? What's Flawed, What's Missing, What's Needed," *Wildlife Professional* (Summer 2011): 59.

180 *"Hunters support wildlife conservation":* Valerius Geist, "The North American Model of Wildlife Conservation: A Means of Creating Wealth and Protecting Public Health while Generating Biodiversity," in *Gaining Ground: In Pursuit of Ecological Sustainability*, ed. David M. Lavigne (Guelph, ON: International Fund for Animal Welfare, 2006), 290.

181 *"Why did Dad hunt bears?":* Richard C. Folta, *Of Bench and Bears: Alaska's Bear Hunting Judge* (Anchorage: Great Northwest Publishing, 1986), 88.

181 *"I knew every bear":* John Howe, *Bear Man of Admiralty Island: A Biography of Allen E. Hasselborg* (Fairbanks: University of Alaska Press, 1996), 162.

182 *"It is just about the last frontier":* Harold Bartlett Scott, "Alaska Yacht Hunting Party," *Alaska Sportsman*, March 1937, 6.

182 *Evidently, he was a believer:* Ibid., 25.

182 "Already some 'Fifty-Niners'": "America's Durable Frontier," Life, April 6, 1959, 40.

182 Popular Mechanics hailed: Kenneth Anderson, "Alaska: 'Big Land' of Contrasts," Popular Mechanics, November 1958, 132.

182 "Black, brown, grizzly and polar bears": Marc Taylor, "The Alaska Bears Are Stirring," Sportsman's News, April 2005, 14.

182 "I'd wanted to take my son": Dick Scorzafava, "Creating Memories," Bear Hunting Magazine, January/February 2009, http://www.bear-hunting.com/issue_1_2_2009.cfm.

183 "The successful Alaska brown bear hunter": Christopher Batin, "Where Giants Walk," Outdoor Life, March 1999, 44.

183 "Alaska is largely defined": Susan Kollin, Nature's State: Imagining Alaska as the Last Frontier (Chapel Hill: University of North Carolina Press, 2001), 92.

183 "I hunt for the pure combative spirit": Interview of Juneau guide by Merry Ellefson.

185 "Hunting submerges man deliberately": José Ortega y Gasset, Meditations on Hunting (New York: Scribner, 1986), 98.

185 "To sum up, one does not": Ibid., 96–97.

185 Most nonhunters don't understand: Sarkis Atamian, The Bears of Manley: Adventures of an Alaskan Trophy Hunter in Search of the Ultimate Symbol (Anchorage: Sarkis Atamian, 1995), Kindle edition, foreword.

185 "Killing is not the goal": Ibid., introduction.

186 "Since my boyhood": Ibid., "Grizzly before Breakfast."

186 "I felt sorry for the noble Old Kodiak": Don DeHart, All about Bears (Boulder, CO: Johnson Publishing, 1971), 64–65.

186 "Even with as little knowledge": Marvin H. Clark Jr., Pinnell and Talifson: Last of the Great Brown Bear Men (Spokane, WA: Great Northwest Publishing, 1980), 19.

187 These include "the harsh confrontation": Ortega y Gasset, Meditations on Hunting, 95.

187 "There he had his breakfast": Clark, Pinnell and Talifson, 178.

187 When shot, the second-place: Eldon L. ("Buck") Buckner, Jack Reneau, and Ryan Hatfield, eds., Boone and Crockett Club's 26th Big Game Awards, 2004–2006 (Missoula, MT: Boone and Crockett Club, 2007), 53.

187 The third-place brown bear: Ibid., 59.

187 The hunter who killed: Ibid., 35.

188 The bow hunter who killed: Ibid., 37–41.

188 He'd had to borrow against: Brad Spychalski, "The North American 28," North American Hunter, Special Bowhunting Enthusiast Section, September 2005, B.

188 "As far as excitement": Susan Shemanske, "Target in Sight: Yorkville Man Aiming for Big-Game Record," Racine Journal Times, February 14, 2008.

188 A blurb for the show: Dangerous Game, preview for September 25, 2009, on Versus network.

188 *An episode of:* Lynn Burkhead, "ESPN2 TV: Lucky 13 Alaskan Brown Bear," *ESPN Outdoors* online, September 24, 2004, http://espn.go.com/outdoors /tv/s/g_fea_ESPN2_Wildlife-Qest_040924.html.

189 *"One misconception that hunters":* Clark, Pinnell and Talifson, 177–178.

189 *They have been responsible:* Larry Van Daele, "Kodiak Bear Fact Sheet," http:// www.adfg.alaska.gov/index.cfm?adfg=brownbear.trivia.

190 *"Somehow, my reactions":* Brien T. King, "Alaska Holiday," *Alaska Sportsman,* May 1937, 9.

190 *"In that instant, I realized":* Brien T. King, "Alaska Holiday II," *Alaska Sportsman,* June 1937, 10.

190 *"I think that in the end":* Jans, *Grizzly Maze,* 182.

190 *"We never shot a bear just to shoot 'em":* Interview of Tlingit hunter by Merry Ellefson.

190 *That's a lot of dead bears:* Clark, Pinnell and Talifson, 178.

190 *"I've had about enough of killing":* Dodge, *Kodiak Island,* 179.

190 *"If I had my preference":* Ibid., 221.

191 *"Now I'm saying, geez":* Ellefson interview with Juneau guide.

191 *Almost 90 percent of participating Alaskans:* Suzanne Miller, Sterling D. Miller, and Daniel W. McCollum, "Attitudes toward and Relative Value of Alaskan Brown and Black Bears to Resident Voters, Resident Hunters, and Nonresident Hunters," *Ursus* 10 (1998): 364.

192 *Note, however, that the number:* Buckner, Reneau, and Hatfield, *Boone and Crockett,* 3.

193 *A promoter of:* James Curley, *Secrets of an Alaskan Master Guide,* http://www .biggamehuntingvideos.com.

193 *The Alaska Peninsula alone:* Lem Butler, "Game Management Unit 9, Alaska Peninsula," in *Region II Briefing Book* (ADF&G Division of Wildlife Conservation, February 2009), 26.

194 *In an Outdoor Life piece:* Christopher Batin, "Cub Killer: Hunting down a Bear Who Slays His Own," *Outdoor Life,* April 2002, 60.

194 *"I couldn't help but admire":* Ibid., 61.

196 *"When I think of wildlife":* Tom Kizzia, "Game Board: Famous McNeil River Bruins Are at Risk, Critics Say, as Panel Mulls Opening Adjacent Lands to Hunting," *ADN,* March 4, 2005.

197 *"It was greed, pure and simple":* Thomas McIntyre, "The Last Bear," *American Hunter,* June 2003, 60.

198 *Still, wildlife managers estimate:* Sterling Miller, "Population Management of Bears in North America," *Int. Conf. Bear Res. Mgmt.* 8 (1990): 361.

201 *To a Native hunter:* Thornton, *Subsistence Use,* 78.

201 *"They don't care what happens":* Fall and Hutchinson-Scarbrough, *Subsistence Use,* 13.

201 *Maybe, as Matt Cartmill argued:* Matt Cartmill, *A View to Death in the Morning: Hunting and Nature through History* (Cambridge, MA: Harvard University Press, 1996), 226.

201 *Today, stripped of narrative:* Records at http://collections.mnh.si.edu/search /mammals/.

THE DISAPPEARING ICE BEAR

204 *This was the last field season:* See Susanne Miller, Kelly Proffitt, and Scott Schliebe, *Demographics and Behavior of Polar Bears Feeding on Bowhead Whale Carcasses at Barter and Cross Islands, Alaska, 2002–2004* (Anchorage: USFWS Marine Mammals Management, April 2006).

205 *Generally, researchers are an aerial bunch:* Steven Amstrup, "Polar Bear, Ursus maritimus," in *Wild Mammals of North America: Biology, Management, and Conservation,* ed. George Feldhamer, Bruce C. Thompson, and Joseph A. Chapman (Baltimore: Johns Hopkins University Press, 2003), 593.

206 *Bears are pagophilic:* Ibid., 587.

207 *The period from 2005 to 2010:* John E. Walsh, James E. Overland, Pavel Y. Groisman, and Bruno Rudolf, "Arctic Climate: Recent Variations," in *Snow, Water, Ice and Permafrost in the Arctic (SWIPA): Climate Change and the Cryosphere* (Oslo: Arctic Monitoring and Assessment Programme, 2011), 4.

207 *People who live here tell the story:* Henry Huntington and Shari Fox, "Changing Arctic: Indigenous Perspectives," in *Arctic Climate Impact Assessment* (New York: Cambridge University Press, 2005), 68–71; Paul Wassmann, Carlos M. Duarte, Susana Agustí, and Mikael K. Sejr, "Footprints of Climate Change in the Arctic Marine Ecosystem," *Global Change Biology* 17 (2011): 1239–1242.

207 *Villagers no longer rely:* Victoria Barber, "Warming Permafrost Threatens Arctic Ice Cellars," *Arctic Sounder,* June 9, 2010.

207 *Tundra yields to advancing:* Andrea H. Lloyd, "Ecological Histories from Alaskan Tree Lines Provide Insight into Future Changes," *Ecology* 86, 7 (July 2005): 1692.

207 *Gray whales overwinter:* Sue E. Moore and Henry Huntington, "Arctic Marine Mammals and Climate Change: Impacts and Resilience," *Ecological Applications* 18, 2 Supplement (2008): S160.

207 *Walrus by the tens of thousands:* Chadwick J. Jay and Anthony S. Fischbach, "Pacific Walrus Response to Arctic Sea Ice Losses," USGS Fact Sheet 2008-3041.

207 *"The current reduction in Arctic ice":* Leonid Polyak, Richard B. Alley, John T. Andrews, Julie Brigham-Grette, Thomas M. Cronin, Dennis A. Darby, Arthur S. Dyke, Joan J. Fitzpatrick, Svend Funder, Marika Holland, Anne E. Jennings, Gifford H. Miller, Matt O'Regan, James Savelle, Mark Serreze, Kristen St. John, James W. C. White, and Eric Wolff, "History of Sea Ice in the Arctic," *Quaternary Science Reviews* 29 (2010): 1757.

208 *"The major point is"*: Julienne C. Stroeve, Mark C. Serreze, Marika M. Holland, Jennifer E. Kay, James Malanik, and Andrew P. Barrett, "The Arctic's Rapidly Shrinking Sea Ice Cover: A Research Synthesis," *Climatic Change* 110 (2012): 1016.

208 *"The reduction of the age"*: Walter N. Meier, Sebastian Gerland, Mats A. Granskog, and Jeffrey R. Key, "Sea Ice," in *Snow, Water, Ice and Permafrost in the Arctic (SWIPA): Climate Change and the Cryosphere* (Oslo: Arctic Monitoring and Assessment Programme, 2011), 10.

208 *In 2012 scientists reported:* "Arctic Sea Ice Shatters Previous Low Records; Antarctic Sea Ice Edge to Record High," press release, National Snow and Ice Data Center, October 2, 2012, http://nsidc.org/news/press/20121002_Mini mumPR.html; "Poles Apart: A Record-Breaking Summer and Winter," National Snow and Ice Data Center, October 2, 2012, http://nsidc.org/arcticsea icenews/2012/10poles-apart-a-record-breaking-summer-and-winter/.

208 *That same year, eighty polar bears:* Ben Anderson, "Rotting Whale Meat Lures Record 80 Polar Bears to Kaktovik," *Alaska Dispatch*, September 23, 2012.

209 *"Polar bears are the original"*: Andrew Derocher, *Polar Bears: A Complete Guide to Their Biology and Behavior* (Baltimore: Johns Hopkins University Press, 2012), 5.

209 *The abstract began:* Ian Stirling and Andrew E. Derocher, "Possible Impacts of Climatic Warming on Polar Bears," *Arctic* 46, 3 (September 1993): 240.

209 *By 2004, when they published:* Andrew E. Derocher, Nicholas J. Lunn, and Ian Stirling, "Polar Bears in a Warming Climate," *Integrative and Comparative Biology* 44 (2004): 163.

209 *Observers surveying bowhead whales:* Jeffrey S. Gleason and Karyn D. Rode, "Polar Bear Distribution and Habitat Association Reflect Long-Term Changes in Fall Sea Ice Conditions in the Alaskan Beaufort Sea," *Arctic* 62, 4 (December 2009): 412.

210 *An increasing proportion of bears:* Scott Schliebe, Karyn D. Rode, Jeffrey S. Gleason, Jim Wilder, Kelly Proffitt, Tom J. Evans, and Susanne Miller, "Effects of Sea Ice Extent and Food Availability on Spatial and Temporal Distribution of Polar Bears during the Fall Open-Water Period in Southern Beaufort Sea," *Polar Biology* 31, 8 (2008): 1007.

210 *"Because Polar Bears depend"*: Steven Amstrup, "Polar Bears and Climate Change: Certainties, Uncertainties, and Hope in a Warming World," in *Gyrfalcons and Ptarmigan in a Changing World*, vol. 1, ed. R. T. Watson, T. J. Cade, M. Fuller, G. Hunt, and E. Potapov (Boise, ID: Peregrine Fund, 2011), 16.

210 *People who believe:* Peter Dykstra, "Magic Number: A Sketchy 'Fact' about Polar Bears Keeps Going . . . and Going . . . and Going," *SE Journal* (Summer 2008), http://www.sejarchive.org/pub/SEJournal_Excerpts_Su08.htm.

210 *These bears are loosely grouped:* For detailed information on each population, see "Population Status Reviews," IUCN/SSC Polar Bear Specialist Group, http://pbsg.npolar.no/en/status/.

211 *If you divide polar bear habitat:* Steven C. Amstrup, Bruce Marcot, and David C. Douglas, "A Bayesian Network Modeling Approach to Forecasting the 21st Century Worldwide Status of Polar Bears," in *Arctic Sea Ice Decline: Observations, Projections, Mechanisms, and Implications,* Geophysical Monograph 180, ed. Eric T. DeWeaver, Ceclia M. Bita, and L.-Bruno Tremblay (Washington, DC: American Geophysical Union, 2008), 224–226.

211 *Between 1987 and 2004:* Eric V. Regehr, Nicholas J. Lunn, Steven C. Amstrup, and Ian Stirling, "Effects of Earlier Sea Ice Breakup on Survival and Population Size of Polar Bears in Western Hudson Bay," *Journal of Wildlife Management* 71, 8 (November 2007): 2679.

211 *"Future reduction of sea ice":* "Future Retreat of Arctic Sea Ice Will Lower Polar Bear Populations and Limit Their Distribution," news release, USGS, September 7, 2007.

211 *Scientists have since linked:* For an overview, see Ian Stirling and Andrew E. Derocher, "Effects of Climate Warming on Polar Bears: A Review of the Evidence," *Global Change Biology* 18, 9 (September 2012): 2694–2706.

211 *That sounds a bit abstract:* Ian Stirling, Evan Richardson, Gregory W. Thiemann, and Andrew E. Derocher, "Unusual Predation Attempts of Polar Bears on Ringed Seals in the Southern Beaufort Sea: Possible Significance of Changing Spring Ice Conditions," *Arctic* 61, 1 (March 2008): 21.

211 *"During 24 years of research":* Steven Amstrup, Ian Stirling, Tom Smith, Craig Perham, and Gregory Thiemann, "Recent Observations of Intraspecific Predation and Cannibalism among Polar Bears in the Southern Beaufort Sea," *Polar Biology* 29, 11 (October 2006): 997.

212 *Occasional incidents of infanticide:* Bob Weber, "Polar Bears Eating Young Due to Shrinking Sea Ice: Scientists," *Toronto Star,* November 27, 2009.

212 *Such problems will be delayed:* Amstrup et al., "Bayesian Network Modeling," 239–240.

212 *"If the climate continues to warm":* Stirling and Derocher, "Effects of Climate Warming," 2694.

212 *Especially disturbing, however:* Muyin Wang and James E. Overland, "A Sea Ice Free Summer Arctic within 30 Years: An Update from CMIP5 Models," *Geophysical Research Letters* 39, 18 (September 2012): 1.

212 *"The perception that nothing":* Steven C. Amstrup, Eric T. DeWeaver, David C. Douglas, Bruce G. Marcot, George M. Durner, Cecilia M. Bitz, and David A. Bailey, "Greenhouse Gas Mitigation Can Reduce Sea-Ice Loss and Increase Polar Bear Persistence," *Nature* 468 (December 16, 2010): 955.

213 *Still, cutting emissions would:* Ibid., 957.

213 *Some Alaska bears too large:* Amstrup, "Polar Bear, Ursus maritimus," 588.

213 *A Kotzebue Sound trophy:* Keith Sutton, "The Outdoor Life Book of World Records," *Outdoor Life,* September 2007, http://www.outdoorlife.com/articles/hunting/2007/09/outdoor-life-book-world-records.

213 Radio-collaring, tracking: Ian Stirling, Polar Bears (Ann Arbor: University of Michigan Press, 1998), Google eBook, 66.

214 A typical female: Amstrup, "Polar Bear, Ursus maritimus," 593.

214 The bear's life history: "NOAA Lists Ringed and Bearded Ice Seal Populations under the Endangered Species Act," news release, National Oceanic and Atmospheric Administration, December 21, 2012.

214 "There's been a sort of evolutionary war": Steven Amstrup, "Natural History," transcription of presentation, San Diego, February 5, 2004, www.polar bearsinternationalorg/pbhc/Amstrup/transcript.htm.

214 A bear that spots a seal's dark shape: Stirling, Polar Bears, 116–117.

215 Even a 450-pound polar bear: Scott Schliebe, Thomas Evans, Kurt Johnson, Susanne Miller, Charles Hamilton, Rosa Meehan, and Sonja Jahrsdoerfer, Range-Wide Status Review of the Polar Bear (Ursus maritimus) (Anchorage: USFWS, December 21, 2006), 17.

215 "This ability could make polar bears": Amstrup, "Polar Bear, Ursus maritimus," 598.

215 Throughout the North, most bears: Ibid., 595–596.

215 But as the sea ice continues to shrink: Scott Bergen, George M. Durner, David C. Douglas, and Steven C. Amstrup, Predicting Movements of Female Polar Bears between Summer Sea Ice Foraging Habitats and Terrestrial Denning Habitats of Alaska in the 21st Century: Proposed Methodology and Pilot Assessment (Reston, VA: USGS, 2007), 6.

216 Meanwhile, warming conditions will: Schliebe et al., Range-Wide Status, 87.

216 Though the chronology varies: Ibid., 18–22.

216 In 1992 a female bear traversed: George M. Durner and Steven C. Amstrup, "Movements of a Polar Bear from Northern Alaska to Northern Greenland," Arctic 48, 4 (December 1995): 339.

216 Tourists aboard the Russian: Rinie van Meurs and John F. Splettstoesser, "Farthest North Polar Bear," Arctic 5, 3 (September 2003): 309.

216 One radio-collared bear: Alister Doyle, "Polar Bear Makes Huge 74 km One-Day Arctic Swim," Reuters, August 12, 2005.

216 A long way, reported a 2012 study: Anthony Pagano, George M. Durner, Steven C. Amstrup, Kristin S. Simac, and Geoff S. York, "Long-Distance Swimming by Polar Bears (Ursus maritimus) of the Southern Beaufort Sea during Years of Extensive Open Water," Canadian Journal of Zoology 90, 5 (May 2012): 667.

216 It's impossible to say: "New Observations of Swimming Polar Bears Presented at International Bear Conference," press release, USGS July 20, 2011.

217 Researchers captured and collared: George M. Durner, John P. Whiteman, Henry J. Harlow, Steven C. Amstrup, Eric V. Regehr, and Merav Ben-David, "Consequences of Long-Distance Swimming and Travel over Deep-Water Pack Ice for a Female Polar Bear during a Year of Extreme Sea Ice Retreat," Polar Biology 34, 7 (July 2011): 978–979.

217   "Their ability to engage": Ibid., 983.

217   Drowning comes to mind: Charles Monnett and Jeffrey Gleason, "Observations of Mortality Associated with Extended Open-Water Swimming by Polar Bears in the Alaskan Beaufort Sea," *Polar Biology* 29, 8 (2006): 681.

217   Four bears that swam: Tim MacDonald, "Polar Bears Are Back, Tired," *Arctic Sounder*, September 9, 2004.

217   One traveled more than: "Wayward Polar Bear Tours the Dalton Highway," *Alaska*, March 2003, 12.

217   The USFWS called this: Tim Mowry, "Why Did the Polar Bear Cross the Brooks Range? Biologists Are Baffled," FDNM, March 28, 2008.

217   Inupiaq hunters from Bering Sea: Susanne B. Kalxdorff, *Collection of Local Knowledge Regarding Polar Bear Habitat Use in Alaska*, Technical Report MMM 97-2 (Anchorage: USFWS Marine Mammals Management, August 1997), 8–10.

218   A polar bear excited residents: Kyle Hopkins, "Polar Bear Causes a Stir in Yukon Delta Village," ADN, July 22, 2010.

218   Ringed seals accounted for: Gregory W. Thiemann, Sara J. Iverson, and Ian Stirling, "Polar Bear Diets and Arctic Marine Food Webs: Insights from Fatty Acid Analysis," *Ecological Monographs* 78, 4 (2008): 599.

218   In 1999 a Canadian researcher:"Breaking the Ice about Sassats," *The Science and the Environment Bulletin*, March/April 2000, Environment Canada online, www.ec.gc.ca/science/sandemaroo/article1_e.html.

218   From a helicopter, Canadian biologists: Thomas G. Smith and Becky Sjare, "Predation of Belugas and Narwhals by Polar Bears in Nearshore Areas of the Canadian High Arctic," *Arctic* 43, 2 (June 1990): 100.

218   "When polar bears are hunting seals": Susan Georgette, *Brown Bears on the Northern Seward Peninsula, Alaska: Traditional Knowledge and Subsistence Uses in Deering and Shishmaref*, Technical Paper No. 248 (Juneau: ADF&G Division of Subsistence, March 2001), 14.

218   Wainwright hunters advised anthropologist: Richard K. Nelson, *Hunters of the Northern Ice* (Chicago: University of Chicago Press, 1969), 201.

219   Brown bears are more skilled: Susan Georgette, "Left-Handed Bears: How Kuuvangmiit See the Grizzly," *Alaska Fish & Game* 26, 2 (November–December 1989): 8.

219   "All I can say is that": Stirling, *Polar Bears*, 117–118.

219   Perhaps temper tantrums: Ibid., 136.

219   This idea began with scientists: Daniel W. Koon, "Power of the Polar Myth," *New Scientist* 158, 2131 (April 25, 1998): 50.

219   When the future of polar bears: Kalxdorff, *Collection of Local Knowledge*, 6–7; Derocher, *Polar Bears*, 84–90.

220   "Polar bears are large animals": Ian Stirling and Andrew E. Derocher, "Melting under Pressure: The Real Scoop on Climate Warming and Polar Bears," *Wildlife Professional* 1, 3 (September 2007): 26.

220 *To survive as a vegetarian:* Karla Dutton, Susanne Miller, and Terry DeBruyn, eds., *Polar Bear Diversionary Feeding Workshop Report, June 8–9, 2011* (Anchorage: USFWS and Defenders of Wildlife, February 29, 2012), 10.

220 *At least a dozen different:* Miller, Schliebe, and Proffitt, *Demographics and Behavior,* 10.

220 *Eight grizzlies and twenty-four polar bears:* "Summary of 2005 Survey Activities," USFWS, Arctic National Wildlife Refuge.

221 *Usually U. arctos ousted:* Doug O'Harra, "Frozen Feast," ADN, April 24, 2005.

221 *Predictably, news that grizzlies:* "Bear Fight! Grizzlies Are Creeping into Polar Bears' Canadian Turf," *Discover* magazine online, 80beats blog, February 25, 2010.

221 *Then an Idaho man:* "Strange Bear Was Grizzly-Polar Hybrid, Tests Show," CBC News, May 10, 2006.

221 *An Inuvialuit hunter:* "DNA Testing Confirms Hybrid Bear Shot Near Ulukhaktok," news release, government of the Northwest Territories, April 3, 2010.

221 *In 2012 two Northwest Territories:* Ed Struzik, "Hybrid Polar Bear–Grizzly Sightings Common in Arctic," *Edmonton Journal,* July 27, 2012.

221 *Research that pegged the divergence:* Charlotte Lindqvist, Stephan C. Schuster, Yazhou Sun, Sandra L. Talbot, Ji Qi, Aakrosh Ratan, Lynn P. Tomsho, Lindsay Kasson, Eve Zeyl, Jon Aars, Webb Miller, Ólafur Ingólfsson, Lutz Bachmann, and Øystein Wiig, "Complete Mitochondrial Genome of a Pleistocene Jawbone Unveils the Origin of Polar Bear," *Proceedings of the National Academy of Sciences* 107 (2010): 5053.

221 *Then a research team that used:* Webb Miller, Stephan C. Schuster, Andreanna J. Welch, Aakrosh Ratan, Oscar C. Bedoya-Reina, Fangqing Zhao, Hie Lim Kim, Richard C. Burhans, Daniela I. Drautz, Nicola E. Wittekindt, Lynn P. Tomsho, Enrique Ibarra-Laclette, Luis Herrera-Estrella, Elizabeth Peacock, Sean Farley, George K. Sage, Karyn Rode, Martyn Obbard, Rafael Montiel, Lutz Bachmann, Ólafur Ingólfsson, Jon Aars, Thomas Mailund, Øystein Wiig, Sandra L. Talbot, and Charlotte Lindqvist, "Polar and Brown Bear Genomes Reveal Ancient Admixture and Demographic Footprints of Past Climate Change," PNAS 109, 36 (July 23, 2012): E2389.

222 *"We also found, perhaps unsurprisingly":* "Polar Bear Evolution Tracked Climate Change, New DNA Study Suggests," news release, University at Buffalo, State University of New York, July 23, 2012.

222 *"How much Styrofoam":* Yvonne Zipp, "Steven Amstrup Says It's Not Too Late to Save Polar Bears—and Ourselves," *Christian Science Monitor,* October 19, 2012.

222 *Around the world:* Camille Parmesan, "Ecological and Evolutionary Responses to Recent Climate Change," *Annual Review of Ecology, Evolution, and Systematics* 37 (2006): 657.

222 *"The direct impacts of anthropogenic":* Ibid., 639.

222 *The polar bear:* Jeffrey Kluger, "A Big Win for Polar Bears?" *Time* magazine online, December 27, 2006.

223 *Norsemen called them:* "Polar Bear Names," Polar Bears International, http://www.polarbearsinternational.org/about-polar-bears/essentials/polar-bear-names.

223 *When the Dutch navigator:* Gerrit De Veer, *The Three Voyages of William Barents,* ed. Charles T. Beke (London: Hakluyt Society, 1853), Google eBook, 15.

223 *Engraver Thomas Bewick:* Thomas Bewick, *A General History of the Quadrupeds,* 3rd ed. (Newcastle: Hodgson, Beilby, & Bewick, 1792), Google eBook, 270.

224 *The chronicler of this episode:* Anonymous journal cited in Ann Savours, "'A Very Interesting Point in Geography': The 1773 Phipps Expedition towards the North Pole," *Arctic* 37, 4 (December 1984): 418.

224 *A white bear:* J. Donald Hughes, "Europe as Consumer of Exotic Biodiversity: Greek and Roman Times," *Landscape Research* 28, 1 (2003): 24.

224 *But those were definitely polar bears:* Vernon N. Kisling, ed., *Zoo and Aquarium History: Ancient Animal Collections to Zoological Gardens* (Boca Raton, FL: CRC Press, 2001), 22, 77, 275.

224 *Even priests coveted:* Richard C. Davids, *Lords of the Arctic: A Journey among the Polar Bears* (New York: Macmillan, 1982), 7.

224 *King Henry III muzzled:* Phillip Drennon Thomas, "The Tower of London's Royal Menagerie," *History Today,* August 1996, 30.

224 *James could not resist:* William Andrews, *England in the Days of Old* (London: William Andrews, 1897), Google eBook, 216.

224 *"One white cub was spared":* Barbara Ravelhofer, "'Beasts of Recreacion': Henslowe's White Bears," *English Literary Renaissance* 32, 2 (March 2002): 293.

225 *About 400 journalists attended:* Kate Connolly, "Rejected at Birth, Knut Becomes Berlin Zoo's Bear Essential," *Guardian,* March 23, 2007.

225 *"Knutmania" celebrated him:* Andrea Zammert, "Knutmania Sweeps the Globe," *Bloomberg Businessweek,* May 8, 2007; Mike Swanson, "Knut the Bear Draws Record Number of Visitors to Berlin Zoo," *Deutsche Presse-Agentur,* April 5, 2007.

225 *Mourning fans protested:* Michael Slackman, "For Mourners of Knut, a Stuffed Bear Just Won't Do," *New York Times,* April 11, 2011.

225 *People whose existence depended:* Anne Fienup-Riordan, *Boundaries and Passages: Rule and Ritual in Yup'ik Eskimo Oral Tradition* (Norman: University of Oklahoma Press, 1994), 51–52.

225 *"This paradox appears to characterize":* John C. Russell, *Nanuq: Cultural Significance and Traditional Knowledge among Alaska Natives* (Nome: Alaska Nanuuq Commission, May 2005), 17.

226 *A bear's carcass:* Ibid., 65–68; Ronald Brower Sr., "Cultural Uses of Alaska Marine Mammals" (paper presented at the 29th Alaska Science Conference,

Fairbanks, August 1978), http://www.Alaskool.Org/Projects/Traditionalife
/Brower/Brower-Pt1.Htm.

226 *Contemporary Uqqurmiut elders*: Michele Thierren and Frederic Laugrand, *In-terviewing Inuit Elders: Perspectives on Traditional Health* (Arviat, NU: Nunavut Arctic College, 2001), 167–168.

226 *"Men and the beasts are much alike"*: Knud Rasmussen, *Across Arctic America: Narrative of the Fifth Thule Expedition* (reprint, Fairbanks: University of Alaska Press, 1999), 25.

226 *Navigating this complicated cosmos*: Russell, *Nanuq*, 103–106; Jean Blodgett, *The Coming and Going of the Shaman: Eskimo Shamanism and Art* (Winnipeg: Winnipeg Art Gallery, 1978), 89–91.

227 *"The fact that Eskimos"*: Nelson, *Hunters of Northern Ice*, 189.

227 *Inupiaq men who worked as guides*: *Proceedings of the First International Scientific Meeting on the Polar Bear, September 6–10, Fairbanks, Alaska* (Washington, DC: US Department of Interior and University of Alaska, 1966), 47.

227 *The late Harry Brower Sr.*: Karen Brewster, ed., *The Whales, They Give Themselves: Conversations with Harry Brower, Sr.* (Fairbanks: University of Alaska Press, 2004), 104.

227 *"That's how come the polar bears"*: Ibid., 59.

228 *"If an ordinary stalk is impossible"*: *Proceedings of First International Scientific Meeting on the Polar Bear*, 47.

228 *The annual harvest quickly escalated*: Big Game Investigations, Bear Studies (Polar Bear), January 1, 1968–December 1, 1968 (Federal Aid in Wildlife Restoration, Work Plan Segment Report, W-15-R-3 and W-17-1, 1969), i.

228 *In 2006 a Barrow man*: Beth Ipsen, "Barrow Man Gets Five Years in Jail for Selling Polar Bear Hide," *Arctic Sounder*, November 30, 2006, 1.

228 *The Alaska harvest of thirty-four bears*: Terry D. DeBruyn, Thomas J. Evans, Charles Hamilton, Susanne Miller, Craig J. Perham, Christopher Putnam, Eric Regehr, Karyn Rode, Michelle St. Martin, and James Wilder, *Summary of Polar Bear Management 2009/2010*, Report to the Canadian Polar Bear Technical Committee, Winnipeg, Manitoba, Canada (Anchorage: USFWS Marine Mammals Management, 2011), 5.

229 *The US-Russia Joint Commission*: *Questions and Answers about Polar Bear Management in the Chukchi Region under the U.S.-Russia Agreement* (Anchorage: USFWS Marine Mammals Management, May 2011).

229 *At the turn of the twenty-first century*: James A. Fall and Robert J. Wolfe, *Subsistence in Alaska: A Year 2010 Update*, rev. ed. (Anchorage: ADF&G Division of Subsistence, January 2012), 2.

229 *"'Is it Fat?' is a commonly asked question"*: Josh Wisniewski, *"We're Always Going Back and Forth": Kigiqtaamiut Subsistence Land Use and Occupancy for the Community of Shishmaref* (Anchorage: US Army Corps of Engineers Alaska District, 2005), 25.

229 *"We don't separate ourselves"*: Brower, "Cultural Uses."

230 *She wrote that the islanders*: Maria Williams, "To Dance Is to Be: Heritage Preservation in the 21st Century," *Alaska Park Science* 4, 1 (June 2005): 37.

230 *"The dancer's experience"*: Paul Shepard, *The Others: How Animals Made Us Human* (Washington, DC: Island Press/Shearwater Books, 1997), 161.

233 *Preliminary results showed*: Dutton, Miller, and DeBruyn, *Polar Bear Diversionary Feeding Workshop Report*, 20.

233 *"Only [when] they hungry"*: Pete Sovalik, "Two Hunters at Point Hope," transcription of interview with Don Kimball and Vic Hessler, 3, tape H88-26D, Naval Arctic Research Laboratory Collection, Barrow file, box 137, Alaska Polar Regions, Rasmuson Library, University of Alaska–Fairbanks.

233 *"The polar bear is cowardly"*: Anatoly A. Kochnev, Vladimir M. Etylin, Vladilen I. Kavry, Evgeny B. Siv-Siv, and Ivan V. Tanko, *Traditional Knowledge of Chukotka Native Peoples Regarding Polar Bear Habitat Use* (Anchorage: National Park Service, July 2003), 44–45.

234 *In 1990 a bear attacked*: Charles Wohlforth, "Man Dies Saving Wife from Polar Bear," ADN, December 10, 1990; Charles Wohlforth, "Starvation Spurred Polar Bear's Attack," ADN, December 12, 1990.

234 *Similarly, a 305-pound male bear*: David Hulen, "Polar Bear in Attack Young, Famished," ADN, December 3, 1993.

234 *"If you've ever seen pictures"*: Ibid.; David Hulen, "Polar Bear Mauls Mechanic: Bloody Attack at North Slope Ends with Two Shotgun Blasts," ADN, December 2, 1993.

234 *"Polar bears are one"*: Rachel Duncan, ed., *Polar Expeditions*, 4th ed. (London: Royal Geographical Society, 2003), 79.

235 *The USFWS trains oil-field workers*: *Polar Bear News* (Anchorage: USFWS Marine Mammals Management, 2010), 9–10.

235 *In Alaska the number*: Scott Schliebe, Thomas J. Evans, Susanne Miller, Craig Perham, James Wilder, and Lisa J. Lierheimer, "Polar Bear Management in Alaska 2000–2004," in *Proceedings of the 14th Working Meeting of the IUCN/SSC Polar Bear Specialist Group* (Seattle, June 20–24, 2005), 66.

235 *"This is something our grandchildren"*: Rebecca Luczycki, "Last Chance," *Alaska*, February 2010, 35.

236 *They lost their appeal*: Ben Anderson, "Appeals Court Ruling Determines Polar Bears Will Retain 'Threatened' Listing," *Alaska Dispatch*, March 1, 2013.

236 *In January 2013*: Ella Foley Gannon and Camarin E. B. Madigan, "Federal District Court Vacates Critical Habitat Designation for Polar Bears," *Bingham Legal Alerts*, January 24, 2013.

236 *Even as 5 million gallons*: John M. Broder, "Obama to Open Offshore Areas to Oil Drilling for First Time," *New York Times*, March 31, 2010.

236 *Royal Dutch Shell began*: "Shell Begins Preliminary Drilling in Beaufort Sea," *Alaska Dispatch*, October 3, 2012.

236 *If Shell taps into 25 billion:* Jill Burke and Tony Hopfinger, "Arctic Ocean vs. ANWR: A Hard-Earned Quest to Drill in the Icy Abyss," *Alaska Dispatch*, September 26, 2012.

237 *If their onshore fasting period:* Péter K. Molnár, Andrew E. Derocher, Gregory W. Thiemann, and Mark A. Lewis, "Predicting Survival, Reproduction and Abundance of Polar Bears under Climate Change," *Biological Conservation* 143, 7 (2010): 1612.

237 *"We can say with a very":* Bartley Kives, "Churchill Bears Doomed?" *Winnipeg Free Press*, June 7, 2010.

237 *Oceans have already absorbed:* "Ocean Acidification," State of the Science Fact Sheet, National Oceanic and Atmospheric Administration, May 2008 and January 2013.

THE WATCHED BEAR

242 *They hoped, Bass wrote:* Rick Bass, *The Lost Grizzlies: A Search for Survivors in the Wilderness of Colorado* (New York: Houghton Mifflin, 1995), 13.

242 *About 2,200 bears live in Katmai:* Tamara L. Olson and Judy A. Putera, *Refining Monitoring Protocols to Survey Brown Bear Populations in Katmai National Park and Preserve and Lake Clark National Park and Preserve*, Alaska Region Natural Resources Technical Report NPS/AR/NRTR-2007-66 (Anchorage: National Park Service, November 2007), 2.

243 *"As we sat and watched":* Cecil E. Rhode, "When Giant Bears Go Fishing," *National Geographic*, August 1954, 195.

243 *"He quite rightly wanted":* Ibid.

243 *"I wanted a place":* Tom Walker, *The Way of the Grizzly: The Bears of Alaska's Famed McNeil River* (Stillwater, MN: Voyageur Press, 1993), 59.

243 *"There were no controls":* Riley Woodford, "Larry Aumiller: Bridging the Worlds of Bears and People," *Alaska Fish & Wildlife News* online magazine, July 2003.

243 *Faro took charge:* Walker, *Way of the Grizzly*, 61.

244 *Concessioner Ray Petersen:* Frank B. Norris, *Tourism in Katmai Country: A History of Concessions Activity in Katmai National Park and Preserve* (Anchorage: National Park Service, Alaska Regional Office, 1992, rev. 2004), chap. 2, http://www.nps.gov/history/history/online_books/katm/.

244 *Far fewer bears:* Frank B. Norris, *Isolated Paradise: An Administrative History of the Katmai and Aniakchak NPS Units, Alaska* (Anchorage: National Park Service, 1996), chap. 9, http://www.nps.gov/history/history/online_books/katm/adhi/.

244 *The danger of food-conditioning bears:* Ibid.

244 *"The camper was sleeping":* Memorandum from Gary Lillie to Darrell Coe, July 17, 1967, cited in Frederick C. Dean, *Brown Bear–Human Interrelationship Study*, NPS PO 126-301 (unpublished report, National Park Service, 1968).

245 *"They are matter-of-fact":* Memorandum from Clifford Estabrook to Darrell Coe, July 4, 1967, cited in Dean, *Brown Bear–Human Interrelationship Study*.

245 *"The visitor takes"*: Dean, Brown Bear–Human Interrelationship Study, 20.

245 *"Some of the older"*: Estabrook memorandum.

245 *Among those who took bears*: Unsigned memorandum, July 15, 1967, cited in Dean, Brown Bear–Human Interrelationship Study.

245 *Of three bear charges*: Tamara L. Olson, Eric M. Groth, Katja W. Mocnik, and Carlton I. Vaughn, *Bear Management at Brooks River, Katmai National Park, 2003–2006*, Alaska Region Natural Resources Technical Report NPS/AR/ NRTR-2009-73 (Anchorage: National Park Service, January 2009), 7.

246 *A trail from Dumpling Mountain*: Terry D. DeBruyn, *A Review of Bear-Human Interactions over Time and the Overall Implications to Management of the Brooks River Area, Katmai National Park and Preserve*, Technical Report NPS/KAT/99-004 (National Park Service, 1999), 19–21.

246 *Dean urged a philosophical shift*: Dean, Brown Bear–Human Interrelationship Study, 14–20.

246 *"When the bear begins"*: Ibid., 15.

246 *In the 2000s*: See National Park Service Visitor Use Statistics, https://irma .nps.gov/Stats/Reports/ReportList; Brooks River Visitor Access Final Environmental Impact Statement, *Katmai National Park and Preserve* (Anchorage: National Park Service, January 2013), 110.

246 *Between 1993 and 2000*: Terry D. DeBruyn, Tom S. Smith, Kelly Proffitt, Steve Partridge, and Thomas D. Drummer, "Brown Bear Response to Elevated Viewing Structures at Brooks River, Alaska," *Wildlife Society Bulletin* 32, 4 (2004): 1139.

246 *Bears "trespassed"*: Olson et al., *Bear Management*, 1.

247 *Perhaps the most surprising*: Brooks River Visitor Access, 20.

247 *Yet in the past fifty years*: Norris, Isolated Paradise, chap. 9; Steve Rinehart, "Bears, People Face Changes at [sic] Brooks River Plan Moves Camp, Limits Visitors," ADN, April 18, 1994.

248 *"Exactly what is the behavior"*: Dean, Brown Bear–Human Interrelationship Study, 38.

248 *"I'd seen how he handled himself"*: Woodford, "Larry Aumiller."

248 *But bear expert Tom Smith*: Tom S. Smith, "Effects of Human Activity on Brown Bear Use of the Kulik River, Alaska," *Ursus* 13 (2002): 266.

248 *Highly habituated bears*: Larry Aumiller and Colleen Matt, "Management of McNeil River State Game Sanctuary for Viewing of Brown Bears," *Int. Conf. Bear Res. Mgmt.* 9 (1994): 53–54.

249 *Only thirteen serious charges*: Memorandum from Larry Aumiller to Joe Meehan, "2004 McNeil River Field Report," December 20, 2004.

249 *"We found that, in the absence"*: Aumiller and Matt, "Management of McNeil River," 53.

250 *One bear that inadvertently*: Rhode, "When Giant Bears Go Fishing," 96.

250 *They identified the innate*: Tom S. Smith, Stephen Herrero, and Terry D.

DeBruyn, "Alaskan Brown Bears, Humans, and Habituation," *Ursus* 16, 1 (2005): 1–3.

250 *"We maintain that"*: Ibid., 8.

250 *"There's no doubt about it"*: Interview with Patricia Owen.

251 *Park managers must be aware*: Smith, Herrero, and DeBruyn, "Alaskan Brown Bears," 9.

251 *Smith and his colleagues described*: Ibid., 4.

254 *"It is my greatest fear"*: Timothy Treadwell and Jewel Palovak, *Among Grizzlies: Living with Wild Bears in Alaska* (New York: Random House, 1999), 191.

254 *"Failure to make that distinction"*: Smith, Herrero, and DeBruyn, "Alaskan Brown Bears," 8.

255 *Homer businesses estimated*: Data provided by Ken and Chris Day.

255 *About thirty people visited*: Olson and Putera, *Refining Monitoring Protocols*, 3.

256 *The superintendent reported*: Ralph Moore, Superintendent's Annual Report, Fiscal Year 2010, Katmai National Park and Preserve, Aniakchak National Monument and Preserve, Alagnak Wild River (National Park Service, 2010), 23.

256 *People who visit Alaska*: Steve Colt and Darcy Dugan, *Spending Patterns of Selected Alaska Bear Viewers: Preliminary Results from a Survey* (Institute of Social and Economic Research, University of Alaska–Anchorage, March 17, 2005), 3.

256 *The Alaska Department of Fish and Game estimated*: Lem Butler, "Game Management Unit 9, Alaska Peninsula," in *Region II Briefing Book* (ADF&G Division of Wildlife Conservation, February 2009), 26.

256 *In contrast, one economic analysis*: Ginny Fay and Neal Christensen, *Katmai National Park and Preserve Economic Significance Analysis and Model Documentation* (prepared for National Park Conservation Association and National Park Service, Katmai National Park and Preserve, 2010), 4.

257 *The guidelines recommended*: *Best Practices for Viewing Bears on the West Side of Cook Inlet and the Katmai Coast* (ADF&G and National Park Service, 2003).

257 *More than 80 percent of groups*: Carissa Turner, *Evaluating the Use and Effectiveness of the "Best Bear Viewing Practices" Guidelines in Katmai National Park and Preserve*, Investigator's Annual Report, KATM-00082 (National Park Service, 2011), 3.

257 *At Wolverine Creek and Cove*: "Wolverine Creek Management Committee Charter," ADF&G; Troy N. Tollefson, Colleen Matt, Joe Meehan, and Charles T. Robbins, "Quantifying Spatiotemporal Overlap of Alaskan Brown Bears and People," *Journal of Wildlife Management* 69, 2 (April 2005): 810.

259 *Fishing activity at Wolverine Creek*: Tollefson et al., "Quantifying Spatiotemporal Overlap," 815–816.

259 *Nonhabituated bears delayed*: Tamara L. Olson, Barrie K. Gilbert, and Ronald C. Squibb, "The Effects of Increasing Human Activity on Brown Bear Use of an Alaskan River," *Biological Conservation* 82 (1997): 98.

259 *Bears avoided sections*: Smith, "Effects of Human Activity," 267.

259 *On the Chilkoot River near Haines*: Anthony P. Crupi Jr., "Foraging Behavior and

Habitat Use Patterns of Brown Bears (*Ursus arctos*) in Relation to Human Activity and Salmon Abundance on a Coastal Alaskan Salmon Stream" (M.S. thesis, Utah State University, 2003), iv.

259 *A long-term study:* Gregory A. Wilker and Victor G. Barnes Jr., "Responses of Brown Bears to Human Activities at O'Malley River, Kodiak Island, Alaska," *Ursus* 10 (1998): 560.

259 *Time-lapse cameras:* Carissa Turner and Troy Hamon, "Describing Brown Bear Activity Patterns Using Time-Lapse Photography in Katmai National Park and Preserve," *Alaska Park Science* 10, 2 (December 2011): 25.

259 *However, the number of bears:* Carissa Turner, "Bear Use of a Coastal Foraging Area in Katmai National Park: Understanding Bear Use through Time-Lapse Photography" (presented at the 2011 Southwest Alaska Park Science Symposium, Anchorage, November 2–14).

259 *Let's not forget:* DeBruyn, *Review of Bear-Human Interactions*, 11.

259 *During an experiment conducted:* Karyn A. Rode, Sean D. Farley, and Charles T. Robbins, "Behavioral Responses of Brown Bears Mediate Nutritional Effects of Experimentally Introduced Tourism," *Biological Conservation* 133, 1 (2006): 78–79.

260 *At a British Columbia site:* Owen T. Nevin and Barrie K. Gilbert, "Perceived Risk, Displacement and Refuging in Brown Bears: Positive Impacts of Ecotourism?" *Biological Conservation* 121, 4 (2005): 620–621.

260 *"An over-arching principle":* Terry D. DeBruyn and Tom S. Smith, "Managing Bear-Viewing to Minimize Human Impacts on the Species in Alaska," in *Ecotourism and Environmental Sustainability: Principles and Practices,* ed. Jennifer Hill and Tim Gale (Burlington, VT: Ashgate Publishing, 2009), 112.

260 *Allowing bears to define:* Ibid., 120.

260 *The researchers also recommended:* Ibid., 112–113.

260 *Still, bear-human habituation:* Stephen Herrero, Tom Smith, Terry D. DeBruyn, Kerry Gunther, and Colleen A. Matt, "From the Field: Brown Bear Habituation to People—Safety, Risks, and Benefits," *Wildlife Society Bulletin* 33, 1 (2005): 366.

261 *In 2009 a young brown bear:* Jenny Neyman, "Road Kill," *Redoubt Reporter,* October 7, 2009.

261 *"If that was hunting":* Jenny Neyman, "Bear Death under Scrutiny," *Redoubt Reporter,* October 28, 2009.

261 *One of the hunters:* Jenny Neyman, "Bear Hunter Regrets Shooting," *Redoubt Reporter,* November 11, 2009.

261 *Yet land management:* DeBruyn and Smith, "Managing Bear-Viewing," 118.

261 *Bear habitat, behavior, and needs:* Ibid., 119.

261 *Hunters killed ten:* Derek Stonorov, *Bears of Katmai National Park Preserve and Kamishak Special Use Area* (prepared for Jim Stratton, regional director, National Parks Conservation Association, Anchorage, January 19, 2007), 5.

261 *Later, when the state:* Tom Kizzia, "Permit-Winners Say They'll Spare the Bear," ADN, July 13, 1995; Steve Rinehart, "Game Board Cancels McNeil River Bear Hunt," ADN, October 28, 1995.

262 *However, Governor Frank Murkowski:* Doug O'Harra, "Game Board Gives McNeil Grizzlies Room to Roam," ADN, March 11, 2005.

263 *"To purposely and knowingly":* Larry Aumiller, "McNeil Bears Need Governor's Support," ADN, October 15, 2005.

263 *Two years of negative publicity:* Alex deMarban, "Board of Game Kills Hunt for McNeil Area Bears," ADN, March 7, 2007.

263 *"The bears simply dodged":* Carey James, "Bear Battle Not over, Say Advocates," Homer Tribune, March 14, 2007.

263 *About 75 percent:* Butler, "Game Management Unit 9," 26.

264 *Since 1995 the Days:* Interview with Ken and Chris Day.

264 *Other viewing guides:* Stonorov, Bears of Katmai, 14–16.

264 *Between 2001 and 2010: Finding of No Significant Impact. Hunting Guide Concessions Environmental Assessment, Katmai National Preserve, Alaska* (Anchorage: National Park Service, Alaska Region, September 2012), B-4.

264 *The state considers:* Lem Butler, "Unit 9 Brown Bear," in *Brown Bear Management Report of Survey and Inventory Activities 1 July 2004—30 June 2006,* ed. Patricia Harper (Juneau: ADF&G, 2007), 112.

264 *In 2007 the Days:* "Groups Seek Shorter Grizzly Hunting Season," Wildlife Policy News 17, 5 (October 2007): 6.

264 *The ethics of hunting:* Peter Porco, "Cameras Show Katmai Bear Kills," ADN, October 6, 2007; Megan Baldino, "Sides Face off over Katmai Bear Hunt," October 5, 2007, http://www.ktuu.com/Global/story.asp?S=7177433; Megan Baldino, "Katmai Hunt and Story Surrounded by Controversy," October 8, 2007, http://www.ktuu.com/Global/story.asp?S=7186391.

264 *The hunters complained:* Megan Baldino, "Troopers Say Cameras Didn't Interfere with Hunt," October 9, 2007, http://www.ktuu.com/Global/story .asp?S=7192100.

265 *"This was a once-in-a-lifetime":* Michael D. Faw, "Media Ruin Alaskan Bear Hunt," January 9, 2008, updated October 21, 2009, http://www.NRAhunt ersrights.org/Article.aspx?id=162.

265 *Guide Jim Hamilton defended:* Jim Hamilton, statement on Katmai bear hunts, http://www.ktuu.com/Global/story.asp?S=7176905.

265 *Fair chase is a concept:* "Katmai National Preserve Brown Bear Hunts," ADF&G Division of Wildlife Conservation, http://www.wc.adfg.state.ak.us/index .cfm?adfg=game.katmai; "Katmai Bear Data Reviewed," news release, Alaska National Parks, National Park Service, October 19, 2007.

265 *Park superintendent Ralph Moore:* Bill Sherwonit, "The Bears of Katmai," Anchorage Press, February 18, 2009.

266 *Nobody mentioned the role: Hunting Guide Concessions Environmental Assessment,*

Public Review (Anchorage: National Park Service Alaska Region, June 2012), 3–27.

266 *"Because some claim"*: Smith, Herrero, and DeBruyn, "Alaskan Brown Bears," 8.

266 *The National Park Service: Hunting Guide Concessions*, 1-1.

266 *Alaska state troopers reported*: Alaska State Troopers, Department of Public Safety, Daily Dispatches, Case Number 09-60940, Kodiak, posted March 29, 2010, http://dps.alaska.gov/PIO/dispatch/.

266 *The total number: Finding of No Significant Impact*, 2.

266 *"Does the NPS"*: Derek Stonorov to Bud Rice, National Park Service, July 31, 2012.

267 *The NPS avoided discussing: Finding of No Significant Impact*, A-1.

267 *"It's not much of a hunt"*: Sherwonit, "Bears of Katmai."

268 *"How much more informative"*: Terry D. DeBruyn, *Walking with Bears: One Man's Relationship with Three Generations of Wild Bears* (Guilford, CT: Globe Pequot Press, 1999), 214.

268 *"Because populations"*: DeBruyn and Smith, "Managing Bear-Viewing," 121.

269 *The loss of such a bear*: Memo from Aumiller to Meehan.

269 *A year later*: DeBruyn, *Walking with Bears*, 249.

269 *In a passionate rant*: Charles Jonkel, "Idiots to Icons," *Bear News* 19, 3–4 (2004): 3.

270 *Paul Shepard wondered about*: Paul Shepard, *The Others: How Animals Made Us Human* (Washington, DC: Island Press/Shearwater Books, 1997), 6.

THE PREDATORY BEAR

273 *By early 2013*: "Intensive Management in Alaska: Alaska's Predator Control Programs," ADF&G Division of Wildlife Conservation, http://www.adfg.alaska.gov/index.cfm?adfg=intensivemanagement.programs; "Intensive Management Area Big Game Population Status," Department of Fish and Game–Wildlife Conservation, Office of Management and Budget, State of Alaska, http://omb.alaska.gov/html/performance/details.html?p=63.

273 *"The role of the hunter"*: Mark Richards, "Wolf Control Expansion Plan Is Shortsighted at Best," FDNM, May 28, 2006.

273 *They include snaring bears: Unit 16 and Unit 19D Bear Predator Control Programs, 2012–2013* (ADF&G Division of Wildlife Conservation).

273 *"Most represent practices"*: Karen Noyce, letter to Alaska Board of Game, February 20, 2004.

274 *To speed things along*: "Brown Bear Control Program Approved," news release 11-17, ADF&G, March 11, 2011; Tim Mowry, "Alaska Board of Game OKs Baited Grizzly Kills," FDNM, March 8, 2012.

274 *No matter what you call it: Predator Management in Alaska* (Juneau: ADF&G Division of Wildlife Conservation, November 2007), 5–6.

275 *"Predators have to bear"*: Statement by Bert Sharp, Intensive Management of

Game Resources: Hearings on SB77, February 16, 1994, before the House Resources Committee, 18th Alaska State Legislature.

275 *"Since Statehood, the controversy":* Don Russell, *A Review of Wolf Management Programs in Alaska, Yukon, British Columbia, Alberta and Northwest Territories* (Yukon Wolf Conservation and Management Plan Review, November 6, 2010), 22.

275 *Historian Morgan Sherwood:* Morgan Sherwood, *Big Game in Alaska: A History of Wildlife and People* (New Haven, CT: Yale University Press, 1981), 38.

275 *"Like it or not":* Mark Richards, comments on online Alaska Outdoors Forum.

275 *A prominent supporter:* Ralph Seekins, "SFW Alaska President's Message," Sportsmen for Fish and Wildlife Alaska Chapter, fall 2009, http://sfwalaska .com/web/index.php?option=com_content&view=category&layout=blog&i d=9&Itemid=12.

276 *"This isn't about wolves":* Joel Gay, "No One Budges at Wolf Debate," ADN, December 4, 2003.

276 *To generalize: Opponents:* Rodney D. Boertje, Mark A. Keech, and Thomas F. Paragi, "Science and Values Influencing Predator Control for Alaska Moose Management," *Journal of Wildlife Management* 74, 5 (2010): 924–926.

276 *Nobody wants to eradicate:* Rod Arno, "Which Side Are You On?" *Outdoor Alaska* (Winter 2008): 3.

276 *"We know this land":* Joel Gay, "Chairman Uses Personal History as Guide," ADN, May 30, 2005.

277 *Subsistence practically defines:* James A. Fall and Robert J. Wolfe, *Subsistence in Alaska: A Year 2010 Update,* rev. ed. (Anchorage: ADF&G Division of Subsistence, January 2012), 1–4.

278 *The governor appoints citizens: Predator Management,* 8–9.

278 *The amount of work:* Tim Mowry, "Board of Game: No Interior Alaska Bear Trapping for Now," FDNM, March 10, 2012.

278 *The board sets population: Intensive Management Protocol* (ADF&G Division of Wildlife Conservation, December 2011), 2.

278 *A persistent criticism:* "The Sportsman's 'Crown Jewel' Joins the SFW/SFH Family," Sportsmen for Fish and Wildlife Alaska Chapter, www.sfwalaska .org.

279 *To many wildlife biologists:* Donald D. Young, Rodney D. Boertje, C. Tom Seaton, and Kalin A. Kellie, "Intensive Management of Moose at High Density: Impediments, Achievements, and Recommendations," *Alces* 42 (2006): 42–43.

279 *That phenomenon is suggested:* Tom Paragi, "Overview of Intensive Management with Emphasis on Region III Moose" (ADF&G presentation to Alaska Board of Game, March 2008), 13.

280 *"When I look at the bear":* Cliff Judkins, Alaska Board of Game meeting, March 11, 2007.

281 *From a scientific standpoint:* Boertje, Keech, and Paragi, "Science and Values," 919; Wayne L. Regelin, Patrick Valkenburg, and Rod D. Boertje, "Management of Large Predators in Alaska," *Wildlife Biology in Practice* 1, 1 (June 2005): 77.

281 *Not even the professionals:* Kris Hundertmark, "Message from President Kris Hundertmark," *Alaskan Wildlifer*, November 2011, 1.

281 *"The relative importance":* Intensive Management Protocol, 33.

281 *Boertje and colleagues reviewed:* Boertje, Keech, and Paragi, "Science and Values," 926, 924.

282 *"Predator control really":* Mark Keech, Alaska Board of Game meeting, March 2, 2012.

282 *"In the short term":* Mark A. Keech, Mark S. Lindberg, Rodney D. Boertje, Patrick Valkenburg, Brian D. Taras, Toby A. Boudreau, and Kimberlee B. Beckman, "Effect of Predator Treatments, Individual Traits, and Environment on Moose Survival in Alaska," *Journal of Wildlife Management* 75, 6 (2011): 1377.

282 *The department spent:* Corey Rossi, Craig Fleener, Patrick Valkenburg, and Ted Spraker, "Alaska's Intensive Management Policy: The View from the State," *Wildlife Professional* (Winter 2011), http://joomla.wildlife.org/index .php?option=com_content&task=view&id=951.

282 *Returns may already:* "Intensive Management Area Big Game Population Status."

282 *"However, there are no":* Sterling D. Miller, John W. Schoen, Jim Faro, and David R. Klein, "Trends in Intensive Management of Alaska's Grizzly Bears, 1980–2010," *Journal of Wildlife Management* 75, 6 (2011): 1248–1249.

283 *"Such programs can lead":* Victor Van Ballenberghe, "Intensive Management— Or Mismanagement?" *Wildlife Professional* (Winter 2011): 74.

283 *For example, under one plan:* Operational Plan for Intensive Management of Moose in Unit 24(B) during Regulatory Years 2012–2017 (ADF&G Division of Wildlife Conservation, February 2012), 1.

283 *The estimated cost:* Feasibility Assessment for Intensive Management Program: Game Management Unit 24B (ADF&G Division of Wildlife Conservation, February 25, 2011), 10.

283 *But in nine of twenty winters:* Ibid., 15.

284 *Although board and department leadership:* Rossi et al., "Alaska's Intensive Management Policy."

284 *The panel of scientists found evidence:* Committee on Management of Wolf and Bear Populations in Alaska, National Research Council, *Wolves, Bears, and Their Prey in Alaska: Biological and Social Challenges in Wildlife Management* (Washington, DC: National Academy Press, 1997), 183–188.

285 *"Variations in weather":* Ibid., 88.

285 *"Indeed, recent predator control":* Miller et al., "Trends in Intensive Management," 1248.

285 *One reason definitive answers: Management of Large Mammalian Carnivores in North America*, Technical Review 12-01 (Bethesda, MD: Wildlife Society, March 2012), 57.

286 *Wildlife managers undertake:* Caryl L. Elzinga, Daniel W. Salzer, and John W. Willoughby, *Measuring & Monitoring Plant Populations* (US Bureau of Land Management, 1998), 2.

286 *"While social considerations":* Teresa Sager Albaugh, Alaska Board of Game statewide meeting, January 13, 2012.

286 *What frustrates many Alaskans:* "License Sale Statistics 2011 Calendar Year," State of Alaska Division of Administrative Services, License Accounting, February 10, 2012.

287 *Ironically, fears that:* Deborah Weisberg, "Windfall Spent on Recruiting New Hunters," *Pittsburgh Post-Gazette*, March 29, 2012.

287 *One obstacle was opposition:* Cindy McKinney, Lauren Ris, Heather Rorer, and Sara Williams, "Investing in Wildlife: State Wildlife Funding Campaigns" (M.S. project, University of Michigan, April 2005), 32.

288 *"Wildlife management":* Alaska Constitutional Convention minutes, December 14, 1955, http://www.law.alaska.gov/doclibrary/conconv/37.html.

288 *"In response to these findings":* Miller et al., "Trends in Intensive Management," 1243.

288 *"That's a place I don't":* Elizabeth Manning, "Unexpected Results of Study Show Grizzlies Are Killing Moose Calves," ADN, June 24, 2001.

289 *"My directive to them":* "Murkowski Appoints Six to Game Board," news release, Office of the Governor, State of Alaska, January 17, 2003.

289 *"[The appointments] are a step":* Sean Cockerham, "Murkowski Game Board Heavy on Hunting Advocates," ADN, January 18, 2003.

289 *"ISSUE: Declining moose":* Allen Dubord, "Proposal 73," in *Alaska Board of Game Spring 2004 Proposal Book* (Juneau: ADF&G Boards Support Section, 2004), 59–60.

289 *Moose were uncommon there:* James B. Faro, "Moose, Unit 16," in *Federal Aid in Wildlife Restoration Annual Report of Survey-Inventory Activities 1 July 1988–30 June 1989* (Juneau: ADF&G Division of Wildlife Conservation, August 1990), 165.

290 *Fish and Game had demonstrated:* Victor Van Ballenberghe, "Predator Control, Politics, and Wildlife Conservation," *Alces* 42 (2006): 6.

290 *"Biologists also don't know":* Elizabeth Manning, "Predators and Moose: Why Aren't Moose Calves Surviving?" *Alaska Fish & Wildlife News* online magazine, January 2007.

291 *"It's really true we're not":* Ron Somerville, Alaska Board of Game meeting, March 11, 2007.

291 *"Allowing the harvest":* Jake Jefferson, "Written Comments Regarding BOG Proposals for March 2nd 2007 Meeting," RC 18, Alaska Board of Game spring 2007 meeting.

291 *"I don't believe in fair chase"*: Elizabeth Manning, "Predators Face Another Hard Hit," ADN, March 15, 2003.

292 *Killing more than 2,600*: James Halpin, "Hunters Organize to Help State Kill off Bears," ADN, March 11, 2008.

292 *They approved a snaring*: "Experimental Foot-Snaring Program," news release, ADF&G, September 4, 2009.

292 *Between 2009 and 2012*: Olin Anderson, Alaska Board of Game meeting, February 13, 2013.

292 *By then, hunters*: Annual Report to the Alaska Board of Game on Intensive Management for Moose with Wolf, Black Bear, and Brown Bear Predation Control in GMU 16 (ADF&G Division of Wildlife Conservation, February 2013), 8–10; Annual Report to the Alaska Board of Game on Intensive Management for Moose with Wolf, Black Bear, and Brown Bear Predation Control in GMU 16 (ADF&G Division of Wildlife Conservation, February 2012), 6–7.

293 *As research biologist Lou Bender*: Lou Bender, Alaska Board of Game meeting, February 13, 2012.

293 *"Almost without exception"*: Management of Large Mammalian Carnivores, 61.

293 *Instead, they doubled down*: "Brown Bear Control Program."

293 *"We're really changing"*: Ted Spraker, Alaska Board of Game meeting, March 6, 2011.

294 *"Probably the greatest"*: Ben Grussendorf, Alaska Board of Game meeting, March 6, 2011.

294 *"I think we ought to"*: Cliff Judkins, Alaska Board of Game meeting, March 6, 2011.

294 *The game board and predator control advocates*: Jason Lamb, "Board of Game Turns down Proposal to Limit Non-Resident Hunters," KTUU-TV, February 1, 2010.

294 *"Everybody loves to beat"*: Mary Pemberton, "Herds up in Areas of Wolf Control," ADN, September 14, 2009.

294 *"Alaska hunters and nonresident"*: Rod Arno, letter to the editor, ADN, September 23, 2009.

294 *"Much of the available surplus"*: David McHoes, "Proposal 94," in Alaska Board of Game Spring 2011 Proposal Book (Regions II and IV) (ADF&G Boards Support Section, 2011).

295 *During the snaring project's*: David McHoes, "27 and Done," Alaska Trapper, n.d.

295 *Trappers had snared*: Olin Anderson, Alaska Board of Game meeting, February 13, 2013.

296 *The grand "experiment"*: Annual Report on Intensive Management (February 2013), 12.

297 *He failed to point out*: Keech et al., "Effect of Predator Treatments," 1361.

297 *Eight years of wolf control*: Annual Report to the Alaska Board of Game on Intensive Management for Moose with Wolf, Black Bear, and Grizzly Predation Control in Game

Management Unit 19A (ADF&G Division of Wildlife Conservation, February 2013), 8.

298 In the spring of 2013 and 2014: "Bear Control Program Approved on Middle Kuskokwim River," news release, ADF&G, March 5, 2012.

298 As the Wildlife Society's carnivore review: Management of Large Mammalian Carnivores, 58.

298 In the early 1960s: Harry B. Dodge III, Kodiak Island and Its Bears: A History of Bear/Human Interactions on Alaska's Kodiak Archipelago (Anchorage: Great Northwest Publishing, 2004), 312–316.

298 "I really look forward": Ted Spraker, Alaska Board of Game meeting, February 26, 2010.

299 She not only continued: Rachel D'Oro, "Judge Halts 'Bounty' on Wolves," Seattle Times, March 31, 2007.

299 Two weeks before the election: Mary Pemberton, "Campaigns over Measure 2 Get Heated," Juneau Empire, August 20, 2008.

299 A record 56,000: Mary Pemberton, "Voters Reject Predator Control Program Changes," ADN, August 27, 2008.

299 Palin also introduced: Mark Richards, "Wildlife Management Bill Goes Too Far," ADN, March 8, 2008; "Governor Palin Introduces Bill to Streamline Predator Management Laws: HB 256/SN 176 Clarify, Clean up Statutes, Encourages Abundance-Based Management," news release 07-14, ADF&G, May 11, 2007.

299 And Palin invented a position: Craig Medred, "The Spectacular Rise of Alaska Wildlife Manager Corey Rossi," Alaska Dispatch, January 15, 2012.

300 "It'll be our opportunity": Sarah Palin, "Re: KTUU," e-mail to Michael A. Nizich, February 5, 2009, http://www.documentcloud.org/documents/309316-pra -gsp02–0027220.html.

300 "I'm honestly getting": Sarah Palin, "Re: Predator Control and Re: Utility," e-mail to Michael Nizich, February 7, 2009, http://www.documentcloud.org /documents/310077-pra-gsp02–0022294.html#search/p1/Palin.

300 In a rebuttal: Rossi et al., "Alaska's Intensive Management Policy."

300 The board approved: Amanda Coyne, "Season of Snaring Bears Starts," Alaska Dispatch, June 3, 2009.

301 "A lot of people": Ralph Seekins, interview with Shoup Shepherd, "America the Wild" podcast, show 122, March 15, 2008, http://www.americathewild .com/031508/atwo31508seg2finalmixdown.mp3.

301 In 2010, with no public notice: "Proposal 39," preliminary actions, Alaska Board of Game statewide meeting, January 29–February 1, 2010.

301 Valkenburg also discussed plans: Patrick Valkenburg, Alaska Board of Game Interior Region meeting, March 6, 2010.

301 These often led to skirmishes: ADF&G Report (Western Association of Fish and Wildlife Agencies, 2013 Winter Meeting, Tucson, AZ), http://www.wafwa

.org/documents/commissioners/Summary%20SOS%20Report%200113
.pdf.

301   *endangered population of beluga whales:* Hundertmark, "Message from President," 1.

301   *refusals to let the state:* "NPS, ADFG Meet on Wolf Protocol," news release, March 30, 2010.

301   *"Let legislators know we'll":* Rudy Wittshirk, "Leaked Email Reveals How Wildlife Is Being Mismanaged from the Governor on Down," ADN, April 10, 2012.

301   *"I think it high time":* Riptide, "SFH Attacks ADF&G," Alaska Game Management Forum, Outdoors Directory website, October 1, 2009, http://forums .outdoorsdirectory.com/showthread.php/64653-SFH-Attacks-ADF-amp-G.

302   *SFW claimed credit:* Tim Mowry, "Critics Decry New Alaska Wildlife Director," FDNM, March 16, 2010.

302   *That can-do attitude seemed:* Craig Medred, "Alaska Wildlife Conservation Director Charged with Helping Illegally Kill Bears," Alaska Dispatch, January 12, 2012; Craig Medred, "Alaska Wildlife Official Faces New Allegations of Illegal Hunting," Alaska Dispatch, January 12, 2012.

302   *He resigned immediately:* Craig Medred, "Illegal Alaska Bear Hunter Gets off Easier Than Rocker Ted Nugent," Alaska Dispatch, May 4, 2012.

302   *Many Fish and Game employees:* Rick Sinnott, "Wildlife Chief's Resignation Resonates with Biologists," Alaska Dispatch, January 12, 2012.

302   *After Rossi's resignation:* Medred, "Alaska Wildlife Official."

302   *Rossi was also criticized:* "Alaska Auction and Raffle Permits, 2012–13" (ADF&G Division of Wildlife Conservation, June 28, 2011).

302   *Most damaging were revelations:* Richard Mauer, "Hunting Rights for Landowners Weighed," ADN, March 3, 2012.

303   *Eventually, the board voted against:* Mowry, "Board of Game."

303   *"I don't think anyone":* Ted Spraker, Alaska Board of Game Interior Region meeting, March 9, 2012.

304   *But in 2012 the game board:* Mowry, "Alaska Board of Game."

304   *"If you can bait a black bear":* Ted Spraker, Alaska Board of Game meeting, February 13, 2013.

304   *"It's not a different-colored bear":* Bob Mumford, Alaska Board of Game meeting, March 19, 2013.

304   *Within days, his outfitter:* "Alaska 2014 Brown Bear over Bait!!!" Bowsite.com online forum, April 21, 2013.

305   *"Environmental groups did their part":* Bob Hayes, Wolves of the Yukon (Bob Hayes, 2010), Kindle edition.

306   *"Strong concerns from the public":* Yukon Wolf Conservation and Management Plan (Whitehorse: Yukon Environment, 2012), 10–11.

307   "*Predators are just that*": Akres, Alaska Hunting Forums, September 17, 2009, http://forums.outdoorsdirectory.com/showthread.php/63716-Why-quot -calf-killer-quot/page2.

307   "*Bears are brutal, mean*": Maximum Penetration, Alaska Hunting Forums, September 13, 2010, http://forums.outdoorsdirectory.com/showthread.php / 86700-ADFG-Recommends-to-LEGALIZE-BEAR-TRAPPING/page8.

307   "*I guess my perception*": BrentC, Alaska Hunting Forums, June 18, 2009, http:// forums.outdoorsdirectory.com/showthread.php/56899-Getting-Browns -off-your-bait-rubber-bullets.

307   "*Perhaps F&G needs*": Akres, Alaska Hunting Forums, March 3, 2010, http:// forums.outdoorsdirectory.com/showthread.php/74402-How-d-you-like -to-snare-black-and-grizzly-bears/page3.

308   "*Permitting the baiting and snaring*": Dave Klein, "Bear Snaring Defies Our Values: Management Should Be Based on Respect for the Bruin's Role," FDNM, February 26, 2012.

309   *When the board approved*: Alaska Professional Hunters Association, "Board of Game News," Bare Facts (Spring 2006): 3.

309   "*Predator control leads us*": Karl Braendel, "'Predator Control' Demeans Us All," ADN, February 4, 2012.

309   *Board of Game member*: Teresa Sager Albaugh, Alaska Board of Game meeting, March 19, 2013.

THE STORY OF BEARS

312   *JJI was the official name*: "Godspeed Bruno: Brown Bear Meets Tragic End," Spiegel International online, June 26, 2006.

313   "*There's no room here*": "Fruitless Search for Wild Bear," Spiegel International online, June 15, 2006.

313   *Though Italy asked*: "Famous Stuffed Bear Goes on Display," Spiegel International online, March 26, 2008.

313   "*True wilderness, even in mountainous*": Matthew Rooney, "Bruno's Last Stand," June 30, 2006, Spiegel International online, December 3, 2010.

314   "*Wilderness is not a single*": Marilynne Robinson, The Death of Adam: Essays on Modern Thought (New York: Picador, 2005), 247.

315 "*The place where we are*": William Cronon, "The Trouble with Wilderness," in Uncommon Ground: Rethinking the Human Place in Nature, ed. William Cronon (New York: W. W. Norton, 1996), 81.

bibliography

ABBREVIATIONS

ADF&G	Alaska Department of Fish and Game
ADN	*Anchorage Daily News*
FDNM	*Fairbanks Daily News-Miner*
Int. Conf. Bear Res. Mgmt.	*International Conference on Bear Research and Management*
USFWS	US Fish and Wildlife Service
USGS	US Geological Survey

Adams, Layne G., Francis J. Singer, and Bruce Dale. "Caribou Calf Mortality in Denali National Park, Alaska." *Journal of Wildlife Management* 59, 3 (1995): 584–594.

ADF&G news release. March 16, 2004.

ADF&G Report. Western Association of Fish and Wildlife Agencies, 2013 Winter Meeting, Tucson, AZ. http://www.wafwa.org/documents/commissioners/Summary%20SOS%20Report%200113.pdf (accessed May 6, 2013).

"Alaska Auction and Raffle Permits, 2012–13." ADF&G Division of Wildlife Conservation. June 28, 2011.

Alaska Constitutional Convention minutes. December 14, 1955. http://www.law.alaska.gov/doclibrary/conconv/37.html.

"Alaska Population Projections 2010 to 2035." Alaska Department of Labor and Workforce Development. http://labor.alaska.gov/research/pop/popproj.htm (accessed September 24, 2012).

Alaska Professional Hunters Association. "Board of Game News." *Bare Facts* (Spring 2006): 1–12.

Alaska State Troopers, Department of Public Safety. Daily Dispatches, Case Number 09-60940, Kodiak. Posted March 29, 2010. http://dps.alaska.gov/PIO/dispatch/ (accessed May 27, 2010).

Albert, David M., R. Terry Bowyer, and Sterling D. Miller. "Effort and Success of Brown Bear Hunters in Alaska." *Wildlife Society Bulletin* 29, 2 (Summer 2001): 501–508.

"America's Durable Frontier." *Life*, April 6, 1959, 40.

Amstrup, Steven C. "Natural History." Transcription of presentation, San Diego, February 5, 2004. www.polarbearsinternationalorg/pbhc/Amstrup/transcript.htm (accessed June 18, 2005).

———. "Polar Bear, *Ursus maritimus.*" In *Wild Mammals of North America: Biology, Management, and Conservation,* ed. George Feldhamer, Bruce C. Thompson, and Joseph A. Chapman, 587–610. Baltimore: Johns Hopkins University Press, 2003.

———. "Polar Bears and Climate Change: Certainties, Uncertainties, and Hope in a Warming World." In *Gyrfalcons and Ptarmigan in a Changing World,* vol. 1, ed. R. T. Watson, T. J. Cade, M. Fuller, G. Hunt, and E. Potapov, 11–20. Boise, ID: Peregrine Fund, 2011.

Amstrup, Steven C., Eric T. DeWeaver, David C. Douglas, Bruce G. Marcot, George M. Durner, Cecilia M. Bitz, and David A. Bailey. "Greenhouse Gas Mitigation Can Reduce Sea-Ice Loss and Increase Polar Bear Persistence." *Nature* 468 (December 16, 2010): 955–958.

Amstrup, Steven C., Bruce Marcot, and David C. Douglas. "A Bayesian Network Modeling Approach to Forecasting the 21st Century Worldwide Status of Polar Bears." In *Arctic Sea Ice Decline: Observations, Projections, Mechanisms, and Implications,* Geophysical Monograph 180, ed. Eric T. DeWeaver, Ceclia M. Bitz, and L.-Bruno Tremblay, 213–268. Washington, DC: American Geophysical Union, 2008.

Amstrup, Steven C., Ian Stirling, Tom Smith, Craig Perham, and Gregory Thiemann. "Recent Observations of Intraspecific Predation and Cannibalism among Polar Bears in the Southern Beaufort Sea." *Polar Biology* 29, 11 (October 2006): 997–1002.

Anchorage Bear Committee. *Guidelines for Maintaining Bear Habitat while Reducing Bear-Human Conflicts in the Municipality of Anchorage and Chugach State Park.* June 2004.

Anderson, Ben. "Appeals Court Ruling Determines Polar Bears Will Retain 'Threatened' Listing." *Alaska Dispatch,* March 1, 2013.

———. "Rotting Whale Meat Lures Record 80 Polar Bears to Kaktovik." *Alaska Dispatch,* September 23, 2012.

Anderson, Kenneth. "Alaska: 'Big Land' of Contrasts." *Popular Mechanics,* November 1958.

Andrews, William. *England in the Days of Old.* London: William Andrews, 1897. Google eBook.

Annual Report to the Alaska Board of Game on Intensive Management for Moose with Wolf, Black Bear, and Brown Bear Predation Control in Game Management Unit (GMU) 16. ADF&G Division of Wildlife Conservation, February 2012.

Annual Report to the Alaska Board of Game on Intensive Management for Moose with Wolf, Black Bear, and Brown Bear Predation Control in GMU 16. ADF&G Division of Wildlife Conservation, February 2013.

Annual Report to the Alaska Board of Game on Intensive Management for Moose with Wolf, Black Bear, and Grizzly Predation Control in GMU 19A. ADF&G Division of Wildlife Conservation, February 2013.

"Arctic Sea Ice Shatters Previous Low Records; Antarctic Sea Ice Edge to Record High." Press release, National Snow and Ice Data Center, October 2, 2012. http://nsidc.org/news/press/20121002_MinimumPR.html (accessed October 21, 2012).

"Arctic Sea Ice Volume Anomaly, Version 2." Polar Science Center, University of Washington, October 2012.

Arno, Rod. Letter to the editor. ADN, September 23, 2009.

———. "Which Side Are You On?" Outdoor Alaska (Winter 2008): 3.

AR No. 2011-100. "A Resolution of the Anchorage Municipal Assembly to Foster Bear Awareness, Outdoor Safety Practices, Minimizing Bear Attractants Around Homes, Campsites, and Cabins, Building a Sense of Personal Responsibility and Stewardship for Our Bears and All Our Wildlife Resources." March 29, 2011.

Associated Press. "Bear Encounter Gives Swedish Exchange Student Tale to Take Home." ADN, May 19, 2004.

———. "Necropsy Yields No Clues about Why Bear Killed Alaska Couple." Seattle Post-Intelligencer, July 6, 2005.

Atamian, Sarkis. The Bears of Manley: Adventures of an Alaskan Trophy Hunter in Search of the Ultimate Symbol. Anchorage: Sarkis Atamian, 1995. Kindle edition.

Aumiller, Larry. "McNeil Bears Need Governor's Support." ADN, October 15, 2005.

———. Memorandum to Joe Meehan. "2004 McNeil River Field Report." December 20, 2004.

Aumiller, Larry, and Colleen Matt. "Management of McNeil River State Game Sanctuary for Viewing of Brown Bears." Int. Conf. Bear Res. Mgmt. 9 (1994): 51–61.

Austin, M. A., M. E. Obbard, and G. B. Kolensoky. "Evidence for a Black Bear, Ursus americanus, Killing an Adult Moose, Alces alces." Canadian Field-Naturalist 108, 2 (1994): 236–238.

Bacon, Ellis S., and Gordon M. Burghardt. "Learning and Color Discrimination in the American Black Bear." Int. Conf. Bear Res. Mgmt. 3 (1974): 27–36.

Bailey, Edgar P., and Nina H. Faust. "Distribution and Abundance of Marine Birds Breeding between Amber and Kamishak Bays, Alaska, with Notes on Interactions with Bears." Western Birds 15 (1984): 161–174.

Baldino, Megan. "Katmai Bear Hunt Debate Rages On." October 5, 2007. http://www.ktuu.com/Global/story.asp?S=7177267 (accessed October 12, 2007).

———. "Katmai Hunt and Story Surrounded by Controversy." October 8, 2007. http://www.ktuu.com/Global/story.asp?S=7186391 (accessed February 22, 2009).

———. "Sides Face off over Katmai Bear Hunt." October 5, 2007. http://www.ktuu.com/Global/story.asp?S=7177433 (accessed February 13, 2009).

———. "Troopers Say Cameras Didn't Interfere with Hunt." October 9, 2007. http://www.ktuu.com/Global/story.asp?S=7192100 (accessed February 13, 2009).

Ballard, Warren B. "Bear Predation on Moose: A Review of Recent North American Studies and Their Management Implications." *Alces* Supplement 1 (1992): 162–176.

Barber, Kim R., and Frederick G. Lindzey. "Breeding Behavior of Black Bears." *Int. Conf. Bear Res. Mgmt.* 6 (1987): 129–136.

Barber, Victoria. "Warming Permafrost Threatens Arctic Ice Cellars." *Arctic Sounder*, June 9, 2010.

Barnes, Victor G., Jr. "Brown Bear–Human Interactions Associated with Deer Hunting on Kodiak Island." *Int. Conf. Bear Res. Mgmt.* 9, 1 (1994): 63–73.

Barringer, Felicity. "Bears' Taste for Chicken Sets up Collision Course." *New York Times*, July 6, 2012.

Barten, Neil. Memorandum to Maria Gladziszewski, January 24, 2003.

———. "Unit 1C Black Bear Management Report." In *Black Bear Management Report of Survey and Inventory Activities, 1 July 2004–30 June 2007*, ed. Patricia Harper, 30–47. Juneau: ADF&G Division of Wildlife Conservation, 2008.

Baruch-Mordo, S., S. W. Breck, K. R. Wilson, and J. Broderick. "The Carrot or the Stick? Evaluation of Education and Enforcement as Management Tools for Human-Wildlife Conflicts." *PLoS ONE* 6, 1 (2011), e15681.

———. "Urban Black Bear Ecology: Fluctuating Synanthropy and Its Implications for Management." Poster presented at the 20th International Conference on Bear Research and Management, Ottawa, Canada, July 17–23, 2011.

Baskin, Leonid. "Bear Behaviors Potentially Contributing to the Fatal Mauling of Two Photographers." *International Bear News* 15, 2 (May 2006): 17–18.

Bass, Rick. *The Lost Grizzlies: A Search for Survivors in the Wilderness of Colorado*. New York: Houghton Mifflin, 1995.

Batin, Christopher. "Cub Killer: Hunting down a Bear Who Slays His Own." *Outdoor Life*, April 2002.

———. "Where Giants Walk." *Outdoor Life*, March 1999.

"Bear Control Program Approved on Middle Kuskokwim River." News release, ADF&G, March 5, 2012.

"Bear Fatally Mauls Hiker." *Whitehorse Daily Star*, July 8, 1996.

"Bear Fight! Grizzlies Are Creeping into Polar Bears' Canadian Turf." *Discover* magazine online, 80beats blog, February 25, 2010.

Bear-Human Conflict Management Plan. Rev. Wildlife Team, Center for Resources, Science and Learning, Denali National Park and Preserve, June 2003.

Beckmann, Jon P. "Bears Will Be Bears: Conserving Black Bears by Altering Human Behavior." *Wildlife Professional* (Winter 2009): 50–52.

Beckmann, Jon P., and Joel Berger. "Rapid Ecological and Behavioural Changes in Carnivores: The Responses of Black Bears (*Ursus americanus*) to Altered Food." *Journal of Zoology London* 261 (October 2003): 207–212.

———. "Using Black Bears to Test Ideal-Free Distribution Models Experimentally." *Journal of Mammalogy* 84, 2 (2003): 594–606.

Beckmann, Jon P., Lesley Karasin, Cecily Costello, Sean Matthews, and Zoë Smith. *Co-existing with Bears: Perspectives from Four Case Studies across North America*. Working Paper No. 33. Bozeman, MT: Wildlife Conservation Society, March 2008.

Beckmann, Jon P., and Carl W. Lackey. "Carnivores, Urban Landscapes, and Longitudinal Studies: A Case History of Black Bears." *Human-Wildlife Conflicts* 2, 2 (Fall 2008): 168–174.

Beckmann, Jon P., Carl W. Lackey, and Joel Berger. "Evaluation of Deterrent Techniques and Dogs to Alter Behavior of 'Nuisance' Black Bears." *Wildlife Society Bulletin* 32, 4 (2004): 1141–1146.

Bekoff, Marc. *Animal Passions and Beastly Virtues: Reflections on Redecorating Nature*. Philadelphia: Temple University Press, 2006.

Bell, Tom. "The Primal Fear: If We Are Much More Likely to Be Killed by a Car, Why Are We So Terrified of Bears?" *ADN*, July 14, 1995.

Bellemain, Eva, Jon E. Swenson, and Pierre Taberlet. "Mating Strategies in Relation to Sexually Selected Infanticide in a Non-Social Carnivore: The Brown Bear." *Ethology* 112, 3 (2006): 238–246.

Bellemain, Eva, Andreas Zedrosser, Stéphanie Manel, Lisette P. Waits, Pierre Taberlet, and Jon E. Swenson. "The Dilemma of Female Mate Selection in the Brown Bear, a Species with Sexually Selected Infanticide." *Proceedings of the Royal Society B* 273, 1584 (2006): 283–291.

Ben-David, Merav, Kimberly Titus, and LaVern R. Beier. "Consumption of Salmon by Alaskan Brown Bears: A Trade-off between Nutritional Requirements and the Risk of Infanticide?" *Oecologia* 138 (February 2004): 465–474.

Bergen, Scott, George M. Durner, David C. Douglas, and Steven C. Amstrup. *Predicting Movements of Female Polar Bears between Summer Sea Ice Foraging Habitats and Terrestrial Denning Habitats of Alaska in the 21st Century: Proposed Methodology and Pilot Assessment*. Reston, VA: USGS, 2007.

Berger, Joel, Peter B. Stacey, Lori Bellis, and Matthew P. Johnson. "A Mammalian Predator-Prey Imbalance: Grizzly Bear and Wolf Extinction Affect Avian Neotropical Migrants." *Ecological Applications* 11, 4 (August 2001): 947–960.

Berns, Vernon D., Gerry C. Atwell, and Daniel L. Boone. "Brown Bear Movements and Habitat Use at Karluk Lake, Kodiak Island." *Int. Conf. Bear Res. Mgmt.* 4 (1980): 293–296.

Bertram, Mark R., and Michael T. Vivion. "Black Bear Monitoring in Eastern Interior Alaska." *Ursus* 13 (2002): 69–77.

Best Practices for Viewing Bears on the West Side of Cook Inlet and the Katmai Coast. ADF&G and National Park Service, 2003.

Bewick, Thomas. *A General History of the Quadrupeds*. 3rd ed. Newcastle: Hodgson, Beilby, & Bewick, 1792. Google eBook.

Biel, Alice Wondrak. *Do (Not) Feed the Bears*. Lawrence: University Press of Kansas, 2006.

Big Game Investigations, Bear Studies (Polar Bear), January 1, 1968–December 1, 1968.

Federal Aid in Wildlife Restoration, Work Plan Segment Report, W-15-R-3 and W-17-1, 1969.

Biro, Peter A., and Judy A. Stamps. "Are Animal Personality Traits Linked to Life-History Productivity?" *Trends in Ecology and Evolution* 23, 7 (July 2008): 361–368.

Black, Lydia. "Bear in Human Imagination and in Ritual." *Ursus* 10 (1995): 343–347.

Bledsoe, Thomas. *Brown Bear Summer: Life among Alaska's Giants.* New York: E. P. Dutton, 1987.

Blodgett, Jean. *The Coming and Going of the Shaman: Eskimo Shamanism and Art.* Winnipeg: Winnipeg Art Gallery, 1978.

Board of Game Bear Conservation, Harvest, and Management Policy. Findings of the Alaska Board of Game, 2012-198-BOG. Expiration date June 30, 2016.

Boertje, Rodney D., William C. Gasaway, Daniel V. Grangaard, and David G. Kellyhouse. "Predation on Moose and Caribou by Radio-Collared Grizzly Bears in East Central Alaska (USA)." *Canadian Journal of Zoology* 66, 11 (1988): 2492–2499.

Boertje, Rodney D., Mark A. Keech, and Thomas F. Paragi. "Science and Values Influencing Predator Control for Alaska Moose Management." *Journal of Wildlife Management* 74, 5 (2010): 917–928.

Bon, Céline, Véronique Berthonaud, Philippe Fosse, Bernard Gély, Frédéric Maksud, Renaud Vitalis, Michel Philippe, Johannes van der Plicht, and Jean-Marc Elalouf. "Low Regional Diversity of Late Cave Bears Mitochondrial DNA at the Time of Chauvet Aurignacian Paintings." *Journal of Archaeological Science* 38, 8 (2011): 1886–1895.

Boone, William R., M. Elaine Richardson, and Jennifer A. Greer. "Breeding Behavior of the American Black Bear *Ursus americanus*." *Theriogenology* 60, 2 (July 2003): 289–297.

Boots, Michelle Theriault. "Bear Mauling Victim Believed 'This Is the End.'" ADN, May 15, 2012.

———. "Grizzly Sow Attacks Woman on Eagle River Trail." ADN, June 16, 2012.

———. "Owners of Urban Chickens Battle Predators." ADN, July 8, 2012.

Brackenridge, Henry Marie. *Journal of a Voyage up the Missouri River, in 1811.* Pittsburgh: Cramer, Spear & Eichbaum, 1814. http://user.xmission.com/~drudy/mtman/html/Brackenridge/Brackenridge.html.

Braendel, Karl. "'Predator Control' Demeans Us All." ADN, February 4, 2012.

Bragg, Beth. "Eagle River Trail Would Be Bear Road, Biologist Warns." ADN, July 18, 2008.

"Breaking the Ice about Sassats." *The Science and the Environment Bulletin*, March/April 2000. Environment Canada online. www.ec.gc.ca/science/sandemaroo/article1_e.html (accessed June 18, 2007).

Breining, Greg. "The Secret Lives of Bears." *Minnesota* (Fall 2012): 18–23.

Brewster, Karen, ed. *The Whales, They Give Themselves: Conversations with Harry Brower, Sr.* Fairbanks: University of Alaska Press, 2004.

Brinkley, Douglas. *The Wilderness Warrior: Theodore Roosevelt and the Crusade for America*. New York: Harper Perennial, 2010.

Broadbent, Noel D., Jan Storå, Britta Wennstedt Edvinger, and Katherine Rusk. "Ritual Sites." In *The Search for a Past: The Prehistory of the Indigenous Saami in Northern Coastal Sweden*. Arctic Studies Center, National Museum of Natural History, Smithsonian Institution, 2004. http://www.mnh.si.edu/arctic/features/saami/ritualsites.html (accessed June 18, 2007).

Broder, John M. "Obama to Open Offshore Areas to Oil Drilling for First Time." *New York Times*, March 31, 2010.

Brooks River Visitor Access Final Environmental Impact Statement, Katmai National Park and Preserve. Anchorage: National Park Service, January 2013.

Brower, Ronald, Sr. "Cultural Uses of Alaska Marine Mammals." Paper presented at the 29th Alaska Science Conference, Fairbanks, August 1978. http://www.Alaskool.Org/Projects/Traditionalife/Brower/Brower-Pt1.Htm (accessed September 6, 2008).

Brown, Caroline L. *Customary and Traditional Use Worksheet, Brown Bear, Game Management Units 20A, 20B, and 20C*. Special Publication BOG 2012–02. Fairbanks: ADF&G Division of Subsistence, 2012.

Brown, Molly. "Brown Bear Kills, Feeds on Ketchikan Man, State Says." ADN, July 18, 2000.

"Brown Bear Control Program Approved." News release 11-17, ADF&G, March 11, 2011.

Bryson, George. "Is 'Rogue Grizzly' on the Loose? Not Likely." ADN, July 3, 2008.
———. "The Final Days of Michio Hoshino." *We Alaskans* magazine, ADN, October 13, 1996.

Buchanan, Minor Ferris. *Holt Collier: His Life, His Roosevelt Hunts, and the Origin of the Teddy Bear*. Jackson: Centennial Press of Mississippi, 2002.

Buckner, Eldon L. ("Buck"), Jack Reneau, and Ryan Hatfield, eds. *Boone and Crockett Club's 26th Big Game Awards, 2004–2006*. Missoula, MT: Boone and Crockett Club, 2007.

Bunnell, Fred L. "Rapporteur's Report." In *Bear-People Conflicts: Proceedings of a Symposium on Management Strategies, April 6–10, 1987*, ed. Marianne Bromley. Yellowknife: Northwest Territories Department of Natural Resources, 1989.

Burke, Jill. "Are Backyard Chickens Too Dangerous for Urban Bear Country?" *Alaska Dispatch*, October 25, 2012.

Burke, Jill, and Tony Hopfinger. "Arctic Ocean vs. ANWR: A Hard-Earned Quest to Drill in the Icy Abyss." *Alaska Dispatch*, September 26, 2012.

Burkhead, Lynn. "ESPN2 TV: Lucky 13 Alaskan Brown Bear." *ESPN Outdoors* online, September 24, 2004. http://espn.go.com/outdoors/tv/s/g_fea_ESPN2_Wildlife-Qest_040924.html (accessed July 25, 2005).

Burroughs, John. *The Writings of John Burroughs: Far and Near*, vol. 13. Boston: Houghton, Mifflin, 1904. Google eBook.

Burroughs, John, and John Muir. *Alaska: The Harriman Expedition, 1899.* Reprint. New York: Dover Publications, 1986.

Burroughs, Raymond Darwin, ed. *The Natural History of the Lewis and Clark Expedition.* 2nd ed. East Lansing: Michigan State University Press, 1995.

Burstein, Mara. Letter to the editor. *ADN,* July 2, 2004.

Butcher, Gregory S., and Daniel K. Niven. "Combining Data from the Christmas Bird Count and the Breeding Bird Survey to Determine the Continental Status and Trends of North America Birds." National Audubon Society, June 14, 2007. http://stateofthebirds.audubon.org/cbid/content/Report.pdf.

Butler, David R. "Human-Induced Changes in Animal Populations and Distributions, and the Subsequent Effects on Fluvial Systems." *Geomorphology* 79 (2006): 448–459.

Butler, Lem. "Game Management Unit 9, Alaska Peninsula." In *Region II Briefing Book,* 25–31. ADF&G Division of Wildlife Conservation, February 2009.

———. "Unit 9 Brown Bear." In *Brown Bear Management Report of Survey and Inventory Activities 1 July 2004–30 June 2006,* ed. Patricia Harper, 109–120. Juneau: ADF&G, 2007.

Campbell, Bruce H. "Activities of Brown Bears on the Copper River Delta, Alaska and Their Impact on Nesting Dusky Canada Geese." *Northwestern Naturalist* 72 (Winter 1991): 92–99.

Campbell, J. Michael. "The Effect of Education in Reducing Bear Attractants on Cottage Properties: Manitoba's 'Bear Smart' Program." *Forest Policy and Economics* 19 (2012): 56–65.

Campbell, Mike. "Risking a Run-in?" *ADN,* September 22, 2009.

Carlson, Stephanie M., Ray Hilborn, Andrew P. Hendry, and Thomas P. Quinn. "Predation by Bears Drives Senescence in Natural Populations of Salmon." *PLoS ONE* 2, 12 (2007): e1286.

Carroll, Tony. "Glacier Bear Shot in Thunder Mountain Park." *Juneau Empire,* July 17, 2003.

Cartmill, Matt. *A View to Death in the Morning: Hunting and Nature through History.* Cambridge, MA: Harvard University Press, 1996.

Catton, Theodore. *Inhabited Wilderness: Indians, Eskimos and National Parks in Alaska.* Albuquerque: University of New Mexico Press, 1997.

Celizic, Mike. "Teen Who Survived Bear Attack: 'Mostly It Was Scared.'" *Today Show,* MSNBC, October 20, 2008. http://www.today.com/id/27276527/site/today show/ns/today-today_news/t/teen-who-survived-bear-attack-mostly-it-was -scared/#.UPXinYnjmkI (accessed November 20, 2012).

Chaney, Rob. "Bear Conflicts a Continentwide Challenge." *Missoulian,* March 21, 2012.

Chowder, Ken. "North to Alaska." *Smithsonian,* June 2003.

Christie, Katie S., and Thomas E. Reimchen. "Presence of Salmon Increases Passerine Density on Pacific Northwest Streams." *Auk* 125, 1 (2008): 51–59.

Chugach State Park Trail Management Plan. Public Review Draft, Issue Response Summary. Alaska Department of Natural Resources, August 2011.

City and Borough of Juneau. "An Ordinance Repealing and Reenacting the Urban Bear Ordinance." CBJ 03.30.0353 Ordinance 2004-11.

Claar, James, and Doug Zimmer. *Bear Spray Report.* Interagency Grizzly Bear Committee, June 2008.

Clark, Douglas A., and D. Scott Slocombe. "Respect for Grizzly Bears: An Aboriginal Approach for Co-existence and Resilience." *Ecology and Society* 14, 1 (2009): article 42. http://www.ecologyandsociety.org/vol14/iss1/art42/ (accessed October 7, 2011).

Clark, Marvin H., Jr. *Pinnell and Talifson: Last of the Great Brown Bear Men.* Spokane, WA: Great Northwest Publishing, 1980.

Clément, Gilles. "The Musculo-skeletal System in Space." *Fundamentals of Space Medicine* 23 (2011): 181–216.

Cockerham, Sean. "Murkowski Game Board Heavy on Hunting Advocates." *ADN,* January 18, 2003.

Colby, Merle. *A Guide to Alaska. Last American Frontier.* New York: J. J. Little & Ives, 1939. Google eBook.

———. *What Has Alaska to Offer Postwar Pioneers?* Office of War Information, August 1944. http://www.historians.org/projects/giroundtable/Alaska/Alaska_TOC (accessed May 17, 2010).

Colt, Steve, and Darcy Dugan. *Spending Patterns of Selected Alaska Bear Viewers: Preliminary Results from a Survey.* Institute of Social and Economic Research, University of Alaska–Anchorage, March 17, 2005.

Coltrane, Jessica. "Unit 14C." In *Brown Bear Management Report of Survey and Inventory Activities 1 July 2008–30 June 2010,* ed. Patricia Harper, 158–162. Juneau: ADF&G, 2011.

Committee on Management of Wolf and Bear Populations in Alaska, National Research Council. *Wolves, Bears, and Their Prey in Alaska: Biological and Social Challenges in Wildlife Management.* Washington, DC: National Academy Press, 1997.

Connolly, Kate. "Rejected at Birth, Knut Becomes Berlin Zoo's Bear Essential." *Guardian,* March 23, 2007.

Coppock, Mike. "The Cowboy Kings of Kodiak." October/November 2008, 57–61. www.Americancowboy.com.

Costello, Pat. "Garbage Problem Poses Risk to People, Bears." *Juneau Empire,* November 18, 2001.

Côté, Steeve D. "Extirpation of a Large Black Bear Population by Introduced White-Tailed Deer." *Conservation Biology* 19, 5 (October 2005): 1668–1671.

Coues, Elliott, ed. *History of the Expedition under the Command of Lewis and Clark,* vol. 1. Mineola, NY: Dover Publications, 1979. Google eBook.

Coyne, Amanda. "Season of Snaring Bears Starts." *Alaska Dispatch,* June 3, 2009.

Craighead, John J., Jay S. Sumner, and John A. Mitchell. *The Grizzly Bears of Yellowstone: Their Ecology in the Yellowstone Ecosystem, 1959–1992*. Washington, DC: Island Press, 1995.

Crane, Ralph. "Alaska: The Hard Country." *Life*, October 1, 1965, 64–88.

Creel, Eileen M. "Effectiveness of Deterrents on Black Bear (*Ursus americanus*) to Anthropogenic Attractants in Urban-Wildland Interfaces." M.S. thesis, Humboldt State University, 2007.

Cronon, William. "The Trouble with Wilderness; or, Getting Back to the Wrong Nature." In *Uncommon Ground: Rethinking the Human Place in Nature*, ed. William Cronon, 69–90. New York: W. W. Norton, 1996.

Crupi, Anthony P., Jr. "Foraging Behavior and Habitat Use Patterns of Brown Bears (*Ursus arctos*) in Relation to Human Activity and Salmon Abundance on a Coastal Alaskan Salmon Stream." M.S. thesis, Utah State University, 2003.

Cummins, James L. "New Refuge in Mississippi Protects Birthplace of Fair Chase." Boone and Crockett Club, October 24, 2008. http://www.boone-crockett.org/news/featured_story.asp?area=news&ID=31.

Cunningham, Tom. Letter to the editor. *Juneau Empire*, June 29, 2001.

Curley, James. "Secrets of an Alaskan Master Guide." http://www.biggamehuntingvideos.com (accessed January 7, 2010).

Curwen, Thomas, and David Petersen. "The Nature of the Beast." *Los Angeles Times*, August 2, 2005.

Czetwertynski, Sophie M., Mark S. Boyce, and Fiona K. Schmiegelow. "Effects of Hunting on Demographic Parameters of American Black Bears." *Ursus* 18, 1 (2007): 1–18.

Dahle, Bjørn, and Jon E. Swenson. "Seasonal Range Size in Relation to Reproductive Strategies in Brown Bears *Ursus arctos*." *Journal of Animal Ecology* 72 (2003): 660–667.

Dall, William H. "First Lessons in Natural History." In *The Harriman Alaska Expedition: Chronicles and Souvenirs May to August 1899*. W. Averell Harriman Papers, American Memory Digital Collections, Library of Congress. http://memory.loc.gov/mss/amrvm/vmh/vmh.html.

Davids, Richard C. *Lords of the Arctic: A Journey among the Polar Bears*. New York: Macmillan, 1982.

Davidson, Dan. "Bear Mauling in Tent City." *Klondike Sun*, July 23, 1999.

Davison, John, Simon Y. W. Ho, Sarah C. Bray, Marju Korsten, Egle Tammeleht, Maris Hindrikson, Kjartan Østbye, Eivind Østbye, Stein-Erik Lauritzen, Jeremy Austin, Alan Cooper, and Urmas Saarma. "Late-Quaternary Biogeographic Scenarios for the Brown Bear (*Ursus arctos*), a Wild Mammal Model Species." *Quaternary Science Reviews* 30 (2011): 418–430.

Dean, Frederick C. *A Land Use Philosophy Proposal for Bear Management*. Fairbanks: Department of Wildlife and Fisheries and Alaska Cooperative Park Studies Unit, University of Alaska, 1975.

———. *Brown Bear–Human Interrelationship Study.* NPS PO 126–301, unpublished report. National Park Service, 1968.

Dean, Frederick C., Rick McIntyre, and Richard A. Sellers. "Additional Mixed-Age Brown Bear, *Ursus arctos*, Associations in Alaska." *Canadian Field-Naturalist* 106, 2 (1992): 257–259.

DeBruyn, Terry D. *A Review of Bear-Human Interactions over Time and the Overall Implications to Management of the Brooks River Area, Katmai National Park and Preserve.* Technical Report NPS/KAT/99–004. National Park Service, 1999.

———. *Walking with Bears: One Man's Relationship with Three Generations of Wild Bears.* Guilford, CT: Globe Pequot Press, 1999.

DeBruyn, Terry D., Thomas J. Evans, Charles Hamilton, Susanne Miller, Craig J. Perham, Christopher Putnam, Eric Regehr, Karyn Rode, Michelle St. Martin, and James Wilder. *Summary of Polar Bear Management 2009/2010.* Report to the Canadian Polar Bear Technical Committee, Winnipeg, Manitoba, Canada. Anchorage: USFWS Marine Mammals Management, 2011.

DeBruyn, Terry D., and Tom S. Smith. "Managing Bear-Viewing to Minimize Human Impacts on the Species in Alaska." In *Ecotourism and Environmental Sustainability: Principles and Practices,* ed. Jennifer Hill and Tim Gale, 109–124. Burlington, VT: Ashgate Publishing, 2009.

DeBruyn, Terry D., Tom S. Smith, Kelly Proffitt, Steve Partridge, and Thomas D. Drummer. "Brown Bear Response to Elevated Viewing Structures at Brooks River, Alaska." *Wildlife Society Bulletin* 32, 4 (2004): 1132–1140.

Deecke, Volker B. "Tool-Use in the Brown Bear (*Ursus arctos*)."*Animal Cognition* 15, 4 (July 2012): 725–730.

DeGayner, Eugene J., Marc G. Kramer, Joseph G. Doerr, and Margaret J. Robertsen. "Windstorm Disturbance Effects on Forest Structure and Black Bear Dens in Southeast Alaska." *Ecological Applications* 15, 4 (August 2005): 1306–1316.

DeHart, Don. *All about Bears.* Boulder, CO: Johnson Publishing, 1971.

deMarban, Alex. "Board of Game Kills Hunt for McNeil Area Bears." ADN, March 7, 2007.

———. "Life and Values Twine in Native Priest's Stories." ADN, October 24, 2006.

Demer, Lisa. "Big Bruin Chases Hiker up a Tree on Bird Creek Trail." ADN, June 11, 2012.

———. "Victim Startled Sow with Cubs." ADN, July 23, 2012.

Derocher, Andrew. *Polar Bears: A Complete Guide to Their Biology and Behavior.* Baltimore: Johns Hopkins University Press, 2012.

Derocher, Andrew, Nicholas J. Lunn, and Ian Stirling. "Polar Bears in a Warming Climate." *Integrative and Comparative Biology* 44 (2004): 163–176.

De Veer, Gerrit. *The Three Voyages of William Barents,* ed. Charles T. Beke. London: Hakluyt Society, 1853. Google eBook.

Dingemanse, Niels J., and Denis Réale. "Natural Selection and Animal Personality." *Behaviour* 142, 9–10 (2005): 1159–1184.

Ditmer, Mark A., Karen V. Noyce, Timothy G. Laske, and Paul A. Iaizzo. "Creating a Metabolic Map to Assess Potential for Range Expansion of American Black Bears." *International Bear News* 21, 4 (November 2012): 28–30.

"DNA Testing Confirms Hybrid Bear Shot Near Ulukhaktok." News release, government of the Northwest Territories, April 3, 2010.

Doak, Daniel F., and Michael G. Loso. "Effects of Grizzly Bear Digging on Alpine Plant Community Structure." *Arctic, Antarctic, and Alpine Research* 35, 4 (2003): 421–428.

Dodge, Harry B., III. *Kodiak Island and Its Bears: A History of Bear/Human Interactions on Alaska's Kodiak Archipelago.* Anchorage: Great Northwest Publishing, 2004.

"Dog Bites and Human Deaths from Dog Attack in Alaska: A Public Health Tragedy." *State of Alaska Epidemiology Bulletin*, April 17, 1981.

D'Oro, Rachel. "Judge Halts 'Bounty' on Wolves." *Seattle Times*, March 31, 2007.

Doyle, Alister. "Polar Bear Makes Huge 74 km One-Day Arctic Swim." Reuters, August 12, 2005.

"Drunk Bears Looking for a Fight." *Croatian Times*, November 14, 2008.

Dubord, Allen. "Proposal 73." In *Alaska Board of Game Spring 2004 Proposal Book*, 59–60. Juneau: ADF&G Boards Support Section, 2004.

Duncan, Rachel, ed. *Polar Expeditions.* 4th ed. London: Royal Geographical Society, 2003.

Durner, George M., and Steven C. Amstrup. "Movements of a Polar Bear from Northern Alaska to Northern Greenland." *Arctic* 48, 4 (December 1995): 338–341.

Durner, George M., John P. Whiteman, Henry J. Harlow, Steven C. Amstrup, Eric V. Regehr, and Merav Ben-David. "Consequences of Long-Distance Swimming and Travel over Deep-Water Pack Ice for a Female Polar Bear during a Year of Extreme Sea Ice Retreat." *Polar Biology* 34, 7 (July 2011): 975–984.

Dutton, Karla, Susanne Miller, and Terry DeBruyn, eds. *Polar Bear Diversionary Feeding Workshop Report, June 8–9, 2011.* Anchorage: USFWS and Defenders of Wildlife, February 29, 2012.

Dykstra, Peter. "Magic Number: A Sketchy 'Fact' about Polar Bears Keeps Going . . . and Going . . . and Going." *SE Journal* (Summer 2008). http://www.sejarchive.org/pub/SEJournal_Excerpts_Su08.htm (accessed May 16, 2013).

Edwards, Mark A., Andrew E. Derocher, Keith A. Hobson, Marsha Branigan, and John A. Nagy. "Fast Carnivores and Slow Herbivores: Differential Foraging Strategies among Grizzly Bears in the Canadian Arctic." *Oecologia* 165, 4 (April 2011): 877–889.

Egbert, Allan L. "The Social Behavior of Brown Bears at McNeil River, Alaska." Ph.D. diss., Utah State University, 1978.

Egbert, Allan L., and Allen W. Stokes. "The Social Behaviour of Brown Bears on an Alaskan Salmon Stream." *Int. Conf. Bear Res. Mgmt.* 3 (1974): 41–56.

Eide, Sterling, and Sterling Miller. "Brown Bear." Revised by Larry Van Daele. In *Alaska Wildlife Notebook Series*. ADF&G, 2008. http://www.adfg.alaska.gov /static/education/wns/brown_bear.pdf (accessed May 16, 2013).

Elzinga, Caryl L., Daniel W. Salzer, and John W. Willoughby. *Measuring & Monitoring Plant Populations*. US Bureau of Land Management, 1998.

Erdbrink, Dirk Pieter. *A Review of Fossil and Recent Bears of the Old World*, vol. 1. Deventer, Netherlands: Jan de Lange, 1953.

"Experimental Foot-Snaring Program." News release, ADF&G, September 4, 2009.

Fagen, Robert, and Johanna Fagen. "Individual Distinctiveness in Brown Bears, Ursus arctos L." *Ethology* 102, 2 (1996): 212–226.

———. "Juvenile Survival and Benefits of Play Behaviour in Brown Bears, Ursus arctos." *Evolutionary Ecology Research* 6, 1 (2004): 89–102.

Fall, James A., and Lisa B. Hutchinson-Scarbrough. *Subsistence Uses of Brown Bears in Communities of Game Management Unit 9E, Alaska Peninsula, Southwest Alaska*. Technical Paper No. 235. Juneau: ADF&G Division of Subsistence, 1996.

Fall, James A., and Robert J. Wolfe. *Subsistence in Alaska: A Year 2010 Update*. Rev. ed. Anchorage: ADF&G Division of Subsistence, January 2012.

"Famous Stuffed Bear Goes on Display." *Spiegel International* online, March 26, 2008.

Farley, Sean, Herman Griese, Rick Sinnott, Jessica Coltrane, Chris Garner, and Dave Battle. *Brown Bear (Ursus arctos) Minimum Population Count, Habitat Use, Movement Corridors, and Food Resources across Fort Richardson Army Post, Elmendorf Air Force Base, Campbell Tract Area, and the Municipality of Anchorage, Alaska*. Department of the Army, October 2007.

Farmer, Mark. "We Still Haven't Solved the Bear Problem." *Juneau Empire*, July 30, 2001.

Farnsworth, Clyde H. "After Fatal Mauling in Canada: Too Many Bears?" *New York Times*, August 4, 1996.

Faro, James B. "Moose, Unit 16." In *Federal Aid in Wildlife Restoration Annual Report of Survey-Inventory Activities 1 July 1988–30 June 1989*, 165–170. Juneau: ADF&G Division of Wildlife Conservation, August 1990.

"Fatal Car Crashes and Road Traffic Accident Statistics for 2008." http://www .city-data.com/accidents/acc-Anchorage-Alaska.html (accessed January 14, 2013).

Faw, Michael D. "Media Ruin Alaskan Bear Hunt." January 9, 2008, updated October 21, 2009. http://www.NRAhuntersrights.org/Article.aspx?id=162 (accessed January 10, 2013).

Fay, Ginny, and Neal Christensen. *Katmai National Park and Preserve Economic Significance Analysis and Model Documentation*. Prepared for National Park Conservation Association and National Park Service, Katmai National Park and Preserve, 2010.

Feasibility Assessment for Intensive Management Program: Game Management Unit 24B. ADF&G Division of Wildlife Conservation, February 25, 2011.

Fienup-Riordan, Anne. *Boundaries and Passages: Rule and Ritual in Yup'ik Eskimo Oral Tradition.* Norman: University of Oklahoma Press, 1994.

Finding of No Significant Impact. Hunting Guide Concessions Environmental Assessment, Katmai National Preserve, Alaska. Anchorage: National Park Service, Alaska Region, September 2012.

Flanzraich, Annie. "Lake Tahoe Bear Season Down, but Maybe Not Out." *Sierra Sun,* September 9, 2009.

Flores, Dan. *The Natural West: Environmental History in the Great Plains.* Norman: University of Oklahoma Press/Red River Books, 2003.

Folta, Richard C. *Of Bench and Bears: Alaska's Bear Hunting Judge.* Anchorage: Great Northwest Publishing, 1986.

Fortin, Jennifer K., Sean D. Farley, Karyn D. Rode, and Charles R. Robbins. "Dietary and Spatial Overlap between Sympatric Ursids Relative to Salmon Use." *Ursus* 18, 1 (2007): 19–29.

Fowler, Joe. Technical Board of Investigation. Case Incident 03-109. National Park Service, convened November 20, 2003.

Francis and Ives v. United States. "Findings of Fact, Conclusions of Law, and Order." Case 2:08CV244 DAK. US District Court, District of Utah, Central Division, May 3, 2011. http://courtweb.pamd.uscourts.gov/courtwebsearch/utdc/FFSS 7TXIiH.pdf (accessed January 10, 2013).

Frey, Kevin, Sam Shepard, Kerry Gunther, Stephen Herrero, Chris Servheen, Dan Tyers, and Mark Bruscino. *Investigation Team Report: Attacks by a Grizzly Bear in Soda Butte Campground on the Gallatin National Forest on July 28, 2010.* August 13, 2010.

"Fruitless Search for Wild Bear." *Spiegel International* online, June 15, 2006.

"Future Retreat of Arctic Sea Ice Will Lower Polar Bear Populations and Limit Their Distribution." News release, USGS, September 7, 2007.

Gannon, Ella Foley, and Camarin E. B. Madigan. "Federal District Court Vacates Critical Habitat Designation for Polar Bears." *Bingham Legal Alerts,* January 24, 2013.

Garshelis, D. L., D. Crider, and F. van Manen. "*Ursus americanus.*" IUCN Red List of Threatened Species. Version 2012.2 (2008). http://www.iucnredlist.org /details/41687/0.

Garshelis, David L., and Hank Hristienko. "State and Provincial Estimates of American Black Bear Numbers versus Assessments of Population Trend." *Ursus* 17, 1 (2006): 1–7.

Gau, Robert J., Ray Case, David F. Penner, and Philip D. McLoughlin. "Feeding Patterns of Barren-Ground Grizzly Bears in the Central Canadian Arctic." *Arctic* 55, 4 (December 2002): 339–344.

Gay, Joel. "Chairman Uses Personal History as Guide." *ADN,* May 30, 2005.

———. "No One Budges at Wolf Debate." ADN, December 4, 2003.

Gebhard, James G. "Annual Activities and Behavior of a Grizzly Bear (Ursus arctos) Family in Northern Alaska." M.S. thesis, University of Alaska, 1982.

Geist, Valerius. "The North American Model of Wildlife Conservation: A Means of Creating Wealth and Protecting Public Health while Generating Biodiversity." In Gaining Ground: In Pursuit of Ecological Sustainability, ed. David M. Lavigne, 285–293. Guelph, ON: International Fund for Animal Welfare, 2006.

Geist, Valerius, Shane P. Mahoney, and John F. Organ. "Why Hunting Has Defined the North American Model of Wildlife Conservation." Transactions of the North American Wildlife and Natural Resources Conference 66 (2001): 175–185.

Gende, Scott M., Richard T. Edwards, Mary F. Willson, and Mark S. Wipfli. "Pacific Salmon in Aquatic and Terrestrial Ecosystems." BioScience 52, 10 (October 2002): 917–928.

Gende, Scott M., Thomas P. Quinn, Ray Hilborn, Andrew P. Hendry, and Bobette Dickerson. "Brown Bears Selectively Kill Salmon with Higher Energy Content but Only in Habitats That Facilitate Choice." Oikos 104, 3 (2004): 518–528.

Gende, Scott M., Thomas P. Quinn, and Mary F. Willson. "Consumption Choice by Bears Feeding on Salmon." Oecologia 127, 3 (2001): 372–382.

Gende, Scott M., Thomas P. Quinn, Mary F. Willson, Ron Heintz, and Thomas M. Scott. "Magnitude and Fate of Salmon-Derived Nutrients and Energy in a Coastal Stream Ecosystem." Journal of Freshwater Ecology 19, 1 (March 2004): 149–160.

Georgette, Susan. Brown Bears on the Northern Seward Peninsula, Alaska: Traditional Knowledge and Subsistence Uses in Deering and Shishmaref. Technical Paper No. 248. Juneau: ADF&G Division of Subsistence, March 2001.

———. "Left-Handed Bears: How Kuuvangmiit See the Grizzly." Alaska Fish & Game 26, 2 (November–December 1989): 8–10.

Gilbert, Barrie. "Emerging from the Dark Side: A Re-interpretation of Grizzly-Human Relationships Based on Current and Historical Evidence." Abstract, 14th International Congress on Bear Research and Management, Steinkjer, Norway, July 28–August 3, 2002.

———. "Opportunities for Social Learning in Bears." In Mammalian Social Learning: Comparative and Ecological Perspectives, ed. Hilary O. Box and Kathleen Rita Gibson, 225–235. Cambridge: Cambridge University Press, 1999.

Gill, Ian D., and James M. Helfield. "Alternative Foraging Strategies among Bears Fishing for Salmon: A Test of the Dominance Hypothesis." Canadian Journal of Zoology 90, 6 (June 2012): 766–775.

Gleason, Jeffrey S., and Karyn D. Rode. "Polar Bear Distribution and Habitat Association Reflect Long-Term Changes in Fall Sea Ice Conditions in the Alaskan Beaufort Sea." Arctic 62, 4 (December 2009): 405–417.

Gmelch, George. Resource Use in Glacier Bay National Preserve. US Department of the Interior, National Park Service, 1982.

"Godspeed Bruno: Brown Bear Meets Tragic End." *Spiegel International* online, June 26, 2006.

Goetzmann, William H., and Kay Sloan. *Looking Far North: The Harriman Expedition to Alaska, 1899.* Princeton, NJ: Princeton University Press, 1983.

Gomendio, Montserrat, and Eduardo R. S. Roldan. "Implications of Diversity in Sperm Size and Function for Sperm Competition and Fertility." *International Journal of Developmental Biology* 52, 5 (2008): 439–447.

Gore, Meredith L., Barbara Knuth, Paul Curtis, and James Shanahan. "Education Programs for Reducing American Black Bear–Human Conflict: Indicators of Success?" *Ursus* 17, 1 (2006): 75–80.

Gosling, Samuel D., and Oliver P. John. "Personality Dimensions in Nonhuman Animals: A Cross-Species Review." *Current Directions in Psychological Science* 8, 3 (June 1999): 69–75.

Gosling, Samuel D., and Simine Vazire. "Are We Barking up the Right Tree? Evaluating a Comparative Approach to Personality." *Journal of Research in Personality* 36, 6 (2002): 607–614.

"Governor Palin Introduces Bill to Streamline Predator Management Laws: HB 256/SN 176 Clarify, Clean up Statutes, Encourages Abundance-Based Management." News release 07-14, ADF&G, May 11, 2007.

Grass, Jonathan. "Woman Punches Bear to Save Her Dog." *Juneau Empire,* August 30, 2011.

Griffin, Donald R. *The Question of Animal Awareness: Evolutionary Continuity of Mental Experiences.* Rev. ed. New York: Rockefeller University Press, 1981.

Griffin, Thomas, and Edward W. Weiss. *McNeil River State Game Sanctuary Annual Management Report.* Special Areas Management Report. ADF&G Division of Wildlife Conservation, 2010, 2011, 2012.

"Grizzly Attacks Woman on Admiralty Island." *Juneau Empire,* August 10, 2008.

"Grizzly Bear Recovery." USFWS Endangered Species. http://www.fws.gov /mountain-prairie/species/mammals/grizzly/ (accessed January 14, 2013).

"Grizzly Bears (*Ursus arctos*)." In *Alaska's North Slope Oilfields,* 1–3. Technical Brief, BP Exploration, June 2001.

"Groups Seek Shorter Grizzly Hunting Season." *Wildlife Policy News* 17, 5 (October 2007): 6.

Grove, Casey. "San Diego Man Dies in Denali Grizzly Attack." *ADN,* August 25, 2012.

Hallowell, A. Irving. "Bear Ceremonialism in the Northern Hemisphere." *American Anthropologist* 28, 1 (January–March 1926): 1–175.

Halpin, James. "Hunters Organize to Help State Kill off Bears." *ADN,* March 11, 2008.

Hamilton, Jim. Statement by Jim Hamilton on Katmai bear hunts. http://www .ktuu.com/Global/story.asp?S=7176905 (accessed February 13, 2009).

Harlow, Henry J. "Climate Change Influence on Hibernation Patterns of Bears."

Video presentation at Questioning Greater Yellowstone's Future: Climate, Land Use, and Invasive Species, the 10th Biennial Scientific Conference on the Greater Yellowstone Ecosystem, Yellowstone National Park, Wyoming, October 11–13, 2010. http://vimeo.com/30752553.

Harlow, Henry J., Tom Lohuis, R. C. Anderson-Sprecher, and Thomas D. I. Beck. "Body Surface Temperature of Hibernating Black Bears May Be Related to Periodic Muscle Activity." *Journal of Mammalogy* 85, 3 (June 2004): 414–419.

Harlow, Henry J., Tom Lohuis, Thomas D. I. Beck, and Paul A. Iaizzo. "Muscle Strength in Overwintering Bears." *Nature* 409 (February 22, 2001): 997.

The Harriman Alaska Expedition: Chronicles and Souvenirs May to August 1899. W. Averell Harriman Papers, American Memory Digital Collections, Library of Congress. http://memory.loc.gov/mss/amrvm/vmh/vmh.html.

Hayden, Brian. *Shamans, Sorcerers, and Saints: A Prehistory of Religion.* Washington, DC: Smithsonian Books, 2003.

Hayes, Bob. *Wolves of the Yukon.* Bob Hayes, 2010. Kindle edition.

Hayes, Ernestine. *The Story of the Town Bear and the Forest Bear.* Juneau: Hazy Island Books, 2011.

Hechtel, John. "Activity and Food Habits of Barren-Ground Grizzly Bears in Arctic Alaska." M.S. thesis, University of Montana, 1985.

———. "Review of 'On Nature's Terms: Predators and People Co-existing in Harmony.'" *International Bear News* 14, 2 (May 2005): 40.

Heino, Margaret Ludwig. "American Black Bear Hibernating in Bald Eagle Nest." *International Bear News* 14, 1 (February 2005): 27.

Held, Suzanne D. E., and Marek Špinka. "Animal Play and Animal Welfare." *Animal Behaviour* 81 (2011): 891–899.

Helfield, James M., and Robert J. Naiman. "Salmon and Alder as Nitrogen Sources to Riparian Forests in a Boreal Alaskan Watershed." *Oecologia* 133 (2002): 573–582.

Helton, Kendall. "Memories from Alberta." *Bear Hunting Magazine*, January/February 2010. http://www.bear-hunting.com/issue_01_02_2010.cfm.

Herrero, Stephen. *Bear Attacks: Their Causes and Avoidance.* Rev. ed. Guilford, CT: Globe Pequot Press, 2002.

———. "Conflicts between Man and Grizzly Bears in the National Parks of North America." *Int. Conf. Bear Res. Mgmt.* 3 (1976): 121–145.

———. "Man and the Grizzly Bear (Present, Past, but Future?)." *BioScience* 20, 21 (November 1, 1970): 1148–1153.

Herrero, Stephen, and David Hamer. "Courtship and Copulation of a Pair of Grizzly Bears, with Comments on Reproductive Plasticity and Strategy." *Journal of Mammalogy* 58, 3 (August 1977): 441–444.

Herrero, Stephen, Andrew Higgins, James E. Cardoza, Laura I. Hajduk, and Tom S. Smith. "Fatal Attacks by American Black Bear on People: 1900–2009." *Journal of Wildlife Management* 75, 3 (2011): 596–603.

Herrero, Stephen, Tom Smith, Terry D. DeBruyn, Kerry Gunther, and Colleen A. Matt. "From the Field: Brown Bear Habituation to People—Safety, Risks, and Benefits." *Wildlife Society Bulletin* 33, 1 (2005): 362–373.

Herzog, Werner. *Cave of Forgotten Dreams*. Documentary. Creative Differences Productions, 2010.

Hessing, Pauline, and Larry Aumiller. "Observations of Conspecific Predation by Brown Bears." *Canadian Field-Naturalist* 108, 3 (1994): 332–336.

Hickock, Bryan. Comment on Rick Sinnott, "Educating Bears by Educating People." *Alaska Dispatch*, May 23, 2011. http://www.alaskadispatch.com/article/educating-bears-educating-people (accessed May 28, 2011).

Hilderbrand, Grant V., Sean D. Farley, Charles C. Schwartz, and Charles T. Robbins. "Importance of Salmon to Wildlife: Implications for Integrated Management." *Ursus* 15, 1 (2004): 1–9.

Hilderbrand, Grant V., Thomas A. Hanley, Charles T. Robbins, and Charles C. Schwartz. "Role of Brown Bears (*Ursus arctos*) in the Flow of Marine Nitrogen into a Terrestrial Ecosystem." *Oecologia* 121, 4 (1999): 546–550.

Hilderbrand, Grant V., Stacy G. Jenkins, Charles C. Schwartz, Thomas A. Hanley, and Charles T. Robbins. "Effect of Seasonal Differences in Dietary Meat Intake on Changes in Body Mass and Composition in Wild and Captive Brown Bears." *Canadian Journal of Zoology* 77, 10 (1999): 1623–1630.

Hilderbrand, Grant V., Charles C. Schwartz, Charles T. Robbins, and Thomas A. Hanley. "Effect of Hibernation and Reproductive Status on Body Mass and Condition of Coastal Brown Bears." *Journal of Wildlife Management* 64, 1 (2000): 178–183.

Hilderbrand, Grant V., Charles C. Schwartz, Charles T. Robbins, M. E. Jacoby, Thomas A. Hanley, S. M. Arthur, and Christopher Servheen. "The Importance of Meat, Particularly Salmon, to Body Size, Population Productivity, and Conservation of North American Brown Bears." *Canadian Journal of Zoology* 77, 1 (1999): 132–138.

Hirsch, Andrea. "Indianapolis Zoo Becomes Haven for Orphaned Bear Cubs." *Hendricks County Flyer*, September 5, 2008.

Histand, Ben. "A Heavy Yoke." *Anchorage Press*, August 17, 2011.

Hoagland, Edward. "Dogs and the Tug of Life." In *Heart's Desire: The Best of Edward Hoagland*. New York: Simon & Schuster, 1991.

Holland, Megan. "Bear Attacks Bicyclist on Anchorage Trail." *ADN*, June 15, 2010.

———. "Bear Encounters Create Dispute over Trail Status." *ADN*, June 16, 2010.

———. "Biologist Rick Sinnott Wounded in Drive-by in Anchorage." *ADN*, October 20, 2006.

———. "Biologist Shoots Grizzly in Eagle River," *ADN*, June 27, 2004.

———. "Mauling Victim Recounts Attack on City Trail." *ADN*, August 10, 2008.

———. "Neighborhood Awakes to Sound of Calf Killing." *ADN*, June 24, 2004.

———. "Woman Lost for Five Days Braved Bears, Lives on Snow." ADN, July 2, 2005.

Holzworth, John M. *The Wild Grizzlies of Alaska*. New York: G. P. Putnam's Sons, 1930.

Homstol, Lori. "Applications of Learning Theory to Human-Bear Conflict: The Efficacy of Aversive Conditioning and Conditioned Taste Aversion." M.S. thesis, University of Alberta, 2011.

Hopkins, Kyle. "Anchorage Bears Lose Frequent Confrontations." ADN, June 5, 2010.

———. "Game Board Allows Bear Snares," ADN, March 9, 2009 (modified March 10, 2009).

———. "Polar Bear Causes a Stir in Yukon Delta Village." ADN, July 22, 2010.

———. "Reality TV Invades Alaska." ADN, February 2, 2011.

Hornaday, William T. *Our Vanishing Wild Life: Its Extermination and Preservation*. New York: Charles Scribner's Sons, 1913. http://www.gutenberg.org/dirs /1/3/2/4/13249/13249-h/13249-h.htm.

Hoshino, Michio. *The Grizzly Bear Family Book*. New York: North-South Books, 1997.

Howard, Charles. Letter to the editor. ADN, August 6, 2005.

Howe, Eric J., Martyn E. Obbard, and Heather Smith. "Literature Review of Factors Affecting Nuisance Bear Activity." In *Nuisance Bear Review Committee Report and Recommendations*, appendix 9. Ontario: Minister of Natural Resources, August 28, 2003.

Howe, John. *Bear Man of Admiralty Island: A Biography of Allen E. Hasselborg*. Fairbanks: University of Alaska Press, 1996.

Hristienko, Hank, and John E. McDonald Jr. "Going into the 21st Century: A Perspective on Trends and Controversies in the Management of the American Black Bear." *Ursus* 18, 1 (2007): 72–88.

Hughes, J. Donald. "Europe as Consumer of Exotic Biodiversity: Greek and Roman Times." *Landscape Research* 28, 1 (2003): 21–31.

Hulen, David. "Grizzly Mauls Hiker Near Visitor Center." ADN, May 17, 1995.

———. "Polar Bear in Attack Young, Famished." ADN, December 3, 1993.

———. "Polar Bear Mauls Mechanic: Bloody Attack at North Slope Ends with Two Shotgun Blasts." ADN, December 2, 1993.

Hundertmark, Kris. "Message from President Kris Hundertmark." *Alaskan Wildlifer*, November 2011, 1–6.

Hunt, Carrie L. "Behavioral Responses of Bears to the Tests of Repellents, Deterrents, and Aversive Conditioning." M.S. thesis, University of Montana, 1984.

Hunting Guide Concessions Environmental Assessment, Public Review. Anchorage: National Park Service Alaska Region, June 2012.

Huntington, Henry, and Shari Fox. "Changing Arctic: Indigenous Perspectives."

In *Arctic Climate Impact Assessment*, 61–98. New York: Cambridge University Press, 2005.

Hutchison, Kristan. "Bear Shot in Tussle." *Juneau Empire*, September 5, 2000 (correction September 6, 2000).

Iaizzo, Paul A., and Timothy G. Laske. "The Heart of the Hibernating Bear: Medical Possibilities from Bear Den to Hospital Bed." Video presentation to Young Scientist Roundtable, Wayzata Public Schools, February 1, 2011. http://vimeo .com/29373040.

Iaizzo, Paul A., Timothy G. Laske, Henry J. Harlow, Carolyn B. McClay, and David L. Garshelis. "Wound Healing during Hibernation by Black Bears (*Ursus americanus*) in the Wild: Elicitation of Reduced Scar Formation." *Integrative Zoology* 7, 1 (2012): 48–60.

"Intensive Management Area Big Game Population Status." Department of Fish and Game–Wildlife Conservation, Office of Management and Budget, State of Alaska. http://omb.alaska.gov/html/performance/details.html?p=63 (accessed May 13, 2013).

"Intensive Management in Alaska: Alaska's Predator Control Programs." ADF&G Division of Wildlife Conservation. http://www.adfg.alaska.gov/index .cfm?adfg=intensivemanagement.programs (accessed May 13, 2013).

"Intensive Management Plan 6, Unit 16 Predation Control Area." Alaska Statutes 2012, Title 5 AAC 92.122.

Intensive Management Protocol. ADF&G Division of Wildlife Conservation, December 2011.

"Investigation Continues in Fatal Bear Attack." News release, Denali National Park and Preserve, National Park Service, August 29, 2012.

Ipsen, Beth. "Barrow Man Gets Five Years in Jail for Selling Polar Bear Hide." *Arctic Sounder*, November 30, 2006.

James, Carey. "Bear Battle Not over, Say Advocates." *Homer Tribune*, March 14, 2007.

Jamison, Michael. "Neurosurgeon: Griz Are Sniffing Champs of the Wild." *Missoulian*, July 29, 2007.

Janhunen, Juha. "Tracing the Bear Myth in Northeast Asia." *Acta Slavica Iaponica* 20 (2003): 1–24.

Jans, Nick. *The Grizzly Maze: Timothy Treadwell's Fatal Obsession with Alaskan Bears*. New York: Dutton, 2005.

Jay, Chadwick J., and Anthony S. Fischbach. "Pacific Walrus Response to Arctic Sea Ice Losses." USGS Fact Sheet 2008-3041.

Jefferson, Jake. "Written Comments Regarding BOG Proposals for March 2nd 2007 Meeting." RC 18, Alaska Board of Game spring 2007 meeting.

Johnson, Kathryn R. "Examining the Frequency and Characteristics of Human-Bear Conflicts in the Native Villages of the Kodiak Archipelago." M.S. thesis, University of Alaska Anchorage, 2008.

Johnson, Loyal, and Paul LeRoux. "Age of Self-Sufficiency in Brown/Grizzly Bear in Alaska." *Journal of Wildlife Management* 37, 1 (January 1973): 122–123.

Jones, Clive G., John H. Lawton, and Moshe Shachak. "Organisms as Ecosystem Engineers." *Oikos* 69, 3 (April 1994): 373–386.

Jonkel, Charles. "Idiots to Icons." *Bear News* 19, 3–4 (2004): 3.

The Journals of the Lewis and Clark Expedition. University of Nebraska Press/University of Nebraska–Lincoln Libraries Electronic Text Center. http://lewisandclark journals.unl.edu.

Juneau Police Department. "JPD Urban Bear Activity Summary." September 3–9, 2002.

Kalxdorff, Susanne B. *Collection of Local Knowledge Regarding Polar Bear Habitat Use in Alaska.* Technical Report MMM 97-2. Anchorage: USFWS Marine Mammals Management, August 1997.

Kaniut, Larry. "'Los Anchorage' Is Too Soft on Bears." *ADN*, April 19, 2009.

"Katmai Bear Data Reviewed." News release, Alaska National Parks, National Park Service, October 19, 2007.

"Katmai National Preserve Brown Bear Hunts." ADF&G Division of Wildlife Conservation. http://www.wc.adfg.state.ak.us/index.cfm?adfg=game.katmai (accessed November 6, 2007.

Keech, Mark A., Mark S. Lindberg, Rodney D. Boertje, Patrick Valkenburg, Brian D. Taras, Toby A. Boudreau, and Kimberlee B. Beckman. "Effect of Predator Treatments, Individual Traits, and Environment on Moose Survival in Alaska." *Journal of Wildlife Management* 75, 6 (2011): 1361–1380.

King, Brien T. "Alaska Holiday," *Alaska Sportsman*, May 1937.

———. "Alaska Holiday II." *Alaska Sportsman*, June 1937.

Kisling, Vernon N., ed. *Zoo and Aquarium History: Ancient Animal Collections to Zoological Gardens.* Boca Raton, FL: CRC Press, 2001.

Kitchener, A. C. "Taxonomic Issues in Bears: Impacts on Conservation in Zoos and the Wild, and Gaps in Current Knowledge." *International Zoo Yearbook* 44 (2010): 33–46.

Kives, Bartley. "Churchill Bears Doomed?" *Winnipeg Free Press*, June 7, 2010.

Kizzia, Tom. "Game Board: Famous McNeil River Bruins Are at Risk, Critics Say, as Panel Mulls Opening Adjacent Lands to Hunting." *ADN*, March 4, 2005.

———. "Permit-Winners Say They'll Spare the Bear." *ADN*, July 13, 1995.

———. "Victims of Bear Attack Were Wilderness Vets." *ADN*, June 28, 2005.

Klein, Dave. "Bear Snaring Defies Our Values: Management Should Be Based on Respect for the Bruin's Role." *FDNM*, February 26, 2012.

Kluger, Jeffrey. "A Big Win for Polar Bears?" *Time* magazine online, December 27, 2006.

Kochnev, Anatoly A., Vladimir M. Etylin, Vladilen I. Kavry, Evgeny B. Siv-Siv, and Ivan V. Tanko. *Traditional Knowledge of Chukotka Native Peoples Regarding Polar Bear Habitat Use.* Anchorage: National Park Service, July 2003.

Kollin, Susan. *Nature's State: Imagining Alaska as the Last Frontier*. Chapel Hill: University of North Carolina Press, 2001.

Koon, Daniel W. "Power of the Polar Myth." *New Scientist* 158, 2131 (April 25, 1998): 50.

Kovach, Adrienne I., and Roger A. Powell. "Effects of Body Size on Male Mating Tactics and Paternity in Black Bears, *Ursus americanus*." *Canadian Journal of Zoology* 81, 7 (2003): 1257–1268.

Kovach, Steven D., Gail H. Collins, Michael T. Hinkes, and Jeffrey W. Denton. "Reproduction and Survival of Brown Bears in Southwest Alaska, USA." *Ursus* 17, 1 (2006): 16–29.

Kurtén, Björn, and Elaine Anderson. *Pleistocene Mammals of North America*. New York: Columbia University Press, 1980.

Lamb, Jason. "Board of Game Turns down Proposal to Limit Non-Resident Hunters." KTUU-TV, February 1, 2010.

Larivière, Serge. "*Ursus americanus*." *Mammalian Species* 647 (2001): 1–11.

Larivière, Serge, and Steven H. Ferguson. "Evolution of Induced Ovulation in North American Carnivores." *Journal of Mammalogy* 84, 3 (2003): 937–947.

Laske, Timothy G., David L. Garshelis, and Paul A. Iaizzo. "Monitoring the Wild Black Bear's Reaction to Human and Environmental Stressors." *BMC Physiology* 11, 11 (2011): 1–14.

Lee, Jeannette J. "Grizzly to Grace Alaska Quarter." *Juneau Empire*, April 24, 2007.

Leung, Rebecca. "Not in My Backyard. . . ." *60 Minutes*, February 11, 2009. http://www.cbsnews.com/8301–18560_162–699622.html (accessed November 27, 2012).

Lewis, Larry. "X3W Wildlife Protection and Control Webcast." http://www.taser.com/videos/events/larry-lewis-video.

Lewis, Larry, Donald Dawes, Andrew Hinz, and Phil Mooney. "Tasers for Wildlife?" *Wildlife Professional* (Spring 2011): 44–46.

Libal, Nathan S., Jerrold L. Belant, Bruce D. Leopold, Guiming Wang, and Patricia A. Owen. "Despotism and Risk of Infanticide Influence Grizzly Bear Den-Site Selection." *PLoS ONE* 6, 9 (September 2011): e24133, 1–10.

"License Sale Statistics 2011 Calendar Year." State of Alaska Division of Administrative Services, License Accounting, February 10, 2012.

Limerick, Patricia Nelson. *The Legacy of Conquest: The Unbroken Past of the American West*. New York: W. W. Norton, 1988.

Linderman, Spencer. *Ground Tracking of Arctic Grizzly Bears*. Juneau: ADF&G Division of Game, 1974.

Lindqvist, Charlotte, Stephan C. Schuster, Yazhou Sun, Sandra L. Talbot, Ji Qi, Aakrosh Ratan, Lynn P. Tomsho, Lindsay Kasson, Eve Zeyl, Jon Aars, Webb Miller, Ólafur Ingólfsson, Lutz Bachmann, and Øystein Wiig. "Complete Mitochondrial Genome of a Pleistocene Jawbone Unveils the Origin of Polar Bear." *Proceedings of the National Academy of Sciences* 107 (2010): 5053–5057.

Linnell, John D. C., Jon E. Swenson, Reidar Andersen, and Brian Barnes. "How Vulnerable Are Denning Bears to Disturbance?" *Wildlife Society Bulletin* 28, 2 (2000): 400–413.

Livingston, John. *The John Livingston Reader*. Toronto: McClelland & Stewart, 2007.

Lloyd, Andrea H. "Ecological Histories from Alaskan Tree Lines Provide Insight into Future Changes." *Ecology* 86, 7 (July 2005): 1687–1695.

Loon, Hannah, and Susan Georgette. *Contemporary Brown Bear Use in Northwest Alaska*. Technical Paper No. 163. Juneau: ADF&G Division of Subsistence, 1989.

Lowenfels, Jeff. Letter to the editor. *ADN*, August 6, 2005.

Luczycki, Rebecca. "Last Chance." *Alaska*, February 2010, 32–35.

Luque, Michael. "Fishing Behavior of Alaska Brown Bear *Ursus arctos*." M.S. thesis, Utah State University, 1978.

MacDonald, Tim. "Polar Bears Are Back, Tired." *Arctic Sounder*, September 9, 2004.

Mallory, J. P., and D. Q. Adams, eds. *Encyclopedia of Indo-European Culture*. Chicago: Fitzroy Dearborn, 1997.

"Man Pleads for Help in 911 Call during Alaska Grizzly Mauling." *Alaska Dispatch*, September 25, 2012.

Management of Large Mammalian Carnivores in North America. Technical Review 12-01. Bethesda, MD: Wildlife Society, March 2012.

Managing Alaska's Wildlife. ADF&G Division of Wildlife Conservation, 2010.

Manning, Elizabeth. "Predators and Moose: Why Aren't Moose Calves Surviving?" *Alaska Fish & Wildlife News* online magazine, January 2007.

———. "Predators Face Another Hard Hit." *ADN*, March 15, 2003.

———. "Unexpected Results of Study Show Grizzlies Are Killing Moose Calves." *ADN*, June 24, 2001.

Markell, Joanna. "Bear Patrol Takes to Street." *Juneau Empire*, August 3, 2001.

———. "Bear Snubs Cheese Pinwheels for Bath." *Juneau Empire*, October 27, 2002.

———. "City Bear Committee Is Back." *Juneau Empire*, August 15, 2001.

———. "Garbage Law Limited by Privacy Concerns." *Juneau Empire*, August 5, 2002.

Marshall, H. D., and K. Ritland. "Genetic Diversity and Differentiation of Kermode Bear Populations." *Molecular Ecology* 11, 4 (2002): 685–697.

Massey, Ray. Letter to the *Oklahoma Sun*, July 31, 2006.

Matt, Colleen. Letter to Mayor Mark Begich, June 30, 2004.

———. *Summary of 3rd International Bear-People Conflicts Workshop*. Canmore, AB, November 15–17, 2009.

———. *Summary of 4th International Human-Bear Conflicts Workshop*. Missoula, MT, March 20–22, 2012.

Mattson, David J., Marilynn G. French, and Steven P. French. "Consumption of Earthworms by Yellowstone Grizzly Bears." *Ursus* 13 (2002): 105–110.

Mattson, David J., Katherine C. Kendall, and Daniel P. Reinhart. "Whitebark Pine,

Grizzly Bears, and Red Squirrels." In *Whitebark Pine Communities: Ecology and Restoration*, ed. Diana F. Tomback, Stephen F. Arno, and Robert E. Keane, 121–136. Washington, DC: Island Press, 2001.

Mauer, Richard. "Hunting Rights for Landowners Weighed." ADN, March 3, 2012.

Mazur, Rachel L. "Does Aversive Conditioning Reduce Human–Black Bear Conflict?" *Journal of Wildlife Management* 74, 1 (2010): 48–54.

McCarthy, Thomas M., and Roger Seavoy "Reducing Nonsport Losses Attributable to Food Conditioning: Human and Bear Behavior Modification in an Urban Environment." *Int. Conf. Bear Res. Mgmt.* 9, 1 (1994): 75–84.

McClannahan, Dave. Letter to the editor. ADN, August 6, 2005.

McHoes, David. "Proposal 94." In *Alaska Board of Game Spring 2011 Proposal Book (Regions II and IV)*, 117–119. ADF&G Boards Support Section, 2011.

———. "27 and Done." *Alaska Trapper Magazine*, n.d., 10–12.

McIntyre, Thomas. "The Last Bear." *American Hunter*, June 2003, 58–62.

McKinney, Cindy, Lauren Ris, Heather Rorer, and Sara Williams. "Investing in Wildlife: State Wildlife Funding Campaigns." M.S. project, University of Michigan, April 2005.

McLellan, Bruce N. "Implications of a High-Energy and Low-Protein Diet on the Body Composition, Fitness, and Competitive Abilities of Black (*Ursus americanus*) and Grizzly (*Ursus arctos*) Bears." *Canadian Journal of Zoology* 89, 6 (2011): 546–558.

———. "Sexually Selected Infanticide in Grizzly Bears: The Effects of Hunting on Cub Survival." *Ursus* 16, 2 (2005): 141–156.

McLellan, Bruce N., and Frederick W. Hovey. "Natal Dispersal of Grizzly Bears." *Canadian Journal of Zoology* 79, 5 (2001): 838–844.

McLellan, Bruce N., Chris Servheen, and Djuro Huber (IUCN SSC Bear Specialist Group). "*Ursus arctos*." IUCN Red List of Threatened Species, Version 2012.2 (2008). http://www.iucnredlist.org/details/41687/0.

McQueeney, Kerry. "'It Came so Close It Sniffed His Hoodie': Tourists Reveal the Terrifying Moment a Grizzly Bear Charged at Them. And They Didn't Even Flinch." *Daily Mail* online, February 28, 2012.

Medred, Craig. "Alaska Wildlife Conservation Director Charged with Helping Illegally Kill Bears." *Alaska Dispatch*, January 12, 2012.

———. "Alaska Wildlife Official Faces New Allegations of Illegal Hunting." *Alaska Dispatch*, January 12, 2012.

———. "Battling Bearanoia," ADN, July 12, 1992.

———. "Bear Behavior." ADN, May 30, 1993.

———. "Bear Savaging Swift, Deadly, Unique," ADN, February 10, 1998.

———. "Bears of Last Summer Will Be Back Shortly." ADN, January 29, 2009.

———. "Campfire Whopper Balloons to New Dimensions on the Web." ADN, November 5, 2006.

———. "Denali Park Bear Bites Backpacker." ADN, July 7, 1987.

———. "DNA Test IDs Grizzly in Mauling Jogger." ADN, October 23, 2008.

———. "Girdwood Hiker Battles, Races Bears." ADN, July 20, 2003.

———. "Hiker Scares off Three Bears." Associated Press version, Peninsula Clarion, June 2, 2003.

———. "How Could NOLS Students Have Avoided Bear Attack?" Alaska Dispatch, March 26, 2012.

———. "Illegal Alaska Bear Hunter Gets off Easier Than Rocker Ted Nugent." Alaska Dispatch, May 4, 2012.

———. "New Report Details 2011 Alaska Grizzly Bear Attack on Outdoors School Students." Alaska Dispatch, March 25, 2012.

———. "No Bear, Ax to Back up Hiker's Tale." ADN, August 23, 2004.

———. "The Spectacular Rise of Alaska Wildlife Manager Corey Rossi." Alaska Dispatch, January 15, 2012.

———. "Treadwell: 'Get Out Here, I'm Getting Killed.'" ADN, October 9, 2003.

———. "When It Comes to Bears, Reason Often Disappears." ADN, August 6, 2000.

Medred, Craig, and James Halpin. "2nd Woman Mauled in Bicentennial Park." ADN, August 9, 2008.

Meehan, Erin, Elizabeth E. Seminet-Reneau, and Thomas P. Quinn. "Bear Predation on Pacific Salmon Facilitates Colonization of Carcasses by Fly Maggots." American Midland Naturalist 153, 1 (January 2005): 142–151.

Meehan, Joe. Status of Brown Bears and Other Natural Resources in the McNeil River State Game Sanctuary and Refuge in 2005. Annual Report to the Alaska State Legislature. ADF&G, January 2006.

Meier, Walter N., Sebastian Gerland, Mats A. Granskog, and Jeffrey R. Key. "Sea Ice." In Snow, Water, Ice and Permafrost in the Arctic (SWIPA): Climate Change and the Cryosphere, 1–87. Oslo: Arctic Monitoring and Assessment Programme, 2011.

Merriam, C. H. "Review of the Grizzly and Big Brown Bears of North America (Genus Ursus) with the Description of a New Genus, Vetularctos." North American Fauna 41 (1918): 1–136.

Mikkelson, Barbara, and David P. Mikkelson. "Playground Bears." Snopes.com. April 24, 2010. http://www.snopes.com/photos/animals/playgroundbears.asp (accessed September 27, 2011).

Miller, Sterling. Brown Bears in Alaska: A Statewide Management Overview. Wildlife Technical Bulletin No. 11. Juneau: ADF&G Division of Wildlife Conservation, December 1993.

———. "Denning Ecology of Brown Bears in Southcentral Alaska and Comparisons with a Sympatric Black Bear Population." Int. Conf. Bear Res. Mgmt. 8 (1990): 279–287.

———. "Detection of Differences in Brown Bear Density and Population Composition Caused by Hunting." Int. Conf. Bear Res. Mgmt. 8 (1990): 393–404.

———. "Population Management of Bears in North America." Int. Conf. Bear Res. Mgmt. 8 (1990): 357–373.

———. "The Slow Revival of America's Grizzlies." National Wildlife Federation blog *Wildlife Promise*, March 19, 2012. http://blog.nwf.org/2012/03/the-slow-revival-of-americas-grizzlies/.

Miller, Sterling D., and Warren Ballard. "Homing of Transplanted Alaskan Brown Bears." *Journal of Wildlife Management* 46, 4 (October 1982): 869–876.

Miller, Sterling D., and John W. Schoen. "Status and Management of the Brown Bear in Alaska." In *Bears: Status Survey and Conservation Action Plan*, ed. Christopher Servheen, Stephen Herrero, and Bernard Peyton, 39–46. IUCN/SSC Bear Specialist Group, 1999.

Miller, Sterling D., John W. Schoen, Jim Faro, and David R. Klein. "Trends in Intensive Management of Alaska's Grizzly Bears, 1980–2010." *Journal of Wildlife Management* 75, 6 (2011): 1243–1252.

Miller, Sterling D., Richard A. Sellers, and Jeffrey A. Keay. "Effects of Hunting on Brown Bear Cub Survival and Litter Size in Alaska." *Ursus* 14, 2 (2003): 130–152.

Miller, Sterling D., and V. Leigh Tutterrow. "Characteristics of Nonsport Mortalities to Brown and Black Bears and Human Injuries from Bears in Alaska." *Ursus* 11 (1999): 239–252.

Miller, Sterling D., Gary C. White, Richard A. Sellers, Harry V. Reynolds, John W. Schoen, Kimberly Titus, Victor G. Barnes Jr., Roger B. Smith, Robert R. Nelson, Warren B. Ballard, and Charles C. Schwartz. "Brown and Black Bear Density Estimation in Alaska Using Radiotelemetry and Replicated Mark-Resight Techniques." *Wildlife Monographs* 133 (January 1997): 3–55.

Miller, Suzanne M., Sterling D. Miller, and Daniel W. McCollum. "Attitudes toward and Relative Value of Alaskan Brown and Black Bears to Resident Voters, Resident Hunters, and Nonresident Hunters." *Ursus* 10 (1998): 357–376.

Miller, Susanne, Kelly Proffitt, and Scott Schliebe. *Demographics and Behavior of Polar Bears Feeding on Bowhead Whale Carcasses at Barter and Cross Islands, Alaska, 2002–2004.* Anchorage: USFWS Marine Mammals Management, April 2006.

Miller, Webb, Stephan C. Schuster, Andreanna J. Welch, Aakrosh Ratan, Oscar C. Bedoya-Reina, Fangqing Zhao, Hie Lim Kim, Richard C. Burhans, Daniela I. Drautz, Nicola E. Wittekindt, Lynn P. Tomsho, Enrique Ibarra-Laclette, Luis Herrera-Estrella, Elizabeth Peacock, Sean Farley, George K. Sage, Karyn Rode, Martyn Obbard, Rafael Montiel, Lutz Bachmann, Ólafur Ingólfsson, Jon Aars, Thomas Mailund, Øystein Wiig, Sandra L. Talbot, and Charlotte Lindqvist. "Polar and Brown Bear Genomes Reveal Ancient Admixture and Demographic Footprints of Past Climate Change." *PNAS* 109, 36 (July 23, 2012): E2382–E2390.

Molnár, Péter K., Andrew E. Derocher, Gregory W. Thiemann, and Mark A. Lewis. "Predicting Survival, Reproduction and Abundance of Polar Bears under Climate Change." *Biological Conservation* 143, 7 (2010): 1612–1622.

Moment, Gairdner B. "Bears: The Need for a New Sanity in Wildlife Conservation." *BioScience* 18, 12 (December 1968): 1105–1108.

Monnett, Charles, and Jeffrey Gleason. "Observations of Mortality Associated with Extended Open-Water Swimming by Polar Bears in the Alaskan Beaufort Sea." *Polar Biology* 29, 8 (2006): 681–687.

Moore, Ralph. *Superintendent's Annual Report, Fiscal Year 2010, Katmai National Park and Preserve, Aniakchak National Monument and Preserve, Alagnak Wild River.* National Park Service, 2010.

Moore, Sue E., and Henry Huntington. "Arctic Marine Mammals and Climate Change: Impacts and Resilience." *Ecological Applications* 18, 2 Supplement (2008): S157–S165.

Mosolov, Vladimir, and Tatiana Gordienko. "His 33rd Field Season." *International Bear News* 13, 1 (February 2004): 6–7.

Mowat, Garth, and Douglas C. Heard. "Major Components of Grizzly Bear Diet across North America." *Canadian Journal of Zoology* 84, 3 (2006): 473–489.

Mowry, Tim. "Alaska Board of Game OKs Baited Grizzly Kills." FDNM, March 8, 2012.

———. "Board of Game: No Interior Alaska Bear Trapping for Now." FDNM, March 10, 2012.

———. "Critics Decry New Alaska Wildlife Director." FDNM, March 16, 2010.

———. "Denali Park Ranger Gets Creative to Fend off Brazen Bear." FDNM, August 16, 2000.

———. "Former Alaska Biologists Want State's New Wildlife Director Rossi Ousted." FDNM, March 23, 2010.

———. "North Pole Woman Uses Insect Repellent to Fend off Granite Tors Grizzly." FDNM, July 15, 2012.

———. "Why Did the Polar Bear Cross the Brooks Range? Biologists Are Baffled." FDNM, March 28, 2008.

Mueller, Larry, and Marguerite Reiss. *Bear Attacks of the Century: True Stories of Courage and Survival.* Guilford, CT: Lyons Press, 2005.

Muir, John. *Edward Henry Harriman.* New York: Doubleday, Page, 1912. http://www.sierraclub.org/john_muir_exhibit/writings/edward_henry_harriman.aspx.

Municipality of Anchorage. Title 21 Rewrite, Exhibit A, Assembly Committee Draft, Title 21 Chapters. December 18, 2012.

Murie, Adolph. *The Grizzlies of Mount McKinley.* Seattle: University of Washington Press, 1981.

"Murkowski Appoints Six to Game Board." News release, Office of the Governor, State of Alaska, January 17, 2003.

Murphy, Kim. "Alaska Officials Expand Aerial Shooting of Bears." *Los Angeles Times*, January 18, 2012.

Nash, Roderick Frazier. *Wilderness and the American Mind.* 4th ed. New Haven, CT: Yale University Press, 2001.

National Park Service Visitor Use Statistics. https://irma.nps.gov/Stats/Reports/ReportList.

Nawaz, Muhammad Ali. "Ecology, Genetics and Conservation of Himalayan Brown Bears." Ph.D. diss., Norwegian University of Life Sciences, 2008. http://www.bearproject.info/uploads/publications/PhD%20thesis%20Nawaz.pdf.

Nelson, Michael P., John A. Vucetich, Paul C. Paquet, and Joseph K. Bump. "An Inadequate Construct? What's Flawed, What's Missing, What's Needed." *Wildlife Professional* (Summer 2011): 58–60.

Nelson, Ralph A., G. Edgar Folk Jr., Egbert W. Pfeiffer, John J. Craighead, Charles J. Jonkel, and Dianne L. Steiger. "Behavior, Biochemistry, and Hibernation in Black, Grizzly, and Polar Bears." *Int. Conf. Bear Res. Mgmt.* 5 (1983): 284–290.

Nelson, Richard K. *Hunters of the Northern Forest: Designs for Survival among the Alaskan Kutchin.* Chicago: University of Chicago Press, 1986.

———. *Hunters of the Northern Ice.* Chicago: University of Chicago Press, 1969.

———. *Make Prayers to the Raven: A Koyukon View of the Northern Forest.* Chicago: University of Chicago Press, 1983.

Nettle, Daniel. "The Evolution of Personality Variation in Humans and Other Animals." *American Psychologist* 61, 6 (September 2006): 622–631.

Nevin, Owen T., and Barrie K. Gilbert. "Perceived Risk, Displacement and Refuging in Brown Bears: Positive Impacts of Ecotourism?" *Biological Conservation* 121, 4 (2005): 611–622.

"New Observations of Swimming Polar Bears Presented at International Bear Conference." Press release, USGS July 20, 2011.

Neyman, Jenny. "Bear Death under Scrutiny." *Redoubt Reporter*, October 28, 2009.

———. "Bear Hunter Regrets Shooting." *Redoubt Reporter*, November 11, 2009.

———. "Road Kill." *Redoubt Reporter*, October 7, 2009.

"NOAA Lists Ringed and Bearded Ice Seal Populations under the Endangered Species Act." News release, National Oceanic and Atmospheric Administration, December 21, 2012.

Norris, Frank B. *Isolated Paradise: An Administrative History of the Katmai and Aniakchak NPS Units, Alaska.* Anchorage: National Park Service, 1996. http://www.nps.gov/history/history/online_books/katm/adhi/.

———. *Tourism in Katmai Country: A History of Concessions Activity in Katmai National Park and Preserve.* Anchorage: National Park Service, Alaska Regional Office, 1992 (rev. 2004). http://www.nps.gov/history/history/online_books/katm/.

Noyce, Karen. Letter to Alaska Board of Game, February 20, 2004.

"NPS, ADFG Meet on Wolf Protocol." News release, March 30, 2010.

"Ocean Acidification." State of the Science Fact Sheet, National Oceanic and Atmospheric Administration, May 2008 and January 2013.

O'Harra, Doug. "Biologist Loves Wildlife, Hates Killing Bears." ADN, August 21, 2005.

———. "Frozen Feast." ADN, April 24, 2005.

———. "Game Board Gives McNeil Grizzlies Room to Roam." ADN, March 11, 2005.

Ohnuki-Tierney, Emiko. "Ainu Sociality." In *Ainu: Spirit of a Northern People*, ed. W. W. Fitzhugh, and C. O. Dubreuil, 240–248. Washington, DC: National Museum of Natural History, Smithsonian Institution, 1999.

Olsen, Jack. *Night of the Grizzlies*. New York: G. P. Putnam's Sons/Signet Classics, 1969.

Olson, Tamara L., Barrie K. Gilbert, and Ronald C. Squibb. "The Effects of Increasing Human Activity on Brown Bear Use of an Alaskan River." *Biological Conservation* 82, 1 (1997): 95–99.

Olson, Tamara L., Eric M. Groth, Katja W. Mocnik, and Carlton I. Vaughn. *Bear Management at Brooks River, Katmai National Park, 2003–2006*. Alaska Region Natural Resources Technical Report NPS/AR/NRTR-2009-73. Anchorage: National Park Service, January 2009.

Olson, Tamara L., and Judy A. Putera. *Refining Monitoring Protocols to Survey Brown Bear Populations in Katmai National Park and Preserve and Lake Clark National Park and Preserve*. Alaska Region Natural Resources Technical Report NPS/AR/NRTR-2007-66. Anchorage: National Park Service, November 2007.

Operational Plan for Intensive Management of Moose in Unit 24(B) during Regulatory Years 2012–2017. ADF&G Division of Wildlife Conservation, February 2012.

Ordiz, Andrés, Ole-Gunnar Støen, Jon E. Swenson, Ilpo Kojola, and Richard Bischof. "Distance-Dependent Effect of the Nearest Neighbor: Spatiotemporal Patterns in Brown Bear Reproduction." *Ecology* 89, 12 (2008): 3327–3335.

Orellana, Roxana. "Utah Judge Dismisses Bear-Attack Wrongful Death Lawsuit." *Salt Lake Tribune*, October 14, 2011.

Ortega y Gasset, José. *Meditations on Hunting*. New York: Scribner, 1986.

Owen, Patricia A., and Richard D. Mace. "Grizzly Bear Population Ecology in Denali National Park and Preserve." *Alaska Park Science* 6, 2 (2007): 66–68.

Pagano, Anthony, George M. Durner, Steven C. Amstrup, Kristin S. Simac, and Geoff S. York. "Long-Distance Swimming by Polar Bears (*Ursus maritimus*) of the Southern Beaufort Sea during Years of Extensive Open Water." *Canadian Journal of Zoology* 90, 5 (May 2012): 663–676.

Palin, Sarah. "Re: For Your Review and Approval—Polar Bear Release." E-mail to Sharon Leighow, August 4, 2008. *Wall Street Journal* online. http://online.wsj .com/public/resources/documents/palin08042008.pdf (accessed January 13, 2013).

———. "Re: KTUU." E-mail to Michael A. Nizich, February 5, 2009. http://www .documentcloud.org/documents/309316-pra-gsp02–0027220.html (accessed January 13, 2013).

———. "Re: Predator Control and Re: Utility." E-mail to Michael Nizich, February 7, 2009. http://www.documentcloud.org/documents/310077-pra-gsp02 –0022294.html#search/p1/Palin (accessed January 13, 2013).

Paragi, Tom. "Overview of Intensive Management with Emphasis on Region III Moose." ADF&G presentation to Alaska Board of Game, March 2008.

Parmesan, Camille. "Ecological and Evolutionary Responses to Recent Climate Change." *Annual Review of Ecology, Evolution, and Systematics* 37 (2006): 637–669.

Partnow, Patricia. "Ursine Urges and Urban Ungulates: Anchorage Asserts Its Alaskanness." *Western Folklore* 58, 1 (Winter 1999): 33–56.

Partridge, Steve, Tom Smith, and Tania Lewis. *Black and Brown Bear Activity at Selected Coastal Sites in Glacier Bay National Park and Preserve, Alaska: A Preliminary Assessment Using Noninvasive Procedures.* Open-File Report 2009-1169. Reston, VA: USGS, 2009.

Pasitschniak-Arts, Maria. "*Ursus arctos.*" *Mammalian Species* 439 (April 23, 1993): 1–10.

Patten, Laura A. "Seed Dispersal Patterns Generated by Brown Bears (*Ursus arctos*) in Southeast Alaska." M.S. thesis, Washington State University, 1993.

Pederson, Kay. Letter to the editor. ADN, July 2, 2004.

Pemberton, Mary. "Campaigns over Measure 2 Get Heated." *Juneau Empire,* August 20, 2008.

———. "Herds up in Areas of Wolf Control." ADN, September 14, 2009.

———. "Rossi to Head State Division of Wildlife Conservation." ADN, March 12, 2010.

———. "Voters Reject Predator Control Program Changes." ADN, August 27, 2008.

Pesznecker, Katie. "Curious Holiday Crowd Dooms Young Grizzly." ADN, July 6, 2007.

———. "Woman, Bear Trade Blows." ADN, July 12, 2002.

Petersen, David. "Old Ephraim's Last Stand." *Mother Earth News,* March/April 1985.

Peterson, Chris. "Grizzlies Have Great Sniffers." *Hungry Horse News,* August 3, 2005.

Pettitt, Paul. *The Paleolithic Origins of Human Burial.* New York: Routledge, 2011. eLibrary edition.

Phillips, Natalie. "Legend Brewin'." ADN, December 16, 2001.

Pinney, Amy. "Brown Bear Research in Alaska." *Alaska Fish & Wildlife News* online magazine, April 2012.

Pitblado, Bonnie L. "A Tale of Two Migrations: Reconciling Recent Biological and Geological Evidence for the Pleistocene Peopling of the Americas." *Journal of Archaeological Research* 19, 4 (2011): 327–375.

Plenda, Melanie. "Concern Grows about Official Bear Shootings." *Juneau Empire,* August 23, 2002.

Polar Bear (Ursus maritimus). USFWS Fact Sheet, May 2012.

Polar Bear (Ursus maritimus): Chukchi/Bering Seas Stock. USFWS Marine Mammals Management, rev. January 2010.

Polar Bear (Ursus maritimus): Southern Beaufort Sea Stock. USFWS Marine Mammals Management, rev. January 2010.

"Polar Bear Evolution Tracked Climate Change, New DNA Study Suggests." News release, University at Buffalo, State University of New York, July 23, 2012.

"Polar Bear Names." Polar Bears International. http://www.polarbearsinterna
tional.org/about-polar-bears/essentials/polar-bear-names.

Polar Bear News. Anchorage: USFWS Marine Mammals Management, 2010.

"Poles Apart: A Record-Breaking Summer and Winter." National Snow and Ice Data
Center, October 2, 2012. http://nsidc.org/arcticseaicenews/2012/10/poles-apart
-a-record-breaking-summer-and-winter/ (accessed October 21, 2012).

Polson, Shannon Huffman. *North of Hope: A Daughter's Arctic Journey.* Grand Rapids,
MI: Zondervan, 2013.

Polyak, Leonid, Richard B. Alley, John T. Andrews, Julie Brigham-Grette, Thomas M.
Cronin, Dennis A. Darby, Arthur S. Dyke, Joan J. Fitzpatrick, Svend Funder,
Marika Holland, Anne E. Jennings, Gifford H. Miller, Matt O'Regan, James
Savelle, Mark Serreze, Kristen St. John, James W. C. White, and Eric Wolff. "His-
tory of Sea Ice in the Arctic." *Quaternary Science Reviews* 29 (2010): 1757–1778.

Porco, Peter. "Cameras Show Katmai Bear Kills." ADN, October 6, 2007.

———. "Forest Service Details Give the Lie to Monster Hunting Myth." ADN, May
7, 2003.

Predator Management in Alaska. Juneau: ADF&G Division of Wildlife Conservation,
November 2007.

"The Price Paid by the Bears." Conservation Officer Service Bear Statistics. http://
records.viu.ca/www/discover/rmot/tblbear.htm (accessed November 2, 2012).

*Proceedings of the First International Scientific Meeting on the Polar Bear, September 6–10,
Fairbanks, Alaska.* Washington, DC: US Department of the Interior and University of Alaska, 1966.

Promisco, Mike. 2008 testimonial. Litzen Guide Service. http://www.litzenguide
service.com/testimonials.htm.

"Proposal 39." Preliminary actions, Alaska Board of Game statewide meeting,
January 29–February 1, 2010.

Quammen, David. *Monster of God.* New York: W. W. Norton, 2003.

*Questions and Answers about Polar Bear Management in the Chukchi Region under the U.S.-
Russia Agreement.* Anchorage: USFWS Marine Mammals Management, May 2011.

Quinn, Thomas P., Stephanie M. Carlson, Scott M. Gende, and Harry B. Rich Jr.
"Transportation of Pacific Salmon Carcasses from Streams to Riparian Forests
by Bears." *Canadian Journal of Zoology* 87, 3 (2009): 195–203.

"Rabies Risk from Bear Attacks." *State of Alaska Epidemiology Bulletin,* October 17,
2002.

Randall, Gail. "Killer Bear a Mystery to Experts." ADN, July 10, 1992.

Rasmussen, Knud. *Across Arctic America: Narrative of the Fifth Thule Expedition.* Reprint. Fairbanks: University of Alaska Press, 1999.

Rausch, Robert L. "Geographic Variation in Size in North American Brown Bears,
Ursus arctos L., as Indicated by Condylobasal Length." *Canadian Journal of Zoology* 41, 1 (1963): 33–45.

———. "Notes on the Nunamiut Eskimo and Mammals of the Anaktuvuk Pass Region, Brooks Range, Alaska." *Arctic* 4, 3 (December 1951): 147–195.

———. "On the Status of Some Arctic Mammals." *Arctic* 6, 2 (July 1953): 91–148.

Ravelhofer, Barbara. "'Beasts of Recreacion': Henslowe's White Bears." *English Literary Renaissance* 32, 2 (March 2002): 287–323.

Rearden, Jim. *Alaska's Wolf Man: The 1915–55 Wilderness Adventures of Frank Glaser.* Missoula, MT: Pictorial Histories Publishing, 1998.

Regehr, Eric V., Nicholas J. Lunn, Steven C. Amstrup, and Ian Stirling. "Effects of Earlier Sea Ice Breakup on Survival and Population Size of Polar Bears in Western Hudson Bay." *Journal of Wildlife Management* 71, 8 (November 2007): 2673–2683.

Regelin, Wayne L., Patrick Valkenburg, and Rod D. Boertje. "Management of Large Predators in Alaska." *Wildlife Biology in Practice* 1, 1 (June 2005): 77–85.

Reimchen, Tom. "Salmon Nutrients, Nitrogen Isotopes and Coastal Forests." *Ecoforestry* 16, 3 (Fall 2001): 13–16.

———. "Some Ecological and Evolutionary Aspects of Bear-Salmon Interactions in Coastal British Columbia." *Canadian Journal of Zoology* 78, 3 (2000): 448–457.

Resolution on the Harvest of Wolves in Alaska. American Society of Mammalogists, June 2006.

Responsive Management. Anchorage Residents' Opinions on and Experiences with Bears and Other Wildlife. Focus Group Report, 2009.

Responsive Management. Anchorage Residents' Opinions on Bear and Moose Population Levels and Management Strategies, 2010.

Revenko, Igor. "Life Devoted to Brown Bears." *International Bear News* 13, 1 (February 2004): 6.

Reynolds, Harry V. *Effects of Harvest on Grizzly Bear Population Dynamics in the Northcentral Alaska Range, July 1, 1996–June 30, 1998.* ADF&G Division of Wildlife Conservation, 1999.

Reynolds, Harry V., James A. Curatolo, and Roland Quimby. "Denning Ecology of Grizzly Bears in Northeastern Alaska." *Third International Conference on Bears* 3 (1974): 403–409.

Reynolds, Patricia E., Harry V. Reynolds, and Richard T. Shideler. "Predation and Multiple Kills of Muskoxen by Grizzly Bears." *Ursus* 13 (2002): 79–84.

Rhoads, Samuel N. *A Reprint of the North American Zoology, by George Ord.* 2nd ed. Haddonfield, NJ: Samuel Rhoads, 1894. http://archive.org/details/reprintof northamooordg.

Rhode, Cecil E. "When Giant Bears Go Fishing." *National Geographic*, August 1954.

Richards, Mark. "Wildlife Management Bill Goes Too Far." ADN, March 8, 2008.

———. "Wolf Control Expansion Plan Is Shortsighted at Best." FDNM, May 28, 2006.

Riggs, Thomas, Jr., letter to H. C. Copeland, June 3, 1920. State of Alaska Archives, Office of the District and Territorial Governor, RG 101, box 178, series 130, file 25, Fish & Game: Alaska Game Commission 1920.

Rinehart, Steve. "Bears, People Face Changes at [sic] Brooks River Plan Moves Camp, Limits Visitors." ADN, April 18, 1994.

———. "Game Board Cancels McNeil River Bear Hunt." ADN, October 28, 1995.

Riptide. "SFH Attacks ADF&G." Alaska Game Management Forum. Outdoors Directory website, October 1, 2009. http://forums.outdoorsdirectory.com/show thread.php/64653-SFH-Attacks-ADF-amp-G.

Robbins, Charles T., Merav Ben-David, Jennifer K. Fortin, and O. Lynne Nelson. "Maternal Condition Determines Birth Date and Growth of Newborn Bear Cubs." Journal of Mammalogy 93, 2 (2012): 540–546.

Robbins, Charles T., Jennifer K. Fortin, Karyn D. Rode, Sean D. Farley, Lisa A. Shipley, and Laura A. Felicetti. "Optimizing Protein Intake as a Foraging Strategy to Maximize Mass Gain in an Omnivore." Oikos 116, 10 (2007): 1675–1682.

Robbins, Charles T., Charles C. Schwartz, and Laura A. Felicetti. "Nutritional Ecology of Ursids: A Review of Newer Methods and Management Implications." Ursus 15, 2 (2004): 161–171.

Robinson, Donald H., and Maynard C. Bowers. "Visitation Statistics, Appendix D." In Through the Years in Glacier National Park: An Administrative History. Glacier Natural History Association, May 1960. http://www.gov/history/history /online_books/glac/.

Robinson, Marilynne. The Death of Adam: Essays on Modern Thought. New York: Picador, 2005.

Rode, Karyn D., Sean D. Farley, and Charles T. Robbins. "Behavioral Responses of Brown Bears Mediate Nutritional Effects of Experimentally Introduced Tourism." Biological Conservation 133, 1 (2006): 70–80.

Rode, Karyn D., and Charles T. Robbins. "Why Bears Consume Mixed Diets during Fruit Abundance." Canadian Journal of Zoology 78, 9 (2000): 1640–1645.

Roodenburg, Jane. Letter to the editor. Juneau Empire, August 30, 1999.

Rooney, Matthew. "Bruno's Last Stand." June 30, 2006. Spiegel International online, December 3, 2010.

Roosevelt, Theodore. The Wilderness Hunter: An Account of the Big Game of the United States and Its Chase with Horse, Hound and Rifle. New York: G. P. Putnam's Sons, 1893. Google eBook.

Roosevelt, Theodore, and George Bird Grinnell, eds. American Big-Game Hunting: The Book of the Boone and Crockett Club. New York: Forest and Stream, 1893. Google eBook.

Rossi, Corey, Craig Fleener, Patrick Valkenburg, and Ted Spraker. "Alaska's Intensive Management Policy: The View from the State." Wildlife Professional (Winter 2011). http://joomla.wildlife.org/index.php?option=com_content&task=view&id=951 (accessed February 18, 2012).

Rozell, Ned. "Early Death May Benefit Bear-Pressured Salmon." Alaska Science Forum, September 19, 2005, article 1768.

Russell, Don. A Review of Wolf Management Programs in Alaska, Yukon, British Columbia,

Alberta and Northwest Territories. Yukon Wolf Conservation and Management Plan Review, November 6, 2010.

Russell, John C. *Nanuq: Cultural Significance and Traditional Knowledge among Alaska Natives.* Nome: Alaska Nanuuq Commission, May 2005.

"Salazar Announces Almost $34 Million to Alaska for Fish and Wildlife Projects." News release, USFWS, February 18, 2011.

Sanders, Jack. "Conservation Officers Review Base Bear Policy after Incident." Joint Base Elmendorf-Richardson, June 9, 2010.

Savours, Ann. "'A Very Interesting Point in Geography': The 1773 Phipps Expedition towards the North Pole." *Arctic* 37, 4 (December 1984): 402–428.

Schaul, Jordan Carlton. "Bears of the Last Frontier: Interview with Chris Morgan (Ecologist, Author, TV Host)." May 5, 2011. http://newswatch.nationalgeograph ic.com/2011/05/05/bears-of-the-last-frontier-chris-morgan/ (accessed September 8, 2011).

Schliebe, Scott, Thomas Evans, Kurt Johnson, Michael Roy, Susanne Miller, Charles Hamilton, Rosa Meehan, and Sonja Jahrsdoerfer. *Range-Wide Status Review of the Polar Bear (Ursus maritimus).* Anchorage: USFWS, December 21, 2006.

Schliebe, Scott, Thomas J. Evans, Susanne Miller, Craig Perham, James Wilder, and Lisa J. Lierheimer. "Polar Bear Management in Alaska 2000–2004." In *Proceedings of the 14th Working Meeting of the IUCN/SSC Polar Bear Specialist Group,* Seattle, June 20–24, 2005.

Schliebe, Scott, Karyn D. Rode, Jeffrey S. Gleason, James Wilder, Kelly Proffitt, Tom J. Evans, and Susanne Miller. "Effects of Sea Ice Extent and Food Availability on Spatial and Temporal Distribution of Polar Bears during the Fall Open-Water Period in Southern Beaufort Sea." *Polar Biology* 31, 8 (2008): 999–1010.

Schoen, John W. "Bear Habitat Management: A Review and Future Perspective." *Int. Conf. Bear Res. Mgmt.* 8 (1990): 143–154.

———. "Conserving Alaska's Bears: Challenges and Opportunities." Presented at the 7th Alaska Bear Forum, Anchorage Museum of History and Art, April 19, 2005.

Schoen, John W., LaVern R. Beier, Jack W. Lentfer, and Loyal J. Johnson. "Denning Ecology of Brown Bears on Admiralty and Chichagof Islands." *Int. Conf. Bear Res. Mgmt.* 7 (1987): 293–304.

Schoen, John, and Scott Gende. "Brown Bear (*Ursus arctos*)." In *A Conservation Assessment and Resource Synthesis for the Coastal Forests and Mountains Ecoregion in the Tongass National Forest and Southeast Alaska,* ed. John W. Schoen and Erin Dovichin, 1–23. Anchorage: Audubon Alaska and Nature Conservancy of Alaska, 2007. eBook.

Schoen, John W., Jack W. Lentfer, and LaVern R. Beier. "Differential Distribution of Brown Bears on Admiralty Island, Southeast Alaska: A Preliminary Assessment." *Int. Conf. Bear Res. Mgmt.* 6 (1986): 1–5.

Schoen, John W., Sterling Miller, and Harry V. Reynolds III. "Last Stronghold of the Grizzly." *Natural History*, January 1987, 50–59.

Schullery, Paul. *Lewis and Clark among the Grizzlies: Legend and Legacy in the American West*. Guilford, CT: Globe Pequot Press, 2002.

Schwartz, Charles C., and Albert W. Franzmann. "Dispersal and Survival of Subadult Black Bears from the Kenai Peninsula, Alaska." *Journal of Wildlife Management* 56, 3 (July 1992): 426–431.

Schwartz, Charles C., Mark A. Haroldson, and Gary C. White. "Hazards Affecting Grizzly Bear Survival in the Greater Yellowstone Ecosystem." *Journal of Wildlife Management* 74, 4 (2010): 654–667.

Schwartz, Charles C., Kim A. Keating, Harry V. Reynolds III, Victor G. Barnes Jr., Richard A. Sellers, Jon E. Swenson, Sterling D. Miller, Bruce N. McLellan, Jeff Keay, Robert McCann, Michael Gibeau, Wayne F. Wakkinen, Richard D. Mace, Wayne Kasworm, Rodger Smith, and Steven Herrero. "Reproductive Maturation and Senescence in the Female Brown Bear." *Ursus* 14, 2 (2003): 109–119.

Schwartz, Charles C., Sterling D. Miller, and Albert W. Franzmann. "Denning Ecology of Three Black Bear Populations in Alaska." *Int. Conf. Bear Res. Mgmt.* 7 (1987): 281–291.

Schwartz, Charles C., Sterling D. Miller, and Mark A. Haroldson. "Grizzly Bear." In *Wild Mammals of North America: Biology, Management, and Conservation*, ed. George A. Feldhamer, Bruce C. Thompson, and Joseph A. Chapman, 556–586. Baltimore: Johns Hopkins University Press, 2003.

Schwartz, Charles C., Jon E. Swenson, and Sterling D. Miller. "Large Carnivores, Moose, and Humans: A Changing Paradigm of Predator Management in the 21st Century." *Alces* 39 (2003): 41–63.

Scorzafava, Dick. "Creating Memories." *Bear Hunting Magazine*, January/February 2009. http://www.bear-hunting.com/issue_1_2_2009.cfm (accessed March 14, 2011).

Scott, Harold Bartlett. "Alaska Yacht Hunting Party." *Alaska Sportsman*, March 1937.

Seekins, Ralph. Interview with Shoup Shepherd. "America the Wild" podcast, show 122, March 15, 2008. http://www.americathewild.com/031508/atwo31508seg2finalmixdown.mp3 (accessed February 20, 2009).

———. "SFW Alaska President's Message." Sportsmen for Fish and Wildlife Alaska Chapter, Fall 2009. http://sfwalaska.com/web/index.php?option=com_content&view=category&layout=blog&id=9&Itemid=12 (accessed August 20, 2010).

Sellers, Richard A., and Larry Aumiller. "Brown Bear Population Characteristics at McNeil River, Alaska." *Int. Conf. Bear Res. Mgmt.* 9, 1 (1994): 283–293.

Servheen, Chris. "Status and Management of the Grizzly Bear in the Lower 48 United States." In *Bears: Status Survey and Conservation Action Plan*, ed. Christopher Servheen, Stephen Herrero, and Bernard Peyton, 50–54. IUCN/SSC Bear Specialist Group, 1999.

Servheen, Christopher, Stephen Herrero, and Bernard Peyton, eds. *Bears: Status Survey and Conservation Action Plan*. IUCN/SSC Bear Specialist Group, 1998.

Sharp, Bert. Intensive Management of Game Resources: Hearings on SB77, February 16, 1994, before the House Resources Committee, 18th Alaska State Legislature. Sponsor statement.

"Shell Begins Preliminary Drilling in Beaufort Sea." *Alaska Dispatch*, October 3, 2012.

Shemanske, Susan. "Target in Sight: Yorkville Man Aiming for Big-Game Record." *Racine Journal Times*, February 14, 2008.

Shepard, Paul. "The Biological Bases of Bear Mythology and Ceremonialism." *Trumpeter* 23, 2 (2007): 74–80.

———. *The Others: How Animals Made Us Human*. Washington, DC: Island Press/Shearwater Books, 1997.

Shepard, Paul, and Barry Sanders. *Sacred Paw: The Bear in Nature, Myth, and Literature*. New York: Viking Penguin, 1985.

Sherwonit, Bill. "The Bears of Katmai." *Anchorage Press*, February 18, 2009.

Sherwood, Morgan. *Big Game in Alaska: A History of Wildlife and People*. New Haven, CT: Yale University Press, 1981.

Shideler, Richard T. "Denning Ecology of Grizzly Bears in the Oilfield Region of Alaska's North Slope." Presented at the Wildlife Society's 13th Annual Conference and Trade Show, Anchorage, September 2006.

Shinohara, Rosemary. "State Hogties Bear Expert over Remarks." ADN, July 28, 2005.

Shockey, Jim. "Black Bears—Simple Fools or Cunning Killers." *Outdoor Life* online, September 2007.

Shuster, Stephen. "Sexual Selection and Mating Systems." *Proceedings of the National Academy of Sciences* 106, Supplement 1 (June 16, 2009): 10009–10016.

Signor, Kari. "Investigating Methods to Reduce Black Bear (*Ursus americanus*) Visitation to Anthropogenic Food Sources: Conditioned Taste Aversion and Food Removal." M.S. thesis, Utah State University, 2010.

Simberloff, Daniel. "Biodiversity and Bears—A Conservation Paradigm Shift." *Ursus* 11 (1999): 21–28.

Simpson, Sherry. "Another Way of Saying." In *Living Blue in the Red States*, ed. David Starkey, 17–38. Lincoln: University of Nebraska Press/Bison Books, 2007.

———. "The Bear Beside Me." *Superstition Review* 5 (Spring 2010). http://superstitionreview.asu.edu/n5/bio.php?author=sherrysimpson&bio=nonfiction.

———. "Is It Really Us or Them?" *Anchorage Press*, September 1, 2005.

———. "The Sad Tale of Juneau's Garbage Bears." *Juneau Empire*, August 26, 1991.

———. "The Scrimmage of Appetite." *Anchorage Press*, October 3, 2003.

———. "A Short, Happy Life." *We Alaskans* magazine, ADN, October 13, 1996.

Sinnott, Rick. "Case Histories: Recounting Some Terrible Alaska Bear Attacks." *Alaska Dispatch*, April 12, 2012.

———. "Community Forum: Bears, Be Aware." Interview by Nellie Moore, KSKA-FM, July 9, 2008.

———. "Educating Bears by Educating People." *Alaska Dispatch*, May 23, 2011.

———. "Is Alaska's Largest City Bear-Infested, as Some Residents Seem to Think?" *Alaska Dispatch*, August 23, 2012.

———. "Is Bear Population Growing in Anchorage, Alaska?" *Alaska Dispatch*, August 22, 2012.

———. "Kaniut Has Changed Advice on Bears." ADN, May 11, 2009.

———. "Mayor Sullivan Is Betting Anchorage Bears Will Behave." *Alaska Dispatch*, May 30, 2011.

———. "Wildlife Chief's Resignation Resonates with Biologists." *Alaska Dispatch*, January 12, 2012.

Sisson, Dan. "Bear Hunt at Terror Bay." *Field & Stream*, January 1985, 50.

Slackman, Michael. "For Mourners of Knut, a Stuffed Bear Just Won't Do." *New York Times*, April 11, 2011.

Smith, Thomas G., and Becky Sjare. "Predation of Belugas and Narwhals by Polar Bears in Nearshore Areas of the Canadian High Arctic." *Arctic* 43, 2 (June 1990): 99–102.

Smith, Todd. "A Bear in the Dark." *Outdoor Life*, April 2004, 11.

Smith, Tom S. *A Century of Bear-Human Conflict in Alaska: Analyses and Implications.* Alaska Science Center, USGS. http://www.absc.usgs.gov/research/brownbears /attacks/bear-human_conflicts.htm (last reviewed May 31, 2007; accessed April 4, 2009).

———. "Attraction of Brown Bears to Red Pepper Spray Deterrent: Caveats for Use." *Wildlife Society Bulletin* 26, 1 (1998): 92–94.

———. "Effects of Human Activity on Brown Bear Use of the Kulik River, Alaska." *Ursus* 13 (2002): 257–267.

Smith, Tom S., Terry D. DeBruyn, Tania Lewis, Rusty Yerxa, and Steven Partridge. "Bear-Human Interactions at Glacier Bay National Park and Preserve: Conflict Risk Assessment." *Alaska Park Science* (Summer 2003): 20–25.

Smith, Tom S., Stephen Herrero, and Terry D. DeBruyn. "Alaskan Brown Bears, Humans, and Habituation." *Ursus* 16, 1 (2005): 1–10.

Smith, Tom S., Stephen Herrero, Terry D. DeBruyn, and James M. Wilder. "Efficacy of Bear Deterrent Spray in Alaska." *Journal of Wildlife Management* 72, 3 (2008): 640–645.

Smith, Tom S., Stephen Herrero, Cali S. Layton, Randy T. Larsen, and Kathryn R. Johnson. "Efficacy of Firearms for Bear Deterrence in Alaska." *Journal of Wildlife Management* 76, 5 (July 2012): 1021–1027.

Smith, Tom S., and Steven Partridge. "Dynamics of Intertidal Foraging by Coastal Brown Bears in Southwestern Alaska." *Journal of Wildlife Management* 68, 2 (2004): 233–240.

Sovalik, Pete. "Two Hunters at Point Hope." Transcription of interview with Don

Kimball and Vic Hessler. Tape H88–26D, Naval Arctic Research Laboratory Collection, Barrow file, box 137, Alaska Polar Regions, Rasmuson Library, University of Alaska–Fairbanks.

Spartz, India. *Eight Stars of Gold: The Story of Alaska's Flag.* Juneau: Alaska State Museums, 2001.

Spencer, Rocky D., Richard A. Beausoleil, and Donald A. Martorello. "How Agencies Respond to Human–Black Bear Conflicts: A Survey of Wildlife Agencies in North America." *Ursus* 18, 2 (2007): 217–229.

"The Sportsman's 'Crown Jewel' Joins the SFW/SFH Family." Sportsmen for Fish and Wildlife Alaska Chapter. www.sfwalaska.org (accessed March 9, 2009).

Spychalski, Brad. "The North American 28." *North American Hunter*, Special Bowhunting Enthusiast Section, September 2005.

Stahl, Lesley. "Bears in the Backyard." *60 Minutes*, June 2005. http://www.cbs news.com/video/watch/?id=6997300 (accessed August 21, 2011).

"Statewide Moose-Vehicle Crashes by Severity, 1977–2007." In *Revised Environmental Assessment, Parks Highway: MP 44-52*, "Appendix F: Moose Vehicle Collision Analysis." Anchorage: Alaska Department of Transportation and Public Facilities, September 2010.

Status of Brown Bears and Other Natural Resources in the McNeil River State Game Sanctuary in 2006. Annual Report to the Alaska State Legislature. Anchorage: ADF&G Division of Wildlife Conservation Lands and Refuges Program, January 2007.

Staying Safe in Bear Country: A Behavioral-Based Approach to Reducing Risk. Atlin, BC: Wild Eye Productions, Safety in Bear Country Society, 2001, rev. 2008. http://www.bearsmart.com/video/206.

Stenhouse, Gordon, John Boulanger, John Lee, Karen Graham, Julie Duval, and Jerome Cranston. "Grizzly Bear Associations along the Eastern Slopes of Alberta." *Ursus* 16, 1 (2005): 31–40.

Steyært, Sam, Anders Endrestøl, Klaus Hackländer, Jon Swenson, and Andreas Zedrosser. "The Mating System of the Brown Bear *Ursus arctos*." *Mammal Review* 42, 1 (January 2012): 12–34.

Stirling, Ian. *Polar Bears.* Ann Arbor: University of Michigan Press, 1998. Google eBook.

Stirling, Ian, and Andrew E. Derocher. "Effects of Climate Warming on Polar Bears: A Review of the Evidence." *Global Change Biology* 18, 9 (September 2012): 2694–2706.

——. "Factors Affecting the Evolution and Behavioral Ecology of the Modern Bears." *Int. Conf. Bear Res. Mgmt.* 8 (1990): 189–204.

——. "Melting under Pressure: The Real Scoop on Climate Warming and Polar Bears." *Wildlife Professional* 1, 3 (September 2007): 24–27, 43.

——. "Possible Impacts of Climatic Warming on Polar Bears." *Arctic* 46, 3 (September 1993): 240–245.

Stirling, Ian, Evan Richardson, Gregory W. Thiemann, and Andrew E. Derocher.

"Unusual Predation Attempts of Polar Bears on Ringed Seals in the Southern Beaufort Sea: Possible Significance of Changing Spring Ice Conditions." *Arctic* 61, 1 (March 2008): 14–22.

Støen, Ole-Gunnar, Eva Bellemain, Solve Sæbø, and Jon E. Swenson. "Kin-Related Spatial Structure in Brown Bears *Ursus arctos*." *Behavioral Ecology and Sociobiology* 59, 2 (December 2005): 191–197.

Stonorov, Derek. *Bears of Katmai National Park Preserve and Kamishak Special Use Area*. Prepared for Jim Stratton, regional director, National Parks Conservation Association, Anchorage, January 19, 2007.

———. *Living in Harmony with Bears*. National Audubon Society, 2000.

Stonorov, Derek, and Allen W. Stokes. "Social Behavior of the Alaska Brown Bear." *Int. Conf. Bear Res. Mgmt.* 2 (1972): 232–242.

"Strange Bear Was Grizzly-Polar Hybrid, Tests Show." CBC News, May 10, 2006.

Stricker, Craig A., Steven D. Kovach, Gail H. Collins, Sean D. Farley, Robert O. Rye, and Michael T. Hinkes. "Inter-annual Variation in the Foraging Ecology of a Brown Bear Population in Southwest Alaska." Poster presented at the American Geophysical Union fall meeting, San Francisco, December 2010.

Stroeve, Julienne C., Mark C. Serreze, Marika M. Holland, Jennifer E. Kay, James Malanik, and Andrew P. Barrett. "The Arctic's Rapidly Shrinking Sea Ice Cover: A Research Synthesis." *Climatic Change* 110 (2012): 1005–1027.

Struzik, Ed. "Hybrid Polar Bear–Grizzly Sightings Common in Arctic." *Edmonton Journal*, July 27, 2012.

"Summary of 2005 Survey Activities." USFWS, Arctic National Wildlife Refuge.

Sutkoski, Matt. "Bare Gov. Shumlin Barely Bails on Bothersome Bears." *Burlington Free Press*, April 13, 2012.

Sutton, Keith. "The Outdoor Life Book of World Records." *Outdoor Life*, September 2007. http://www.outdoorlife.com/articles/hunting/2007/09/outdoor-life-book-world-records (accessed October 22, 2012).

Swanson, Mike. "Knut the Bear Draws Record Number of Visitors to Berlin Zoo." *Deutsche Presse-Agentur*, April 5, 2007.

Swenson, J., A. Jansson, R. Riig, and F. Sandegren. "Bears and Ants: Myrmecophagy by Brown Bears in Central Scandinavia." *Canadian Journal of Zoology* 77, 4 (1999): 551–561.

Swenson, Jon E., and Mark A. Haroldson. "Observations of Mixed-Age Litters in Brown Bears." *Ursus* 19, 1 (2008): 73–79.

Tapper, James. "Latest TV Fake Scenes: 'Grizzly Attack' on Survival Show Was Man in Fancy-Dress Bear Costume." *Daily Mail* online, July 28, 2007.

Tardiff, Sandra E., and Jack A. Stanford. "Grizzly Bear Digging: Effects on Subalpine Meadow Plants in Relation to Mineral Nitrogen Availability." *Ecology* 79, 7 (1998): 2219–2228.

Taylor, Marc. "The Alaska Bears Are Stirring." *Sportsman's News*, April 2005, 14–15.

Taylor, Mitchell. "Grizzly Bear Sightings in Viscount Melville Sound." In *Polar*

Bears: Proceedings of the Eleventh Working Meeting of the IUCN/SSC Polar Bear Specialist Group, ed. Øystein Wiig, Erik W. Born, and Gerald W. Garner, 191–192. Copenhagen, Denmark, January 25–27, 1993.

Ternent, Mark A., and David L. Garshelis. "Taste-Aversion Conditioning to Reduce Nuisance Activity by Black Bears in a Minnesota Military Reservation." *Wildlife Society Bulletin* 27, 3 (Autumn 1999): 720–728.

Thiemann, Gregory W., Sara J. Iverson, and Ian Stirling. "Polar Bear Diets and Arctic Marine Food Webs: Insights from Fatty Acid Analysis." *Ecological Monographs* 78, 4 (2008): 591–613.

Thierren, Michele, and Frederic Laugrand. *Interviewing Inuit Elders: Perspectives on Traditional Health.* Arviat, NU: Nunavut Arctic College, 2001.

Thomas, E. Donnall, Jr. *Longbows in the Far North: An Archer's Adventures in Alaska and Siberia.* Mechanicsburg, PA: Stackpole Books, 1993.

Thomas, Phillip Drennon. "The Tower of London's Royal Menagerie." *History Today*, August 1996, 29–35.

Thornton, Thomas F. *Subsistence Use of Brown Bear in Southeast Alaska.* Technical Paper No. 214. Juneau: ADF&G Division of Subsistence, February 1992.

"Threatened Grizzly Bear Populations and Their Recovery." USFWS. Interagency Grizzly Bear Committee online, October 10, 2012. http://www.igbconline.org/index.php/population-recovery/current-status-of-grizzly-populations (accessed February 10, 2013).

Tøien, Øivind, John Blake, Dale M. Edgar, Dennis A. Grahn, H. Craig Heller, and Brian M. Barnes. "Hibernation in Black Bears: Independence of Metabolic Suppression from Body Temperature." *Science* 331, 6019 (February 18, 2011): 906–909.

Tollefson, Troy N., Colleen Matt, Joe Meehan, and Charles T. Robbins. "Quantifying Spatiotemporal Overlap of Alaskan Brown Bears and People." *Journal of Wildlife Management* 69, 2 (April 2005): 810–817.

Townsend, Jim. "The Big Bore Grizzly." *Bear Hunting Magazine*, January/February 2010.

Traveset, Anna, Teresa Bermejo, and Mary F. Willson. "Effect of Manure Composition on Seedling Emergence and Growth of Two Common Shrub Species of Southeast Alaska." *Plant Ecology* 155 (2001): 29–34.

Treadwell, Timothy, and Jewel Palovak. *Among Grizzlies: Living with Wild Bears in Alaska.* New York: Random House, 1999.

Treves, Adrian, Kirsten J. Kapp, and David M. MacFarland. "American Black Bear Nuisance Complaints and Hunter Take." *Ursus* 21 (2010): 30–42.

Troyer, Will. *Into Brown Bear Country.* Fairbanks: University of Alaska Press, 2005.

Turner, Carissa. "Bear Use of a Coastal Foraging Area in Katmai National Park: Understanding Bear Use through Time-Lapse Photography." Presented at the 2011 Southwest Alaska Park Science Symposium, Anchorage, November 2–14.

———. *Evaluating the Use and Effectiveness of the "Best Bear Viewing Practices" Guidelines* in *Katmai National Park and Preserve*. Investigator's Annual Report, KATM-00082. National Park Service, 2011.

Turner, Carissa, and Troy Hamon. "Describing Brown Bear Activity Patterns Using Time-Lapse Photography in Katmai National Park and Preserve." *Alaska Park Science* 10, 2 (December 2011): 22–27.

Turner, Frederick Jackson. "The Significance of the Frontier in American History." In *The Annual Report of the American Historical Association*, 1893, 199–227. http://www.library.wisc.edu/etext/wireader/WER0750.html (accessed January 12, 2013).

Unit 16 and Unit 19D Bear Predator Control Programs, 2012–2013. ADF&G Division of Wildlife Conservation.

"Valkenburg, Rossi Join ADF&G Leadership Team." Press release 08-20, ADF&G, December 30, 2008.

Van Ballenberghe, Victor. "Intensive Management—Or Mismanagement?" *Wildlife Professional* (Winter 2011): 74–77.

———. "Predator Control, Politics, and Wildlife Conservation in Alaska." *Alces* 42 (2006): 1–11.

Van Daele, Larry. *The History of Bears on the Kodiak Archipelago*. Anchorage: Alaska Natural History Association, 2003.

———. "Kodiak Bear Fact Sheet." http://www.adfg.alaska.gov/index.cfm?adfg =brownbear.trivia.

———. "Population Dynamics and Management of Brown Bears on Kodiak Island, Alaska." Ph.D. diss., University of Idaho, 2007.

Van Daele, Lawrence J., Victor G. Barnes Jr., and Jerrold L. Belant. "Ecological Flexibility of Brown Bears on Kodiak Island, Alaska." *Ursus* 23, 1 (2012): 21–29.

van Dijk, Jiska. "Considerations for the Rehabilitation and Release of Bears into the Wild." In *Rehabilitation and Release of Bears*, ed. Lydia Kolter and Jiska van Dijk, 7–16. Köln, Germany: Zoologischer Garten Köln, 2005.

van Meurs, Rinie, and John F. Splettstoesser. "Farthest North Polar Bear." *Arctic* 5, 3 (September 2003): 309.

Villalba, Constanza. "10 Lessons Medicine Can Learn from Bears." *Scientific American*, January 6, 2009. http://www.scientificamerican.com/slideshow.cfm?id =bear-hibernation-science (accessed December 12, 2012).

Walker, Tom. *The Way of the Grizzly: The Bears of Alaska's Famed McNeil River*. Stillwater, MN: Voyageur Press, 1993.

Walsh, John E., James E. Overland, Pavel Y. Groisman, and Bruno Rudolf. "Arctic Climate: Recent Variations." In *Snow, Water, Ice and Permafrost in the Arctic (SWIPA): Climate Change and the Cryosphere*, 1–13. Oslo: Arctic Monitoring and Assessment Programme, 2011.

Wang, Muyin, and James E. Overland. "A Sea Ice Free Summer Arctic within 30 Years: An Update from CMIP5 Models." *Geophysical Research Letters* 39, 18 (September 2012): L18501.

Wassmann, Paul, Carlos M. Duarte, Susana Agustí, and Mikael K. Sejr. "Footprints of Climate Change in the Arctic Marine Ecosystem." *Global Change Biology* 17 (2011): 1235–1249.

Waterman, Jonathan. "ANWR Grizzly Attacks: They Did Everything Right." *National Geographic Adventure*, October 2005, 55–59.

Watson, Emmett. "Menace in Our Northern Parks." *Sports Illustrated*, October 30, 1967, 62–74.

"Wayward Polar Bear Tours the Dalton Highway." *Alaska*, March 2003, 12.

Weber, Bob. "Polar Bears Eating Young Due to Shrinking Sea Ice: Scientists." *Toronto Star*, November 27, 2009.

Weisberg, Deborah. "Windfall Spent on Recruiting New Hunters." *Pittsburgh Post-Gazette*, March 29, 2012.

Welch, Christy A., Jeffrey A. Keay, Katherine C. Kendall, and Charles T. Robbins. "Constraints on Frugivory by Bears." *Ecology* 78, 4 (1997): 1105–1119.

West-Eberhard, Mary Jane. *Developmental Plasticity and Evolution.* New York: Oxford University Press, 2003.

White, Don, Jr., Katherine C. Kendall, and Harold Picton. "Potential Energetic Effects of Mountain Climbers on Foraging Grizzly Bears." *Wildlife Society Bulletin* 27, 1 (Spring 1999): 146–151.

"Whitebark Pine to Be Designated a Candidate for Endangered Species Protection." News release, USFWS, July 18, 2011.

Whiting, John. Letter to the editor. ADN, July 2, 2004.

Wikelski, Martin, and Steven J. Cooke. "Conservation Physiology." *Trends in Ecology and Evolution* 21, 1 (January 2006): 38–46.

Wilbanks, William. *Forgotten Heroes: Police Officers Killed in Alaska, 1850–1997.* Paducah, KY: Turner Publishing, 1999.

"Wildlife Damage Management in the News." *Probe* 216 (May/June 2001): 3. http://digitalcommons.unl.edu/icwdmprobe/75/.

Wilk, Randall J., John W. Solberg, Vernon D. Berns, and Richard A. Sellers. "Brown Bear, Ursus arctos, with Six Young." *Canadian Field-Naturalist* 102, 3 (1988): 541–543.

Wilker, Gregory A., and Victor G. Barnes Jr. "Responses of Brown Bears to Human Activities at O'Malley River, Kodiak Island, Alaska." *Ursus* 10 (1998): 557–561.

Williams, Maria. "To Dance Is to Be: Heritage Preservation in the 21st Century." *Alaska Park Science* 4, 1 (June 2005): 32–37.

Willson, Mary F. "Mammals as Seed-Dispersal Mutualists in North America." *Oikos* 67, 1 (May 1993): 159–176.

Willson, Mary F., and Scott M. Gende. "Seed Dispersal by Brown Bears, Ursus arctos, in Southeastern Alaska." *Canadian Field-Naturalist* 118, 4 (2004): 499–503.

Wilson, E. O. "In Praise of Sharks." *Discover*, July 1985.

———. *Sociobiology: The Abridged Edition.* Cambridge, MA: Harvard University Press, 1980.

Wilson, George. Affidavit, July 8, 1920. Alaska State Archives, Office of the District and Territorial Governor, RG 101, box 183-18, series 130, file 49-4, Predatory Animals & Birds & Bounties.

Winder, Monika, Daniel E. Schindler, Jonathan W. Moore, Susan P. Johnson, and Wendy J. Palen. "Do Bears Facilitate Transfer of Salmon Resources to Aquatic Macroinvertebrates?" *Canadian Journal of Fisheries and Aquatic Sciences* 62 (2005): 2285–2293.

Wisniewski, Josh. *"We're Always Going Back and Forth": Kigiqtaamiut Subsistence Land Use and Occupancy for the Community of Shishmaref.* Anchorage: US Army Corps of Engineers Alaska District, 2005.

Witt, Linda. "The Bear Facts? Dr. Ralph Nelson of the Mayo Clinic Studies the Miracle of Hibernation." *People,* March 27, 1978. http://www.people.com/peo ple/archive/article/0,,20070479,00.html (accessed January 12, 2013).

Wittshirk, Rudy. "Leaked Email Reveals How Wildlife Is Being Mismanaged from the Governor on Down." ADN, April 10, 2012.

Wohlforth, Charles. "Man Dies Saving Wife from Polar Bear." ADN, December 10, 1990.

———. "Starvation Spurred Polar Bear's Attack." ADN, December 12, 1990.

Wolfe, Linnie Marsh. *Son of the Wilderness: The Life of John Muir.* Reprint. Madison: University of Wisconsin Press, 2003.

"Wolverine Creek Management Committee Charter." ADF&G. http://www.adfg .alaska.gov/index.cfm?adfg=wolverinecreek.charter (accessed October 9, 2009).

Woodford, Riley. "Bear Milk." *Alaska Fish & Wildlife News* online magazine, June 2007.

———. "City Gets out of the Business of Killing Bears." *Juneau Empire,* October 7, 2001.

———. "Critter Cam Reveals Bear's Eye View." *Alaska Fish & Wildlife News* online magazine, October 2003.

———. "Fact versus Frenzy Bear Program Burns Biologists." *Alaska Fish & Wildlife News* online magazine, February 2009.

———. "Larry Aumiller: Bridging the Worlds of Bears and People." *Alaska Fish & Wildlife News* online magazine, July 2003.

———. "Testing Bears' Color Vision." *Alaska Fish & Wildlife News* online magazine, April 2005.

———. "Where Sleeping Bears Lie." *Alaska Fish & Wildlife News* online magazine, January 2010.

———. "Who Takes Home Alaska Wildlife?" *Alaska Fish & Wildlife News* online magazine, January 2009.

"World Record Grizzly Bear." Urban Legends online. http://urbanlegends.about .com/library/bl-grizzlybear.htm.

Wright, William Henry. *The Grizzly Bear: The Narrative of a Hunter-Naturalist.* New York: Charles Scribner's Sons, 1909. eBook.

Young, Donald D., Rodney D. Boertje, C. Tom Seaton, and Kalin A. Kellie. "Intensive Management of Moose at High Density: Impediments, Achievements, and Recommendations." *Alces* 42 (2006): 41–48.

Young, E. L., and Thomas McCarthy. "A Problem of Progress: Bear Conflict in Southeast Alaska." *Alaska Fish & Game* 21, 5 (September–October 1989): 32–33, 36.

Yukon Wolf Conservation and Management Plan. Whitehorse: Yukon Environment, 2012.

Zager, Peter, and John Beecham. "The Role of American Black Bears and Brown Bears as Predators on Ungulates in North America." *Ursus* 17, 2 (2006): 95–108.

Zammert, Andrea. "Knutmania Sweeps the Globe." *Bloomberg Businessweek*, May 8, 2007.

Zedrosser, Andreas, Eva Bellemain, Pierre Taberlet, and Jon E. Swenson. "Genetic Estimates of Annual Reproductive Success in Male Brown Bears: The Effects of Body Size, Age, Internal Relatedness and Population Density." *Journal of Animal Ecology* 76, 2 (2007): 368–375.

Zipp, Yvonne. "Steven Amstrup Says It's Not Too Late to Save Polar Bears—and Ourselves." *Christian Science Monitor*, October 19, 2012.

Ziupko, Bill. "A Brown Bear Hunt to Remember." Testimonial, Alaska Wilderness Charters and Guiding, November 25, 2008.

Zorich, Zach. "A Chauvet Primer." *Archaeology*, March/April 2011, 39.

index